KV-116-889

658
. ४

Business Policy and Strategic Management

Charles E. Merrill Publishing Company
A Bell & Howell Company
Columbus Toronto London Sydney

Published by Charles E. Merrill Publishing Co.
A Bell & Howell Company
Columbus, Ohio 43216

This book was set in Serifa.
Text designer: Ann Mirels
Production coordination: Ben Shriver

Copyright © 1982, by Bell & Howell Company. All rights reserved.

No part of this book may be reproduced in any form, electronic or mechanical, including photocopy, recording, or any information storage and retrieval system, without permission in writing from the publisher.

Library of Congress Catalog Card Number: 82–80026
International Standard Book Number: 0–675–09882–3
Printed in the United States of America
   2 3 4 5 6 7 8 9 10—87 86 85 84 83 82

PREFACE

This is a book about strategic management—the management process aimed at improving organizational effectiveness by means of a systematic set of strategic goals, plans, and actions.

In the changing business environment of the 1980s, top management's emphasis has shifted from more routine managerial functions to the development of both the organization's capabilities and managerial styles capable of functioning in varying situations. These new strategies focus upon the manager's style of thought and upon the development of new patterns of relationship among operating executives, to provide an anticipative mode of strategic management.

Strategic management has changed during the recent past because of two emerging forces. First, the manager of today is managing in a dynamic environment. The manager faces an accelerating rate of change in technical, social, political, and economic forces, through all of which he must steer the organization as it meets unprecedented challenges.

A second factor involves the changes in organization forms, which have expanded in scope and complexity. Organizations in the past were often relatively small and were focused on one major product. But today we see tremendous changes in the size and complexity of operations, as firms have diversified into multiple product lines and even multinational markets.

As a result of these changing forces, the management process has also become more difficult, requiring greater skills of analysis, planning, and controlling. These skills aim at controlling the future course of the firm in a changing and uncertain world.

This book has been developed for business policy courses in undergraduate degree programs, graduate degree programs, and executive development programs for practicing managers. All such "capstone" courses study the job of the general manager or chief executive of an organization.

In recent years the field of business policy has emerged as a distinct field of study focusing upon the formulation and implementation of strategy. While these concepts and studies may not yet provide a conclusive theory of how to manage a firm, they do provide the manager with a framework for analyzing strategic problems.

Several new trends in this discipline are reflected in this text, including:

1   A focus on the role of the top manager as a strategist.
2   A view of the organization as an open, sociotechnical system of related subelements.
3   An emphasis on the strategic management process.
4   The separation of strategic management and operational functions.
5   The evaluation of research studies on strategic factors.
6   A focus on the external systems, including social responsibility, business ethics, and multinational issues and problems.

v

The objective of this book is to examine in detail the current state of the art in the field of organization strategy and policy. The book is designed to bring present and potential managers into direct contact with the knowledge currently available in the field.

This volume develops in detail a model for the formulation and implementation of strategy. Text as well as case material consider in depth both the formulation and implementation phases of strategy for both business and nonbusiness organizations.

The text focuses upon key areas of interest on at least three dimensions:

1 *Concern with practical "real world" applications.* The material emphasizes techniques and theory in actual organizational situations. Each chapter contains specific examples of the triumphs and failures of strategic management—the experiences of practicing chief executive officers bring the theories to life.
2 *Research orientation.* Studies utilizing experimental or field designs are included to develop the student's understanding of research in the field.
3 *Conceptual perspectives.* The book's focus throughout is on strategic management—the process of defining business purpose, setting objectives, formulating and implementing a strategic plan, and then monitoring performance and results.

It is our position that strategic management is more than just a collection of experiences from successful practitioners. Rather, strategic management is an organized body of knowledge, with its own concepts, techniques, and necessary skills. In this text, we have attempted to present a complete picture of management's role and responsibilities in steering the course of a business and to demonstrate why these factors are essential in shaping an organization's future success. Moreover, because the practice of management by its very nature concerns people in organizations, emphasis also falls upon developing improved interpersonal skills.

Every successful strategy is the result of a concerted group effort, and each management failure is a failure for all the organization members. Therefore managers, not forces or structures, determine whether any strategy will be implemented effectively or ineffectively. Whether you will manage effectively will be determined not only by the concepts you learn, but also by your managerial style. Consequently, our emphasis is upon the experiential approach to learning about strategic management.

As you progress in the book, the cases will allow you to continually use your growing knowledge and experience to build a foundation of management experience to carry forward into your managerial career. By analyzing and critiquing your successes and failures in case analysis, you will begin to develop your ability to learn from your own experiences and develop insights into organizational functioning that would normally take years to acquire.

The book is designed so that you may assess your own managerial style and begin setting some personal development goals. Also, many opportunities are created whereby you may gain feedback on the effectiveness of your managerial style.

The text also contains a discussion of the case method and suggestions for case analysis, which provides a framework for analyzing and evaluating a company's situation. A checklist of areas to examine in sizing up a company's strategic position, what to look for in identifying company strengths and weaknesses, how to prepare a case for class discussion, and guidelines for written case analyses are included.

We have successfully used the material in this text with undergraduate management majors and MBA's, as well as with graduate administration majors from many fields including public administration, health care administration, and planning. The material has also been used many times for management-training and executive-development programs in a variety of fields with bankers, engineers, teachers, public administrators, military officers, production managers, and marketing managers, at a variety of levels from first-line supervision to top management teams.

Many topical features have been incorporated:

1 The nature of open systems and contingencies are thoroughly covered.
2 The cases are based on topics directly related to the text material.
3 Objectives have been provided at the beginning and review questions at the end of each chapter.
4 A full set of teaching aids can be provided.

The text includes 26 cases, most of them newly published, written by experienced case writers from across the country who have generously contributed to this volume. All of the cases have been class-tested, and they provide an exceptionally well balanced mix of strategic problems and organizational situations. The comprehensive *Instructor's Manual* contains a suggested sequencing of cases, course outlines, transparency masters, and comprehensive teaching aids.

We are grateful to many people who have contributed to making this book a reality. For assistance and encouragement offered throughout the development of the text, a special note of appreciation is extended to Management Chairman Dr. Charles Bown of Eastern Washington University. Our sincere appreciation is also extended to Mr. Gary Bauer of Merrill for timely support and assistance.

Many colleagues in the School of Business at Eastern Washington University have been helpful, but special thanks go to Professor Hugh Hunter, EWU, who directed and coordinated the case material, and to Professor Neal Kneip, Gonzaga University, for support and review suggestions. Many students and managers have been involved in the development of the simulations and cases, but special appreciation goes to Mr. Ed Owens, Ms. Lynn McClure, Ms. Colleen Bunnell, Ms. Martha Jo Messex (Bendix), and Mr. Jim Sayles (IBM) for their suggestions. Assisting greatly in the development of the strategic management style matrix were Capt. Charles Finke (USAF) and Mr. Mike Miller (J. C. Penney).

Reviewers who were greatly helpful were Professor George E. Stevens, Arizona State University; Professor C. W. Millard, Iowa State University; and Professor Herman Waggener, from Wright State University.

EWU's Word Processing Center (especially Ms. Mary Rivera and Ms. Leona Anderson) did an outstanding job of typing the final manuscript and Mrs.

Jenny Gibbs did a valuable job of editing. The photos were provided by the companies involved, and the conception for the art work by Ms. Cynthia Brunk of Merrill Publishing, to whom our appreciation is extended for adding so much.

Finally, my wife, Becky Harvey, and sons Mikie and Scottie have contributed in more ways than I can count—not just in allowing the time for writing, but in a form of involvement that can never be fully appreciated or repaid. As usual the author must accept the responsibility for any problems, in spite of the efforts of all contributors.

Donald F. Harvey

CONTENTS

4 Identifying Strategic Opportunities and Threats *91*

PART TWO: Strategy Evaluation and Decision Making

5 Identifying Strategic Alternatives *125*

6 Conglomerate Diversification Strategies *153*

MINI-STORAGE BUSINESS *347*
is a case of *medium complexity* that deals with the very basics of entrepreneural decision making—finding a suitable business to enter and choosing a suitable location for it.

ITY-BITTY MACHINE COMPANY *355*
focuses on the excitement as well as the hazards of starting a business in a new industry—in this instance, the retail home-computer field. A *less complex* case.

CUMBERLAND CRAFTS *367*
is another *less complex* case that concentrates on the difficulties of managing growth in a small business: the retailing and wholesaling of crafts in the American Southwest.

U AND I, INC. *380*
is the saga of a church-owned enterprise, tracing the Mormons' struggle to establish a viable sugar-processing business down to the troubled present. This case is of *moderate complexity.*

BERVEN CARPETS (A) *390*
is another *moderately complex* case that outlines one medium-sized company's struggle to survive in a highly competitive environment.

PACIFIC WOMEN'S BANK (A) *409*
details the steps necessary to start a very different type of new business enterprise. *Medium complexity.*

PACIFIC WOMEN'S BANK (B) *422*
Again *moderate complexity.* This continuation traces the development of a strategic plan, given the philosophy of that distinctive new business.

BOISE CASCADE *427*
is a *moderately complex* case that outlines the process of changing corporate strategy, again in a highly competitive industry—wood and paper products.

CASES: Planning Stage II

CITY HARDWARE (A) *442*
offers an anatomy of a strategic choice, a relocation decision that is attended by some substantial risk. The case is of *medium complexity*.

JOHNSON ENTERPRISES *453*
is an acquisition analysis that gives equal coverage to the perspectives of the company (a small RV manufacturer) being absorbed and that doing the absorbing. *Medium complexity.*

CASES: Planning Stage III

BENDIX *640*
treats the implementation of change in a large firm, particularly as the personalities and styles of decision makers affect that process. This is a fairly *long, complex* case.

SOUTHERN UNIVERSITY *657*
is another *complex* case, showing the difficulties of leadership in a not-for-profit organization.

GENERAL MOTORS' DOWNSIZING DECISION *669*
is a quite *long, complex* case detailing this industry leader's reaction to environmental shocks. It offers a somewhat surprising picture of the decision-making process at that corporation.

B. J. GUNESS CONSTRUCTION CO. *696*
shows a family-owned and -operated firm in Arizona making hard choices in a constrained business environment. *Complex.*

FIRST CHICAGO CORP. *714*
concentrates on the impact of two leaders as they devised strategies in reaction to their competition among "money center" banks. *Complex.*

POTLATCH CORP. *730*
is about managing the lower-market-share firm. Again the field is the wood- and paper-products industry, dominated by giants of the Pacific Northwest. A *moderately complex* case.

R.T.C. LIBRARY, LETTERKENNY

Strategy Identification and Policy Formulation

C H A P T E R

1

We've got a pretty good agreement on what a business unit is going
to do. These estimates have withstood the criticisms and
arguments of all the people who have something to contribute. . . .
But when we're through, the manager will have a game plan. . . .

Harold Geneen, ITT
quoted in "The Financial Key at ITT,"
Dun's Review, December 1970, 6.

Management Policy and Strategy: An Overview

CHAPTER OBJECTIVES

When you have completed this chapter, you will be able to:

- ☐ *Demonstrate an understanding of strategy, policy, and strategic management.*

- ☐ *Describe the basic stages in the strategic management process.*

- ☐ *Explain the importance of strategic management in achieving the organizational mission.*

THE VIEW FROM THE TOP

Harold S. Geneen

In a conference room high up in the Manhattan headquarters of International Telephone and Telegraph Corporation (ITT), fifty executives from all around the world sit at two long, green felt-covered tables. The mood, as always, will be electric. With the air of a surgeon, ITT's chairman Harold S. Geneen begins another of his famous probes for soft spots in the strategic plans of this vast business empire. The focus of the meeting is ITT's "business plan." This plan sets forth an elaborately detailed map of targets and timetables spanning two years and projected ahead to the fifth. The strategic plan is rewritten every year and reviewed at the monthly meeting chaired by Geneen. The strategic planning meetings provide a constant interplay between corporate goals and ever-changing world economic conditions. The meetings are combative, and the discussion often gets hot and heavy. The pace is grueling, the hours are long, and the demands are stringent. But, on the other hand, there is plenty of excitement, top pay, and sizable bonuses for successful performance.[1]

In meetings like those at ITT, organizations around the world hammer out strategic goals and plans. This is the arena in which the field of strategic management takes place. This is where the strategic decisions are made: decisions that may lead to the thrill of victory or the agony of failure.

Harold Geneen, as ITT chairman, was one of the key leaders who developed a strategic management system that enabled ITT to program and plan to the bottom line. At monthly meetings, like those described, managers were examining financial reports of sales, profits, return on investment, and the status of their competitors on a product-by-product basis. As a result, these managers were analyzing and describing virtually every existing or potential problem ITT was likely to be facing. The emphasis of such meetings is on problem solving for potential problems in an uncertain future. This is what strategic management is all about: developing a game plan for future management actions.

Our focus in this book will be on the most exciting aspect of managing in all types of organizations: *strategic management.* It should provide you with an understanding of the critical importance of policy and strategy in organizations. It is hoped that you will gain an increased awareness of the process which managers in major corporations and government use to determine organizational objectives and strategy. In this chapter, an overview of the strategic management process will be presented. The purpose is to help you understand how and why strategic management is used and to prepare you for a successful career in management. If you gain a thorough understanding of this process, you will be more likely to become an effective manager.

THE GAME PLAN

What makes one organization a winner, while another fails to take advantage of its opportunities? How did Charles B. "Tex" Thornton lead Litton Industries from virtual obscurity to the top 500, while Armour, once the number seven ranked company, is now a subsidiary of another company? What factors allowed Henry S. Singleton to guide Teledyne to the top 500, while during the same period W. T. Grant went into bankruptcy? And how did Richard Goodwin manage to turn around a stagnating Johns-Manville Corporation, while Chrysler, once in the top five, came perilously close to bankruptcy?

The answer lies in the strategic decisions made by top management of these organizations. Harold Geneen was effective in developing a strategic game plan for achieving ITT's objectives. While other managers simply let their organizations drift toward uncertain goals, Geneen was designing an effective, results-oriented system for coordinating a diverse set of endeavors. Some managers are simply unable to focus the resources of their organization, and the results are ineffective performances. In a dynamic, competitive environment, an organization must either move forward with purpose and direction or fall back. There is no standing still. The difference between success and failure depends upon how well the manager is able to perform the strategic management function: to develop an effective, winning game plan.

STRATEGIC MANAGEMENT

Strategic management refers to the process of selecting strategy and policy toward maximizing the organization's objectives.[2] Strategic management includes all the activities leading to the definition of the organization's objectives, strategies, and the development of plans, actions, and policy to accomplish these strategic objectives for the total organization. The focus of strategic management is on the external environment and on future operations. Strategic management determines the long range direction of the organization and is concerned with relating the resources of the organization to opportunities in the larger environment. At ITT, the monthly meetings, chaired by Harold Geneen, focused on the strategic management aspects of the organization: the development of a course of action and the review of progress toward ITT's target objectives.

STRATEGIC MANAGEMENT: THE MACRO LEVEL

The emphasis of strategic management, then, may be distinguished from other levels as shown in Figure 1.1. The strategic (MACRO) level is concerned with the relation of the organization to its external environment and with the total organizational system.[3] The middle and lower (MICRO) levels are more concerned with the accomplishment of internal operating plans and activities at a more detailed level. Their concern is with the implementation of the strategic plan.

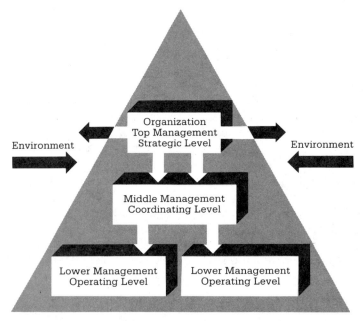

FIGURE 1.1
Levels of Management

THE OPERATING LEVEL (MICRO)

The operating level is concerned with the actual production and marketing of goods and services. Even though operations may involve many large-scale decisions, such as purchasing, hiring, etc., this is at a more detailed or "micro" level compared to decisions which influence the entire system. At General Motors, for example, the production plant managers are making decisions about the development and use of resources, people, facilities, money, etc., necessary to produce Chevrolet automobiles. The operating manager makes decisions involving the allocation of unit resources to produce the desired product, at an acceptable cost and quality, and on a given time schedule.

THE COORDINATION LEVEL (MICRO)

The coordinating level makes decisions influencing the relations among operating units and mediating between the technical operations and other elements, such as customers and suppliers. The decisions at this level determine how the operating units function and control their performance. At General Motors, the president of the Chevrolet division allocates resources among various plant locations, monitors operations, and coordinates activities toward the goals of the Chevrolet division which represent only one segment of total system goals.

THE STRATEGIC LEVEL (MACRO)

While the emphasis of the other levels is on smaller, internal problems, the strategic level is concerned with broad, externally oriented decisions. The strategic manager provides objectives and controls for lower level internal units but not for detailed matters. The strategic level is concerned with long-range planning and makes decisions on the long-range direction of the organization and its interaction with the larger environment, including competitive, governmental, and social concerns. In a word, the macro issues settle questions of organizational purpose.

The top management at ITT was involved with identifying the mission of the organization, selecting strategic objectives, and implementing plans and programs to achieve them. Harold Geneen's job, then, was aimed at allocating the vast resources of ITT through a complex set of plans, procedures, and programs to advance toward long-term goals. This is strategic management.

ORGANIZATIONAL STRATEGY

An *organizational strategy* is a course of action used to achieve major objectives. The term strategy is derived from the Greek *strategos,* meaning general. In a military sense, strategy involves the planning and directing of battles or campaigns. In the business world this term refers to actions by a manager to offset actual or potential actions of competitors. Strategic decisions involve the determination of broad directions and the development of comprehensive plans to attain those objectives.

THE CONCEPT OF STRATEGY

Richard Vancil (Harvard University) defines the concept of strategy as follows: "The strategy of an organization, or the subunit of a larger organization, is a conceptualization expressed or implied by the organization's leader, of (1) the long-term objectives or purposes of the organization, (2) the broad constraints and policies, either self-imposed by the leader or accepted by him from his superiors, that currently restrict the scope of the organization's activities, and (3) the current set of plans and near-term goals that have been adopted in the expectation of contributing to the achievement of the organization's objectives."[4]

The purpose of a strategy is to maintain or gain a position of advantage in relation to competitors. An advantage is gained by seizing opportunities in the environment that enable the organization to capitalize upon areas of strength. During an ITT meeting, the fact that Japanese companies were moving new products into a certain country emerged. The ITT top management team then evolved a strategy to meet this challenge. It selected a course of action meeting this potential threat, leading to the accomplishment of its own objectives for this world market.

STRATEGY AT MEAD CORP.

Another example of strategy in action is Mead Corp. The Dayton-based paper and forest products company feels its six-year-old strategic management system has improved the return on total capital to 12 percent in 1979 from 5 percent in 1972, and increased its industrywide rank among forest product companies to number 2 of 15 (tied with three others) from number 12 in 1972. Mead's strategy involved forming twenty-four strategic business units and moving twenty-four top executives into new managerial positions so that their expertise closely fit the business they run. "If you have a business you want a lot of cash out of instead of growth, don't put a conservative accountant in charge," explains William W. Wommack, Mead's vice chairman.[5] Mead also is allocating its resources differently. Instead of funding all businesses with percentage allocations, it now funds strategic business units (SBUs). This method enables management to phase out "dog" products, to reinvest cash from its mature cash producers, and concentrate investment in high-growth potential fields.

Mead's underlying strategic principle is to devote its investment resources to market segments that are growing and that offer opportunities to build or maintain a position of cost-effective leadership.

ORGANIZATIONAL POLICY

One outcome of strategy is *organizational policy. Policy* is generally used to refer to general guides to actions and decisions within the organization. A policy is often referred to as a standing decision made in advance to cover a prescribed set of conditions, thus setting the limitations or guidelines for making decisions or taking actions. Policies provide organization members with a framework for making decisions so that actions will be consistent throughout the system. At many companies, there is a policy of not acquiring or investing in product lines with a return below a certain level, say 20 percent. Firms may also have policies to deal with recurring situations. For example, most organizations have personnel policies that cover the basic situations of hiring, promoting, or terminating employees. Mandatory retirement at age 70 is a typical policy of many organizations. Weyerhaeuser, for example, has a policy of "promotion from within," while its competition, International Paper, has relied upon hiring from other companies, such as Xerox and Du Pont, as a way of injecting new ideas and values.

At ITT, "There's no lack of communication for setting goals, for following performance, or for taking action between the top echelon of the company and the firing line."[6] Organization policies are intended to provide this communication and consistency through all levels of the organization. The term policy, then, evolves from strategy and includes the procedures, rules, and methods which are used in the implementation of strategic decisions (see Figure 1.2).

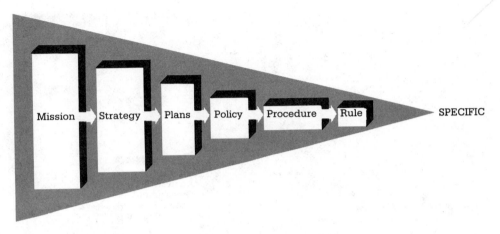

FIGURE 1.2
From Broad Mission/Strategy to Specific Rules/Job

Goals are the overall strategic mission expressed in terms of five-year market share, ROI, etc. The *strategy* and *plans* are designed as directions for achieving attainment of goals and missions, the steps that lead to the attainment of objectives. From strategy and plans, *policies* are then developed to provide guidance for operational decisions and actions. *Procedures* provide direction in handling specific sections but allow for a certain amount of judgmental discretion. *Rules,* which are quite rigid and very specific, deal with certain categories or situations in which little if any discretion is allowed.

THE STRATEGIC MANAGEMENT PROCESS

Because of the success of strategic planning in such organizations as ITT and General Electric, the emphasis has been shifting from policy or operational planning toward strategic management. This emphasis on strategic management reflects the growing importance of the impact of the outside world on the organization. The fast-changing and uncertain world situation is forcing organizations to do more strategic planning.

At ITT, for example, the strategic planning and monthly review meetings are part of the system of management. Once a year, each ITT business is required to develop a complete business plan covering a five-year period. The business plans are then reviewed in the monthly meetings. This adds up to at least fifty top management meeting days per year, so that continual updating of the strategic plan is done to meet possible changes and correct potential problems. The primary reason is that in a rapidly changing and increasingly complex environment strategic decisions based on past conditions may be obsolete almost as quickly as they can be put into operation. Organizations are finding that strategic planning is necessary if they are to anticipate and adapt to changing conditions.

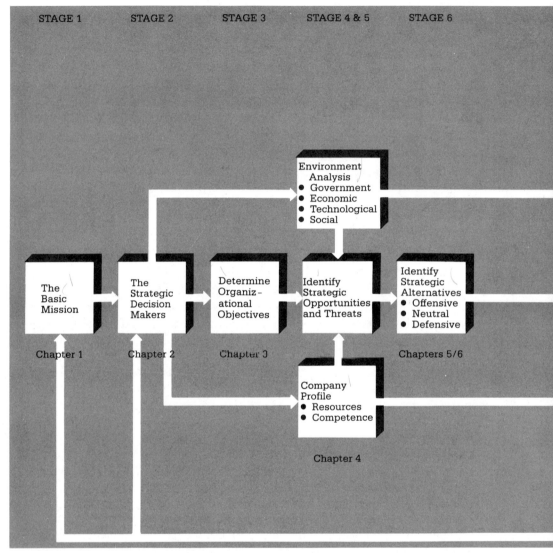

FIGURE 1.3
A Model of Strategic Management

THE STRATEGIC MANAGEMENT MODEL

The evolving strategic management model is based upon the concepts of strategy and of a process for managing strategy. An essential part of this process is the developing of a master strategy for the firm to provide positive, future-oriented direction to its business activities. The strategic management model of ten interrelated stages is shown in Figure 1.3.

Each element of the strategic process is discussed in the following section. Each stage evolves from the prior stage, and an effective strategy is more

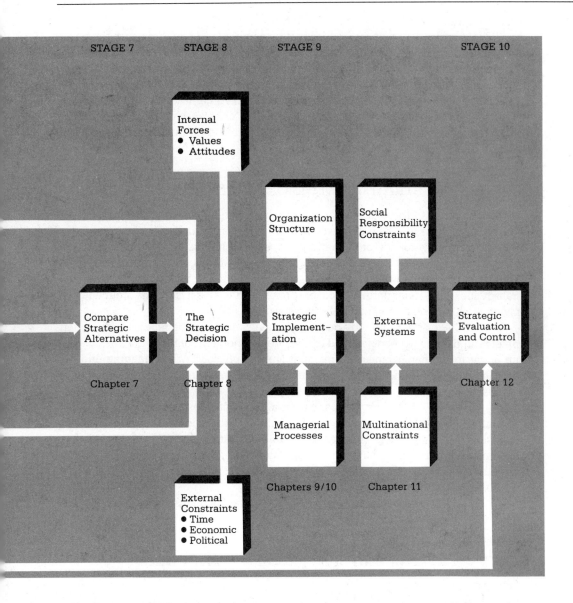

probable when these stages are followed in a logical sequence. It should be under-stood that the elements of the strategic process will be discussed separately, while in fact they often happen simultaneously. Strategic management is a continuing process and the stages are interacting parts of a whole system, However, for purposes of clarity, we will discuss each element separately.

STAGE 1: IDENTIFYING THE BASIC PURPOSE OR MISSION OF THE ORGANIZATION

What is the basic mission or purpose of the organization? Who are its clients or customers? What are its basic products or services? And who are its major competitors? These and other basic questions must be answered clearly to set forth the basic direction and thrust of the organization. Clearly the answers will be different in varying industries, and for public versus private organizations. But the first step in the strategic process is the definition of organization purpose or mission. The mission of an organization provides the long-term view of what the organization is going to be in the future. As an example, IBM defines its mission as solving problems, not selling computers. Clear and accurate identification of mission is crucial: all elements of strategy depend on this factor.

STAGE 2: THE STRATEGIC DECISION MAKERS

The second stage of the strategic process involves the impact of the strategic decision makers. These are the individuals who are responsible for determining the basic strategy and policy for the organization, probably including the top managers, the board of directors, and corporate planning groups. The impact of their personal styles is reflected in strategic decisions. There are a whole set of factors which influence strategy including managerial philosophy, roles, and values. Decisions are made not only on facts, but on a range of other forces as well.

President Kennedy had a certain vision and set of beliefs which, when implemented, and further developed by President Lyndon B. Johnson, led this country into a war in Vietnam. Similarly, President Nixon's philosophy of managing and his personal values encouraged the problems of Watergate which led to the erosion of his presidency.

At ITT, the system tends to bring good people to the top very fast. But the kind of people that stay with the company like this momentum and constant expansion. "At most companies you have to wait until somebody dies before you have an opportunity to run things . . . " one manager comments. "We believe that if a product line doesn't return eight percent after taxes, you should get the hell out of that business."[7]

The personal values of the strategy makers greatly influence the strategy of the organization.

STAGE 3: DETERMINING SPECIFIC ORGANIZATIONAL GOALS AND OBJECTIVES

The third step in the strategic process is defining organizational goals and objectives. Strategic goals refer to the performance results which an organization seeks to attain. Here the organization's mission is translated into specific objectives, targets, and action plans. The strategic goals are broad guides for action leading to more specific and detailed objectives at lower levels of the organization.

STAGE 4: IDENTIFYING ORGANIZATIONAL STRENGTHS AND WEAKNESSES

In the determination of what the organization should do, we must not overlook what it can do. What are the unique strengths, competencies, and capabilities of the organization and what are its areas of vulnerability or weakness? Two key areas are, of course, financial and technical capability.

Two Key Areas   An organization may seek to move in to solid-state electronics and see this as a potential market, but its financial resources may be too limited, or its technical capability may not be strong enough for such a move. In analyzing a diverse set of alternative strategies, the manager, like Harold Geneen of ITT, must also consider his corporation's competitive position in a given market, and the marketing strengths of his organization in a given product line relative to others. This usually includes a critical evaluation of each product's strengths and weaknesses versus those of the major competitors.

Strategy at Eaton   During the last decade, most big auto parts producers followed similar strategies aimed at diversifying into new technologies. At Eaton Corp., for example, it took four years to bring new strategies into focus. The $2.1 billion automotive and industrial parts maker began its form of strategy planning four years ago by creating 400 "product market segments" within its twenty-six divisions. Eaton's system identifies two primary factors affecting strategy planning—"push" and "pull." The pull factors, which are largely uncontrollable, include inflation, exchange rates, and the growth rate of one business as compared with others. All operating divisions monitor the impact of such factors on their businesses, then contribute data on them to a 10-year benchmark report. The push factors are actions the company can take to control operations: increase R and D, build a new plant, or aggressively pursue market share growth. To influence the push factors, explains corporate development chief Robert C. Brown, each division and market segment unit creates a five-year plan, as does the corporation. To date, Eaton attributes rapid growth in its automatic cruise control product line to the planning system.[8]

This analysis enables a company to identify and capitalize on its strengths in certain markets and to withdraw from markets where profits are marginal.

STAGE 5: IDENTIFY STRATEGIC OPPORTUNITIES AND THREATS

In determining a strategy, other factors are the opportunities and threats which exist in the environment. What economic and demographic factors have been important and will be important in the future? Almost all organizations use economic forecasting and indicators to predict future conditions. The airlines, for example, must base future strategic moves on such factors as growth trends in air travel, overall economic conditions, and the future price of fuel. The strategic decision maker evaluates options based on the information about probable future situations which influence the attainment of strategic objectives. This includes an analysis of economic and market conditions. The strategy must take into account both the potential opportunities which exist and the possible threats which may impede future actions.

The ability to read or recognize changing economic conditions or markets will have an influence on the choice of strategy. For example, Sewell Avery, then chairman of Montgomery Ward and Company, was certain that a severe economic recession was going to follow World War II. Therefore, Montgomery Ward followed a strategy of limiting growth and hoarding cash. Meanwhile, his competitor Sears,

Roebuck was rapidly expanding, since the top management of Sears read the economic conditions differently. It took years for Wards to overcome the results of this strategic decision.

STAGE 6: IDENTIFYING STRATEGIC ALTERNATIVES

The next step is to identify and evaluate alternative strategies or options. There is rarely only one strategy to pursue. There are usually many possible ways to allocate the resources of the organization and many possible strategies. Depending upon the analysis of the firm and the environment, these may generate aggressive-offensive strategies aimed at attacking the market or specific market segments, or they may generate alternatives for defensive purposes, for reducing spending, cutting costs, limiting growth, and even possibly selling off business units. The key here is the generation of many possible options or courses of action. What are the possible alternatives which could be used in developing a new strategic approach?

STAGE 7: COMPARING STRATEGIC ALTERNATIVES

Once the strategic alternatives and the possible actions have been identified, then the relative advantages or disadvantages of each can be compared against some set of criteria. The alternatives can be examined to determine which strategy best matches the firm's resources and capabilities, and which offers the best competitive advantage, in terms of potential opportunities or threats. Each strategic alternative will have advantages and disadvantages. Often there are conflicting alternatives: Should ITT concentrate on growth or on earnings? Should it invest more in European operations or in North America? Should one subsidiary get a larger share of resources or should another? At this point in the decision process, management must analyze the alternatives and compare them on the basis of certain criteria in order to screen out the more promising options from less likely alternatives.

STAGE 8: THE STRATEGIC DECISION

After the process of strategic evaluation, the next step is the most critical factor in the strategic management process: the strategic decision. A decision is a choice from among possible alternative strategies. As the old saying goes, "The buck stops here!" The purpose of decision making is to direct resources toward objectives, and a decision to pursue one strategy usually means there are other possible actions that are not being taken. The decisions may be good decisions, or they may be terrible decisions, but they must be made. At Boeing Co., Chairman T. A. Wilson's decision to invest $3 billion in designing two new airliner series (757, 767) has placed the concern in a commanding lead among aircraft companies. But a decision by Rolls-Royce to design a new jet engine led that company into bankruptcy.

STAGE 9: IMPLEMENTING THE STRATEGIC DECISION AND PLANS

The decision alone is valueless until it is implemented. The decision must be implemented in order to achieve the strategic objectives. The strategic decision is implemented by developing specific and detailed policies, plans, and action programs aimed at the attainment of objectives. Once the strategic decision is made, then the next step is the implementation of the action plan: the actual performance and activities which commit the organization's resources toward the desired goals.

Many strategists feel the implementation stage may be even more critical than the decision itself. For example, President Carter made a decision early in 1980 to attempt an armed rescue of the United States' hostages in Iran. Unfortunately, the implementation of that decision was inadequately carried out, with a resulting failure of the strategy. Regardless of the merit of the decision, unless it it is properly carried out and executed, it may end up as an ineffective strategic decision.

STAGE 10: STRATEGIC EVALUATION AND CONTROL

The purpose of strategic evaluation and control is critical to any plan. If actual results do not track with planned results, then changes must be made. As noted in the ITT example, managers are continually reviewing the progress of strategic moves so that they can take corrective action or countermoves if the original plan is not working or if conditions have changed. This final step involves the strategic review and evaluation of the game plan. This involves the monitoring of activities and plans to determine how well these moves are working and to introduce changes if problems have emerged.

This is the strategic management process which will determine future performance. How effectively managers are able to deal with these complex and changing factors of market, competition, and economic conditions is what strategic management is all about.

As you can see, the Strategic Management Model describes the activities of Mr. Geneen and his associates at ITT as they were reviewing and determining the current and future status of operations, planning future actions, and making strategic decisions. From these meetings, ITT's strategy and policy emerged. At ITT, this process forms a system of management relating strategic decisions to the long-range planning process, so that strategic decision making is intertwined with strategic planning. Strategic Management, then, is a process that begins with goals and objectives and selects strategies, policies, and detailed plans and controls to achieve them.

Each of the strategic management elements and decisions in the strategic management process is explained in more detail in Chapters 2 through 12, as indicated in Figure 1.3. This model is used throughout the book to relate the material to that covered previously and that which follows.

THE BOTTOM LINE

The strategic decisions made by top managers are the most critical decisions in the organization. Lower-level managers also make decisions, but from a more segmented or specialized viewpoint. Therefore, the role of the Chief Executive Officer is unique. The CEO, such as Geneen of ITT, is responsible for determining the strategic objectives and for the allocation of resources among various divisions, products, and functions. He must consider all of the possible options and then decide upon a course of action that, in his judgment, is best for the organization. The CEO is responsible for that decision and for the results which occur. It is not an easy job.

A strategy begins with an idea of how to use the resources of the firm most effectively to accomplish the basic mission and goals of the firm.

THE BASIC MISSION

The first step in the strategic process is the definition of organizational purpose or mission. The mission of an organization presents a long-term idea of what that organization is striving to become in the future. The mission includes the basic thrust of the company, including its basic products, businesses, and markets. The identification of the mission is an awareness of a sense of purpose, the competitive environment, and the degree to which the firm's mission fits its capabilities and the opportunities which the environment offers.

The mission provides a starting point as to how the firm will deal with such issues as technological innovation, product quality, customer service, employee satisfaction, and socially responsible conduct. The answer to these issues of mission have a significant impact on future strategy. As an example, William Hewlett and Dave Packard founded Hewlett-Packard in 1939. They evolved a basic mission of (1) technological leadership; (2) high quality products; and (3) good employee relations. Because of these basic premises, Hewlett Packard does not use time clocks and bases its marketing approach on innovative design and product quality. In fact, it prefers not to use "price" as a strategy at the expense of quality.[9]

Strategic decisions are aimed at optimizing future performance rather than dealing with the past. Harold Geneen developed a strategic planning system at ITT involving a highly refined system of goals and controls. When he was hired away from Raytheon Company in 1959 to take the top spot at ITT, he faced nothing but difficulties. His strategic decisions resulted in added sales of $1.8 billion and profits of $560 million, along with an increase in the number of executives from 450 to 2,200. Geneen reassessed the basic mission of ITT and started on a program of acquisition and expansion.

THE BASIC STRATEGIC GOALS

The purpose of organizational goals is to translate the broad mission or purpose into workable terms. These basic goals serve as guides to action for all levels of the organization. From these basic goals, strategic decisions are made. These strategies represent the actions to be made by the organization in achieving its basic mission. These include several basic goals.

Profitability   The goal of profitability is to maintain and improve the return on investment realized from existing resources.

Opportunity   The goal of opportunity is to find opportunities for additional investments which can be profitable (beneficial) for the organization.

Efficiency (Survival)   The goal of efficiency is to protect the financial integrity of the organization.

The strategies represent the basic decisions, the game plan, which will determine the direction to be taken by the organization in achieving these basic goals and mission. The performance of management's strategic decisions can be measured by the results which are achieved, that is, by the bottom line.

RESPONSIBILITY FOR RESULTS

All strategic decisions take into account the concepts of revenues (income, funding, etc.), costs (expenditures), and the resulting profit or loss (surplus-deficit). For example, note Table 1.1.

TABLE 1.1

Chrysler's Reported Daily Figures	
Revenue	$20,000,000
Costs	$25,000,000
Loss	($ 5,000,000)

Revenues represent the ability of the organization to take advantage of a market or service opportunity which exists in the environment. Costs represent the commitment or sacrifice of resources. Therefore, costs are a measure of the extent of sacrifice which is involved in a given decision.

STRATEGY INVOLVES RISKS

Strategic decisions, then, attempt to weigh the potential benefits against the cost to be incurred. For example, when Sohio Chairman Charles Spahr decided to embark on the strategic decision to develop the Alaskan oil fields, costs were estimated to be about $900 million. Costs actually ran up to about $6.2 billion before the first oil was shipped. "We . . . wanted to be remembered as men of courage and judgment, as risk takers on a grand scale," says Charles Spahr. Those risks brought his company closer to disaster than most people ever suspected.[10]

As you can see, decisions always involve costs. Consequently, the goal of strategic decision making is to increase revenues at a rate higher than the increase in cost, thus improving the overall return.

For one example of bottom-line analysis, it has been reported that Chrysler, in the first quarter of 1980, had daily revenues of $20 million, and daily costs of $25 million, resulting in a loss of $5 million per day, and a loss of some $445 million for the quarter. This is in addition to the billion dollar loss for 1979 alone.

MAKE YOUR NUMBERS

One example of bottom-line emphasis is given by Richard Beeson, former President of Canada Dry, on the decision making of David Mahoney of Norton Simon, Inc.[11]:

"I had been on the job only a couple of weeks," Beeson says, "when we had a Canada Dry board meeting. I said to Mahoney, 'Dave, we're a little bit below budget now, and I think we can hold that for the rest of the year.'

"Dave looked at me, smiled, and said, 'Be on budget by the six-month mark; be on by the year.'

" 'But Dave,' I said, 'there isn't enough time to get on by the *half*. I inherited this situation, after all.'

"Still smiling, Dave looked at me and said, 'Do I pay you a lot of money? Do I argue with you over what you want to spend? Do I bother you? Then don't tell me what the goals should be. Be on by the half; be on by the end of the year.'

" 'What if I can't, Dave?', I asked.

" 'Then clean out your desk and go home.' "

Beeson . . . says he began running through the reasons why he could not meet the goals, but Mahoney said, "Not interested. My board and my stockholders want me to make my numbers. The way I make my numbers is for you guys to make *your* numbers. Make your numbers!"

The pressure to show fast, short-term results, "to make your numbers," can also have an unfavorable effect on longer-range strategy. Research by Bruce and Judith Kirchhoff (of the University of Nebraska-Omaha) indicates that short-run optimization is not best for long-term results.[12]

In fact, long-term success may involve reduced return in the short-run. The Boston Consulting Group has suggested that sacrificing short-run profits to gain market share will yield the highest long-term gain.[13]

Therefore, while all strategic decisions involve the concepts of revenues and cost, such decisions usually are complex decisions involving multiple forces, factors, and time frames.

The performance of management's strategic decisions, or game plan, can be measured by the results which are achieved; that is, by the bottom line.

THE PAYOFF

The payoff for these strategic choices is how effective the organization is in accomplishing its basic mission. The task of the CEO is to allocate resources so as to optimize their efficiency in achieving certain goals: to maximize potential return and to minimize costs and risks. Profitability, however, is only one criterion of broad responsibility. The bottom line, as we use the term, refers to the broader concept of organizational performance on a range and scope of objectives including growth, profitability, market share, employee satisfaction, and corporate responsibility as well. The bottom line simply suggests that strategic management is concerned with the total performance of the organization, and those responsible for strategic decisions are ultimately responsible for the final outcomes.

Most organizations have multiple goals each of which is important in determining and measuring performance. *Effectiveness* refers to the accomplishment of the basic goals or mission. *Efficiency* refers to the ratio of output to input, or benefit

3548 9362

to cost; thus it is possible to be effective but not efficient and vice versa. Measures of efficiency seek to determine how well resources are being used. Thus a ratio such as return on sales or return on investment (ROI) when compared to similar organizations provides management with an indication of how efficient its operations are.

Another element is *employee development and satisfaction*. The human resources of the organization must be considered if long-term goal accomplishment is to be achieved. Well-managed organizations maintain objectives of quality of management and satisfying their people, etc., all of which are important to long-term survival.

This is what makes strategic management such an exciting and dynamic field. In many decisions, the management team is placing the entire organization's assets on the line in selecting a certain course of action. This might be termed "you bet your company!" IBM in developing its new computer line, Boeing in the development of its new 767 and 757 series of planes, and others are typical of the bold and daring strategic decisions which are being made in organizations.

WHY IS STRATEGIC MANAGEMENT IMPORTANT?

Strategic management encompasses all the decisions and actions leading to the attainment of long-range objectives. The total organization is considered as an open system in determining the allocation of resources, the direction of organizational forces, and the plan of strategic actions. The open-system perspective emphasizes that an organization has a number of interacting elements and can be considered only in relation to its external environment. Without this system perspective, managers tend to see problems in isolation, often failing to recognize the dynamic interrelationship among subsystems of the organization and with other external systems.

The strategic manager's job, then, is one of managing systems. The strategist identifies system and subsystem relationships, develops goals, objectives and plans, and integrates these activities into a broad course of action. The systems view recognizes the independent forces, both internal and external, which directly influence the organization. These include: (1) external constraints; (2) opportunities for growth and survival; (3) internal processes, such as structure and climate; and (4) the degree of freedom which exists in strategic choice. The external environment includes those economic, political, and cultural systems which affect the firm. Because this external environment is becoming more unpredictable and complex, it is essential for the strategist to develop skills needed in coping with these changing forces.

Organizations are never completely static. They are in continuous interaction with external forces (see Figure 1.4). Changing consumer attitudes, new legislation, and technological breakthroughs all act on the organization to cause it to change. The degree of change may vary from one organization to another, but all face the need for adaptation to external forces. Many of these changes are forced upon the organization, while others are generated internally.

Because changes are occurring so rapidly, these put even more pressure on top management. The increased use of strategic planning and management pro-

658
.4

vides one way to aid managers in dealing with this uncertain future. There are many reasons why we see an increased emphasis upon strategic management. On this, see Figure 1.4.

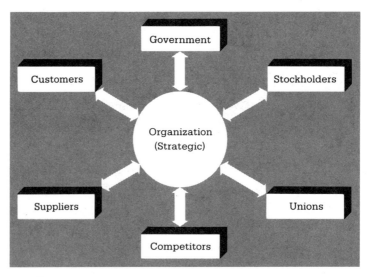

FIGURE 1.4
The Organizational Environment of Strategic Management

PLANNING FOR AN UNCERTAIN FUTURE

Economic conditions change so fast that strategic management is the only way to anticipate future opportunities and problems. Given this increasingly complex environment, it becomes even more critical for management to identify and respond to forces of social and technical change.

Many executives in attempting to manage today's organizations are finding that insufficient consideration of the changing environment in the past is creating problems for them today. For example, Singer Corporation lost a substantial portion of the sewing machine market because it reacted too slowly to technological changes in its product line and has now been bypassed by its competitors.[14] U.S. Steel, frequently criticized as "slow-moving, parochial, and autocratic," now finds itself with some of the oldest facilities in the industry and is experiencing plant shutdowns because of exorbitant operating costs.[15]

IMPROVING DECISIONS IN A HIGH RISK ENVIRONMENT

Risk taking might be characterized as riskier than ever, and strategic planning offers the possibility of preparing contingency plans and "worst case scenarios" to provide greater flexibility in decision making.

As Alfred Sloan, former chairman at General Motors, once noted, "An organization does not make decisions; its function is to provide a framework, based upon established criteria, within which decisions can be fashioned in an orderly manner. Individuals make the decisions and take the responsibility for them. . . . The task of management is not to apply a formula but to decide issues on a case-by-case basis. No fixed, inflexible rule can ever be substituted for exercise of sound business judgment in the decision-making process."[16]

ORGANIZATIONS WHICH USE STRATEGIC MANAGEMENT ARE MORE EFFECTIVE

Not only are decisions harder to make but the stakes keep getting higher. As a result, several studies have presented data to support the contention that strategic management tends to provide better sources of data and more reasoned decisions than more intuitive-type decision making. Consider the research studies on the impact of strategic planning.

The Ansoff Study   This group studied ninety companies which had made important strategic decisions. It found that firms using strategic management outperformed those that did not on such financial measures as earnings growth, sales growth, earnings-per-share growth, and others.[17]

The Eastlack and McDonald Study   This study examined 211 companies, 105 of which were in the Fortune 500 largest companies. It found that the Chief Executive Officers who used strategic management concepts had the fastest growing companies.[18]

The Herold Report   This researcher conducted a seven-year study of firms using strategic planning and firms not using formal planning methods in the drug and chemical industries. Those firms utilizing strategic management techniques significantly outperformed those firms that did not use them. The study concluded that strategic planning should be considered a strong indicator of a firm's future success.[19]

The Karger and Malik Study   This study examined the impact of strategic management in 273 firms. The success of these efforts was compiled on the basis of generally accepted financial performance measurements. The results indicated improved performance of those firms employing strategic planning methods over those firms that did not. The researchers concluded that management is negligent if strategic planning is not implemented.[20]

The PIMS Study (Schoeffler, Buzzell, and Heany)   In a study of fifty-seven corporations in 620 diverse businesses, the researchers measured the effects of strategic decisions upon a company's return on investment. The Profit Impact of Market Strategies (PIMS) is a model comprising thirty-seven variables that reflect the profitability of a company in terms of its competitive position. The three most significant factors determining return on investment were market share, investment intensity, and certain company factors, such as diversification and specialization. Their data indicate that the PIMS model provides management with a very useful tool for assessing corporate and divisional objectives and strategic choices and suggests that use of such models can result in strategic benefits.[21]

The Stanford Research Institute Study   SRI studied 210 firms with higher than average growth rate in sales and earnings and compared them with 169 firms whose growth rate was significantly below average. The institute concluded that successful companies engage in broad participation in planning and the entire corporation is aware of the significance of the planning function.[22]

The Thune and House Study   Utilizing an economic performance criterion, these researchers compared companies using formal planning with those who did not. They found that the greatest success among companies that used planning occurred in rapidly changing industries and among medium-sized companies. Their study suggests a strong correlation between economic performance and the use of strategic management.[23]

They studied eighteen matched pairs of medium- to large-sized companies in the petroleum, food, drug, steel, chemical, and machinery industries. They found that the firms which initiated formal strategic planning significantly outperformed not only their own past results but those of the nonplanners on most measures of success, such as return on equity, earnings-per-share growth, and return on investments. On no measure of success did the planners underperform the nonplanners.

The Wood and LaForge Study   The authors' study of seventy large commercial banks examined the effect of strategic management on financial performance, using such measures as return on investment and increase in net income. They found that banks using strategic management systems reported higher performance measures than those not using formal planning systems.[24]

STRATEGIC MANAGEMENT PROVIDES FOR MORE DECENTRALIZED AND UNIFIED OBJECTIVES FOR THE ORGANIZATION UNITS AND MEMBERS

John DeLorean, former general manager of the Chevrolet Division, resigned from General Motors, leaving a job that paid more than $550,000 allegedly because "GM's sheer size had led to a mind-dulling bureaucracy leaving no room for an individualist."[25] In this case, GM lost a valuable individual because top management had become too rigid in its structure and methods of operation. It failed to perceive the need for allowing individuals to fulfill personal objectives as well as attaining company goals. The loss of key managers can greatly impact on the effectiveness of an organization and alter its ability to attract and develop new leadership.

STRATEGIC MANAGEMENT IS WIDELY PRACTICED IN INDUSTRY AND GOVERNMENT

The concepts which you will be learning in strategic management are being used more extensively at all levels by large, medium-sized, and even by more sophisticated small businesses.[26]

When Richard B. Madden took over in 1970 as president and chief executive officer, Potlatch was floundering badly. The economy was in the grip of a recession, and Potlatch was trailing its competitors with an 83 percent decline in profits. New top managers commonly approach this type of situation with an eye toward reorganization and restaffing. Madden chose to do things differently. Instead of shaking up Potlatch's management team, he decided to reform it. His reform program consisted of comprehensive training in sophisticated strategic planning. As Potlatch's top managers became better strategic planners, the situation began to improve and the firm's return on investment went from unsatisfactory to excellent. Strategic planning produced handsome returns for Potlatch.[27]

Strategic management allows top executives to adapt to changes, to innovate in time to take advantage of new opportunities, and to reduce risk because of anticipated threats. Thomas H. Naylor (Duke University) suggests that nearly 2,000 firms in the United States, Canada, and Mexico are using or developing some form of corporate planning model.

WHY STUDY STRATEGIC MANAGEMENT?

Even though strategic management deals with the generalist or top management view of the organization, it is still of value for all of us.

AT LOWER LEVELS

First, the decision skills and analytical techniques that you will develop are just as useful at lower levels of an organization. For example, a department store buyer must make decisions, allocate resources, etc., just as a top manager does. When Raymond F. Good took over the Consumer Products Group Managership at Pillsbury Company, he immediately instituted a strategic management system. The outcome was a strategic game plan enabling his product group to move more aggressively into convenience food lines.[28] As these examples suggest, strategic concepts are useful at many levels of the organization.

FOR SMALL BUSINESS

Second, some of you may end up managing your own smaller business and will be applying the same strategic concepts, although on a smaller scale. Nolan K. Bushnell, for example, a 33-year-old computer whiz, turned an idea for a video ping-pong game into his own company, Atari, Inc. Three years after graduating from the University of Utah, Bushnell founded his company with $250 from a savings account in 1971. In 1976 he sold Atari, Inc., for $28 million.[29] So smaller businesses also offer an opportunity for application of strategic management concepts. Although the basic functions of small and large companies are essentially the same, the larger the organization, the greater the need for strategic management and planning.

NONPROFIT SECTOR

Third, you may also be applying these strategic concepts in the public or not-for-profit sector. Most of the fundamental approaches, methods, and procedures of corporate management are directly applicable to the public sector. There are, of course, also differences. But in general, there is a growing trend to make use of strategic planning and budgeting concepts in the public management area. Although there is a greater amount of interaction between public and private, there is disagreement over whether the two sectors should be managed differently. There is certainly evidence to suggest that they have a large number of managerial problems and characteristics in common.

YOUR OWN CAREER

And finally, it is possible to use these same approaches to managing your own career or personal resources. You will very likely be making a series of strategic decisions about your life, career, and personal finances. What kind of job do you want and in what career field? Will you want to pursue a graduate degree? If so, what is the return on investment of an MBA? Questions like these are not unlike the strategic choices a firm must make.

Most of you are in continual contact with a large number of organizations: schools, businesses, churches, hospitals and governmental departments. All of them need to be well managed in order to be effectivo. Thus, strategic management is an important, exciting and challenging field, and one that offers applications and rewards in numerous areas of activity and responsibility.

MANAGING CHANGE

Today executives manage in a changing and dynamic environment. This fact has important implications for organizations and strategic managers. Preparing managers to cope with today's accelerating rate of change is the central concern of this book. The modern manager must not only be flexible and adaptive in a changing environment but also be able to diagnose problems, make strategic decisions, and implement strategic plans.

Because change is occurring so rapidly, this puts more pressure on top management. The strategic decisions are harder to make, and the stakes keep getting higher. Strategic management provides one way for organizations to become more effective in adapting to these changes.

Today's managers exist in shifting organizational structures and can be the central force in initiating strategic direction and establishing the means for adaptation. Most organizations strive to be creative, efficient, and highly competitive, maintaining a leading edge in their respective fields rather than following trends set by others. Effective strategic planning is vital to the continuing self-renewal and ultimate survival of the organization. The manager must recognize when changes are occurring in the external environment and possess the necessary competence to bring about changes in strategy when it is needed.

THE OBJECTIVES OF THE POLICY STRATEGY COURSE

This book introduces the practicing manager and the student to the field of strategic management and policy. Its purpose is twofold: first, to create an awareness of the changing environmental forces confronting the strategic manager; and second, to provide a foundation of knowledge and skills for those who will be pursuing a career in management.

The policy course has a number of objectives involving learning about strategic decision making at the top management level. These involve learning how to deal with business and organizational problems in a systematic way. These objectives include:

1   An understanding of the basic concepts of strategy and policy.

2   An opportunity for the integration of functional areas of business.

3   An increased ability to analyze facts and logically identify critical factors.

4   An increased ability to diagnose problem situations.

5   An increased decision-making ability and skill and practice at making strategic decisions.

6   Increased communication and presentation skills.

7   Development of a strategic management style.

THE PLAN OF THE BOOK

Strategic management is a fundamental process for solving complex organizational problems. The central focus of this book involves the perspective of the top manager and his role in strategic planning and decision making.

THE STRATEGIC MODEL

Earlier a strategic management model was presented in Figure 1.3. The organization of this text follows the flow of this *strategic management model,* with each segment building on the earlier foundations.

In Chapter One, we examine the basic mission of the firm and present an overview of the strategic management process. The strategic decision maker and the importance of this role is presented in Chapter Two.

In Chapter Three, we discuss the formulation of goals and objectives giving direction to the organization and serving as a means for channeling multiple interests into a unified effort.

The open system perspective is presented in terms of the analysis of internal subsystem capabilities and of external opportunities and threats in Chapter Four.

In Chapters Five and Six, we deal with the generation of strategic alternatives, of how to develop a range of possible strategies that might be followed.

The major techniques for comparing and evaluating these alternative strategies will be discussed in Chapter Seven.

In Chapter Eight, we focus on the strategic decision: deciding which course of action will be chosen from all available alternatives.

After the decision, the strategy must be implemented. Several important factors involved in the implementation of the strategy, including organization structure and climate, are presented in Chapters Nine and Ten.

In Chapter Eleven, the interface between strategic implementation and external systems, both governmental and international, are discussed.

Finally in Chapter Twelve, we present the final stage of the strategic process: the review and evaluation of the strategy. Here we ask, did the strategy work as planned?

BRINGING MANAGEMENT TO LIFE

The goal of the book is to help you as a manager develop an improved way of thinking about problems and form a broader point of view. Throughout the book the emphasis is on strategic practices, analysis, and theory, rather than on description and lists of advantages and disadvantages. The aim of the policy course is the stimulation of thought processes rather than the memorization of answers. Throughout the text there is an emphasis on new techniques and ideas that hold promise for the future development of strategic management rather than following the inadequate and unsystematic methods often used in the past.

The first chapter has presented an overview of the strategic management process. The remainder of the book examines each element of the strategic process. Chapter Two deals with the importance of strategy making in the strategy process, and the following chapters deal with the analysis of environment, developing alternatives, making the strategic decision, and implementing of the strategy.

In summary, this book is about strategic management. It attempts to bring this field and the job of the manager into sharper focus for the reader. The emphasis throughout the book is on the application of systematic management processes to achieve optimal performance in organizations.

MANAGERIAL IMPLICATIONS

This chapter has developed the basic concepts of strategic management. At ITT, for example, the overall strategic planning of the company has caused it to change directions as economic conditions have changed. ITT, under Geneen, has become a giant in its field because of good strategic management systems. The most important strategic questions are "What, if . . ?" questions when making decisions, because strategic decisions directly impact on the future effectiveness and results of the organization.

THE STATE OF THE ART

In this text, we present the field of management strategy and policy—both theory and practice. The material has been selected to provide you with most of what is known at this time about strategic management: the current state of the art.

The text is intended to assist the participant, manager, and student in understanding the process and techniques of strategic management, and it follows a movement from the more basic elements to the more complex. The topic coverage is shown in Figure 1.3 (see p. 10).

STRATEGIC IMPLICATIONS

Keystone   Strategic management is the keystone of the critical management function. All other organizational activities and functions are derived from strategic management.

Changing Environment   Strategic planning is becoming increasingly important because of the rapidly changing environment that managers must face. Strategic planning provides the means for anticipating the future and defining new strategic directions.

Implementing Mission   The strategic management process offers a series of stages that translates the basic mission into objectives, strategy, plans, and policy which are then implemented to achieve stated goals.

Basic Objectives   Basic objectives of the organization include profitability, opportunity, and efficiency.

Manager's Performance   The manager's performance is based on achieving strategic objectives: the bottom line.

Organizational Strategies   Organizational strategies are the general approaches that are selected as a means to achieve the overall objectives.

Effectiveness   There is a direct relationship between strategic management and the effectiveness of the organization.

The purpose of this book is to help you in understanding how and why strategic management is used and to make you a more effective manager. It is aimed at making the transition from the classroom to the "real world" by allowing you an opportunity to develop your own strategic management process.

REVIEW QUESTIONS

1 Define strategic management.

2 What are the major elements of the strategic management process?

3 As discussed in the Chapter, Boeing risked $3 billion in developing its new series of planes (757, 767). Use the strategic management model to consider some of the important factors Boeing should have analyzed prior to this decision.

4 What is the bottom line? How would you measure performance?

5 What objectives do you feel are important for the business policy course?

PERSONAL OBJECTIVES

Outside of class list some of the specific objectives and expectations you have for this class. These objectives should describe what you will be able to do or demonstrate at the end of this course.

1. _____
   _____

2. _____
   _____

3. _____
   _____

4. _____
   _____

ENDNOTES

1 Based upon articles: Jack B. Weiner, "ITT Can Profit as Programmed?" *Dun's Review,* November 1965, 39–41, 103–104, 106; "ITT Takes the Profit Path to Change," *Business Week,* May 9, 1970.

2 For further discussion of topic, see William E. Glueck, *Business Policy and Strategic Management* (New York: McGraw-Hill, 1980); George A. Steiner and John B. Miner, *Management Policy and Strategy: Text, Readings, and Cases* (New York: Macmillan, 1977); Hugo E. R. Uyterhoeven, Robert W. Ackerman, and John W. Rosenblum, *Strategy and Organization: Text and Cases in General Management* (Homewood, Ill.: Irwin, 1973); and Arthur A. Thompson, Jr., and A. J. Strickland, III, *Strategy and Policy: Concepts and Cases* (Dallas, Texas: Business Publications, 1978).

3 Various authors suggest different levels. For example, J. Thomas Cannon refers to result strategy, action strategy, and commitment strategy in *Business Strategy and Policy* (New York: Harcourt, Brace and World, 1968), figure 2. McNichols classifies strategies as root strategy, operating strategy, organizational control strategy, and recovery strategy in *Policy Making and Executive Action,*

New York: McGraw-Hill, 1977) pp. 11–13. Hofer and Schendel suggest three levels of strategies—corporate strategy, business strategy, and functional area strategy—in *Strategy Formulation: Analytical Concepts* (St. Paul, Minn.: West, 1978).

4   Richard F. Vancil, "Strategy Formulation in Complex Organizations," *Sloan Management Review,* Winter 1976, 1–18.

5   "Making the Concept Fit a Company's Needs" *Business Week,* Mar. 27, 1978, 104–9.

6   "ITT Takes the Profit Path."

7   Ibid.

8   "Making the Concept Fit a Company's Needs," 105, and "Eaton: Poised for Profits," *Business Week,* June 8, 1981, 133.

9   "Hewlett-Packard: Where Slower Growth is Smarter Management" *Business Week,* June 9, 1975, 50–54, 56, 59.

10   "Alaskan Oil—or Bust," *Fortune,* August 1977, 173.

11   "The Way I Make My Numbers," *Forbes,* Feb. 15, 1972, 26.

12   Bruce Kirchhoff and Judith Kirchhoff, "Empirical Assessment of the Strategy/Tactics Dilemma," *Academy of Management Proceedings,* 1980, 7.

13   Boston Consulting Group, *Perspectives on Experience,* Boston: The Boston Consulting Group, 1968.

14   "Behind the Snafu at Singer," *Fortune,* Nov. 5, 1979, 76–78, 80.

15   See "Getting by Without a Tin Cup," *Fortune,* Dec. 31, 1979, 13, and "Getting in Trim," *Wall Street Journal,* Jan. 21, 1980, 1.

16   A. Sloan, *My Years at General Motors* (New York: Doubleday, 1964), p. 443.

17   H. Igor Ansoff et al., *Acquisition Behavior of U.S. Manufacturing Firms,* 1946–65 (Nashville, Tenn.: Vanderbilt University Press, 1971).

18   Joseph Eastlack, Jr., and Philip McDonald: "CEO's Role in Corporate Growth," *Harvard Business Review,* May–June 1970, 150–63.

19   David Herold, "Long Range Planning and Organizational Performance: A Cross Validation Study," *Academy of Management Review,* March 1972, 91–102.

20   Delmar Karger, and Zafar Malik: "Long Range Planning and Organizational Performance," *Long Range Planning,* December 1975.

21   Sidney Schoeffler et al. "Impact of Strategic Planning on Profit Performance," *Harvard Business Review,* March–April 1974, 137–45.

22   Stanford Research Institute: as reported in "Why Companies Grow," *Nation's Business,* November 1957, 80–82, 84–86.

23   Stanley Thune and Robert House, "Where Long Range Planning Pays Off," *Business Horizons,* August 1970, 81–87.

24   D. Robley Wood, Jr., and R. Lawrence LaForge, "The Impact of Comprehensive Planning on Financial Performance," *Academy of Management Journal,* 22, no. 3 (1979), 516–26.

25   Rush Loving, Jr., "The Automobile Industry Has Lost Its Masculinity," *Fortune,* September 1973, 187–91.

26   See Parmand Kumar, "Long Range Planning Practices by U.S. Companies," *Long Range Planning,* January/February 1978, pp. 31–38; also Thomas Naylor and Daniel Gattis, "Corporate Planning Models," *California Management Review,* 18, no. 4 (Summer 1976), 69–78.

27   "At Potlatch, Nothing Happens Without a Plan," *Business Week,* November 10, 1975, 129–31, 133, 134.

28   "A New Face Jolts Pillsbury," *Business Week,* May 2, 1977, 92, 97.

29   "Atari Sells Self to Survive Success," *Business Week,* November 15, 1976.

CHAPTER

2

The successful organization has one major attribute that sets it apart from unsuccessful organizations: dynamic and effective leadership.

Paul Hersey and Kenneth Blanchard
Management and Organizational Behavior, 2nd ed.
(Englewood Cliffs, N.J.: Prentice-Hall, 1972).

The Strategic Decision Makers

R.T.C. LIBRARY, LETTERKENNY

CHAPTER OBJECTIVES

Upon completion of this chapter, you will be able to:

☐ *Demonstrate an understanding of strategic decision making techniques.*

☐ *Recognize the impact of managerial values and decision styles on strategy.*

☐ *Identify your own executive style and assess its impact upon others.*

CREATIVE TENSION IN A GROWTH COMPANY[1]

Wilfred J. Corrigan

"Steering his sleek, silver $14,000 Jensen Interceptor into his reserved parking stall at Fairchild Camera & Instrument Corp., in Mountain View, California, Wilfred J. Corrigan has definitely 'arrived.' At 37, he is president and chief executive of a $385-million-a-year company, the third largest in the semiconductor industry behind only Texas Instruments, Inc., and Motorola, Inc." In 1979 the company was getting clobbered in its digital watch division to the tune of a $24.5-million pre-tax loss. Fairchild had what looked like a turn-round in 1973–74 but never quite recovered from the recession in semiconductor sales, largely because of the digital watch problems. But Corrigan is now optimistic: "We have now gotten rid of a bunch of subcritical businesses and are going to refocus on the high technology areas," he commented. But he has made such promises ever since he became president in 1974. As chief executive, Corrigan is responsible for defining what business the firm is in and matching the company's resources with the emerging product and market opportunities. He works, on the average, about a 60–hour week and his annual salary including bonuses comes to a reported $175,000. "Once you are through the middle-management level and as your tax base goes up," says Corrigan, "material rewards become less of a driving factor." Far more important to this supremely self-confident chief executive is running a growth company and "*managing change.*"

But for Fairchild the problems remain. Corrigan needs to move quickly into the MOS (metal-oxide-silicon) product area where technology is now shifting.

A TOUGH STYLE

Every chief executive officer (CEO) has his own particular managerial style which is most effective in accomplishing organizational goals. Corrigan, for example, believes in "*creative tension,*" a state in which workers are under enough pressure to get their jobs done but not so much that it panics them. "I want to create enough tension to keep the adrenalin flowing, but I don't want to overdo it," says Corrigan. Often the job of the CEO requires the making of tough or unpopular decisions, but decisions which must be made. One former division vice president claims that Corrigan is not only bright and gutsy but also *"very calculating and ambitiously ruthless—he is effective in cutting costs and people, but there is ice water in his veins."* Says vice president Thomas A. Longo: "Wilf makes sure people don't get comfortable in their jobs."[2]

THE MANAGERIAL IMPACT

The job of the CEO of a major organization is not an easy one. There have been many success stories of managers who have rescued seriously troubled companies and led them to a program of consistent growth. However, for every manager who becomes a winner, there are probably just as many who fail to turn their company around or even those who guide them from a leading position to a losing one. For when we talk about organizational strategy we are really talking about the managers who make the strategic decisions.

MANAGERIAL STYLE AT FIRST CHICAGO

Business Week sums up the relationship between strategy and style in the recent appointment of a new CEO at First Chicago Corp. "Barry F. Sullivan could well credit his style with giving him 'the best job in banking today.' That job—chairman and chief executive at First Chicago Corp., the holding company for First National Bank of Chicago—which Sullivan assumed on July 28, 1980, distinctly needed a change of style from that of Sullivan's predecessor, A. Robert Abboud. When the bank's board fired Abboud after his five-year reign, the reasons centered on the domineering and abrasive style that made Abboud banking's most controversial executive and that produced endless management turmoil and turnover. Sullivan, a well-liked executive vice president of Chase Manhattan Corp., has been deemed to have the 'people skills' that Abboud lacked."[3]

DIFFERENCES IN ENVIRONMENT

There are literally thousands of organizations in the United States, large and small, public and private, yet no two management systems are exactly alike. Each organization has its own unique techniques and approaches, its own strong and soft spots, and its own values and traditions. Each organization also has its own culture and tradition. The corporate culture includes ways of behaving, solving problems, and making decisions, functions that influence strategy and operations. Therefore, the manager must recognize that a given strategy or managerial style may not fit in all situations. As a result, either the strategy or the culture must be changed. These differing organizational environments and cultures each require differing managerial styles and approaches.

DIFFERENCES IN INDIVIDUALS

Managers' values and management styles also have great variations. Clearly the personal style of any one manager may differ greatly from that of another. Managers emerge from differing backgrounds, with various skills and a unique set of values. Yet each manager's individual style and values influence the nature of the strategic decision process. Currently, it is generally recognized that social values are rapidly changing. A manager who grew up in the 1920s or 1930s (a person in the 50- to 60-age group now moving into top management) may have a distinctly different value system from one who grew up in the 1960s era.

Morris Massey, of the University of Colorado, proposed that people are "*value programmed*" during their early years; therefore, there is a "*value gap*" between people who acquire their values during different time periods. For example, those now in top management were shaped by the value forces of the Depression and World War II (including thrift, patriotism, etc.). An entirely different set of forces influenced the values of those growing up in the hard rock, drug and antiwar background of the 1960s.

The individual values and style of the top management can greatly influence strategy and the way it is developed within the organization.

MANAGERIAL STYLE AND STRATEGY

The strategic manager's job, however, is extremely complex. How managers choose to deal with the rapidly changing and uncertain decisions which confront them is basically a matter of their management style. Corrigan, it may be noted, believes in "creative tension", and it is said he has the "uncanny ability to make the right decisions." These decisions, then, which determine the strategic direction for the organization are the most critical decisions with which managers are faced. Other managers, with different styles, will not necessarily make the same strategic choices as Corrigan would. These differences in managerial styles are a critical factor in the strategic process because they exert a significant and fundamental influence in strategy and policy formation.

The top manager must first be able to identify a gap between the current situation and some desired condition. Strategies are then aimed at improving effectiveness, efficiency, and participant well-being. Too often short-run, expedient programs, aimed solely at cost savings, are introduced. Such programs often have unintended dysfunctional effects on participant satisfaction and the long-term goals of the organization. The manager, then, has an impact on organization strategy by identifying differences between "*where it is*" and "*where it would like to be,*" and in designing and implementing appropriate strategic plans.

Top managers, then, are those in charge of the organization and responsible for the design and development of strategic direction for the firm. These managers must ensure that the organization produces its products and services efficiently. They must also design and maintain the stability and continuity of operations, as well as adapt its strategy to an ever-changing environment. The top managers also ensure that the results of these moves of the game plan meet the needs of those persons who own and control it: the stockholders, the board, etc. In this sense, the top manager's role is analogous to the conductor of a symphony orchestra, attempting to integrate and coordinate many differing factors into a synchronized musical performance. To examine this complex set of interacting forces, we will look at three major elements in the following sections: managerial tasks, managerial roles, and managerial styles.

THE MANAGER AS STRATEGIST

The most successful organizations in the years ahead will be the ones that best match their competitive strengths to the changing demands of the environment. The competitive environment which an organization must deal with varies as a function of the particular organization and the type of industry. Wilf Corrigan of Fairchild, for example, is a relatively young manager in the relatively dynamic electronics industry. One central factor in the success of strategic decision making, then, is the role of the manager. The manager is responsible for making strategic decisions and then for making the strategy work. This job involves a number of related activities.

SETTING ORGANIZATIONAL OBJECTIVES

The manager points out the basic directions and objectives of the organization. The objectives set the standard of performance for the organization and point at the areas of key activity. The manager defines the results that must be achieved. Corrigan, for example, sets the peformance goals for the MOS divisions.

DEVELOPING AND ALLOCATING INTERNAL RESOURCES

The organization's strategic objectives, then, form a basis for the development and allocation of internal resources. Managers like Corrigan must use their leadership to develop the management, financial, and technical resources of the organization, or as Corrigan has put it, inject a "creative tension," or pressure toward improvement. Similarly, the manager determines and sets priorities. What results do we want to achieve? What objectives are most critical? And what percentage of our total efforts should be allocated to each of our various objectives?

INTEGRATING STRATEGIC PLANS

Some organizations specialize in narrow and distinct fields, while others engage in a variety of products and businesses. The position of the general manager is to tie those multiple activities together into a coherent, comprehensive strategy and an integrated strategic plan. Corrigan spent fully a quarter of his time in financial and planning meetings doing just this.

CONTROLLING EFFECTIVE PERFORMANCE

One basic part of the CEO's job is measuring and controlling performance. It is not enough to set forth a strategic plan. The manager must also know where the organization is in terms of accomplishing its strategic plan. At ITT, Harold Geneen held monthly meetings with his top management team to review the status of plans on a product-by-product basis. At Fairchild, Wilf Corrigan held monthly review meetings for each of the eleven divisions, each product line, and each individual product. The strategic manager is involved in setting objectives, assigning responsibility for results, and measuring performance toward the strategic plan.

INFLUENCING MANAGERIAL STYLE

It is the CEO who sets the tone for managerial style throughout the organization. The CEO develops a certain style of working with others on his management team, and this filters down through the organization. This interpersonal model sets the degree to which leadership style is authoritative or collaborative. The degree of toughness or laxity, and the degree of delegation to subordinates all flows from the top. "If Corrigan doesn't see results in 18 months, he assumes it must be the guy who's running it," says a Fairchild manager.[4]

This is important strategically in terms of commitment toward organizational goals. At Fairchild, Corrigan felt he was adept at delegating authority without abandoning it. The CEO must also gain the support of organization members, and make sure that everyone has a complete understanding of the basic strategic thrust of the organization. If this is not done, organizational elements may be working at cross purposes, or failing to place the same priority on various projects, leading to ineffective strategic performance.

The CEO, by individual style, represents the managerial moral, ethical, and personal behavior that is valued in the organization. Thus, the managerial style of the CEO influences the organization's climate and interrelationships in all the interdependent activities that must be integrated into the organization's strategy.

DEVELOPING POLICY AND PROCEDURE

Fairchild's Corrigan developed certain ideas about how a strategy should be implemented, and those ideas carry on down through the organization in the form of policies and procedures. The intent of the organization policy is to provide automatic decision guidelines for how certain problems should be handled. The policy and procedures set by top management promote uniformity and continuity of behavior and decisions throughout the organization. Corrigan could not possibly handle every problem or every decision that arose in his eleven divisions, or each of the numerous product lines. The policy, however, presents guidelines for how managers should deal with these problems and is necessary for internal efficiency.

THE STRATEGY MAKERS

Who makes the strategic decisions for an organization? Three groups of individuals are generally involved in the strategic decision making of most organizations: the top manager (CEO) or top management team; the board of directors; and the corporate planning group.[5]

While the board of directors has ultimate authority, as indicated in Figure 2.1, the CEO (and top management team, who are often members of the board) plays a very central role, and the corporate planning group is usually responsible for the strategic plan itself. Consequently, each of these groups has some influence on corporate decision making. Top management, in most cases the president, gives final approval to the strategic plans. However, after this approval, the complete program is usually placed in broad outline before the board of directors. A financial plan is submitted to the board stating what management intends to accomplish, and what the probable outcome will be. The president points out that the plan is based on certain economic forecasts regarding the future. The presentation of the strategic program to the board is something of a formality, but the board members must understand and approve of its major aspects.

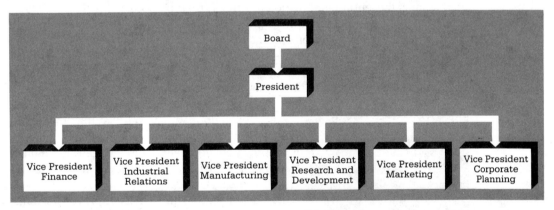

FIGURE 2.1
The Organization Chart

THE TEAM AT THE TOP

The top management team of a firm includes those corporate managers who are responsible for the success of the organization. The chief executive (who may also be chairman of the board) is responsible for the performance of the organization.[6] It is the CEOs, the Geneens and Corrigans, who make the strategic decisions in most organizations, and this is what they get paid for (usually, very handsomely). Strategic management would not be effective without the involvement and leadership of the CEO. The job also involves tremendous pressures. Almost every strategic decision involves conflicting courses of action and options. Each of the options has some relative degree of risk and some potential rates of return. The selection of strategy is the job of the CEO.[7]

STRATEGIC DECISIONS AT EXXON

At Exxon Corporation (number one in the *Fortune* 500), chairman and CEO Clifton C. Garvin and the seven members of the executive committee meet monthly to make the major strategic decisions.

The room is half the size of a tennis court, lined in uninterrupted walnut and carpeted in quiet luxury. The table is long and tapered, pieced from six massive sections of Indian laurel. The eight men who sit in the swivel chairs around it are a blur of blue, gray, and tan suits. They are here to make what for them is a routine decision involving the expenditure of several hundred million dollars. They run the Exxon Corp., the biggest industrial concern in the world.[8]

The committee listens to presentations by key managers on why Exxon should invest heavily in a new petrochemical plant, make a major acquisition, or invest in a research project. The managers show slides and charts with graphs, ratios, and diagrams presenting information to support their proposals.

In theory, the ultimate power of a corporation lies with its board of directors. In the case of Exxon, the board consists of these eight men, who are employees, and the ten men and one woman who are outside directors. It meets once a month to review the company's activities. But it is the eight men around this table, members of what is known as the management committee, who really rule Exxon.[9]

Clifton C. Garvin, Jr.

The committee also reviews and evaluates performance to see that the firm is profitable and in a broader sense is adapting to its changing environment. At Exxon, they put a great deal of emphasis upon developing managerial talent—the Exxon man—a manager who has repeatedly demonstrated the ability to solve problems, make decisions, and manage resources effectively.

At the top is Clifton Garvin, the epitome of the Exxon man. A chemical engineer by training, the 58-year-old executive has spent his entire professional life with the company, zigzagging his way up through the system—managing a refinery, holding down headquarters staff jobs, running the company's chemical business. He got the top post in 1975. A gruff but personable sort who speaks his mind, Garvin is nonetheless a consummate pragmatist.[10]

INITIATIVES OF THE CEO

Invariably the top management team and the CEO are the executives at the highest level who are responsible for the survival and success of the organization. They significantly influence the major strategic direction of the firm. The chief executive must initiate several strategic actions.

The CEO is responsible for creating a strategic planning system   The management review which Geneen implemented so successfully at ITT is one example of such a system.

The CEO must assess the degree of risk which is acceptable   Singer Company, under Donald Kircher, underwent an overly ambitious program of acquisition, which resulted in large losses to the corporation and led to his replacement as CEO.[11] On the other hand, an overly cautious strategy may allow competitors to take over market share.

The CEO decides in which direction the corporation will move   When Roy Ash took over as CEO of Addressograph-Multigraph (now AM International), his first move was to strengthen the product mix by adding new electronic products while weeding out the older mechanical lines which were past maturity.

The CEO is responsible for results   To the CEO goes the glory and rewards when the strategic decisions are successful, such as Geneen's at ITT, but it is also the CEO's neck if the strategy fails. Jonathan Scott of A & P was hired to turn around the sliding fortunes of the giant food retailer, but his retrenchment strategy of closing unprofitable stores did not halt the decline of A & P. So, Scott is gone: replaced by another CEO, who will again try to design a strategy for change.[12]

UNSUCCESSFUL STRATEGIC APPROACHES

There are also unsuccessful strategic moves. Danny Miller (of McGill University) set forth several dysfunctional approaches, including:

- The firm fails when a power-hoarding strategist creates overambitious, incautious strategies which ignore environmental signals. This strategist has not developed adequate strategic management systems.

- The firm fails when power-hoarding strategists refuse to change the strategy which was successful in the past. Again the fault is this strategist does not accept advice from subordinates or search the environment himself.

- The firm fails when the chief strategist creates no strategy. This strategist expects the firm to run itself without a strategy.

- The firm fails because the strategist creates an overambitious strategy given the weakened resource base of the firm. In this case, the strategist has not adequately analyzed his strategic advantages.[13]

WELCOME TO THE CLUB

The board of directors in business and other institutions is responsible to the stockholders or constituencies of the organization. It hires the CEO, rewards effective strategy, and fires the CEO if the strategy doesn't work. However, there have been many studies, including the work of Myles L. Mace (Professor Emeritus, Harvard Business School), that have questioned the true authority of the board, suggesting that it often rubber stamps management's decisions.[14] Even so, the board has important functions.

THE BOARD'S FUNCTIONS

Hiring, rewarding, and replacing the CEO   The major responsibility of the board is to ensure that the stockholders' interests are being protected. The actual strategic operation of the organization is in the hands of the CEO. At Johns-Manville, sales grew slowly at an average annual rate of 4 percent between 1950 and 1970, lower than the nation's GNP. In a word, the company was stagnant. As a result, Richard Goodwin was hired by the Board to get JM moving. But five years later, Mr. Goodwin became involved in some conflicts with the Board and he was asked to resign.[15]

Approving major decisions   The major strategic and financial decisions are generally approved by the board. At Scovill Mfg. Co., for example, Malcolm Baldridge, the CEO, wanted to sell off the company's copper interests and move into consumer products. Because it was a major decision, he had to sell this to the Board which approved this strategy.[16]

Protecting financial integrity   The board oversees operations and guards against actions that may place the company in jeopardy. One of the criticisms of the board of directors is that it often fails to do so. For example, at Singer, after a major acquisition program was approved under one CEO, another CEO was hired to carry out a strategy of selling off these same acquisitions.

Guarding against unethical actions by the CEO   The board of directors must exert control over the ethics of the company; several CEOs have been forced to resign because of this. In one example, corporate bribery involved Lockheed's payment of over $9 million in bribes in connection with overseas sales. This resulted in the resignation of key corporate executives.[17] Another example was Eberhard Faber Inc. (pencil manufacturer), where the president, Mr. Faber, wanted to enter into a joint interest agreement with a subsidiary in a foreign country. However, the Board (including his own mother) turned this venture down because of possible unethical practices by the foreign subsidiary. This resulted in the company losing a profitable strategic move, but also avoiding possible ethical problems.[18]

A changing role   While in the past the board of directors may not have been actively involved in strategic management, William R. Boulton (of the University of

Georgia) suggests that current problems are leading to a more active role for board members, including increasing involvement in business strategy issues.[19]

There is evidence that a change is taking place, especially in corporations where stock is widely held. The forces underlying this change are both legal challenges by stockholders and social reform movements which deal with civil rights, women's rights, the ecology, nuclear power, questionable payments, etc., all of which have added pressure on the duties of the board members.

THE CORPORATE PLANNERS

Most large organizations now use corporate planning staffs to coordinate the strategic function. George A. Steiner (UCLA Business School professor) suggests there will be an increasing use of corporate planners as professionals who are responsible for the development and integration of company-wide strategic plans.[20] The corporate planners may consist of an individual, a small group, or, as in the case of General Electric, there may be as many as 100 planners involved in handling this function. These individuals are staff specialists trained in planning techniques, and they include economists, statisticians, computer modeling experts, and futurists who provide direction and support for overall planning efforts. The planners are most active in assessing the firm's capabilities, analyzing environmental forces, and generating strategic alternatives. However, there is evidence indicating that planners seldom take an active role in the actual strategic decision.[21]

THE EXTENT OF PLANNING

In 1974, Thomas H. Naylor (of Social Systems, Inc.) conducted a survey of 1,880 companies to determine the use of corporate planning models. Out of 346 corporations who returned responses, 73 percent reported using some form of strategic planning model, and another 15 percent indicated the intention to develop such a model.[22]

One major difference seems to be the emphasis placed on contingency planning. Where before a company would have one master strategic plan, now companies often have five or more separate tracks plotted to meet a variety of possible future conditions. These strategic plans are aimed at accommodating a wider divergence of possible economic environments.

THE ROLE OF THE PLANNER

Corporate planners have important roles and functions to perform.[23]

Developing a framework for strategic planning and providing the data base   The corporate planning group usually designs the strategic information system. This activity provides the information and forecasts, creates planning procedures, and integrates the multiplicity of plans into a single plan.

Identifying and evaluating new product and market opportunities   The time frame for planning has telescoped. The life cycle of a product is much shorter, yet the time frame for new product research and development is growing. Consequently, the planning staff must keep tabs on new market trends.

Monitoring, reviewing, and revising the strategic plan   Companies now have to revise plans more frequently because of unpredictable and changing conditions. Many companies have a dynamic five-year plan, which is "rolled over" each month.

Forecasting new economic conditions and trends   Many of the large companies subscribe to national economic forecasting services, or run their own econometric models including pricing, cost, supply, and demand factors.

Developing contingency plans and alternate scenarios   Rather than developing only a single strategic plan, many firms now set up multiple contingency plans.

Predicting the uncertain future   Many companies have futurists, or groups of intuitive thinkers, who try to predict long-range social forces which may have an impact on the business, such as changing consumer preferences, demographic changes, energy shortages, etc.

In summary, then, three groups are involved in strategic decision making: the corporate planner in an advising and coordinating role; the board of directors, in overseeing and approving major decisions; and the top management team who make most of the key strategic decisions. At General Electric, for example, the final decisions are made by the corporate policy committee, made up of the chairman, three vice chairmen, five senior vice presidents, and the vice president for finance.

THE MANAGERIAL ROLE

There have been a number of studies which have examined what managers actually do and how they spend their time. Wilf Corrigan of Fairchild, for example, found that he was becoming a "workaholic," so he adjusted his schedule to spend all weekends with his family. It has been said of Harold Geneen that his job was his family. He reportedly spent some eighty hours a week on the job, often calling people at all hours of the day or night. Henry Mintzberg studied the role of chief executive and found several basic roles which are shown in Figure 2.2.[24]

THE INTERPERSONAL ROLE

In the interpersonal role, the manager builds a network of interpersonal contacts and communication links. Corrigan, for example, performs many roles requiring interpersonal interaction, acting as figurehead, as leader, and in a liaison role. At the strategic level, the manager's liaison contacts are made outside of the organization, with external systems. Corrigan also represents Fairchild to external systems including government, industry, etc.—a boundary spanning role.

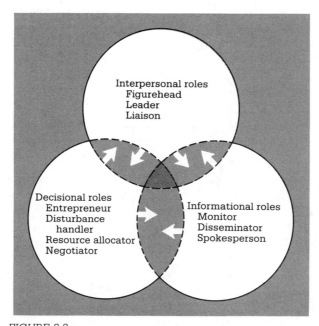

FIGURE 2.2
The Role of the Manager

SOURCE: Copyright © 1975 by the President and Fellows of Harvard College; all rights reserved. Reprinted by permission of the Harvard Business Review. "The Manager's Job" by H. Mintzberg, July-August 1975, 49–61.

THE INFORMATIONAL ROLE

In the informational role, the manager is acting as an information center: as a focal point for the receiving and sending of information among units and levels. This role involves processing information. At his monthly meetings, Wilf Corrigan gathers and disseminates information throughout the organization; he is acting as a nerve center for communications. At the strategic level, much of the information gathering is derived from outside sources and is aimed at attempting to anticipate possible effects other forces may have on the internal strategy and operations.

THE DECISIONAL ROLE

Finally, the third managerial role, decisional, involves the decision-making activities of the manager. As noted, it has been said of Wilf Corrigan: "He has the uncanny ability to make the right decisions." He sets goals, solves problems, and makes decisions. At the strategic level, the manager must solve problems, handle conflicts, and allocate resources among alternative, often competing demands, thus determining the firm's long range direction.

     In summary, the top manager's job is complex and stressful. It is estimated that from 60 to 80 percent of a top manager's time is spent in communicating, so communication skills are very important. And some 60 to 70 percent of a manager's job involves meetings, both scheduled and unscheduled. As a result, the ability to operate effectively and make decisions in a group setting is also extremely important to the manager. In terms of the managerial roles which are used, the variation depends upon the individual manager, the managerial style, and the varying situations in which he and his team are placed.

THE MANAGERIAL STYLES

One of the most critical factors in organization strategy is the managerial style of the CEO. This sets the tone for the whole organization and influences the communication, decision making, and leadership patterns of the entire system.

Earlier, we have seen the impact that the style of Harold Geneen had on ITT and that of Wilf Corrigan on Fairchild. Robert Abboud was brought aboard as chairman at First Chicago to correct problems which had emerged from banking practices in the early 1960s. He was trying to correct the bank's situation regarding ill-advised loan positions without sufficient collateral. In correcting these problems at First Chicago, Robert Abboud reportedly emphasized a very domineering, abrasive, and highly centralized style which had an impact on the firm's market. First Chicago will be unable to recapture its lost market share until the new chairman rebuilds the bank's demoralized and depleted management ranks. In certain areas, First Chicago's turnover has been so massive that some customers believe that this is largely responsible for lost corporate business.[25]

Clearly, the style and approach of one manager may vary widely from that of another. How any particular manager handles this role depends in part on the conditions of the job and in part on the personality of the individual. One manager may be very decisive, aggressive, and fast moving, while another may be calm and analytical, and slow to take action. Many managers prefer direct face-to-face communication and many meetings, while others prefer less direct contact, fewer meetings, and greater reliance on written reports. These differences in personal style can result in major differences in a manager's approach to strategic decision making.

Before continuing with our discussion of managerial style, let us review some of the basic models, including the Decision Grid and Maccoby's Four Basic Types.

THE DECISION-MAKING GRID

The Decision-Making Grid, developed by Jay Hall, Vincent O'Leary, and Martha Williams, provides a model for examining the decision-making style of group members.[26] The Grid is based on two basic dimensions:

1 The concern for decision adequacy experienced by the individual decision maker.

2 The concern for commitment of others to the decision.

The matrix formed by these two dimensions and five decision-making styles can be identified as shown in Figure 2.3.

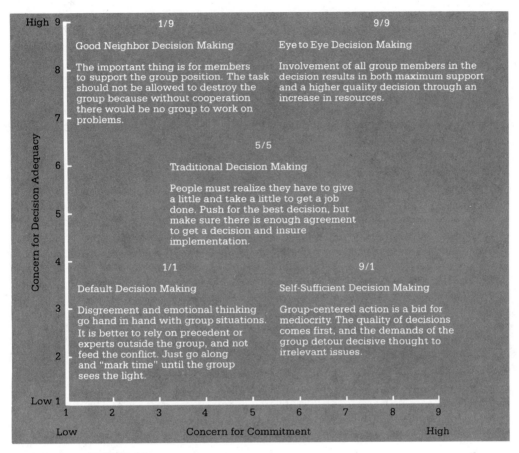

FIGURE 2.3
The Decision-Making Grid
SOURCE: © 1964 by the Regents of the University of California. Reprinted from CALI-FORNIA MANAGEMENT REVIEW, volume VII, no. 2, pp. 43 to 54 by permission of the Regents

1,1 Default Decision Making   This style has a low concern on both dimensions, resulting in a suppression of one's own self-interests or going along with the group.

1,9 Good Neighbor Decision Making   This style requires a high concern for commitment and an atomosphere of cooperation, with low concern for the issues, resulting in the avoiding or minimizing of conflict.

5,5 Traditional Decision Making   This style expresses a moderate level of con-cern in both dimensions, but essentially involves a compromise or bargaining ap-proach to decision making.

9,1 Self-Sufficient Decision Making   This style is characterized by a maximum concern for the adequacy of the decision (results oriented) and minimal concern for commitment.

9,9 Eye-to-Eye Decision Making   This style is characterized by maximum concern on both dimensions and is based on conflict and open expression of opinions, feelings, and ideas until an optimum solution is rendered.

The basic assumption underlying this model is that the 9,9 style should be more effective and is probably practiced by most top managers.

A strategic decision is good when it implements a quality solution and is accepted by those whom it affects. Thus, it is important for managers to be aware of their decision style.

MACCOBY'S FOUR BASIC TYPES

Michael Maccoby recently interviewed managers in twelve major corporations and he suggests that a new type of manager is taking over the leadership role.[27] This new manager, says Maccoby, is driven not to build empires, but to organize a winning team. Maccoby summarizes his findings on the type of manager who holds the leadership in large American companies into four basic types.

The Craftsman   He holds traditional values and is concerned with the *process* of making something. He sees others in terms of whether they will help or hinder him in doing a craftsman-like job. He is dedicated to his field but unable to lead changing organizations.

The Jungle Fighter   He lusts for power and experiences life and work as a jungle. He sees others as either accomplices or enemies.

The Company Man   He bases his identity on being part of the organization. He tends to sustain an atmosphere of cooperation, but lacks the daring to be innovative or competitive.

The Gamesman   He sees life in terms of options and possibilities as if he were playing a game. He likes to take calculated risks and is fascinated by new technologies and methods. His main goal is to be known as a winner, his deepest fear to be labeled a loser.

To some degree, Maccoby's four basic types represent a mixture of achievement and power motivations, but without any concern for people, which many have questioned. In general, there will be managers who fit into some of Maccoby's characteristic patterns, but in part these are formed by the needs, drives and ambitions of the organizational environment. The gamesman, says Maccoby, is cooperative but competitive, detached and playful but compulsively driven to succeed, a team player but a would-be superstar, a team leader but often a rebel against bureaucratic hierarchy, fair, and unprejudiced but contemptuous of weakness, tough and dominating but not destructive. Competition and innovation in modern business require these game-like attitudes, and of all the character types, only the gamesman is emotionally attuned to the environment.

The modern manager, in Maccoby's view, is molded by the requirements of the organization, presenting an emotional and spiritual underdevelopment. Maccoby suggests that managers become so proficient in applying analytical techniques that they lose sight of values beyond winning the game. Consequently, Maccoby asks, "Where will we find future leaders who possess moral strength to know right from wrong and the courage to act on those convictions?"

AN INTEGRATIVE APPROACH TO STRATEGIC STYLE

Harold Geneen (former Chairman of ITT) once said, "If I had enough arms and legs and time, I would do it all myself." But he conceded that it would be impossible for any manager to do it all. The manager must achieve strategic objectives by managing the organization.

In general, these earlier models, with the exception of Maccoby, suggest that a participative or Theory Y managerial style is probably most used and most effective. However, there are reasons to question whether or not this is actually the case with CEOs, the managers at the top. In an article in *Fortune,* "The Ten Toughest Bosses," Hugh Menzies questions which style is most effective.

"During his nineteen-year tenure as chief executive of ITT, Geneen earned a legendary reputation for setting incredibly high goals, driving his managers to meet them, and humiliating those who failed, often in front of their peers," Menzies says. "Yet, for all the talk of Theory Y management and sensitivity training over the past couple of decades, the nation's executive suites are obviously still populated by some very tough bosses."[28]

On the basis of interviews with subordinates, Menzies compiled a list of the ten toughest bosses in American business:

1   A. Robert Abboud, Chairman, First Chicago
2   Thomas Mellon Evans, Chairman, Crane Corp.
3   Maurice Greenberg, Chairman, American International Group, Inc.
4   Richard Jacob, Chairman, DayCo Corp.
5   David Mahoney, Chairman, Norton Simon, Inc.
6   Alex Massed, Executive Vice President, Mobil Corp.
7   Andrall Pearson, President, PepsiCo, Inc.
8   Donald Rumsfeld, President, G. D. Searle, Inc.
9   Robert Stone, Executive Vice President, Columbia Pictures, Inc.
10   William Ylvisaker, Chairman, Gould, Inc.

Do their methods pay off? Menzies suggests that there is no overwhelming evidence, pro or con. Several have done very well; others have not. At this point, one could surmise that such a style would have good short-term results, but with longer-term problems.

There are several common assumptions underlying these models of managerial style which may or may not fit organizational reality. If such articles as the "Ten Toughest Bosses," are any guide, then probably a high percentage of top managers would fit the 9,9 or 9,1 styles, rather than 5,5, 1,9, or 1,1 styles which, one would suspect, are relatively rare at the top.

STRATEGIC MANAGEMENT STYLES

What can we suggest about managerial styles of the strategist then? First, there seems to be a lack of consideration of the element of power. The job of a CEO, unless it is in a family-dominated business with an owner-manager, is subject to relationships with others, including the board of directors and subordinate managers. The manager must use his style as a means of gaining strategic ends.

David McClelland and David Burnham (Harvard) suggest that the power dimension is more important to the manager than affiliative or achievement motives and that a concern for power is essential to an effective managerial style. ". . . managers are primarily concerned with influencing others . . . [and] a high need for Power. . . . Thus, leadership and power appear as two closely related concepts, and if we want to understand better effective leadership, we may begin by studying the power motive in thought and action."[29] Consequently, an effective strategic style may more accurately reflect the need for achievement and need for power dimensions, resulting in some basic typology of managerial styles as shown in Figure 2.4.

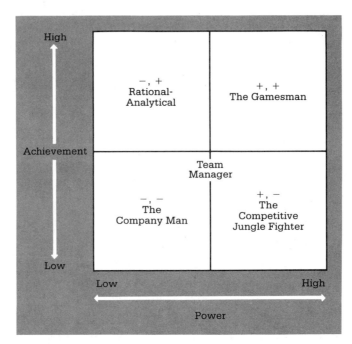

FIGURE 2.4
Four Strategic Managerial Styles

THE COMPANY MAN (LOW RISK)

The manager with a low concern for achievement and a low concern for power tends to fit best in a slow-changing, conservative organization. The company-man style emphasizes low-risk, low-profile, low threat approaches, with survival as the primary goal. Often companies which prefer no change and low-risk strategies will prefer this style of manager. As an example, when Johns-Manville was operating at a low 4 percent growth rate during a period of rapid economic expansions, this would have been a likely managerial style.

THE RATIONAL-ANALYTICAL MANAGER

The manager with high concern for achievement and low concern for power tends to fit into a more highly rational, low-key approach. Decision making is based on the analytical process and the logical analysis of information.

This style is perhaps exemplified by Roy Ash, formerly of Litton, now of AM International. His style is more cool and intellectual. It is results-oriented, but with a low level of confrontation except around factual information. The emphasis is on the rational process and on detailed plans and programs.

THE AGGRESSIVE-COMPETITIVE MANAGER

This managerial style is more aggressive and has a higher concern for personal control. While there is also concern with analysis, there is more open conflict and confrontation. Decison making emerges from the cauldron of conflicting viewpoints argued through until the dominant strategy emerges.

This style might be similar to that of Harold Geneen of ITT, although there are many other managers who use this style. The style is results-oriented, uses a high level of confrontation, and exerts a high level of pressure. Geneen has three fundamental laws[30]:

1 *Problems must be highlighted.* It is his view that for problems to be solved, there must be an early recognition of danger signals.

2 *Facts must by unshakeable.* Analysis and research on problems must be pains-takingly accurate. "I don't believe a man's opinion until I believe his facts," says Geneen.

3 *Face-to-face communication must be relied upon.* Like many executives, Geneen likes to see the expression on the person's face as well as hear the information being presented.

This managerial style involves setting high, almost unattainable goals, having a demanding review and control process, and forcing people to make decisions and defend their position.

THE COLLABORATIVE MANAGER

The collaborative style is concerned with results, a winning team and a balance between achievement and power. There is more reliance on confrontation or conflict in decision making than in the analytical style, but a less aggressive and competitive approach than in the more power-oriented manager.

THE GAMESMAN

According to Michael Maccoby, the most successful executive seems to be the "gamesman," the manager who sees business as a game like chess, and whose motivation is to be a winner. The gamesman is moderately high on both power and achievement motivation, but low on affiliation needs or concern for people, who represent pawns on the field of play. He has high standards tempered by the recognition of political realities. His interpersonal skills are used in persuading others and in negotiating positions of advantage; conceptual thinking emphasizes the long run and total system aspects of the situation. As noted, affiliation and emotional needs are underexpressed, a point of concern for Maccoby.

Donald Frey, who left a senior executive post at Ford Motor Company to become president of Bell & Howell, expresses the gamesman orientation: "I just have to run a whole business—it's in here (clutching his abdomen). In the crudest sense, you could say it's a need for power. In an esoteric sense, it's a need for completeness. I'm not happy unless I'm dealing with all the pieces. All through the years, regardless of what function I was performing, I had a desire to find out the broader aspects of what I was doing—to see what the next guy was going to do."[31]

The gamesman's high performance standards are tempered by a recognition of political realities. The time perspective of this type of manager is longer run and more directed to climbing upward on a fast track.

AN EFFECTIVE STYLE

All of these managerial styles can be effective. There is no one best style, but rather an adapting to the style that works best in each organization. In general, an effective style is results-oriented. There is tremendous pressure to achieve results in a hostile and competitive environment. A CEO must have interpersonal skills, because no one operates alone. A large percentage of the CEO's time is spent in meetings and in external relationships. Therefore, he must be able to deal with people effectively. However, he may not necessarily have many warm relationships in maintaining the role.

The emphasis here is upon developing smooth, working teams with open communication. There is conflict, but less confrontation and less pressure, although there is still emphasis on overall results. Perhaps there is a less threatening climate under the collaborative style.

The position of a top executive is often a perilous one. If things go well, he is well rewarded. If the strategic decisions turn out badly, then he is often held responsible. Since many of the factors that influence strategic outcomes are beyond his control, his only hope for survival is to exert influence through an effective managerial style toward accomplishing strategic objectives. His motives are not always idealistic but they have one basic goal: to ensure his chances of survival.

MANAGERIAL IMPLICATIONS

The organization strategists formulate a strategy to accomplish goals based on their estimates of organizational strengths and environmental opportunities and threats. The strategy makers include the top management team, the board of directors, and corporate planners. Research suggests that in most firms the strategic decision process is normally dominated by the CEO or a coalition of high-ranking corporate officers.

As we have noted, the managerial style of the strategic decision maker has an impact on the strategic management system of the organization. The CEO's job is to make decisions and to gain effective performance from members. Harold Geneen, for example, had an impact on the way ITT was run and on the managers who worked there. He was reported to be a hard man to work for. "I left because of hellish pressure I could not endure." "He goes too far, he drives people up the wall." "He sets almost unattainable standards that either stretch a person or break them. It stretched me!" says one former manager.[32]

The key to all of these managerial styles is to bring the organization's managerial resources to focus on the biggest problems and biggest potential opportunties. The two biggest problems in most organizations are communication and planning. An effective style must have impact in these two areas. Each manager must examine his own decision-making style and critique it. Thus, an effective manager can become more effective.

Some individuals thrive in a setting of harmonious teamwork, others prefer to work alone. Certain individuals like a great deal of autonomy, while others need direction and control. Some individuals enjoy challenging, competitive confrontation; for others this is uncomfortable, and a more rational approach is preferred. All of this suggests that a contingency or flexible style is probably most appropriate, based upon a diagnosis of the specific organization, individuals, and situations. In effect, there is no one best way for managing in all situations or organizations.

As an example of the fortunes of the top manager, Wilfred Corrigan is no longer the CEO for Fairchild. Since his earlier successes, Fairchild has slipped from second to sixth in its industry and, apparently, Corrigan's "creative tension" style, and "uncanny decision making" didn't always work.[33]

Shortly after the $397-million acquisition of Fairchild by Schlumberger Ltd. in October of 1979, Fairchild's chairman, Wilfred J. Corrigan, explained that the French company was not only financially solid but had pledged to give Fairchild complete autonomy. Less than a week later, Corrigan announced his resignation as president and chief executive.

Corrigan was never able strategically to position Fairchild as a strong factor in the MOS (metal-oxide-silicon) technology market, which is in the most important growth market. And apparently the blame for these strategic failures must fall on Corrigan. As one competitor commented, "If there ever was a one-man show, it was Wilf."

As William K. Hall (University of Michigan) has pointed out, strategic planning is conducted by general managers in an unstable, highly political environment.[34] The strategic plans are developed by managers who are responsible for performing multiple tasks under continuous time pressures. As a result, most planning is done using a "bottom up" process, so that management does not generate and evaluate alternative plans. Instead, the role of top management often becomes one of approving or disapproving a plan "pushed up" through the organization. Because such processes are at work, the strategic decisions are often political in nature. Rarely can the strategist make a decision without considering whether or not it will be politically acceptable and be implemented.

Perhaps this process has led to the success of the "gamesman" style manager. Strategic decisions, then, are made by mutual adjustment and negotiation within the rules of the game, until an acceptable decision is agreed upon. Consequently, the manager must know how to pick and choose a style and to use political tactics in order to be effective.

In this chapter, we have looked at several approaches to managerial style and its importance to strategic decision making. We have attempted to present a theoretical framework for understanding the complete effect of the managerial system on strategy. As a manager working within an organization on a day-to-day basis, there is no one best way to manage. Rather there are more effective and less effective styles, depending upon the forces which exist in the specific organizational environment.

REVIEW QUESTIONS

1 Compare and contrast the basic managerial style approaches.

2 What are the relative impacts of the board, top management, and other planners on strategy?

3 Imagine yourself as CEO of an organization which would involve you in strategic decisions. How would you go about gaining support for your strategy?

4 Most universities use boards to govern. How does the board operate in your school? Who appoints them? Perhaps you can observe the board in action and evaluate its actions.

5 How would you describe your own managerial style?

ENDNOTES

1 Based upon, "At Long Last," *Forbes*, Vol. 123, April 2, 1979, p. 80, and "Young Top Management," *Business Week*, October 6, 1975, 58.

2 Ibid.

3 First of Chicago, "New Management to Bring Back the Past," *Business Week*, August 4, 1980, 64.

4 "Young Top Management."

5 The people involved in the process, their titles, and their duties vary. For discussion, see Russell L. Ackoff, *A Concept of Corporate Planning* (New York: Wiley-Interscience, 1970), pp. 128–38.

6 The president of a company is considered an organization leader, a personal leader, and an architect of organization purpose whose central concept is making of corporate strategy. See C. Roland Christensen, Kenneth R. Andrew, and Joseph L. Bower, *Business Policy: Text and Cases* (Homewood, Ill.: Irwin, 1978), pp. 15–22.

7 For further discussion, see Myles L. Mace, "The President and Corporate Planning," in *Harvard Business Review on Management* (New York: Harper and Row, 1975), pp. 119–38.

8 "Inside Exxon" by Anthony J. Parisi, for *The New York Times Magazine*, August 3, 1980. © 1980 by The New York Times Company. Reprinted by permission.

9 Ibid.

10 Ibid.

11 "Behind the Snafu at Singer," *Fortune*, November 5, 1979, 7.

12 "A & P," *Fortune Magazine*, November 6, 1978, 35–36, 38, 40, 42, 44.

13 Danny Miller, "Common Syndromes of Business Failure," *Business Horizons*, November 1977, 43–44.

14 See Mace's study, based on extensive research and interviews, in *Directors: Myth and Reality* (Cambridge, Mass.: Harvard University Press, 1971), especially, p. 4.

15 Herbert Meyer, "Shoot out at Johns-Manville Corral", *Fortune*, October 1976, 146–51.

16 "Scovill," *Business Week*, May 2, 1977, 46, 50–51.

17 For a discussion of overseas payoffs, see Peter Nehemkis, "Business Payoffs Abroad: Rhetoric and Reality," *California Management Review*, Winter 1975, 5–20. For comments on the Foreign Corrupt Practices Act of 1977, see Hurd Baruch, "The Foreign Corrupt Practices Act," *Harvard Business Review*, January–February 1976, 32–50.

18 Eberhard Faber, "How I Lost Our Great Debate About Corporate Ethics," *Fortune Magazine*, November 1976, 180–182, 186, 188.

19 William Boulton, "The Evolving Board: A Look at the Board's Changing Roles & Information Needs," *Academy of Management Review*, October 1978, 827–36.

20 George A. Steiner, "Rise of the Corporate Planner," *Harvard Business Review*, September-October 1970, 133.

21 See, for example, M. Leontiades, "What Kind of Corporate Planner Do You Need?" *Long Range Planning*, April 1977; and P. Lorange, "The Planner's Dual Role," *Long Range Planning*, March 1973.

22 Thomas H. Naylor and Horst Schavland, *A Survey of Users of Corporate Simulation Models* (Durham, N.C.: Social Systems, Inc., 1975). See also Naylor and Gattis, "Corporate Planning Models," *California Management Review*, Summer 1976, 69.

23 "Corporate Planning: Piercing Future Fog in the Executive Suite," *Business Week*, April 28, 1975, 46–50, 52, 54.

24 H. Mintzberg, "The Manager's Job," *Harvard Business Review*, July–August 1975, 49–61.

25 "New Management," *Business Week* (August 4, 1980), p. 69.

26 J. Hall et al., "The Decision Grid," *California Management Review*, Vol III, No. 2, 1964, 43–54.

27 M. Maccoby, *The Gamesman* (New York: Simon & Schuster, 1976).

28 Hugh D. Menzies, "The Ten Toughest Bosses," *Fortune*, April 21, 1980, 62.

29 D. McClelland and D. Burnham, "Power Is the Great Motivator," *Harvard Business Review*, March–April 1976, 13.

30 "The Financial Key at ITT," *Dun's Review*, December 1970, 6f.

31 Arthur M. Louis, "Donald Frey Had a Hunger for the Whole Thing," *Fortune*, September 1976, 140.

32 "They Call It 'Geneen II,' " *Forbes*, May 1, 1966.

33 "A Worried Industry Watches Fairchild," *Business Week*, December 3, 1979, 69.

34 William K. Hall, "Strategic Planning Models: Are Top Managers Really Finding Them Useful?" *Journal of Business Policy*. Winter 1973, 33.

APPENDIX

THE STRATEGIC MANAGEMENT STYLE MATRIX

A. Purpose   The purpose of this survey is to enable you to identify and to get feedback on your strategic decision making and managerial style.

When you are a member of a team, what is your leadership behavior like? In what ways do you try to influence other team members toward accomplishing the team's goals? The purpose of the survey below is to get a description of your behavior in teams in order to examine your executive style.

There is no right or wrong way to manage, therefore the best choice is the way you try to handle situations. Answer honestly, because the more accurate your response the more accurate the result.

B. Procedures   You will find in this survey ten situations that call for your response. Each of the ten situations presents five alternative ways of responding. Because you will be asked to rank order these five responses to the situation, it is important that you read through all the responses before answering. Once you have read through all five responses, select the response that is most similar to the way you think you would actually behave or think in such a situation. Place the letter corresponding to that response (a, b, c, d, or e) somewhere on the "Most Similar" end of the ten-point scale appropriate to the intensity of your feeling. Next select the response that is least similar to the way you would actually act or think. Again place the letter corresponding to that response somewhere on the "Least Similar" end of the scale. Complete the answers by placing the remaining three responses that reflect your actions or thoughts for those responses within the range of previously selected most-least points.

As an example, the answer to a situation could be:

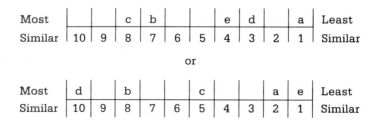

STRATEGIC MANAGEMENT SURVEY

In answering these questions, think of how you would actually handle or act in the situation or how you think about the nature of strategic management.

COPYRIGHT © 1980 by CMS, and Donald F. Harvey, Rt. 1, Box 123, Colbert, WA 99005. Not to be reproduced or copied without the express permission of D. F. Harvey, and is available from CMS.

1. STRATEGIC GOALS

In determining strategic goals for the organization:

a. Clear-cut directions need to be spelled out, "stretching" people to higher performances, by establishing goals, the first step in pushing a change into new strategies.

b. One specifies the goals and values toward which effort should be directed and by which success will be measured. Develop a collective viewpoint as to what makes a company great, and then translate these visions into broad goals.

c. A quantitative set of results should be detailed. Define the firm's capabilities and weaknesses, then develop logical criteria and standards for future accomplishment.

d. Set high standards for accomplishment, aiming at being the best in the field. Announce that our team is going to be a winner, then determine goals that represent a negotiated position among the important power centers in the company.

e. Pursue attainable goals. Stay with past approaches and seek to have everyone pulling together when we do set our course.

| Most Similar | 10 | 9 | 8 | 7 | 6 | 5 | 4 | 3 | 2 | 1 | Least Similar |

2. STRATEGIC MANAGEMENT STYLE

My style of management relies upon:

a. Rational emphasis, setting high standards, and launching trial concepts to see what will "fly." Get managers to analyze their differences, but try to keep options open until substantive alternatives can be analyzed.

b. Developing a sense of urgency to accomplish and create, because it takes results to make us a winning team. Take charge, giving directions and creating a winning climate.

c. Formal procedures, written reports and the chain-of-command, keep my own exposure low, to keep a low profile.

d. Frequent contact, participation and delegation of responsibility, and gaining a consensus among subordinates.

e. Pushing managers to set high standards, driving subordinates toward demanding goals, and using competition between groups and individuals as a means of improving total results.

| Most Similar | 10 | 9 | 8 | 7 | 6 | 5 | 4 | 3 | 2 | 1 | Least Similar |

3. STRATEGIC PLANNING

The formal strategic planning system should:

a. Emphasize confrontations between strategic options, improve short term results against targets, and drive out weaker alternatives.

b. Provide dynamic leadership toward achieving major goals. Individual managers must be chosen, motivated and assigned roles.

c. Use quantitative, analytical techniques and "bottom up" approaches to coordinating cross-divisional goals.

d. Result in detailed, budgetary plans done by a planning group, which set forth some basic criteria.

e. Specify goals and values.

4. ORGANIZING FOR STRATEGIC ACTION

The organization structure should:

a. Provide decentralized and flexible task responsibility. Keep decision makers informed on a person-to-person basis.

b. Provide an effective means of control, by directing managers constructively, and use discipline.

c. Follow organization strategy, and focus on results.

d. Provide a logical chain of command to analyze and implemont strategy by means of clearly defined channels of information flow.

e. Clearly define areas of authority and responsibility.

5. STRATEGIC ANALYSIS

The analysis of strategic factors should:

a. Allow the firm to develop extensive quantitative data and econometric models by careful, logical analysis.

b. Use the open confrontation between opposing factions, analyze the "real facts" of a situation by means of argument, controversy, and conflict between managers.

c. Attempt to get team members involved in constructive analysis of different ideas, options, and approaches.

d. Be part of a political process because a winning strategy can be formed among these coalitions which is superior to any quantitative approach.

e. Be handled through formal procedures so that each manager's performance can be compared to standards.

6. STRATEGIC DECISION MAKING

Strategic decisions are made

a. By using quantitative, result-oriented techniques of rational analysis.

b. By limiting your exposure to risk after a careful assessment of the alternatives.

c. As the result of performance "shoot-outs" between competing strategic proposals, with face-to-face communication and confrontation.

d. As the result of power-political interplays.

e. After working through new ideas, capabilities, and reactions of key principals affected.

7. STRATEGIC IMPLEMENTATION

In implementing the strategic decision,

a. Put an emphasis on communication, participation, and commitment to a team effort.

b. Gain the full support of organizational elements, by persuasion, negotiation, or cooperation.

c. Make things happen by pressuring team members to perform and by providing feedback.

d. Move slowly, maintaining the enterprise's ongoing stengths while shifting its posture in new directions.

e. A strategic plan with budgetary targets is communicated to each responsible manager.

8. MANAGERIAL PROCESSES

In putting strategic plans into operation,

a. Individual goals must be sacrificed to maintain productivity and an optimal performance level. The proper reporting system and tightening up of controls will lead to effectiveness and efficiency.

b. A managerial system that is open and charismatic, with a warm, human operating system provides the best results.

c. Optimal performance must be achieved whatever the cost. A balancing of conflicting viewpoints is necessary for an effective operation.

d. Continue existing procedures, emphasizing low levels of conflict, and careful low risk strategies.

e. The needs of the organization come first and managers must sacrifice their personal goals, to maintain a high level of performance.

9. STRATEGIC EVALUATION

Strategic Evaluation:

a. Should be accomplished on the basis of comparisons of performance results with plans, by the numbers.

b. Provides a means to measure performance toward goals and provide for rewards.

c. Uses a shared responsibility approach, with team members getting together to critique, evaluate, and make revisions or improvements on the plan.

d. Challenges past assumptions with new ideas and potentials.

e. Is used to keep on the strategic plan and control any deviations quickly.

10. STRATEGIC CONTROLS

In controlling strategic action, the strategist should

a. Operate through questioning and fact gathering, and measure quantitatively against standards of profitability.

b. Have a frequent review of company performance to determine if the manager's estimates are realistic.

c. Ask for suggestions from managers for improving problem areas, without making any drastic changes to the plan.

d. Meet with subordinate managers, with others as a team in solving problems.

e. Provide a tough, rigorous review, maintaining control over the problems so that a winning performance will be achieved.

STEP 1. SCORING INSTRUCTIONS

On the question sheets you wrote your answers (a, b, c, d, and e) above a number. Now transfer from each of the ten situations your number values for each letter to the table below. You will have to look for each letter score for all questions and complete filling in the scoring spaces. Once all values have been entered, total up the score for each column.

		Games	Team	Analytical	Power	Company
				SCORING FORM		
1.		d. _____	b. _____	c. _____	a. _____	e. _____
2.		b. _____	d. _____	a. _____	e. _____	c. _____
3.		b. _____	e. _____	c. _____	a. _____	d. _____
4.		c. _____	a. _____	d. _____	b. _____	e. _____
5.		d. _____	c. _____	a. _____	b. _____	e. _____
6.		d. _____	e. _____	a. _____	c. _____	b. _____
7.		b. _____	a. _____	e. _____	c. _____	d. _____
8.		c. _____	b. _____	a. _____	e. _____	d. _____
9.		d. _____	c. _____	a. _____	e. _____	b. _____
10.		e. _____	d. _____	a. _____	b. _____	c. _____
TOTALS		_____	_____	_____	_____	_____

STEP 2. ENTER THE SCORES ON THE SUMMARY FORM AS FOLLOWS:

1 Transfer the numerical sums from the score sheet to the summary form in *descending* order. (Enter in column 3.)

2 In column 2 write the appropriate Word Description of Approach to Change beside the score.

3 In column 4 place the numerical difference of your adjacent scores found in column 3. (The difference between the scores on the first and second lines of column 3 will be placed on the first line of column 4.)

EXECUTIVE STYLE SUMMARY			
Your Choice	Word Description of Style	Score	Difference between Scores of Adjacent Lines
1st	_____	_____	_____
2nd	_____	_____	_____
3rd	_____	_____	_____
4th	_____	_____	_____
5th	_____	_____	_____

COPYRIGHT © 1980 by CMS, and Donald F. Harvey, Rt. 1, Box 123, Colbert, WA 99005. Not to be reproduced or copied without the express permission of D. F. Harvey, and is available from CMS.

Place scores from Scoring Form:

```
┌──────────────────────────────────────────────────────────────┐
│                                                                │
│  4. ┌────┐  ┌────┐           5. ┌────┐  ┌────┐                  │
│     └────┘  └────┘              └────┘  └────┘                  │
│     Analytical                  Gamesman                       │
│                                                                │
│                  3. ┌────┐  ┌────┐                             │
│                     └────┘  └────┘                             │
│                     Collaborative—                            │
│                     Team Manager                              │
│                                                                │
│  1. ┌────┐  ┌────┐           2. ┌────┐  ┌────┐                  │
│     └────┘  └────┘              └────┘  └────┘                  │
│     Company man                 Competitive—                  │
│                                 Jungle Fighter                │
│                                                                │
└──────────────────────────────────────────────────────────────┘
```

THE STRATEGIC MANAGEMENT STYLE MATRIX

COPYRIGHT © 1980 by CMS, and Donald F. Harvey, Rt. 1, box 123, Colbert, WA 99005. Not to be reproduced or copied without the express permission of D. F. Harvey, and is available from CMS.

EXECUTIVE STYLE PROFILE

You have just completed and scored your Executive Style. Following is a brief explanation of the five styles.

1. The Gamesman   He sees life in terms of options and possibilities as if he were playing a game. He likes to take calculated risks and is fascinated by new technologies and methods. His main goal is to be known as a winner, his deepest fear is to be labeled a loser. The Gamesman is concerned with winning at all costs. He seeks competition, sets a standard of excellence, and is results-oriented.

2. The Aggressive-Competitive Style   This managerial style is more aggressive and has a higher concern for personal control. While there is also concern with analysis, there is more open conflict and confrontation. Decision making emerges from the cauldron of conflicting viewpoints argued through until the dominant strategy emerges. The style is results-oriented, uses a high level of confrontation, and exerts a high level of pressure.

3. The Rational-Analytical Style   The manager with the higher concern for achievement and lower concern for power tends to fit into a more rational, low key and highly rational approach. Decision making is based on the analytical process and the logical analysis of information. His style is more cool and intellectual. It is results-oriented, but with a low level of confrontation except around factual information. The emphasis is on the rational process and on detailed plans and programs. The analytical manager is concerned with achievement of long-term goals and with the application of rational, quantitative analysis to problems. He prefers responsibility for results, and taking calculated risks.

4. The Company Man   He bases his identify on being part of the organization. He tends to sustain an atmosphere of cooperation, but lacks the daring to be innovative or competitive. The company man is concerned with maintaining harmony, and order, and with solid low-risk decisions. He prefers group harmony, avoids conflict, and prefers slow, long-term goal attainment, without drastic changes.

5. The Collaborative Team Style   The collaborative style is concerned with results and a winning team and a balance between achievement and power. There is more reliance on confrontation or conflict in decision making than the analytical style, but a less aggressive and competitive approach than the more power-oriented manager.

All of these styles can be effective. There is no one best style, but rather an adapting to the style that works best in each organization.

A person does not operate using one type of executive style to the exclusion of the other styles. The purpose of the scoring was to give you an indication of the importance you place on each of the five styles relative to each other. The difference between your first and second styles indicates the strength of your performance and how quickly you will fall back on another style. Little difference between scores could indicate a tendency to vacillate between styles or vague thoughts about how you handle decisions. A large difference could indicate a strong reliance on the predominant style.

This survey should be used as a point of departure for further reflection and observation concerning the way you attempt to manage and influence others. To obtain a better understanding of your style, try to become aware in your associations with friends, peers, and working associates as to how you handle problems. It may also be helpful to observe other people when they try to influence your behavior and become aware of how you react to their methods.

In plenary session, discuss the five change styles. Does your score for your primary and backup change style seem congruent with the way you think you operate in decision situations? Share your scores with class members with whom you have been working and get their feedback.

C H A P T E R

3

The essential task of modern management is to deal with change. Management is the agency through which most changes enter our society, and it is the agency that then must cope with the environment it has set in turbulent motion.

Max Ways, "Tomorrow's Management"
Fortune, July 1, 1966, 84.

Organizational Strategy in a Changing World

CHAPTER OBJECTIVES

When you complete this chapter, you will be able to:

- ☐ *Demonstrate an understanding of the basic concepts of strategy and factors contributing to the development of strategic goals, objectives, and plans.*

- ☐ *Understand and apply the contingency approach to strategic planning.*

- ☐ *Identify the ways an organization may adapt to change.*

- ☐ *Apply these concepts in analyzing a comprehensive management case.*

THE SHOOTOUT AT THE JOHNS-MANVILLE CORRAL[1]

W. Richard Goodwin

"When W. Richard Goodwin boarded a private jet on Wednesday, September 1, 1967, to fly from Denver to New York City, he felt more confident and more assured than he had ever been during his five and three-quarter years as president and chief executive of Johns-Manville Corp. Goodwin, fifty-two, who combines a low-key personal manner with an uncommon flair for corporate showmanship, was looking forward to meeting with his board of directors Friday morning. With considerable justification, he believed that he had accomplished virtually everything the directors had hired him to do.

"He had reorganized and rejuvenated the once torpid building-materials company. Sales had risen 91 percent, from $578 million in 1970 to $1.1 billion in 1975. Net profits had gone up 115 percent between 1970 and 1974, and although last year's recession wiped out almost all of that gain, earnings had rebounded sharply during the first half of 1976 to set a company record." Goodwin, a former professor and consultant, had also been instrumental in moving the company headquarters from a drab building in New York City to a beautiful 10,000-acre ranch just outside of downtown Denver. The relocation was the cornerstone of Goodwin's corporate overhaul, and it was proving to be a roaring success. Johns-Manville's new style and performance were drawing public attention to the company for the first time in decades. Wall Street analysts were beginning to turn out reports praising J-M's prospects."

STAGE 3: DETERMINING ORGANIZATIONAL GOALS AND OBJECTIVES

The strategic management process involves the formulation of a set of goals and objectives for organizational performance. Strategic management is based on results, so goal formulation initiates the strategic formulation process. This is true because it is difficult to develop strategy if the manager does not know what results he is seeking to achieve. After the goals and objectives are set, then strategy can be formulated, evaluated, and implemented. The development of goals and objectives is influenced by three factors.

THE GOAL FORMULATION PROCESS

Goal formulation is a complex *process*. The process may involve a rational analysis of economic factors, a political process of bargaining and negotiation among organizational power centers, and the formal strategic planning system of the organization. At Johns-Manville each of these forces interacted in the formulation of the strategic goals and objectives for the organization. Richard Goodwin, the CEO, designed a strategic planning system, imposed a system of rational analysis for setting goals and resource allocation among units, and engaged in bargaining with the various powers of the organization to set and achieve strategic goals.

In general, goal formulation may be said to involve four elements:

1 Defining specific goals and objectives for the organization.

2 Setting forth these goals clearly and explicitly.

3 Assigning responsibility for goals to individuals or units.

4 Developing performance measures to control progress toward goals.

GOAL SETTING PRACTICES

However, James B. Quinn (Professor of Management, Amos Tuck School, Dartmouth College), suggests that this approach is not necessarily followed by top managers; instead he contends, their practices are "purposeful, politically astute, and effective."[2] Quinn argues that setting specific goals leads to undesired centralization, a focusing of opposition to top management, and rigidity. Instead, Quinn found that broad, general goals led to cohesion, identity, and elan.

H. Edward Wrapp argues the same point: Managers should have objectives but should avoid being committed publicly to specific objectives for the following reasons:[3]

● It is impossible to set down specific objectives which will be relevant for any reasonable period of time (things change too fast to do that).

● It is impossible to state objectives clearly enough so that everyone in the organization understands what they mean.

● Detailed objectives complicate the task of reaching them. If employees will not accept the strategist's objectives, it is useful to be vague and avoid this problem.

As can be seen, goal formulation is a complex process, often involving politics and conflicts, yet it is central to the strategic management process.

CHANGE IS A FACT OF MANAGERIAL LIFE

Change is the name of the game in management today. Market, product, and competitive conditions are rapidly changing. For instance, over 20 million digital watches were sold in 1979, a market that did not even exist three years before. Management in the future is likely to be even more dynamic and challenging. Therefore, the focus of strategic management is on changing organizational systems to meet new economic conditions. This approach stresses the situational nature of problems and their systemwide impact. Consequently, in solving a given problem, managers must analyze the organization, its subsystem interrelationships, and the possible effects of the external environment as well.

CHANGING CONDITIONS

As an example of these *changing conditions,* look at the sudden decline in the market for sewing machines along with the projected increase in the demand for home computers. Singer Company has had to reorganize, sell off unprofitable units, and change its marketing strategy because the percentage of women buying sewing machines has declined drastically. The market for home computers, on the other hand, was virtually nonexistent a few years ago, but Texas Instruments is now predicting that a several billion dollar market will soon emerge.

As a result of these shorter product life cycles, firms are confronted with early technological obsolescence of products. In the past, companies could grow during the long life span of a proprietary invention, but they are now finding that innovations are being quickly overtaken by competitors. As Roy Ash, former president of Litton Industries, found when he took over Addressograph-Multigraph, the most immediate task was to catch up in technology. Ash noted that "AM missed a series of technological boats over the years and now we've got to charter a jet airplane to get out in front.[4]

INCREASING CHANGES

These problems are symptoms of *an increasing rate of change* and its impact upon strategic management. The result is that managers, like Dick Goodwin of JM, are facing risk situations unlike those faced before. In an era of accelerating change, management's degree of excellence is judged by its ability to cope with these changes. Organizations either become more adaptive, flexible, and anticipative or they become rigid, stagnant, and react to change after the fact, often when it is too late. Seldom can strategic management decisions be based solely upon the extrapolation of historical experience. Many decisions are unique, innovative, and risky, involving new products and new areas of opportunity. And putting a new product or a new process into production is a major strategic decision.

Since an organization exists in a changing environment, it must have the capacity to adapt. As one consultant points out, "Nobody is moving faster on the experience curve than the high technology electronic companies, and the consequences of being late are most severe in that business.[5]

As a result, the strategist searches the environment determining what forces pose threats to organizational objectives, and determining what factors open up new opportunities for attaining added objectives.

THE TYPE OF ORGANIZATION AND ENVIRONMNENT

Finally, the *type of organization and environment* also influence the goal formulation process. For example, a public utility, a business firm, a hospital, and a university all differ greatly in their basic mission and purpose. One way of dealing with such differences is termed "the contingency approach." The contingency approach suggests that for any given type of organization and set of circumstances, a "best" strategy exists. There is research evidence suggesting that environmental and organizational variables, such as the life cycle stage of products, the rate of technological change in the industry, economic factors, and other factors tend to impact goal formulation in the organization.

In summary, then, the basic purpose or mission implies a goal or direction toward which the organization attempts to move. Without goals, strategic planning would be impossible because these are the ends strategy is intended to attain.

In the following sections, those factors influencing goal formulation will be examined in greater detail.

DETERMINING ORGANIZATIONAL DIRECTION

T. A. Wilson

All organizations need a sense of direction, goals, and objectives as guides to strategic action. Strategic management is based on goals and objectives because they give identity, purpose, and mission to the strategy. Strategic goals give meaning to the general direction, and allow the strategy to be converted into specific actions, programs, and targets. The objectives usually include expected targets for internal performance such as profitability, sales, cash flow, etc., as well as anticipated impact on external factors including rate of growth, innovation, market penetration, and market share.

Boeing, for example, under chairman T. A. Wilson set as a strategic goal the development of a new generation of fuel-efficient aircraft—the 757 and 767—while McDonnell-Douglas has no new generation of planes to introduce in the early eighties. Recently, Delta Airlines placed an order for sixty of Boeing's new 757, worth about $3 billion. Delta's order is just the beginning in the race to replace aging aircraft with new fuel efficient planes, like the 757, which burns about 40 percent less fuel per seat than the planes it will succeed.

WHAT GOALS AND OBJECTIVES ARE

Organizational goals and objectives refer to the results which an organization seeks to achieve. An organization usually pursues many goals including primary or strategic objectives, and secondary or subunit objectives.

Organizational goals are desired future states which the organization seeks to achieve. The goals are broad general guidelines to thinking which provide levels of attainment that are relatively timeless. Goals are aimed at the broad purpose and mission of the organization, and include survival, efficiency, and profitability.

Organizational objectives, on the other hand, are the statements that help guide the activities of groups and members toward the overall goals. Objectives are more specific and time-bound than goals, and are: 1) time-limited, 2) measurable, and 3) quantifiable. In Figure 3.1, the relationship between goals, objectives, plans and controls is shown. The plans and controls flow from the goals and objectives. The strategic goals are selected by the strategist and are influenced by environmental forces.

The objectives are the end results or the end state toward which an organization is striving, for example, a 20 percent rate of growth or a 12 percent rate of return. The strategy is the plan or program for accomplishing the objectives, for example, an acquisition strategy, or a cost-cutting strategy. There are many different objectives which may be pursued.

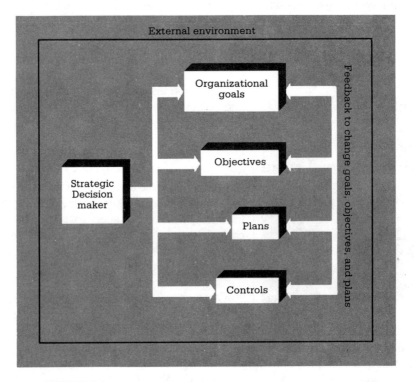

FIGURE 3.1
The Relation of Goals to Objectives, Plans and Controls
SOURCE: Adopted from Edgar F. Huse, *The Modern Manager* (Minneapolis: West Publishing, 1979).

MULTIPLE GOALS

Organizations often have multiple goals rather than one single goal and these goals may even be at cross purposes, such as seeking growth and minimizing costs. Peter Drucker (a leading management consultant) has suggested the importance of managing by objectives and indicated a number of areas in which objectives should be set, including:[6]

1 Profitability
2 Market share
3 Efficiency or productivity
4 Increasing physical and financial resources
5 Innovation
6 Member satisfaction and development
7 Responsibility to shareholders, individuals, etc.
8 Public and social responsibility.

Most firms pursue multiple objectives. Some are short-run targets while others are based on a longer-time horizon. The strategist must set priorities among conflicting goals and objectives. Many retail firms stress shorter-run goals, while others, like Weyerhaeuser, aim at longer-term results.

STRATEGY AT PILLSBURY

Pillsbury Company provides an example of the role of strategic goal setting during a period of organizational transition. William Spoor took over as CEO and set out to develop a new set of goals in order to revitalize the company. After an analysis of the firm's strengths and weaknesses, Spoor and his management team designed a new set of goals and a five-year strategic plan they termed the "Pillsbury Dream."

By his own admission, Bill Spoor, intensely hates to lose. But he loves to play the game—buying and selling businesses for his company, recruiting much-heralded executives from outside, bouncing candidates off one another to determine who gets which top spot. "He's not a manager," said one vice president recently, "—he's a builder."[7] But Spoor has moved the Pillsbury organization toward those strategic goals.

The goals of the firm, then, provide a long-term directional purpose for the organization and company members. The objectives provide more specific guidelines for managerial actions. In the next section, we shall examine why and how objectives are formulated.

WHY USE GOALS AND OBJECTIVES

Just as the environment is subject to change, internal or external forces can cause change in the objectives of any organization as well. For example, a university may pursue an objective of seeking very high-quality students for its graduate programs.

However, if the total number of students available begins to decrease, then the organization may be forced to shift its objectives, by lowering its standards, to meet these new conditions. Generally, there are several reasons why goals are important:

To define the organization's mission   Goals give purpose to the organization. Strategists then initiate actions designed to focus organizational resources toward these objectives.

Goals and objectives perform an integrating function   They provide a means for setting priorities and resolving conflicts between organizational elements. Marketing units may seek one set of objectives, R and D departments another, and financial groups yet another. The strategic goals provide a means of integrating and coordinating these diverse activities and functions.

Objectives provide measures of organizational performance   Objectives set out a target to be achieved and also provide a measure of how well these goals have been accomplished. The objectives enable the organization to set strategy directly around the basic targets of the business. The emphasis is on the combination of factors and functions needed to accomplish the end results.

HOW GOALS ARE FORMULATED

Organizations have not one but multiple sets of goals and objectives. Some objectives are very important; others are less urgent. H. Igor Ansoff of The European Institute for Advanced Studies in Management has suggested that the firm formulates goals which are distinct and different from those of individual participants in the firm. He further notes that, "In our main area of interest, the strategic problem, objectives are used as yardstricks for decisions on changes, deletions, and additions to the firm's product/market posture."[8]

According to Ansoff, these objectives can take the form of a *"threshold objective"* (the minimum acceptable level of achievement) or a *"goal"* (the desired outcome or level of aspiration) and they are ranked in order of priority to form a goal hierarchy.

OPERATIVE VS. OFFICIAL GOALS

Charles A. Perrow has also noted the difference between official goals and operative goals.[9] The *operative goals* are the end results which managers seek to achieve and which actually guide the activities of the organization. The *official goals,* on the other hand, are those which are publically announced by the firm. These are often termed "motherhood and apple pie" goals, statements which no one can really take issue with but are of little practical use in actual operations.

How are these strategic goals and objectives formulated? While there are a number of ways in which goals can be formulated, three major theoretical explanations are discussed here.

GOAL COALITIONS

Earlier economic theorists proposed a single owner-entrepenuer with a single goal: profit maximization. Others, such as Richard M. Cyert and James G. March, have described the organization as a set of forces and interests each seeking to influence goals. Cyert and March contend that goals emerge from a *coalition of interests* and individuals who bargain with each other over objectives using money, status, and power to press their views.[10] Henry Mintzberg's power configuration model describes a situation where individual players seek to exert power within the rules of the game to attain goals acceptable to them as individuals.

Another explanation by Frank Heller proposes that goals evolve as a response to the values of top managers, in terms of what group or type of person is dominant and in turn will strongly influence the choice of goals.[11] Finally, James D. Thompson and William J. McEwen have argued that goals are dynamic variables evolved from review and adjustment and as such are formed as responses to external pressure.[12] These factors, which have major influence on the goal formulation process, will be discussed in the next sections.

POWER AND COALITIONS

The strategic goals, then, are the outcome of coalitions of interests and bargaining among mutually influencing forces. Mintzberg (McGill University) has advanced a model suggesting that goal formation is the result of power and the translation of present goals into organizational desires and actions.[13] Mintzberg's model includes two forces of influence: external and internal, resulting in several different power configurations.

THE EXTERNAL COALITION (EC)

The external forces have the power and influence to affect the goals through what Mintzberg terms the external coalition. This includes four main groups: the owners, suppliers, unions, and the public. The influence of these groups depends upon the degree to which they are concentrated and to which the organization is dependent upon them. These groups influence the firm by social norms, specific constraints (law, etc.), pressure campaigns, direct controls, and membership on the board of directors.

Mintzberg proposes three kinds of external coalitions (ECs):

- Dominated EC: a single individual or group holds most of the power in the EC.
- Divided EC: power is shared among a few main individuals or groups.
- Passive EC: larger numbers of individuals or groups share the power.

THE INTERNAL COALITION (IC)

It is by the efforts of the internal coalition that action is taken and goals emerge. This is the heart of the organizational power system.

The internal coalition includes five main groups: top managers, middle managers, technical staff, support staff, and operators. These groups influence goals by the personal control system, the bureaucratic control system, the political control system, and the ideological system.

There are five basic internal coalitions (ICs):

- Bureaucratic IC: power remains mostly with top management, but some goes to analysts who design the system.

- Autocratic IC: power is controlled by top management alone.

- Ideologic IC: power resides in the top manager because the top manager embodies the ideology.

- Meritocratic IC: power follows expertise. Therefore, it is widely dispersed throughout the organization.

- Politicized IC: power resides with political energy and skills—devoted to power games.

ORGANIZATIONAL POWER CONFIGURATIONS

Mintzberg has proposed six basic power configurations as shown in Figure 3.2. The configurations which he identifies are based on the relation of external and internal coalition forces. Power is derived from the role of the individual and the support of the two coalitions.

POWER CONFIGURATION	EXTERNAL COALITION	INTERNAL COALITION
Instrument	Dominated	Bureaucratic
Closed System	Passive	Bureaucratic
Autocracy	Passive	Personalized
Missionary	Passive	Ideologic
Meritocracy	Passive	Professional
Political Arena	Divided	Politicized

FIGURE 3.2

Six "Pure" Power Configurations

SOURCE: Henry Mintzberg, "Organizational Power and Goals: A Skeletal Theory," in Charles Hofer and Dan Schendel, *Strategic Management: A New View of Business Policy and Planning* (Boston: Little, Brown, 1979).

1. The Instrumented Power Configuration   In this configuration, goals are dominated by one external individual (usually the owner) who controls the internal, bureaucratic organization. This system tends to rely on top-down, highly formalized procedures and is associated with stable environments.

2. The Closed System   This system is similar to the first with one difference: Bureaucratic power rests with the internal manager, usually the president, and the external forces are passive. This system is found in large organizations in which external control is dispersed and ineffective.

3. The Autocracy   This system is similar to the prior one. An internal autocratic manager dominates goals over a passive external coalition. This system is frequently found in electronics firms, in a dynamic environment and with one dominant energizer.

4. The Missionary   In the missionary power configuration, objectives are strongly influenced by past ideology and a charismatic leader. The charisma dictates the objectives.

5. The Meritocracy   In the meritocratic power configuration, the goals are set by a consensus of the members, most of whom are professionals. The internal coalition, the professionals, tends to dominate goal formulation. This system is often found where the work is complex, such as in hospitals, universities, etc.

6. The Political Arena   Here both internal and external power is divided and fragmented. The goal formulation is often vague and conflicting. It is a purely political arena.

The formulation of objectives is not a simple process: According to Mintzberg, goals are set by a complex interplay of internal and external role players and are the results of the play of power.

Organizational goals then, change as a result of:

- The changing demands from the coalition groups that make up the organization
- The changing power levels of members.

MANAGERIAL VALUES

Another factor influencing the formulation of strategic goals is the value system of the strategic decision maker. William Guth (New York University) and Renato Tagiuri (NYU) reported on the role of personal values in corporate strategy and found, "It is quite clear, on the basis of both observation and systematic studies of top management in business organizations, that personal values are important determinants of the choice of corporate strategy."[14] The manager develops a value system from education and experience, and these become part of his management style. A value may be defined as "a conception, explicit or implicit, of what an individual or group rewards as desirable. . . ." Values in this sense act as a guidance system which the manager uses when faced with a decision.

GOALS AND VALUES

Organizational goals, then, are formulated from the confluence of individual values and motivations of members. Therefore, organizational goals represent changing coalitions and shifting compromises among internal value orientations and the changing demands made by the outside environment. As social psychologist Robert Katz says: "Every strategic action must strike a balance between so many conflicting values, objectives, and criteria that it will always be suboptimal from any single viewpoint. Every decision or choice affecting the whole enterprise has negative consequences for some of the parts."[15]

VALUE ORIENTATIONS

Value orientations have been examined by a number of researchers who have found that values play an important role in decision making. Guth and Tagiuri found that American managers tend to place a higher value orientation on certain values than others, from among six major value orientations:

- Theoretical: an orientation toward truth and knowledge.
- Economic: an orientation toward what is useful and powerful.
- Political: an orientation toward power.
- Aesthetic: an orientation toward form and harmony.
- Social: an orientation toward love of people.
- Religious: an orientation toward unity in the universe.

Guth and Tagiuri found that American executives have a major orientation toward economic, theoretical, and political values rather than the other three.

Another study by George England on managerial values reported that successful American managers tend to favor more pragmatic, dynamic, interactive and achievement-oriented values, while those less successful tended to prefer static and passive value orientation.[16]

SIX VALUE AREAS

Douglas T. Hall has suggested six value areas that are important to managing people in modern organizations[17]:

1 There is now more concern about values per se, not just different values.
2 Action is more important. Merely talking about values is not enough. One's values must be backed by action.
3 Values such as integrity, honesty, openness, and realness are more important.
4 In general, values are more humanistic. There are different motivating factors.
5 There is increased concern for the ultimate social value of one's work.
6 Authority based on expertise, personal style, and convictions, or accomplishments is more legitimate than authority based on age or position.

In summary, there is a growing awareness of the impact of the manager's value systems on goal formulation. Goals emerge from the conflicting values and goals of various individuals and groups, as a result of a bargaining, negotiation, and the power process.

EXTERNAL FACTORS

Setting strategic goals and objectives is one of the critical management functions. While some organizations operate in a less dynamic environment than others, no organization can afford to stand still or drift. If the organization is to succeed, it must deal with the uncertainty of the environment. Strategic goal setting and planning are the major tools utilized to cope with the changing environment.

EXTERNAL FORCES

Obviously, some organizations must cope with greater rates of change than others. In any case, the major tools of the strategist are those that anticipate and adapt to changes beyond the control of management.

Many intervening variables outside the control of the manager influence the formulation of objectives.

Unions   One factor which can influence strategic planning is the relationships with unions. Archie R. McCardill, for example, arrived at International Harvester and began to tighten every bolt in the huge and outmoded operation. However, McCardill initiated a confrontation with the union (UAW) about overtime which resulted in a six-month-long strike, which hurt both sides. What did the company get out of the strike? It got nothing concrete but hopes that the new system will work better than the old.[18]

Competition   One firm's strategic moves can be drastically affected by a competitor's actions. When Texas Instruments started to cut prices in hand calculators, it forced Hewlett Packard to revise its marketing goals and strategy.

Suppliers   Each organizational system is dependent upon its suppliers for various types of materials, etc., and its effectiveness is dependent upon how the relationship is handled. Boeing, for example, buys jet engines for its commercial aircraft. If defense contracts are expanded, it is possible that that factor could delay delivery of engines to Boeing. To ensure a dependable and highly reliable supply, Hewlett Packard now makes its own semiconductors, which it is used to buy outside.

Energy   Because of the increasing cost of energy, management must place greater emphasis on this factor. Almost every organization is attempting to control costs and become more energy efficient. Many companies, such as Dow Chemical, use energy derived from production processes, whereas others use waste products, wood, paper, etc., as a fuel source.

Change   When change occurs too rapidly, the capacity of management to react is strained, thereby creating the danger of being surpassed by competitors. As a result, managers must become more adaptable and flexible than ever before. As an example, fast-changing technology has spurred growth and change in the semiconductor industry, including a bewildering array of manufacturing processes and new techniques to build more and more electronic circuitry onto a quarter-inch-square silicon chip. Yet industry leaders expect to see more changes in the next decade than have been seen in the past ten years.

"If you think what we have today is amazing, just wait for Very Large-Scale Integration (VLSI)," says George H. Heilmeier, vice president of corporate research, development, and engineering at Texas Instruments. Continuing, Mr. Heilmeier says, "We must get ourselves out of the rut that says VLSI is simply going to make existing quantitative computation applications smaller, faster and cheaper—a straight-line projection of future trends based on the past. VLSI technology is the key to . . . machine intelligence that represents not a straight-line projection but a quantum leap in opportunities."[19]

And as more and more circuits and functions are built into the microscopic chips, there are impacts on other industries and technologies: calculators, communications, etc. The expected rate of change and problems of "future shock" will lead to managers who are more innovative, adaptive, and flexible and who will develop strategy in such a dynamic environment.

INTERNAL FORCES

Managers must develop effective internal communications to allocate resources intelligently, if strategic plans are to be workable.

Financial   The financial resources which are available to the manager also place constraints on the selection of possible goals. For example, at Chrysler, top management had an investment in large car plant and equipment, yet demand for small cars such as Omni and Horizon was growing. Chrysler decided to purchase a limited number of engines for its smaller cars, and to continue on a full-scale product line. Unfortunately, the market for large autos shrank drastically, while small car demands increased. Consequently, Chrysler could not supply the smaller cars which would have sold, and was left with high inventory levels of big cars, which it could not sell.

Technical   The technical resources are also factors in selecting a strategy. At Hewlett Packard, for example, the decision to move into the microcomputer field (HP3000) was made because H/P already had the technical resources available in other projects. It was a matter of putting them to use, whereas for another company it might have meant developing an advanced technical capability which it did not already possess.

POLITICAL COALITIONS

Strategic objectives are also influenced by the power relationships or political coalitions within the organization.

The degree of conflict   Some organizations are relatively cohesive, others have conflicting elements which influence strategic objectives. Lee Iacocca, formerly with

Ford, and John Bache of CBS are two examples of executives with good performance records, but who were replaced because they were involved in conflicts within the organization.

The level of support   A strategy must receive support and acceptance from members at all levels of the organization if it is to be a benefit. Harold Geneen and Roy Ash were able to gain support for their goals at ITT and AM, respectively. Richard Goodwin, who set JM on new strategic directions, lost the support of the board of directors and was replaced. Robert Abboud, formerly Chairman of First Chicago (also one of the "ten toughest managers"), replaced some 200 managers, but lost the support and confidence of his board members and also was forced to resign.

In summary, strategic goals and objectives are not the result of any one individual's ideas, but rather result from a coalition of external and internal forces. Thus, managers attempt to develop strategic directions that are acceptable to these external and internal power groups. Also, strategic objectives are derived from past activities and performance. Strategies which pay off are continued, while if there is a lack of results, new strategic objectives are identified.

ADAPTING TO A CHANGING ENVIRONMENT

Change is inevitable. Executives are adapting to changing market conditions and, at the same time, facing the need for creating an "anticipative" rather than a "reactive" managerial system. They are searching for ways to manage an increasingly complex technology and a more sophisticated work force. To accomplish these diverse goals, managers need more than piecemeal, ad hoc decisions dealing only with current crises. They require long-term strategic planning to prepare for future organization requirements.

Given an environment of rapid change, a static organization can no longer be effective. Managers such as Dick Goodwin of Johns-Manville are able to recognize when changes are needed, and possess the necessary skills and competency to implement these changes. Organizations such as Johns-Manville adapt to a dynamic environment by introducing internal changes that will allow the organization to become more effective and competitive. Sometimes this means moving into new product lines, or like J-M, even moving from New York to a ranch near Denver to change its outdated image.

Since the environment is composed of systems outside the immediate influence of the organization, the organization attempts to adapt itself to these forces by introducing internal changes that will allow the organization to be more effective. To be successful, an organization has to develop a management strategy that will adequately handle the challenges and opportunities which it faces. The strategy adequate at one point in time under one set of conditions may become progressively less effective under changing circumstances. At J-M, Richard Goodwin was ultimately interested in developing a strategic plan for resource allocation and in designing organizational policy and processes to create a more adaptive and flexible organization.

Why is change so difficult? Possibly because the culture of the organization becomes a part of the people who perform the work. At Johns-Manville, the organization structure, procedures, and relationships continued to reinforce prior patterns of behavior and to resist the new ones. As a result, strategic change sometimes results in upheaval and dissatisfaction, and possibly even resignation, dismissals, or transfers. Consequently, an organization must develop an adaptive orientation and management strategy which is geared to its environment. Managers in different organizations deal with situations which may be dramatically different. Some organizations exist in relatively stable environments, while others operate in highly dynamic settings. Each requires a different orientation to the environment.

ORIENTATIONS TO STABILITY AND ADAPTATION

Every organization must have enough stability to continue to function satisfactorily and still prevent itself from becoming too static or stagnant to adapt to changing conditions. Both stability and adaptation are essential to continued survival and growth.

An organization which operates in a mature field with a stable product and relatively few competitors needs a different adaptive orientation than a firm operating in a high-growth market, among numerous competitors, and with a high degree of innovation. The former operates in an environment which is relatively stable, while the latter is facing a more dynamic and turbulent set of conditions. A stable environment is characterized by unchanging basic products and services, a static level of competition, a low level of technological innovation, a formalized and centralized structure, and a steady, slow rate of growth. Such an environment remains relatively stable over long time periods.

A dynamic environment, on the other hand, is characterized by rapidly changing product lines, an increasing and changing set of competitors, rapid and continual technological innovation, and rapid market growth. For today's organization, the idea of change is clear. A static organization can no longer survive. Yesterday's accomplishments amount to little in an environment of rapidly advancing markets, products, and life-styles.

In order to survive, organizations must devise methods of continuous self-appraisal. Managers must recognize when it is necesssary to make strategic changes, and they must develop the systems capable of implementing these changes. To meet these conditions, many companies have created specialized strategic planning units whose primary purpose is planning for organizational changes. These units are developing new programs to help the organization improve its level of adaptation to its environment, and policies to maintain a stable identity so that change is not overwhelming. To achieve successful change, both goals must be satisfied.

A MODEL OF ADAPTIVE ORIENTATION

A simplified model of environmental stability and adaptive orientation is shown in Figure 3.3. One dimension represents the degree of stability in the organization's environment, and the second represents the degree of adaptiveness or flexibility present in the internal orientation of the organization.

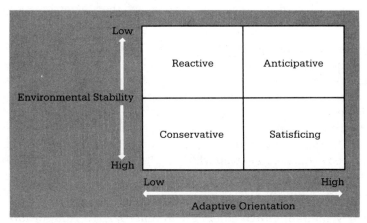

FIGURE 3.3
A Model of Environmental Adaptation Orientation in Organizations

Organizations can vary greatly on these dimensions and the various combinations of these orientations can lead to differing adaptive styles. Certain types of orientations are possible.

Conservative Management (Stable Environment, Low Adaptation)

Conservative management refers to a style of management based on low risk, with formalized procedures and a high degree of structure and control. Typically these organizations have very stable goals and a highly centralized structure. They also tend to have more managerial levels, a higher ratio of superiors to subordinates, and an emphasis upon formal control systems. There may be a tendency to value tradition, to keep on doing things as they have always been done, to value seniority more than performance, and an aversion to accepting new ideas. Johns-Manville, for example, had failed to keep pace with a changing environment.

While this is a low-risk style of managing, it may lead to serious problems in the long run. A competitor has observed of Ray-O-Vac Corporation's declining share of the battery market. "Their technical people came up with new ideas but management didn't come out with the product. . . . They maintained the *status quo* and now they are in the follower's position."[20]

Reactive Management (Dynamic Environment, Low Adaptation)

Organizations with a low level of adaptation, but existing in a rapidly changing environment, tend to deal with problems on a short-run, crisis basis. *Reactive management* refers to a style of reacting to a stimulus after conditions in the environment have changed. It is a short-term, crisis type of adaptation often involving replacement of key people, hasty reorganization, and drastic cutting of people and product lines.

A major food corporation, for example, was feeling the pressures of changing business conditions, losing momentum, experiencing product failures, and reporting decreased earnings. The new chief executive instituted some massive changes, including a major management reorganization, a companywide efficiency drive, cutting salaried pesonnel by 10 percent, and taking a very hard look at all marketing programs. The reactive approach to change implies waiting until serious problems emerge which can no longer be ignored and then taking drastic corrective measures.

Satisficing Management (Stable Environment, High Adaptation) *Satisficing* (accepting something that is "good enough" rather than reaching for the optimum) *management* refers to a style of managing which emphasizes a more centralized decision-making structure with problems being referred to the top. Because of the stable environment, there tend to be more levels of management with coordination done by formal committees. Planning and decision making are usually concentrated at the top, with high clarity of procedures and roles. Change is accomplished at a rate that is "good enough" to keep up with the industry, but certainly well behind the state of the art. Such organizations often tend to accept strategies that are "good enough," because of the low level of pressure for change from the environment.

Anticipative Management (Dynamic Environment, High Adaptation) Organizations with a high level of adaptation existing in a rapidly changing environment tend to utilize the anticipative management style. *Anticipative management* refers to planning for changes to deal with future conditions before they actually come about. Examples of anticipative management would include the innovations of corporations like ITT, Texas Instruments, TRW Systems, and Xerox, which have actively initiated programs of improvement before conditions became critical.

To illustrate the difference between these approaches, let us look at the U.S. railroad industry. In the first half of the 1970s, records were set for freight tonnage, yet earnings did not keep pace. This resulted in bottlenecks, car shortages, and the breakdown of physical plants. It is predicted that tonnage will double within a decade, yet it is currently unclear how the railroads will meet this challenge. The reactive management approach is to wait until after the freight tonnage has doubled to deal with car shortages, physical plant deficiencies, and lack of adequate numbers of trained personnel. This approach operates on a crisis basis, waiting for a problem to reach a critical stage before making internal realignments. The anticipative approach is to recognize that changes in railroad technology, organizations, and people will be required within a decade and initiate planned changes now to deal with predicted future conditions.

There are, then, four basic orientations. A conservative management orientation has little ability to adapt to changes but there is also little pressure to change because of the stable environment. A reactive management orientation has the need to respond to a rapidly changing environment but does not have the flexibility to adapt. A satisficing management orientation has the ability to respond to changing situations but finds itself in a relatively slow-changing environment. An anticipative management orientation has both the ability and need to respond to a dynamic environment. It seems that most modern organizations are increasingly finding the need for the anticipative orientation.

CONTINGENCY THEORIES AND STRATEGIC MANAGING

The increasing rate of environmental change and the increasing size and complexity of organizations have led to changes in strategic management practices. One of the newer practices is termed the "contingency approach."

The contingency theory emerges from the idea that there are many differing organizational and environmental factors which influence strategy and seeks to determine a relationship in which organizational strategy is dependent upon specified environmental conditions.

THE CONTINGENCY APPROACH

The contingency approach to strategy suggests that, for a certain set of organizational and environmental conditions, an optimal strategy exists. Contingency approaches are based upon the idea of contingent relationships between an independent variable: environmental conditions; and a dependent variable: the organization's strategic response. While this approach is in its formative stages, it offers some interesting insights into future developments.

THE CONTINGENCY THEORY

The contingency theory suggests that there is no one "silver bullet solution" for all of the varied problems of strategic management. The managers of Apple Computer, a small manufacturer of personal computers, for example, cannot follow the same strategy as giant IBM uses, even though they are both in the same industry. The managers of Apple Computer, Stephen P. Jobs, 25, and Stephen G. Wozniak, 29, have devised a strategy to fit their particular company based on a special market segment—personal computers—and a strategy of product quality in a field aimed at cutting prices: Apple builds the "Cadillac" of personal computers. *Fortune* tells the Apple story this way:

STRATEGY AT APPLE CORPORATION

"Graduates of Santa Clara's Homestead High School, Jobs and Wozniak dropped out of college. The self-taught computer whizzes went to work for local electronics companies. The two began collaborating five years ago at the Home Brew Computer Club in Palo Alto. They designed their first machine in Job's bedroom, built it in his parents' garage, and showed it to a local computer-store owner, who promptly ordered 25. Demand for the "personal" computer, mainly from hobbyists, soon outstripped the young men's ability to produce, so they began looking for help.

"Enter A. C. Markkula, Jr., 38, who had been marketing manager at Intel, the fast-growing producer of integrated circuits. "Mike" Markkula was soon convinced that the two Steves, as they are known at Apple, were on to something big. He put up $91,000, secured a line of credit, and later raised some $600,000 from venture capitalists. Markkula became chairman of the company in May 1977, and Micheal Scott, 37, signed on as president a month later, taking a 50 percent cut from his job as a director of manufacturing at National Semiconductor."

"You don't need an Apple computer to tell you that at least four new multimillionaires are now roaming the Silicon Valley. The four men own 40 percent of the company, which earned $11.7 million in sales of $117 million last year. At the public-offering price, Scott's shares were worth $62 million, Wozniak's $88 million,

Markkula's $154 million, and Jobs' $165 million."[21] Not bad for a couple of college dropouts!

As a result of the success of Apple Computer, other major firms including IBM are now entering this dynamic market, which will add new variables and unknowns to strategic planning in the future. Although strategic management may be largely situational, there are still certain variables upon which strategic decisions are contingent.

CONTINGENCY VIEWS

While systems theory may provide a conceptual overview of organizational functioning, the strategic manager needs to know how the subsystems of a particular organization are uniquely related in that specific environment, and how best to deal with its particular problems. Contingency theory recognizes that such differences do exist, and that what constitutes effective management in one system may not in another setting. Contingency views tend to emphasize the characteristics of a specific organization, and suggest that to organize and manage a strategic program one must consider the set of conditions in that particular setting.

The contingency approach, then, seeks to identify a relationship between an organization's strategic response and certain environmental variables. The contingency approach has evolved from the work of Paul Lawrence and Jay Lorsch of Harvard, in which they found that there is no one best way to organize different firms in differing industries and that environmental forces require differing structures for different stages of growth. What is new in this approach is that it seeks to describe structures and strategic actions as they best fit the organization's goals for a given set of circumstances.

HOFER'S MODEL

The recent work of Charles W. Hofer (New York University) seeks to identify many of the important variables involved in selecting a strategy. He suggests that "The most fundamental variable in determining an appropriate business strategy is the stage of the product life cycle."[23] The variables considered are:

1 *Market and consumer behavior variables*
2 *Industry structure variables*
3 *Competitor variables*
4 *Supplier variables*
5 *Broader environmental variables*
6 *Organizational characteristic and response variables*

Hofer then presents contingency hypotheses using these determinants. In the maturity stage, for example: When

1   the degree of product differentiation is low,

2   the nature of buyer needs is primarily economic,

3   the rate of technological change in process design is high,

4   the ratio of distribution costs to manufacturing value added is high,

5   the purchase frequency is high,

5   the buyer concentration is high, and

7   the degree of capacity utilization is low;

then businesses should:

1   allocate most of their R and D funds to improvements in process design rather than to new product development,

2   allocate most of their plant and equipment expenditures to new equipment purchases,

3   seek to integrate forward or backward in order to increase the value they add to the product,

4   attempt to improve their production scheduling and inventory control procedures in order to increase their capacity utilization,

5   attempt to segment the market, and

6   attempt to reduce their raw material unit costs by standardizing their product design and using interchangeable components throughout their product line in order to qualify for volume discounts.

SUMMARY OF THE CONTINGENCY APPROACH

The *contingency approach* suggests that there is no one best way of managing in all situations. Given certain combinations of contingencies (such as a stable external environment and a low adaptive orientation to change), one can specify general strategic approaches that are likely to be more effective than others. In other words, the *contingency approach* identifies various types of "If-then" relationships and suggests general directions for change, depending on the situation. The contingency approach is also based on certain conceptual skills, such as diagnosing, forecasting, and understanding the various types of situations that are likely to confront the organization.

As noted, the contingency theory is in its early stages and because of the complexity of the variables no comprehensive contingency strategy has yet been perfected. This suggests that one of the major uses of contingency approaches may lie in the identification of critical variables and possible strategic alternatives. However, the contingency theories do present valuable guidelines for practicing managers by providing a framework for considering which strategy may be preferable in a given industry or situation.

CONTINGENCY PLANNING

Contingency planning involves planning events whose occurrences is uncertain but meant to be anticipated in the strategic plan. The probability of occurrence and the severe impact should they come about call for anticipative planning in specifying alternative actions and strategic regrouping to meet possible contingencies.

A contingency plan is a part of a company's strategic planning process. The basic purpose is to achieve a state of anticipation to counteract possibile problems and to reduce risks.[23] Contingency planning forces management to identify critical assumptions, to review the implementation of strategy and to respond rapidly to contingencies. One of the basic factors affecting the use of contingency planning is the environment of an organization.[24] The organization facing new problems and frequent changes needs flexible strategies that are highly adaptive, responsive, and open to innovation.

NEW PROCEDURES

The development of contingency planning requires new procedures. The first step is to identify critical environmental factors over which the company has little control: A possible downturn of the economy, a shortage of critical parts, a competitor's movement into the market, or labor problems are such contingency factors. The next step involves estimating the impact and scope of possible problems. A slowdown in the economy may affect all business areas of a company, but with differing impacts on each segment. Contingency planning, then, provides alternatives, changing objectives, options for strategic adjustment, and, if necessary, a revision of the basic strategy.

Consequently, the very nature of strategic planning is undergoing a dramatic change. Instead of relying on a narrow strategic plan, managers are now developing a whole range of contingency plans and alternate scenarios. A wood products company, such as Boise Cascade or Potlatch, might develop a whole series of strategies based upon varying levels of housing demand. For example, at 2 million housing starts per year, a growth strategy might be pursued, while at 1.5 million starts, a retrenchment plan might be selected.

WORST CASE SCENARIOS

Many organizations also develop alternate plans for drastic changes, so called "*worst case*" *scenarios*: if things go completely wrong, what can we do to maximize our objectives? Added to this, the economic and political uncertainty in the international situation causes many organizations to try to forecast possible economic or political hot spots or upheavals, such as the Iranian overthrow in 1979.

The contingency view suggests that managers in differing organizations face situations which may be very different on a number of dimensions. There may be varying degrees of structure, differing motivation levels, and a diverse potential for conflict. The manager, then, must recognize that there is "no one best way" for all organizations. The contingency approach suggests that the effectiveness of various strategies will vary according to the circumstances. The contingency variables that need to be considered and the relative emphasis will depend on the type of problem being considered.

COMPLEX PLANNING

As a result, the development of strategic planning is becoming more complex. Successful organizations in the future will be the ones that adapt most quickly to these new techniques of planning. Instead of relying on a single basic plan, managers are now formulating a whole selection of contingency plans and alternative scenarios. The contingency planning method offers multiple options based upon a given set of conditions. A series of possible plans, plan A, plan B, plan C, etc., are formulated based upon a relative economic outlook. Plan A may be based upon a high growth economy, the most optimistic view, with each alternate plan keyed to a different level of economic activity.[25] At the lowest level are the "worst case scenarios," contingency plans based on possible economic or political upheavals, developing plans of action if everything should go wrong.

At Dow Chemical Company, 140 separate cost inputs are fed into an economic simulation model to provide possible strategic scenarios, often involving as many as 100 separate cost/price variables. The effect of potential new chemical plants can be analyzed in terms of capacity, demand, etc., to provide an estimated return on investment, given different economic situations or demand levels. Dow also has a product management team that analyzes social and political pressures around the world and forecasts the possible impact on its business of such things as overthrow of governments, etc. Dow calls this its ESP (economic, social, political) report.

For corporate planners and top managers, the environment has never seemed so turbulent as it is today. The very uncertainties, from the unsettled economic outlook to the energy crisis, make accurate planning for the future much more difficult. In such a rapidly changing environment, the corporate plan may be out of date within six to twelve months, and new strategic plans and goals must be devised to meet these changing conditions.

KEY FACTORS IN STRATEGIC PLANNING[26]

One of the major reasons for the rapid adoption of strategic planning models is the fact that the absence of corporate planning efforts will result in organizational performance that is lower than potential. The experiences of managers and consultants in many industries and firms suggest that the following factors are important keys to a successful planning system.

1. INVENT THE FUTURE

Comprehensive long-range planning is not solely an attempt to blueprint the future by extrapolating from the present. If an organization plans by a statistical projection of current activities, it tends to make it difficult to adapt to changing conditions. Instead the firm must test assumptions, and invent its future position. As Mead Corporation's William Wommack says, "Operating people depend too much on trade association forecasts, and the economists that trade associations hire are too optimistic. When you get two sets of data you tend to believe the one you want."

2. STAY FLEXIBLE

Any organizational plan that is more than one year old is probably obsolete, given the rapidly changing environment of most organizations. To achieve maximum value, strategic planning needs accurate information and timely updating. Dow Chemical Co.'s director of corporate planning, J. E. Mitchell, says too many plans "are too inflexible and involve too many numbers. We stress fast response time. We worry about getting too bureaucratic." Avoid communicating through computer printouts, says Mitchell. Use people-to-people contact instead.

3. AVOID GETTING INTO A NUMBERS GAME

There is currently an increasing reliance on more sophisticated quantitative tools at corporate levels. Often these systems tend to translate broad organizational goals into specific financial targets. Unfortunately, these elements of financial performance are invariably related to time. However, many of the key intervening variables (interest rates, technical innovation, etc.) are not controlled by a rigid time horizon. Consequently, the plan should not attempt to overemphasize "forced" numerical targets, at the expense of broad goals.

4. INVOLVE TOP MANAGERS

Corporate planning must be a way of life, and a part of the corporate culture, not merely an annual exercise in number-crunching. The top managers of the organization need to develop a climate of effective corporate planning by active support and involvement. Harvard's Professor James P. Baughman says the chief executive office has more influence on the planning process than any other variable. "He can make or break a plan depending on the vibes he sends out in a crisis," says Baughman. Says Planmetrics, Inc.'s Gary L. Neale: "The real planner—whatever his title—should be reporting to the CEO, or be the CEO."

5. CONTINGENCY PLANNING APPROACHES

Strategic planning is done on the basis of predicting future conditions and which events are most likely to occur. There are, however, many other possible conditions or events which may pose serious threats, or provide access to great opportunities. The planner must ask some "what-if" questions regarding the future and then derive likely responses from each possible scenario. For example, "what if there is a shortage of a critical raw material?" or "what if a new competitor enters the field?" etc. As a result, contingency planning should identify events that can occur during the planning time frame, their effect on strategy, and what actions the organization may take in the occurrence of such events. "The point is not to overreact, to understand that when the business cycle is at its maximum rate of change, it is probably the worst possible time to start making changes in your strategy," says General Electric Co.'s Reuben Gutoff. In a year like this, he says, the trick is to position yourself for an upturn in the economy.

6. THE PLANNING IS NOT AN END IN ITSELF

Although the strategic planning process may produce a written document on a periodic basis, the process should be a continuous activity of top management. It is rare that the plan assesses future changes with complete accuracy. Therefore, the plan provides a framework and guideline for managerial action, but managers must be able to deal with changes if they are to maintain the needed flexibility of operation.

7. ANTICIPATE FUTURE PROBLEMS

Strategic planning deals with the future effect of current decisions. This involves the examination of cause-and-effect relationships among variables over time of an actual or proposed strategic decision. Consequently, an early warning of danger signals must be part of the planning process. "The toughest thing to get rid of is the Persian messenger syndrome, where the bearer of bad tidings is beheaded by the king," says William S. Woodside, American Can Co. executive vice president. "You have to lean over backwards to reward the guy who is first with the bad news. Most companies have all kinds of abilities to handle problems, if they only learn about them soon enough."

8. PLANNING SHOULD FLOW FROM LONG-RANGE GOALS

Strategy precedes planning. Therefore, strategic goals should be established before the planning takes place. Strategy deals with the directions the firm desires to follow: planning focuses on how these goals will be attained. Otherwise, short term, crisis management takes over. "The pressure to show short-term earnings-per-share gains," says Cresap, McCormick & Paget, Inc.'s Donald Miller, "is one of the biggest deterrents to effective long-range planning."

In the past, strategists could be reasonably confident about long-term economic projects and plan accordingly. Today this is not true. The degree of risk is higher than ever. The strategic decision maker must deal with changing variables. He must anticipate future conditions which makes strategic planning and management even more critical.

MANAGERIAL IMPLICATIONS

Strategic goals and objectives emerge from a coalition of internal and external forces. Despite the success of Richard Goodwin in rebuilding the fortunes of Johns-Manville, he ran into problems. He had designed a new strategic management and planning system, initiated new goals, shifted JM out of unprofitable businesses and moved aggressively into higher growth areas. He developed a management team and a participative style at JM. In short, he did it the way the textbooks say it should be done.

Then what wrong? Unfortunately, many of his ideas for change conflicted with the more conservative philosophy of the board of directors. And with the company in a more secure position he wasn't as indispensible as he had been in the past. As Mintzberg's model suggests, when the external coalition is powerful, then the chief executive cannot be too strong or a conflict will emerge. This happened at the J-M board meeting, when a coalition of nine of the twelve directors agreed to ask for Goodwin's resignation. He was replaced by John A. McKinney who said, "It all happened so fast, I almost missed it."[27]

AFTER THE SHOOTOUT

Twenty-two months after W. Richard Goodwin was fired as president of Johns-Manville Corp., the controversial and flamboyant executive is once again standing on the top rung of a corporate ladder. It is, however, a very short and precarious ladder. Goodwin has become the founder, chairman, and president of a tiny conglomerate called, aptly, the Goodwin Companies, Inc. It is involved, or trying to become involved, in the insulation, real-estate, construction, steel-pipe, expansion-bolt, and industrial-fuel businesses.

The fledgling company is based in a Denver suburb, about ten miles east and a billion dollars south of the 10,000-acre ranch that Goodwin once roamed when he was riding high as chief executive of Johns-Manville. It was Goodwin, of course, who engineered JM's exodus from New York to Denver a few years back, and who converted that ranch into one of the corporate world's most spectacular headquarters sites. He was just completing that $89-million project when the board of directors ambushed him in September 1976 (see "Shootout at the Johns-Manville Corral," *Fortune*, October 1976).

No one is more surprised to find Goodwin still in Denver, scrambling to pump life into his own little company, than Goodwin himself. "This is not what I expected I'd wind up doing," he says ruefully. An exceptionally candid man, Goodwin concedes that he formed G.C.I. only because none of the wonderful job offers he expected to receive following his ouster from J-M ever materialized. "I spoke with people at nearly every major executive-search firm in the country," he recalls. "Everybody said I'd be running another *Fortune* 500 company within six months. Everybody was wrong. Finally I said the hell with it, I'd start my own company."[28]

POWER POLITICS

The spectacular rise and fall of Dick Goodwin presents a graphic example of the complexity of the strategic process and the influence that *power politics* play in the formulation of *strategic goals and plans.*

Goals and *objectives* are a central element in a strategic process. They determine the direction in which the organization will move and position itself in a rapidly changing environment. The strategic goals come about from a series of negotiations and tradeoffs among both internal and external forces.

Finally, the strategic manager must realize that there are no clear, unified solutions that can be applied to all situations. Instead, there are contingent strategies which may work best under a given set of circumstances. Certainly contingency approaches can provide guidelines for identifying strategies which are preferable in a specific situation over others.

REVIEW QUESTIONS

1 What are the factors which influence goal formulation?

2 What is an organizational goal? How does it differ from an objective?

3 Explain the use of contingency approaches in planning.

4 Compare and contrast the four types of management orientations used in relating to the environment. Can you name some firms or industries which fit these four types?

5 Select an organization and interview members at several differing levels. How does the perception of goals and objectives differ between levels?

ENDNOTES

1 Herbert E. Meyer, "Shoot Out at the Johns-Manville Corral," *Fortune,* October, 1976, 146.

2 James Quinn, "Strategic Goals: Process and Politics," *Sloan Management Review,* Fall 1977, 21–37.

3 H. Edward Wrapp, "Good Managers Don't Make Policy Decisions," *Harvard Business Review,* September–October 1967, 95.

4 "Addressograph Gets the Roy Ash Treatment," *Business Week,* March 22, 1977, 78.

5 "Hewlett-Packard, Where Slower Growth is Smarter Management," *Business Week,* June 9, 1975, 50.

6 Peter Drucker, *The Practice of Management* (New York: Harper Brothers, 1954) p. 63.

7 Walter Kiechel, "Now for the Greening of Pillsbury," *Fortune,* Nov. 5, 1979, 128.

8 H. Igor Ansoff, *Corporate Strategy* (New York: McGraw-Hill, 1965).

9 C. Perrow, "The Analysis of Goals in Complex Organizations," *American Sociological Review,* December 1961, 854–66.

10 Richard Cyert and James March, *A Behavioral Theory of the Firm* (Englewood Cliffs, N.J.: Prentice-Hall, Inc. 1963).

11 Frank Heller, *Managerial Decision-Making: A Study of Leadership Styles and Power Sharing Among Senior Managers,* (London: Tavistock Publications, 1971).

12 James Thompson and William McEwen, "Organizational Goals and Environment: Goal-Setting as an Interaction Process," *American Sociological Review,* February 1958, 23–30.

13 Henry Mintzberg, "Organizational Power and Goals: A Skeletal Theory," pp. 64–80, in Charles Hofer and Dan Schendel, *Strategic Management: A New View of Business Policy and Planning* (Boston: Little, Brown, 1979).

14 William D. Guth and Renato Tagiuri, "Personal Values and Corporate Strategy," *Harvard Business Review,* September–October 1965, 123.

15 Robert L. Katz, *Management of the Total Enterprise* (Englewood Cliffs, N.J.: Prentice-Hall, 1970), p. 13.

16 George England, "Personal Value Systems of Managers and Administrators," *Academy of Management Proceedings,* August 1973.

17 Douglas T. Hall, "Potential for Career Growth," *Personnel Administration,* May–June 1971, 18–19.

18 "The Strike That Rained on Archie McCardells' Parade," *Fortune,* May 19, 1980, 91.

19 "The Super Chip" *Wall Street Journal,* April 27, 1979.

20 "ESB Ray-O-Vac: Decentralizing to Recharge Its Innovative Spirit," *Business Week,* March 12, 1979, 116.

21 "Whom the Apples Fell On," *Fortune,* January 12, 1981, 68.

22 C. W. Hofer, "Toward a Contingency Theory of Business Strategy," *Academy of Management Journal,* December 1975, 784–810.

23 See: John Argenti, *Systematic Corporate Planning,* (New York: Wiley 1974), pp. 238–40. Also D. E. Hussey, *Introducing Corporate Planning* (Oxford: Pergamon Press, 1971), pp. 71–76.

24 (Three Environmental Types are: Stable; Regulated Flexibility; and Adaptive.) See William H. Newman, and E. K. Wannen. *The Process of Management,* 4th ed. Englewood Cliffs, N.J.: Prentice-Hall, Inc. 1977. Part VI.

25 The development of a series of conditional propositions about strategy selection in a given situation is suggested by Charles W. Hofer in "Toward a Continuing Theory of Business Strategy," *Academy of Management Journal,* December 1975, 784–810.

26 Managerial quotes from "Piercing the Future Fog in the Executive Suite," *Business Week,* April 28, 1975, 52.

27 Meyer, "Shoot Out," p. 148.

28 Herbert E. Meyer, "Dick Goodwin Has to Build His Own Comeback Road," *Fortune,* June 19, 1978, 76.

C H A P T E R

4

The skill of limiting risk comes from identifying and formulating criteria on which to judge a new business. That is the most critical step.

Charles E. Reed
Senior V.P. General Electric
quoted in "The Opposites," *Business Week,*
January 31, 1977, 64.

Identifying Strategic Opportunities and Threats

CHAPTER OBJECTIVES

When you have completed this chapter, you will be able to:

☐ *Demonstrate an understanding of strategic factors by preparing an environmental analysis.*

☐ *Analyze the internal functioning of a firm by preparing a company analysis profile.*

☐ *Identify the various techniques used in environmental analysis.*

☐ *Analyze a management case using the concepts in this unit.*

THE CORPORATE TURNAROUND AT A M[1]

Roy L. Ash

"Roy Ash is staking his managerial reputation and a substantial part of his personal fortune—$2.7 million—on an effort to turn around the troubled company that Wall Street analysts privately dubbed "Addressogrief-Multigrief." As both the chief executive and the largest individual stockholder, he has been engaged for the past seventeen months in what he calls 'a classic case of corporate renewal.' The full recovery of Addressograph-Multigraph, he says, will take another four or five years, but the performance so far suggests that he probably won't come to grief.

"Ash seems determined to recapture the luster he had in the 1960s as president of glamorous Litton Industries and one of the brightest stars on the U.S. business scene. In Washington, he created the idea of an Office of Management and Budget, a considerable accomplishment that was obscured in the general ruin of the Nixon Administration. Now Ash seems eager to prove that the managerial success of the glory days at Litton was not a fluke. . . .

"Rescuing a creaky maker of mechanical office equipment seems a very different kind of challenge from founding and running a high-technology conglomerate, but Ash believes that the right executive decisions can shape up any organization. "At a sufficiently high level of abstraction," he says, "all businesses are the same."

"Ash's plans for testing that theory are summed up in the notes that he continually pencils on yellow legal pads. One of the most revealing of these notes says: 'Develop a much greater attachment of everybody to the bottom line—more agony and ecstasy.' As he sees it, the really important change in a company is a process of psychological transformation. So far, he has flushed out unpromising products, outmoded plants, and surplus personnel . . . But these are only the surface signs of what Ash insists is a much deeper process, a deliberate attempt to change a corporate culture.

"In trying to do that, Ash employs what he calls 'immersion manage-ment.' To reach the core of problems, he probes deeply into operations through re-lentless questioning, which one executive calls "excruciating." Ash batters down bureaucratic practices in the belief that they tend to become an end in themselves. He forbids long memos, which managers submit, he says, 'to have the record show the right thing for a defense later.' And to make managers fully aware of the impact of their decisions, he demands a penetrating financial analysis of everything the company does or considers doing.

"Ash found plenty that seemed to need changing. AM, in his words, was 'slow in pace, conservative in attitude, and living in the past.' Its once-dominant line of "clanking machinery" for offset printing and addressing was being over-whelmed by quiet, more efficient electronic products of rivals that include Xerox, IBM, and Eastman Kodak. The previous management had floundered about, never coming up with a clear plan for the company's future. Inertia had almost paralyzed its board, which according to one member "kept wishfully thinking that something is going to happen to improve things."

THE DETERMINANTS OF STRATEGY

The starting point in strategic management involves the definition of organizational purpose and mission and setting future goals: the determination of what the business will be like in the future. The strategist is concerned with the fit between corporate purpose and mission and the realities of market and competition. Therefore, a nec-essary next step in strategic formulation is the analysis of the potential fit between external conditions and internal capabilities.

FOUR AREAS TO TARGET

There are four potential areas of opportunity which strategists, like Roy Ash of AM, try to target:

1 New technological or product innovation opening new markets.

2 New product or market opportunity due to growth in underlying demand.

3 New opportunities in existing product or market segments in which the firm has a competitive advantage.

4 New opportunities in expanding into additional market segments or geographic areas.

At AM, for example, Roy Ash examined the areas of product and market opportunity, and as he observed the AM managers in action, he was making notes of important problems on yellow pads. These notes on strategic and operating problems became his analysis of the internal organization, including over 200 items ranging from prob-lem products and markets to organizational red tape and inefficiencies. As a result,

Ash decided to move the firm into new electronic equipment product lines. The first step for the strategist, then, is to examine the determinants of strategy: to analyze the internal and external factors that exert a primary influence on the current and future position of the firm.

TWO MAJOR ELEMENTS

The strategist today is concerned with events external to the firm because these have an important impact on future results. Further, for most organizations, the ability to control these external forces is considerably less than the ability to control operations inside the firm. The formulation of a formal, strategic plan essentially involves two elements which clearly interact, but which can be separately described and examined. These elements are:

1 Strategic environmental analysis
2 Competitive advantage appraisal.

If either of these activities is inadequately performed, then the organization is taking the risk of operating with an ineffective strategy. The result of inadequate analysis may include loss of market share, loss of profits, and possibly even bankruptcy or liquidation.

This, then, is the field of action for the strategic decision maker. The manager is attempting to position his firm in relation to an uncertain future environment. As a result, the strategic decision maker (like Roy Ash at AM) must analyze two basic determinants of strategy: the external environment and the firm's internal capabilities.

STAGE 4: ENVIRONMENTAL ANALYSIS

The first problem facing the strategist is to determine the relationship of the firm to its broader environment. When the USC Trojans are preparing to play the University of Washington Huskies in Seattle, Coach John Robinson must consider the likely defenses his team will face, and also the likelihood of inclement weather. Consequently, he has his team practice passing and handling a wet football. The organization strategist must consider a similar set of environmental factors.

Environmental analysis may be termed the process of seeking "information about events and relationships in a company's outside environment, the knowledge of which would assist top management in its task of charting the company's future course of action."[2] According to Philip S. Thomas, effective environmental analysis is crucial to corporate planning.[3] Factors needing analysis include the global context of governmental, economic, technological, and social conditions as they affect strategic planning. There are two factors to be considered which make environment analysis a critical stage in the management process.

First, the organization does not exist in isolation, rather it is interrelated with other elements that make up its environment. And to make this even more complex, the environment is constantly changing: new products, new technologies and new economic conditions are constantly emerging. In the past twenty-five years there have been many changes in the firms on the *Fortune* 500. The big companies do not just keep getting bigger and bigger. Many smaller companies, seizing new opportunities, have managed to take over spots in the top group. *Fortune* reported that only 262 (52.4%) of the original top 500 firms appeared in the 1980 ranking. Most of the missing companies were taken over by merger or acquisition, but several went out of business. Of the new additions to the top 500 in 1980, 147 (30%) were too small to even make the list of 1955.[4] In many cases, this failure to survive stems from an inability to analyze and adapt to changing environmental conditions. There is some research evidence to suggest that firms which do environmental analysis are more successful than those that do not.[5]

Second, environmental influence is complex and can affect many different parts of the organization. There is an increasing demand for energy by consumers, leading to the construction of new power plants. Yet environmental groups often delay the construction by demonstrations or legal delaying tactics. As a result, the lead time and cost for new plant construction is now almost double what it was previously. For example, Dow Chemical planned for several years to develop a new chemical complex in northern California but decided to cancel the plan because of the environmental protests and delays which kept stretching its lead time and increasing the end costs.

Environmental analysis, then, is the process by which strategists analyze factors outside the firm to determine possible opportunities and threats.

SEIZE THE OPPORTUNITY

The recognition of potential product or market opportunity is always an important factor. As one manager has noted, "If you see an opportunity, put the plan on ice and seize the opportunity."[6] There will always be new product and market opportunities as long as there are unsatisfied needs among consumers. The task of the manager is to recognize the shifting trends and to seek out markets where demand is rapidly growing. For instance, certain demographic trends emerged from the baby boom of the 1950s and as this age group moves into the home- and car-buying age segments, one can predict increased demand in these markets in the next few years.

The United States, however, is going through some fundamental demographic changes that forecasters and policymakers will have to take into account. The economy is already feeling the impact of these shifts, and there is more—much more—to come in the future. "Demographic statistics make dull reading," says economist Michael L. Wachter of the University of Pennsylvania's Wharton School, "but they helped lay the groundwork for our current economic problems."[7]

The most obvious change in the U.S. population is simply that it is growing older. In 1970 the median age was just under 28. By 1982 it will reach 30, and by the turn of the century, it will hit 35. Such a change means a shift in patterns of consumption and incomes, and inevitably, changes in social attitudes as well.

The strategic decision maker must first be aware of the potential growth areas; his second concern is to identify those segments where the firm will be in a position to exert some form of competitive advantage. Roy Ash, for example, recognized that AM's strengths were in mature markets. He then proceeded to seek out the high growth areas where AM could compete with its sales force and distribution system. As a result, he has moved AM into new high technology fields.

IDENTIFY THREATS

The strategic decision maker must also search the environment to identify factors that may pose potential threats to the organization's strategy. The more dynamic the environment, the greater the threat to strategy. As noted in Chapter Three, many organizations react to environmental changes, rather than adopting a more proactive, anticipative approach. There are many forces in the environment which can have an impact on future strategy. One force involves new technological developments. In the airline industry, for example, the introduction of newer, more fuel-efficient planes by competitors is a significant threat to TWA, which is still flying older, less efficient planes.

"Maybe 95 percent of all companies really don't pay much attention to the future," says Dale H. Marco, who heads the industrial management group at Peat, Marwick, Mitchell and Co., one of the big eight auditing firms that makes available management consulting services as well as accounting. "They react to history—history that is anywhere from one day to a few centuries old."[8]

THE "JEANNE DIXON SYNDROME"

In addition, many companies are afflicted with what may be termed the "Jeanne Dixon syndrome"; that is, they see planning as an effort to predict the future. In reality, planning is a complex, sophisticated process of isolating developments that may have an impact on the future; monitoring the growth—or death—of these developments; and making adjustments as new facts are made available and placed alongside assumptions.

The economic conditions can also present adverse forces in times of recession when consumer spending decreases, and during times of inflation when operating costs may rise drastically. The strategist must also be aware of changing consumer values and buying patterns. A few years ago hardly anyone owned a hand-held calculator, but now almost everyone has one.

Finally, one must be aware of governmental and international influences upon future strategic moves. Factors such as the steadily rising price of energy and the impact of OPEC must be considered in all strategic planning. The airlines must base their planning on a number of possible supply and pricing situations, because the cost of jet fuel is such an important element in predicting their future financial position. Strategic managers must therefore not only recognize and be aware of these potential threats, they must also develop strategic contingency plans for a number of possible conditions.

Among the possible threats are economic recession, product obsolescence, unexpected new product innovation, unexpected price changes, and decline in a particular market segment. At any rate, strategists like Roy Ash at AM seek to determine how best to allocate scarce resources in order to minimize possible threats and take advantage of new opportunities.

WHY STRATEGISTS DO ENVIRONMENTAL ANALYSIS

In the past, executives could be relatively confident about the long-term outlook and plan accordingly. This is no longer true. The strategist today is confronted with unexpected and unanticipated changes. The environment has never seemed so turbulent and unpredictable. These uncertainties make strategic analysis a critical stage in the planning process.

THE ACCELERATING RATE OF CHANGE

The external environment is changing so rapidly that the strategist can no longer afford to ignore it or guess at future trends. Demographic changes caught many universities unprepared for the declining enrollments of the 1980s. This demographic change in the size of the 18-year-old age group has created financial problems at many schools and even forced some to close, even though environmental analysis revealed this trend was coming several years earlier.

THE LEVEL OF OPPORTUNITY AND THREAT

In a changing environment, new technological, cultural, and economic forces continually pose new opportunities and threats. In the watch industry, for example, the emergence of the solid state digital watch provided an opportunity for U.S. and Japanese watch companies to move into a market long dominated by the Swiss watch industry. The Swiss, on the other hand, using a reactive management style, failed to recognize this change and as a result their once dominant market share has eroded away.

COMPANIES WHICH USE ENVIRONMENTAL ANALYSIS TEND TO BE MORE EFFECTIVE

There is research which tends to support the use of formal analysis. Danny Miller and Peter Friesen (McGill University), for example, found that in most cases the firm's level of effectiveness is related to the amount of environmental analysis.[9] Peter H. Grinyer and David Norburn (of the London Graduate Business School) also concluded, in a study of twenty-one United Kingdom companies, that the more environmental information was analyzed in strategic decisions, the more effective was the firm's financial performance.[10]

A MODEL FOR ENVIRONMENTAL ANALYSIS

The single most important factor in the strategic process is the analysis of the environment. The more dynamic the environment, the greater its impact on strategy. There are a number of significant relationships which need to be examined in formulating a plan of strategic action. A model of these interrelationships between the strategist and the key external and internal factors is shown in Figure 4.1. First, the strategist must examine the fit between the firm's current strategy and the environment, and then predict probable future conditions.

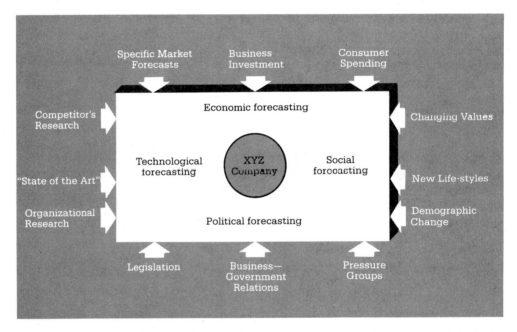

FIGURE 4.1

A Model for Environmental Analysis

SOURCE: Adapted from Ian H. Wilson, "Socio-Political Forecasting: A New Dimension to Strategic Planning," *Michigan Business Review,* July, 1974, 19–20. Reprinted by permission from the July, 1974, issue of the *University of Michigan Business Review,* published by the Graduate School of Business Administration, The University of Michigan.

AN OPEN SYSTEM VIEW

The model indicates that environmental analysis is a complex endeavor. The organization may be viewed as an open system in interaction with its environment. The firm has an impact on the environment as well, and it operates in several environments at once. Thus, governmental forces may exert one influence, while social forces may exert another. For example, the government exerted pressure on automobile manufacturers to incorporate air bags as a safety feature or option in new autos. The consumer, on the other hand, resisted this safety feature, perhaps because of higher cost or lack of understanding.

THE GETS MODEL

There are many ways to structure the external environment, but one easily useable method is to separate the outside influences into those dealing with Government, Economy, Technology, and Sociology—termed GETS for short. The organization is also influenced by the constituent demands which are placed upon the organization, including customers, competitors, suppliers, employees, regulatory agencies and special interest groups. The interaction of these elements is shown in Figure 4.2[11]

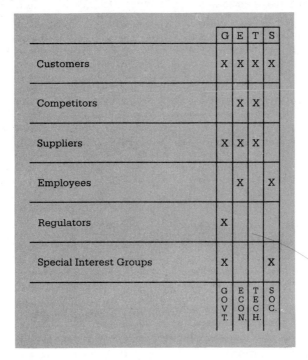

	G	E	T	S
Customers	X	X	X	X
Competitors		X	X	
Suppliers	X	X	X	
Employees		X		X
Regulators	X			
Special Interest Groups	X			X
	GOVT.	ECON.	TECH.	SOC.

FIGURE 4.2
The GETS Model of Environment Analysis

SOURCE: Reprinted with permission from *Long Range Planning* 11, Louis E. DeNoya, "How to Evaluate Long-Range Plans," 36, Copyright 1978, Pergamon Press, Ltd.

GOVERNMENT

As government gets bigger and bigger, federal, state and local governments have an increasing effect on how business operates. Governmental forces influence a range of factors including wage and price controls, equal employment opportunity, safety and health at work, consumer credit, environmental constraints, plant location, and other similar factors. These laws and regulations all influence how companies operate on a strategic basis.

In 1979, the government's budget of $365.6 billion made up almost a quarter of our total GNP, and one-third of the U.S. labor force is now employed in the public sector. As a result, goverment impacts strategy in at least two ways:

FINANCIAL POLICY

The government is a large purchaser of goods and services. It has been reported that about 20 percent of all purchases are made by the government, and in many fields, such as in aerospace, electronics, and defense industry, it is the major purchaser.

Government subsidies and loans   The government plays an expanding role in supporting certain strategic industries: farm supports, natural resources, the railroad industry, and of course, ailing companies like Lockheed Aircraft and Chrysler Corp.

Government import policies   The government can influence the level of foreign competition by use of import restrictions, tariffs, etc. Recently, the steel and auto industries have been urging such restrictions.

LAWS AND REGULATIONS

Environmental compliance laws   The large manufacturing industries—chemicals, steel, oil, etc.—have added costs due to environmental laws; automobile companies have been required to design safer, pollutant-free, higher-mileage autos.

Antitrust regulations   The antitrust laws have affected many large firms, particularly those contemplating mergers. Several airlines have been blocked from merger because of these laws, and IBM has been battling an antitrust suit for several years, at the cost of many thousands of dollars.

Governmental regulations   Many regulations have an impact on business operations. For example, the OSHA safety regulations and the EEO equal opportunity hiring regulations require extensive plans, programs, reports, etc. Consequently, firms must be aware of governmental forces in the environment that may offer opportunities or pose threats for future strategy.

ECONOMIC FORCES

Economic forces have a significant effect on the organization's strategy. The condition of the economy has a direct bearing on what strategies are likely to be selected, and upon the outcomes. A strategy that is successful in economic prosperity may well be a failure in a recession. Economic factors include:

1 The Gross National Product (GNP)

2 The state of the economic cycle (i.e., recession, prosperity, etc.)

3 Income of consumers

4 Monetary policy—money supply, interest rates, etc.

Each of these basic economic factors must be examined and evaluated in terms of potential impact upon the firm and upon future strategic moves. High interest rates, for example, have a significant effect upon the housing and auto industries.

In general, strategic analysis and forecasting begins with the general economic situation, then moves to the industry as a whole, and finally to the economic situation for the specific firm.

MARKET FORCES

A second key area of economic concern for the strategist includes factors in the competitive market place. The most important factors are outlined below.

DEMAND FACTORS

These factors include the total market, and market segments such as age, sex, income distribution, etc., including total population growth and trends.

The strategist attempts to determine how demand factors in the market will affect the future of the firm. A number of important factors affect the market.

Population   As the characteristics of the total population shift, i.e., age, size, needs, etc., demand for products or services will also change.

Income distribution   This dynamic factor impacts on the firm's future.

Age of the population   As total population changes, the age distribution changes. The most dramatic demographic change of the decade will be the sharp decline of people between 15 and 35. Over the next decade, the post-war babies will move into the 25-to-45 age bracket. By 1990, 41 percent of the population will be in that age group, 24 percent between 45 and 64, while 15- to 24-year-olds will comprise only 18 percent (see Figure 4.3).

Product life cycles   The demand for a product moves through a life cycle. At first, the product has a high rate of sales growth. Then it matures and later declines.

COMPETITIVE FACTORS

Market share   It is important to recognize the competitive structure of the industry. What market share does your firm hold? What share do competing firms hold? And what are the trends? Is your firm gaining or losing share?

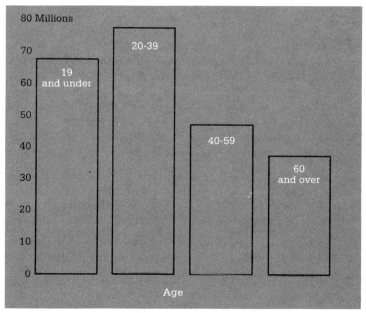

FIGURE 4.3
Age Distribution in 1985
SOURCE: U.S. Census

Pricing   What are the pricing strategies of competitors, and what effect will this have on strategy.

SUPPLIER FACTORS

Another set of factors may be termed supply factors. These include sources of supply for raw materials, assemblies, energy, transportation, labor, etc. These are important because changes in any major element will have an impact on future production and pricing strategies.

1. Availability and cost of raw materials   Strategists must examine long-run trends in availability and cost of materials.

2. Availability and cost of labor   Strategists need to determine whether skilled employees are available and at what cost.

TECHNOLOGICAL FORCES

The strategist must also be aware of changing technology which may affect the firm's future raw materials, production processes, and its products and services. Changing technology can open up vast opportunities, or threaten the dominance of a firm in an industry or product. It can even threaten the survival of a firm, if it fails to adapt. The rapid rate of technological innovation not only is likely to continue, but may even accelerate. Technological advances can suddenly cause a firm's products to become obsolete, as Roy Ash found at Addressograph-Multigraph.

Technology can also change the life-style and behavior patterns of the consumer. Texas Instruments is risking a large-scale investment in the field of home computers because it feels that in the future the computer will take its place with the telephone and television in every home. Whether or not this is true remains to be seen. Do you think you will have your own home computer, or do you already?

NEW TECHNOLOGY AT TI

Texas Instruments, Inc., the Dallas-based electronics giant, is a fearsome competitor in all its businesses, from semiconductors to geophysical services to bonded metals. But it has been a holy terror in the consumer electronics market. Though most other semiconductor houses have abandoned the field, TI keeps right on launching new calculators, electronic watches, and calculator-based "learning aids" that teach spelling and arithmetic—and can even talk. The company's traditionally savage price cutting has driven off many domestic competitors and kept the marketers of the Far East at bay. In fact, with consumer-product sales of about $400 million, TI leads the world in the calculator market and is the largest U.S. maker of electronic watches. *Fortune* magazine details their methods in the following words:

RIDING THE LEARNING CURVE

"TI's unique performance is closely linked to its special *management methods*. President J. Fred Bucy, a fanatically hard-driving engineer, has likened his company's approach to that of his Japanese competitors." Bucy uses an elaborate, intensive planning system that forces line managers to take strategic responsibility, and looks at its markets over the very long term, much as the Japanese do. Bucy "is willing, and financially able, to tolerate slim margins for the sake of acquiring larger market shares. Getting a larger market share is important because TI is a leading domestic exponent of 'riding the learning curve' [see Ch. 7] . . . [TI] prices very close to high volume cost in order to build up volume, and hence experience, that will eventually enable the company to drive costs well below prices.

"To date, *this aproach has worked* brilliantly. In 1977, for example, TI was able to cut its competitors off at the knees by launching a digital watch that sold for just $9.95. Until recently, at least, the company has kept ahead by passing cost savings on to consumers. For example, the SR-51, a popular scientific calculator, listed for $225 back in 1975, when it was introduced. Partly because the original number of electronic components—128—has been reduced to a mere twelve, a comparable model can be had for less than $40 today."[12]

Texas Instruments has been able to recognize the forces of technological change and take advantage of those opportunities. Other firms have not been aware, and have watched others take over the emerging markets.

SOCIAL-CULTURAL FORCES

The social-cultural factor focuses on the values and attitudes of people, both customers and employees. Ian H. Wilson, in charge of General Electric's Business Environment Research and Forecasting unit, says "It really began in 1967. A business environment studies unit was established as part of the personnel and industrial relations section of the company. There is no real logic to its emerging in that part of the company, except that the type of policy analysis, trend analysis, and forecasting that we were set up to do was essentially people-oriented rather than economics-oriented or technology-oriented. The charter that evolved for this work was the identification and analysis of the long-term social, political and in a broad sense, economic trends influencing the corporation, with particular emphasis on their impact on personnel relations, management style, organization of work, union relations—the subfunctions of the major component to which we were attached.

"Since 1972, we have done really two things each year: a quick checklist updating of the whole environment—what are some of the things that have gone right or gone wrong in our forecast, what new things have come up on the horizon? And the other thing is zeroing in on particular areas. Those scenarios are so general that they're not a great deal of help to a planner. You can only contribute that help as you focus in on a particular area like the whole question of energy. Where is the technology going? Where are the economics going? Where is the national energy policy going? What impact are these going to have on the company's businesses? How much attention should we pay to energy conservation—is that going to be the wave of the future? What effect are public attitudes about nuclear power likely to have on our business, and how do we respond to it? When you get that sort of specific question, to which an answer is required and on which a decision would be based, then you can start to pull together your environmental analyses into a much tighter web, and much more useful data can flow from it."[13]

SOCIAL FACTORS

There are a number of social factors to consider.

Family size   Formerly, it was the normal thing for a family to have two to four children. Today not all members of society accept this as a norm and family size is shrinking.

Married women in work force   In the past, most married women stayed home. Now, most work (see Figure 4.4). Walter Guzzardi, Jr., points out yet another surprise—"the degree to which married women joined the march. They have come to the job market in waves—first those beyond childbearing age, then younger married women without children, and finally, in unbelievable numbers, those with children at home. Twenty-three million wives now work. Some 16.1 million women with children under eighteen, or more than half of their total number, are now in the labor force; of them, six million have children under six."[14]

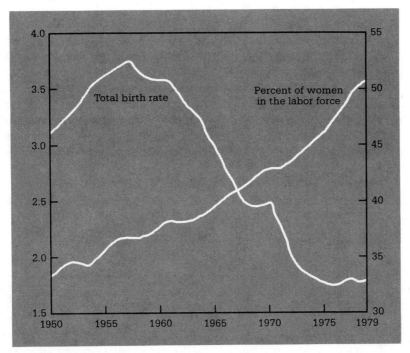

FIGURE 4.4
Changing Attitudes—Women and Work
SOURCE: U.S. Census.

Mobility   In the first part of this century people used to live and die in one place. Now there are thousands of workers who move from city-to-city as jobs open up and families are spread out across the United States.

Consumer attitudes   As society changes, new attitudes about what is acceptable emerge. In the past, many people were against legalized gambling. But this has changed in such places as Las Vegas and Atlantic City. Also with cars, some interesting crosscurrents will be flowing. Fewer people will be turning sixteen, the traditional used-car-buying age, and since the labor force will be growing more slowly, fewer new workers will need a set of wheels to get to the job. On the other hand, the smaller, older family will have more money to spend on new cars that meet its fancy. Size, style, quality, and gasoline consumption are what will make the auto race interesting.

Normal Krandall of Ford's corporate strategy department says: "Attitudinal and life-style changes are important in our business. And we have to ask—what are the consequences of the oil shortage, and long lines, *occasional* long lines, at the gas pumps? Is this going to alter the nature of what people do? And of how they get to the places where they do it?"[15]

EMPLOYEE ATTITUDES

Attitudes are also changing on the part of the workers about the hours they wish to work, the quality of life at work, and the benefits they expect to receive.

In this section, we have discused the major factors to be considered in the analysis of the environment. By analyzing these factors, the strategist can recognize the potential opportunities and threats which must be faced. In addition, the strategist can compare the current strategy of the firm with the environment and identify which factors appear to continue to be important and which factors may have changed.

THE TECHNIQUES OF ENVIRONMENTAL ANALYSIS

It is important that the strategist be able to predict probable future conditions, prior to selecting strategic actions. Changes may emerge from unanticipated sources which will force disruption of a particular strategy. The introduction of new technology, a new pricing strategy by competitors, or decreased supplies of energy or materials, will have an impact on the advantages or disadvantages associated with each possible strategic alternative. As Don Lebell and O. J. Krasner have commented: "Environmental forecasting in a dynamic and competitive business arena is challenging in concept and implementation. It is essential to remember the fundamental limitations of confronting the unknowable future: (1) We cannot always be certain of future purposes, objectives, and strategies. (2) We may not even know what questions to ask. (3) We may not know crucial cause-and-effect relationship, coefficients of those relationships, or impact coefficients which relate concerns to model outputs. Given such formidable obstacles, one might ask: "Why bother to forecast?" Of course, that question is pointless, because forecasts are an inescapable part of rational decision making."[16] The external environment of the firm is one of the major determinants of strategy. Yet the tools and techniques used to monitor this important determinant are still relatively undeveloped in most firms. Basil W. Denning suggests that environmental forecasts are used primarily in order to provide assumptions on which strategic planning can take place, and presents a summary of techniques which may be used (see Table 4.1).[17] What, then, are some of the techniques and methods strategists may use to anticipate the impact of environmental forces upon the firm?

SCANNING AND INFORMATION GATHERING

This includes all sources of information gathering outside the firm, both informal and formal, and structured and unstructured methods. These sources include external contacts outside the firm with customers, suppliers, competitors, bankers, consultants, and others. Information may also be gained by means of surveys, questionnaires, or interviews. Finally, there is a great deal of information available in published material such as trade journals, newspapers, and general publications.

TABLE 4.1

Environmental Forecasting for Planning Assumptions

	Sources of Information	Techniques
Economic Forecasts (a) National Economy (b) Sector Forecasts	(i) Government and Private forecasts. (ii) Industry association, government, private forecasts. (iii) Market Research.	(a) Critical appreciation of published forecasts. (b) Development of models or relationships for sector forecasts. (c) Input-output analysis. (d) Large number of quantitative techniques.
Technological Forecasts	(i) Technical intelligence service reports. (ii) Technical market research. (iii) Research into competitors' developments.	(a) Demand and conditional demand analyses. (b) Opportunity identification techniques. (c) Theoretical limits testing. (d) Parameter analysis. (e) Various systems analysis methods. (f) Discipline reviews. (g) Expert opinion.
Sociological Forecasts	Wide variety of sources of data, including government reports, educational forecasts, population forecasts, regional forecasts, skilled labour forecasts, institutional changes, etc.	(a) National models such as built by Battelle (unlikely to be done in any one corporation). (b) Expert opinion.
Political Forecasts	Political intelligence services and government reports.	Expert opinion.
Forecasting Competitors' Actions	Any intelligence about competitors.	Any relevant technique to give information from intelligence.

SOURCE: Printed with permission from *Long Range Planning,* vol. 11, March 1973, Basil W. Denning, "Strategic Environmental Appraisal". Copyright © 1973, Pergamon Press, Ltd.

EXPERT OPINIONS

Another source of information may be gained by contacting experts in various fields. These may be economists, university professors, consultants, or others with specialized expertise. One technique which has been used to systematically gain expert opinion is the *"delphi"* method. This method, originally developed by the RAND Corporation, involves using a group of knowledgeable people who make anonymous predictions which are then summarized by computer and fed back to the panel until a consensus opinion is achieved.

FORECASTING—TREND ANALYSIS

Forecasting is another technique used in analyzing the environment and is usually concerned with predicting, projecting, or extrapolating future events or conditions. There are several types of forecasts.

1. Economic forecasts   Economic forecasting involves general surveillance of the economy, including gross national product, consumer expenditures, income, etc., and usually includes sales, cash flow, and manpower forecasts for short- to long-range terms.

2. Market/competitive forecasts   These forecasts are based on surveys, market research and industry analysis.

3. Technological/supplier forecast   These forecasts, based on specific product market areas, are often made by "futurists."

4. Social forecasts   These forecasts, performed by "futurists" or social scientists looking at the longer term social and political trends, use nonquantitative techniques to forecast demographic changes, life-style shifts, political attitudes, and other socio-political developments.

Social forecasting intended to supplement traditional forecasting provides a view of the complete socio-economic-political-technological environment, so that strategic plans can be based on a more comprehensive set of premises. According to Kenneth E. Newgren (Indiana State University) in a survey of *Fortune* 500 firms, sixty-three, or 34.4 percent were classified as fully engaging in social forecasting, and these were the firms involved in very long-range forecasting. Newgren found that companies in the electronic computing and food preparation industries were least likely to use this technique.[18]

COMPETITIVE INTELLIGENCE

Another source of information involves active intelligence or "spying" to gather information on competitors. Generally such information is gathered from suppliers, customers, or employees of the competitor. Often a firm will hire someone from a competitor to gain more information about its activities. According to Robert Hershey, some of the activities a company of any size can normally afford to do include:[19]

- Buying a competitor's product, tearing it down, and evaluating it. (This is entirely legal and ethical.)

- Implementing a report system that requires field sales personnel to provide feedback on the activities of customers, suppliers, distributors, and competitors.

- Assigning every key officer to spend several days per year talking to customers. These are end-user contacts and should provide valuable information about a competitor's product and service.

- Calling in all sales personnel once every quarter for a two-way debriefing with key officers in a face-to-face reporting and planning conference on competitive matters.

- Studying internal security to ensure that competitors cannot gain access to company secrets.

- Keeping aware of the inroads of overseas companies. (Frequently, foreign competitors have the full support of their governments.)

- Appreciating that giants are often clumsy. A smaller company's response time to user needs can frequently offset a larger competitor's advantage in advertising power, distributive competence, or cash flow.

- Questioning your vice-president of marketing about the kind of marketing data needed to enhance this function when drawing up the annual sales plan.

ECONOMETRIC MODELS

Econometric models predict the effects of decisions by management or changes in the environment. Robert H. Turner sees the focus of such models as "the identification of relatively consistent economic relationships over a past period of time. Quantification (reduction to equations) of these relationships is the principal advantage of econometric models. To the extent that the equations remain valid, the computerized model can solve mathematical problems beyond the capabilities of the human brain. But such quantification is often the biggest liability of econometric models."[20] Such models are designed to allow management to forecast the effects of various strategies, without actually trying them. The models allow managers to ask "what if" questions. For example, if we raise our prices on product x by 10 percent, then what would be the impact on profitability, or on market share? At Ralston Purina, for example, a one percent change in the price of a prime commodity triggers a change in the company's cost models and the whole corporate plan may change as a result. The econometric methods, then, are computerized models which aid managers in strategic decision making.

ENVIRONMENTAL ANALYSIS RELATIONSHIPS

What, then, are the relationships between environmental analysis techniques and other factors? Two proposed sets of relationships have been set forth. First, James Utterback (M.I.T.) has suggested that a firm's environment largely determines its strategic planning process.[21] The relationship between environmental complexity and change and techniques is shown in Figure 4.5.

Environmental Change	Environmental Complexity	Type of Strategy	Forecasting Methods
Static	Simple	Cost-minimizing	No methods, or expert opinion
Static	Complex	Mixed and sales-maximizing	Expert opinion, monitoring, and trend extrapolation
Dynamic	Simple	Mixed and sales-maximizing	Expert opinion, monitoring, and trend extrapolation
Dynamic	Complex	Performance-maximizing	Above and simulation, quantitative and probabilistic models

FIGURE 4.5

Types of Environment Related to Forecasting Methods.

SOURCE: James Utterback, "Environmental Analysis and Forecasting," in Charles Hofer and Dan Schendel (eds.), *Strategic Management: A New View of Business Policy and Planning* (Boston: Little, Brown, 1979).

Utterback identifies four possible relationships.

Simple-static   Firms in a simple-static environment usually do not use formal forecasting techniques, but may use simpler informal and expert opinion methods.

Complex-static   Firms facing a complex-static environment use information scanning, monitoring and expert opinion methods.

Simple-dynamic   Firms in a simple-dynamic environment use such techniques as economic forecasting, trend analysis, delphi and other means suited to a limited data base.

Complex-dynamic   Firms facing a more complex and dynamic environment would be expected to use the more sophisticated forecasting methods, including the use of simulation models.

In summary, Utterback suggests that a firm's environment conditions its strategy and its choice of forecasting methods.

Don LeBell and O. J. Krasner have proposed a similar relationship between the developmental stage of the firm and its choice of forecasting techniques, as shown in Figure 4.6.[22]

The techniques suggested are similar to those described above including:

- *Single-variable extrapolation* such as linear extrapolation, life-cycle curves, exponential smoothing, power series expansion, and others.

Maturity phase \ Forecasting techniques	Single-variable extrapolation	Theoretical limit envelope	Dynamic models	Mapping	Multivariable interaction analysis	Unstructured expert opinion	Structured expert opinion	Structured inexpert opinion	Unstructured inexpert speculation
Product technology	Moderately or occasionally appropriate	Moderately or occasionally appropriate	Inappropriate	Inappropriate	Inappropriate	Appropriate	Inappropriate	Inappropriate	Inappropriate
Capital resources	Moderately or occasionally appropriate	Appropriate	Moderately or occasionally appropriate	Appropriate	Moderately or occasionally appropriate	Moderately or occasionally appropriate	Appropriate	Inappropriate	Moderately or occasionally appropriate
Production and distribution	Moderately or occasionally appropriate	Moderately or occasionally appropriate	Moderately or occasionally appropriate	Inappropriate	Inappropriate	Appropriate	Inappropriate	Inappropriate	Inappropriate
Marketing	Moderately or occasionally appropriate	Inappropriate	Moderately or occasionally appropriate	Moderately or occasionally appropriate	Moderately or occasionally appropriate	Appropriate	Moderately or occasionally appropriate	Moderately or occasionally appropriate	Moderately or occasionally appropriate
Competition	Moderately or occasionally appropriate	Inappropriate	Moderately or occasionally appropriate	Moderately or occasionally appropriate	Moderately or occasionally appropriate	Appropriate	Moderately or occasionally appropriate	Moderately or occasionally appropriate	Moderately or occasionally appropriate
Sociopolitical	Inappropriate	Appropriate	Inappropriate	Appropriate	Appropriate	Moderately or occasionally appropriate	Appropriate	Appropriate	Appropriate
Diversification	Moderately or occasionally appropriate	Moderately or occasionally appropriate	Appropriate	Appropriate	Appropriate	Appropriate	Appropriate	Inappropriate	Appropriate

Appropriate | Moderately or occasionally appropriate | Inappropriate

FIGURE 4.6

Analyzing the Environment Relationship Between Enterprise's Development Phase and Forecasting Techniques at Policy/Strategic Planning Level

SOURCE: Don LeBell and O. J. Krasner, "Selecting Environmental Forecasting Techniques from Business Planning Requirements," *Academy of Management Review,* July 1977, 379.

- *Theoretical limit envelopes* include methods such as worst case analysis, high- and low-limits estimation, and sizing calculations.
- *Dynamic models* include historical analogs, time lags, and stochastic modeling.
- *Mapping* includes relevance trees and morphology analysis.
- *Multivariable interaction analysis* includes methods such as input/output models, probability networks, factor analysis, and regression analysis.
- *Unstructured expert opinion* techniques include "what if" interviews, role playing, consensus panels, and scenario generation.
- *Structured expert opinion* techniques include delphi, highly structured interviews, and on-line computer interaction.
- *Structured inexpert opinion* includes interviews, questionnaires, and surveys.
- *Unstructured inexpert speculation* includes techniques such as person-in-the-street interviews, scenario generation, and brainstorming.

Their model proposes that as the firm moves into a more advanced stage of development, a wider range of forecasting techniques are appropriate, and more sophisticated forecasting methods tend to be used.

THE USE OF ENVIRONMENTAL ANALYSIS

We have discussed a number of techniques which can be used to gather environmental data for analysis and prediction. Of these techniques which are actually used by strategists in environmental analysis? The studies cited vary from a small number of intensive case studies to large-scale surveys. Informal planning in strategy formulation is still widely used. This may be satisfactory under stable conditions but in a dynamic environment it is not sufficient for good management.

TECHNOLOGICAL FORECASTS

Despite uncertainty about the future and problems in accurate forecasting, it is still necessary to take environmental forces into account in making strategic decisions.
As James B. Quinn (Dartmouth College) has noted "To be useful, technological forecasts do not necessarily need to predict the precise form technology will take in a given application at some specific future date. Like any other forecasts, their purpose is simply to help evaluate the probability and significance of various possible future developments so that managers can make better decisions."[23]

RESEARCH FINDINGS

We have much yet to learn, but some of the findings at present are:

1   Most firms are not doing as well in environmental forecasting as they could or should do.

2   A number of firms, such as General Electric and Xerox, are beginning to experiment with models of the external environment, and we can expect to see this type of forecasting becoming much more important and widely used during the next decade.

3   According to one researcher's survey of 358 large corporations, the most important factors mentioned were:[24]

Changes in the economy or economic policy	45%
New product innovation (internal)	32%
New product innovation (competition)	28%
Major new government regulations	19%
Major shifts in consumer preferences	18%

As we can see, environmental analysis is a critical stage in the strategic decision process and interacts with the next stage: the analysis of internal competitive advantages.

STAGE 5: COMPETITIVE ADVANTAGE ANALYSIS[25]

Together with analyzing the environment, the strategist must assess the internal capabilities of the organization. What can the firm do, given the resources that it has available? An opportunity, no matter how attractive, is simply wishful thinking unless the organization has the resources to take advantage of it. Consequently, there must be an analysis which compares the strengths and weaknesses of the organization and its competitors.

The strategist must determine the fit between organizational resources and potential opportunities. An organization's strategic advantages may present a strong position so that it may seize an opportunity which exists at a particular point in time. Similarly, certain weaknesses, such as a lack of financial resources, may limit the possible avenues of opportunity to be sought out.

Every organization can analyze its strengths and weaknesses compared with those of its competitors. Some firms may excel in marketing and distribution channels, while others may possess unique R and D or technical competence, or some other special attribute. The strategist must attempt to determine how best to utilize these strengths in taking advantage of the opportunities which exist; that is, what sets this firm apart and provides a possible strategic advantage?

According to Bruce Henderson of the Boston Consulting Group, taking advantage of this distinctive competence may include[26]:

1 following a course of action different from those of rival firms;

2 developing a strategy which will provide different and better outcomes than those of its competitors;

3 making it difficult for other firms to duplicate the strategy or enter the area of opportunity, if the strategy works.

THE BRICK PILE FOR REDESIGN—INTERNAL ANALYSIS

The second major determinant of strategy is the internal analysis of the firm's resources and capabilities. This is essentially the same procedure used by Roy Ash when he took over at Addressograph-Multigraph. Ash assembled and analyzed all available information on the company including company, division, and product reports, interviews with operating managers, and his own observations. From this information, he prepared a profile of the organization that enabled him to pinpoint AM's strengths and weaknesses. Based upon his analysis, Ash made a detailed list of problems including some 200 items ranging from problem products to organizational difficulties. Ash termed this his "brick pile" for redesigning AM.[27]

WHAT CAN WE DO?

Primarily this analysis enabled Ash to determine what AM was capable of accomplishing and what it *could do* with its available resources. This internal analysis provided a basis for future strategic determination by matching AM's resources with potential market opportunities. For example, Ash felt that AM's 13,000-man sales and service team represented a real strength, one that he wanted to build upon by developing new advanced technology products which could be marketed through the existing distribution system.

Every organization has distinct strategic advantages and disadvantages. One firm may excel at technical expertise but lacks money. Another may have a cash surplus, but lacks innovation. Unless the strategist is aware of these factors, he may be unable to exploit possible opportunities fully.

Just as the strategist must investigate the opportunities and threats in the environment, he must also examine the strengths and weaknesses of the firm's ability to meet these challenges and threats. This process of internal analysis may be termed capability or resource audit, competitive advantage analysis, or strategic advantage analysis, but all refer to the same thing: an assessment of the firm's resources.

AN ORGANIZATIONAL SYSTEM

The organization may be viewed as a system of interrelated parts. One may examine each of the subunits separately, then analyze the way the parts are incorporated into a functioning unit. In the analysis of the organization it is customary to review each of the key functional areas—marketing, finance, production, etc.—as well as the managerial system that ties them together. Westinghouse, for example, recently found itself in trouble because of two basic failings—the lack of a strategic planning system and an absence of financial controls.[28]

MARKETING

The marketing area is perhaps the most crucial of the functional areas because marketing brings in revenues—the life blood of the organization. The marketing function also provides a vital interface and communication link between the organization and the external environment. Information on customers, pricing, demand, and competition can all be gained through the marketing activity.

The primary marketing factors include:

1 Competitive position and market share: does the firm have a strong market share in the total market or its segments?

2 Product life cycle: do they have new product leadership? In what phase of the life cycle are the main products?

3 The product mix: what are the range and quality of products and services?

4 How effective is the pricing strategy for products and services?

5 Does the organization have an effective sales force, or is there a dependence on a few customers?

6   Are there effective channels of distribution with broad geographic coverage, including multinational?

7   Advertising: has it established the company's product and brand image?

8   Does the firm have an effective market research system?

FINANCIAL

The financial area determines the availability of cash resources to implement strategic actions. The firm's financial situation is important because it directly relates to the amount of resources it will be able to commit and to the degree of cost control over existing programs.

The primary purpose of financial analysis is to determine the strength of the firm's relationship to its needs and to competition. The primary factors include:

1   Financial capacity: the availability of capital relative to industry and competitors.

2   The capital structure, does it allow effective use of financial leverage?

3   Is there a solid base of financial reserves and cash flow?

4   Is it using tax forms advantageously?

5   Is there access to new fields because of available resources?

6   How efficient are financial planning and budgeting procedures?

7   Are there effective accounting systems for cost, budget and profit planning, and auditing procedures?

8   How efficient is the use of debt (debt-equity ratio)?

PRODUCTION

Production, the nuts-and-bolts aspect of the organization, represents the firm's ability to produce goods and services. The production area contributes greatly to the firm's profitability through efficiency in the use of capital and human resources.

The primary production factors include:

1   An efficient cost control of operations in comparison with those of its competitors.

2   An adequate capacity and modern facilities: are the capacities overutilized or underutilized given the current and potential demand levels?

3   What is the relative level of raw materials cost and availability?

4   Are there effective inventory control and purchasing systems?

5   Is there a strategic location of plant facilities?

6   How efficient are operations procedures: production control, design, scheduling, testing, tooling, and quality control?

7   Are there effective management information and production control systems?

RESEARCH AND DEVELOPMENT

Research and development is an important function, because it often determines the degree of innovation which a firm is able to apply in its strategic decisions.

American companies spend large amounts of money on R and D, depending of course on the nature of the industry. Annual expenditures on R and D amounted to over $35 billion in 1975, for example. R and D usually includes scientific research, both basic and applied, and the engineering capabilities.

According to *Fortune*, "the obstacle that Smith Richardson, Jr., of Richardson-Merrell judged to stand in his way is the problem invariably described in the pharmaceutical industry as that of *critical mass*.' The term is borrowed from the world of nuclear physics and refers to the amount of fissionable material necessary to create a chain reaction. In an atomic bomb, for example, fissionable material the size of a golf ball would be too small—'subcritical.' But if the mass is of baseball size, a self-sustaining reaction becomes possible.

"In the pharmaceutical business today, the equivalent of that baseball is widely perceived to be an annual research budget of about $75 million. At that level and up, the proposition goes, a company can fund research on a broad spectrum of products, allow for the inevitable disappointments—the "dry holes" of this business— and, over time, very likely develop enough new products to support a sizable marketing operation. Each of these products, the conventional wisdom continues, will have taken years to get to market, at a cost of perhaps $50 million—the price imposed by tough laws concerning safety and efficacy, and by a rough-riding Food and Drug Administration.

"Another piece of conventional wisdom in the industry is that a company cannot rationally spend much more than 10 percent of its sales on research, a proposition suggesting that a $75-million research budget can be supported only by a company with at least $750 million in sales. Merrell, at $280 million, was not in that league, and its research spending in 1980 was correspondingly subcritical: $30 million."[29]

The primary strategic questions about R and D include:

1 The amount of R and D spending. Does it reach the critical mass?
2 What is the level of technical expertise, relative to key competitors?
3 How modern and efficient are R and D facilities, laboratories, equipment, etc?
4 How well are the R and D efforts organized and managed?
5 What is the mix of R and D projects between basic, long-term projects and applied, short-term projects?

HUMAN RESOURCES

The organization is no more effective than its human resource capabilities. These capabilities all consider the factors that go into recruitment, training, selection, development, promotion, and compensation of the members of the organization, including:

1 How healthy is the organizational climate?

2 Is the company competitive with regard to salary, benefits, etc.?

3 How effective are the channels of communication and direction?

4 What managerial style is used and to what degree is delegation used?

5 Are there programs to gain involvement, such as MBO?

When all the internal factors have been analyzed, the strategist has an awareness of the firm's capabilities: what the organization can do. Then the manager can realistically determine how these resources can best be applied to take advantage of environmental opportunities.

COMPETITIVE ADVANTAGE ANALYSIS

In summary, competitive advantage analysis is a basic step in the formulation of corporate strategy. Competitive advantage analysis is the process of examining the organization's marketing, financial, production, research, and human resource factors. Then, to enable it to meet possible threats or to dominate potential areas of opportunity, the organization can determine where the firm has critical strengths (advantages) or weaknesses. Primarily, the competitive advantage analysis determines what the firm is capable of doing and what it has the resources to accomplish.

AN EXAMPLE: PLAYBOY'S STRATEGIC MOVE TO ATLANTIC CITY[30]

There are always strategic factors to be considered that will determine the success or failure of a company in a particular industry and at a given point in time. After assessing the strategic factors, both internal and external, the strategist makes decisions to accomplish desired future goals. These decisions always involve some degree of risk. The strategist attempts to reduce this risk by getting as much information as possible on the strategic forces in the environment and in the firm.

The purposes of the strategic analysis are to maintain a position of advantage in relation to competitors, capitalize on one's own competitive strengths, and minimize weaknesses. One example of the environmental analysis process was the decision of Playboy Enterprises, Inc., to seek entry into the gambling casino field in Atlantic City, New Jersey.

A HIGH STAKES RACE

In 1976, Playboy's management personnel, including chairman Hugh Hefner, were examining possible strategic alternatives. They felt the economy was recovering, but Playboy had not been performing as well financially as they had hoped. Playboy's management analyzed their own internal resources: the management, marketing, image, their people, the Bunnies, the Playboy Club experience, and Playboy's financial resources. They also looked at several possible opportunities for investment in the United States and abroad.

Playboy's analysis indicated that Atlantic City had only three casinos under way, compared to more than one hundred gaming clubs in Las Vegas. It also noted that Resorts International (a New Jersey casino) had average gross winnings of nearly $600,000 a day, about double that of Las Vegas firms. It felt that $600,000 per day looked like a good return; therefore, based on the analysis, a strategic decision was made to build a Playboy Club casino in Atlantic City. Playboy's management decided to implement this decision at an estimated cost of $50 million, an amount their financial analysis indicated it could handle.

THE LAND

The first problem was getting a piece of land suitable for building a casino and 500-room hotel. Playboy management found that land in Atlantic City was not cheap. It finally found a site on Boardwalk (obviously a high-rent area) of three-quarters of an acre, costing about $7 million, with another $2 million for plans. Unfortunately, the site was not large enough, so they ended up designing a three-tiered casino. To illustrate the difficulty of getting land in Atlantic City, Penthouse International (one of Playboy's competitors) later bought all the parcels of land except for that of one small landowner whose price was exorbitant. The result: they are building their casino complex around the one small house which still sits there.

As costs escalated, Playboy found their own financial resources were drained: they could no longer handle the rising costs, estimated from $100 to $110 million, more than double the original estimate. Fortunately, they were able to work out a joint venture with Hyatt Corporation for some $45 million, because bank loans for gambling casinos are hard to come by. This illustrates the complex forces, internal and external, which influence strategic decisions and the uncertainty which emerges in bringing plans into fruition.

MANAGERIAL IMPLICATIONS

The analysis of the organization's external and internal environments is one of the most important activities performed by the strategic manager. It is important not only because this analysis provides an evaluation of the current state of the firm, but also because the resulting strategic decisions will have long-term impact on the future of the organization.

Managers must view the external environment as an open system of government, economic, technical, and social components, each of which has interacting impacts on the organization. The analysis of the environment presents the opportunities, demands, and constraints on the firm; in essence, it spells out what the firm might be able to do.

Businesses and other organizations as well can survive only if they are able to manage in an environment of change and constraint. As the rate of change in the external environment increases, the manager must find new and more sophisticated ways to analyze, forecast, and plan for an unpredictable future. As Harold Koontz (UCLA) has commented, "Long-range planning is not planning for future decisions, but planning for the future impact of present decisions."[31] The major concerns, then, of environmental analysis in the strategic process are to identify opportunities and threats in the future, and to develop courses of action that will achieve desired corporate goals.

CONTINGENCY PLANNING

The internal analysis, the competitive advantage analysis, focuses on the resources of the organization—marketing, financial, technical, and managerial—which established the competencies and capabilities of the firm—what the firm can do.

Although environmental analysis is an important element in strategic formulation, it must be related to an internal competitive advantage analysis in determining what can be done with a given and limited set of resources. The advantages which are revealed will provide the chance to exploit opportunities in the environment; and similarly, weaknesses, whether technical, financial or others, will prevent the strategist from moving in other directions. There is an increasing emphasis on environmental analysis and forecasting and on the development of contingency plans to meet an uncertain future. Although larger organizations generally use more sophisticated techniques, there are indications that all firms are placing more and more emphasis on this aspect of strategic planning.

WATCH OUT FOR THOSE SPECIAL BOARD MEETINGS

On February 20, 1981, at a special meeting of the AM International Board of Directors held in New York City away from the Los Angeles headquarters, Roy L. Ash resigned as chairman. Despite his promises and efforts, Ash was unable to move AM into new high technology markets after five years at the helm. Director John P. Birkelund put together a coalition of board members to seek Ash's resignation after manufacturing snafus and several ill-fated new products had resulted in an operating loss of $1.5 million and the debt level was getting dangerously high. Ash, who plans to invest in another high technology company, said of AM, "The harvest time was coming and I wanted to be around when it did."

Sometimes in strategic management, no matter how carefully the strategy is analyzed, no matter how many variables are considered, things just don't work out the way they were planned.

MANAGERIAL SKILLS AND JUDGMENT

While a variety of forecasting techniques are available to the manager for predicting future conditions, including scanning, time series analysis, technological forecasting, and econometric models, it is important to remember that it is still a question of judgment. Managerial skills and judgment are important elements in the analysis stages, because no matter how good quantitative methods are, as Roy Ash found at AM, there is still the power-political process, requiring creativity, flexibility, and entrepreneurial spirit in setting future directions for the firm.

REVIEW QUESTIONS

1   Of the primary environmental factors, which do you feel are the most critical?

2   In the years 1985 to 1990, managers in the 45 to 65 year age bracket will only be 11 to 17 percent of the total population segment in management. How does this affect your career goals?

3   What environmental analysis techniques do you feel would be most useful to you, if you were a manager in a strategic position?

4   Do you agree with Roy Ash's approach to internal assessment at AM? What factors seem most important to you?

5   What are some of the major published sources of information in which you might find environmental analysis information?

6   Assume that your local real estate dealers ask you to forecast the future for your city or area. What key factors should be used to anticipate growth or decline for this?

ENDNOTES

1   Louis Kraar, "Roy Ash is Having Fun at Addressogrief-Multigrief," *Fortune*, February 27, 1978, 47.

2   Francis Aguilar, *Scanning the Business Environment* (New York: MacMillan, 1967).

3   Philip S. Thomas, "Environmental Analysis for Corporate Planning," *Business Horizons*, October 1974, 27.

4   Linda Hayes, "Twenty-five Years of Change," *Fortune*, May 5, 1980, 88.

5   See Danny Miller and Peter Friesen, "Strategy Making in Context: Ten Empirical Archetypes," *Journal of Management* Studies, October 1977, 253–80.

6   Henry Wriston, in the *Chronicle of Higher Education*, August 25, 1980, 72.

7   "Americans Change," *Business Week*, February 20, 1978, 64.

8   Arthur Roalman, "Why Corporations Hate the Future," *MBA*, November 1975.

9   Miller and Friesen, "Strategy Making in Context."

10   Peter H. Grinyer and David Norburn, "Strategic Planning in 21 U.K. Companies," *Long Range Planning*, August 1974, 80.

11   Louis E. DeNoya, "How to Evaluate Long-Range Plans," *Long Range Planning*, June 1978, 36.

12   Bro Uttal, "Texas Instruments Wrestles with the Consumer Market," *Fortune*, December 3, 1979, 50–51.

13 "Does GE Really Plan Better?" *MBA,* November 1975, 42–46.

14 Walter Guzzardi, Jr., "Demography's Good News for the Eighties," *Fortune,* November 5, 1979, 3.

15 Ibid. 106.

16 Don LeBell and O. J. Krasner, "Selecting Environmental Forecasting Techniques from Business Planning Requirements," *Academy of Management Review,* July 1977, 373–83.

17 Basil W. Denning, "Strategic Environmental Appraisal," *Long Range Planning,* March 1978, 22; see also Liam Fahey and William King, "Environmental Scanning for Corporate Planning," *Business Horizons,* August 1977.

18 Kenneth Newgren and Archie Carroll, "Social Forecasting," *Proceedings Academy of Management* (1978).

19 Robert Hershey, "Competitive Intelligence for the Smaller Company," *Management Review,* 66, no. 1 (Jan. 1977) 18–22.

20 Robert H. Turner, "Should You Take Business Forecasting Seriously?" *Business Horizons,* April 1978, 68.

21 James Utterback, "Environmental Analysis and Forecasting," in Charles Hofer and Dan Schendel (eds.), *Strategic Management: A New View of Business Policy and Planning* (Boston: Little, Brown, 1979).

22 LeBell and Krasner, "Selecting Environmental Forecasting," 373–83.

23 James Brian Quinn, "Technological Forecasting," *Harvard Business Review,* March/April 1967, 89.

24 William F. Glueck, *Business Policy,* 3rd ed. (New York: McGraw-Hill, 1980), 106.

25 For two excellent articles see: Robert B. Buchele, "How to Evaluate a Firm," *California Management Review,* Fall 1962, 5–76; and Howard H. Stevenson, "Defining Corporate Strengths and Weaknesses," *Sloan Management Review,* Spring 1976, 51–68.

26 Bruce D. Henderson, "Construction of a Business Strategy," in *Business Policy and Strategy: Concepts and Readings* (Homewood, Ill.: Irwin 1975), 290.

27 Kraar, "Roy Ash," 48.

28 "The Opposites," *Business Week,* January 31, 1977, 60.

29 Carol J. Loomis, "Richardson-Merrell Unswallows a Pill," *Fortune,* January 12, 1981, 54–55.

30 Based on "Playboy's Work on Atlantic City Casino," *Wall Street Journal,* April 15, 1980, 48.

31 Harold Koontz, "Making Strategic Planning Work," *Business Horizons,* 19 (April 1976), 39.

Strategy Evaluation and Decision Making

C H A P T E R

5

"If you define the business too broadly, you pour resources into so many things that you don't do anything effectively. You have to have the right balance."

John A. Georges, vice chairman, International Paper, quoted in "International Paper Tries Managing for the Long Run," *Business Week,* July 28, 1980, 98.

Identifying Strategic Alternatives

CHAPTER OBJECTIVES

When you have completed this chapter, you will be able to:

☐ *Demonstrate an understanding of the basic strategic alternatives.*

☐ *Describe the basic strategic alternatives and why they are used.*

☐ *Use strategic analysis in determining which alternatives are best selected under varying conditions.*

☐ *Analyze a management case using these techniques.*

MANAGING FOR THE LONG RUN[1]

Edwin A. Gee

Chairman Edwin A. Gee (pronounced with a hard "g") of International Paper Co. is developing a new strategic game plan for one of the nation's largest manufacturers of paper products. Gee's strategic game plan has evolved into a fundamental change in both operating strategy and corporate philosophy. He has initiated a large-scale reorganization and embarked on an unprecedented capital spending program. This corporate upheaval has changed the very culture of the old line company, one that has been slow to adapt to changes.

Gee is a Ph.D. in Chemical Engineering (University of Maryland). His expertise in water-pollution control, corporate development, and strategic planning coincide with subjects of major concern at IP.

"'Gee is very human,'" says a former IP manager. "'He likes to talk and listen to people. He will get more information than Smith and Brennan, who scare hell out of people.'" But despite the collegial atmosphere that he is creating, Gee is a forceful, decisive man. He has instructed his mangers not to give him what one man calls 'silver-bullet solutions'—direct specific recommendations on what to do about a problem. He wants them to offer 'viable alternatives' from which he can select what he deems is the right decision."[1] For example, Gee was considering several alternative proposals for actions involving the General Crude Oil subsidiary. He decided to sell it off (a divestment strategy) when he found that drilling expenses were exceeding its own cash flow.

The changing strategic direction of International Paper under Gee exemplifies a reaction to a conservative management that lost its leadership and its hold on market share. "'IP had its head in the sand,'" says a executive at Georgia-Pacific Corp. 'It didn't keep pace with the changing scenario in the pulp and paper business, and it didn't keep up with the "renegades" from the wood products industry who were moving into the paper market.'"[2]

THE SEARCH FOR ALTERNATIVES

There is no perfect strategy. There are only strategies that work at a certain point in time and those that don't. No organization can continue to apply the same strategy or game plan indefinitely, because conditions are constantly changing. International Paper was but one example of a successful company that became complacent, failing to change to meet new economic conditions and competition. In order to continue meeting these new and changing conditions, the manager needs to be developing an awareness of the various options which are open to him. In the strategic management process, the identification of strategic alternatives is an important element.

Sooner or later every strategy becomes ineffective. Because of this each organization must constantly reappraise its own strategic plans and make necessary revisions and changes. There are times when only minor revisions will have to be made; a fine tuning of an existing strategy. At other times, the strategic plan may need a wholesale overhauling to revitalize and redirect organizational fortunes. Because strategic management involves the selection of a corporate "game plan," the strategic decision process begins with an analysis of possible moves and countermoves. One strategist, Henry E. Singleton of Teledyne, has been described in these terms, "Everything he does has lots of deliberate thought behind it. He doesn't know what his opponent is going to do, but whatever the opponent does Henry has three possible moves."[3]

A CRITICAL STEP

The first step in the formulation of strategic alternatives is an analysis of the environment for potential opportunities or threats, and an assessment of internal resources and capabilities as discussed in the preceding chapter. The next stage involves the search for strategic alternatives. As Edwin A. Gee has suggested, rarely are there any magic answers or "silver bullet solutions" to strategic problems. Instead there must be a careful, logical analysis of many possible options and the examination of the possible consequences and risks associated with each potential strategy.

The examination of strategic alternatives is a critical step in strategy making. At International Paper, Edwin Gee is attempting to develop a new strategy and to revitalize what had become a stagnant, poorly managed operation. In his approach to new strategic directions, Gee is developing a strategy to become more cost competitive in paper (IP's major product), and at the same time move into a new market: lumber and building products (see Table 5.1).

DIFFERENT STRATEGIC APPROACHES

As may be noted, each of the major forest product companies employs a slightly different strategic approach, with varying degrees of success. Georgia-Pacific, for example, has used a strategy of diversification by moving into chemicals and other fields, while Weyerhaeuser relies upon size, forest management, and large timber resources to expand in a more intensive and focused strategy. Although International Paper is among the leaders in sales volume with $4.5 billion, it is also among the lowest in return on equity (14.9 percent). Therefore, Edwin Gee will attempt to select those strategic alternatives which he feels will improve IP's position relative to its competitors, and best achieve the long-term goals of IP.

TABLE 5.1
The Top Ten in the Forest Products Industry

Company	Sales Billions of Dollars	Net Income Millions of Dollars	Return on Equity Percent	Pulp, Paper, Packaging		Lumber, Building Products	
				Percent of Sales	Percent of Operating Income	Percent of Sales	Percent of Operating Income
Georgia-Pacific	$5.2	$327.0	18.3%	24%	24%	64%	52%
International Paper	4.5	347.5	14.9	76	71	16	27
Weyerhaeuser	4.4	512.2	20.4	33	22	57	76
Champion Intl.	3.7	247.1	19.1	51	58	49	42
Boise Cascade	2.9	174.9	15.7	55	69	44	30
Crown Zellerbach	2.8	133.5	13.8	76	57	23	42
Mead	2.6	140.9	20.4	100	100	—	—
St. Regis Paper	2.5	158.5	13.7	75	59	14	19
Kimberly-Clark	2.2	314.4	29.0	99	100	—	—
Scott	1.9	137.1	14.5	92	88	—	—

SOURCE: Standard & Poor's Reports, 1979.

ALTERNATE DECISIONS AT IP

One of the alternative decisions facing Gee, for example, involved three highly inefficient paper mills (representing about 17% of production). He needed to determine whether to close down the mills (a retrenchment strategy) or to invest the large amount of capital necessary to modernize them (a growth strategy). These strategic alternatives and decisions are the most critical issues facing the strategic decision maker. Edwin Gee's answers to these strategic questions will determine how well International Paper will compare with its competitors in the future.

In this chapter, we will examine how strategic decision makers, like Gee, generate alternative strategies in order to identify the courses of action most likely to result in an increased level of performance for their firm.

The search for strategic alternatives involves two essential elements:

1 the identification of those factors which provide the development of an appropriate strategy

2 the specification of strategic alternatives for consideration in the evaluation and decision stages.

In the next sections, we shall examine how the strategic decision maker searches out alternatives and describe the major strategies.

DEVELOPING STRATEGIC ALTERNATIVES

The development of strategic alternatives emerges out of the analysis of the environment (Stage 4) and the firm's competitive position (Stage 5), and merges with strategic evaluation (Stage 7) and strategic choice (Stage 8). Yet for our purposes we shall discuss it as if it were a separate stage in the strategic formulation process.

STRATEGIC CHANGE

A strategic change is necessary whenever potential actions by competitors threaten to affect the firm's future goals. Although decision theorists suggest that the decision maker should consider all possible alternatives, in fact strategists rarely do this. Generally, the pressures of time and money limit the search, but in most situations several alternatives should be considered. This is true because a consideration of several options usually provides a superior comparison of trade-offs, advantages, weaknesses, etc., for strategic selection.

The consideration of strategic alternatives involves several factors. First, the alternatives which will be considered are a function of the firm's resources and capabilities. If, for example, the firm is in a tight cash situation and has a shortage of capital, then major expenditure alternatives are unrealistic.

A second consideration is the firm's past strategy: What strategy has the firm used and with what results? Generally, strategists start with the past strategy and continue until conditions change and they are forced to change. James B. Quinn (Dartmouth College) suggests that strategy is formed as an incremental process.[4] He suggests that successful strategists constantly reassess the future, find new directions as events unfurl, and direct the organization's skills and resources into new balances of dominance and risk aversion by incrementally modifying previous strategies. In the next sections, we will examine some of the forces influencing the development of alternatives.

THE INERTIA OF PAST STRATEGY

For most organizations, like International Paper, strategy is an ongoing and continuing process. In fact, there is research evidence to suggest that past strategic choices strongly influence later strategic choices.[5] Consequently, it is likely that a firm will continue with its previous strategy unless something changes, such as management, the environment, or products. Therefore, the starting point in strategic search is always the past strategy.

At ITT, for example, Harold Geneen was acclaimed for his aggressive program of acquisition and growth. Now, however, new CEO Rand V. Araskog is faced with sluggish profits and needs for internal growth as well as acquisition. The risk is that following both growth plans may be impossible.

"The areas in which ITT wants most to grow internally—energy and electronic office equipment among them—would be major draws on cash. Making acquisitions at the same time would strain ITT's financial capability. If Araskog is led nonetheless into a Geneen-like acquisition program, it may be mainly because of the powerful imprint the former chief made during a generation in office. And with Geneen still active, Araskog must work out his goals for ITT under the scrutiny of a strong leader who still believes in his own original vision." So says *Business Week.*[6]

As noted, each strategist must assess the conditions and strategic options to determine which among an array of possible alternatives will be most beneficial for the organization.

THE BASIC STRATEGIC ALTERNATIVES

One of the critical steps in the strategic process is the development of strategic alternatives. It is an important step because it allows a systematic comparison of the various tradeoffs, risks, and rewards associated with each possible strategy. Therefore, the final strategic choice, such as the strategy of International Paper, is likely to be more effective in terms of long-run performance.

THE KEY STRATEGIC VARIABLE

The first question to be asked (often termed the key strategic variable), is "what business are we in?" Peter Drucker (a leading management consultant) has suggested that this question can only be answered "by looking at the business from the outside, from the point of view of customer and market."[7] As Jacques Maisonrouge, a senior IBM executive, has stated:

"We want to be in the problem-solving business—this is our mission. Our business is not to make computers. It is to help solve administrative, scientific, and even human problems. If your mission is broad enough, you do not find one day that a competitor's new product has outmoded all your equipment."[8]

STRATEGIC DIRECTION AT GREYHOUND

Greyhound Corporation, for example, originally defined itself as a bus company. It later broadened this view to include the transportation field, and then more broadly to the "people satisfaction" business. As a result, Greyhound is now a diversified corporation, and Greyhound buses represent only one segment of its total business concerns. *Fortune* tells the story this way.

Gerald H. Trautman (Chairman and CEO) "had built Greyhound Lines, the nation's largest bus carrier, into a profitable conglomerate. Soon after taking command in 1966, he established his management style by firing half a dozen vice-presidents who did not share his conviction that the company could be revamped. . . ." His strategic decision moved "the Phoenix-based company into mortgage financing, insurance, car leasing, computer leasing, and a variety of other businesses—mostly through acquisitions."

Trautman, a Stanford economics major and Harvard Law graduate, maintains that his acquisition strategy was "plotted as scrupulously as a moon shot."

Others, including former senior officers, argue that the company used an ad hoc strategy and level the charge at Trautman that he has imparted no ennobling sense of Greyhound's mission or direction.

One former manager said, "'If Greyhound needs anything, it's strategic direction. It's got to decide which businesses it ought to grow and which to divest.' Adds a former division chief: 'There is not now, never has been, and won't be while Jerry Trautman is there, a strategic plan for the Greyhound Corp. It's grown in reaction to events.'"[9]

THE STRATEGIC ALTERNATIVE MATRIX

From this basic strategic question, "what business are we in?" follow other questions such as "should we stay in this business or should we get out?" These strategic issues involve a number of fundamental strategic alternatives as shown in The Strategic Alternative Matrix (Table 5.2). There are many possible strategic alternatives and each of the basic strategies will be discussed in the following sections.

The matrix is designed as a framework for the identifiction and comparison of strategic actions and also indicates the relative frequency of use and the

TABLE 5.2
The Strategic Alternative Matrix

Strategy	Frequency (of Use)	Goals	Uses	Examples
1. *Aggressive-Growth* Intensive Concentric Diversification Conglomerate Diversification Vertical Integration	54.4%	To increase sales/ earnings	High market growth Economic prosperity	H. Geneen (ITT)
2. *Mixed-Combination*	28.7%	To increase earnings Cut costs	In economic transition multi-division companies	Roy Ash (AM)
3. *Neutral* Holding Harvesting	9.2%	To increase profitability	In mature industry Stable environment	Roger Smith (General Motors)
4. *Defensive* Turnaround Divestment Liquidation	7.5%	Survival To cut costs To eliminate losses	In crisis Severe losses, etc.	Lee Iacocca (Chrysler)

basic goals associated with each of these strategic alterntives. Each strategy can be effective depending upon the competitive position of the firm, its resources, the type of market, the competition, etc. In general, large multiproduct firms tend to take a more aggressive strategic approach than firms in weaker, less dominant positions.

A TYPOLOGY OF STRATEGIC APPROACHES

One typology of strategic approaches proposed by Raymond E. Miles and Charles C. Snow (Harvard University) suggests a continuum of strategic positions.[10]

Defenders   These are firms which operate in a narrow product/market domain and guard it. They plan intensively, have centralized control, use limited environmental scanning, and are cost-efficient. This is one end of the strategic continuum.

Prospectors   At the other end of the continuum are the firms which use broad planning approaches, decentralized controls and broad environmental scanning, and have some underutilized resources. The prospectors aggessively seek new product/market segments.

Analyzers   In between the two extremes are two midpositions, one of which is termed analyzer. Analyzers have some characteristics of prospectors and some of defenders—in other words a mixed strategic approach.

Reactors   The other in-between position is termed the reactor. This firm realizes the environment is changing but is unable to effect the necessary change of strategy to meet the competition. The reactor either moves into one of the other three positions or fails. It is an unstable strategic posture.

Usually large, dominant firms will be most effective if they develop aggressive strategic alternatives in their major market segments. Smaller firms will usually do best when they use defensive strategies toward the larger firms' major markets and aggressive strategies toward those market segments not saturated by the dominant firm(s) in which they can expand.

In the following sections, each of the basic strategic alternatives will be described.

THE AGGRESSIVE-GROWTH STRATEGY

One of the most popular and frequently used strategic options is the aggressive or growth strategy. In a study of 358 *Fortune* 500 companies, William Glueck found that over 50 percent chose growth as a primary strategy.[11] The aggressive strategy seeks to attack the market and dominate its product/market segment. This strategy involves attempting to increase the level of sales and market share at a higher rate than in the past, and usually at a higher rate than competitors. In highly competitive industries with high rates of technological change (i.e., electronics), firms that do not use aggressive strategies will likely be left far behind.

To stand still in a dynamic environment is to move backward. RCA Corp., for example, announced a plan "to market its long-awaited Selectavision videodisc player nationally in early 1981—a $100-million effort to give viewers still another chance to forego network and station shows for those on record-like discs." *Business Week* tells this RCA story.

STRATEGY AT RCA

"Although its actions seem paradoxial, RCA has plenty of company. Along with individualistic entrepreneurs who arrived on the TV scene only recently, numerous well-entrenched companies are scrambling to get in on the ground floor of a technological revolution that will change the face of the TV industry in the next decade. Many are turning their backs on areas that made them properous and are jumping wholeheartedly into new ventures. Others, uncertain which of a half-dozen technological innovations has the greatest potential, are hedging bets by moving gingerly in several new directions at the same time," as shown in Figure 5.1.[12]

DYNAMIC GROWTH

Not surprisingly, many firms feel that growth is a highly desirable, necessary objective. There are many examples of dynamic-growth strategies: Harold Geneen of ITT,

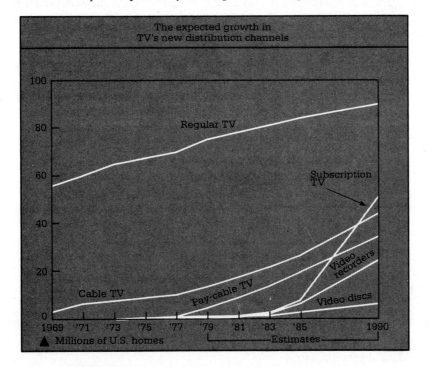

FIGURE 5.1
New Growth Markets in the TV Industry

Data: Television Bureau of Advertising, National Cable Television Assn., *Television Digest*

for example, led his company into a pattern of rapid growth that moved ITT to number 11 in the *Fortune* top 500. Charles B. "Tex" Thornton started Litton Industries when Hughes Aircraft was the dominant firm in electronics, but Thornton used an aggressive growth-oriented strategy to move Litton into one of the leading firms in the industry and to number 81 in the top 500.

One of the primary advocates of the growth strategy approach is Bruce Henderson of the Boston Consulting Group. The BCG supports getting the biggest market share as early as possible, and then holding costs and prices down to reduce the attractiveness of the market to other possible entrants.[13]

WHY USE AGGRESSIVE STRATEGIES

There are many reasons why an aggressive-growth strategy may be selected. *First, many studies indicate that growth is associated with effectiveness* (as measured by profitability and other standard measures).[14]

Second, there is much support for "experience curve" theories (see Chapter Seven) which suggests that as the firm grows in size and experience there is an increase in effectiveness, including economies of scale.[15]

Growth strategy is one of the most difficult to manage. Growth often hides serious underlying problems which do not come to light until the growth rate stops or a decline is experienced. At Litton, for example, there were several management problems which developed during periods of rapid growth, which caused an impact on later profitability. Fred Wittenbert has found that as the rate of growth accelerates, there tends to be a corresponding decline in profitability,[16] although more recent data suggest that this is not true.

Finally, there is the ego involvement of the manager. Most managers have "paid their dues"; that is, they have worked their way up through years of hard work. They want to be remembered as the individual who led their company to new successes, not as some one who only occupied the office for five years.

SOME RESEARCH FINDINGS

In support of the popularity of the aggressive-growth strategy, there are a number of research findings which reinforce the effectiveness which strategic managers intuitively strive to grasp.

In a study of fifty-three leading growth companies, Peter Gutman (CCNY) found that growth rates ranged up to 76.7 percent annually.[17] Gutman's findings include the following:

The firms with the highest growth rates:

1 chose industries where sales increased more rapidly than the economy as a whole;
2 concentrated on the market segments within the industries which grew more rapidly than the industry;
3 entered the marker earlier than competing firms;
4 operated in multinational markets.

Michel Chevalier and Bernard Catry studied three U.S. industries and found that some growth strategies were more effective than others, namely:

1   Focus on products whose markets are growing. Never focus on slow-growth products unless there is technical or market know-how you can learn to apply to more promising markets.

2   It is better to be a big fish in a small pond if the pond (market segment) is growing. Get out of small nongrowth markets. Don't be a follower.

3   Select specific market segments to compete in. Don't try to compete against larger firms.[18]

These studies suggest that a growth strategy, when properly selected and implemented, can be very effective. In the following sections, each of the major aggressive strategic options will be described.

INTENSIVE GROWTH: CONCENTRATION ON SPECIALIZED PRODUCT OR MARKET

One widely used growth strategy is to increase the sales and market share of a concentrated product line or market at an increasing rate. This involves doing only one thing but doing it very well.

1. INCREASE MARKET SHARE IN A HIGH-GROWTH FIELD.

One strategy is to concentrate resources in a high-growth field, and attempt to dominate it.

McDonald's   McDonald's is an example of a high-growth strategy based on specializing in one product and doing it well. Its strategy was to lead the growth in the fast-food field—then a high-growth area.

Deere and Co.   Another case is Deere and Co., the farm equipment company. While conventional wisdom might dictate a cautious approach to expansion or even a program of wholehearted diversification, Deere is plowing an unprecedented $2 billion back into its core businesses over the next five years. The new plan, however, represents a determined effort to boost manufacturing capacity and efficiency, even though Deere already is the low-cost producer in farm equipment and among the leaders in construction machinery. Deere executives will not discuss precise goals, but it is clear that their strategy is to gain market share during the coming period of adversity.[19]

2. INCREASE SALES INTO ADDITIONAL GEOGRAPHIC AREAS.

If your market stops growing, then one strategy is to expand the area of operation. Coors, for example, was a highly growing regional brewing corporation, with a strong market share in the West. However, it decided to shift into a national geographic market in order to expand its total market.

3. INCREASE SALES BY FOCUSING ON DIFFERENT MARKET SEGMENTS.

When a market begins to slow, another way to continue growth is to seek separate market segments, distinctive product quality, etc. Polaroid, for example, started in a high-growth field, and has since expanded from the low end (the One-Step) up to the high end (the SX-70) in instant photography. McDonald's sought to expand its market by moving into the breakfast segment, a move which other competitors are likely to follow as the basic market growth rate slows.

Philip Morris   When Philip Morris, Inc., eight years ago tapped John A. Murphy, a lawyer turned tobacco executive, to head its newly acquired Miller Brewing Co., it marked the beginning of what has since become a classic study on how sophisticated marketing can work miracles for a consumer product going nowhere. By introducing a host of new products such as Lite beer, upgrading Miller's distribution network, and throwing advertising dollars around so freely that it stunned other brewers, Murphy increased Miller's sales more than ninefold to $1.8 billion last year and moved to within striking distance of his goal of knocking off Anheuser-Busch, Inc., as the nation's king of beers. Under Murphy, Miller jumped from seventh place, with 4 percent of the beer market, to second place, with 19 percent.[20]

4. INCREASE SALES BY NEW PRICING STRATEGIES.

This is not a widely used strategy, because the competition will rarely let you take market share on pricing moves: If you can do it, they will do it. However, it can be used in certain instances, where one firm has a pricing advantage. One example was Texas Instruments, which used a learning curve pricing strategy to move into the watch market. It was able to assemble solid-state watches at an extremely low cost and, with high volume, was able to gain a significant share in a market dominated by others by offering a $10 digital watch. It is now attempting to apply a similar strategy to the computer market.

CONCENTRIC DIVERSIFICATION

At some point in time, a firm can no longer expand in its basic market. When the firm can no longer grow through market penetration, then it must seek to add new products or markets. When a firm grows by adding related products, this is termed a *concentric diversification strategy.*

There are a number of factors underlying the selection of the concentric diversification strategy.

1 *Market saturation.* The firm may be in an industry or market which is already saturated, or one in which the growth has stabilized.

2 *Cash flow.* Another reason for diversification is that the existing business is producing a high positive cash flow, and outside opportunities present a favorable rate of return.

3 *Countercyclical trends.* The firm in one industry may be subject to business cycles and thus may wish to diversify in order to smooth out the earnings flow.

4 *Access to new technical expertise.* The firm may also use diversification as a means to gain entry into new products, new markets, or new technology, or to gain managerial expertise in a new field. One typical reason might be to move into a new geographic area, particularly into overseas markets quickly.

Studies of the effectiveness of internal diversification have found that entry into a diversified line on a large scale is related to eventual success and growth.[21]

CONGLOMERATE DIVERSIFICATION

Another approach to diversifying, which will be discussed in detail in Chapter Six, is conglomerate diversification. The difference here is that the firm seeks to diversify into products completely unrelated to the current product line. ITT is one example of a firm using a conglomerate strategy, as it manages some 265 different companies in a range of industries. Conglomerate diversification takes place for the same reasons as concentric diversification.

DEFINITION

Norman Berg (Harvard University) has identified some of the differences between diversified firms and conglomerates. His definition of a conglomerate is a firm which has at least five or six divisions which sell different products principally to external markets, rather than to each other. Berg points out that conglomerates have diversified rapidly, primarily through mergers and acquisitions, into products unrelated to their prior business. In terms of growth in sales and earnings over the past ten years, Berg suggests many conglomerates have far out-paced their older and more mature counterparts.

DIFFERENT STYLE

Berg also suggests that conglomerate management style is different as follows:

1 Conglomerates have much smaller central offices than diversified firms.

2 Conglomerates tend to place most major operating decisions at decentralized divisional levels.

3 Conglomerates' division managers are autonomous as long as the division "delivers."[22]

By placing responsibility where it belongs—at the divisional level—conglomerate managers can evaluate performance better and do not become involved in operating decisions at lower levels of the organization.

The conglomerate strategy allows rapid growth primarily by purchasing (acquiring) other companies for stock, when the conglomerate's stock is at a much higher price-earning ratio than that of the target company's stock. A merger occurs when two organizations literally "merge" all resources (human included). Acquisition occurs with outright purchase or through a stock-swap take-over as described.

VERTICAL INTEGRATION

Vertical integration, another approach to strategic alternatives, is a growth strategy that involves the expansion of the business by moving backward or forward from the present product level.

Backward integration refers to moving lower on the production process scale, so that the firm is able to supply its own raw materials or basic components. If McDonald's Hamburgers decides to buy cattle ranches and supply its own beef, this would represent backward integration. Another example of a primarily retail firm integrating down the scale is Revco's move into manufacturing.

VERTICAL INTEGRATION AT REVCO

Since 1947, when Revco D.S., Inc., started out as a single drugstore in Detroit, the company's growth has been phenomenal. During the past decade alone, Revco, now based in Twinsburg, Ohio, has increased its revenues more than eightfold, to $928 million. With 1,174 outlets, it is the nation's largest discount drugstore chain, ranking No. 4 among drug merchants in total sales, after Jack Eckerd, Skaggs, and Walgreen.

And according to President and Chief Executive Officer Sidney Dworkin, growth for the sake of growth defines Revco's retailing strategy rather well. Yet Dworkin is now quietly but forcefully moving Revco to become a producer of drugs and related items, making the Ohio-based chain the first drug vendor to launch a major push into drug manufacturing. While the company first dipped its toe cautiously into production eight years ago, when it bought a tiny maker of vitamins and food supplements, it today is poised for a genuine attempt to join the ranks of substantial drugmakers. Through an aggressive program of internal expansion and acquisitions, Dworkin plans to triple the size of Revco's drug-making business to $100 million within three years.[23]

Forward integration is the other side of the coin, and refers to moving higher up on the production/distribution process, toward the end consumer. If someone who owned a cattle ranch were to open his own meat market, or fast food restaurant, and sell directly to the consumer, then this would be forward integration. For example, Xerox Corporation recently launched a nationwide chain of plushly appointed office-equipment retail stores. The stores, which sell small copying machines, word-processing equipment, small computers and telephone-answering devices, are aimed at the huge market of small businesses.

WHY USE VERTICAL INTEGRATION

There are a number of reasons why firms might use this strategy including:

1 *Economies of scale.* Firms may feel that by increasing scope they may reduce overall costs.

2 *Supplier dependability.* This lessens the influence of uncertain supplies and of price variation in raw materials.

3 *Better cost and quality control.* Cost efficiencies of stable operating level and quality level improve.

4 *Less dependence on uncertain suppliers.* Preventing possible shortages or loss of supply sources. For example, some firms who buy solid-state electronic components from Texas Instruments often find orders are delayed because TI cannot fill all orders and meet internal requirements.

5 *Increase in overall profit margins.*

Joseph Vesey (Harvard University) found that certain characteristics were associated with companies making successful use of vertical integration. They were

- Firms with sales of $1 to $2 billion which were highly diversified.
- Relatively few new products were introduced.
- Firms which had a low investment per employee.
- Firms with relatively concentrated customers: 40 or more customers represented 50 percent of the business.
- Low product value—the products produced are "unimportant" financially to the customers.[24]

Vesey also found that backward integration led to higher profit performance than forward integration.

As can be seen, firms which wish to achieve rapid expansion will usually follow one of the growth strategies.

THE NEUTRAL STRATEGY

A neutral, or "satisfying," strategy involves a continuation of past strategy or an incremental improvement in performance. In essence, these companies are satisfied with the way things are going, so hesitate to make drastic changes. Such strategies are usually implemented by companies who are dominant in their field, or by those who exist in a relatively stable external environment. These strategies may be termed "don't rock the boat," or "steer a steady course" approaches to strategic decisions.

This strategy is often used by companies like General Motors, Coca Cola or Anheuser Busch, where one company holds a commanding lead in the industry, and the strategists want to "keep on doing what we have been doing." However, such firms are also often what might be termed "counter punchers." They are satisfied with the way things are going, but if a corporation starts to cut into their market share, then watch out because they will react aggressively.

Often a neutral strategy is adapted after a company has been through a period of rapid growth. For example, John B. Fery of Boise Cascade and Robert Kirby of Westinghouse attempted to solidify their firms' positions following high growth eras. Now the emphasis is more on profitability than on growth.

When General Motors recently named Roger B. Smith as Chairman, Smith said he planned no major changes. "I'd be very surprised if there were any dramatic changes," he said.[25]

WHY FIRMS USE THE NEUTRAL STRATEGY

The neutral or satisfying strategy is used when a firm is satisfied with its past performance (sometimes unwisely so) and decides to continue with objectives in line with prior achievements. This is a relatively low-risk approach. The reasons for this are several.

1 *The firm is already doing well.* Why change or tamper with success?

2 *Low-risk taking.* The management may not wish to take the risk of greatly modifying its strategy but just keeps on doing what it has been doing. Some researchers have noted that too much growth too fast can lead to ineffectiveness.[26]

3 *The firm is in the satisfying mode, and the current level of change is good enough.* If the level of change for the industry is low, then a high-growth strategy may not be necessary. Arnold Cooper (Purdue University) found that in many industries, firms with steady growth are more effective.[27]

4 *The firm is unaware of changes in its environment.* This is also sometimes termed "having your head in the sand." Sometimes a firm is simply unaware that it is not keeping up with the competition and so continues on a neutral course (i.e., Chrysler, Ford, etc.).

There are two variations of the neutral strategy termed holding and harvesting.

A HOLDING STRATEGY

A holding, or sustainable growth, strategy may be defined as a steady rate of growth but at a slower rate than the external environment. This strategy is usually followed by large, dominant firms in a mature industry, where the goal is maintenance of position rather than rapid growth.

Often, a firm pursuing this strategy concentrates on one product but does this well. The firm grows slowly and incrementally by means of greater market penetration and slowly adding new products.

One example is PPG Industries, Inc., where executives "are abuzz with final preparations to build a $100-million headquarters. Lavishly sheathed in glass, the edifice not only will house the company but will also describe its business.

"PPG, also a maker of chemicals and coatings, remains dependent on glass production for more than one-third of it revenues. . . ." The danger of reliance on low-growth markets has seldom seemed more apparent. Both "auto and housing markets are depressed. And for the long term, the two markets are changing in a way threatening to" PPG.

According to *Business Week,* since 1973, auto downsizing already has reduced the amount of glass used in the average car by about 10 pecent. In construction, ordinary flat glass, of which PPG is the leading U.S. producer, is synonymous with energy loss. Although an orderly retreat from these markets might seem prudent, PPG is launching an aggressive marketing and capital investment program that will maintain the company's existing dependence on them by expanding its position in a few healthy niches of otherwise sickly fields.

Management, credited by outsiders as top-notch in the fields it knows, has picked an essentially conservative path under L. Stanton Williams, chairman and chief executive since last January. "We see no need to risk diversifying into industries we know nothing about," says Williams.[28]

LOW-MARKET SHARE

Some firms that use a holding strategy do so to pursue a low market share in their industry as a whole. Richard Hamermesh (Harvard University) found that firms like Union Camp and Burroughs achieve excellent return-on-invested-capital objectives by effective market segmentation and operating efficiency, and by lowering production and distribution costs. A low-market-share firm is defined as one with less than half the industry leader's share. A characteristic of successful low-market-share companies is that they are content to remain small and emphasize profits rather than growth.[29]

HARVESTING STRATEGIES

No product or market can grow indefinitely. A *harvesting strategy* is followed when the main objective of the firm is to generate cash for the corporation or stockholders. Harvesting is a decision to reduce investment in a business in the hopes of cutting costs and/or improving cash flow. Often market share is sacrificed to generate cash for other purposes. Firms using a harvesting strategy try to limit the amount of investment provided and instead attempt only to maintain market share.

HARVESTING AT B. F. GOODRICH

B. F. Goodrich, for example, is harvesting from its tire business while expanding in plastics and chemicals. Continuing to emphasize profitability rather than market share in its tire business, B. F. Goodrich plans to drop out of the original-equipment automotive market at the end of the 1981 model year. Goodrich currently holds about a 10 percent share of that low-margin, $1.2 billion market. Chairman John D. Ong is using cash from Goodrich's tire operations to expand faster-growing businesses, such as polyvinyl chloride and conveyors.[30]

CONDITIONS FOR HARVESTING

Philip Kotler (Northwestern University) suggests that a harvesting strategy will work if these conditions are present:

1   The business entity is in a stable or declining market.
2   The business unit doesn't provide sales stability or prestige to the firm.
3   The business entity's market share is small and it would be too costly to increase.
4   The business does not contribute a large percentage to total sales
5   The corporation has better uses for the freed-up resources.
6   Sales will decline less rapidly than the reduction in corporate support.[31]

The strategist must be aware of the fact that the market does not remain static. The nature of market and competitors can change rapidly. Products mature or are surpassed by innovations. The firm may achieve a dominant position in one segment but still may be forced to look elsewhere for growth.

THE ENDGAME

Kathryn Harrigan and Michael Porter (Harvard University) have described the harvesting strategy as an *"endgame"* strategy. They indicate that some firms have successfully profited from careful management of products which most firms felt were obsolete.

The functional strategies used by the successful endgame players include:

1   Dominate market share.
2   Hold market share (relative to competitors).
3   Shrink selectively (get out of unprofitable segments).
4   Milk the investment (harvest strategy.)
5   Divest now (sell before asset value shrinks too much).[32]

A comparison of these strategies with industry traits is shown in Figure 5.2

Characteristics	Possess Relative Corporate Strengths	Have Relative Corporate Weaknesses
Favorable Industry Traits for Endgame	"Dominate market" or "hold market share."	"Shrink selectively" or "milk."
Unfavorable Industry Traits for Endgame	"Shrink selectively" or "milk."	"Get out now!"

FIGURE 5.2
Conditions for Using Endgame Strategies
SOURCE: Kathryn Harrigan and Michael Porter, "A Framework for Looking at Endgame Strategies," *Proceedings,* Academy of Management, August 1976, 14.

The neutral strategy, such as holding or harvesting, can be implemented by a company or by business units or divisions within the firm. The neutral strategy is used when a firm is dominant in an industry or where the environment is not extremely dynamic. This is a low-risk, conservative strategy, but can be effective.

THE DEFENSIVE STRATEGY

The defensive strategy is the least used strategy, selected by only 7.5 percent of the firms studied. The use of defensive strategies, also termed retrenchment, is generally a reaction to operating problems stemming from either internal mismanagement or unanticipated actions by competitors. These strategies are used when the market is saturated or declining, the company is in trouble, during economic recession or financial crisis. Survival is often the goal of a defensive strategy. In general, this is a short-run strategy used to weather the storm during periods of recession, financial strain, or inadequate performance.

WHY FIRMS USE DEFENSIVE STRATEGIES

These strategies are generally used because of necessity, not by choice. There are reasons for using defensive strategies.

1 *The firm is doing poorly.* When A & P, the giant retailer, suffered lower earnings and profits, it closed down unprofitable stores and operations. In this way the company closed over one-third of its stores to halt the decline.

2 *The firm suffers major losses on one product.* General Electric, doing very well as a company, was losing heavily, about $100 million per year, in its computer business. Consequently, it got out of this business.

3 *The firm's survival is threatened.* At times a firm may find its very survival is in doubt, and some very drastic actions must be taken. Two recent examples of such firms include Lockheed and Chrysler, both of whom obtained government-backed loans to stay in business. When James H. Maloon become CEO of Itel, his top priority was *"survival, period."*

There are a number of possible alternatives within the defensive strategy mode which will be discussed in the following sections.

THE TURNAROUND STRATEGY

The turnaround strategy, as the name implies, is aimed at halting a firm's decline and improving its long-term efficiency. As a result, the short-term strategy is focused on cost reduction, while longer-run strategy may be aimed at growth or holding strategies. The turnaround strategy usually emphasizes cost-cutting, personnel reductions, closing inefficient plants, or even closing out unprofitable products.

INTERNATIONAL HARVESTER—A TURNAROUND

Business Week tells of such a strategy at International Harvester Co.: "Chairman Archie R. McCardell savored a momentary taste of the fatter profits he covets for the $8.4 billion manufacturer of trucks, farm implements, and construction equipment. Thanks to a surge in all three key markets—and the success of a cost-cutting campaign that McCardell says has saved $460 million in two years—the company's earnings soared 98 percent in 1979 to $370 million, producing an aftertax margin of 4.4 percent, a 15-year high. Buoyed by such initial results, McCardell, who was lured to Harvester from the presidency of Xerox Corp. in 1977 with a $1.5-million bonus, proclaimed just last September that his five-year plan to invigorate the sluggish giant was a full year ahead of schedule."[33]

Turnaround strategy may also include selling off assets in order to improve short-term cash flow. In fact, any measure that gives the firm some immediate breathing room may be undertaken, because the goal of the turnaround is to relieve current ailments, and get the firm on the road to improved performance.

SCHLUMBERGER LTD.

For example, when Schlumberger Ltd., acquired Fairchild Camera and Instrument Corp., "Schlumberger also bought far more problems than even its careful managers had anticipated. Over the past six years, the Mountain View (Calif.) company has dropped from No. 2 to No. 6 in the world rankings of integrated circuit producers, after having been the industry pioneer and market leader," writes one leading business periodical in 1980. ". . . Fairchild diversified disastrously into consumer products. That, plus an ill-fated computer development, cost the company $70 million or more. Even worse, it diverted the company's attention from more important markets such as metal oxide semiconductor (MOS) circuits. That prompted analysts such as James R. Berdell of Montgomery Securities to describe the company as 'the lousiest of the majors.' "[34]

Dan Schendel (Purdue University) found in a study of some fifty-eight firms that only about 20 percent of them actually changed prior strategy, while the majority (about 80 percent) applied some form of cost-cutting techniques.[35]

THE DIVESTMENT STRATEGY

If cost reduction methods don't solve the problems, then the next strategic move may be necessary: the divestment, or selling, of part of the business in order to increase overall profitability. The divestment strategy is often the outgrowth of previous expansion or acquisition strategies which have resulted in a serious decrease in profits or cash flow for the firm.

General Electric, for example, entered the computer industry because it was a high-growth field. However, General Electric found that it could no longer afford the heavy drain on its financial resources and so decided to exit from that industry. As might be expected, divestment, like the turnaround strategy, is aimed at improving long-term efficiency by selling off unprofitable segments of the business.

There are many reasons for selecting this strategy. Profits may be lower than in alternative sources of investment, the market share may be too low, the market growth potential too low, the cash investment required to stay in the game too high, or the product may not fit with the total product line.

A DIFFICULT DECISION

Divestment is often a difficult decision to make. This is because (as was the case at GE), there has usually been much effort, investment, and commitment put into making the project succeed. GE had several plants with thousands of loyal employees and was reputed to have some of the strongest technical expertise in the field. Michael Porter (Harvard University) has pointed out several of the factors which inhibit a decision to divest, including that it is often taken as a sign of failure, or as a setback or a loss, and no one likes that.[36] This is why divestment is often selected after there is a change in the management. The new manager does not have a proprietary interest in earlier decisions or in defending past errors in judgment. A study by Stuart Gilmore of three divestment case histories found that in all three cases a change in top management was required before the companies would divest unprofitable businesses.[37]

NATIONAL CAN—DIVESTMENT STRATEGY

National Can Corp., the country's third largest can producer, provides an example of a divestment strategy. "Following an unsuccessful stab at diversification, the big Chicago-based company is selling off outside businesses while investing heavily to expand and upgrade its can, bottle, plastic container, and bottle-cap operations," writes *Business Week* (1979). "Just last year, National Can sold a pet food division and a food processing unit, which together generated some $150 million in sales.

"It is now trying to unload a dormant speciality protein division that made soybean pet food additives. 'We're clearing the decks,' says President Frank W. Considine. 'We are investing only in businesses that we know, and where there is a reliable profitability.' "[38]

THE LIQUIDATION STRATEGY

The most drastic defensive strategy is *liquidation:* the selling off of the entire company or liquidation of its assets. Although there are rare situations in which a company is "worth more dead than alive," and management chooses to sell out, this is generally a strategy of last resort. There simply is no other way out. This is obviously the least popular strategy and is used only when there are no other feasible alternatives. For example, W. T. Grant, once a successful discount store with over 1,100 stores was forced to liquidate.

ALLIED SUPERMARKETS, INC.

Allied Supermarkets, Inc., is another firm trying a comeback from eighteen months of bankruptcy reorganization, "slimmed down from a peak of more than 450 stores in 1970—when it was the nation's eleventh largest food chain—to eighty-four."

Any potential partner "is sure to be stunned by Allied's past management blunders. Allied became one of the fastest-growing food chains in the country in the 1960s when it agreed with rapidly expanding K-Mart Corp. to open a supermarket alongside each new discount outlet. By the end of the decade, moreover, it had built a mammoth warehouse just outside Detroit, a building of 1.3 million square feet that also housed a bakery, dairy, and meat-packing plant.

"Such moves propelled Allied too far too fast. Although the sites picked by K-mart were fine for department stores, many locations meant stiff competition for Allied without offering the hoped-for rewards of K-Mart's high traffic. Sales per store began to sag, yet the company continued to operate the warehouse at far below capacity. In a last-ditch attempt to bolster volume, Allied in 1975 bought ailing Great Scott Super Markets, Inc., but the new operation itself soon slipped into the red. Allied lost $9.2 million on sales of $763 million in the year ended June 24, 1978."[39]

DEFENSIVE ALTERNATIVES

The defensive strategies which have been described are among a range of possible alternatives. In general, this is the hardest strategy to follow because it suggests that earlier strategies have failed. However, often firms that are reluctant to use such strategies are taken over by other companies whose first move is to apply these approaches as a means of turning a "loser" into a "winner."

THE MIXED STRATEGY

The mixed or combination strategy involves using elements of two or more basic strategies at the same time in different segments of the organization. If a firm is operating in several markets which are changing at different rates, or its products are in varying stages of the product life cycle, then a mixed strategy may be necessary.

The mixed strategy was the second most popular strategy among *Fortune* 500 firms (28.7%), according to a study by the late William Glueck.[40] It is most frequently used in large, multidivision companies. It is typically selected in order to optimize the firm's profitable elements and minimize the effect of its losers. Therefore, such a strategy usually involves a growth strategy in certain divisions or product lines, and harvesting, or defensive strategies in others. Westinghouse, for example, under Robert Kirby is adapting to changes in its environment after a period of growth, which emphasized increasing volume without regard to risk. Kirby has tightened up operations, so that businesses with returns of less than 15 percent are candidates for divestiture and those with a return below 7 percent are certain to be spun off.[41]

DIAMOND SHAMROCK'S STRATEGY

A second example of mixed strategy is the approach of William H. Bricker, the controversial chairman of Diamond Shamrock Corp. who has a reputation of riding roughshod over people to get what he wants. Bricker's strategy has been to move the $2.3-billion Diamond Shamrock, one of the country's oldest chemical firms, out of mature and capital-intensive chemical lines and into oil, gas, and coal production. According to *Business Week,* he has more often than not bulldozed over opposition from both board members and his own executives in such strategic decisions as transplanting the company in 1979 from its long-time Cleveland headquarters to Dallas and acquiring coal-producer Falcon Seaboard, Inc.

Meanwhile, Bricker has marked six divisions as divestiture candidates among Diamond Shamrock's chemical and plastics businesses. Behind Bricker's determination to de-emphasize such specialty chemical businesses as metal coatings and functional polymers, even if they are profitable or hold leading positions, is his belief that the company must be better able to cope with—and, indeed, to profit from—persistent high inflation. "All of our new corporate goals reflect our expectation that we will have to cope with at least a 10 percent inflation rate through the 1980s," says Bricker. "Historically, if your assets are in natural resources, you are able to keep pace, and our perception of the 1980s is that such resources will keep us ahead of the inflation rate," he says.[43]

Time is the enemy of all strategic plans. From the time a strategic decision is made and implemented, it begins to become outdated. Therefore, for some firms, the mixed strategy provides a suitable approach for adapting to changing market conditions.

WHY FIRMS USE MIXED STRATEGY

As noted earlier, mixed strategy is more appropriate in large multiproduct firms, because often a single strategy does not fit all products or markets. The times for using mixed strategies might include:

1   *When the firm has many different products and they are in different stages of the life cycle.* The strategy for an innovative, high growth product should be different from that of a mature, or declining product.

2 *During times of economic recession.* There is often a need to tighten the belt in marginal or losing areas, and concentrate on growth areas.

3 *When a firm reaches a certain size.* There are often more opportunities than there are available resources, and it is not possible to attack all markets with aggressive or growth strategies.

The mixed strategy, then, is usually used when a company has several businesses or products in differing stages of maturity. The purpose is to allocate resources to the high growth and the high potential areas of business, while reducing investment, or selling off less profitable endeavors.

A COMPARISON OF STRATEGIC ALTERNATIVES

In the strategic decision process, the manager must consider a range of possible alternatives. As you have seen, these alternatives range from extremely aggressive and dynamic growth strategies to very defensive positions, including getting out of the business. Generally speaking the appropriate strategy depends on the firm's position relative to external market and competitive positions, and, of course, the firm's financial resources. A firm that has low cash resources will find it difficult to implement certain strategies, even though it might like to. In Figure 5.3 a comparison of strategic alternatives is shown based upon two key variables: the potential market growth and the firm's competitive position.

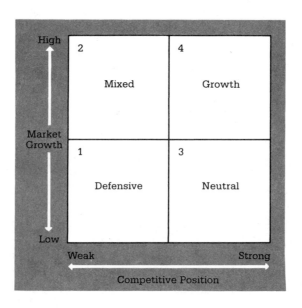

FIGURE 5.3
Matching Strategy and External Factors

1. DEFENSIVE POSITION

Firms fitting the characteristics of quadrant 1, with weak competitive position and low growth potential, would most likely select a defensive strategy. Because of the low probability for future growth, firms might look toward retrenchment or divestiture strategies and invest excess cash in areas where profit potential is greater.

2. MIXED POSITION

Those firms falling into quadrant 2, with a high market potential but with a weak competitive position, would most likely select some form of mixed strategy. In a high-growth field, there is an opportunity for the application of aggressive strategies, such as market penetration, or even diversification if the firm has the necessary resources. However, if the firm is not able to exploit such an opportunity, then it must consider the possibility of moving into other fields. In other words, in this situation, a firm must either aggressively seize the opportunity presented by the growth market and carve out a market segment, or it should consider getting out of the field altogether.

3. NEUTRAL, HOLDING POSITION

Firms in quadrant 3, with strong competitive position and low market growth, are most likely to select some form of neutral strategy, either a holding or harvesting approach, and use excess cash to invest in areas offering higher growth and return. In general, the firm tries to maintain its position and market share, with a minimum of investment, thereby generating cash for other strategic manuevers.

4. AGGRESSIVE-GROWTH POSITION

Those firms in quadrant 4, high-growth and strong competitive position, generally should be using growth strategies, seeking to maximize market share, and make it unattractive for competing firms to gain a foothold.

There are many factors to consider in the development of strategic alternatives, and each firm must consider the trade-offs, risks and rewards which are associated with each possible option. Strategists like Edwin A. Gee of International Paper must consider the opportunities which are presented by the various markets, the firm's competitive strength, its financial resources, and possible moves and coun-termoves of its main competitors in shaping a master strategy.

MANAGERIAL IMPLICATIONS

In this chapter, we have discussed one stage in the strategic management process: the development of strategic alternatives. Strategy precedes planning. It deals with the options and directions that the organization will follow in the future. If more than one alternative is selected, then this strategy must be integrated into the cohesive framework. Once the strategist is able to compare the possible courses of action, then it is possible to assess the likely outcomes and select that strategy which provides the best fit for that particular organization.

The identification of strategic alternatives emerges from the analysis done in preceding stages. From the environmental analysis, areas of growth and threat have been identified, and these are matched with the firm's competitive advantage profile. Out of this analysis evolves an assessment of the firm's current position and an evaluation of the past strategy. The strategist must then decide whether to continue with a similar strategy or to change the game plan. Because the competitive environment is constantly changing and new areas of opportunity are emerging, new strategic alternatives need to be identified and evaluated.

If a change is necessary, there are a number of possible strategic *approaches.* Four different types of strategic alternatives have been presented: aggressive-growth, neutral, defensive, and mixed. Each strategy provides the firm with differing choices of action to meet differing situations and goals. These major strategic alternatives have been presented to enhance the reader's knowledge of possible strategic directions which organizations may pursue; however, there are many differing approaches, and those suggested should not be considered as all inclusive.

The strategist makes many decisions: decisions about goals, decisions about markets and products, and decisions about strategies. The major strategic decisions, however, are important and far reaching, and are often made under conditions of uncertainty. The strategic decision is a good one only if it is successful in achieving company goals. Better decisions are likely to be made, we feel, when a range of possible strategic alternatives are examined as a means to selecting a most appropriate strategy.

Often *pressures toward* short-term results create a tendency to concentrate only on current *problems and crises,* at the expense of longer-term performance. One of the advantages of strategic alternative evaluation is a consideration of these and other tradeoffs and the possible consequences of each option.

Contingency approaches have grown in popularity because many strategic plans fail to take into account the changing environment. The crucial "what if" questions have caused strategic managers to include contingency approaches as a major factor in strategy selection.

The selection of a strategy is essentially a contingency decision. The best strategy will vary from industry to industry, from company to company, and from situation to situation. There is no simple set of strategic rules from which the manager can choose. Instead, the effect of many complex variables must be considered. There is an increasing emphasis on the development of contingency plans or scenarios for many possible future conditions, with varying strategic alternatives, depending upon the competitive situation.

Here we have presented a range of strategic alternatives to highlight the variety of strategic options available, and to provide a framework for identifying and generating alternatives in a changing environment.

REVIEW QUESTIONS

1 Identify the basic strategic alternatives and their relative frequency of use.

2 Under what conditions might a strategist use a neutral strategy? What might be some of the advantages and disadvantages?

3 How would you compare the use of mixed strategy with the use of a defensive or turnaround strategy?

4 Given the rate of potential market growth and relative competitive position for any firm, suggest likely strategic moves for it.

5 Many analysts have pointed out the fact that the fast foods industry is in a slow growth stage. What strategy might McDonald's or Burger King use to meet the changing conditions?

ENDNOTES

1 "International Paper Tries Managing for the Long Run," *Business Week,* July 28, 1980, 98; "A Paper Giant Protects Its Homeland," *Fortune,* September 10, 1979, 23.

2 "International Paper," 94

3 A. F. Ehrbar, "Henry Singleton's Mystifying $400 Million Flyer," *Fortune,* January 16, 1978, 66–67.

4 James B. Quinn, *Strategies for Change* (Homewood, Ill.: Irwin, 1980).

5 Henry Mintzberg, "Research on Strategy Making," *Proceedings, Academy of Management* (1972).

6 "ITT Groping for a New Strategy," *Business Week,* December 15, 1980, 66.

7 Peter F. Drucker, *Management: Tasks, Responsibilities, Practices* (New York: Harper and Row, 1974), p. 77.

8 Jacques Maisonrouge, then president of IBM World Trade Corporation, quoted in *Harvard Business Review,* January–February 1972, 45.

9 John Quirt, "How a Greyhound Made a U-Turn," *Fortune,* March 24, 1980, 139; Alexander Stuart, "Greyhound Gets Ready for a New Driver," *Fortune,* December 15, 1980, 59.

10 Raymond E. Miles, and Charles C. Snow, *Organizational Strategy: Structure and Process* (New York: McGraw-Hill, 1978).

11 See William Glueck, *Business Policy and Strategic Management* (New York: McGraw-Hill, 1980), p. 290.

12 "Television's Fragmented Future," *Business Week,* December 17, 1979, 60.

13 Bruce Henderson, *Henderson on Corporate Strategy.* (Cambridge, Mass.: Abt Books, 1979).

14 Robert Buzzell et al., "Market Share: A Key to Profitability," *Harvard Business Review,* January–February 1975, 97–106, see also William Hall, "Strategic Planning, Product Innovation and the Theory of the Firm," *Harvard Business Review,* Spring, 1973.

15 Patrick Conley, "Experience Curves as a Planning Tool," in Robert Rothenberg, ed., *Corporate Strategy and Product Innovation* (New York: Free Press, 1977).

16 Fred Wittenbert, "Bigness vs. Profitability," *Harvard Business Review,* January–February 1970.

17 Peter Gutman, "Strategies for Growth," *California Management Review,* vol. 6, no. 4, Summer 1964.

18. Michel Chevalier and Bernard Catry, "Don't Misuse Your Market Share Goal," *European Business,* Winter–Spring 1974, 43–50.

19 "Deere: A Counter-Cyclical Expansion to Grab Market Share," *Business Week*, November 19, 1979, 79.

20 "Philip Morris: Turning 7Up into the Miller of Soft Drinks," *Business Week*, April 2, 1979, 66.

21 Ralph Biggadike, "Entry Strategy and Performance," *Proceedings, Academy of Management* (1977); Charles Berry, *Corporate Growth and Diversification* (Princeton, N.J.: Princeton University Press, 1975).

22 Norman A. Berg. "What's Different About Conglomerate Management," *Harvard Business Review*, November–December 1969, 112–20.

23 "Revco: A Discount Drug Retailer Expands into Manufacturing," *Business Week*, November 12, 1979, 122.

24 Joseph Vesey, "Vertical Integration: Its Affect on Business Performance," *Managerial Planning*, May–June 1978, 11–15.

25 Spokesman Review (Spokane), September 10, 1980.

26 David Gerwin and Douglas Tuggle, "Modeling Organizational Decisions Using the Human Problem Solving Paradigm," *Academy of Management Review*, October 1978, 762–73.

27 Arnold Cooper et al., "Strategic Responses to Technological Threats," *Proceedings, Academy of Management* (1973).

28 "PPG Industries: Still Relying on Glass—But Now in Growth Areas," *Business Week*, January 21, 1980, 94.

29 R. G. Hamermesh et al., "Strategies for Low Market Share Businesses," *Harvard Business Review*, May–June 1978, 95–102.

30 "Goodrich's Cash Cow Starts to Deliver," *Business Week*, November 14, 1977, 78, 83, 84.

31 Philip Kotler, "Harvesting Strategies for Weak Products," *Business Horizons*, August 1978, 17–18.

32 Kathryn Harrigan and Michael Porter, "A Framework for Looking at End-Game Strategies," *Proceedings, Academy of Management* (1976); Kathryn Harrigan, "Structural Factors on the Exit Decisions," *Proceedings, Academy of Management*, 1980.

33 "International Harvester: When Cost-Cutting Threatens the Future," *Business Week*, February 11, 1980, 98.

34 "Schlumberger's Troubles with Ailing Fairchild," *Business Week*, August 11, 1980, 66.

35 Dan Schendel et al. "Corporate Turnaround Strategies: A Study of Profit Decline and Recovery," *Journal of General Management*, Spring 1976, 3–11.

36 Michael Porter, "Please Note Location of Nearest Exit," *California Management Review*, Winter 1976, 21–33.

37 Stuart Gilmore, "The Divestment Decision Process" (unpublished D.B.A. dissertation, Harvard Business School, Boston, 1973).

38 "National Can: Getting Back to the Business It Knows Best," *Business Week*, April 30, 1979, 92.

39 "Allied Supermarkets: Will Upgrading Pull It Out of Reorganization?" *Business Week*, May 26, 1980, 93.

40 Glueck, *Business Policy*, p. 290.

41 "The Opposites: GE Grows While Westinghouse Shrinks," *Business Week* Jan. 31, 1977, 60–64, 66.

42 "AM International: The Cash Bind That Threatens a Turnaround," *Business Week*, August 18, 1980, 118.

43 "Diamond Shamrock: Looking for Energy Plays to Beat Inflation," *Busines Week*, December 8, 1980, 73, 76.

C H A P T E R

6

"His organization is well managed, it moves quickly, efficiently and intelligently. I guess you could call the trademark of Evans' operations ruthlessness and efficiency."

Robert A. Charpie, President, Cabot Corporation, quoted in "Thomas Mellon Evans—A Corporate Entrepreneur Hits the Jackpot," *Business Week,* October 15, 1976, 81.

Conglomerate Diversification Strategies

CHAPTER OBJECTIVES

When you have completed this chapter, you will be able to:

☐ *Recognize the various strategies which may be used to diversify an organizational system.*

☐ *Identify some of the techniques used in merger and acquisition strategies.*

☐ *Demonstrate an understanding of the conglomerate diversification strategy.*

☐ *Use these concepts in the analysis of a management case.*

WHAT MAKES HARRY GRAY RUN?[1]

Harry Gray

"What makes Harry Gray run so hard? Gray, CEO of United Technology Corp., normally begins each day at 6 A.M. and exercises for 30 minutes, as therapy for his legs. An armed chauffeur picks him up about an hour later. He usually arrives at his office by 7:30 A.M., often for breakfast meetings, rarely goes home before 8 P.M., and frequently has working suppers. He has a phobia about paper-littered desks, and the top of his own small, circular desk is invariably bare. At least half his time is spent traveling outside Hartford in one of eighteen planes in the corporate fleet. At least once a week a Sikorsky helicopter flies him to New York, mostly for meetings with investment bankers and airline executives. He plays golf poorly and tennis respectably and likes to ski crosscountry. His tennis is played with the same ferociously competitive vigor that he displays in fighting reluctant merger mates."

Harry Gray, the hard-driving, extraordinarily ambitious chairman and president of United Technologies, once a Litton manager under "Tex" Thornton, is now known as "Mr. Takeover" because of the series of acquisitions he has accomplished. Crosscountry motocycling was once his hobby and he plays the game of business with the same intensity.

Hidden in his office are bulky dossiers on about 50 industrial companies. The files contain annual reports, financial analyses, newspaper clippings, and other data on each company. A staff of five maintains the files, contstantly updating the contents and occasionally discarding some dossiers or starting new ones. Gray began to assemble the files in late 1972, a year after he was recruited from Litton Industries, Inc., to diversify the operations of what was then known as United Aircraft Corp. They make up what might be termed his "hit list" of potential merger targets. Gray's reported goal is to build a second General Electric Company.

Gray has assembled a strong assortment of companies, but his strategy also entails considerable risks. For one thing, the cash and preferred stock he paid out for the acquired companies have leveraged United's finances to a degree normally associated with electric utilities. On June 30, the company's debt equaled 62 percent of total assets. If preferred stock is included in debt, as it should be from the perspective of the owners of common stock, the debt amounted to 75 percent of assets.

His name has become a byword for aggressive merger making. When McDonnell Douglas Corp. failed last year to acquire Data 100 Corp., which manufactures computer terminals, a Wall Street analyst said scornfully: "That's not the way Harry Gray buys companies." In explaining an unsuccessful bid to take over McGraw-Hill, Inc., earlier this year, American Express Co. Chairman James D. Robinson, III, was quoted as saying that he was only trying to follow "Harry Gray's approach."

THE CONGLOMERATE STRATEGY

One widely used strategy for growth is the conglomerate diversification strategy. There are, as noted, two distinct types of corporate diversification: concentric and conglomerate. Concentric diversification, on the one hand, involves adding new product lines, but in a related field. Boeing and Dow Chemical have diversified, but both built upon their existing technical expertise by staying in related businesses.

Conglomerate strategy, on the other hand, involves diversification into fields which are not significantly similar or related to the primary business mission. Conglomerates refer to businesses that are loosely related, often in completely different fields. Under Harold Geneen, ITT acquired and operated a multiple line of businesses including Sheraton (hotel), telephone companies, Levitt (home building), Hartford Insurance, Avis (car rental) and Canteen (vending). This is an example of a conglomerate diversification strategy.

Conglomerate diversification is an attempt to diversify outside of an industry. It can offer rapid growth, broader stability, and greater profit potential. On the other hand, there are higher risks and potentially greater losses. A successful diversification requires management depth to develop a strategy for managing complex, unrelated businesses.

RAPID GROWTH—UNITED TECHNOLOGIES CORP.

At United Technologies Corp., Harry Gray has added seven key acquisitions which diversified the corporation into a more varied combination of industries but all of which contributed to the firm's overall growth. Gray added to the basic Pratt and Whitney business such diverse businesses as Mostek Semiconductors and Otis Elevators.

STABILITY—TWA

Trans World Airlines, on the other hand, under Chairman L. Edwin Smart, has attempted to reduce its dependence on the volatile airline business with a strategy of conglomerate diversification, by acquiring Hilton Hotels, Spartan Foods, Century 21 Real Estate, and Canteen Corp. However, this strategy has forced Smart into making some tough choices to survive, including some difficult strategic decisions. The reason is that Trans World, by far the most diversified of airline companies, may have to choose whether to remain a major air carrier or focus instead on its more stable nonairline operations, which offer better growth potential. Conglomerate diversification, initially seen as a way to make TWA a more viable airline, now provides some compelling reasons for the company to pullback—or even withdraw altogether—from that business.[2]

TWA's strategic objective—then and now—has been to develop non-airline businesses that would smooth out the wide cyclical fluctuations common in the airline industry.

WHY CONGLOMERATE STRATEGIES ARE USED

There are many reasons why managers like Harry Gray choose to use a conglomerate diversification strategy. Several underlying reasons have been suggested by H. Igor Ansoff, including:

1 selecting greater growth, which can no longer be realized by expansion;

2 achieving better use of financial resources when retained earnings exceed planned investment needs;

3 exploiting new potential opportunities for greater profitability wherein company resources can be better used;

4 achieving distinct competitive advantages and broader stability.[3]

TABLE 6.1
Growth of Selected Conglomerates

Company	Sales in $ millions		Approximate number of acquisitions	Fortune's "500" rank	
	1958	1968	1958–1968	1958	1968
Bangor Punta	18	257	20	—	326
City Investing	5	207	12*	—	380
Gulf & Western	8	1,300	80+	—	69
Indian Head	43	370	36	—	252
ITT	687	4,100	50+	49	11
Kidde (Walter)	31	566	50+	—	176
Litton	83	1,900	60+	395	40
LTV	7	2,800	25	—	25
Ogden	299	1,000	30+	†	94
Textron	244	1,700	60+	174	47
#250 on Fortune's "500" list	161	370	—	250	250

*Period covered in 1967–1968 only.
†Ranked as a merchandising company (#29) in 1958.

SOURCE: Norman Berg: "What Is Different about Conglomerate Management."
Harvard Business Review, November–December 1969. Copyright © (1969) by the President and Fellows of Harvard College; all rights reserved.

THE MAJOR REASON

The major reason is probably *growth.* Many firms feel that the maximum growth rate possible by internal growth is simply not fast enough. Obviously, by using carefully chosen acquisitions, that growth rate can be multiplied many times over. Charles Berry (Princeton University), for example, found that the 500 largest firms in the United States used a diversification strategy and Norman Berg (Harvard University) found that conglomerates far outstripped the growth of the median firm on *Fortune's* 500 list (see Table 6.1).[4]

At United Technologies, Harry Gray's conglomerate strategy has doubled sales growth in five years, and with sales now at $10 billion his goal is to reach $20 billion by 1985 (as shown in Figure 6.1).

THE BOTTOM LINE

Another primary reason for selecting a conglomerate strategy is the *bottom line:* that is, to improve sales, earnings, and the profit picture for the entire corporation. Therefore, the first question is, will the proposed acquisition meet minimum objectives for return on investment? Each organization has an expected standard of profitability and one criterion is whether the proposed business can meet this level. Harry Gray's strategy at United Technologies has resulted in an increase in common stock of four times in value, and dividends have increased two and one-half times. So, Gray's conglomerate diversification strategy shows results at the bottom line.

EXPLOIT NEW OPPORTUNITIES

A third reason is to *exploit new potential opportunities.* The strategist may ask, if it isn't profitable now can we make it profitable? Many organizations, such as Litton

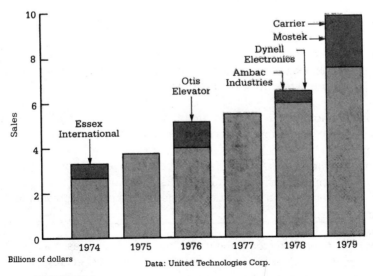

FIGURE 6.1
The Growth Strategy of United Technology

and ITT, feel that their system of management is so strong that many problems of mismanagement and poor control can be overcome, thus making the acquisition acceptable.

Such situations are ruled out by Harry Gray who says, "I don't know how to turn around ailing companies and I don't get along well with people who do know how to do that." Northwest Industries' CEO, Ben W. Heineman, is also "particularly leery of turnaround situations. 'It always takes longer than anyone believes to turn a company around,' he explains. Heineman specifically looks for companies that are earning at least 12 percent on capital and whose markets are growing by 10 percent a year or more. He is willing to pay up to 15 times earnings, and he expects to get a 12 percent annual return on investment after taxes and any charges for goodwill."[5]

A LONG-TERM PROGRAM

Finally, a company with a clear strategy will consider diversification as a long-term program, proceeding systematically with a common purpose running through various diversification actions. When diversifying, a company should capitalize on its strengths—its overall production capacity, access to markets, and technological capability.[6]

One strategic decision, then, is the choice between internal development or external development through acquisition and merger. Internal development offers a slower rate of growth and lower risks, but it provides a company with a solid base. External development provides a means for more rapid growth with a corresponding increase in risk.

FACTORS IN CONGLOMERATE STRATEGY

There are a number of factors to be considered in selecting the conglomerate strategy.

Growth   One very important factor is the potential growth rate of the market in which the new business operates. Since a primary reason for a conglomerate strategy is growth, it is always best to seek high growth fields.

Market or Technology   An opportunity to buy into an emerging market or technology is certainly one factor to be considered in the strategy.

Competitive position   Another factor is competitive position. It is always better to take over a business with higher market share than one with marginal strength—for example, Norton Simon's acquisition of Avis which held a 28 percent market share in the car rental field.

Cash flow   Another factor is the size of the cash flow or assets of the proposed new business. As we shall see later, many of the takeover specialists seek out cash-rich companies, and for a very obvious reason. Often it is possible to take over a company with large cash reserves, for a relatively small investment, and then use that cash for other more lucrative ventures.

THE OBJECTIVES OF CONGLOMERATE STRATEGY

There are many possible objectives underlying the selection of a conglomerate diversification strategy.[7] The company may feel too dependent on one industry, such as the case of TWA, or may wish to move into higher growth areas. Large-scale acquisition for the purpose of planned entry into a new industry is often a major strategy for corporate growth. Through forcing structural changes of business and management, it creates a synergistic condition—the addition of the parts is greater than the whole.

To gain an increased rate of growth   It is an exceptional company that can grow internally at a 20 percent annual rate, yet the LTV Corporation averaged a 51 percent rate of growth over a ten-year period by using a conglomerate strategy.

To increase the value of the company's stock   An effective acquisition can often result in an improved price/earnings ratio and a higher stock price. Litton's stock, during Tex Thornton's acquisition period, increased from about $15 per share to about $150 per share, including several stock splits.

Using excess cash to buy into high growth or high technology markets Harry Gray's acquisition of Mostek, a small but highly innovative semiconductor company is an example of buying into a new technology. He believes that a semiconductor company will give United's product designers a winning edge on the competition. "In the long run, every piece of equipment we manufacture is going to be controlled by microprocessors," says Gray. "The main reason we bought Mostek is to let the designers know what it's possible to do now and what it will be possible to do, at what cost, in the next three, five, or ten years."[8] Others simply use excess cash to acquire other companies, as Mobil Corp., for example, acquired Montgomery Ward.

To gain increased financial synergy   Sometimes a highly leveraged company can merge with a low-debt company to the benefit of both. Also, experts on takeovers often seek companies with high cash positions.

To spread risk or gain increased stability   A company in the defense industry may seek to diversify into consumer products to spread the risk of economic down turn, or diversify into countercyclical fields to reduce essential or cyclical fluctuation and stabilize earnings. TWA's diversification program was aimed at smoothing out the wild, cyclical fluctuations of the airline industry.

Improving product line by expanding into new products or markets   Norton Simon's diversification into beverages allowed it to expand its product line and yet build on its existing marketing skills and techniques.

To take any acquisition when its earnings and profit level will meet or exceed the desired level   Some companies with the advantage of wide diversification, preferably in totally unrelated industries, have been able to offset an earnings decline in one division with higher earnings elsewhere. Clearly, one of the tricks in managing a successful conglomerate is to place the investment risk on more than one race horse.

The strategy of diversification is, at best, a risky affair. What might seem a good move today can turn out, for the most unexpected reasons, to be tomorrow's disaster. But the more skilled conglomerate strategists apply sound management practices. They carefully study each acquisition rather than plunging precipitously into every possible deal. They select profitable enterprises with a substantial market share, even if a premium price has to be paid. And they are concerned with a comprehensive growth plan rather than with diversification for its own sake.

THE ADVANTAGES

The advantages, then, of conglomerate diversification are improved revenues, profits, and growth. In other words, a synergistic effect is sought, that is, $2 + 2 = 5$, or the combination of resources is more effective than either alone. The disadvantages are that the increase often takes place only on paper and poor management continues; also, the price paid for the acquisition may be too high. Harry Gray, for example, paid 32 times earnings for Mostek which is a premium, but which he considered a bargain.

THE CONCEPT OF SYNERGY

Synergy may be defined as the processs of combining elements so that the whole becomes greater than the sum of its individual parts. Synergy emerges when two actions performed collaboratively produce a better output than if they were performed independently. It is a concept that considers each acquisition as a significant contribution to the total profitability of the firm.[9] In each acquisition, the combined outcome is computed to show increases in the total rate of return on investment based on sales, costs, and equity. An acquisition can develop its synergistic effects from four areas: marketing, production, finance, and management. The possible contribution of each part logically leads to the synergy of the whole system. An example of a synergistic effect is the joint-venture of Albertson (the supermarket chain) with Skaggs (the drug store chain) being located together on the same premises and thereby providing one-stop shopping.

As former Du Pont chairman Irving Shapiro said about the acquisition of Conoco, "We expect that by combining their skills and our skills we can add two and two and get five or six."[10]

MERGERS AND ACQUISITIONS

The major method of conglomerate diversifiction is by merger or acquisition, although these methods may also be used in a concentric growth strategy. In this sense, merger or acquisition is a technique for accomplishing an accelerated level of growth by acquiring other firms. A *merger* refers to combining two firms into one, while an *acquisition* is where one company purchases the assets of another and absorbs it into its own operations.

TYPES OF MERGERS

Mergers include several basic types.

Horizontal Merger   A horizontal merger involves a combination of two firms within the same basic industry and product field. For example, Potlatch Corporation (a forest products company), led by chairman Richard B. Madden, diversified or expanded its investment in paper mills by acquiring additional companies in the field. It is often more efficient to acquire existing facilities than it is to build a new plant. Developing a new production plant or distribution center can be very costly, both in terms of capital investment and losses during the start-up period. Therefore, acquiring an ongoing operation is often a much easier and less costly diversification strategy.

Vertical Merger   A vertical merger involves a combination of firms involved with different stages of the manufacturing process, for example, a manufacturer acquiring a raw material supplier. Hewlett-Packard acquired its own semiconductor division to increase the quality and dependability of its source of components which it uses in its computers, calculators, and instruments. Another example would be a restaurant firm such as the Black Angus acquiring a cattle ranch in order to have its own supply of beef.

Market Extension Merger   This type of merger is derived by combining firms to increase geographic coverage. As noted, often it is difficult and costly to establish a new set of distribution centers or retail outlets, and one way to move rapidly is to merge or acquire a firm already covering that geographic area.

Product Extension Merger   This form of concentric diversification uses the combining of firms as a means of adding to the product line. For example, Norton Simon's acquisition of Canada Dry Co. enabled it to move quickly into the soft drink product line.

Conglomerate Merger   The conglomerate merger involves a combining of firms in different or unrelated fields. Harry Gray, for example, acquired such diverse companies as Mostek (semiconductors) and Otis Elevator.

MERGER AND ACQUISITION TECHNIQUES ·

Mergers and acquisition can be accomplished in a number of ways and by several different techniques. The biggest single distinction is probably between cooperative (friendly) and hostile (takeover) mergers or acquisitions. The *friendly merger* is between two companies who agree upon the benefits of the acquisition and work together to achieve it. The *hostile merger,* often called a takeover, involves one firm forcefully acquiring another firm that is resisting the attempt. In this case, the "raider" gains control of the majority of the stock, displaces the current management, and puts its own plans into effect.

TAKE-OVER ATTEMPTS

Harry Gray (United Technologies), for example, was unsuccessful in his attempts to acquire Babcock and Wilcox Co. and ESB Ray-O-Vac. The price for B & W was over a half-billion dollars. George G. Zipt, B & W's Chairman, asked coldly, "Why don't you go after one of our competitors?" And Gray responded, "Because you're better and cheaper." But Gray was not successful in this takeover attempt.[11] Dictaphone Company was the target of mergers by Litton in 1965 and Gould, Inc., in 1971, and warded off another take-over attempt in 1974. However, in 1978 Dictaphone was agreeable to a friendly merger proposed by Pitney-Bowes, Inc. Usually these take-over attempts involve proxy battles, bidding competition, and court battles. Because of this, many companies will back off if the target for the merger is not agreeable to the proposal.

Mergers that were once negotiable are suddenly turning unfriendly as management searches for better offers elsewhere. Some corporate officers admit that they are now shying away from making bids because the contests can become so fierce. "We considered bidding for a company," says one chief executive, "but a banker confided that once we did, he would have another company offering more money right away. It's getting so we will only do a merger if we can negotiate it."[12]

One example of this was the attempted take-over of Conoco by Seagram Corp. in 1981. The management of Conoco resisted the Seagram offer and negotiated for a friendly take-over by Du Pont. Du Pont acquired 56 percent of Conoco's stock for $7.3 billion, when Conoco was valued at $17.9 billion.

THE METHODS OF ACQUISITION

There are several acquisition methods.

Purchase of stock on the open market   One company may be able to go out on the open market and buy up a sizeable amount of stock in the target company.

A tender offer   An offer to purchase all or a controlling interest in the company stock at an agreed upon price, usually somewhat over the current trading price.

Purchase of assets   One firm may pay a fixed amount of cash for the assets of the target company.

An exchange of stock   Frequently, the relative values of the two firm's stock prices are considered or an equitable exchange worked out. For each two shares of company Y, one will receive three shares of company Z, etc. The result is a share of ownership in the combined company, hopefully of equal or greater value than that held in the former corporate entities.

In using external expansion, however, a clear-cut business purpose is only part of a successful acquisition strategy. The takeover climate has become so competitive that every corporation interested in acquisitions is finding it necessary to arm itself with the best advice and manpower available and to proceed in a careful, systematic manner.

THE USE OF FINANCIAL SYNERGY

Charles B. Thornton

The key advantage of a conglomerate diversification strategy is the use of financial synergy. To gain such an advantage, the acquiring company must have a higher price-earnings multiple than the acquired company. Charles B. "Tex" Thornton developed Litton Industries into a giant conglomerate by this method. Thornton rarely used cash to acquire these new companies. Instead, he used the growth value of Litton stock to acquire increased earnings, assets and profits which in turn raised the price of Litton stock. Litton stock rose from around $15 per share to as high as $150 per share during the 1960s.

The way financial synergy works is presented in Table 6.2 (a and b). There are two companies, company A and its merger target, company B. Company A with a price/earning ratio of 20 and a price of $100 acquires B for an exchange of stock, two shares of A for three of B, forming a revised set of numbers for company A as shown in Table 6.2(b). The acquiring company, like Litton, usually has a good image and growth record, so that the price earnings multiple will continue to improve in value as a result of the merger, thus opening up another possible merger with company C, etc.

TABLE 6.2(A)
Late 1960s Synergism

Company	Earnings	Shares	Earnings P/S	P/E	Stock Price
A	$1 M	200 K	$5	20	$100
B	$1 M	200 K	$5	10	$ 50

TABLE 6.2(b)

A buys B at two shares for three and you have . . .					
A	$2 M	333 K	$6	20	$120

A POPULAR STRATEGY

What has become evident in this uncertain economic and political climate is that acquisitions clearly stand out as about the best investments many corporations can make. Thus, investment bankers report that the subject of acquisitions is being brought up in virtually every corporate boardroom.

"In the 1960s, financial strategies were the thing that all the chief executives were getting involved in," says J. Ira Harris, the merger specialist at Salomon Bros. "Now acquisition strategies are replacing them and getting the chief executive's attention." Further, with most stocks selling at bargain prices, with the dollar continuing to fall against most foreign currencies, and with the climate for corporate investment in physical assets unlikely to improve markedly, the acquisition movement continues to pick up steam.[13] Table 6.3 shows the impact of merger attempts on stock prices of several firms involved in bidding competitions.

TABLE 6.3
The Effect of Take-overs on Stock Prices

WHAT TAKEOVER BATTLES DO TO STOCK PRICES						
			Price of Target Before Bidding	Initial Bid	Winning Bid	Price-Earnings Multiple of Winning Bid
Winning Bidder	Losing Bidder	Target Company				
Racal Communications	Applied Digital Data Systems	Milgo Electronic	19⅛	28½	36	28
J. Ray McDermott	United Technologies	Babcock & Wilcox	34¾	42	65	15
Norton Simon	Fuqua Industries	Avis	14	15½	22	9
Allegheny Ludlum Industries	Crane	Chemetron	30½	40	55	30
Northwest Industries	MCA	Coca-Cola Bottling of L.A.	21¾	30	40	16

Data: First Boston Corp.

SOURCE: Reprinted from the November 14, 1979, issue of *Business Week* by special permission, © 1977 by McGraw-Hill, Inc., New York, NY 10020. All rights reserved.

GUIDELINES FOR MERGERS

Because acquisitions involve complicated financial transactions and the restructuring of organizations and cause adjustments, managerial shakeups, and other changes, a careful approach is suggested. First, a specific plan and program are needed to assure a smooth transition. Second, a careful realignment of managerial responsibilities is needed to execute the program. Often power or personality clashes cause operating problems. Finally, a new managerial information system needs to be implemented so that top managers can stay on top of critical problem areas.

Based upon his own experience in a number of mergers, Willard Rockwell, Jr. (Chairman, North American Rockwell), has set forth his guidelines for mergers or acquisitions:

1   Pinpoint and spell out the merger objectives, especially earnings objectives.

2   Specify substantial gains for stockholders of both companies.

3   Convince yourself that acquired companies' management is—or else can be made—competent.

4   Certify the existence of important dovetailing resources—but do not expect perfection.

5   Spark the merger program with the chief executive's involvement.

6   Clearly define the business you are in.

7   Check strengths, weaknesses, and key performance factors for both companies.

8   Create a climate of trust by anticipating problems and discussing them early with the other company.

9   Do not let cave man "advances" jeopardize the courtship. Do not threaten the current management.

10 Make people your number one consideration in structuring your plan.

According to Rockwell, "One factor in particular transcends, encompasses, and overrides all others. In buying a company, you acquire its plant, its equipment, its methods and systems, its patents and know-how, its distribution, and research facilities.

"But these are secondary, I believe. What you acquire first of all when you buy a company are its people. They are the precious asset that can keep it imaginative, aggressive, inspired, and dynamic. In my view, if you keep this thought well in mind, you will not go wrong."[14]

THE TAKE-OVER STRATEGY

A *take-over* refers to a surprise attempt by one company to acquire control of another company against the will of the current management. *Business Week* describes one such attempt.

THE CORPORATE "JAWS"

"Late in the afternoon of August 7, 1975, Thomas Mellon Evans, chairman of Crane, Co., telephoned John B. M. Place, chairman of Anaconda Co., the copper giant that had fallen on hard times. Almost simultaneously, the Dow Jones wire service reported that Crane's directors had approved a $125-million investment to buy 5 million shares of Anaconda stock. Anaconda's shares were at $15, near their historic low, and Crane offered $25 subordinated debentures per share. The phone call was the first notice that Place had received of Evans' interest in his company."[15]

Place, who perhaps had heard of Evan's reputation as the "corporate embodiment of *Jaws,* the great white shark," fought the takeover attempt. "He filed lawsuits, pressuring for congressional hearings to generate unfavorable publicity about the bid, bought a company competitive with Crane, and made an abortive plan to merge with Tenneco, Inc. But Evans outmaneuvered Place at every turn, eventually acquiring 4.1 million shares, or 18.6 percent of Anaconda for his company—at 20 percent less than he originally offered. Evans then proceeded to stimulate Atlantic Richfield Co.'s interest in Anaconda, which produced an ARCO tender for 27 percent of the copper company. Evans said, 'It's one of the best investements I've ever made.' "[16]

THE TAKE-OVER STRATEGY

The *take-over strategy* is usually an attempt to use leverage to gain control of a firm that is either having problems or is perhaps mismanaged. A company may become a target of a take-over if

1　Its assets are worth more than current stock market value (for example, Conoco traded at approximately $45 per share, but its asset value was estimated to be $150 per share);

2　Its performance is poor relative to comparable firms;

3　It holds large cash surpluses or unusual borrowing capacity.

　　　　Consequently, firms like Anaconda are often vulnerable to a takeover. First, the takeover target must be selected: Harry Gray, as noted earlier is reported to maintain fifty company dossiers which he is evaluating as potential acquisition targets. Second, an analysis of the target is made to determine its value and to select an appropriate offer price. This is usually just high enough over the current stock price to make it acceptable to stockholders, but low enough to make the merger profitable.

THE LTV CONGLOMERATE STRATEGY

One of the most famous practitioners of the takeover was James Ling. Ling, who was the former CEO of LTV (Ling-Temco-Vought), started with $2,000 in a small electronics company in Dallas, Texas, and through a series of takeovers built the LTV (a $3.7-billion conglomerate) corporation.

JAMES L. LING

His office is on the thirty-first floor of the LTV Tower in Dallas. But these days James L. Ling is rather like a parent watching the progress of an estranged child as he follows the fortunes of LTV. By agreement with the Justice Department, Ling is barred from having either a voice or any significant financial stake in the enterprise he built from a small electrical contracting firm into what was, for a time, the nation's fourteenth-largest company. It is now number thirty-one in *Fortune's* list of the 500 largest industrial corporations.[17]

During this series of takeovers, LTV averaged a growth rate of 51 percent a year for ten years. This, of course, is one of the advantages of the conglomerate strategy: It allows a greater rate of growth. Along the way Ling acquired control of four companies already in the top 500 when he took them over[18]:

1　Temco Aircraft, No. 432, in 1961

2　Chance Vought Aircraft, No. 206, in 1961

3　Wilson Co., No. 37, in 1967

4　Jones and Laughlin Steel, No. 55, in 1967

This was an impressive array of acquisitions. As you might imagine each of these top 500 acquisitions increased the earnings and stock value of LTV. This was pretty fast company for a small-town boy who started out with an insignificant electronics company.

THE LING APPROACH

How did Jimmy Ling accomplish all this? Well, it wasn't easy, although at times he made it look easy. Basically, his approach to acquisition involved maximizing the use of leverage; that is, borrowing money and then getting a higher return than his interest cost. Ling's method involved the following steps:

1　*Borrowing under favorable terms.*

2　*Careful analysis and selection of a takeover target.*

3　The *take-over*—acquiring a controlling interest in the target company.

4　*Splitting the acquired company into several autonomous parts.*

5　*Keeping any desired (profitable) segments, then spinning off, or divesting, the remaining parts.* In other words, turning them into cash.

6　*Using the acquired cash to pay back the loan.*

Sounds easy doesn't it? Unfortunately, it's not quite so easy in actual practice. Even James Ling made a mistake or two. One example of his method in action is in the Wilson takeover in 1967.

THE WILSON TAKEOVER—"JONAH SWALLOWS THE WHALE!"

One of Ling's more remarkable moves was the takeover of the Wilson Company.[19] At the time, Wilson was a major meat packing company (number 37 in the top 500) with sales of over one billion dollars per year: a giant company. Ling's company was much smaller with earnings about half as large, which is why it is referred to as "Jonah swallowing the whale." Ling borrowed $80 million and purchased a controlling interest in Wilson, a rather stagnant company, for about $62 per share. He then split Wilson into three autonomous divisions—Wilson Meat, Wilson Sporting Goods, and Wilson Chemicals (see Figure 6.2).

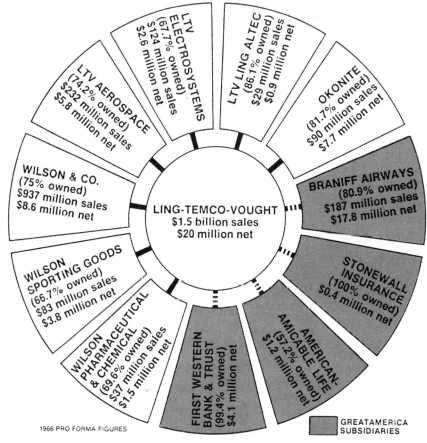

1966 PRO FORMA FIGURES

FIGURE 6.2

The Ling Take-over of Wilson Co.—Redeployment Strategy

SOURCE: Reprinted from information in the November 1, 1967 (p. 45), issue of FORBES Magazine.

Ling then sold stock in these units, and spun off any others which did not fit into his plans. As a result, LTV nearly tripled its sales and then used $74 million of Wilson cash and money from the sale of stock in the divisions to pay back the loan. The net cost for a billion dollar corporation: $6 million.

THOMAS MELLON EVANS OF CRANE CO.[20]

Another widely known expert at the takeover is Thomas Mellon Evans of Crane Co. As Figure 6.3 indicates, Crane is a conglomerate and is particularly adept at the takeover as exemplified by the attempted takeover of Anaconda Copper Co. Evans, like Ling and Gray, does a careful analysis of the target company:

1 *He seeks companies with undervalued assets and a low book value, such as Anaconda.* In other words, its stock is undervalued.

2 *He tries to buy up about 5 percent of the stock on the open market prior to making his move.* That way he stands to make a profit, even if his takeover is unsuccessful.

3 *He then makes a tender offer.* In the case of Anaconda, the stock was selling at $15 per share and he offered $25 per share in subordinated debentures.

In the Anaconda venture, Evans then acquired 18.6 percent of shares (4.1 million) and control for about $82.5 million. In less than one year, he spun off the Anaconda stock to ARCO with an expected profit of some $140 million in cash and stock.

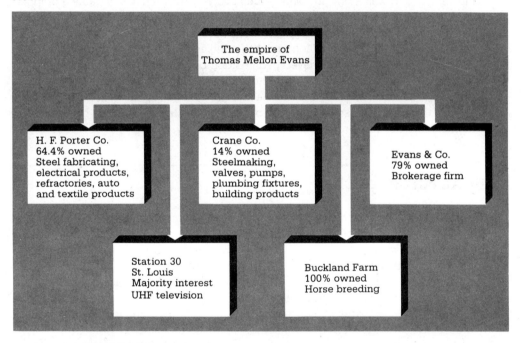

FIGURE 6.3
Thomas Mellon Evans Holdings

Evans and Ling are generally known for their trademark of ruthless efficiency. They are known as "100% bottom line" people. When they take over a company, their first moves are usually to reorganize and cut costs. They chop out all the corporate deadwood and waste that prior management was unwilling to eliminate. They then analyze the various business segments and sell off, liquidate, or shut down the unprofitable or marginal operations.

These are but a few examples of the conglomerate strategy in action. As you can see from the success of many of these companies, it can be an effective strategy for rapidly expanding and accelerating the growth of the organization. But like all strategies, it is no magic formula. It takes proper analysis, planning and execution. And even then things don't always go according to plan. As mentioned earlier, Harry Gray of United Technologies tried unsuccessfully to take over Babcock and Wilcox. After he failed, they were hit with the "Three Mile Island" disaster. "It's good to be born lucky," said Gray.

A BRIDGE TOO FAR

And James Ling went one merger too many. To finance his quest for new acquisitions, Ling devised "project redeployment." He divided his earlier acquisitions into parts and sold some of the stock in each part to raise cash. The equity he put into the market set a value for the shares LTV still held, and Ling used this as collateral for further loans. It was a brilliant plan, but as everyone now knows, it came a cropper.

Since 1968, when Ling borrowed heavily to buy control of Jones & Laughlin and Greatamerica Corp., another Dallas conglomerate, LTV had been burdened by more than $800 million in debt and fixed charges that totaled as much as $60 million a year. His highly leveraged position betrayed him during a tight money, recession period, and he was forced to resign from LTV, the company he had helped to build. A second conglomerate that he started, Omega-Alpha, went bankrupt. Ling is now the CEO of a small Texas company called Matrix Inc., but he has yet to demonstrate the same merger magic.[21]

MANAGERIAL IMPLICATIONS

The search for improved profits and growth has led most major corporations to try diversification strategies. *During the past twenty years, a new breed of aggressive and imaginative entrepreneurs have built conglomerate corporations by following a strategy of expansion by acquisition. Conglomerate diversification is an attempt to diversify outside of an industry.* On the one hand, it offers rapid growth, broader stability, and greater profit potential. On the other hand, there are higher risks and potentially greater losses. A successful diversification requires management depth to develop a strategy for managing complex unrelated business.

In selecting a growth strategy, a firm may either grow through internal or external means. One external strategy, conglomerate diversification, provides for acquiring firms or units not necessarily related to the firm's existing lines of business. The effective strategist must find a balance between these internal and external growth methods. Effective management is more than the accomplishment of immediate short-term results. Because the firm must continue operating in the future, effective management includes creating the potential for achieving results over the longer run as well.

Over a period of twenty years, it is possible for a company to experience numerous changes in its business, its products and markets, and competition. To meet these changes the organization must also change, by increasing the complexity of its products and markets and by diversifying its business and customer groups. The firms that grow fastest, such as conglomerates, tend to change with these rapidly changing conditions.

Merger or acquisition can be a useful technique for implementing a growth strategy. The acquired company may provide access to wider markets, make it possible to expand with a less costly scale of operation, or improve technology or resources.

There are many reasons why managers choose to use a conglomerate diversification strategy. Four major reasons are: (1) selecting greater growth, which can no longer be realized by internal expansion; (2) achieving better use of financial resources; (3) exploiting new potential opportunities for greater profitability; and (4) achieving distinct competitive advantages and broader stability.

The underlying reason for the use of acquisition strategies is to keep pace with the rapid rate of change, and often it is cheaper to buy or acquire than it is to build a new business, plant, or market from scratch. When companies are undervalued on the market, then opportunities for the effective use of these external growth strategies are apparent. But an even more fundamental reason lies in the fact that today companies are finding it even harder to grow from internal sources. Of course, as we have seen from the experience of James Ling, not all acquisition programs are successful. Some are opportunities which seek only short-term financial gains. An unwieldy debt situation, depletion of cash reserves, or unhealthy financial condition can cause acquisition problems. Therefore, an acquisition strategy needs both careful planning and execution.

The conglomerate strategy offers no magic answers, and many firms have run into operating difficulties as a result of unwise moves. However, this approach offers many advantages and has been used successfully as one possible strategic alternative.

REVIEW QUESTIONS

1   What are the objectives of using a conglomerate strategy?

2   In the Du Pont acquisition of Conoco, what were some of the key factors involved? For example, how did the management of Du Pont compare with that of Conoco? How did this acquisition turn out?

3   What is a take-over? What are some of the steps in such a move?

4   Many firms feel that the take-over is a raider's device aimed at milking cash or liquidating the company taken over. Do you agree? What are some advantages and disadvantages to each group of stockholders?

5   What are some guidelines on mergers?

6   Synergy has been explained as a "2 + 2 = 5" phenomenon. With regard to Du Pont's acquisition of Conoco, do you see any synergistic effects?

ENDNOTES

1 See "What Makes Harry Gray Run," *Business Week*, Dec. 10, 1979; A. F. Ehrbar, "United Technologies' Master Plan," *Fortune*, September 22, 1980, 96.

2 "The Strategy Squeeze in the Airlines," *Business Week*, May 19, 1980, 104–107, 110, 115.

3 H. Igor Ansoff, *Corporate Strategy* (New York: McGraw-Hill, 1965), p. 127.

4 See Charles Berry, *Corporate Growth and Diversification*, (Princeton: N.J.: Princeton University Press, 1973), Chap. 7; Norman Berg, "What's Different About Conglomerate Management?" *Harvard Business Review*, November–December, 1969, 112–20.

5 "The Great Takeover Binge," *Business Week*, November 14, 1977, 176.

6 Paul Brown, "Diversifying Successfully," *Business Horizons*, August 1975, 84–87.

7 There has been a large collection of literature on the subject. For books, see David F. Linowes, *Managing Growth Through Acquisition* (New York: American Management Association, 1968), p. 105; Myles L. Mace and George G. Montgomery, Jr., *Management Problems of Corporate Acquisition* (Cambridge, Mass.: Harvard University, 1962).

8 Ehrbar, "United Technologies' Master Plan."

9 Ansoff, *Corporate Strategy*, pp. 75–102.

10 "A Triumph for Du Pont," *Business Week*, August 17, 1981, 38.

11 "The Takeover Wave," *Fortune*, May 1977, 61.

12 "The Great Takeover Binge," 177.

13 Ibid.

14 Willard Rockwell, Jr., "How to Acquire a Company," *Harvard Business Review*, September–October 1968.

15 "Thomas Mellon Evans."

16 Ibid.

17 Lewis Beman, "Jim Ling Tries His Wings One More Time," *Fortune*, June 1977, 139, 232–34.

18 Arthur M. Louis, "Ten Conglomerates and How They Grew," *Fortune*, May 15, 1969, 152–53.

19 See Rush Loving, Jr., "LTV's Flight From Bankruptcy," *Fortune*, June 1973, 134–45; "The Conglomerate Commotion," *Fortune*, May 15, 1969.

20 "Thomas Mellon Evans," *Business Week*, October 15, 1976, 80.

21 "Razzle-Dazzle," *Fortune*, May 7, 1979, 48.

CHAPTER

7

This company is in good shape. It's got the money, resources, brand names, and opportunities, I've bet my life on it. I've got my blood all over these bricks, for good or bad.

David Mahoney, Chairman and Chief Executive Officer, Norton Simon, Inc., quoted in "Frustration and Turmoil Plague a Marketing Prodigy," *Business Week,* April 7, 1980, 71.

- OBJECTIVES
- STRATEGY AT NORTON SIMON
- ANALYZING STRATEGIC OPTIONS
- A FRAMEWORK FOR COMPARING ALTERNATIVES
- THE BOSTON CONSULTING GROUP (BCG) MODEL
- THE GROWTH-SHARE MATRIX
- THE GENERAL ELECTRIC "STOP-LIGHT STRATEGY"
- THE DIRECTIONAL POLICY MATRIX (DPM)
- THE APPLICATION OF STRATEGIC ANALYSIS MODELS
- MANAGERIAL IMPLICATIONS

Comparing Strategic Alternatives

CHAPTER OBJECTIVES

When you have completed this chapter, you will be able to:

- ☐ *Demonstrate an understanding of techniques for comparing alternative strategies.*

- ☐ *Make a comparison of the major strategic alternatives and understand how these techniques are used.*

- ☐ *Develop a framework for determining which alternative strategies are best for varying conditions.*

- ☐ *Analyze a complex management case using the concepts in this unit.*

STRATEGY AT NORTON SIMON[1]

David Mahoney

"David Mahoney, the chairman and chief executive officer of Norton Simon, Inc., takes considerable pride in his reputation as a marketing prodigy, established during two decades as a Madison Avenue adman and as a top executive with such consumer packaged-goods companies as Good Humor, Colgate-Palmolive, and Canada Dry. Since 1969 he has been piecing together Norton Simon, which heralds itself as a marketing powerhouse with a lineup of brands that include Hunt-Wesson foods, Avis car rentals, Max Factor cosmetics, Johnnie Walker Scotch, and Canada Dry beverages."

"At NSI's executive quarters a visitor may meet with Mahoney in any of three strikingly decorated offices. An elegant dresser with good looks and elan, the 6 ft. 1 in. Mahoney exudes the charm that has made him popular with the jet set."

As noted earlier, the strategist must seek to gain the best fit between internal capabilities and environmental opportunities. Each business, product, or division of the company has varying strengths and weaknesses. Unless the executive, like Dave Mahoney, is fully aware of these competitive advantages, he may not allocate resources to the product areas which are likely to lead to the greatest success.

At Norton Simon, the strategy has been to spend heavily on brand advertising to obtain market leadership. Unfortunately, something appears to be going wrong with these strategic choices, because NSI's market shares in food, cosmetics, and beverages are all declining, and management is troubled with defection of key people. Although NSI's earnings have been increasing, the gains lag far behind the rise in sales and have been derived as much from financial tactics as from prowess in the marketplace.

"Norton Simon appears troubled by an inability to strike a balance between its needs for short-term profit gains and longer-range investment and growth. Mahoney seems hung up on a desire to maximize current earnings, even at the expense of funding new products," analyzes *Business Week.*.

"Mahoney has little patience with people who lament the changing economic conditions. 'I think that's a copout,' he snaps. 'We're paid handsomely to figure out what to do. If we don't, some guys who take advantage of the times will.' "

But Mahoney contends that his company has significantly outperformed the economy in the past decade, when Norton Simon's sales rose from about $1 billion to more than $3 billion, and earnings per share rose from 98 cents to $2.49. "We entered the 1980s with 17 brands that rank either Number 1 or Number 2 in their markets, compared with only 11 a decade earlier." he says.

The Norton Simon chairman says his company sticks to a strict discipline of asset management, particularly in an environment of continued high inflation. "We will continue to examine each of our businesses to reassess its fit in the corporation's future. Where appropriate, we will invest heavily to improve operations. And, if it is in our best interest, we are willing to divest ourselves of other operations."

"Credibility is important," Mahoney stresses, believing that he has to tell it as it is to win the respect of the financial community.

ANALYZING STRATEGIC OPTIONS

In a turbulent and changing environment, managers like David Mahoney are concerned not only with managing organizations as they exist at a point in time, but also with developing new strategies to meet future conditions. New strategies do not happen accidentally. Instead strategic alternatives are considered as options for allocating resources to best achieve overall corporate goals. These strategic decisions, such as the diversification strategy at Norton Simon, often represent a major alteration in organization directions and programs. Therefore, strategic alternatives must be compared and analyzed prior to selecting the strategy to be pursued: Stage 7 of the strategic management process.

No organization can go on indefinitely by continuing to apply the same strategy. In an environment of change, over time a strategy will become ineffective or dysfunctional in accomplishing organizational goals. Therefore, the organization, be it profit or nonprofit, must be constantly assessing the environment for opportunities and reappraising its current strategic options.

Corporate strategy, as opposed to business unit strategy, is aimed at a higher level and is broader in scope. Top management is concerned with developing a total system of businesses—all contributing to strategic position. This requires a careful allocation of resources. Some products will be increased, others harvested or liquidated, and new products will be added. Because this allocation process is similar to mangement of a financial portfolio, the term "portfolio management" is widely used to identify this form of managing.

MULTIPLE STRATEGIC OPTIONS

When Roy Ash assumed the leadership at Addressograph-Multigraph, his first move was to analyze the profitability of each product. He discovered that no one knew precisely which products were profitable. Based on this assessment, Ash began a strategy aimed at phasing out older product lines and strengthening AM's position in new technologies. Similarly, when Dick Goodwin took over a president of Johns-Manville, he initiated a study to determine which products could gain larger market share and which could not. From this study of strategic alternatives, a series of eleven major acquisitions and twelve divestitures were undertaken, leading to new strategic directions.

These examples suggest that the evaluation of strategy in a complex organization is usually a multiple series of decisions, rather than one single decision. Strategic decision making, then, involves examining various tradeoffs and comparing alternatives in order to determine how best to allocate one's resources to maximize the return.

ALLOCATING RESOURCES

At Norton Simon, David Mahoney is known for his quick decision making, or "hip shooting," as some would call it, his aggressive tactics, tough management style, and as a "bottom line" manager. Over a 10-year span Mahoney has built Norton Simon into a marketing powerhouse and a diversified conglomerate rated in the top 120 of U.S. firms. Norton Simon has nine operating companies and five basic businesses.

Like every strategist, Mahoney must consider how to allocate resources among these basic businesses to attain overall objectives. "Can I go after Procter and Gamble in the food oil business and Del Monte in tomato sauce at the same time?" he asks. "I have to ask where is the best juice for my money. Can I cover everybody? The answer is no."[2]

In a nutshell, this is the problem facing strategic management. There are many products, many competitors, and may possible actions. How does the manager select from among the possible alternative strategies?

How does he identify the various strategic alternatives, before making a strategic decision? In the following sections, a framework for comparing strategic alternatives will be presented.

A FRAMEWORK FOR COMPARING ALTERNATIVES

After the manager has analyzed the opportunities and resources, how does he determine how to allocate the resources into the most effective strategic pattern? As noted earlier, Trans World Corporation (see Figure 7.1) acquired a diversified set of businesses to reduce its dependence on the fluctuation of the airline industry, and now includes TWA, Century 21, Hilton Hotels, Quincy Steak Houses and Canteen (vending) among its component companies. Now the strategic problem facing Trans World management is that each company needs investment capital in order to compete and gain market share, yet the corporation has only limited capital resources.

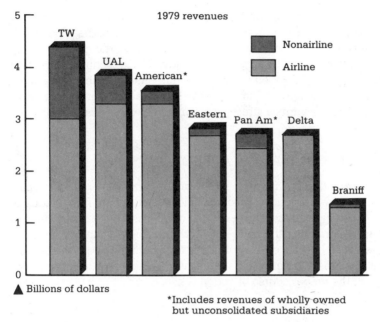

FIGURE 7.1
TWA's Diversification from Basic Business
SOURCE: TWA Annual Reports and *Standard & Poors Reports*, 1980

TWA'S STRATEGIC PROBLEM

Moreover, the acquired businesses now are looking to spend surprisingly large amounts of capital to seize growth opportunities or respond to competitive challenges in their markets. At the same time, however, TWA, which operates one of the oldest and most fuel-inefficient fleets among trunk carriers, has been forced to embark on a massive $1.2-billion equipment purchase program to meet the two major challenges of its business in the early 1980s—price competition and fuel conservation. "We will have as efficient, if not the most efficient, aircraft of any company in the industry by 1985," boasts Chairman Smart.

If it strains to buy all the equipment TWA needs, the corporation seems certain to restrain growth at its other subsidiaries, all of which have ambitious expansion plans of their own. Canteen wants to acquire a youth-oriented restaurant chain, and Century 21 wants to buy back regional franchises it sold in the 1970s to speed its nationwide development. Meanwhile, Hilton is trying to follow an industry trend among foreign hotel chains by building luxury units in the United States.[3]

As a result, top management must carefully consider all of its various alternatives, and select a course of action which will best achieve long-term goals. This provides one example of the complexity and importance of the strategic evaluation stage in portfolio management.

In large corporations, such as TWA, ITT, or Norton Simon, the strategist is dealing with several hundred distinct businesses and perhaps hundreds of differing countries and markets. Even in a smaller business, there are alternatives among products, customers, marketing methods, advertising techniques, pricing strategies, etc., which must be decided. From these numerous possible strategies, a course of action must be selected and implemented. In this chapter, the process of exploring and comparing the various strategic alternatives will be discussed.

STRATEGIC EVALUATION APPROACHES

Strategic evaluation provides a mechanism for integrating the functional areas of the smaller firm and the various products and businesses in multi-industry firms. The evaluative comparison of alternatives and options is a major determinant of long-term economic performance, because these choices play a major role in allocating the firm's resources. Because of the impact on existing and potential strategies, it is essential that the evaluation of alternatives be accurate and complete in order to ensure that the proper course of action is selected.

TWO BASIC ISSUES

The process of strategic evaluation deals with two basic issues:

1   How effective is the firm's existing strategy likely to be, given our analysis of emerging environmental conditions?
2   Which of the possible strategic alternatives will be more effective in achieving desired goals, given the expected environmental conditions?

The outcome of the strategic evaluation process, then, is a strategy or strategic game plan that will be most effective in positioning the firm in an uncertain future.

MANY POSSIBLE OPTIONS

The strategist, then, is usually faced with a number of possible directions for channeling the critical resources and energies of the firm. There may be many elements of each proposed strategy that offer advantages, are attractive, and potentially profitable. It takes, however, only one major drawback or disadvantage to cause a strategy to backfire and become ineffective. One major problem is measuring alternatives by an inaccurate or incomplete set of criteria or standards.

EVALUATION CRITERIA

What are some of the criteria which can and should be used in comparing alternatives? Seymour Tilles has suggested the following six criteria for evaluation:

1 *Does the strategy involve an acceptable degree of risk?* The strategist should be totally aware of the nature of risk—the extent of financial exposure, duration of commitment, and the size of the stakes.

2 *Is the strategy internally consistent?* In a well-planned strategy, each move fits into an integrated approach.

3 *Is the strategy consistent with the environment?* A good strategy fits the environment in both its static and its dynamic (projected) aspects.

4 *Is the strategy appropriate in view of available resources?* The strategist must seek a balance between strategic goals and available resources.

5 Does the strategy have an appropriate time horizon?

6 Is the strategy workable?[4]

Richard P. Rumelt (UCLA) has proposed a similar set of four essential tests a strategy must meet:

1 Be internally consistent.

2 Provide for consonance between the firm and its environment.

3 Be based on the gaining and maintenance of competitive advantage.

4 Be feasible in the light of existing skills and resources.[5]

A strategy which fails one or more of these tests possesses quite serious flaws. While a strategy which passes all four tests cannot be guaranteed to succeed, it is without question a better starting place than one that is known to be unsound.

A TEST OF REALITY

A solid strategy is evaluated by its probability of producing the desired short- and long-range results. A strategy that fails to consider changes is one that lacks future credibility. A strategy that is not supported by organizational activities at the coordinating and operational level is only partially effective and likely to suffer from weak implementation. As a result, in addition to the criteria cited above, an effective strategy must meet the test of reality—*is it workable?*

HOW TO SELECT A STRATEGY

How, then, do managers select certain strategies from an array of possible options? The purpose of critically comparing strategic alternatives is to ensure accuracy, feasibility, and compatibiilty between strategy and goals and to seek advantages that may be gained or synergies that may result from the way the firm deploys its resources. The managers of companies having a variety of products with differing life cycles, growth rates, and market shares are searching for strategies that will optimize the company's long-run profits.

MARKET SEGMENTATION

The Exxon Corp. doesn't really sell oil, chemicals, electronic typewriters and motors; rather, it owns an array of companies that sell those things. It is, in effect, a fabulously wealthy investment club with a limited portfolio. Each year, it makes investments in thirteen affiliated companies that are expected to return that money plus a suitable profit. Those who can show they can make more with more, get more. Those who cannot, do not. It is just that simple, and just that complicated.[6]

The portfolio management strategy for a diversified corporation, such as Exxon, integrates several diverse considerations. The long-run strength and direction of combined businesses are the dominant criteria. Each of the various businesses is assigned a role derived from overall corporate goals. In the strategic plan, some businesses are aiming at rapid growth, while others are used to support this goal. Some businesses will be taking high risks, because the potential gains are high.

There are several approaches or models that can be used to evaluate strategic alternatives. In the next section, a number of these analytical/conceptual models will be described with a focus on the strengths and weaknesses of each and their application in the strategic evaluation process.

THE BOSTON CONSULTING GROUP (BCG) MODEL

The first of these analytical conceptual models which may be used to assist managers in making decisions about the overall deployment of resources is termed the "growth-share matrix," the portfolio concept, or the Boston Consulting Group model.

The underlying concept of portfolio planning involves the allocation of resources according to a corporate strategic perspective of each of the businesses within the total portfolio. This model and others like it represent the first major advances in systematically identifying the main, underlying strategic characteristics of specific business segments. By carefully analyzing each product and market segment as a separate business to determine its potential for sales growth and profitability, each business may be assigned to a specific substrategy, for example, growth, harvesting, divestment, etc., within a comprehensive corporate plan (such as the Exxon example cited earlier). The resulting corporate portfolio of businesses should then be managed to optimize the allocation of resources within the firm.

At the center of a firm's business strategy is the issue of product and market segmentation. The analysis of a firm's scope of business interests provides a set of guidelines for developing present and future increases through the development and realignment of business segments. The BCG model is not confined to large corporations. The concept applies to small firms as well. In large firms, the portfolio can consist of businesses and products in several industries and markets. In a small firm, the portfolio revolves around products and markets.

Almost every company can find its businesses falling into one of the four basic types. Each type represents a firm's business interests. The specific form of a portfolio mix, however, affects the choice of strategic planning. These four types are summarized as follows:

1 *Single business:* Companies that are committed to a single business.

2 *Dominant business:* Companies that have diversified, but still focus the bulk of their resources into a single business.

3 *Related business:* Concentrically integrated firms in which diversification has been primarily accomplished by relating new lines to the major business.

4 *Unrelated business:* Companies that have diversified without regard to relationship between the new business and present activities. Conglomerate companies fall into this category.[7]

USES OF THE MODEL

Bruce D. Henderson

The Boston Consulting Group, under chairman Bruce D. Henderson, uses the model to focus clients' strategy toward gaining the cost advantages of high market share. According to Henderson, "The BCG growth/share matrix cannot be applied to a company, administrative unit, or even a product line. To be of any value, it must be applied to the specific segments of a business. The segments must be defined as that combination of products, services, customers and geography with respect to which that specific competitor has an absolute advantage compared to all other competitors. Even small business are composed of multiple segments with quite different characteristics."[8]

Henderson, a 62-year-old Tennessee native, believes that each market segment can support only about three competitors profitably. Thus BCG advises its clients to concentrate their businesses only in product areas where they are—or have a chance of becoming—number one or number two (or perhaps number three). If a product can't meet this test, it should be abandoned. Although Henderson and BCG have been arguing this case since 1966, it has become increasingly popular recently. Says one marketing professor at a midwestern university: "Market dominance is the magic word in every management seminar today."[9]

THE BCG FRAMEWORK

The BCG model examines the structure of a firm's businesses in a continuous progression and is dynamic in nature. An optimal strategy enables a firm to position its resources to fully exploit business opportunities available as a function of competitive position in a given industry, market, or product. The BCG framework also provides a powerful tactical model. The strategist can estimate cash flows under a variety of pricing, cost and growth conditions. In its design, the BCG model provides for a balanced strategic approach so that products have the synergistic force to resist business slowdowns and sustain long-term growth. In its management, the BCG model necessitates constant environmental scanning on the part of management over the changing characteristics and trends of industry and market needs so the strategist is able to redesign and realign business strategy as necessary.

The BCG model is based on the application of two interrelated concepts, the experience curve and growth-share matrix.

THE EXPERIENCE CURVE

The primary element underlying the model is the *experience curve theory.* This theory is based on the relationship between total cost per unit and the number of units produced (experience). The theory predicts that the unit costs of production, marketing, and distribution will decrease by 20 to 30 percent each time total output doubles. This decrease in cost with experience comes from economies of scale, improvements in labor, technology, etc. The BCG also found a relationship between cost and market share. The company that is able to produce more units than its competitors is bound to become the market share leader. Because of the greater volume of production, the market leader is farther down on the production curve than its competitors and therefore can turn out its product at the lowest cost.

According to the BCG, "Strategy is based upon competitive differences. If the experience curve permits you to confidently predict that one competitor can and should have a lower cost than another one, then the experience curve also permits you to predict that the low-cost competitor can and should displace the higher cost competitor if he provides identical products to identical customers with identical margins. That is the implication of the relationship between market share and the experience curve.

It is an observable fact that companies make most of their profit from a very limited portion of their total business. It is less obvious but equally certain that most of the profit is earned where the competitive advantage is the greatest."[10]

WHAT IS THE EXPERIENCE CURVE?

The experience curve is a rule of thumb. Its characteristic pattern is observable. "*Value added* net production costs will characteristically decline 25 to 30 percent each time the total accumulated experience has been doubled." (This plots as a straight line on logarithmic coordinates.)

The experience curve is based on the concept that people repetitively performing a task get better at it. In more technical terms, labor costs per unit decrease in a predictable manner with an increased volume of production.

In the mid 1960s, Bruce Henderson and his colleagues at the Boston Consulting Group took this experience curve concept and expanded it. They concentrated on total cost so that the vertical axis can be used as an index of total cost per unit. The horizontal axis, then, is used to plot the number of units produced or cumulative experience. The resulting slope, labeled the experience curve, can then be used to evaluate relative costs at various levels of production.

In order to establish market share, the product should be priced according to learning curve costs based on estimated volume. (Texas Instruments uses this pricing strategy.) This factor is *most* important for gaining large market share early.

The factors in this experience curve model, then, include: costs, volume, and market share. The greater the volume, the lower the unit cost. And the larger the market share the larger the production volume.

This leads to a relationship between unit cost and the dynamics of market share. Therefore, the company that has the greatest volume of production is operating farther down on the experience curve than its competitors. Consequently, the market share leader should be able to steadily increase its share at the expense of its competitors whose unit cost should theoretically be higher. As an example, the relative production levels at Chrysler, Ford, and General Motors are plotted on an experience curve in Figure 7.2. Actually, of course, each firm is on its own experience curve, but, as Figure 7.3 suggests, GM's profits have been about double those of Ford, while Chrysler has been reporting large losses.

SOURCES OF THE EXPERIENCE CURVE EFFECT

The BCG claims that the cost of most value-added items declines quite significantly each time accumulated experience doubles. Gerald Allan (Harvard University) has suggested a number of factors that influence experience curves as outlined below:

1   Labor efficiency
2   New processes and improved methods
3   Product redesign
4   Product standardization
5   Scale effect
6   Substitution in the product

The experience curve effect may be derived by dividing the accumulated costs by the accumulated product output. The economies of scale, the learning curve, critical masses of knowledge, and specializations all contribute to the result. The more experience a company has in producing a product, the lower its unit costs.[11]

COMPETITIVE IMPLICATIONS

The experience curve may be used as a basis for developing several strategic alternatives.

1. Growth   Expand market share as fast as possible so that one can attain a dominant position in the market.

2. Knowing when to divest   *If you can't expand market share and are operating from a weaker cost position, then get out.*

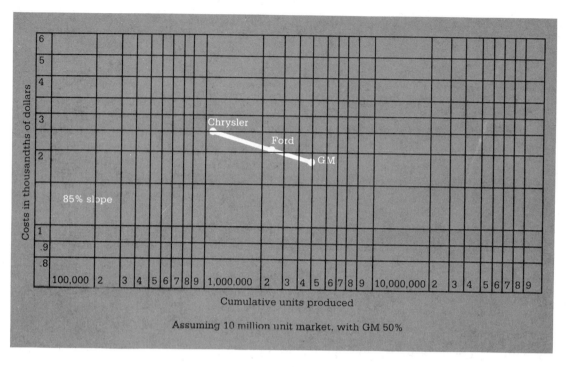

FIGURE 7.2

The Experience Curve Effect—An Illustration of Auto Companies.

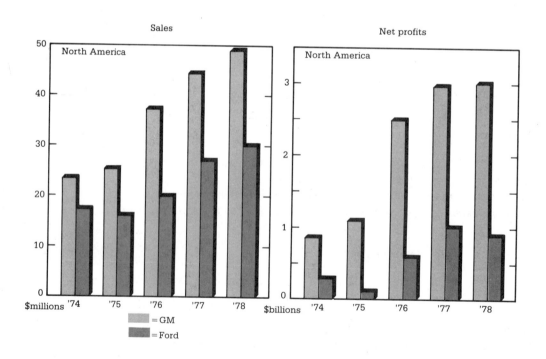

FIGURE 7.3

Comparison of Auto Makers' Profits (GM is about double that of Ford.)

SOURCE: Adapted from *Forbes*, April 2, 1979, p. 45

3. Pricing down the curve   By using the experience curve, a company can estimate probable costs at any given level of cumulative production. This then leads to a strategy of accepting lower profit margins in the short run in order to expand market share and perhaps the total market as well. The eventual outcome is an anticipated long-term increase in profitability.

Texas Instruments employs a pricing strategy based on high sales volume and relies on the concept of the experience curve. One example of pricing along the learning curve by Texas Instruments was its entry into the low-price digital watch market.[12] The watch had to be simple in design and easy to assemble because millions had to be made annually to make a reasonable profit. This strategy of pricing down on the learning curve was an attempt to gain market penetration and maximize market share in a market long dominated by others.

As Richard Rumelt (UCLA) has noted, while the underlying factors of "experience curve" theory are well established, the application is not so straightforward.[13] The electronics industry appears to be an environment where the reality fits this model, but it is not so clear in other areas characterized by highly segmented markets, with heavy branding and promotion.

THE GROWTH-SHARE MATRIX[14]

The second element in the BCG model is termed the *growth-share matrix*. The growth-share matrix is a framework designed to provide a comparative analysis of businesses according to expected growth rates and relative market dominance. In most instances, it is not possible for any one firm to gain full market dominance in all of its businesses. It is possible, however, to divide the market into a series of market segments and apply competitive advantages by concentrating on strategic market segments. A balanced strategy should include two basic features: (1) the identification and strengthening of the major market segments; and (2) a common strategic pattern that relates the varied businesses into a total portfolio.

FOCUS ON MAJOR MARKET STRENGTHS

A firm's strengths lie in the main market segments from which it obtains its major revenues and in which it dominates the competition. This simple fact suggests that a firm should develop the main business segments for revenue, stability, and growth. For this reason, no firm should allow these major markets to be neglected or unprotected, or it will find its position vulnerable and its growth and stability threatened.

As Bruce Henderson has noted, "All misperceptions by competitors are strategy opportunities. The major unknown variable in strategy is the probable behavior and perceptions of competitors. If this were not true, all strategy would be merely an exercise in mathematical analysis. The ultimate creation of strategy depends upon the commitment of resources and reserves as investments in the future. The interaction of "competitive segmentation" and "experience curves" can provide a powerful insight into the most critical strategy factor of all: competitors' behavior."[15]

AN INTEGRATED STRATEGY

The main strength of the BCG approach is the assignment of a specific role or function for each product or segment, and its integration into a total company strategy. Each product is evaluated in terms of its cash flow and growth potential, and the differences determine which products represent cash investment opportunities and which represent sources of funds. The underlying strategy for relating varied businesses is the exploitation of competitive advantage. A company's advantages may consist of its production capability, its dominance of a specific market, its technological excellence, its financial strength, or it management excellence.

One dimension of the BCG approach involves balancing cash flows, or putting your money on the faster racehorse. The model seeks to shift cash from mature cash-generating units to high growth products in the early product development stage, which are cash users.

A second dimension is to balance the degree of risk and profit fluctuation which is acceptable. For example, companies in mature markets try to shift investment into newer growth fields.

The growth-share matrix is based upon the idea that high market share in rapidly growing market segments leads to higher profitability and a strong competitive situation. If, on the other hand, the firm has markets in slow-growth areas, then increasing its market share requires large investments, often with diminishing returns. Therefore, the BCG approach recommends removing cash flow from these slow-growth areas and placing it in higher-growth market segments, even at the expense of market share.

WHAT IS THE GROWTH-SHARE MATRIX?

The growth-share matrix is a model for analyzing how market share, market growth, and cash flow are related. The BCG model proposes that the organization should be managed as a portfolio of businesses giving each a clearly defined strategy. The growth-share matrix is used to evaluate business strategy in multi-industry firms, where a large array of businesses demand advanced techniques in selection and management. The BCG's use of growth-share analysis is based upon the well-known relationship between market share and profitability. The central thrust of matrix analysis is its emphasis on achieving balanced, long-term growth in volume, revenue, cash flow, and resource allocation.

The basic element of the technique is the construction of a matrix that relates market growth or its attractiveness to a firm's relative competitive position. When a series of such matrices or charts are constructed, a company's product positions are diagrammed to show the changing relationship of these product segments at any critical time. To use growth-share analysis, a series of studies must be made to assess market attractiveness and competitive position, and to plot the overall portfolio balance on charts. Once the plotting of the product portfolio chart is completed, growth-share management is perhaps the most challenging part of the whole scheme. Managing the portfolio of markets requires both economic considerations and a concern for people and the resources of the organization.

HOW THE GROWTH-SHARE MATRIX WORKS

Each of the various businesses or products develops a strategy which best meets its competitive position and objectives.

Because high-market share and higher profitability are correlated, the competitive objective is market dominance in high-growth areas. In low-growth markets, where it is difficult and expensive to increase share, the strategy should be one of holding or harvesting, maximizing cash flow to other areas, even if this results in loss of existing market share. Therefore, the strategic alternative that is selected depends upon the assessment of competitive strength, the costs of gaining market leadership in various segments, and the amount of capital that is available for investment.

The total organization, then, is managed to allocate resources in such a way as to maximize total profitability and to achieve the overall corporate goals. There are four steps in the application of the growth-share matrix.

1 *Identification of the corporations's businesses or products.* Also called strategic business units or "SBUs."

2 *Analysis of competitive position.* The businesses are arrayed to ascertain market share and potential market growth.

3 *Identify the best business strategy given their positioning in the market-share matrix.*

4 *Strategic reappraisal and review.*

In the following sections, these steps will be described.

STEP ONE—IDENTIFICATION OF MARKET SEGMENTS

The first step in using the growth-share matrix is to identify the distinct businesses, market segments, or product lines which make up the organization. However, the concept of what constitutes a market or business is often not easily defined in working terms. In fact, a product/market segment can be defined in a variety of ways. These units should identify the natural businesses or markets of the organization, usually by product or profit center units. For example, General Electric has forty-three business units while Union Carbide has 150 strategic units. In general, a natural business should have primary responsibility for managing such basic functions as marketing, production, and research and development.

One problem in the identification phase involves the number of separate units which can be effectively managed. Research by Richard Bettis (SMU) and William Hall (University of Michigan) suggests that managers tend to group businesses (SBUs) into a manageable numbers of units, so that instead of several hundred product groups, these units tend to range from six to forty-three major business units.[16] The key in each situation is to identify the economically distinct product/market segments of the firm's total operation as strategic business units. A second concern is that this number of businesses be manageable at the strategic level.

STEP TWO—ANALYSIS OF COMPETITIVE POSITION

Each of the basic business units identified in Step One are then distributed into a matrix position based upon two criteria: (1) *market growth potential;* and (2) relative market share as shown in Figure 7.4. As a result, there are four possible categories based on the SBU's position in the product portfolio chart.

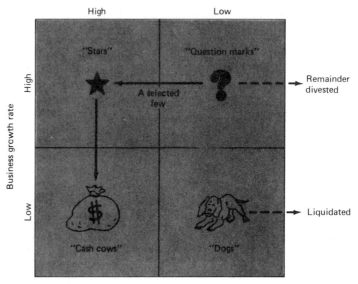

Relative competition position (market share)

FIGURE 7.4.
Growth-Share Matrix

SOURCE: Reprinted with permission from *Long Range Planning,* vol. 10, Barry Hedley, "Strategy and the 'Business Portfolio,' " Copyright 1977, Pergamon Press, Ltd.

Low Growth Potential/Low Market Share   A business in this category is typically termed a *"dog"* or *"cash trap."* The reason for this is that the low market share places this business at a competitive disadvantage and with a low-growth rate it suggests a low probability for improvement. Therefore, how do we manage this business? The answer is: we manage this business to maximize short-term cash flow which includes cost cutting, divestiture, or liquidation.

Low Growth/High Market Share   These businesses have a strong competitive position, but in a stabilized market and are termed *"cash cows."* Because these businesses are already in a strong competitive position, the strategy is to invest only enough to maintain your present market share while using the competitive advantage to build cash flow for use in higher-growth areas.

High Growth/Low Market Share   Businesses in this category are typically termed *"question marks"* or *"problem children"* because they are in potentially lucrative market segments but are operating at a competitive disadvantage. Consequently, these businesses must either be expanded to increase market share to take advantage of the growth or suffer competitive disadvantage. However, if it is impossible to improve competitive position, then it may be strategically advantageous to withdraw from this business. This is because cash demand is high, but cash generation is low.

High Growth/High Market Share   Businesses in this capacity are called *"stars"* and are the business segments where the firm's resources should be allocated. These businesses are attempting to use strong competitive position so that they can grow at a faster rate than competitors in sales and profits.

The use of the growth-share matrix as a management tool permits management to array all of the businesses on one graph, called a "product portfolio chart." BCG's use of product portfolio charts is based upon the relationship between market share and profitability, so that market dominance is the major strategic objective in high-growth markets.[17]

STEP THREE—IDENTIFY THE STRATEGY

Given the relative position on the growth-share matrix, a business strategy is selected. For example, at Norton Simon, David Mahoney (CEO) must decide which of his products or businesses are "cash cows," to be managed to maintain current share, and which are rated as "stars," and should be allocated the majority of resources. At one company, it is reported that 80 percent of its resources are allocated to products in the "star" category.

PORTFOLIO MANAGEMENT—MEAD CORP

Mead Corp. has twenty-four strategic business units, and it has moved managers into new slots so that their expertise matches the strategy of the unit they run. Richard Bettis and William Hall have suggested a similar approach, that managerial style should be matched to the business unit.[18] For example, they report on one company where a "star" mission is associated with an "analytical" type of manager, a "cash cow" with an "engineer" type, a "problem child" with a "salesman" type, and a "dog" with a "cost accountant" type. The important point is the fit between the style and the strategic mission.

MANAGE EACH BUSINESS

William W. Wommack, vice-chairman of Mead, is also allocating money differently. Instead of funding projects with "fair share" allocations, he now funds strategies, a method that lets the company weed out "dog" products, milk its mature cash producers, and concentrate investment on potential growth lines. "If you have a business you want a lot of cash out of instead of growth, you don't put a high-powered marketing man in charge, and if you want growth, don't put a conservative accountant in charge," explains Wommack.[19]

STEP FOUR—STRATEGIC REVIEW

Each month, top managers, like David Mahoney of Norton Simon, must review the status of the strategic plan in light of economic conditions and competitors' countermoves and determine how well the portfolio plan is working. If there is a gap between plan and actual situation, then some corrective action must be put into effect. For example, at NSI the market share is declining in several product lines, resulting in short-term profit pressures and requiring a review of strategic decisions.

While the BCG model has had wide application in industry, there are problems associated with the identification of market segments, the number of units which can be managed, and the idea that growth rate is always associated with profitability. There is no doubt, however, that such models do offer a useful tool for strategic evaluation and decisions.

THE GENERAL ELECTRIC "STOP-LIGHT STRATEGY" FOR PLANNING

A second strategic planning model is the *business planning matrix,* or *"stop-light strategy"* approach, developed by General Electric and McKinsey & Company. The business planning matrix provides a means of relating the multiple factors forming the firm's competitive advantage profile to its environmental opportunities and risks.

General Electric uses stop-light strategy (a Strategic Business Planning Grid—see Figure 7.5) to evaluate critical factors in strategic planning for its forty-three SBUs or strategic business units.

What Is the GE Grid?   The business planning matrix, as used at GE, provides a means of monitoring industry characteristics and has served to protect developing business units during business downturns.

In the planning review, each business is rated on a multiple set of strategic factors.

GE Business Strength Factors   Size, growth rate, market share, position, profitability, technology position, image, and people are GE business strength factors.

Industry Attractiveness Factors   Factors enhancing industry attractiveness are size, market growth, planning, market chemistry, technical role, competitive structure, social, environmental, legal, and human factors.

How Does the GE Grid Work?   The outcome of these ratings is high, medium, or low in both industry attractiveness and GE's position in the field, as shown in Figure 7.5. If the product falls into the green section, then it has a *"green light"* and a "go," the strategic decision to invest and grow. Products in the *"yellow light"* or caution section are "question marks": these are borderline situations that might go either way. If the product falls in the red zone, this indicates a *"red light"* or "stop" strategy, such as a retrenchment, consolidation, or divestment strategic decision.

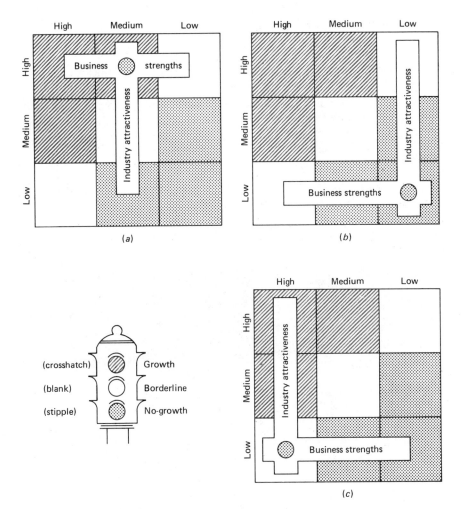

FIGURE 7.5
General Electric's Planning Grid
SOURCE: Reprinted from information in the March 15, 1975, issue of FORBES Magazine.

"We don't give definitive weights to the nonnumerical factors," says Reuben Gutoff, corporate planner, "but they do have weights. At the end of our discussion there is a good consensus on what's green, red, or yellow."[20]

The elaboration of the "stop-light" model specifies the functional areas and management styles for each major strategic alternative, thus providing a set of contingent actions for use in directing the strategic actions for each business unit.

THE DIRECTIONAL POLICY MATRIX (DPM)[21]

A third strategic planning model, the *Directional Policy Matrix (DPM)* has been developed by Royal Dutch Shell. This model, like the GE model, uses a weighted multivariate analysis to position a business on a three by three matrix, thus allowing for greater complexity than the BCG model.

What Is the DPM?   The major technique of the DPM is to identify:

1   the main criteria by which the prospects for a business sector may be judged to be favorable or unfavorable;

2   the criteria by which a company's position in a sector may be judged to be strong or weak.

These criteria are then used to construct separate ratings of "sector prospects" and of "company's competitive capabilities" and the ratings are plotted on a matrix. The matrix can be used to display all the competitors in one particular business sector, since the method lends itself to evaluating competitors' ratings as well as those of one's own company.

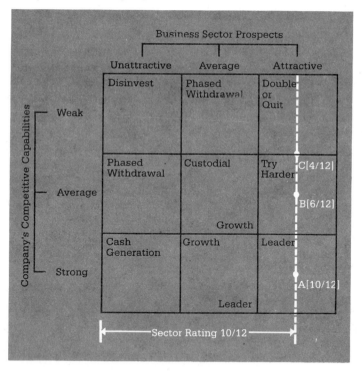

FIGURE 7.6

Comparison of Competitive Capabilities—Product X

SOURCE: Reprinted with permission from *Long Range Planning,* vol. 11, S. Robinson and others, "The Directional Policy Matrix," Copyright 1978, Pergamon Press, Ltd.

How Does the DPM Work?   This model, as indicated in Figure 7.6, is developed by the positioning of each product/market unit within a nine-cell matrix. The basic technique analyzes each product on two primary factors and the results are plotted on the matrix. Since the various zones of the matrix are associated with different combinations of sector prospects and company strength or weakness, different product strategies are appropriate to them. These are indicated by the various key words which suggest the type of strategy or resource allocation to be followed for products falling in these zones.

Leader   Competitor A, the largest producer with the lowest unit costs and a commanding technical situation, is in the highly desirable position of leader in a business sector with attractive prospects. His indicated strategy is to give absolute priority to the product with all the resources necessary to hold his market position.

Try Harder   Competitor B is in this position. It implies that products located in this zone can be moved down toward at least an equality position by the right allocation of resources.

Double or Quit   This is the zone of the matrix from which products destined to become the future high fliers should be selected. A company should not normally seek to diversify into any new sector unless the prospects for it are judged to be attractive.

Growth   Products will tend to fall in this zone for a company which is one of two to four major competitors (four-star market position) backed up by commensurate production capability and product R and D.

Custodial   A product will fall in the custodial zone of the matrix when the company concerned has a position of distinct weakness either in respect of market position (below three star), process economics, hardware, feedstock, or two or more of these in combination.

Cash Generation   A company with a strong position in such a sector can still earn satisfactory profits and for that company the sector can be regarded as a cash generator.

Phased Withdrawal   A company with an average-to-weak position in a low-growth sector is unlikely to be earning any significant amount of cash and the key word in this sector is phased withdrawal. This implies that efforts should be made to realize the value of the assets and put the money to more profitable use.

Disinvest   Products falling within this zone are likely to be losing money already. Even if they generate some positive cash flows when business is good, they will lose money when business is bad. It is best to dispose of the assets as rapidly as possible and redeploy more profitably the resources of cash, feedstock, and skilled manpower so released.

        This overall comparison of business units allows the development of a strategic plan within each SBU. At the corporate level, hard decisions about the relative future prospects are used as a basis for allocating scarce resources among the business units.

In general, the DPM may present a useful tool in strategic planning in narrowing the set of possible alternatives from which to choose.

THE APPLICATION OF STRATEGIC ANALYSIS MODELS

During the past decade there has been a widespread adoption of strategic analysis models in which resources are being allocated according to a strategic perspective of each business segment within the total portfolio of the firm.

The BCG model is one widely used technique for analyzing a company's strategic alternatives. One source estimates that over 40 percent of the *Fortune* top 500 firms are using the portfolio planning concept while another research study suggests that about 40 percent of firms studied use this technique.[22] Others have estimated that as many as 80 percent of the top 500, and a sizable portion of the second 500, are using some element of the BCG techniques. It has also been reported that at least seven major forest product companies are BCG clients, including Hammermill Paper, International Paper, Mead, Crown-Zellerbach, Boise Cascade, Great Northern Nekoosa, and Potlatch.

However, in the application of these concepts a number of problems have emerged. These problems may apply with varying degrees to different models or within differing firms, but should be recognized by the strategist.

TIME FRAME: LONG RUN VS. SHORT RUN

The BCG growth-share model for strategic analysis is based on the relationship between cash generation and market share, and is derived from the effect of the experience curve. In other words, the firm with the greatest experience (market share), also has the lowest cost and the greatest cash generation. It is important to recognize, however, that the BCG approach is based on long-term relationships and is not a short-term adjustment technique.

Many organizations find it difficult to balance both short-term and longer-range strategies. Norton Simon, for example, seems to have an inability to strike a balance between its needs for short-term profits and longer-range investment and growth. President David Mahoney has been criticized for his desire to maximize current earnings at the expense of funding new-growth products.

Norton Simon has five basic product segments as shown in Figure 7.7. NSI's market share is declining in foods, cosmetics, and beverages, basically because of a failure to meet competition. The Hunt-Wesson Foods product is highest in revenues and profits but has a declining market share. Hunt-Wesson is thus being managed as a "cash cow." As a result, however, NSI's market share in tomato sauce, for example, has declined from 48 to 39 percent in five years. The beverage business also has suffered. Canada Dry now has only a 2.9 percent share of market. Consequently, one strategy would be to divest this business unless it has a high-growth

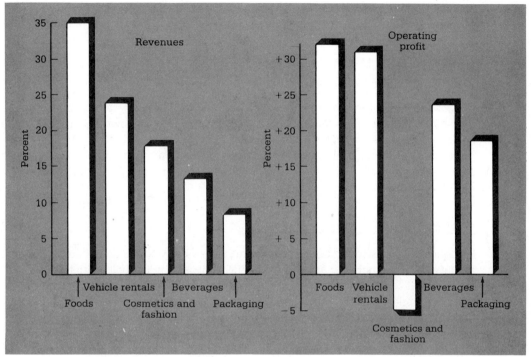

FIGURE 7.7
Norton Simon's Market and Earnings Mix
SOURCE: Norton Simon Inc. Annual Report, 1979.

potential. Avis Car Rental, on the other hand, has a 28 percent market share but needs more investment in order to shift its rental fleet to a more fuel-efficient mix as well as to provide increased advertising budgets.

In cosmetics, NSI's Max Factor lost $30 million and market share. Does a manager decide to keep pouring money in, or is it wiser to retrench and shift resources into other, more profitable areas? David Mahoney says, "The reason I won't sell Max Factor is that I won't have it turned around fast enough to get what I think it's worth."[23]

In fact, divestments are often decided upon too slowly. Even successful firms are often reluctant to get rid of their losing businesses or "dogs." Mahoney is reluctant to sell Max Factor. RCA stayed in the computer business until losses in the hundreds of millions forced them to divest. The primary cause, of course, is usually hope for a turnaround or waiting for the opportunity to improve the selling price, which often never comes.

MARKET-SHARE DEFINITION

One of the main problems of strategic analysis is the definition of market share. It is difficult to precisely determine the exact boundaries of any specific market and errors here can make the analysis invalid. Similarly, there is often a serious problem of accurate product/market segmentation and relation of market share to strategy.

MARKET SHARE/GROWTH

Market share and growth rate are directly related to the generation of strategic alternatives. Market share as it affects volume, profitability, growth, and cash flow reflects management's judgment of the company's future opportunities. Market share is the percentage of industry sales made by a company over some specific time period. The strategist is concerned with both the size and quality of its share.

MARKET SHARE PROFITABILITY

Evidence suggests that a direct relationship exists between market share and profitability. A high-market-share firm can usually outperform its rivals with low-market-share. It was found in one study that "on an average, a difference of ten percentage points in market share is accompanied by a difference of about five points in pretax ROI."[24] The explanation was threefold: (1) economies of scale—the ability to capitalize on size; (2) marketing power—the capacity to apply power for competitive advantages; and (3) quality of management—the underlying strength for performance.

QUALITY OF SHARE

The quality of the share is important because the firm's position is not vulnerable to competitive countermoves. When a firm has quality of share, a low-market-share business can be as attractive as a high-market-share business. High market share provides power and implies financial strength. But within a corporation, it is often necessary to seek high market share for certain businesses, while accepting low market share for other businesses. In either situation market share significantly affects profitability. A study by Richard Hammermesh and others (Harvard University) showed that low-market-share firms can outperform high share competitors.[25]

PROCTER AND GAMBLE

To be successful, a low market share company must compete in the segments where its own strengths will be most highly valued and where its large competitors will be most unlikely to compete. But it is often possible to compete with large competitors. Procter and Gamble under CEO John G. Smale, for example, entered the disposable diaper market with Pampers, even though the market was controlled by Scott. This was a costly and riskly action, but it paid off—Pampers has become the market leader despite the slow start. And Johnson & Johnson, who held 20 percent of the market, decided to pullout altogether as their share dropped to a meager 8 percent.

PHILIP MORRIS

Similarly, in 1970, Philip Morris, Inc., purchased the remaining outstanding shares of Miller Brewing Company and began transforming the staid and conservative brewing company into an aggressive, consumer-product-oriented industry giant. To accomplish this goal, PM brought in John A. Murphy, the executive vice president in charge of Philip Morris's International Operations, to head the brewing company. Murphy recognized that beer is essentially a homogeneous product, distinguished primarily as a result of product consumer advertising strategy. Subsequently, Miller became the fastest growing brewer. Between 1970 and 1975, Miller rose from seventh to fourth in sales and passed Pabst to become third in 1976, taking over second place in 1978 as shown in Figure 7.8.[26]

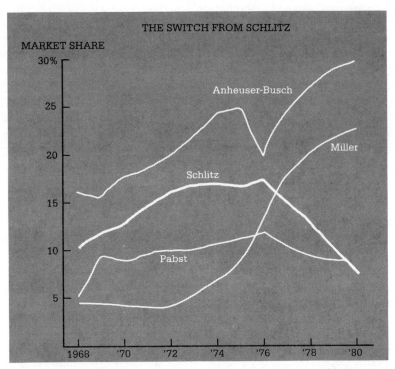

FIGURE 7.8
Market Share Performance

TURNING DOGS INTO WINNERS

There have also been examples of "dogs," money-losing businesses, in one company which were bought and turned into winners. For example, a group bought Helena Rubenstein, a cosmetics company, even through Colgate-Palmolive lost $50 million there in 1979, and another businessman bought Remington from Sperry despite losses of $30 million in five years.

A recent *Fortune* article questioned, "Why would anyone want such intractable losers? They were certainly cheap; some corporate dogs went for less than their presumed liquidation value. Still, the sellers were happy to get rid of them, which means that the buyers must have seen something in the losers that some pretty classy managements hadn't." "In a few cases what the buyers saw seems fairly clear. Large companies with tremendous overhead and burdensome bureaucracies simply are not built to manage small businesses. An entrepreneur can make quick decisions, intuitively respond to changing market pressures, fire staff, and ignore Wall Street's need for ever-increasing quarterly profits. All this might be enough to turn a laggard into a champ."[27]

UNSUCCESSFUL TURNAROUNDS

In a study of sixty-four companies, William K. Hall (University of Michigan) found no successful turnarounds among the most troubled companies in eight basic industries. "Competitors who end up last in mature, hostile environments ultimately must fail or be subsidized." He was specifically referring to Chrysler and Kaiser Steel.[28]

As William Hall has suggested, "For general managers guiding their companies into the economic environments of the 1980s, the implications of these findings are clear. The laws of the jungle change as maturity comes and hostility intensifies. In such a jungle, the range of strategic options narrows, requiring both an early warning of the coming hostility and an early strategic repositioning for a company to survive and prosper."[29]

IDENTIFYING GROWTH RATE

Another problem lies in the identification of the actual underlying growth rate of the market segment, a problem compounded by the impact of inflation. In the first place, there are no exact ways to determine the growth rates of new innovations, and forecasting methods often miss the mark. For example, how was one to determine the market for hand-held calculators, or digital watches? Today we recognize the scope of these markets, but at one time the Swiss watch industry felt that the digital watch was only a small, insignificant segment of the entrenched mechanical watch industry. How quickly things can change! Similarly, what is the market potential for home or personal computers? Texas Instruments and others are betting that this will be a tremendous growth market, but it has yet to fully emerge.

This problem is especially important for strategic models where growth rate is a primary variable in developing strategy for various business elements. An inaccurate estimate makes strategic evaluation unreliable.

MANAGERIAL MOTIVATION

Finally, there is the problem of management and employee satisfaction which emerges when a business is labeled as a "dog" or "cash cow." How motivated could you get if you were working on or managing a product identified as a target for divestment, or for no growth? This poses a special problem in attempting to apply the portfolio concepts as a strategic management tool.

Despite these problems, the use of strategic analytical models is increasing, and they offer a useful approach to the evaluation of strategic alternatives.

MANAGERIAL IMPLICATIONS

Two important elements in the strategic management process are the comparison and evaluation of strategic alternatives. There are always a number of possible strategic moves for allocating available resources to achieve organizational goals. These possible strategies must then be evaluated to determine whether they are consistent with environmental opportunities and competitive advantages. The final choice is aimed at optimizing the total return to the firm, subject to market and competitive constraints. Therefore, the evaluation of strategy in a complex organization is usually a multiple series of decisions rather than a single choice. Strategic decision making, then, involves the comparison of various tradeoffs in order to select the most appropriate strategy.

THE USE OF ANALYTICAL MODELS

In this chapter, several analytical/conceptual models that may be used to analyze strategic alternatives have been described. The use of these analytical models has grown rapidly over the past decade, and many of these techniques are being used as integral components of the strategic evaluation and decision process in large companies. These models represent the first major advances in systematically identifying the critical factors in strategic planning.

The use of these models provide one of the most detailed and important techniques in strategy selection. One of the keys to the successful application of these tools is accurate market segmentation. Another is the participation of lower-level managers in its development. The models should not be used as rigid, inflexible instruments. On the contrary, they must be used as flexible guides to action in meeting changing market and competitive conditions. It is also important to recognize that successful short-term strategies may not necessarily guarantee improved long-term performance.

The analytical models are used to examine the current state of the organization and to analyze important trends that may be emerging. The manager's diagnostic skills, then, are particularly important in making these determinations.

Strategic evaluation involves developing and selecting a course of action for the future. At the higher levels of the organization this tends to be broader in scope, but managers at all levels must be involved in determining how best to allocate the firms' resources. The use of strategic models reduces the extent of intuitive planning and "management by crisis" and provides a tool for the optimal use of various product/market business units within the firm.

There is no doubt that these models have not yet been perfected. They do not provide a simple mathematical solution to strategic questions but rather a framework for a rational comparison of complex factors. However, there are still a number of problems associated with their use including the time frame, definition of market, identification of growth markets, and motivation of managers.

One problem is that financial performance is invariably related to time. However, many of the key factors in the model are not controlled by a rigid time horizon. Innovation does not usually occur on a planned orderly basis. In other words, the strategist should not force fit the strategy to meet a set of numbers, but rather must temper the analysis with commonsense and business judgment.

In spite of these problems and shortcomings, it would appear that strategic analysis models are a useful and growing element in evaluating strategies in large, diversified firms.

The fundamental idea of a flexible strategic analysis system is one of regular review and evaluation. For maximum value, don't overlook the requirement for timely and accurate information and the element of managerial skill. The analytical models, then, simply provide a means of managing future ventures with reduced risks and uncertainties.

REVIEW QUESTIONS

1   Texas Instruments moved into the digital watch market a few years ago and now has about 50 percent of the market. How was this done? And what do you feel were the long-term outcomes? That is, is it successful? Describe experience curve theory and how it affects strategy.

2   Singer is a leader in the sewing machine field, but it is also a diversified corporation (including power tools and aerospace products). In view of the changing demographics and life styles, how would you manage your portfolio of businesses in this field? Explain the growth-share matrix and its role in strategic analysis.

3   Why do managers need to do strategic analysis, and what is the difference between portfolio strategy and SBU strategy?

4   Describe GE's stop-light strategy and its use.

5   What are some of the problems of strategic analysis models?

6   At Norton Simon, David Mahoney was pondering what to do with Max Factor. Using the BCG Model, what would you do? Look up NSI's annual report and see which strategic move might be most effective.

ENDNOTES

1   "Frustration and Turmoil Plague a Marketing Prodigy," *Business Week*, April 7, 1980, 70.
2   Ibid, 72.

3 "The Strategy Squeeze on the Airlines," *Business Week,* May 19, 1980, 104.

4 Seymour Tilles, "How to Evaluate Corporate Strategy," *Harvard Business Review,* July-August 1963.

5 Richard Rumelt, "Evaluation of Strategy: Theory and Models," in Dan Schendel and Charles Hofer (eds.), *Strategic Management: A New View of Business Policy and Planning* (Boston: Little, Brown, 1979).

6 Anthony J. Parisi, "Exxon: An Empire," *New York Times,* August 3, 1980.

7 For more on this, see Richard P. Rumelt, *Strategy, Structure, and Economic Performance* (Cambridge, Mass.: Graduate School of Business Administration, Harvard University, 1974), 11–32.

8 Personal Correspondence from Bruce Henderson, November 25, 1980.

9 "Markets: It's Better to Be Big," *Forbes,* October 15, 1977, 132

10 Boston Consulting Group, "The Experience Curve Revisited," *Perspectives,* Boston Consulting Group, 1980.

11 Gerald Allan, "A Note on the Use of Experience Curves in Decision Making," *ICCH #9-175-174,* June 1976.

12 "How TI Beat the Clock on Its $20 Digital Watch," *Business Week,* May 31, 1976, 62

13 Rumelt, "Evaluation of Strategy."

14 Based on Gerald Allan, "A Note on the Boston Consulting Group Concept of Competitive Analysis and Corporate Strategy," *ICCH#9-175-175,* June 1976.

15 *Perspectives,* Boston Consulting Group, 1980.

16 See Richard Bettis and William Hall, "Implementing the Portfolio Concept," paper presented at *Academy of Management,* Detroit, Michigan, 1980.

17 Robert D. Buzzell, T. Gale Bradley, and Ralph G. M. Sultan, "Market Share—A Key to Profitability," *Harvard Business Review,* January-February 1975, 97–106.

18 Bettis and Hall, "Implementing the Portfolio Concept."

19 "Olin's Shift to Strategy Planning," *Business Week,* March 27, 1978, 102.

20 "Piercing the Future Fog," *Business Week,* April 28, 1975, 49.

21 S. J. Q. Robinson *et al,* "The Directional Policy Matrix-Tool for Strategic Planning," *Long Range Planning,* June 1978, 8.

22 Richard Bettis and William Hall, "Strategic Portfolio Management in the Multinational Firm," *Working Paper,* Southern Methodist University, 1980; see also research by Philippe Haspeslagh presented at the Academy of Management, Detroit, 1980, to be published in the *Harvard Business Review.*

23 "Frustration and Turmoil," 104.

24 Gale Buzzell and Ralph Sultan, "Market Share," 97–106.

25 R. G. Hammermesh, M. J. Anderson, Jr., and J. E. Harris, "Strategies for Low Market Share Businesses," *Harvard Business Review,* May-June 1978, 95–102.

26 "Make Way for Miller," *Forbes,* May 15, 1976, pp. 45–47.

27 Peter W. Bernstein, "Who Buys Corporate Losers?" *Fortune,* January 26, 1981, 60.

28 William K. Hall, "Survival Strategies in a Hostile Environment," *Harvard Business Review,* September-October, 1980, 75.

29 Ibid.

C H A P T E R

8

The fine art of executive decision consists in not deciding questions that are not now pertinent, in not deciding prematurely, in not making decisions that cannot be made effective, and in not making decisions that others should make.

Chester Barnard, *Functions of an Executive*
(Cambridge, Mass.: Harvard University Press, 1939).

The Strategic Decision

CHAPTER OBJECTIVES

When you have completed this chapter, you will be able to:

- ☐ *Demonstrate an understanding of the strategic choice process.*

- ☐ *Develop your own analytical and technical skills in decision making.*

- ☐ *Increase your awareness of how managers make strategic decisions.*

- ☐ *Analyze a complex management case using the concepts in this unit.*

MAKING BIG DECISIONS[1]

Dr. Henry E. Singleton

Henry Singleton started Teledyne, Inc., in 1960, reportedly betting some $400,000 of his own money that he could repeat what Charles "Tex" Thornton had done at Litton. He did. Starting from scratch in 1960, Singleton built his company to *Fortune* 500 proportions (126) in just six years.

"Over the last two years or so, Henry E. Singleton, the gifted founder and chaiman of Teledyne, Inc., has quietly moved more than $400 million of his corporation's funds into the market and bought up some remarkably large positions in eleven *Fortune* 500 companies. Through his far-flung conglomerate, he is now the largest shareholder in nine of those companies and, incredibly, he has effective control of six."

Singleton has managed to acquire the image of an Olympian personage shielding some mysterious business strategy by the simple device of not talking much to the press or Wall Street. "Henry's not like that at all," says an acquaintance. "He's just a great executive who does not need publicity." Besides buying large blocks of its own stock, Teledyne presciently invested a lot of its insurance subsidiaries' money in undervalued companies like Litton rather than buying fixed-income securities. Now Singleton looks like a genius, with a paper profit of about $200 million on Litton alone (and some $320 million in Apple Computer stock). "The big positions, however, look like more than mere investments. Indeed, they have all the earmarks of a complicated gambit of some sort, and this view of the holdings is furthered by Singleton's reputation as an avid chess player who delights in elaborate stratagems. 'He's like Bobby Fischer,' one former associate explains. 'Everything he does has lots of deliberate thought behind it. He doesn't know what his opponent is going to do, but whatever the opponent does, Henry has three possible moves.' "

Managers make decisions to accomplish strategic goals. Unfortunately, the future is not always safe and predictable and managers must assume risks when making strategic choices. Singleton's willingness to risk so much in the stock market doesn't seem out of character. "He is a lean, sixty-one-year-old Texan whose brilliance is said to be matched only by his integrity and arrogance. A man who likes to be called 'Doctor' (he received the doctor of science degree from M.I.T.), he never doubted that he would become a famous industrialist when he started Teledyne. He also seems to be disdainful of the capabilities of other men, and downright contemptuous of the denizens of Wall Street."

"Those holdings are rather unusual, to say the least. They give Singleton an astonishing amount of power over some very large pieces of corporate America. And that influence clearly is Singleton's alone. Though he owns only 6 percent of the company, he runs it like a personal fiefdom, and he made the investment decisions personally. Not even George A. Roberts, Teledyne's president, learned of the purchases until after they had been made."

STRATEGIC DECISION MAKING

The strategic manager is a decision maker. Henry Singleton of Teledyne has made a series of strategic choices which have resulted in the success of his firm to date. There are always a number of possible strategies and a number of courses of action that might be taken, but the executive must make the strategic choice. As John H. Patterson of NCR has been quoted as saying, "An executive is a man who decides; sometimes he decides right, but always he decides."

The purpose of this chapter is to explore the nature of the strategic decision process. The first section examines decision making and outlines the stages of the decision process. This is followed by a discussion of the constraining forces which influence decision making. Finally, some behavioral implications of the decision process will be discussed.

STAGE 8: THE STRATEGIC DECISION

After the process of strategic evaluation, the next step (Stage 8) is the most critical factor in the strategic management process: *the strategic decision*. A decision may be defined as a choice from among possible alternative strategies. As the old saying goes, "The buck stops here." The purpose of decision making is to direct resources toward objectives, and a decision to pursue one strategy usually means there are other possible actions that are not being taken. The strategic decisions may be good decisions or they may be terrible decisions, but they must be made. Boeing's decision to design a new generation of airliners, the 757 and 767, has placed them in a commanding lead among aircraft companies. But a decision by Rolls-Royce to design a new jet engine, the RB-211, led that company into bankruptcy.

CALLING THE SHOTS

After all the analysis of alternatives, there comes a point when the strategic decision must be made. The strategic decision is a process of systematically comparing how each possible strategy will impact the market and the firm. There are always several possible alternatives and there are always trade-offs to be considered between differing courses of action.

But in the end the strategic decision narrows down to the business judgment of one person: the Chief Executive Officer of the firm. The CEO finally makes the decision of how the firm's resources shall be committed at that point in time. At Chrysler, for example, a decision needed to be made regarding the source of motors for their small car lines, the Omni and Horizon. They had a choice between building a new plant or buying the engines from Volkswagen. Top management at Chrysler made the decision to buy the engines rather than build the plant. A few years later, however, the Omni and Horizon became Chrysler's hottest selling cars. The factor limiting the number of cars which could be produced turned out to be the shortage of engines. That one decision had a significant impact on Chrysler's competitive position for the next few years, and was a contributing factor to its heavy losses.

WHAT IS A DECISION?

A *strategic decision* is the choice by the decision maker of a course of action from among the alternatives available. Strategic management involves making the decisions which will ultimately determine the organization's survival. As Herbert Simon has noted, "If *all* behavior results from decision making and if management is a particular kind of behavior, then managing is decision making."[2]

The purpose of the strategic decision is the accomplishment of organizational goals and objectives. Consequently, the decision process is a fundamental part of strategic management. Many of these decisions require consideration of an uncertain and unpredictable set of future conditions. Therefore, the strategist must make a calculated judgment of what his future will be, and then select a strategy that will enhance the firm's competitive position. But because of the uncertainty of the future, there is always an element of risk in such decisions. As an example, cigarette companies often spend between $50 and $100 million on the introduction of new brands, many of which fail, and Gillette spent over $100 million on the introduction of a new dry antiperspirant.

At A & P, Jonathan Scott (CEO) needed to make a strategic decision. One choice was to close down the company's worst operating units, store by store, warehouse by warehouse, plant by plant. A second more radical course of action was to shut down entire operating divisions. Scott opted for the first alternative. "We made a conscious decision to close down on a store-by-store basis," he recalls. "We decided to weed out the very worst and try to turn around the rest. We wanted to save as much as we could."[3]

DECISION FACTORS

There are a range of strategic decisions which must be made. Sometimes these decisions involve relatively low levels of risk, but other times, the risk is substantial. One way to clarify decision elements is to examine the following factors[4]

What is the impact of the decision on the goals and objectives of the organization?   As we have seen from previous illustrations, effective decisions lead to a successful organization. The decisions by Henry Singleton at Teledyne and Harold Geneen at ITT, for example, led to growth and profitability for their companies. At Penn Central Railroad, W. T. Grant, and Rolls-Royce, on the other hand, strategic decisions led to disaster and failure.

What is the scope of the decision?   A decision affecting one product or department in a small business will have a greater effect than one involving the same number of elements in a large organization.

What level of financial outlay is involved?   The financial impact of a decision is, of course, relative to the size of the firm. A $100,000 purchase by a small business may be very important, yet the same amount for General Motors may be routine.

What is the relative frequency of this type of decision?   Decisions which need to be made frequently often tend to be routine. The decision to buy materials or hire workers is made routinely in most organizations. But a decision to build a new research laboratory or chemical complex is made less frequently and is not a routine decision.

What is the time frame?   Important decisions must often be made under conditions of urgency and the time given to make the decision may be short. Frequently, deadlines are forced by the situation or by other people; buyers, suppliers, etc. A sudden breakdown of the supply of raw material may force a quick decision and action. In other decisions there may be enough time to study the situation in detail and determine alternative ways to solve the problems.

INADEQUATE DECISIONS

Inadequate decisions are frequently the result of (1) not analyzing carefully enough the impact of the decision on the organization's objectives, (2) the tendency to ignore problems in the hope they may disappear, (3) insufficient evaluation of alternatives, and (4) the avoidance of risk.

AN END AND A BEGINNING

The strategic decision is both an end and a beginning. It marks the end of the strategy formulation phase, and the beginning of the implementation phase. The role of the strategist in strategic choice is to analyze all information on the firm and the environment, and using a rational process translate the organization's mission and goals into action. The strategic choice signals the commitment of resources toward a specific goal: a new product, increased market share, or even acquiring or selling off a business. Henry Singleton analyzed Teledyne's resources and the opportunities available. There were many possible choices but, at that point in time, he made a decision to invest some $400 million into other company's stocks: a commitment to action.

THE STRATEGIC DECISION PROCESS

Strategic choice is a deliberate attempt to modify the functioning of the organization in order to bring about increased future effectiveness. Managers sometimes assume that a decision is an isolated phenomenon. However, if we view the strategic decision from a systems viewpoint, then we find a number of interrelated factors. Decision making may be described as a sequential process of stages that enable the decision maker to structure the problem in a meaningful way as shown in Figure 8.1.

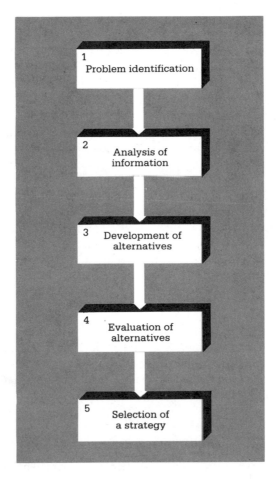

FIGURE 8.1
The Decision Process—The Rational Model

MANAGERIAL DECISION MAKING: GENERAL ELECTRIC

General Electric, the largest diversified company in the world, has long been known for its strategic planning excellence, timely decision making, and the seemingly endless stream of competent managers. An example is Tom Vanderslice, formerly senior vice president and head of GE's power systems business.

To this difficult task, "Vanderslice brought skills acquired in a varied career with GE. Like many managers, he has spent virtually his entire professional life inside the company, growing and learning new skills along the way. With degrees in chemistry and physics, he has progressed from scientific research to managing scientific research, and then from managing scientific businesses to the general management of business. . . . A meticulous decision maker, Vanderslice is more interested in figures than in words or their pronounciation. In conferences with his subordinates, he says, 'I listen to the war stories, but then I go back to check the data.' " For some time, he has even kept a computer terminal at home so that he can summon up real-time financial results anytime he is not at his corporate office.[5]

MULTIPLE FORCES

An organization is a dynamic system and major decisions often involve multiple . forces. Decisions are also likely to have both intended and unintended consequences and these must be anticipated. The decision made by the strategist today may have major ramifications on the future survival of the firm. Edwin Gee, CEO of International Paper, made the major decision of moving his company into lumber and building materials and is aiming at long-range market trends and the improvement of IP's competitive position.

THE RATIONAL PROCESS

Because making major strategic decisions involves a high level of risk, the decision process can be quite complex. The strategist may have limited alternatives and information, and frequently he is operating under rigid time pressures. Many theorists have proposed a rational decision process, beginning with John Dewey who outlined a three stage process: First, there must be a controversy consisting of opposite claims regarding the same objective situation. Second, there must be a process of defining and elaborating these claims. Finally, a decision is made which closes the matter in dispute and serves as a rule or principle for the future.[5]

SIMON'S PROCESS

Herbert A. Simon, one of the best-known decision theorists, conceptualizes three major phases in the decision-making process.

1. Intelligence activity Borrowing from the military meaning of intelligence, this initial phase consists of searching the environment for conditions calling for decision.

2. Design activity In this second phase, inventing, developing, and analyzing possible courses of action take place.

3. Choice activity   The third and final phase is the actual choice, selecting a particular course of action from those available.[7]

WITTE'S FIVE-STAGE MODEL

However, Eberhard Witte (West Germany) has researched the application of a five-stage model as follows (see Figure 8.1).

1. Problem identification   A necessary condition for a decision is a problem, or a gap between the desired level of achievement and the existing level.

2. Analysis of information   A search process is undertaken for relevant internal and external information.

3. Develop alternatives   A number of possible alternative solutions are identified. These alternative strategies are the possible courses of action from which choices can be made. Obviously, the broader the range of alternatives which are considered, the more likely an effective strategy will emerge.

4. Evaluation of alternatives   The relative worth of the various alternatives is examined and rated against some criteria or standard.

5. Selection of a strategy   The strategy that best meets the decision criteria is selected. The decision is not an end in itself, but rather the means to the end. The strategic choice also depends on the comparison of objectives and alternatives by the decision maker. There is a range of forces which influences the judgments which will be made including the values of the decision maker, the risk-taking attitudes, and the internal policies of the situation.[8]

CHOICES/TRADE-OFFS

In the rational model of decision making, it is assumed that the decision maker has a full range of alternatives and a criteria for making the decision. However, in actual situations the manager often has limited information, and may not have the time to systematically search out all possible alternatives. Eberhard Witte has investigated the actual decision process in some 230 cases in three large international corporations, including IBM and Univac. He reported, not surprisingly, that his research failed to support the five-phase decision process, and he reported the following conclusions.

1   A complex innovative decision is a multi-operational process;

2   a complex decision process consists of not one final decision, but rather a series of subdecisions;

3   the rational process can be found in actual decisions; however, they do not form distinct phases in time, but rather are distributed over the total duration of the process.[9]

In the broadest sense, then, managers do follow a decision process, but tend to rely more on action than diagnosis and frequently shortcut the decision process by combining the steps. As James B. Quinn (Dartmouth College) has commented, "Any organization's ultimate direction is the result of many such choices and trade-offs. . . . The attempt to find an acceptable and motivating compromise among multiple competing goals is what forces much of the coalition behavior observed in large organizations, including major businesses."[10]

WHO MAKES THE DECISION

But the final and perhaps most significant difference between a simplistic model of decision making and the complex reality of the decision process in modern organizations lies in who makes the strategic decisions. In theory, the manager often seems to be an isolated commander making strategic plans, but in reality the strategist is part of the action—interacting with the internal and external forces that determine the final decision. These interactions are an important element in better understanding decision making, and we shall examine these external and internal constraining forces in the next sections.

CONSTRAINING FORCES

The survival of a firm in a competitive environment depends on the decision which its executives make. These strategic decisions determine the amount and type of resources available and the allocation of those resources. These are often life or death choices for the firm—if the executive's decisions are effective, then the firm will be successful and profitable. If, however, the choices are inferior to the competition's, then not only will the firm's market position deteriorate but the company may go out of business.

In a world of rising prices and increasing shortages of energy and other resources, the manager has to manage within constraints. The firm's strategic decision, then, is dependent upon a multitude of constraining elements including competitors, customers, suppliers, etc., which act to influence the decision. These forces impact the decisions and usually involve the assessment of various trade-offs. These trade-offs occur because there are many objectives which the organization seeks to achieve, and many forces which limit the effectiveness of a given strategy. Obviously, the greater the dependence on these elements, the less independent is the range of possible strategies.

INTRAORGANIZATIONAL FORCES

There are also intraorganizational forces which place constraints upon the development of strategy, including the values and attitudes of the decision makers. Jules Schwartz examined managerial risk and found that lower-level management prepared proposals for decisions and evaluated the risks. The evaluations tended to suggest alternatives to top management that were less risky, incremental choices, rather than risky, breakthrough decisions.[11]

CARTER'S FINDINGS

Eugene Carter also reported on strategic decisions in a medium-sized firm. His major findings included:

- Lower-level managers suggest strategic choices that will likely be accepted and withold suggestions that have less probability of approval.

- Various departments evaluate strategic choices differently, usually in their own interest when suggesting a proposed strategic choice.

- The greater the uncertainty of outcome in the environment of the organization, the larger the number of criteria which will be developed to make the strategic decisions.

- The number of criteria considered in evaluating a strategic choice is directly related to the degree of uncertainty in the project's forecasts.[12]

In the mid 1970s, for example, General Motors made the strategic decision to down-size its line of cars to meet the threat of imports. Ford and Chrysler, on the other hand, reacted differently, each with a differing set of values, attitudes and resources, and were slower to make strategic changes. As a result, GM led in the market while Ford and, especially, Chrysler were losing market share as consumer demand shifted toward more fuel efficient autos.

MINTZBERG'S MODEL

Henry Mintzberg (McGill) suggests the process of strategy formulation may be thought of as the interplay among three basic forces: (1) an *environment* that changes continuously but irregularly, with frequent discontinuities and wide swings in the rate of change; (2) an organizational operation system, or *bureaucracy*, which above all seeks to stabilize its actions, despite the characteristics of the environment it serves; and (3) a *leadership* whose role is to mediate between these two forces to maintain the stability of the organization's operating system while at the same time adapting it to environmental change. *Strategy* can then be viewed as the set of consistent behaviors by which the organization establishes for a time its place in its environment; *strategic change* can be viewed as the organization's response to environmental change, constrained by the momentum of the bureaucracy and accelerated or dampened by the leadership.[13]

Decision making is one of the critical elements in the whole strategic process. There are internal forces as well as external constraints which act to influence the strategic decision. In the next section some of the constraining factors which have a critical influence upon the strategic decision will be discussed.

EXTERNAL CONSTRAINTS

Organizations do not exist in isolation. They interact with other elements of the environment as we pointed out in Chapter Three. These forces include the board of directors, stockholders, customers, suppliers, competitors, government, and the broader society. The weaker the organization is in relation to these external forces, the less flexible it is likely to be in its strategic choice. For a firm in Chrysler's position, for example, the range of possible alternatives tends to become more limited. The external constraints include the past strategy, time, and information.

THE INERTIA OF PAST STRATEGY

There is always some inertia effect from previous strategies. This is because prior strategies are usually the starting point in formulating new strategies. As a result, certain alternatives may not be explored as thoroughly as they might be; some strategic choices may even be eliminated.

MINTZBERG'S FINDINGS

Henry Mintzberg concluded that past strategy strongly influenced current strategic choice. He found that:

- *The older and more successful a strategy, the harder it is to change.* The present strategy evolves from a past strategy developed by a single, powerful leader. This original and tightly integrated strategy (a Gestalt strategy) is a major influence on later strategic choices.

- *Once a strategy gets underway, it becomes exceedingly difficult to change,* and the bureaucratic momentum keeps it going. Mintzberg calls this the *"push-pull phenomenon"*: the original decision maker "pushes" the strategy, then lower management "pulls" it along.

- *When past strategy begins to fail because of changing conditions, the enterprise reacts in discrete steps,* grafting new substrategies onto the old and only later seeking out a new strategy.

- *If the environment changes even more radically, then the leadership begins to consider initiating a new cycle of strategic change.*[14]

AT GULF & WESTERN

At Gulf & Western Industries, Inc., the momentum of an aggressive acquisition strategy carried out by the "first generation" leadership of chairman Charles G. Bluhdorn slowly eroded its rate of return until the leaders were forced to reappraise and change this strategy.

"In fact, G & W is finally undergoing the significant streamlining process already under way at other conglomerates welded together in the 1960s. G & W, mainly known in the past for its slick acquisitions of assets, is now going to refocus its efforts on managing those assets to improve its return on equity. When completed, the process at G & W could eliminate at least five areas with total sales close to $850 million," writes *Business Week*.

The streamlining stems from a recognition at G & W that the company has stayed too long in businesses that are either drains on cash or unlikely ever to yield satisfactory returns.

"The company has been criticized for not weeding out unprofitable elements sooner. Unlike such other diversified giants as General Electric Co., which expeditiously sold off cash-draining operations, such as its computer business, 'Gulf & Western appears not to manage its way out of cash traps,' says W. Walker Lewis, president of Strategy Planning Associates, a Washington consulting firm."[15]

DEEPER IN THE BIG MUDDY

Barry Staw (Northwestern University) also found that as decision makers committed larger and larger amounts to strategic decisions, they tended to become personally involved with the decision, thus influencing later strategic choice[16] When the decision maker feels personally responsible, he tends to increase the amount of investment to a prior course of action, even though the results were negative (see Figure 8.2).

In Staw's experiment, it seems that once the strategist becomes committed to a certain strategy, that strategy tends to be followed. In organizational situations, this may support the tendency to replace top executives when a change in strategy is needed. At A & P, for example, even though the strategy of Jonathan Scott to cut unprofitable stores failed to reverse losses, this strategy was continued until a new manager was named to replace Scott.

TIME CONSTRAINTS

Time is always a factor in the decision process. There are schedules and due dates, a time when a loan must be repaid, a time when a union contract must be signed. Generally, there are two types of time constraints. First, there are the time pressures on the decision itself, the deadlines for making the decision. Decision deadlines, such as, "the bid is due on the 30th of the month," etc., force action. Time deadlines pressure the manager into making a choice either by action or inaction, and people deal with pressure in different ways. Some people like pressure and don't really feel comfortable until the "late innings of the game." Others function poorly, if at all, in time pressure situations. A second constraint involves the time frame of the decision itself.

TIME DEADLINES

Under time pressure, strategic decision making may be different. There may be a conflict between those who favor a fast decision, who feel that to wait is to lose the

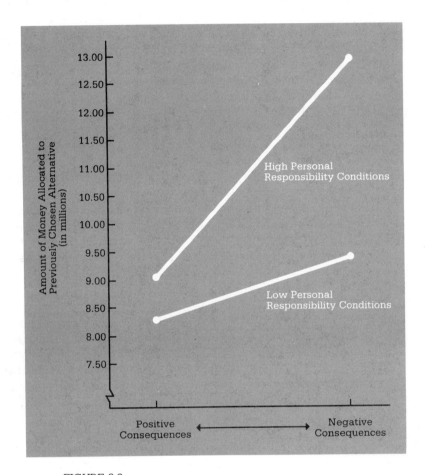

FIGURE 8.2

The Amount of Money Allocated to Previously Chosen Alternative by Personal Responsibility and Decision Consequences

SOURCE: Adopted from Barry M. Staw, "Knee-Deep in the Big Muddy: A Study of Escalating Commitment to a Chosen Course of Action," *Organizational Behavior and Human Performance 16*, June 1976, 27–44.

opportunity, and others who may suggest more time and study. Deadlines may pressure the manager into an either-or choice. Under these conditions, there is often a tendency to give greater weight to highly negative information, and there is a tendency to consider fewer aspects of the problem.[17]

In writing about the Cuban missile confrontation, Robert Kennedy said: "The time that was available to the President and his advisors to work secretly, quietly, privately, developing a course of action and recommendations for the President, was essential. If our deliberations had been publicized, if we had had to make a decision in twenty-four hours, I believe the course that we ultimately would have taken would have been quite different and filled with far greater risks. The fact that we were able to talk, debate, argue, disagree, and then debate some more was essential in choosing the utlimate course. Such time is not always present, although, perhaps surprisingly, on most occasions of great crisis it is; but when it is, it should be utilized."[18]

When strategic decisions are made under time pressure, there may be more unknowns involved in the outcome. When Rolls Royce made the decision under time pressure to bid on the RB-211 jet engine for the L-1011 airplane, it overemphasized certain aspects of the situation and failed to consider all of the technical difficulties, delays, and costs which might arise. As a result, Rolls Royce ended up by going bankrupt over this one decision.

THE TIME FRAME

A second time frame aspect is the time frame of the strategic decison itself: the impact upon near- and long-term results. Often the reward systems of a company are set up to inhibit the maximizing of long-term goals because of an overemphasis upon short-range objectives. The managers who show the best short-term results are generally the ones who tend to receive rapid promotion. Executive incentive compensation is often related to short-term earnings performance which penalizes longer-term strategic considerations.

FAIRCHILD

As an example, Wilfred Corrigan (CEO, Fairchild) had to try to rebuild the new Metal Oxide Semiconductor (MOS) technology, but lost about four years on his competition and fell far behind. "But the time lost was precious. Even now, Fairchild is 50 percent MOS in such advanced areas as large-scale integration (LSI); and although "bipolar" (the other technique) is better for high performance applications, the MOS markets generally have grown faster than the bipolar; thus Fairchild was squeezed in the total market," says *Forbes*.

"But strategy is one thing, tactics another, and Fairchild has little time to get the tactics under control. 'We've paid our dues,' says Tom Longo. 'The next five years belong to us.' Maybe. But when you fall behind in a business like this, it isn't easy to catch up."[19]

THE TIME HORIZON

A related factor is the time horizon of the decision, whether it is immediate- or long-range. The decision to build a major chemical or power complex, for example, may require from five to ten years lead time because of construction time and environmental delays. This ability to decide about an uncertain future is, of course, the difference between *"anticipative"* or *"reactive"* management styles. Another important consideration is what C. Northcote Parkinson appropriately has termed, *"the law of delay."* Stated in simple terms, he suggests that the longer a decision can be delayed, the lower the probability that it will ever be accepted.[20]

DECISION TIMING

There is also the problem of timing of the decision. Often there is a moment when an opportunity opens up and there is a need to strike while the iron is hot. To wait or to delay a decision may give competitors just enough time to get into the market.

As an example, the auto makers are faced with the introduction of the 60-miles-per-gallon car, but must decide when to get into the market. Detroit says it will eventually build minimites, too. But *when*? The Japanese may hit the market first and capture it, just as they've won most of the market for 30-mpg cars.

"Says Erick Reickert, director of small-car programs at Ford Motor Co.: 'It is a time-frame question. My guess is there will be a market of probably 1 million units, 10% of the market, by 1990.' He also figures the first models could be coming on the market by 1984 or 1985, possibly sooner if the foreign manufacturers move in."[21]

For these reasons, time is always an important constraining factor in making strategic decisions.

INFORMATION CONSTRAINTS—THE CERTAINTY-UNCERTAINTY CONTINUUM

Another constraining factor involves the amount of information available to the decision maker.

The strategist must make decisions to accomplish future objectives. These objectives may be immediate and short-term such as the signing of a union contract by a certain date, or they may be long-term, such as the decision by Texas Instruments to enter the digital watch market. Unfortunately, the future is rarely safe and predictable, but the strategist must make decisions based on the information which is available.

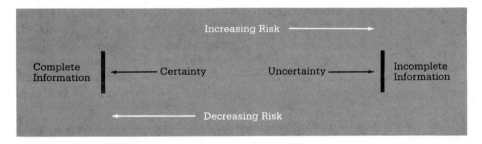

FIGURE 8.3
The Certainty-Uncertainty Continuum

For any major decision a manager will likely have enormous quantities of information available. There are usually many possible alternatives and it would be extremely time consuming and costly to calculate them all. The amount of information available to the decision maker may vary as shown in Figure 8.3. At one extreme is the condition of complete certainty and information, a condition which we rarely find in strategic decisions. At the opposite end is a condition of complete uncertainty, where there is little or no information on which to base a decision. Actually, it is more realistic to consider this as a continuum of possible states of information.

DECISION RISK

This continuum between certainty and uncertainty is called risk. Therefore, the amount of information which the decision maker has becomes a critical factor. Theoretically, if we know all of the variables and their outcomes, then we are taking no risk. When you decide to invest your money in the bank at a fixed rate of interest, you are making a decision under certainty. The greater the amount of information available to the decision maker the lower the level of uncertainty and risk. Conversely, the less information, the greater the risk.

Since managers tend to avoid risk, or more accurately to take calculated risks, then the amount of information which one can bring to bear is an important element in effective strategic choice. Unfortunately, it isn't always that easy. Getting more information usually takes more time and money. And even then it is usually impossible to eliminate all risk. All the manager can do is try to minimize risk as much as possible.

AT XEROX

At Xerox Corp., for example, a failure to assess a growing market cost them valuable market share. "Back in 1972, Xerox shares sold at a price/earnings ratio of 54. Today they sell for seven times earnings.

"Though Xerox probably won't retrieve much of its lost market share— it once had virtually all of the market for plain-paper copiers—it will probably be able to halt the precipitous slide of recent years. That won't be easy, because it will have come, in part, through price-cutting against Japanese competitors. However, Xerox has regained lost momentum and has a strong foothold in some new growth markets. . . . Xerox President David T. Kearns ruefully concurs: 'We really should have been thinking about the market on a much broader basis.' "[22] In this instance, Xerox was operating without complete information on market growth rates, thus increasing their decision risk.

INTERNAL CONSTRAINTS

There is also a set of internal forces and factors which exert constraints upon the decision maker. For example, the manager has a set of personal values and an attitude toward risk taking. There is also a set of organizational constraints which impact the final strategic choice. These forces include attitudes toward risk taking and managerial values.

MANAGERIAL ATTITUDE TOWARD RISK

Research has indicated that individuals vary considerably in their propensity for accepting risk. Managerial attitudes toward risk vary from comfort with high risk to very strong risk aversion. A manager less inclined toward risk taking will set different goals, evaluate alternatives differently, and make different decisions than another manager who prefers risk. These risk attitudes vary by industry and firm so that some managers need to be capable of withstanding higher levels of risk than others.

In industries where decisions need to be made quickly, as in the electronics industry where price levels must be shifted rapidly to meet competitors, risk takers can be expected to outperform low-risk managers because delays are usually associated with higher costs.

RISK TAKING

Strategic decision making usually involves some level of risk. A major decision often involves the commitment of large resources and wrong choice may mean an executive's career. The strategic choice is the commitment of organizational resources to a specific course of action: to build a new plant or not to build, to invest R & D money in a new technology or not to invest, to invest in a large marketing campaign on a product or not. These are the fundamental strategic questions, and making big decisions requires the courage to take a stand. There are many managers who prefer to take the low-risk option of "no decision."

UNITED AIRLINES

President Richard J. Ferris of United Airlines, a 43-year-old marketing whiz, is taking a calculated risk by attempting to raise revenues by eliminating money-losing flights and developing a long-haul route structure, a strategy that contrasts sharply with the rest of the industry.

But the latest results for United can be more accurately read as dramatic evidence of the enormous risk Ferris is taking in radically restructuring the airline in the face of plunging traffic. "Ferris is gambling, however, that he can build traffic on scores of new routes even though the market is soft. He is not moving as recklessly as Braniff Airways, Inc., which has expanded willy-nilly and run itself into a deep financial hole. Instead, United has been careful to add routes from such points as Chicago and Denver, where it has inherent strength. But Ferris is clearly adopting a strategy that contrasts vividly with that of the rest of the industry."[23]

THE RISK-REWARD TRADE-OFF

The major factor in any strategic decision involves the level of risk associated with a given rate of return. The higher the rate of return offered by a strategy, the more attractive that alternative is likely to be perceived. Each manager has developed a set of criteria about which decisions are acceptable or unacceptable for his firm or industry and certain levels of risk which can be taken (for example, Henry Singleton's decisions at Teledyne).

Each organization also has certain minimum rates of return which are attractive and returns below these levels will be rejected. At Westinghouse, for example, a standard rate of return is 20 percent, while at many companies 25 percent or more must be achieved to make it worth going into. Fringe businesses with returns of less than 15 percent are candidates for divestment, and businesses below 7 percent are targets for oblivion.[24]

Sometimes a firm is more concerned with other factors such as growth rate and market share. A cash-rich company, such as Exxon, may decide to get into a high-growth field like word processing even though it may sacrifice short-term rate of return for the longer-term potential. A firm may also place emphasis on gaining market share in a given product, with relatively less concern for profits. At Coors, for example, the company decided to switch its strategy from a relatively low rate of advertising to going head-to-head with the big guys, because they wanted to gain market share.

AT GE

At General Electric, managers are required to use more than just a single number, such as rate of return on investment or assets, to justify proposed programs.

" 'In the past five years we have come to realize that a single number criterion doesn't work,' says Charles E. Reed, senior vice president. 'People can make that number come out any way they want.' Instead, planning now consists of an analysis of the company's basic strengths in attacking the new business. These include relative competitive strength, competitors, economic, social, political, and technological trends, and financial documentation."[25]

YOU BET YOUR COMPANY

A related factor is the degree of risk with which managers feel that they can live. Although management decision making always involves some element of risk, managers, as a rule, try to minimize risk. As a result, the strategic decision process involves taking calculated risks. The difference, of course, is how different managers calculate the degree of risk and how they perceive risk-taking as a strategic factor.

LOW-RISK TAKERS

There are some managers, like bankers, who are very uncomfortable in risk situations. They tend to be very low-risk-takers in strategic decisions. They would prefer low risk, safer options, even though the payoff may not be as great. Similarly, such managers are more comfortable with very low debt situations, and they prefer to be followers rather than innovators in newer, untried fields.

Other managers, like Charles "Tex" Thornton of Litton or James Ling of LTV, by comparison could be classified as "Mississippi River Boat Gamblers." These managers look for high returns in high-growth, less-stable markets. They are comfortable with highly leveraged positions, in fact, would probably not accept a no-debt position. These managers prefer to be the pioneers or innovators, seeking early entry into new high-growth markets.

"BET-A-BILLION" KIRBY

At Westinghouse, Chairman Robert Kirby, called "bet-a-billion Kirby," made a decision to pay the highest price in cable history for Teleprompter, more than $800 million. "The figures are unclear because Teleprompter has just bought out its partner, Hughes Aircraft, in a complicated joint venture and won't discuss the deal." The purchase and debt assumptions make Westinghouse's costs for Teleprompter about $850 million. *Forbes* goes on to say:

"But, of course, Westinghouse isn't buying numbers; it is buying a stake in a dazzling new industry. It argues that its Westinghouse Broadcasting subsidiary (operating earnings of $59 million on revenues of $219 million) and Teleprompter will make beautiful music together.

""Give Westinghouse Chairman Robert Kirby credit for taking a bold gamble to get his $7-billion company off dead center. But Westinghouse's gambles haven't always paid off. There were $1 billion in losses on fixed-price uranium contracts, and much red ink in modular housing and pollution control. So, there's a lot riding on this one. The future of the company, perhaps."[26]

THE INFLUENCE OF VALUES

The personal value system of the individual manager will also influence the manager's perception of strategy and problems. The most extensive analysis of managerial values has been done by George England (University of Minnesota), establishing the role that values play in decision making. In his study, England found that successful managers favor pragmatic, dynamic, achievement-oriented values, while less successful managers prefer more static and passive values.[27]

The strategic decision determines the broad direction of the total firm by balancing the firm's various business interests. Yet there is no single criteria for deciding what this direction should be. Different executives in reviewing the strategic balance may disagree because of different personal values and weightings placed on key factors. To contrast these differing values, let us compare two strategic decision makers: Donald P. Kircher, former CEO of Singer and James S. "Mr. Mac" McDonnell, former chairman of McDonnell Douglas.

A RISK TAKER

"Donald B. Kircher enjoys horseback riding and fox hunting and savors 'the thrill of the risk' of fox hunting in winter, when the horse might hurdle a stone fence and come down on a sheet of ice," wrote *Fortune* (1975). At Singer, he launched an aggressive program of diversification and acquisition.

"Despite his braininess and certitude, Kircher was often wrong. He ultimately contributed to Singer's difficulties and to his own downfall. Aloof, formal, and severe, Kircher once succinctly described his management techniques as the use of 'fear' (a colleague says 'sheer terror' was more like it). His methods recall Patton's approach to dealing with the troops. 'A good cussing out is the only way,' the general once said. 'I've got to make them more scared of me than they are of the Germans.'

"Kircher acknowledges that the most persistent criticism of his management style—'at least by those who have criticized me in my presence'—was that he dominated everything and everyone. 'My own theory,' he adds, 'is that an enterprise requires a single leader, it doesn't require a committee. If the chief executive is not a dominant personality, he ought to get the hell out.' "[28]

JAMES McDONNELL—A CONSERVATIVE STYLE

McDonnell brought a different set of values to his firm. "The chairman's influence, for example, was sharply reflected in the company's agonizing decision during the summer of 1978 to abandon development of so-called 'new-generation' jetliners in the mid-size, medium-range class to compete with Boeing Co. and Europe's Airbus Industrie. In accord with 'Mr. Mac's' well-known bent for frugality and prudence, McDonnell Douglas concentrated on derivative designs of the DC-9 and DC-10, rather than launching costly new development programs to meet the new boom in airline buying. . . .

"The chairman's ultraconservative style also showed up clearly in a corporate diversification strategy that continued to limit new ventures to natural outgrowths of the company's existing aerospace, electronics, and related high-technology operations. McDonnell Douglas is not—and never has been—interested in acquiring companies in general industrial fields, although such deals are brought regularly to its attention."[29]

RELIANCE ON QUALITATIVE VS. QUANTITATIVE

In recent years there has been an increasing reliance on quantitative decision models and techniques at the strategic decision-making level. The 1980s have been termed the "age of the computer" and every major corporation has economic analysts and planners whose job it is to bring to bear these sophisticated techniques. Steven R. Holmberg, for example, surveyed eighty-nine public utilities and found that 60 percent reported the use of simulation models in plant and equipment decisions.[30] *Fortune* magazine describes the problems one company ran into in using such a model:

DOW'S DECISION MODEL

Dow Chemical Company—which uses a corporate model including forty separate cost inputs—recently tried to switch from average-cost to replacement-cost pricing. "A less theoretical problem with replacement-cost pricing is that a company's success is making its prices stick ultimately depends on the dynamics of the marketplace. If demand is slack and producers are running at low utilization rates, it takes quite a bit of fortitude even to approach customers with the notion that they should pay replacement-cost prices. And competitors may feel under pressure to sell at lower prices in order to keep volume high enough just to break even.

"Last year, in the face of low operating rates, Dow tried twice to raise its price for polystyrene. Though other major producers—Dow is the biggest—did not follow, the company stuck to its guns for a while and lost market share. Finally, it had to come down to be competitive. Says James Kerley, executive vice president of Monsanto, which was one of the companies to stand firm: 'We didn't think the increases would stick. That's the fallacy in the concept of replacement-cost pricing. It's great to say you ought to price at replacement cost, and when there's good utilization of capacity, you do it. It's also true that no new capacity will be built unless prices are attractive. But in a product like polystyrene with a lot of producers operating at 65 percent of capacity, replacement-cost pricing is for the college textbooks. It's not the real world.' "[31]

"GUT FEEL" DECISIONS

But the computers don't make decisions, executives do. The CEO faces incredibly complex choices and must consider the impact of each decision on a range of strategic factors. Regardless of how refined the analytical model, the manager must still exercise qualitative, "gut-feel" judgment about which strategic choice will best achieve long-term objectives.

AT GENERAL CABLE CORPORATION

Effective decision making is often the result of the proper integration of detailed analysis and intuition. Consider the case of Robert P. Jensen, chairman of General Cable Corporation, a former tight end for the Baltimore Colts football team. Sensing the need for his company to diversify, he found himself faced with five major decisions that involved over $300 million.

"On each decision," says Jensen, "the mathematical analysis only got me to the point where my intuition had to take over"—as was the case with the $106 million cash purchase of Automation Industries. General Cable's strategic planning department had come with a purchase price based on Automation's future sales. "It's not that the numbers weren't accurate," Jensen recalls, "but were the underlying assumptions correct?"

As an engineer not given to making hasty decisions, he calls patience crucial to the decision-making process. At the same time, he warns that the perfectionist who keeps waiting for new information never gets anything done. "Intuition is picking the right moment for making your move."[32]

One reason that quantitative models are not used more widely is that most strategic decisions are very complex and therefore are not easily amenable to statistical analysis. And generally, the strategist is dealing with difficult trade-offs between strategic choices, rather than a simple choice between two clearly distinct alternatives. Larry Greiner (University of Southern California) found that managers rely more on qualitative than quantitative criteria even when quantitative information is available.[33]

THE IMPORTANT DECISION

The strategist can never know precisely what is going to happen tomorrow. He rarely has complete information about the past or present and seldom about the future. His judgment about the outcome of each potential alternative must be conjectural and contain an element of uncertainty. Strategic choice fundamentally involves judgment.

An example is the style of C. Peter McColough, chairman and CEO of Xerox Corp. " 'If something bothers me,' he says, 'I don't rely on the reports or what other top executives may want to tell me. I'll go down very deep into the organization, into certain issues and certain levels of people, so I have a feel for what they think.' McColough gets deeply involved in the 'important decisions that are really critical to the business' such as the decision by Xerox to purchase Scientific Data Systems."[34]

POWER AND POLITICAL CONSTRAINTS

Among the most critical but least discussed factors in decisions are the power relationships and political influences within the organization. *Power* may be termed the "ability of a person or group, for whatever reason, to affect other persons' or groups' ability to achieve their goals."[35] *Politics,* on the other hand, involves the method and tactics used to gain power over others. Although both of these terms are often given a negative connotation, they are simply realities of organizational life and the strategic decision maker needs to be aware of these forces. William D. Guth (New York University) studied strategic decisions in a major corporation and he concluded that decisions were significantly influenced by interpersonal relations and the power relationships of top managers.[36]

Similarly, Peter Grinyer and David Norburn found that "those involved in the real process of strategic decision making recognized that it is ultimately a political process in which power and influence of individuals change with the nature of the challenges to the company."[37]

WHY POLITICS?

Why are there political or power struggles? Essentially, they are derived from the complex problems and multiple goals of the organization. As a result, there are many differing views and vested interests. To cite only a few examples, marketing has different goals from manufacturing, doctors and administrators' differ as to how hospitals should operate, and professors in the behavioral disciplines and those in the quantitative disciplines often differ over curriculum, etc., in the business schools.

Each of these groups has some special interest it wishes to see advanced, and opposing interests it sees as being of lesser value to the total organization. In one sense such conflicting interests are of value, for they bring different ideas, values, etc., to bear on problems. But in another sense, this tends to create conflict and the politicization of strategic decisions.

A KEEN AWARENESS

The manager who hopes to change a strategy, then, must be aware of the political nature of such a move. The past strategy may have been successful during an earlier time, and the managers who influenced these choices are probably still in positions where their support will be important in gaining acceptance of a new strategy. In order to gain support for a new strategy, the manager needs to win the support of key people, and co-opt or neutralize the major opposing forces. This requires a keen awareness of political forces, a perception of strengths and weaknesses, and persuasiveness on the part of the manager.

These power struggles often involve conflicts between short- and long-run goals. For example, at Memorex Corp., new CEO Clarence W. Spangle, the former president of Honeywell Information Systems, is trying to reverse a downward slide by his firm because of an overemphasis on short-term profits at the expense of its long-term prospects which are looking bleaker by the day.

AT MEMOREX

"But Memorex has worked its way out of trouble in the past. Memorex went outside and recruited Robert C. Wilson, who proceeded to lead Memorex into one of the most dramatic turnarounds in corporate history. From a cash-flow point of view, he bailed Memorex out," says *Business Week*.

Wilson brought annual new income up, by cutting corporate debt by two-thirds and by cutting costs including drastic cuts to the research and development budget. However, the cuts in R and D have put Memorex behind the state of the art in technology, and have hurt their long term technological position as a leader in the field.

"At the same time, however, Wilson may have sown the seeds that grew into the company's current problems by emphasizing these short-term gains at the expense of longer-term payoffs."

THE RESULTS OF CONFLICTING VIEWS

The result of such power conflicts is often bargaining, compromise and coalition. *Bargaining* is simply the negotiation of agreement between two or more parties, and is often necessary in organizations where power is not concentrated. Many strategic decisions are the result of bargaining among power groups. Another likely outcome is *compromise*. It has been said that politics is the art of the possible. Therefore, decisions are often the result of compromise between groups.

Finally, *coalitions* may be formed among two or more groups or persons to increase the likelihood of opposing or supporting a particular decision.

Ian C. MacMillan (Columbia University) has observed, "Coalition members do not join the coalition without bringing with them their demands, and the support of these members could easily be given to alternative coalitions. . . . Each member will, therefore, make a set of demands on the coalition to commit itself to certain goals. . . . However, it is often impossible for the coalition to satisfy all the demands of all its members. . . . A potential member will join only if he feels that the policy commitments of the coalition will promote his own goals, and he will stay only as long as he expects the coalition to be successful."[38]

There are many examples of the importance of power struggles and politics, but one which was mentioned earlier in Chapter Three concerned the forced resignation of Richard Goodwin as CEO of Johns-Manville. There was a difference in strategic choice between Goodwin and the board, and nine of the twelve board members formed a coalition to achieve a majority and force Goodwin out, even though he had done an outstanding job of managing the turnaround of the company.

DON'T ARGUE WITH THE MAN

Another example of power politics is the firing of Lee Iacocca (now CEO, Chrysler) from Ford Motor Company. Iacocca launched a campaign to gather support from outside board members and was fired by Henry Ford after thirty-two years with the company. Power struggles are nothing new at Ford Motor Co., but this one was a stunner. After weeks of futile maneuvering to save his job, Lee Iacocca, 53, the hard-driving, cigar-chomping president of the world's fourth largest manufacturing company, found himself quite bluntly sacked by his equally tough-minded boss, Chairman Henry Ford II. It was the culmination of months of behind-the-scenes quarreling between two of the auto industry's most respected—and often feared—executives. As the saying goes, "don't argue with the man whose name is on the building!"

From the moment Lee Iacocca moved into Gene Cafiero's presidential office at Chrysler headquarters in Highland Park, Michigan, in 1978 his hands were full. But he won't make the mistake that Semon Kundsen made when he moved abruptly from GM to Ford a decade ago and tried to impose his GM-Pontiac ways on the number two automaker. Iacocca understands that a move from the top of one major auto company to another is like the chancellor of Germany becoming premier of France and can be fraught with comparable political pitfalls. Iacocca himself is often credited with sandbagging Kundsen at Ford (he lasted 19 months), so he is likely to staff up with people he knows and trusts to protect his flanks and rear while he attempts to impose his style on the sagging number three. Some of those he'll be able to trust are still at Ford, but at least one moved over to Chrysler ahead of him.[39]

POLITICS: TWO FACTORS

In a study of twenty-four strategic decisions, Mintzberg found that in one-third of the cases power and politics were significant factors, and were important factors in all of the decisions.[40]

Decisions are not always made on the facts of the situation. Generally the more important the decision, the greater the probability that power and politics will be involved. These examples point out that managerial decisions are often influenced by the political realities of the situation and these cannot be ignored. The idea that politics are a factor, however, does not mean that managerial decisions are dishonest—it simply implies that there are multiple forces involved in strategic decisions.

THE INTEGRATION OF MULTIPLE GOALS

Strategic decisions are never easy. That's why top managers get paid big bucks. These choices are based on complex sets of variables and unknown factors in imprecise relationships. If a certain set of economic conditions prevails, and if the competition takes one set of actions, then a given strategy may be very effective. If, however, conditions change or competitors take unanticipated actions, then the same strategy may prove to be disastrous.

While the CEO is responsible for the strategic choice, it is important to recognize that a majority of important decisions take place in management review meetings. The strategic decisions are typically made in the board room as a result of group interaction, after a careful consideration of all available information. When President John F. Kennedy made his famous "Bay of Pigs" decision, he first listened to a range of opinions, facts, viewpoints, and analyses from important members of government. There was no "silver bullet solution." Instead there were a number of proposed plausible arguments from both "Hawks and Doves," including many brilliant minds such as Robert McNamara, MacGeorge Bundy, Maxwell Taylor, and others. After all the meetings, discussion of alternatives, airing of opinions, and sifting of the pros and cons of each proposal, Kennedy made the decision. (Unfortunately, the Bay of Pigs decision is generally regarded as a fiasco.)

DECISION ACCEPTANCE

It is often said that a decision is no better than its implementation, that is, its acceptance by those who must carry it out. Because the strategic decision is influenced by external and internal coalitions, the decision maker needs persuasive and influential skills if he is to gain acceptance. No matter how brilliant the analysis, unless it can be "sold" to important forces (i.e., the board of directors) the decision will not be carried out.

An example of a strategist with these skills would be Charles B. "Tex" Thornton, Chairman of Litton Industries. "Tex was one of the great managers of the Fifties and Sixties. He was a tremendous salesman. He turned on that Texas charm, deliberately using folksy colloquialisms. He had the gift of making everyone feel that they were valuable and important and worth listening to."[41]

This is typical of the strategic decision process also. The problems are complex and controversial. There are facts, data and arguments supporting several possible courses of action. No one man has all the expertise or all the information. Therefore, the decision maker must have the ability to function effectively in a group decision-making situation. The decision is usually based on the fluctuating and often vague realities expressed by experts in other fields, and often based on uncertain information and differing analyses.

MANAGERIAL IMPLICATIONS

The final stage in the strategic formulation process involves making the strategic decision. The strategic manager is a decision maker. Sometimes he decides right, sometimes he decides wrong, but always he must decide. Decision making is the most important activity of the strategic manager. In fact, some theorists suggest the term decision maker instead of manager. Decision making is involved in the entire strategic process, from goal setting and planning to controlling.

Decision making is an integral part of strategic management. More than any other factor, competence in this skill differentiates the effective manager from the ineffective. The manager's success as a strategic decision maker depends upon a combination of analysis, personal values, experience, and intuitive judgment.

Decision making is a dynamic process rather than a fixed, set procedure. Making a strategic decison is a process of systematically comparing strategic options and choosing between alternative courses of action. The actual choosing activity is usually preceded by data gathering and the development of alternatives. Although the rational decision process is sequential in nature, this process is not always followed. Instead, managers take short cuts, use bargaining or other power political techniques to deal with the complex forces involved in strategic decisions.

Decision making does not take place in a vacuum. Important elements in decision making are the external and constraining factors which influence decisions. The amount of information available, the time frame, and other forces place constraints on the decision outcomes. There are three basic intervening variables including external constraints, internal values and attitudes, and political-power relationships. Managerial value systems influence the decision, and often strategic decisions are the result of compromises or coalitions between various power groups.

The strategic decision is the critical point in the strategic process because here the choice is made that sets the direction for the firm's future. The manager needs to be able to analyze the various alternatives, sort out the important considerations which are involved, and make a judgment regarding what to do.

The strategic decision process involves many managerial styles, skills, and roles. Because the strategic decisions are critical and involve risks, this is a particularly crucial stage in the strategic management process.

In many situations, strategic decisions must be made quickly to be effective. However, there are many examples of decisions made under time pressures which resulted in ineffective choices—such as the Bay of Pigs fiasco.

Decision making is essentially a rational process, but as we have noted, there are limits to how orderly the strategic process actually is.

Managers often approach decisions in intuitive, erratic ways, rather than as a mechanical procedure. And because the stakes are high, there are usually differing power groups inside and outside the organization, who have varying degrees of influence on the final choice.

Therefore, strategic decisions are more of an art than a science, and are often the result of bargaining, compromise and other political factors as much as pure rational analysis. In any event, decision making is an integral part of strategic management. And, in the final result, this is what sets apart the successful strategist from the unsuccessful.

REVIEW QUESTIONS

1 Daniel Ludwig recently made a decision to develop a pulp production and timber growing center on the Amazon River in Brazil, based upon high-growth, high-yield trees (six to ten year growth cycle) with an investment of close to $1 billion. What factors would you want to analyze in such a decision?

2 Many consultants advocate cost cutting and sacrificing short-term profit to build market share. (For example, TI's tactics in the digital watch field.) Do you agree with TI's decision? Why or why not?

3 Current research indicates that quantitative methods are not used as much in strategic decision making as was anticipated. Why?

4 What are the impacts of time and risk on strategic decisions?

5 Wilkenson Sword Ltd. (British razor blade company) recently acquired Scripto to compete in the ballpoint pen market. BIC held a 61 percent market share, Gillette about 35 percent, while Scripto had only a 3 percent share. What would you do at this strategic decision point? Why?

6 In the text, it stated that the higher in the organization and the more important the decision, the less likely it is that quantitative methods will be used in the decision. Do you agree?

ENDNOTES

1 Excerpts from: A. F. Ehrbar, "Henry Singleton's Mystifying $400 Million Flyer," *Fortune,* January 16, 1978, 66–76.

2 Herbert A. Simon, *The New Science of Management Decisions* (Englewood Cliff, N.J.: Prentice-Hall, Inc., 1977), p. 1.

3 Peter W. Bernstein, "Jonathan Scott's Surprising Failure at A & P," *Fortune,* November 6, 1978, 36.

4 See F. Shull, A. Delbeque, and L. Cummings, *Organizational Decision Making* (New York: McGraw-Hill, 1970); D. Miller and M. Starr, *Executive Decision and Operations Research* (Englewood Cliffs, N.J.: Prentice-Hall, 1960); S. Beer, *Brain of the Firm* (London: Penguin Books, 1973).

5 Adapted from W. Kiechell, "Tom Vanderslice Scales the Heights at G.E.," *Fortune,* July 30, 1979, 80–84.

6 John Dewey, *How We Think,* (Boston: D. C. Heath, 1933) p. 120.

7 Herbert A. Simon, *The New Science of Management Decision* (New York: Harper & Row, 1960), p. 2.

8 Eberhard Witte, "Field Research on Complex Decision-Making Processes," *International Studies of Management and Organization,* 2 (1972), 156–82.

9 Ibid.

10   James Quinn, *Strategies for Change* (Homewood, Ill.: Irwin, 1980).

11   Jules Schwartz, "The Decision to Innovate" (unpublished D.B.A. thesis, Harvard Business School, Boston, 1973).

12   E. Eugene Carter, "The Behavioral Theory of the Firm and Top Level Corporate Decisions," *Administrative Science Quarterly*, 16, no. 4 (1971), 413–28.

13   Henry Mintzberg, "Strategy Formulations as a Historical Process," *International Studies of Management and Organization*, Summer 1977, 28.

14   Henry Mintzberg, "Research on Strategy Making," *Proceedings Academy Psychology* (1974), 555–61.

15   "Gulf & Western: An Acquisitor Tries Managing Assets to Boost Return," *Business Week*, Oct. 27, 1980, 131.

16   Barry M. Staw, "Knee-Deep in the Big Muddy: A Study of Escalating Commitment to a Chosen Course of Action," *Organizational Behavior and Human Performance*, June 1976, 27–44.

17   Peter Wright, "The Harrassed Decision Maker," *Journal of Applied Psychology*, 59, no. 5 (1974), 555–61.

18   Robert Kennedy, *Thirteen Days: A Memoir of the Cuban Missile Crisis* (New York: Norton, 1969), p. 111.

19   "The Fairchild Jinx," *Forbes*, March 20, 1978, 82.

20   C. Northcote Parkinson, *Parkinson's Law and Other Studies in Administration*, (Boston: Houghton Mifflin, 1957.)

21   "60 Miles to the Gallon," *Forbes*, June 23, 1980, 38.

22   Subrata, N. Chaktavarty, "Xerox—Back on the Road to Success," *Forbes*, July 7, 1980, 40–42.

23   "Richard J. Ferris: Flying A Risky New Route for United," *Business Week*, August 18, 1980, 78–82.

24   "The Opposites," *Business Week*, January 31, 1977, 04.

25   Ibid.

26   Allan Sloan, "Bet-a-Billion Kirby," *Forbes*, November 10, 1980, 33–34.

27   G. England, O. Dhingra, and N. Agarwal, "The Manager and the Man: A Cross Cultural Study of Personal Values," *Organization and Administrative Sciences* 5 (1974), 1–97.

28   "How the Directors Kept Singer Stitched Together," *Fortune*, December 1975, 100–103, 184, 186, 188–90.

29   "Where Management's Style Sets the Strategy," *Business Week*, October 23, 1978, 88–92, 94, 99.

30   Steven R. Holmberg, "Utilizing Strategic Planning," *Management Planning*, January–February 1975.

31   Aimée L. Morner, "Dow's Strategy for an Unfriendly New Era," *Fortune*, May 1977, 312–15, 318, 320, 322, 324.

32   Adapted from Roy Rowan, "Those Business Hunches Are More Than Blind Faith," *Fortune*, April 23, 1979, 111–12.

33   Larry E. Greiner, D. Paul Leitch, and Louis B. Barnes, "Putting Judgment Back into Decisions," *Harvard Business Review*, March–April 1970.

34   "Personal Management Styles" *Business Week*, May 4, 1974, 43.

35   David McClelland and D. Burnham, "Power is the Great Motivator," *Harvard Business Review*, March–April 1976, 100–10. See also D. McClelland, "The Dynamics of Power and Affiliation Motivation."

36   William Guth, "Toward A Social System Theory of Corporate Strategy," *Journal of Business*, July 1976, 374–88.

37   Peter Grinyer and David Norburn: "Strategic Planning in 21 UK Companies," *Long Range Planning*, August 1974.

38   Ian C. MacMillan, *Strategy Formulation: Analytical Concepts* (St. Paul: West Publishing Co., 1978).

39   "It Won't Be Easy," *Forbes*, November 27, 1979, 130.

40   Henry Mintzberg et al., "The Structure of Unstructured Decision Process," *Administrative Science Quarterly*, June 1976, 246–75.

41   "A Rejuvenated Litton," *Fortune*, October 8, 1979, 150.

Strategy Imple- mentation and Review

CHAPTER

9

The successful managers of the eighties will be those who can manage a slower rate of growth and react very quickly to changing opportunities.

William M. Agee, Chairman, Bendix Corp.,
quoted from his "Futurism: A Lesson from the Private Sector,"
Business Horizons 21, June 1978, 16.

- OBJECTIVES
- THE GAME PLAN THAT BACKFIRED AT BENDIX
- STAGE 9: STRATEGIC IMPLEMENTATION
- AN IMPLEMENTATION MODEL
- THE STRATEGIC IMPLEMENTATION SYSTEM
- DIFFERENTIATION
- INTEGRATION-COORDINATION
- INTEGRATING SYSTEMS
- ORGANIZATION DEVELOPMENT
- MANAGEMENT BY OBJECTIVES
- MANAGERIAL IMPLICATIONS

Implementing the Strategic Plan

CHAPTER OBJECTIVES

When you have completed this chapter, you will be able to:

☐ *Identify the stages in the implementation process.*

☐ *Understand the differentiation-integration process of implementing strategy.*

☐ *Understand and use the concept of organization development.*

☐ *Use these concepts in analyzing a complex case.*

THE GAME PLAN THAT BACKFIRED AT BENDIX

William M. Agee

In 1977, William M. Agee, 39-year old Harvard MBA (class of '63) was hired as chairman and CEO of Bendix Corp., after four years as chief financial officer. He immediately set about straightening out the company's operating and managerial problems and the company performed well. Then in June of 1979 Agee hired young Mary Cunningham (29), a newly minted Harvard MBA, as his executive assistant and began to overhaul the strategic game plan at Bendix.

As *Fortune* tells it, Bendix then "embarked on an ambitious and risky scheme to transform itself from a nondescript automotive and aerospace supplier into a glamorous, high-flying, high-technology company. And the metamorphosis isn't going smoothly.

"In mid-September [1980], Agee suddenly ousted Bendix's president and chief operating officer, William P. Panny. Simultaneously, Jerome Jacobson, executive vice president for strategic planning, resigned, opening the vacancy for Cunningham. A week later the company announced two major decisions: it will sell its forest-products operations for $435 million and put up for grabs its 20% stake in Asarco, the nonferrous-metals producer. Selling those shares could bring another $300 million into the company's coffers and give Agee more than $700 million for acquisitions. Later the same week, Bendix unveiled the details of a major reorganization that will trigger the termination or transfer of about 250 of the 800 employees working at the company headquarters in Southfield, Michigan. Finally, in late September 1980 Mary Cunningham resigned.

"In important ways, the Agee-Cunningham association had a lot to do with the changes in Bendix's direction. While Agee is unquestionably the principal architect of the company's new strategy, Cunningham's role in devising it was critical. 'She has been my right and left arm ever since she came into the company,' said Agee not long before Cunningham quit. 'She is the most vital and important person within the company and has played an important part in conceptualizing the strategy.' "[1]

The new strategy involved selling off losers, such as Bendix Forest Products, and acquiring new companies such as Warner & Swasey, a machine tool manufacturer. This strategy was aimed at lessening the company's dependence on the declining automobile business, while deploying its assets into faster growing and more profitable endeavors. Accordingly, Mary Cunningham was placed in charge of a task force of seven to prepare a report on the topic. They were called by the auto-motive people "Snow White and the Seven Dwarfs."

"Agee has been tackling the company's organization chart as boldly as its balance sheet. Under Blumenthal, Bendix evolved into a highly centralized orga-nization with a large corporate staff and strict financial controls. A financial man himself, Agee was comfortable with that style of administration, but he gradually became convinced that the company was too bureaucratic and had to be decentral-ized. His conviction was widely shared. 'There is no question that Southfield is too involved in divisional affairs,' admits one former Bendix executive who is otherwise critical of Agee's decentralization plan.

"The timing and execution of decentralization, however, have been mat-ters of sharp debate. 'Bendix is a complex organization,' argues one executive. 'You just can't do all this decentralization at the speed being talked about.' Bill Panny, who ardently opposed the quick pace of decentralization, would agree. 'I don't think all the guys are ready for it,' he said recently. Characteristically, Agee was impatient to do everything at once. So Bendix has begun to dismantle its corporate superstructure. Two hundred people, most of them engineering research personnel, will be relocated. Others, mainly staff people, will be laid off."[2]

Mary Cunningham's rapid rise to the top was also meeting resistance from a conservative organization culture, for in September 1980, just 15 months after she had graduated from Harvard, she was appointed vice president for strategic planning. Unfortunately, amid rumors about the relationship between Agee and his protege, Cunningham finally resigned from Bendix Corp. Sometimes the implemen-tation of the strategic decision is not as easy as it may sound. As Mary Cunningham commented, "There are certainly no Harvard Business School cases on how to deal with this."

Despite these setbacks, Agee's plan for Bendix now is proceeding smoothly. His strategic goal involves a repositioning designed to move Bendix into ventures with a high-technology focus which will more consistently meet long-term growth goals.

STAGE 9: STRATEGIC IMPLEMENTATION

The next stage in the strategic process is the implementation of the strategic decision and game plan. The strategic plan is only that, a plan, until it is put into action. The strategic decisions, such as those at Bendix, must be put into effect in order to achieve strategic objectives. At Bendix, the strategy was implemented by developing specific policies, plans, and action programs aimed at shifting the firm's competitive position and decentralizing operations. After the decision was made by Agee and his top management team, then the actual performance and activities aimed at achieving this plan, including selling off and acquiring companies and the move to reorganize were put into effect.

IT TAKES TIME

The strategy implementation stage is concerned with the design and management of the organization to achieve long-term objectives. This stage, therefore, is of great importance and is often a difficult and time consuming phase of the strategic process. At Esmark, Inc. for example, Chairman Robert W. Reneker took over an unwieldy business with nineteen vice presidents reporting to him and no one else having authority to make a decision. So Esmark was decentralized into "profit centers," each with considerable operating authority, but with tight financial controls from top down to operating units. It took Reneker six years to carry out this restructuring.[3] This supports the findings of Robert W. Ackerman in a study of two organizations, who found that it took six years to implement new top management policies.[4]

A KEY FACTOR

There is also research that suggests that effective policy implementation is a key factor in the success of the strategy of the firm.[5] The resources of the organization must be allocated to reinforce the strategic plan. Therefore, the implementation phase involves the coordination of many diverse elements, products, and functions into an integrated course of action. The manager, then, must be able to translate the "game plan" into action on the field.

The implementation phase is accomplished through adjustments in two major factors: (1) organization culture: the managerial processes and behavior; and (2) organization structure: departmentation and responsibility. The first of these is discussed in this chapter, the second in the next chapter.

WHAT IS IMPLEMENTATION?

Implementation involves the carrying out or accomplishing of certain plans or goals. George A. Steiner (UCLA) and John B. Miner (Georgia State University) suggest that "the implementation of policies and strategies is concerned with the design and management of systems to achieve the best integration of people, structures, processes, and resources, in reaching organizational purposes."[6]

Daniel J. McCarthy, Robert J. Minichiello, and Joseph R. Curran (all of Northeastern University) argue that strategy implementation "consists of securing resources, organizing these resources, and directing the use of these resources within and outside of the organization."[7] On the other hand, Larry Alexander of Oregon State University suggests that, "implementation generally begins after a strategic decision has been made and carries through all the intermediary steps until performance achieves what the strategic decision had intended."[8]

Implementation, then, involves actually executing the strategic game plan. This includes setting policies, designing the organization structure, and developing a corporate culture to enable the attainment of organizational objectives.

AN IMPLEMENTATION MODEL

Larry Alexander has developed an eleven-step model of the implementation process (see Figure 9.1).[9] Each step is presented in a typical order of occurrence, although the implementation of any specific decision may not follow this exact order.

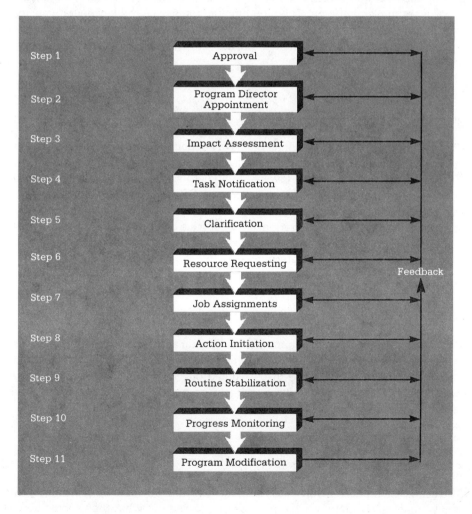

FIGURE 9.1
Key Phases in the Strategic Implementation Process (Alexander).

STEP 1: APPROVAL

The approval phase involves obtaining the formal authorization to proceed with the implementation effort. This consists of getting the approval of key people in top management, including a vote by the board of directors if necessary.

STEP 2: PROGRAM DIRECTOR APPOINTMENT

The program director appointment phase involves the designation of one key person to oversee the entire implementation process. This is often done because the manager making the strategic decision is too busy to also get involved with the details of its subsequent implementation. The program director is usually a key operational manager in top management. The appointment serves to fix responsibility with one individual and to announce to others in the firm the individual who will be heading up the implementation program.

STEP 3: IMPACT ASSESSMENT

The impact assessment phase finds the newly appointed program director determining how the strategic decision will actually effect and change operations in the firm's various departments. He may involve immediate subordinates, staff departments, and key line managers in various departments in this task. It is very important to start this phase early in the implementation process because the actual effect of the strategic decision on the firm's operations may not have been understood by the decision makers. The program director may discuss possible adverse effects on the firm with higher level management to determine how to cope with such situations.

STEP 4: TASK NOTIFICATION

The task notification phase communicates general assignments to the managers in the affected departments. While the overall scope of the task will be communicated, usually the specific details are to be worked out later. This phase may involve a number of levels in the firm and the task may be made more specific as it is passed on to the operating departments.

STEP 5: CLARIFICATION

The clarification phase involves the managers in these lower level operating departments checking back with superiors in order to find out what they should actually do. They may desire a better understanding of the program's intent, ask questions on how to handle specific situations, and present exceptional situations that may require special treatment.

STEP 6: RESOURCE REQUEST

The resource requesting phase involves the releasing of needed finances, manpower, and other resources to the affected operating departments. Although a general discussion of the needed resources will have probably occurred before the strategic decision is made, formal requesting of resources by the operating departments is required later on in most firms. This phase includes the formal requesting of resources, the subsequent negotiating of their specific amounts, and the final releasing of the agreed upon resources. This phase may also include readjusting downward the priorities of other programs and projects in order to implement a new strategic decision on a timely basis.

STEP 7: JOB ASSIGNMENT

The job assignment phase has the managers in the affected operating departments making specific, detailed work assignments to their subordinates. These subordinates are usually not managers themselves; thus they will be personally doing the job assignments.

STEP 8: ACTION INITIATION

The action initiation phase involves the starting up of the plan's requirements by the people in the affected operating departments. This phase takes place over an extended period since the various operating departments probably begin work at different times depending on the nature of their tasks.

STEP 9: ROUTINE STABILIZATION

The routine stabilization phase entails establishing and maintaining rules and procedures to routinely carry out the program requirements on an ongoing basis. Verbal and written procedures are developed within the operating departments as they try to codify the details of how their departmental activities are to be handled. This phase provides reinforcement for the original strategic decision and helps maintain momentum for the new actions being taken.

STEP 10: PROGRESS MONITORING

The progress monitoring phase involves higher level managers checking up on actual performance to determine how the overall program is actually being implemented. It draws upon existing information-gathering procedures as well as new ones that are deemed necessary. These include obtaining regular status reports, reviewing existing performance measures, meeting with the program director or his key subordinates, and assessing reactions of outsiders such as customers. This phase enables the strategic decision makers and the program director to ascertain whether the intent of the earlier decision is actually being met.

STEP 11: PROGRAM MODIFICATION

The program modification phase is the final one and entails making necessary adjustments in the program's original goals. Some changes may be made by the affected departments in order to better achieve the intent of the strategic decision. If some aspects of the implementation program are not working, new ideas are tried. Some other changes may be made in the original goals associated with the strategic decision itself in light of new realities.

As the model suggests, implementation takes place in cascade fashion, moving more or less from the top levels of the organization down to the lower levels. This process requires effective communication among all the managers who are involved. It is clear that the focus is on the integration of managerial actions, that many differing departments, philosophies, and disciplines are involved, and that conflicts are likely to emerge. In the next sections, we shall examine some of the major mechanisms for implementing strategies. In this instance, the strategic decision makers are usually consulted since it may represent a fundamental shift in their original decision.

THE STRATEGIC IMPLEMENTATION SYSTEM

The implementation stage is vital to the success of the organization. Without effective implementation, the strategy may become a set of unobtainable desires rather than a reality. *Business Week,* for example, reported on two major oil companies whose CEOs tried unsuccessfully to implement a new strategy and were replaced.

Each of the CEOs had been unable to implement his strategy, not because it was theoretically wrong or bad but because neither had understood that his company's culture was so entrenched in the traditions and values of doing business as oilmen that employees resisted—and sabotaged—the radical changes that the CEOs tried to impose. Oil operations require long-term investments for long-term rewards; but the new businesses needed short-term views and an emphasis on current returns. Successes had come from hitting it big in wildcatting; but the new success was to be based on such abstractions as market share or numbers growth—all seemingly nebulous concepts to them. Too late did the CEOs realize that strategies can only be implemented with the wholehearted effort and belief of everyone involved. If implementing them violates employees' basic beliefs about their roles in the company, or the traditions that underlie the corporation's culture, they are doomed to fail.[10]

The task of implementation involves a broad range of activities and requires the commitment and cooperation of all units, levels, and members if it is to succeed. William H. Newman (Columbia University) has included planning, organizing, assembling resources, supervising, and coordinating as basic implementation functions, while others include from five to twenty basic activities under implementation.[11] One such list, by Kenneth Andrews (Harvard University), includes twelve major elements of strategy implementation, as shown in Table 9.1.[12]

TABLE 9.1

The Major Elements of Strategy Implementation
1. Once strategy is tentatively or finally set, the key tasks to be performed and kinds of decisions required must be identified.
2. Once the size of operations exceeds the capacity of one person, responsibility for accomplishing key tasks and making decisions must be assigned to individuals or groups.
3. Formal provisions for the coordination of activities thus separated must be made in various ways (hierarchy, committees, task forces, and others).
4. Information systems adequate for coordinating divided functions must be designed and installed.
5. The tasks to be performed should be arranged in a time sequence comprising a program of action or a schedule of targets.
6. Actual performance should be compared to budgeted performance and to standards in order to test achievement, budgeting processes, and the adequacy of the standards themselves.
7. Individuals and groups of individuals must be recruited and assigned to essential tasks in accordance with the specialized or supervisory skills which they possess or can develop.
8. Individual performance should be subjected to influences, constituting a pattern of incentives, which will help to make it effective in accomplishing organizational goals.
9. Since individual motives are complex and multiple, incentives for achievement should range from those that are universally appealing to specialized forms of recognition designed to fit individual needs and unusual accomplishments.
10. A system of constraints, controls, and penalties must be devised to contain nonfunctional activity by individuals and to enforce standards.
11. Provision for the continuing development of requisite technical and managerial skills is a high-priority requirement.
12. Dynamic personal leadership is necessary for continued growth (improves achievement in any organization).

A COMPLEX PROCESS

Essentially, these basic functions may be incorporated in what may be termed the *strategic implementation system*. Peter Lorange (MIT), for example, has commented: "It seems increasingly clear that the systems approach to strategy formulation and implementation, as signified by formal planning systems, is only one of the many aspects relating to effective strategy formulation and implementation . . . several other factors might contribute potentially equally as much or more to a corporation's strategic success . . . Organizational structure and processes is another key area that impacts strategy implementation . . . Finally, formal planning systems cannot function in a vacuum but need to be reinforced by other formal systems such as a management control system, a managerial accounting system, a management information system, and a management incentive/compensation system. . . . In total, formal planning systems is only one part of what seems to be an emerging *strategic administrative system.*"[13]

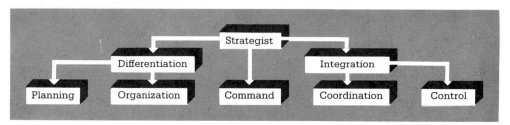

FIGURE 9.2.
The Strategic Implementation System

The strategic implementation process, then, is very complex because it involves two distinct but interrelated task systems as shown in Figure 9.2: (1) *the differentiation,* or organizing task, which involves the segmenting or dividing up of the total project into its subelements or activities; and (2) *the integration,* or coordinating task, which involves coordination of these diverse elements toward the strategic goals. Jay R. Galbraith (Harvard University) has commented on this, "The organizing mode consists first of choices as to how to decompose the overall tasks into subtasks which can be performed by individuals. . . . The organizing choice concerns the means to reintegrate the subtasks into the completion of the whole task."[14]

Strategy must be implemented by dividing up the task among all the sybsystems of the organization: the divisions, departments, products, groups, etc. This will result in a diversity of subgroup goals (marketing vs. engineering, etc.), that may not be totally congruent with total system goals.

AT RALSTON PURINA

At Ralston Purina, for example, chairman R. Hal Dean's strategy had boosted the company to the leading, lowest-cost producer in the pet food industry. However, the company ran into implemention problems. Although well-conceived and successful at first, the strategy late in the 1970s had been poorly executed, and those mistakes were showing up in the company's financial performance.

Dean—convinced that his company's move into high-growth consumer products was basically sound—took steps to implement the strategy again, this time more carefully. Early in 1979, Dean started on the most sweeping management reorganizations in food industry history. Within a nine-month period, he replaced more than a dozen top managers, including Dietrich F. Rosenberg, head of the restaurant group, and Winifred L. Golden, director of new ventures. Their successors, in turn, have replaced scores of subordinates.

By restructuring corporate management, Dean hoped to speed Ralston's recovery of its former dominance in pet food and return his company's consumer products and restaurant divisions to their accustomed 15 percent annual growth rate. To assure closer scrutiny of business decisions, the Ralston chairman also has created four distinct operating groups, with a corporate vice-president appointed as chief operating officer of each one. All four groups have their own boards of directors, which are comprised of executives from other groups. "We've turned rather quickly from darlings to dogs," admits Dean. "We had to pull ourselves up by the bootstraps in all our businesses."[15]

The job of the strategist, then, is to integrate and coordinate these differing subsystems into a total, cohesive strategic system. In the following sections, we shall examine these aspects of strategic implementation.

DIFFERENTIATION

The first phase of the implementation process involves the process of differentiation; that is, dividing the total strategic plan into its component parts: the subunit goals and plans. Differentiation may be defined as "the state of segmentation of the organizational system into subsystems, each of which tends to develop particular attributes in relation to the requirements posed by its relevant external environment."[16]

A TOTAL SYSTEM PLAN

Differentiation is necessary because the overall strategy is a comprehensive plan, but carrying out the plan involves all of the functions and areas of the firm. This includes a multiplicity of activities and at a very detailed level. The purpose of the implementation process is to get organization members working toward accomplishing goals. To do this, a division of tasks, activities and roles must be designed, so as to provide a clear understanding of the responsibility for each part of the plan.

AT OCCIDENTAL

Chief Executive Officer Zoltan Merszei, for example, was trying to bring that kind of system to Occidental Petroleum. "We have to have a system," he declared. "Organization means you're organized." While he praised (Dr. Armand) Hammer (Oxy chairman) for his entrepreneurial success, he was critical of Oxy's lack of management discipline. He made his point in sentences in which he repeatedly emphasized the words "efficient," "lean," "hard-hitting," and "results-oriented." As Merszei viewed it, his job was to consolidate Occidental's diverse businesses, design a management structure, and find top-notch executives to run it. "Dr. Hammer was remarkable in getting the pillars of industry in place," he says. "All I have to do is put on the roof, the walls, and build an edifice."[17]

Therefore, a basic problem facing the manager is how best to organize activities and people to achieve the strategic goals most effectively. This phase involves the organizing and planning functions.

ORGANIZING

One of the first elements of implementation is the assigning of task and responsibility for each primary area of activity. At Boeing Co., for example, a new aircraft project may involve aerodynamic engineering, structural design, electronic and mechanical engineering design, and other special areas such as drafting, production, prototype development, tooling, testing, and marketing functions.

At advanced technology firms, like TRW Systems or Litton, the project system is used to organize the technical and staff specialties. In the project system, a project office is set up for each customer program. The project office reports to a company manager of appropriate rank in the organization with cognizance in the technical area of the project. The overall project organization is similar for each project. The project manager has overall management responsibility for all project activities and directs the activities through the project office, a substructure described in the following terms: The project office is the central location for all projectwide activities such as project schedule, cost and performance control; system planning, system engineering, and system integration; and contract and major subcontract management. Assistant project managers are appointed for these activities as warranted by project scope.

The total project effort is divided into subprojects according to the technical specialty involved, thus matching the basic organization structure. Each subproject has a functional manager who takes project direction from an assistant project manager. The subproject manager is responsible for performance in his functional area (i.e., engineering, design, testing) to the supervisor of the organizational element (engineering, production, etc.) that will perform the subproject work. The subproject manager is the bridge between the project office and this organizational element. The members of the next subordinate level of management in that organization take project direction from him. The work is then further subdivided and performed within their organizations.[18]

PLANNING

Planning is the formal decision process of developing goals and activities through the varied levels of the organization: the linking of detailed subunit plans with the next level, etc. Implementation is typically concerned with:

1 Scheduling of activities
2 Allocating resources
3 Control and integration of operations.

The implementation plan translates strategic goals into operating plans and activities.

SCHEDULING

Scheduling involves the timing of interrelated activities leading toward the total goal accomplishment within a specific time frame. Typically, the planner begins with a start date and completion date, and must then calculate the estimated times for all interrelated activities such as subassembly to assembly, etc. The scheduling activity should involve several differentiation elements, including:

1   Clearly define all task activities and divide subtasks to the lowest operating level.

2   Sequentially lay out activities and identify responsible units for each segment of operations.

3   Specify the time of completion for every task and activity.

The manager must coordinate the departmental actions with those of other functional managers, thus making certain that companywide activities will fit together in the implementation phase.

ALLOCATING RESOURCES

Another important aspect of the planning and implementation phase is the allocation of resources to the operating units. As Peter Drucker has been quoted as saying, "The test of a plan . . . is not how good the plan is itself. The test is whether management actually commits resources to action which will bring results in the future."[19]

SIX TYPES OF ACTION

The allocation of resources is an element in the differentiation stage which includes the following six types of managerial actions:

1   Divides the total operation necessary to achieve objectives into parts (tasks), thus concentrating attention on one task at a time.

2   Plans the necessary sequence and relationship between each of these tasks. Unless the relationships are recognized and monitored closely, individual tasks may cause program inefficiency and delay.

3   Determines who is to be responsible for doing each task. This includes performing units, responsible personnel, and individuals assigned to the program.

4   Decides how each task will be done and what resources will be needed. Program resources may include people, materials and supplies, facilities, and budgets.

5   Estimates the time required for each task, indicating when the task should begin and the time required to complete the operation once it is started.

6   Assigns definite dates when each task is to take place. A fixed date at the end generally governs the schedule, although it is wise to make allowances for sched-

ule slippage. Further, schedule incompatibilities must be accommodated and bottlenecks eliminated.[20]

PERSONAL LEADERSHIP

During the implementation phase, the manager directs operations by means of personal leadership that motivates and directs subordinates' activities. He also is involved in selecting general approaches and assessing the impact of certain actions. However, because implementation also involves human and technical performance, action to secure coordinated effort is equally important. Effective implementation involves a well-defined management plan to ensure the flow of task, schedule, budgetary, and management information for direction and control.

INTEGRATION-COORDINATION

The first phase of strategic implementation facing managers like William Agee (CEO) of Bendix is breaking up the strategic plan into its component parts and allocating resources among the diverse units. But another major function of the strategic manager is to insure the integration of functions and programs among organizational units, over time.

THE INTEGRATION PROCESS

The integration process takes place at three levels:

1 *At the functional level of each business unit* (marketing, manufacturing, etc.);

2 *At the business or product level,* coordinating the various business units (i.e., SBUs); and,

3 *At the corporate level,* where each of the major business plans must be integrated into a total system strategy.

In addition to subdividing activities and responsibility, it is also necessary for the manager to coordinate and integrate these diverse roles and demands into a unified and cohesive approach. This is the integrating function. *Integration* may be termed "the quality of the state of collaboration that exists among departments that are required to achieve unity of effort by the demands of the environment."[21]

Because implementation involves the planning and coordination of processes and resources toward organizational purpose, the organization climate and leadership are important elements. Differentiation among various functional units almost invariably creates a potential for conflict. The integration process, then, is the means by which such conflicts are resolved. In the following sections, we shall examine some of the major aspects of integration.

THE CORPORATE CULTURE

An organization is made up of individual members and each member has unique values, beliefs, and motivations. The leadership style of top management and the norms, values, and beliefs of the organization's members combine to form the *"corporate culture."* Organization effectiveness can be increased by creating a culture that achieves organizational goals and at the same time satisfies members' needs. The CEO's words alone do not produce culture; rather, his actions and those of his managers do, as noted by *Business Week.*

"A corporation's culture can be its major strength when it is consistent with its strategies. Some of the most successful companies have clearly demonstrated that fact, including: *International Business Machines Corp.,* where marketing drives a service philosophy that is almost unparalleled. The company keeps a hot line open 24 hours a day, seven days a week, to service IBM products.

International Telephone & Telegraph Corp., where financial discipline demands total dedication. To beat out the competition in a merger, an executive once called former Chairman Harold S. Geneen at 3 A.M. to get his approval.

Digital Equipment Corp., where an emphasis on innovation creates freedom with responsibility. Employees can set their own hours and working style, but are expected to articulate and support their activities with evidence of progress."[22]

CHANGING THE CULTURE

But the organization culture may also inhibit the implementation of a strategy and prevent a firm from meeting competitive threats or from adapting to changing economic conditions. This can lead to the firm's decline, stagnation or even ultimate demise unless the culture is changed. One company that has systematically changed its cultural emphasis is PepsiCo., Inc. under chairman Donald M. Kendell.

Once the company was content in its No. 2 spot, offering Pepsi as a cheaper alternative to Coca-Cola. But today, a new employee at PepsiCo quickly learns that beating the competition, whether outside or inside the company, is the surest path to success. In its soft-drink, operation, for example, Pepsi's marketers now take on Coke directly, asking consumers to compare the taste of the two colas. That direct confrontation is reflected inside the company as well. Managers are pitted against each other to grab more market share, to work harder, and to wring more profits out of their businesses. Because winning is the key value at Pepsi, losing has its penalties. Consistent runners-up find their jobs gone. Employees know they must win merely to stay in place—and must devastate the competition to get ahead.[23]

Pepsi provides one example of the influence of the corporate culture upon the implementation phase. Another is IBM where new chief executive John R. Opel promises a new aggressiveness. Opel, who picked up the nickname "The Brain" because he asks a lot of probing questions, feels change has been thrust upon IBM. There is more competition than ever, and he intends to maintain IBM's technological leadership.

IBM has been slow to move into new markets, and Opel is concerned that IBM's sheer size makes it difficult to motivate people and adapt to changing conditions. It remains Opel's task to restructure IBM to move into the high-growth markets of the 1980s. One consultant who is optimistic says, "IBM is about as well managed as any company in the industry."[24]

The culture also influences how each member will act toward others and how conflicts will be resolved. The chief executive and others must demonstrate qualities of leadership in this process, because success depends upon individual members' acceptance of the strategic goals and plans.

LEADERSHIP AND IMPLEMENTATION

The importance of leadership and managerial style has been emphasized earlier (see Chap. 2), but is particularly important in the implementation process. Leadership style is a crucial aspect of implementation because it influences a number of other areas: the culture, communications, decision making, and the degree of participation. Therefore, differing managerial or leadership styles have an impact upon how a strategy is implemented. *Business Week* describes one such case.

"At Burroughs Corp., for example, there has been a shift in leadership style as new Chairman W. Michael Blumenthal took over the job of running the Detroit computer firm from Paul S. Mirabito—both of whom represent a dramatic shift from the tough domineering style of former chairman Ray W. Macdonald. Mirabito's quiet, decisive style was in sharp contrast to that of Macdonald, his volatile predecessor. Macdonald ran Burroughs with iron-fisted control, choosing—and sometimes even designing—the products that the company would market. Insiders say the most trivial decisions were made by Macdonald, and one industry executive observes: 'Burroughs has been run like a $100-million company.' "[25]

But if Blumenthal was to succeed, he had to bring a new managerial style to Burroughs' stodgy, inbred management. The leadership style influences the degree of motivation and participation in decision making, which in turn affect the implementation of new strategic direction.

"Perhaps nowhere does Mirabito's determination to change the Burroughs style show up more strongly than in his choice of Blumenthal to succeed him as chairman. Blumenthal's record from 1972 through 1976 as CEO at neighboring Bendix Corp. shows that he chooses his subordinates carefully and lets them run their own business. He stays out of day-to-day operations and delegates that responsibility further down the management ranks than Burroughs management has been accustomed to doing. Those who produced at Bendix got handsome bonuses. Those who did not quickly departed.

"Mirabito was already changing the process of decision making that has kept Burroughs out of so many high-growth areas. 'There's more management participation,' says Donald E. Young, a senior vice president. This shows up now in meetings of the operating committee, where executives now speak as equals with the chairman and where more managers below vice presidential rank are invited to attend the once-secret conclaves."[26]

There are thousands of corporations in the United States, but no two are managed exactly alike. Each company has its own strengths and weaknesses and each chief executive brings his own unique managerial style to bear on system problems. These differences among managers in their approach to the job, as at Burroughs, constitutes the impact of managerial style upon the organization.

INTEGRATING SYSTEMS

The implementation of the firm's strategy, then, involves an interrelationship between strategy and managerial processes. There has been research on the impact of managerial styles and strategic implementation. Pradip N. Khandwalla found that when the leadership style matched the strategy, then the firm was more effective than if it did not. He also noted that under intense competition, decision sharing tends to be much more selective.[27]

Certainly there is no one best way to manage in all situations, but if appears that leadership style is an important factor in effective implementation. Because of the differences in subunit goals and the complexity of strategic activities, conflict is increasingly seen as inevitable. In organizations with complex and interrelated processes, then, there is a need for integrating systems to increase proper coordination and resolution of conflicts that may emerge.

This means that after the strategic plan has been differentiated (that is, broken into specialized parts), it must be integrated and coordinated into a collaborative achievement. The more complex the firm, the greater the need will be for integration.

These integrating activities include such techniques as organization development and management by objectives.

As the late Willian Glueck has commented, "Organizational planning is involved with reviewing and evaluating, on a continuous basis, all organization entities to determine whether the missions, structure, functions, and responsibility relationships are clearly defined and understood, and effectively coordinated to facilitate the overall objectives of the company. Organizational development is providing counsel and guidance that aid and encourage management to develop and clarify its organizational missions; to delineate and group effectively the work to be performed; and to clarify and resolve responsibility relationships that will enable both the organization and its people to realize their mutual objectives. In summary, organizational planning is an approach to organizational problems that places primary emphasis on structured activities and formal analysis of the structures as a way to improve or maintain an effective organization for the company. Organization development is an approach to organization problems that places primary emphasis on behavioral or people activities in attempting to integrate the informal and formal organizations for corporate effectiveness."[28]

In the next section, these integrating methods will be described.

ORGANIZATION DEVELOPMENT

Change is inevitable. Executives are adapting to changing market conditions and, at the same time, facing the need for creating an "anticipative" rather than a "reactive" managerial system. They are searching for ways to manage an increasingly complex technology and a more sophisticated work force. To accomplish these diverse goals, managers need more than piecemeal, *ad hoc* change programs dealing only with current crises. They need long-term efforts to prepare for future organization requirements. One method for bringing about such an anticipated system of management is organization development.

As Richard Beckhard (leading OD practitioner) notes, "Today, there is a need for longer-range, coordinated strategy to develop organization climates, ways of work, relationships, communications systems, and information systems that will be congruent with the predictable and unpredictable requirements of the years ahead."[29]

An organization is made up of individuals. The collective beliefs, values, and motives of these members form the organization culture. Organization development aims at increasing the effectiveness of the organization by improving the collaboration among members and the culture of the organization. The leadership style, the norms, behaviors and values of management all contribute to the culture and influence the way members work together.

As Robert Blake and Jane Mouton have noted, "Organization Development deliberately shifts the emphasis away from the organization's structure, from technical skill, from wherewithal and results *per se,* as it diagnoses the organization's ills. Focusing on organization purposes, the human interaction process, and organization culture, it accepts these as the areas in which problems are preventing the fullest possible integration within the organization.[30]

But a culture that prevents a company from meeting competitive threats, or from adapting to changing economic or social environments, can lead to the company's stagnation and ultimate failure unless it makes a conscious effort to change. These cultural change efforts include activities which are designed to improve the skills, abilities, structure, or motivational levels of organization members. The goals are improved technical skills or improved interpersonal competence. Such implementation efforts may also be directed toward improved leadership, decision making, or problem solving among organization members. The assumption underlying such efforts is that by developing an improved culture, a more effective organization will result.

Because a company's culture is so pervasive, changing it becomes one of the most difficult tasks that any chief executive can undertake. Just as a primitive tribe's survival depended on its ability to react to danger and to alter its way of life when necessary, so must corporations, faced with changing economic, social, and political climates, sometimes radically change their methods of operating.

WHAT IS ORGANIZATION DEVELOPMENT?

Organization development is an emerging discipline aimed at improving the effectiveness of the organization and its members by means of a systematic change program. Chester Barnard and Chris Argyris, among other management theorists, have noted that the truly effective organization is one in which both the organization and the individual can grow and develop. Such an environment may be termed a "healthy" organization and this is what organization development is all about: making organizations healthier and more effective. These concepts apply to all types of organizations including schools, churches, military, government, and industrial concerns.

Change is a way of life in today's organization. But organizations are also faced with maintaining a stable identity and operations in order to accomplish their primary goals. Consequently, organizations involved in managing change have found that the way in which change is handled is critical. There is a need for the use of a systematic approach, discriminating between those features that are healthy and effective and those that are not. Erratic, short-term, unplanned, or haphazard changes may well introduce problems that did not exist before, or the side effects of the change may be worse than the original problem. Managers should also be aware that stability or equilibrium can contribute to a healthy state. Changing just for the sake of changing is not necessarily effective and in fact may be dysfunctional.

A DEFINITION OF ORGANIZATION DEVELOPMENT

Organization development (OD) has been defined as a process designed to increase organizational effectiveness by integrating the desires of individuals for growth and development with organizational goals. Richard Beckhard has suggested that, "organization development is an effort (1) planned, (2) organizationwide, (3) managed from the top, (4) to increase organization effectiveness and health, through (5) planned interventions in the organization's process using behavioral science knowledge.[31]

Organization development efforts then are planned, systematic approaches to change. They involve changes to the total organization or relatively large segments of it. The purpose of OD efforts is to increase the effectiveness of the system, and also to develop the potential of all individual members. Finally, a series of planned behavioral science intervention activities is carried out in collaboration with organization members to help find improved ways of working together toward individual and organizational goals. Another way of gaining an understanding of OD is to explain what it is not.

OD is not a micro approach to change   Management development, for example, is aimed at changing individual behavior, while OD is focused on the macro goal of developing an organizationwide improvement in managerial style.

OD is more than any single technique   While OD change agents use many differing techniques, such as sensitivity training, transactional analysis, or job enrichment, no one technique represents the OD discipline.

OD does not include random or ad hoc changes   OD is based on systematic appraisal and diagnosis of problems, leading to specific types of change efforts.

OD is aimed at more than improving morale or attitudes   OD is aimed at overall organization health and effectiveness. This may include increased participant satisfaction as one aspect of the change effort but also includes other effectiveness parameters, like increased productivity or decreased turnover, etc.

THE CHARACTERISTICS OF ORGANIZATION DEVELOPMENT

To enlarge upon the definition of OD, let us examine some of the basic characteristics of OD programs.

First, as noted, OD is a planned strategy to bring about organizational change   The change effort is aimed at specific objectives and is based on a diagnosis of problem areas.

A second characteristic of OD is the use of an internal or external change agent   Some person or group is responsible for coordinating and facilitating the change effort. In the past few years a growing number of major organizations have created internal OD consulting groups within the organization structure, including Diamond Shamrock, General Electric, General Motors, TRW Systems, Union Carbide, and the U.S. Army. Consequently, the change agent is also either an *external change agent* (an outside consultant called in by the client) or an *internal change agent* (an organization member acting as a change agent). There are advantages and disadvantages involved in both the external and the internal change agent role.

Third, OD always involves a collaborative approach to change   This includes the involvement and participation of those organization members most affected by the changes. Another characteristic of OD is the set of humanistic values about people and organizations aimed at gaining more effective organizations by opening up new opportunities for increased use of human potential.

Finally, OD represents a systems approach   It is concerned with the relationship among various divisions, departments, groups, and individuals as interdependent subsystems of the total organization. Thus, the characteristics of the OD process with an emphasis on people and values should clearly indicate that the OD change agent or practitioner operates differently from more traditional consultants.
     In more general terms, organizational development is based on the notion that an organization, if it is to be effective (accomplish its goals), must be more than merely efficient. It must also be adaptive to change.

OD TECHNIQUES

There are many OD techniques, and any individual change agent may rely on one or a combination of approaches as indicated in Table 9.2. Regardless of the method selected, the objectives are to work from an overall organization perspective which increases the ability of the "whole" to respond to a changing environment.

Team Building   TRW Systems, for example, uses a matrix form of organization. This results in project teams that cut across departmental and even divisional lines, so that employees may be members of several teams at once and report to a number of bosses. "The project office and departmental support group are fundamentally at cross purposes," says D. R. McKell, an industrial relations staffer. "The chief skill

TABLE 9.2
Target Systems and OD Intervention Techniques

Target System	Intervention Technique
1. Personal and interpersonal development	Transactional analysis Behavior modification Gestalt learning Laboratory learning Career planning Managerial grid (phase 1) Stress management
2. Team development	Team building Process consultation Role negotiation Role analysis technique Grid OD (phase 2)
3. Intergroup interface development	Intergroup development Third-party intervention Organization mirror Grid OD (phase 3)
4. Total organization system development	Confrontation meeting Management by objectives Grid OD (phases 4, 5, 6) Survey feedback System 1-4 (Likert) Quality of work life (QWL)

SOURCE: from Donald F. Harvey/Donald Brown, *An Experiential Approach to OD* (2nd ed.). Prentice-Hall, 1982.

needed for matrix is conflict management."[32] From a systematic diagnosis of this situation, TRW initiated an OD program focusing on team-building and intergroup team-building interventions.

Survey Feedback   At Pillsbury, a new executive vice president needed to move quickly to improve the division's performance. With the help of an outside consultant, data were gathered by conducting intensive interviews with top management, as well as with outsiders, to determine key problem areas. Then, without indentifying the source of comments, the management team worked on the information in a ten-hour session until solutions to the major problems were hammered out.[33]

Role Negotiation   *Role negotiation,* a technique developed by Roger Harrison, is directed at the work relationships among group members. The technique basically involves a series of controlled negotiations between participants. In the course of the role negotiation, managers frankly discuss what they want from each other and explain why. The Diamond Shamrock Corporation teaches its managers the art of negotiation with one another during three-day sessions at an off-site, resort setting. Role negotiation seems to be an effective way of improving team performance. At

Diamond Shamrock top management feels the program has produced tangible benefits and more than 200 managers have attended such sessions.[34]

Grid organization development   *Grid organization development* starts with a focus on individual behavior, specifically on the managerial styles of executives. The program then moves through a series of sequential phases involving the work team, the relationships between groups or subunits, and finally to the culture of the organization itself. The Managerial Grid and Grid OD represent one of the most extensively applied approaches to organization improvement and, administered by Scientific Methods, Inc., have been used by such major U.S. corporations as AT&T, Procter & Gamble, Shell Oil, Union Carbide, and Xerox, as well as by a number of foreign organizations. Texas Instruments, for example, has run over 2,200 managers through the Grid, including its president and top executives.

Organizations have objectives—making profits, surviving, growing, etc., while individual members also have desires to achieve, to fulfill unsatisfied needs, and to accomplish career growth in organizations. OD, then, is a process for change whose efforts can benefit both the organization and the individual as well.

MANAGEMENT BY OBJECTIVES

Management by objectives (MBO) is a process aimed at the integration of individual and organization goals.[35] The goals of this approach include an improved level of performance, increased communication and participation, a higher morale and job satisfaction and a better understanding of organization objectives at all levels. MBO may be defined as a system of management implemented to facilitate planning, organizing, problem solving, motivation, and other important management activities. It involves the participation of the subordinate's manager in setting and clarifying the subordinate's goals. George Odiorne (a leading MBO consultant) defines MBO as: "A process whereby the superior and subordinate managers of an organization jointly identify its common goals, define each individual's major areas of responsibility in terms of results expected, and use these measures as guides for operating the unit and assessing the contribution of each of its members."[36]

Anthony Raia (a leading OD consultant and UCLA professor) suggests that management by objectives is a "philosophy of management" that reflects a "proactive" rather than a "reactive" approach to management. It is a philosophy that encourages participative management at all levels of the organization.[37]

THE PURPOSE OF MBO PROGRAMS

There are two underlying purposes for implementing MBO in an organization. One is to clarify organizational goals and plans at all levels; and the other is to gain increased motivation and participation among organization members.

CLARIFYING GOALS

MBO provides a means of increasing the clarity of organization planning and of enhancing the subordinate's knowledge and understanding of his or her job. MBO may be used to identify organization goals at all levels and to encourage participation in setting the standards that will be used to evaluate subordinate performance. Participation in the goal-setting process allows the manager to control and monitor his own performance. He is well able to do this by measuring performance and results against the objectives that he has helped to set. The late Douglas McGregor also suggested a modified approach to MBO under the concept of "management by integration and self control."[38]

MOTIVATION

According to McGregor, the MBO concept could be used to provide an opportunity for managers and subordinates to mutually define and agree upon areas of responsibility, specific performance goals, and the terms of the expected outcomes. He suggested that each manager establish his own performance goals after reaching agreement with his superior regarding his major job responsibilities. After that, his accomplishments would be carefully appraised at the end of a short time period, usually six months. This self-appraisal would be in cooperation with his superior, after which another set of performance goals would be established. McGregor aimed at the commitment of organization members by the "creation of conditions such that the members of an organization can achieve their own goals best by directing their efforts toward the success of the enterprise."[39] He advocated this concept as a means for appraising performance, since it shifted the emphasis from weakness and criticism to an analysis of strength and potential. In this application of MBO the supervisor's role is one of counseling, coaching, or process consultation.

In order for MBO to be used effectively, then, it should include (1) a team approach to setting and reviewing targets; (2) real participation by subordinates in setting goals, with an emphasis upon mutually agreed upon goals; and (3) a real concern for personal career goals as well as for organization goals. When MBO is used in this sense, it can provide individual satisfaction and motivation as well as increased organization attainment.

Among the major premises of MBO are the following:

1 The first step in management is to identify the goals of the organization.

2 Responsibility for achieving these goals is developed among individual managers.

3 Managerial behavior is assumed to be more important than personality, and this should be defined in terms of results. Participation in goal setting and decision making is highly desirable.

4 The successful manager is a manager of situations; thus, there is no one best way of managing. Rather the managerial behavior best calculated to achieve results in each situation will be most effective.

THE MBO PROCESS

The MBO process usually includes the following phases:

1 The top management team studies the operating system.

2 From this study, it sets up measures of organizational performance.

3 Goal setting sessions are then held down through the first-line supervisory level.

Although opinions vary on the specific implementation of MBO, most practitioners emphasize the need for top management's commitment to MBO. The central focus of any MBO program is the development of agreement between supervisor and subordinate about continuing objectives and targets.

Management by objectives may be described as a process consisting of a series of interrelated steps.

Step 1 The subordinate proposes a set of goals for the upcoming time period. This proposal sets forth specific goals and performance measures.

Step 2 The subordinate and the superior jointly develop specific goals and targets. These goals must be specific, measurable objectives for each area of responsibility, and they must be mutually agreed upon by subordinate and superior. The major responsibility, of course, should lie with the subordinate. These objectives should include both performance goals and personal development goals.

Step 3 A period of performance in which actual performance of the individual involved is measured against his individual goals.

Step 4 The feedback of results to the individual and appropriate rewards for performance. This individual performance review involves an appraisal of accomplishments and variances of overall performance compared with targets and is discussed by subordinate and superior.

Step 5 The outcome of the performance review provides the basis for setting new performance goals and recycling of the goal-setting process.

In setting objectives, every effort should be made by the superior and the subordinate to make them as precise and specific as possible. There must be agreement and acceptance of these objectives by both the individual and his superior. These interactions between a manager and a subordinate also provide a counseling and coaching opportunity and in this manner provide for management development. Although these specific steps in the MBO process may vary among organizations and practitioners, the goals are similar, including increased levels of performance and increased understanding at all levels of organization objectives.

THE RESULTS OF MBO

MBO has been tried by many different organizations. One difficulty in appraising this approach is that MBO has become an all-purpose term implying many different things in many different organizational settings. Stephen J. Carroll and Henry L. Tosi, in a study of eighty-seven organizations using MBO, concluded that there are at least ten different approaches to MBO, ranging from motivational to coercive. Most research on MBO programs has reported mixed results. Some studies indicate that MBO has increased organization performance, and others indicate inefficiency and weakness in application. While research on the effectiveness of MBO is not conclusive, the trend of findings is generally favorable. Several studies have found that goal setting results in improved performance and increased motivation and "have found that those managers working under MBO programs were more likely to have taken specific actions to improve performance, than were those who continued with the traditional performance appraisal approach."[40] Other evidence shows that MBO seems to be associated with positive attitudes toward the work situation and that participation by subordinates in decision making can improve performance level and job satisfaction.

Some research on MBO programs indicates that this technique can improve organization performance. In a two-part study at Purex Corporation, Anthony Raia (UCLA) reported that MBO reversed production rates from a .4 percent decline per month to an increase of .3 percent per month. In a second followup study, however, he found that participants felt that the program overemphasized production, was used as a whip, and failed to involve all levels of management.[41]

MANAGERIAL IMPLICATIONS

The strategic manager needs to realize that implementation is an essential stage in the strategic process. The decision alone is valueless until it is put into action. The strategic decision is implemented by developing specific and detailed policies, plans, and action programs aimed at achieving strategic goals. The objectives, plans, and controls enable management to link together the complex yet interrelated functions and activities necessary to accomplish desired goals.

THE STRATEGIC IMPLEMENTATION MODEL

A model for strategic implementation has been presented. Implementation involves the integration of resources, tasks, and goals. The process involves clearly deciding what to do, how to do it, directing performance, and controlling results. The effectiveness of a strategy is often determined by the implementation function.

As William Agee found at Bendix, implementing the strategic plan is often a difficult and costly endeavor. *Fortune* puts it this way:

"Agee may be further along in his thinking than he is willing to disclose. One area that is almost certain to receive an infusion of cash is Bendix's flourishing aerospace business. Says vice president Bill Purple, 'we have in essence unlimited opportunities.' And, as one might suspect, Agee has been spending a lot of time examining potential acquisitions. 'I've been looking at that company for three years,' Agee coyly remarked to some visitors, without disclosing any more information, after hanging up the telephone. He hints that he could announce a major acquisition soon.

"While he is reinventing Bendix, Agee will have to find the right people to help him do the job. With Panny gone, his top priority is finding a new No. 2. And he will be looking for another strategic planner to succeed Mary Cunningham. At best, the job that Agee has begun is only half done. Now that the Mary and Bill soap opera seems to have run its course, Bill Agee had better get back to work."[42]

BACK ON THE JOB

"Mary Cunningham, who resigned as vice president at Bendix Corp. after rumors linked her romantically with the company chairman, has accepted a new job with Joseph E. Seagram & Sons Inc. Miss Cunningham, 29, formerly vice president in charge of strategic planning at Bendix, accepted a similar position, at an annual salary reputed to be in the six figures."

THE IMPLEMENTATION PROCESS

The implementation process involves both differentiation, the breaking down of plans into basic elements, *and integration,* the coordination of diverse functions into a cohesive action. The manager must also be aware of the organizational culture, and understand the use of control systems, organization development, management by objectives and other techniques to effectively carry out the implementation of strategic decisions.

The key to success in implementation involves integrating the component elements into a total organizational system. This suggests a broad-based approach to planning, coordinating, and measuring performance toward strategic goals.

THE CORPORATE CULTURE

Change is an inevitable consequence of operating in a dynamic environment. For strategic managers, it is important to recognize that organization development techniques can be used to change the corporate culture to fit the new strategy. Management by objectives (MBO) can also be a powerful determinant of performance when it is used to tie together the strategic goals, plans, and implementation.

As John A. Young, CEO of Hewlett-Packard has commented, "Every company has kind of a culture to it, in the way it's grown up, it's got peculiar industrial relations things that are part of its history. By no means would I claim that the H-P style, the kind of people-oriented management system, is readily transportable. I think the fundamentals could apply to literally any business but it takes a lot of work to change a company over to a different style. Any style change would be different because the culture of the company is deeply rooted."[43]

Many strategists feel that the implementation is perhaps more critical than the decision itself. As more and more chief executives recognize the importance of the implementation of longer-range strategies, they will have to consider the effect of the strategy upon the organization. It will be up to the CEO to decide whether he must change his strategy to fit corporate culture, or change the culture in order to ensure survival. At any rate, strategic implementation is an important and difficult process.

A CRITICAL PHASE

Effective performance in the implementation phase is complex and requires more than recognition of effectiveness and efficiency: Multiple criteria are involved. There is no one best way to manage, nor to implement a strategy. There are no hard rules or equations. The key to implementation is the ability to analyze each situation, each organization, and each group of members. Managerial skill is as important in this function as in the other stages of the strategic process. In the future, implementation will involve a greater concern over productivity, better ways of allocating resources, and more adaptive leadership styles.

REVIEW QUESTIONS

1   What are some of the important factors in strategic implementation? If you were CEO of an old-line company like Bendix, how would you implement a strategic change?

2   The development of a "corporate culture" calls for continuing action. What type of corporate culture would you like? How does this fit in with your managerial style?

3   What is organization development, and how might it be used?

4   What is MBO, and what are some reasons for the success or failure of such programs?

5   The MBO approach is widely used by major firms. How could it be used in your class? Find a company that uses MBO, and talk to a manager to find out how it works.

ENDNOTES

1   Peter W. Bernstein, "Upheaval at Bendix," *Fortune,* November 3, 1980, 48.

2   Ibid., 52.

3   "Esmark Spawns a Thousand Profit Centers," *Business Week,* August 3, 1974, 48–52.

4   Robert W. Ackerman, *Managing Corporate Responsibility* (Boston, Mass.: Harvard University Press, 1975).

5   Charles Leighton and G. Robert Tod, "After the Acquisition: Continuing Challenge," ICCH #9-378-727, 1977.

6 George A. Steiner and John B. Miner, *Management Policy and Strategy: Text Readings and Cases* (New York: Macmillan, 1977), p. 607.

7 Daniel J. McCarthy, Robert J. Minichiello, and Joseph R. Curran, *Business Policy and Strategy: Concepts and Readings* (Homewood, Ill.: Irwin, 1979).

8 Larry D. Alexander, *"Strategy Implementation: The Neglected Element in the Strategic Process,"* Paper presented at the Academy of Management, August 1980.

9 Ibid.

10 "Corporate Culture," *Business Week,* October 27, 1980, 148.

11. William H. Newman and James P. Logan, *Strategy, Policy, and Central Management* (Cincinnati: South-Western Publishing Co., 1976).

12 Kenneth R. Andrews, *The Concept of Corporate Strategy* (Homewood, Ill.: Dow-Jones Irwin, 1971).

13 Peter Lorange, "Formal Planning Systems: Their Role in Strategy Formulation and Implementation," paper presented at a conference on "Business Policy and Planning Research: The State of the Art," University of Pittsburgh, May 1977.

14 Jay R. Galbraith, *Organization Design* (Reading, Mass.: Addison-Wesley Publishing Co., 1977), pp. 6–7.

15 "Corporate Strategies: Ralston Purina: Turnabout at the Top of Checkerboard Square," *Business Week,* September 10, 1979, 112.

16 Paul R. Lawrence and Jay W. Lorsch. "Differentiation and Integration in Complex Organizations," *Administrative Science Quarterly,* (1967), 3.

17 Susie Nazem, "Occidental Petroleum's Odd Couple," *Fortune,* November 19, 1979, 72.

18 See H. Rush, *Behavioral Science: Concepts and Management Application* (New York: National Industrial Conference Board, 1969), 158–59.

19 David W. Ewing (ed.), *Long Range Planning for Management* (New York: Harper & Row, 1972), p. 5.

20 See Charles C. Martin, *Project Management: How to Make it Work* (New York: AMACOM, 1976), chaps. 4–6.

21 P. Lawrence and J. Lorsch, *Organization and Environment: Managing Differentiation and Integration* (Boston: Harvard University, Graduate School of Business Administration, Division of Research, 1967).

22 "Corporate Culture," 148.

23 Ibid.

24 "No. 1's Awesome Strategy," *Business Week,* June 8, 1981, 84–90.

25 "The Burroughs Syndrome," *Business Week,* November 12, 1979, 82.

26 Ibid.

27 Pradip Khandwalla, "Some Top Management Styles," *Organization and Administrative Sciences,* Winter 1976, 21–51.

28 William Glueck, "Organization Planning and Development," 10–11.

29 Richard Beckhard, *Organization Development: Strategies and Models* (Reading, Mass.: Addision-Wesley, 1969), p. 8.

30 "Corporate Culture," 148. See also Wendell L. French and Cecil H. Bell, Jr., *Organization Development,* 2nd ed. (Englewood Cliffs, N.J.: Prentice-Hall, Inc., 1978), p. 18; Frank Friedlander and Dave L. Brown, *Organization Development,* in *Annual Review Psychology,* 25 (1974), p. 336.

31 Richard Beckhard, *Organizational Development: Strategies and Models* (Reading, Mass.: Addison-Wesley, 1969), p. 9.

32 "Team Work Through Conflict," *Business Week,* March 20, 1971, 44.

33 "A New Face Jolts Pillsbury," *Business Week,* May 2, 1977, 92, 97.

34 "They're Striking Some Strange Bargains at Diamond Shamrock," *Fortune,* January 1976, 142–46, 148–52, 156.

35 This decription is based upon S. Carroll and H. Tosi, Jr., *Management by Objectives, Applications and Research* (New York: MacMillan, 1973); George Odiorne, *Management by Objectives* (New

York: Pitman Publishing Corp., 1965); Anthony Raia, *Managing by Objectives* (Glenview, Ill.: Scott, Foresman, 1974).

36 George Odiorne, *MBO II* (Belmont, Calif.: Feron Pitman Publishing, Inc., 1979), p. 53.

37 Raia, *Managing by Objectives,* p. 11.

38 Douglas M. McGregor, *The Human Side of Enterprise* (New York: McGraw-Hill, 1960), p. 61. Also Douglas McGregor, "An Uneasy Look at Performance Appraisal," *Harvard Business Review,* May–June 1957, 89–94.

39 McGregor, *Human Side,* p. 62.

40 Carroll and Tosi, *Management by Objectives.*

41 See Raia, *Managing by Objectives;* H. Meyer, E. Kay, and J. French, "Split Roles and Performance Appraisal," *Harvard Business Review,* January–February 1965, 123.

42 Bernstein, "Upheaval at Bendix," 53.

43 *Spokesman Review* (Spokane), November 12, 1980.

C H A P T E R

10

The simplest organization structure that will do the job is the best one. What makes an organization structure "good" are the problems it does not create. The simpler the structure, the less that can go wrong.

Peter Drucker, educator and consultant, quoting from his *Management, Tasks, Responsibilities, Practices* (New York: Harper and Row, 1974), pp. 40–41.

Designing a Strategically Effective Organization

CHAPTER OBJECTIVES

When you have completed this chapter, you will be able to:

☐ *Demonstrate, from a contingency perspective, an understanding of the basic types of organizational design and their relationship to environmental uncertainty.*

☐ *Identify the appropriate structure to fit the strategy.*

☐ *Develop your skills in using the concepts of control, communication, delegation, and decentralization as part of the strategic process.*

☐ *Analyze a complex management case using the concepts of this chapter.*

LEARNING THE MATRIX[1]

Robert E. Kirby

Since the mid 1960s, impelled by divergent management and operating philosophies, General Electric and Westinghouse have been heading in two distinctly different directions. Now, the results of those crucial differences in strategy are coming to the surface. And they reveal the perils that even a giant corporation can face when its top management fails to foresee the risks of single mindedly pursuing high-cost markets while placing minimal controls over its divisions. Now the new chairman and CEO of Westinghouse, Robert F. Kirby is trying to reestablish profitability and control to the company. Kirby, who is known for his skill in mathematical games and puzzle-solving, can solve in a few minutes a puzzle that would take the average person several hours. Kirby likes to compete and use his skills at other diversions. A near-par golfer, Kirby occasionally plays in Pro-Am tournaments and is a jazz clarinetist—a profession he almost pursued after getting his chemical engineering degree from Penn State University in 1939. As a manager, he is given particularly high marks for the selection and development of junior executives. "We find people early in their careers, in their early thirties, and review their performance regularly," says Kirby. "For each manager, there are three people identified to replace him and one must be under 40." Kirby has been involved in attempting to transform Westinghouse from a basically domestic company, albeit with substantial foreign business, into a full-fledged multinational.

"The transformation promises to be turbulent. All organizations exist for particular purposes and goals and strive for efficiency in achieving these objectives. To maximize this effectiveness, top mangers attempt to organize and structure their internal resources so as to increase the implementation of strategy and policy. For example, most Westinghouse executives were raised in a management structure based on *product* lines—a structure that was accentuated, if anything, when the company was reorganized five years ago into thirty-seven operating groups known as "business units." Now, however, the business unit managers will have to coordinate their foreign strategies and operations with those of a new international hierarchy organized along geographical lines.

"They will be learning to live, in short, with the more complex "*matrix*" system, which has two chains of command instead of one. Thus, the manager of a factory in Brazil will be reporting to a new Westinghouse manager who oversees the activities of all business units in that country, as well as to a business unit manager in charge of electrical distribution equipment. In effect, he will be reporting to two bosses. Many Westinghouse executives will have trouble adapting to this new arrangement, which requires *considerable interaction* and *consensus decision making at all levels*. Kirby has told the company's top 220 managers that 'some of you will adjust and survive, and some of you won't.' "[2]

Organization structure, then, is one element of strategic implementation. There are many factors which influence the choice of structure, as Robert Kirby of Westinghouse found, including the size, technology, and complexity of the organization. The situation at Westinghouse provides a graphic illustration of the problem facing all companies in program execution. The organization structure must reflect the basic mission, goals, and strategic programs of top management if it is to be effective.

STRATEGIC IMPLEMENTATION: FROM STRATEGY TO ACTION

The strategic choice is both an end and a beginning. It represents the end of the strategy formulation phase and the beginning of the implementation phase. Strategic implementation which involves the development of functional processes, as well as the organization structure and climate, is an extremely important and complex process in all organizations. Formulating policy and strategy and developing a game plan without carrying out the execution of the plan is a wasted effort.

If the strategic choice signals the commitment of resources, then the implementation phase means accomplishing the goals the firm has set out to achieve. This includes the engineers who design the new product, the manufacturing people who convert raw materials into finished products, and the marketing people who must advertise, sell and distribute this product to the customer. Therefore, the implementation involves the coordination of many differing groups and diverse skills into carrying out the strategic game plan.

STRATEGY AND STRUCTURE

Organization structure refers to the logical relationship of functions and authority arranged to accomplish objectives in an efficient manner.

According to Peter Drucker, "Good organization structure does not by itself produce good performance—just as a good constitution does not guarantee great presidents, or good laws, or a moral society. But a poor organization structure makes good performance impossible, no matter how good the individual managers may be. To improve organizational structure . . . will therefore always improve performance."[3] The assumption underlying structural change is that task performance is improved by redefining the separation of tasks and the relationships between functions.

STRUCTURE

Structure involves the pattern of relationships among operating units of the organization. McKinsey & Company studied one company where 223 separate operating committees had to approve an idea before it could be put into production. Can you imagine how long it would take to make decisions and how difficult it would be to use an innovative strategy in such an organization?

The strategist seeks to develop a structural arrangement that allows for the coordination and control of activities. At Westinghouse, for example, Robert Kirby decided upon a strategy of multinational growth. He found that a different structure was necessary to effectively carry out this strategy. Similarly, at Dow Chemical with over 2,300 different products, top management decided to become a global organization in the early 1960s. In a sweeping move, Dow decentralized its operations by using a matrix structure with autonomous geographic units in the expanding overseas markets. The strategist seeks to develop a structural arrangement that allows for the effective coordination and control of activities.

When Joseph B. Flavin, for example, took over as Chairman of the ailing Singer Company, he had to make organizational changes quickly. With the help of a consultant, Flavin examined the existing structure and restructured the relationship between corporate staff and line operations. "Our line people were good," said Flavin, "Our weaknesses were in corporate headquarters."[4]

For years Singer acted as if the sewing machine operation could run without a cohesive plan. Extraordinary latitude was given to top management. Small empires were created in this hands-off atmosphere.

Flavin was late to diagnose the situation when he arrived, and now, assuming he survives as chief executive, he will have to live with it for some time to come.

At Singer, the people were performing well, but the method used to organize the line operations was simply not effective. The emphasis here is placed on altering organization structure as a means of attaining new strategic goals.

AN INTEGRATION NETWORK

An organization may be viewed as an interconnecting network of elements. Through this network or structure flow the resources, information, and materials that allow the major activities to be accomplished. A structural design change attempts to improve organization efficiency by redefining the flow of authority (vertical) and responsibility (horizontal).

J. Thomas Cannon, a former consultant with McKinsey & Company, suggests that: "The experience of McKinsey supports the view that neither strategy nor structure can be determined independently of the other . . . Strategy can rarely succeed without an appropriate structure. In almost every kind of large-scale enterprise, examples can be found where well-conceived strategic plans were thwarted by an organization structure that delayed the execution of the plans or gave priority to the wrong set of considerations. . . . Good structure is inseparably linked to strategy."[5]

"There has been a great deal of research which demonstrates the relationship between strategy and structure." Eric Rhenman, for example, found that in Swedish firms strategic change without corresponding changes in structure led to problems.[6]

WESTINGHOUSE

Westinghouse also found that a strategy of rapid growth without an appropriate organization structure caused problems. In place of an overall corporate design for growth and development, the company ran during most of the 1960s by the output of a computerized planning system that got most of its input from middle management sources. Pervading the whole corporation was the fuzzy philosophy of achieving rapid growth by entering whatever field appeared promising at the moment and gaining volume without regard to risk.[7]

The strategist is concerned with managing systems. The manager designs the organization, establishes objectives, and creates mechanisms to integrate the operation units. All organizations exist to maximize their effectiveness within the constraints of limited resources. Organizational design, then, is one factor of managerial choice. Given a certain strategy or game plan, the manager must then select the system design that best fits this strategic choice.

STRUCTURE FOLLOWS STRATEGY

Alfred Chandler of the Harvard Business School first suggested that structure evolves from strategy in his study of seventy large firms. He found, for example, that when firms shifted to a diversification strategy, they tended to change their structure to a divisional form. There have been other studies which have reported a similar relationship between strategy and structure.[8]

Chandler noted that, "The comparision emphasizes that a company's strategy in time determined its structure and that the common denominator of structure and strategy has been the application of the enterprise's resources to market demand. Structure has been the design for integrating the enterprise's existing resources to current demand; strategy has been the plan for the allocation of resources to anticipated demands."[9]

As the organization's strategy changes from a single-product to multiple-product diversification, the structure in effective organizations also tends to change. There have been several research studies which support this shift as the firm diversifies. Leonard Wrigley (University of Western Ontario) found that almost 86 percent of the *Fortune* 500 companies used the divisional structure,[10] and Richard Rumelt (UCLA) found in a separate study of large companies that 75 percent used a divisional form.[11]

ORGANIZATIONAL GROWTH MODELS

The concept of organizational stages of development has emerged as a result of Chandler's book, *Strategy and Structure*. The organizational growth model suggests that as a firm evolves it tends to go through different stages of growth and development. Firms at different points in the cycle face different economic conditions and competitive situations and therefore require different structural designs to be effective.

There are several stages of development theories, for example, those of Cannon (1968); Thain (1969); and Scott (1973).[12] Although varying in the specific details, each of these models emphasizes that managerial style and organizational structure changes are associated with growth. These basic models propose that there

Characteristics	Entrepreneurial I	Functional Development II	Decentralization III	Staff Proliferation IV	Recentralization V
Strategic decisions	Made mostly by top person	Made more and more by other managers	May have "loss of control"	Corporate staff assists in decisions	Corporate management makes decisions
Organization structure	Informal operations	Specialization based on functions	To cope with problems of functionalization By industry or product divisions	Corporate staff assists chief executive	Similar to Stage II
Communication and climate	From leader down: informal communications	Internal communication is important, is difficult		Conservatism may result in slower communications	
Control system	Minimal need for coordination and control	Concerned with everyday situations	Problems with control	May be problems between line and staff	Tightening of control

FIGURE 10.1

Cannon's Stages of Development

SOURCE: Adapted from J. Thomas Cannon, *Business Strategy and Policy* (New York: Harcourt Brace Jovanovich, 1968), pp. 525–28.

is a continuum of organizational forms from very basic at one extreme to very complex at the other and that as the firm develops there is movement toward more complex forms. Each stage represents an adaptation to changing conditions. In general, the development goes through a three-stage cycle from a small, single-product company (stage 1) to a specialized functional company (stage 2), and finally, to a multiproduct, diversified company (stage 3—see Figure 10.1). These stages will be described in the following sections.

STAGE I ENTREPRENEURIAL

A Stage I firm is a small, single-product company which typically is operated as a one-man show. The top man makes almost all strategic and operating decisions and works through an informal structure and communication network. All functions are handled by the entrepreneur, and most employees report directly to the boss. There is usually little formal strategic planning, and decisions are usually based on intuitive judgment.

As an example of a Stage I firm, Hewlett-Packard was started by Bill Hewlett and Dave Packard in a Palo Alto garage in 1939 to build test equipment: an audio oscillator. The two engineer-managers did it all: they designed, built, tested, and marketed their product. They created the managerial style, set up an informal structure, and made all the decisions.[13]

STAGE II FUNCTIONAL DEVELOPMENT

A Stage II organization is still a single-product company, but with an expanded size and scope of operation. Because of its increased size and complexity, it can no longer be managed by one individual with informal systems. As a result, the company is divided into specialized units and operating decisions are delegated to managers in charge of marketing, production, etc. Group decision making is used in strategic decisions. The planning and budgeting systems are now formalized. The structure is formalized which means that it is based on areas of responsibility. The top manager makes the critical strategic decisions and spends more time on external concerns.

At Hewlett-Packard, as the firm grew out of the garage and began buiding greater volumes and types of test equipment, Hewlett and Packard's role became more of a top management job: making key strategic decisions. Now functional managers were running the various segments of the company in a relatively autonomous manner, although still tying in closely with the owners. At this point, it was impossible for Hewlett and Packard to make all of the myriad of operating decisions that needed to be made. They could no longer become involved in detailed design decisions as they once had. H-P was now a functional organization.

STAGE III DIVISIONAL DIVERSIFIED FIRMS

A Stage III firm has outgrown its single product line and become a multiple-product operation. The organization structure is more complex, divided into semi-autonomous "profit centers" or product groups. The operating decisions are handled by the unit/ division managers, while strategic planning and decisions are typically handled by corporate headquarters. They usually have a formal planning group for gathering information and communication of plans. In the divisionalized structure, the corporate headquarters usually is concerned with financial controls and the allocation of resources, but all other operations are delegated to the units, thus removing routine decision-making chores. In effect, the Stage III firm is a collection of smaller businesses.

HEWLETT-PACKARD

Hewlett-Packard's leadership position in instruments allowed it to diversify into computers, calculators, and components. For Bill H. Hewlett and Dave Packard the task became one of coordinating and controlling the activities of these semi-autonomous units. The responsibility for operating decisions was delegated to plant, product, or division managers, while they retained the responsibility for tight fiscal controls and the strategic planning function.

None of Hewlett-Packards' forty-two divisions ever employs more than 1,200 people so that they maintain a manageable size, and H-P is one of the top five firms in the percentage of sales spent on R & D. The famed decentralized H-P management structure is a direct result of that emphasis on new products. "Nobody could plan that centrally, you'd be crazy to try. That's why we have 42 divisions, because each one of them has a general manager, they have all the marketing resources, they all have a product development team, they're really running a small business."[14]

The move into Stage III may be either by internal development of new products as at Hewlett-Packard, or by acquisition. Donald H. Thain has suggested that, "the key skills necessary to be an outstanding general manager . . . shift from short-term operating ability in Stage I, to product functional emphasis in Stage II, and to broader management abilities, including investment, trusteeship, diversification, and management supervision and development in Stage III."[15]

AMERICAN SIGN & INDICATOR CORP.

As another example of the stages of growth model, consider the American Sign & Indicator Corporation of Spokane. The company was formed in the late 1940s by Luke Williams and his brother Chuck as a commercial sign business, but a major breakthrough occurred in 1951, when Chuck suggested an electrical sign with alternating time and temperature. At that point, AS&I was a *stage one* firm: an entrepreneurial company managed and operated by the two owners.

As the sign business grew, the firm moved into *stage two:* a functionally managed firm. Luke and Chuck Williams focused more on strategic management decisions and planning, while functional managers directed marketing, manufacturing, etc.

By 1980, American Sign has become the largest firm of its kind, building and leasing over 90 percent of the time and temperature displays in the United States.

The firm has also branched into other products in the digital information field, including Sports Information Systems (computer-controlled sports scoreboards) including the Silver Dome in Pontiac, Michigan, and Unex, a computerized display system for airport terminals, shopping centers, etc. As the firm, which now employs approximately 1,500 people, moves into the multiproduct stage, there will probably be a structural change to reflect this move. Perhaps AS&I will soon move into *stage three:* a multidivisional operation with a centralized corporate planning group.[16]

RESEARCH FINDINGS

Research by Bruce Scott indicates that firms moving into Stage III are more profitable than those in Stage I or Stage II. This is supported by the fact that almost 90 percent of the *Fortune* 500 firms are using the divisionalized structural form (Stage III).

Derek Channon (University of Manchester) reported similar results in a study of 100 of the largest firms in Great Britain. From 1950 to 1970 he found that single business firms decreased while dominant firms shifted to a multidivisional structure from only 11 percent in 1950 to 70 percent by 1970.[17] Perhaps the most important results obtained from this research related to the effectiveness of the firms. Comparisons were made for firms whose strategies fit their structures—international divisions or area divisions under conditions of no diversification and worldwide product divisions when there was considerable diversification—and for those that did not. The results suggest that growth in sales is greatest when a diversified growth strategy is coupled with the appropriate structure.

THE CONTINGENCY APPROACH

According to Fremont S. Kast and James E. Rosenzweig (University of Washington), a contingency approach, in a broad definition, "attempts to understand the interrelationships within and among organizational units as well as between the organization and its environment. It emphasizes the complex nature of organizations and attempts to interpret and understand how they operate under varying conditions and in specific situations. The approach strives to aid managers by suggesting organizational design strategies which have the highest probability of succeeding in a specific situation. The success criteria revolve around the accomplishment of organizational goals."[18]

THE ORGANIZATIONAL FIT MODEL

Jay R. Galbraith and Daniel A. Nathanson (of the Wharton School) have extended and revised this model of growth as shown in Figure 10.2. They suggest that the strategy of the firm determines to a large extent the fit with other elements, including the task, structure, information and decision processes, reward systems and people, which then determines the level of performance and results. In total, all these choices must create an internally consistent design. If one practice is changed, the other dimensions must be altered to maintain fit. Similarly, if the strategy is changed, then all the dimensions may need to be altered.[19]

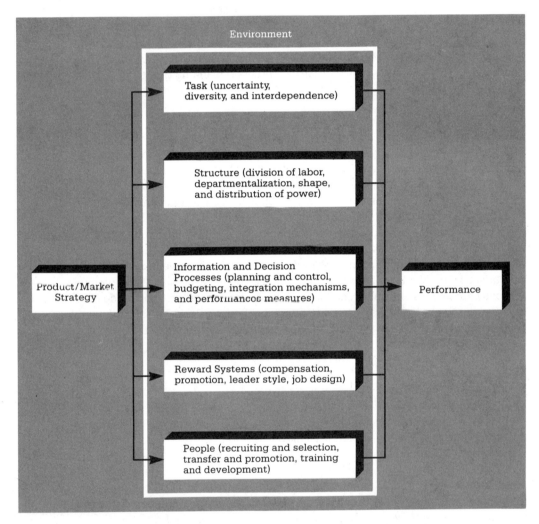

FIGURE 10.2

Flow of Relationships in the Organizational Fit Model

SOURCE: Adapted from Jay R. Galbraith and Daniel A. Nathanson, *Strategy Implementation: The Role of Structure and Process.* St. Paul, Minn.: West, 1978, p. 96.

Galbraith and Nathanson also suggest that a firm may follow one of several tracks of growth, with some firms moving on one track (from functional to divisional), while others may move from holding company to multidivisional, etc., as shown in Figure 10.3—the final result in the stage of evolution being a global multinational firm. Westinghouse, an example of a firm that has moved through these stages of growth, is now moving from the multiproduct divisional form to the multinational matrix organization.

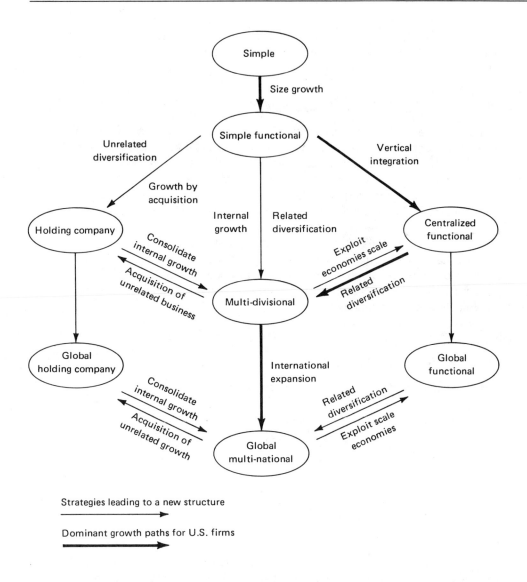

FIGURE 10.3
An Extended Stages-of-Growth Model

A CONTINGENCY MODEL

The early writers on organization structure suggested that there was a best way to design organizations. During the past few years, however, attitudes have changed, and structure has come to be regarded as dependent upon other critical variables. This approach to organization design is called the *contingency approach* and suggests that there is no one best way to structure the organization; instead the design depends upon other factors. The contingency approach suggests that design factors are complex, and that certain designs work best under certain conditions.

THE LAWRENCE AND LORSCH MODEL

Paul Lawrence and Jay Lorsch (Harvard University) have suggested that, "the basic assumption underlying the theory is that organizational variables are in a complex interrelationship with one another and with conditions in the environment."[20] Organizations must be designed according to the tasks they are trying to perform. The high performers in each industry had achieved a fit with their environment. Highly uncertain environments, for example, require a higher degree of both differentiation and integration for effective performance.

Integration, they feel, is most appropriately achieved through confrontation or negotiated problem solving, rather than through either smoothing over differences or forcing resolutions through the use of power or authority. Thus where the demand for integration is high, in uncertain environments, confrontation should prevail in effective organizations.

FOUR BASIC PREMISES

The Lawrence and Lorsch model has four basic premises:

1 There is no single best way to design organizations.

2 The specific design of an organization and/or its subunits must fit both the environment and the technology.

3 The needs of individual organization members are better satisfied when the organization and its subunits are properly designed.

4 Some organizations or their subunits are improperly designed and should be changed or modified.[21]

The effective organization needs both a level of differentiation that matches the diversity of the environment and a similar level of integration. The more differentiation, the greater the need for collaboration and coordination.

FOUR DIMENSIONS

The Lawrence and Lorsch model indicates that differentiation occurs in four basic dimensions.

1. Formality of structure. The degree to which an organization's subsystems have narrow spans of control, rules, regulations, and other formalized procedures. Formality of structure tends to be greater in such departments as manufacturing and finance.

2. Interpersonal orientation.   Members of units that have either highly certain or highly uncertain tasks tend to be more concerned with the tasks than with personal relationships. Members of units with moderately uncertain tasks are concerned about establishing positive social relationships. Manufacturing people tend to be concerned with tasks; sales and marketing people tend to be concerned with relationships.

3. Time orientation.   Subunits that have relatively immediate feedback, such as sales and production, have a much shorter time orientation than do subunits that may not get feedback for months or years, such as research and development. Manufacturing may be highly concerned with meeting daily schedules, while product development may be primarily interested in long-range thinking.

4. Goal orientation.   Different units may have very different goal orientations. Manufacturing may prefer to have a small number of high-volume products, while sales may want a wide variety of products in order to increase the level of overall sales.[22]

RESEARCH FINDINGS

There are other findings which support the contingency approach. Donald K. Clifford, Jr., studied 103 rapidly growing companies and found that: "The 'right' structure for each company at any point in time is a function of five determinants: (1) corporate objectives and plans . . . (2) the number of distinct businesses making up the company . . . (3) the key factors for success in each major line of business . . . (4) organizational principles (adopted by the company) . . . and (5) the management capability, style and personality."[23]

However, there are no theories which fully explain the relationship between design and strategic situation. The manager must attempt to identify which structural elements are most appropriate in the implementation of any specific strategy. However, a number of studies suggest that as a company develops over time there are corresponding changes in its structure.

MOVEMENT TO DECENTRALIZATION

A major emphasis of structural change is the concept of *decentralization,* which refers to moving decision making to lower levels of the organization, thus increasing the authority of lower managers. The real issue is not whether a company needs to decentralize but rather how much. In determining the actual amount of decentralization existing in an organization, the scope and level of decision making must be assessed. In a highly centralized structure, individual managers at lower levels in the organization have a rather narrow range of decisions or actions they can initiate. On the other hand, the scope of authority to make decisions and take actions is rather broad for lower-level managers in a decentralized organization. For example, in a highly centralized organization structure, top management makes all major decisions.

In a decentralized structure, the decision making responsibility is dispersed to business or product management. *Business Week* described one move toward decentralization that came in 1979.

ESB-RAY-O-VAC

"President David C. Dawson of ESB Ray-O-Vac Corporation last month began a massive corporate reorganization aimed at solving the problem that is at the root of the company's declining share of the battery market—its failure to develop and market new products fast enough to keep pace with more aggressive competitors such as Union Carbide Corp., whose Eveready division is the nation's largest battery maker, as well as Gould, Inc. and P. R. Mallory & Co.

"To do that, Dawson is eliminating a major layer of corporate supervision that he believes stifled the marketing of new battery products. His reorganization calls for wholesale decentralization. It divides ESB into four clearly defined and fairly autonomous operating companies and places much greater responsibility for performance on managers in the field. Among other things, each company will now conduct its own research and product development work."[24]

A decentralized organization is possible whenever an organization's tasks are self-contained and centered around products or markets. In a decentralized organization, managers only have to worry about their own product or service. They have the resources to carry out these activities, and they don't have to compete for shared resources.[25]

The strengths of the decentralized structure include:

1 The design is more flexible and suited for quick changes.
2 There is a high product, project, and program visibility.
3 There is a full-time task orientation (i.e., profits, etc.).
4 The task responsibility and contact points are clear to customers.
5 The organization is able to process multiple tasks in parallel, and it is easy to cross functional lines.

The *weakness* of a decentralized structure include:

1 The restriction of innovation and growth to existing project areas.
2 The difficulty of allocating pooled resources.
3 The difficulty of coordinating shared functions.
4 The deterioration of in-depth competence.
5 The possibility of internal task and priority conflicts.
6 The high level of integration required in the organization.

In a study of thirty diverse manufacturing firms in India, Anant R. Negandhi and Bernard C. Reimann found a marked tendency for decentralized firms to be more effective. In the more effective firms, the decentralization was also likely to be accompanied by formalized integrative systems dealing with manpower planning, employee selection, compensation, appraisal, and training.[26]

NESTLÉ'S DECENTRALIZATION

"As Nestlé company's Swiss managers sought to increase U.S. business to 30% of the corporate total, each U.S. operation reported directly to Managing Director Arthur Furer at Nestlé's Vevey headquarters. Unable, however, to reach its goal—despite several acquisitions in the 1970s—Nestlé is now putting together a new, far more aggressive U.S. strategy.

"The company's first step has been to decentralize its operations in the U.S., strengthening management style so that it resembles that of its U.S. food competitors. But there have been other dramatic changes as well, including:

- A centralization of U.S. management authority under David E. Guerrant, the first American-born Nestlé employee to rise quickly through the ranks.
- A new-product blitz.
- A major attempt to increase productivity.
- Expansion of recently acquired nonfood enterprises."[27]

Although such delegation of responsibility is common at U.S. multinational corporations, it represents a dramatic change for Nestlé.

MATRIX ORGANIZATION

One new approach that has evolved out of contingency approaches is the matrix organization. This approach came into prominence during the late 1960s, when the aerospace industry began using it. The matrix combines the functional and project types of structure and is often used to coordinate efforts on large, complex projects. The *matrix organization* may be defined as "any organization that employs a *multiple command system* that includes not only a multiple command structure but also related support mechanisms and an associated organizational culture and behavior patterns."[28]

The matrix organization is formed around specific products or projects (see Figure 10.4), with individuals assigned to a project and a functional department.[29] The advantage of the matrix form is that it provides horizontal groupings of a number of functions to accomplish project objectives under the direction of a project or product manager. It is most effective in large organizations with multiple products, innovative technology, and changing markets. TRW Systems is an example of a company using a matrix design where a team is formed for each special project, cutting across departmental lines. As a result, an employee may be a member of several project teams and report to a number of bosses.

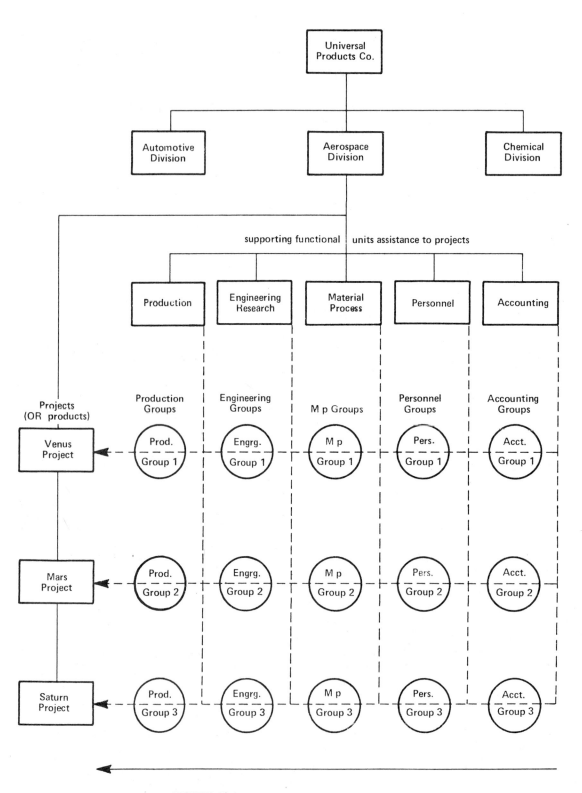

FIGURE 10.4

Diagrammatic Representation: Matrix Organization

SOURCE: Adapted from J. Mee, "Ideational Items: Matrix Organizations," Business Horizons, 7, Summer 1964, 70–72.

STRENGTHS/WEAKNESSES

The *strengths* of the matrix organization include:

1   The full-time focus of personnel on the project or matrix.
2   The matrix manager being the coordinator of functions for each project.
3   The reduction of information requirements and focus on a single product or market.
4   The focus of specialized technical skills to each product or market.

The *weaknesses* of the matrix organization include:

1   The costliness of maintaining a personnel pool to staff the matrix.
2   The participant's experience of dual authority of matrix managers and functional area managers.
3   The small amount of interchange with functional groups outside the matrix, so there may be duplication of effort.
4   The matrix participant's need to have good interpersonal skills in order for it to work.

AT INTERNATIONAL MINERALS AND CHEMICALS

In the mid-1970s, Tony Cascino, vice chairman of International Minerals and Chemicals Corporation (IMC), faced a crisis that threatened to break down the company's problem solving and decision-making processes.

The company's structure had evolved from simple functional design to one that was a complex array of project management and decentralization. Cascino recognized, however, that internal complexities and external environmental turbulence can increase to such a degree that a more effective structure has to be devised. To IMC and Cascino, the answer was a matrix structure.

After six years with matrix management, Cascino learned a number of important lessons from which other managers may benefit. Some of the most important include:

—In the early stages of implementation the structure should not only be put in place in manageable degrees, but minimal concern should be given to rules, titles, and authority. Experience is the best guide to establishing procedures.

—Success rests more on the behavior of people than on structure—the internal operations, therefore, must stress cooperation, not power plays.

—Avoid the condition of "two bosses": the preference was to refer to the "peer group," which minimized authority challenges.

—Keep top management informed but don't let them get too involved in day-to-day activities; whenever this occurred, otherwise good working sessions deteriorated into a series of unproductive meetings and presentations.

—The compensation package for managers must be structured to accommodate both vertical (functional) and horizontal (product) obligations.

—Top management must, in spirit, philosophy, and practice, promote and support the matrix approach.

Matrix structure has helped IMC improve operations, productivity, profitability, and overall working relationships. Its major contribution has been in the development of managers—with the matrix approach improving managerial skills and performance.[30]

In short the matrix offers certain advantages and certain problems, but it can be an effective design under the right conditions. At Westinghouse, for example, top management needs greater flexibility and control in multinational operations, and feel that the matrix is the answer. They recognize, however, that increased interaction skills, consensual decision making, and conflict management will be required if it is to work.

THE DECISION TREE MODEL

It appears that there is no best way to organize that meets the demands of all situations. Management must analyze the relevant factors and develop a structure that

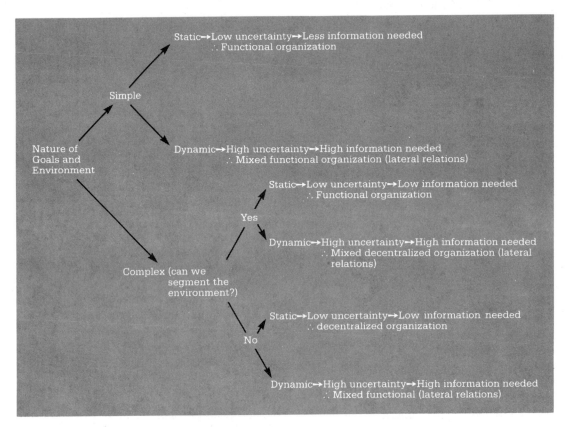

FIGURE 10.5

Organizational Design Decision Tree Model

SOURCE: Robert Duncan, "What Is the Right Organization Structure?" *Organization Dynamics,* Winter 1979.

best fits the situational demands. Robert Duncan (Northwestern University) has developed a decision tree analysis technique which sets forth a process for selecting the right structure to fit the demands of the environment.[31]

As shown in Figure 10.5, the decision analysis indicates when functional, decentralized, or lateral relations (matrix) should be selected. First, the manager must determine the state of the environment, simple or complex, and whether these factors are static or dynamic. Based upon these two factors, the manager can then identify the type of structure which best fits the environment. However, Duncan cautions that managers must be sensitive to the fact that environments are constantly changing, so contingency planning may be useful.

MANAGERIAL IMPLICATIONS

Organizational design is an important factor in the implementation phase—the development of an appropriate structure for the organization.

STRUCTURE FOLLOWS STRATEGY

Chandler's major contribution is the finding that "structure follows strategy." Therefore, the structure is determined, in part, by the type of strategy which is chosen by the organization.

One means of finding a more effective way of allocating resources is the organizational structure. Structural change provides one technique for the strategist, thereby enabling the firm to implement its strategy effectively. The successful use of this element requires that the structure be adapted to fit the environment, the technology, and the stage of growth of the firm.

THE CONTINGENCY APPROACH

The contingency approach offers one approach to organizational design problems. This approach stresses an analysis of the environment, the internal culture, technology, and the strategy as key determining variables in the selection of the best form. *As the environment becomes more complex and dynamic, then a more decentralized structure becomes more appropriate.*

There is no single best design for all organizations. Size, technology, rate of change, complexity, geographic dispersion—all suggest and influence ways of organizing. An organization represents a highly complex open system, with a large number of inputs, processes, and outputs to be managed. Further, managing a large corporation is a constantly changing and dynamic process, because social, economic and technical conditions are constantly changing. The contingency models suggest that relatively static, centralized structures will work under stable, predictable conditions, but under dynamic, uncertain conditions, a more decentralized, flexible structure is appropriate.

THE MATRIX DESIGN

The matrix design, which combines the functional and project structures, is becoming a popular form of organization structure. While it must be recognized that there are problems with this design, it is often found to be effective for firms which operate in a dynamic and complex environment, as is the case for many multinational corporations.

A STRATEGIC DECISION

Coordinating the various departments and divisions of an organization is an extremely important and difficult management activity. Depending on the need for coordination, a number of structural mechanisms are available to the strategist. From the most basic policies to the most complex integrating departments, these structural techniques provide the desired level of managerial control, participant motivation, and organizational resources to the various operating units.

Thus, in the final analysis the selection of an organization structure is a strategic decision. Perhaps the most important lesson of this chapter is that the strategists should not accept the design as a given, without question. Instead the strategist needs to be questioning the design as strategy changes, to determine if the structure and culture fit the current strategy. If it does not, then like Robert Kirby of Westinghouse, the manager must consider changing to more innovative approaches to meet these new and changing conditions.

REVIEW QUESTIONS

1　Identify some of the key factors in designing an organization structure.

2　Explain the contingency theory of design.

2　How might one use a model (such as Duncan's) in determining an appropriate structure?

4　Under what conditions would you recommend the use of a matrix design? How might the matrix design be applied to the business school you attend?

5　Explain the sentence, "There is no one best way to design organizations."

6　How does organization strategy influence structure? For example, when a firm operates internationally, like Westinghouse, what are some of the considerations in selecting an appropriate design?

ENDNOTES

1　See Hugh Menzies, "Westinghouse Takes Aim at the World," *Fortune,* Jan. 14, 1980, 48; "The Luster Dims at Westinghouse," *Business Week,* July 20, 1974, 1, 54; "The Opposites," *Business Week,* January 31, 1977, 60.

2   Ibid.

3   Peter Drucker, *The Practice of Management* (New York: Harper and Row, Publishers, 1954), p. 225.

4   Adapted from Thomas O'Hanlon, "Behind the Snafu at Singer," *Fortune,* November 5, 1979, 76–79.

5   J. Thomas Cannon, *Business Strategy and Policy* (New York: Harcourt, Brace and World, 1968).

6   Eric Rhenman, *Organization Theory for Long-Range Planning,* (New York: Wiley, 1973).

7   "The Opposites."

8   Alfred Chandler, Jr., *Strategy and Structure* (Cambridge, Mass.: M.I.T. Press, 1967) and Richard Hill and James Hlavacek, "Learning From Failures," *California Management Review,* Summer 1977, 5–16.

9   Chandler, *Strategy and Structure.*

10 Leonard Wrigley, "Divisional Autonomy and Diversification," (unpublished D.B.A. thesis, Harvard Business School, Boston, 1977).

11 Richard P. Rumelt, *Strategy, Structure, and Economic Performance* (Boston: Harvard University Press, 1974).

12 Malcolm Salter, "Stages of Corporate Development," *Journal of Business Policy* 1, no. 1 (1970), 23–37.

13 Hewlett-Packard: "Where Slower Growth is Smarter Management." *Business Week,* June 9, 1975, 50–54, 56, 58.

14 *Spokesman-Review* (Spokane) November 12, 1980.

15 Donald H. Thain, "Stages of Corporate Development," *Business Quarterly,* Winter 1969.

16 See Luke Williams, "The American Sign Story," AS&I booklet, November 6, 1975.

17 Bruce Scott, "The Industrial States: Old Myths and New Realities," *Harvard Business Review,* March–April 1973; and Derek F. Channon, *The Strategy and Structure of British Enterprise* (Boston, Mass.: Harvard University, Graduate School of Business Administration, 1973).

18 Fremont S. Kast and James E. Rosenzweig, *"Contingency Views of Organization," Aid Management* (Chicago: Science Research Associates, 1973).

19 Jay R. Galbraith and Daniel Nathanson, *Strategic Implementation: The Role of Structure and Process* (St. Paul, Minn.: West, 1978).

20 Paul Lawrence and Jay Lorsch, *Organization and Environment: Managing Differentiation and Integration* (Boston: Harvard University, Graduate School of Business Administration, Division of Research, 1967).

21 Ibid. p. 157.

22 Ibid.

23 Donald K. Clifford, Jr., *Managing the Threshold Company* (New York: McKinsey and Co. Inc., 1973). p. 26.

24 "ESB Ray-O-Vac: Decentralizing to Recharge Its Innovation Spirit," *Business Week,* March 12, 1979, p. 116.

25 Robert Duncan, "What Is the Right Organization Structure?" *Organizational Dynamics,* Winter 1979.

26 Anant R. Negandhi and Bernard C. Reimann, "Task Environment, Decentralization, and Organizational Effectiveness," *Human Relations,* 26 (1973), 302–314.

27 "Nestlé: Centralizing to Win a Bigger Payoff from the U.S." *Business Week,* February 2, 1981, 56–58.

28 Stanley M. Davis and Paul R. Lawrence, "Problems of Matrix Organizations," *Harvard Business Review,* May–June, 1978, 131–42.

29 Donald Harvey, "Organizational Adaptation and the Matrix Design," *Arizona Business,* Arizona State University, August–September 1972, 19.

30 Adapted from A. E. Cascino, "How One Company Adapted Matrix Management in a Crisis," *Management Review,* November 1979, 57–61.

31 Robert Duncan, "What is the Right Organization Structure?" *Organizational Dynamics,* Winter, 1977.

CHAPTER

11

"Any American corporation, in order to be successful, cannot do business in a way that is socially unacceptable. You won't be permitted to."

William D. Ruckelshaus, Senior Vice President, Weyerhaeuser Company, quoted in Thomas Griffith, "Weyerhaeuser Gets Set for the 21st Century," *Fortune*, April 1977, 75.

Strategic Implementation and External Systems: Social Responsibility and Multinational Forces

CHAPTER OBJECTIVES

When you have finished this chapter, you will be able to:

☐ *Understand the impact of external systems on strategy.*

☐ *Compare and contrast domestic and multinational issues.*

☐ *Assess and anticipate potential problems arising from external system relationships in strategic implementation.*

☐ *Use the concepts of this chapter in analyzing a complex case.*

WEYERHAEUSER'S ENVIRONMENTAL STRATEGY: SEIZE THE DATA BASE

George W. Weyerhaeuser

George W. Weyerhaeuser, President of Weyerhaeuser Company, a giant Pacific Northwest timber company, has earned a reputation for running a tightly managed, but conservative company. The company tries to use its economic forces; it also tries to adapt to social criticism, not just by subtle, low-key PR campaigns, but by genuine efforts to minimize the environmental consequences of its activities.

Two factors make managing the company difficult: first, the timber industry must operate on a long time horizon. Consequently, Weyerhaeuser must do strategic planning for up to 100 years into the future, covering the time it takes to grow a new stand of Douglas fir.

Second, a great deal of effort is put into managing the constant tension between economic land management and the environmentalists who wish to restrict the use of forest lands. Where once about 50 percent of wood used to be left on the ground, Weyerhaeuser now uses 98 percent of the tree: what it doesn't use as chips or wood pulp, it burns at its mills to reduce energy costs. And bringing its mills up to environmental standards has added about 15 percent to its cost of doing business. One environmental group has referred to it as the "best of the SOBs."

"Weyerhaeuser has earned this double-edged compliment by being a well-managed, careful, aggressive company. It throws its weight around when it can. It also mollifies its critics, not just by adroit low-key public relations, but by genuine and expensive efforts to minimize the objectionable effects of its activities. What makes Weyerhaeuser so interesting a company is that its executives share the Pacific Northwest's desire to remain as much as possible like it is, while being driven by an economic impulse that will substantially change the area," *Fortune* reports.

"Weyerhaeuser already has a clear idea of where it intends to be in the twenty-first century. (You get to thinking that way in the forest industry, where the decision you make today, and the tree you plant tomorrow, won't bring in any revenue until fifty years from now.) It hasn't yet sold those intentions to its twentieth-century neighbors, and that's what makes the drama in Weyerhaeuser's well-ordered life."[1]

Yet Weyerhaeuser has not resisted environmental demands and, in fact, has often found that forced changes have led to benefits. This attitude of social responsibility has been reinforced by the arrival of William D. Ruckelshaus, former deputy attorney general.

"Lean, lanky, and low-keyed at forty-four, Ruckelshaus seems to fit easily with Weyerhaeuser's new young top executives. Their soft-voiced manner may in part result from sharing a large luxurious open-floor arrangement where all executives, including George Weyerhaeuser in the center, have their desks and sofas separated only by waist-high partitions and potted plants. Nobody on the executive floor speaks loudly while standing up."[2] Weyerhaeuser's most effective strategy in social issues involves lobbying in Washington, D.C., and supplying accurate data to congressmen, a strategy referred to as *"seizing the data base."* Negative resistance after the fact is not Weyerhaeuser's usual style. Its real gift is for getting on top of an issue before it gets in the papers; to "surface concerns," to participate in any legislation it sees coming, and in George Weyerhaeuser's words "to be ahead of criticism— to be our own advance critics." Because it must operate among the environmentalists and critics, Weyerhaeuser seems genuinely concerned about listening to what its opponents have to say, and in gaining their involvement in the development of the region.

STRATEGY AND POLICY: AN OPEN SYSTEM PERSPECTIVE

Organizations do not exist in isolation. They are continually in contact with other external systems that are exerting forces on them that change over time. These outside pressure groups include governments, customers, and other interest groups. Because of these factors, the strategist must assess the relationship of the firm to these external systems. Just as Weyerhaeuser must deal with environmental groups and governmental standards in its operations, so must each strategist consider the impact of his strategy on the broader society.

EXTERNAL INFLUENCES

These external forces require an open system view or perspective on the part of the strategist, as mentioned earlier in Chapters Three and Four. The external environment directly or indirectly exerts an influence on the firm in several ways:

1 Exerting an influence on internal processes and structure.

2 Presenting opportunities and threats for survival and growth.

3 Affecting the amount of discretionary action, or freedom of activity allowed in strategic decisions.[3]

Today, virtually every major management strategy is affected by some element or pressure group from its external environment (see Figure 11.1). The various

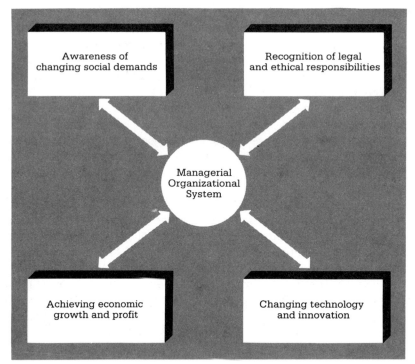

FIGURE 11.1
Strategic Management in a Complex World.

strategies may not be considered as isolated elements, but rather as systems reacting to and impacting the larger environment. Thus, strategic decisions in any one part of the environment, business, government, consumer, etc., will have repercussions throughout the environment, because all of the elements are interrelated and interdependent. A strategic decision by Weyerhaeuser has implications for environmental groups, the public, consumers, homebuilders, governmental agencies, and others, as well as for the organization itself.

AN OPEN SYSTEM PERSPECTIVE

This suggests that corporate strategy must be examined from an open systems perspective, based on the assumption that the firm exists in a complex environment in interaction with organizational elements. Functioning in these situations may be termed *"managing within constraints."* Therefore, one of the essential activities of strategic management is the continuous need to adapt to forces in the external environment. In this chapter we will focus on these external systems, specifically on social responsibility and multinational forces, and their broad implications for strategic management.

SOCIAL RESPONSIBILITY AND STRATEGIC IMPLICATIONS

During the past decade, the sociocultural environment of business has changed significantly, resulting in a new and different role for the business firm in relation to its social environment. Social responsibility is a new and increasingly difficult dimension in strategic management. According to Vernon M. Buehler and Y. K. Shetty, socially responsible management involves several factors:

1 Management must have an awareness of the firm's obligation to solve some of the problems of society.

2 Management must be willing to work on solving these problems.

3 Management must actually be willing to commit resources toward actions involving these problem areas.[4]

As a result of these shifting forces and values, many firms have become very active in large-scale social programs, such as poverty, pollution, etc. Managers of today are being asked to make decisions which attempt to balance the outcomes for a variety of groups including consumers, employees, and the public.

WHAT IS SOCIAL RESPONSIBILITY?

In the past, the responsibility of business involved the most efficient use of resources to provide a high-quality, low-cost standard of living for the larger society through the free enterprise system. There is a growing body of evidence that the social role of business has changed dramatically. This change involves a new role for managers and has changed the nature of the strategic management task within large corporations. Now there is a broader general responsibility for actions for the social good of all beyond the law or demands of social custom. These issues include ecological impact, consumer protection, human development, social justice, and ethics.

Social responsibility may be defined as "actions that protect and improve the welfare of society along with its own interests."[5]

Because of this emerging concept of corporate social responsibility, there has been a change in the relationship between the organization and its environment. The public has devoted an increasing amount of attention to problems such as pollution control, health, safety, impacts of business operations on local communities, product quality and safety, and the like. These concerns have also resulted in a proliferation of new laws and regulatory agencies that restrict business activities as they affect society. The long-term outcome of these problems and restrictions is a dramatic change in the "rules of the game" by which business is expected to operate.

This changing relationship between business and external systems has, of course, had an impact on the managerial task. Managers now have to incorporate social and political concerns into their strategic decision making.

TWO MODELS OF BUSINESS BEHAVIOR

There are two differing models or viewpoints regarding the social responsibility of business. The traditional economic model based on the classical role of business suggests that business should maximize profits and leave social programs to other institutions. The socio-economic model suggests that there are broader social goals, and business obligations in areas other than purely economic.

THE TRADITIONAL ECONOMIC MODEL

Many people question whether social problems should be placed on the door step of the manager. Milton Friedman, the Nobel Prize winning economist from the University of Chicago, suggests that any diversion of resources from the task of maximizing stockholder wealth is unfair to the stockholder.

". . . There is one and only one social responsibility of business—to use its resources and engage in activities designed to increase its profits so long as it stays within the rules of the game, which is to say, engages in open and free competition, without deception or fraud . . . Few trends could so thoroughly undermine the very foundations of our free society as the acceptance by corporate officials of a social responsibility other than to make as much money for their stockholders as possible. This is a fundamentally subversive doctrine."[6]

Friedman's view is that managers' actions are constrained by the economic need of their companies. Profit and positive cash flow are still the report card for most firms. Friedman emphasizes that no manager can afford to jeopardize the firm's financial position for social programs.

One Boise Cascade Corporation program provides an example of this. It backed a minority enterprise which ended up with a loss of approximately $40 million to the firm. The loss resulted in a decreasing stock price and, because of this action, angry stockholders tried to get Boise's officers to resign.

THE SOCIO-ECONOMIC MODEL

The second model proposes that social responsibility is part of corporate "good citizenship" because of the immense power and impact of giant corporations. From this viewpoint, government and business are both contributors and, therefore, must cooperate in solving the larger problems of society. This view, suggesting that when social goals change so does the responsibility of corporations, is expressed by Fletcher Byrom, chairman of the board of Koppers Company, as follows: "You can't continue a business without profit, but profits are not the be-all and end-all of the corporation . . . If it does not at the same time serve the needs of society, then the corporation as an instrumentality of accomplishment will surely perish, and deserves to perish."[7]

There are many arguments supporting this view. As Kenneth Andrews has suggested, ". . . corporate executives of the caliber, integrity, intelligence, and humanity required to run substantial companies cannot be expected to confine themselves to their narrow economic activity and to ignore its social consequences."[8]

Another authority, Neil H. Jacoby, suggests that "There is no conflict between profit maximization and corporate social activity, because the contemporary corporation must become socially involved in order to maximize its profits."[9]

In summary, this model suggests that in the long run it is in the best interest of business to improve the environment in which it exists.

Which of the two models best applies? It is up to each manager and organization to determine which view is most important. In general, most concerns would probably select a balanced approach, as in the case of Weyerhaeuser, attempting to perform against multiple standards. Certainly, no enlightened manager today can simply ignore social demands.

THE STRATEGIC MANAGER

The strategic manager's job, then, can be viewed as one of managing complex systems. The strategist must recognize the contribution and interdependence of each of the interrelated elements, and consider these forces in responding to the external environment. The social responsibility aspects of strategic implementation require even more awareness and skill. These factors include a greater recognition of the external systems, the emergence of political awareness enabling the resolution of conflicting interests, the communication skills to clearly articulate the company's position on complex issues, and the ability to integrate economic goals with external pressures to form a comprehensive framework for strategic decision making and implementation.

THE SOCIOPOLITICAL SYSTEM

An organization is interrelated to the larger society and its external environment. Therefore, the scope of managerial activity and responsibility extends beyond economic exchange. Social involvement is the interaction of the organization as a system with other organizations and with society as a whole. This relationship may be characterized as a system consisting of a set of interrelated subsystems.

In this systems model, the organization can be considered as a micro part of the larger environment. As a result, the organization and society are neither completely free from nor completely controlled by one another, but instead form interdependent units, each affected by the others' actions. Therefore, in strategic implementation the strategist must consider the potential conflicts and impacts arising from these interwoven relationships.

The sociopolitical system is shown in Figure 11.1, and identifies a number of systems which interact with, or even are in conflict with the organization. The major subsystems will be discussed in the following sections.

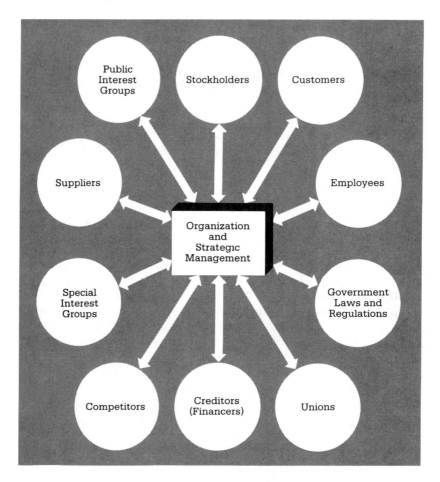

FIGURE 11.2
The Sociopolitical System.

ENVIRONMENTAL GROUP SUBSYSTEM

Environmental groups have emerged in the past few years with a focus on maintaining the quality of the environment. These groups are perhaps characterized by the Sierra Club, which seeks to maintain open, untouched wilderness areas for public use, while other environmental groups are concerned with pollution and control of hazardous wastes. Companies as diverse as Weyerhaeuser, Dow Chemical, and ARCO all must consider the impact of strategies on the environment prior to implementation.

   The environmental groups continue to issue challenges. For example, in the mid-1970s Weyerhaeuser showed the forestry industry a new way of enhancing social relationships. The Weyerhaeuser Co. (and two other companies) collectively donated 19,395 acres of forest land valued at $7,215,000 to public agencies, with instructions that the land be preserved in its natural state. Thousands of individuals will be able to enjoy large areas of unspoiled wilderness as a result of this corporate generosity.

In 1972 Xerox Corporation, on the one hand, continued to pay the salaries of twenty-one employees who were given from six months to one year's leave of absence to work on community development programs of their choice.[10]

Dow Chemical, on the other hand, planned on building a new plant in California. When the plant was held up by environmental protests, it was forced to cancel the plant and change its plans. A California Power Company invested over $30 million during the five-year development of a new coal-fired power complex in Utah, but was forced to write it off because of environmental problems, rising costs, and continuing delays.

Some of the widely published social problems include:

- The recall of over a million Firestone 500 radial tires.
- The pollution of the Niagra River by an Olin plant.
- The recall of Ford Pintos because of safety issues.
- The asbestos-related problems of Johns-Manville workers.

CONSUMER GROUP SUBSYSTEM

Consumer groups of recent emergence have also frankly challenged the older, "let the buyer beware" approach to selling products. The focus of these groups is on the safety and quality of products sold to the consumer. Social response to the consumer movement has resulted in two different approaches. The first approach is reluctant compliance to organized public pressures and emerging consumer legislation. Consumer advocate Ralph Nader has stimulated much of this compliance. The second approach is social awareness, where businesses take the initiative in promoting consumer satisfaction and voluntarily cooperate with consumer demands. One promising development has been the creation of consumer-affairs departments in an increasing number of firms. Polaroid provides one example of this new concern for the consumer: Polaroid Corp., in Cambridge, Massachusetts, maintains a 300-person consumer services department to perform such chores as rewriting ads that might mislead buyers and dropping in on Polaroid camera repair centers to check on quality. And—because small stores sometimes duck customer complaints—the department makes sure that Polaroid's free service phone number is printed in big type on every product.[11] Consumer satisfaction is being emphasized in other, more fundamental, ways as well. For example, concern for product safety is playing a greater role during the product design stage in many industries.

Once again, in today's world the strategist must consider these consumer forces as an element in the implementation of a given strategy.

GOVERNMENTAL SUBSYSTEMS

Government regulations also place important constraints on organizational strategy. There are a multitude of Federal regulations and requirements which influence the operation of the firm. One important influence is legislation, such as Equal Employment Opportunity (EEO) which places pressure on organizations regarding discrimination against minorities in employment and promotion.

Managers must strive continuously to keep up with growing new legal constraints placed on their activities, but merely following the law is not enough. There is a need for increasing compliance and a spirit of affirmative cooperation between government and businesses. Environmental protection, then, is one of the social responsibilities of strategic management. Robert Leone (Harvard University) identifies the crux of the problem: "The incredible array of environmental protection laws passed in the last few years has created its own by-product of confusion that seems every bit as murky as our skies or rivers ever were. My examination of the laws and their effects on several major industries—paper, oil, aluminum, lead, metal finishing and electroplating among them—suggests that even the most diligent managers don't understand the complex and pervasive ways in which environmental controls have affected vast segments of our economy."[12]

Each organization must provide reports and plans to show compliance with the law, especially those that do business with the government. Many companies have been sued for alleged discriminatory practices, and AT&T, for example, had to pay $15 million as a result of one lawsuit. There is also the cost of doing business under such regulations, and it is estimated that firms spend millions of dollars in setting up, maintaining and reporting on such programs. One example is 3M Company's "Pollution Prevention Pays" (3P) program. This innovative ecological program received from the EPA a special commendation. The overall goal of the 3P program is "to get personnel to stop thinking about pollution removal and instead stress product reformulation, equipment changes, process modification, and materials recovery."[13] Once again, the strategist must be aware of possible governmental implications in any strategic move.

Given these changing concepts of social responsibility, and the changing role of business in relation to the larger society, strategy becomes a complex function of the interplay among the external constraints and the organization's goals and resources. It has become necessary for the manager to understand the external systems and to consider their impact in making strategic decisions. Few strategic decisions today can be based solely on economic considerations and be successful.

THE SOCIAL AUDIT

Because of the emerging pressures toward socially responsible management, there has been accompanying movement toward making the company more accountable to the larger society. In general, the response to these pressures has been reports on performance as required by law, such as EEO, and efforts to meet the demands of outside pressure groups. Much of this reporting involves the degree of compliance in minority hiring or product safety levels. Often such reporting tends to emphasize areas where requirements are being met and ignores any areas where performance has been substandard. One response to these pressures is a corporate report on social performance called a *social audit*. More and more investors and the public are seeking to find out what is being done toward socially responsible management.

WHAT IS A SOCIAL AUDIT?

In response to these pressures toward corporate accountability, many firms have considered or are using the social audit. A *social audit* is a report setting forth an evaluation of performance against planned goals in the areas of social responsibility. Many firms include in the annual report a listing and dollar amounts of its social programs. In a survey of 284 firms, John J. Corson and George A. Steiner (UCLA) found that 76 percent were attempting to assess or inventory their social performance.[14]

In order to develop and implement a social audit, the company must identify social improvement goals, allocate resources, and evaluate and review progress toward these goals on a continuing basis. A recent study of 185 firms from *Fortune's* top 500 found that only about half had actually established objectives in the area of external affairs.[15]

Without the development of social responsibility objectives, however, it would seem to be difficult to assess accurately the company's strengths or weaknesses in this area.

PROBLEMS IN SOCIAL AUDIT

At the present time, there is little agreement in terms of what a social audit is, or how it should be accomplished. Since there are no accepted standards or guidelines, there is little commonality among the differing types of reports.

First, there is no clear definition of what is included in social performance and how to measure the actual costs and benefits of such programs. How, for example, do you measure the social benefits of an improved smoke filter, in dollars?

Another problem involves how the audit should be accomplished. For example, some firms simply list all of their social programs, while others include dollar amount costs for each social activity. Other firms attempt to use a cost-benefit approach by attempting to measure cost incurred against social programs and the value of each expenditure.

THE FUTURE OF THE SOCIAL AUDIT

Both the American Accounting Association and the Institute of Certified Public Accountants have established committees to examine social accounting guidelines. Without some accepted reporting standards and without guidelines for performing a social audit, the reports which are presented often lack credibility.

Current research suggests that significant new approaches to social auditing are not being developed and that existing approaches are not being widely adopted. However, in spite of a lack of significant progress in social auditing, social responsibility appears to be alive and well. For example, a 1977 survey of the annual reports of the 500 largest companies in the United States uncovered social responsibility disclosures in 91.3 percent of them. While it appears that social auditing is still in the early stages of development, the public's demand for increased accountability will stress continuing developments in this field.

Certainly there is much more to be done in this area. *Industry Week* describes a pioneering approach by Kaiser Corporation in Oakland.

THE SOCIALLY RESPONSIBLE MANAGER

"Although many executives of large corporations are steering their firms increasingly toward social consciousness, Cornell Meier, chairman of Kaiser Aluminum and Chemical does so with gusto. He goes out of his way to look for ways he and his firm can perform good community deeds. To Mr. Maier, corporate citizenship is a matter of conviction and remarkable personal interest. He feels that business has a clear social responsibility. Business is frequently critical of government involvement, but he believes that if business wants to criticize, it needs to become more involved itself.

"To be sure, Kaiser does all the traditional things expected of a leading community employer. In its Oakland, California, headquarters area, for example, it hires disadvantaged workers, donates money to education, supports the local symphony and downtown renovation efforts, and offers financial and personnel backing to the United Way fund.

"What sets Kaiser Aluminum and Maier apart, however, is their nontraditional activities. One of the newest is the unique "Summer on the Move" work-learn program developed in the summer of 1979 by Kaiser and the Oakland school district. Some 120 high schools students attend morning classes, taught by University of California at Berkeley professors, and work in meaningful jobs in Oakland companies in the afternoon. In a related project, Kaiser has 'adopted' Oakland High School, an aging inner-city school with a heavy enrollment of minority students. The company is buying needed facilities for the school and donating the time of its employees to work directly with the students."[16]

MULTINATIONAL STRATEGY

In an era of rapid technological change and increasing international competition, the multinational firm occupies a unique position. Because of the diversity of national environments, the variety of products and markets, and the greater geographic dispersion, the multinational company faces a more complex array of strategic decisions.

WHAT IS A MULTINATIONAL?

The *multinational* company may be defined as: A number of affiliated business establishments that function as productive enterprises in different countries simultaneously. To have such capacity the firm must possess host-country-based production units such as factories, mines, retail stores, insurance offices, banking houses, or whatever operating facility is characteristic to its business.

THE MULTINATIONAL MANAGER

Zoltan Merszei

"Zoltan Merszei, the fifty-nine-year-old vice chairman of the board of Occidental Petroleum and former president and chief executive officer of the Dow Chemical Company, perhaps represents the new multinational manager. Merszei, a native of Hungary, is fluent in five languages, and claims to have visited every major country in the world. Merszei's daily regimen starts at 5:30 A.M. and includes pushups, a three-mile jog, or 200 rope-jumping steps. His busy routine includes frequent trips to visit Occidental's far-flung operations."

Merszei began his multinational career at Dow Chemical as president of Dow-Europe as reported in *Fortune:* "After Ben Branch, who was a chemical engineer by training and a brilliant strategic planner, took charge of the international business in 1958, he and Merszei built Dow's first overseas plant, in the Netherlands. Though Dow caught the international bug later than many U.S. companies, it grew faster, in part because it set up a highly effective marketing network rather than relying on agents. Dow located its plants near lush supplies of raw materials and on deep-water harbors, which gave them the flexibility to avoid economic downturns by shipping products from counties that were in a slump to those where business was booming. During the past twenty years, Dow's foreign sales exploded, from pin money to $2.6 billion. Three-fifths of that came from Europe, where sales and profits rose nearly 25 percent annually (Merszei ran Dow-Europe until shortly before he was named president and chief executive officer of Dow Chemical Company in May 1976).

"In all, foreign business contributes some 45 percent of Dow's total revenues—more than at Du Pont, Union Carbide, or Monsanto."

THE ADVANTAGES OF DOW'S MANAGERIAL AUTONOMY

"While expanding abroad, Dow developed a management structure that proved to be a fantastic engine for growth. For decades, says Ted Doan, the last family member to run the company, "we had the distinct advantage of never having been organized." But that turned into a disadvantage when foreign sales reached a quarter billion dollars in 1965; in a sweeping move, Doan decentralized operations into autonomous units—the U.S., Canada, Europe, Latin America, and the Pacific—each with a president and an area headquarters.

"The geographic structure, which is unique to Dow among chemical companies, keeps management from becoming entangled in a bureaucratic web.

Each area president has a lot of autonomy. Managers well down the line respond quickly to the needs of the marketplace—unlike those at some chemical companies, which suffer, as one Wall Street analyst puts it, from "arterio-sclerosis."

"In Midland, as president of Dow, Merszei implemented an aggressive growth strategy in the international marketplace. He relied heavily on a corporate products department that sets forth strategic plans and keeps tabs on capacity, demand, and prices for Dow's 2,300 products worldwide. The board of directors is truly an operating entity and is made up almost entirely of insiders—13 top executives, three retired officers, and one university professor. The directors have special incentives for meeting the company's objectives. Collectively they own—or as one of them puts it, "the banks own," through hefty personal loans—Dow stock valued at more than $135 million. And they hold unexercised options on nearly 700,000 shares. The annual bonuses for all top executives are linked to improving profits. . . ."[17]

As president of Dow, Merszei was responsible for developing some half a dozen petrochemical complexes around the world, each with a price tag of well over $500 million. After joining Occidental Petroleum, he continued his emphasis on multinational expansion.

As might be expected of an internationalist like Zoltan Merszei, he was especially eager to expand abroad. The way to do it, he said, is through joint ventures with countries that have promising untapped markets, which he calls "new frontiers." His targets include Yugoslavia, Hungary, Mexico, Brazil, and the Middle East. Each of those opportunities presents a satchelful of difficulties. First of all, it is a slow, painstaking process to line up joint ventures in less developed countries. Second, once a deal is struck, there are dozens of obstacles to doing business, everything from an inadequate supply of skilled labor to outsized construction costs. Merszei tends to gloss over these problems. "The world is a big place," he says. "We will go where we are really wanted." He was quick to point out his past success in Yugoslavia, where he negotiated a $700-million joint venture in petrochemicals for Dow. And he signed a protocol in Hungary, opening the way to possible ventures in oil, coal, and chemicals.[18]

THE EXTENT OF MULTINATIONALS

Dow Chemical, one example of a multinational company with almost half of its revenues coming from outside the United States, demonstrates the increasing importance of the world environment in corporate strategy.

To grasp the growing importance of multinationalism, the extent of the direct investment of the United States abroad increased more than two and one-half times from 1966 to 1976, which is shown in Figure 11.3.

Organizations become multinational in order to expand potential markets and increase the alternatives which are open to them. They may apply a multinational strategy to benefit from cheaper labor costs, to gain access to scarce resources, or to compete more effectively with other companies. Multinational operations require new managerial strategies and more complex decision making than single-country businesses.

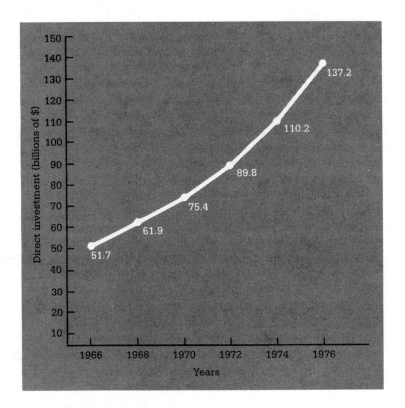

FIGURE 11.3
U.S. Direct Investment Abroad, 1966–1976

SOURCE: Based on Obie G. Whichard, "U.S. Direct Investment Abroad in 1976," Survey of Current Business 57, August 1977, 42.

The expansion of multinational operations has significantly changed the strategic planning of many companies. There is a difference between a *domestic company,* which conducts business in a single country, *an international export operation,* which is based in one country but sells to others, and a *multinational company* which is headquartered in one country but has subsidiary operations in many countries.[19] IBM, for example, markets multiple product lines in over 100 countries and claims about a market share of 60 percent of the overseas data processing market.

As Table 11.1 shows, the percentage of income from overseas generations is a significant factor. Profit potential more than national boundaries dictates the multinational manager's strategies. The rationale for such a multinational conglomeration is profit. This form of multinational interdependence literally explodes with strategic opportunities and threats.

The integration of these diverse operations is an overriding problem. The distance and separation of units are barriers to effective communication and the volume of complex information that must be exchanged makes the nature of their interdependence even more complex. The high degree of differentiation caused by different cultures, languages, and currencies, in addition to the diversity of products and markets, causes integration to be difficult to accomplish. As a result, the multi-

TABLE 11.1

The Extent of Multinational Involvement of Ten Major U.S. Firms

(1980)	
Exxon Corporation	50%
Standard Oil (California)	48%
Dow Chemical	46%
International Business Machines (IBM)	46%
Texaco	45%
Mobil Oil	43%
ITT	42%
General Electric	32%
Ford	26%
Chrysler	24%

national organization must find ways of organizing and managing to overcome these constraints.

THE REASONS FOR MULTINATIONAL OPERATION

Nearly all large companies are involved in internationl or multinational business operations. There are many reasons why multinational operations have expanded, including:

1 An expanding world population with an increasing standard of living.

2 High transportation costs that may make it difficult to compete from abroad.

3 The availability of foreign markets, when domestic markets are saturated.

4 International laws facilitating world trade.

5 Increasing world demand and income levels.

6 The goal of decreasing dependence on a single economy or market.

As these factors suggest, most companies move into multinational operations to increase the strategic alternatives available to them, and to compete more effectively. For example, by moving into new markets, introducing new products, and adding capacity to produce old ones, Dow figures to add some 60 percent to its sales by 1985.

While the multinational operation offers many opportunities for greater efficiency and use of worldwide resources, there are also problems of organization and control.

ORGANIZATIONAL FORMS OF OPERATIONS

There are a number of types of international involvement, depending upon the circumstances which exist, ranging from export sales to full-scale subsidiary operations as indicated in Figure 11.4. Each country and region of the world has its own unique characteristics, the observance of which is critical to operations. Managers must develop, devise, and implement structures, policy and processes that best balance organizational goals with the local situation. The organizational form that is used is important in both an economic and cultural sense.

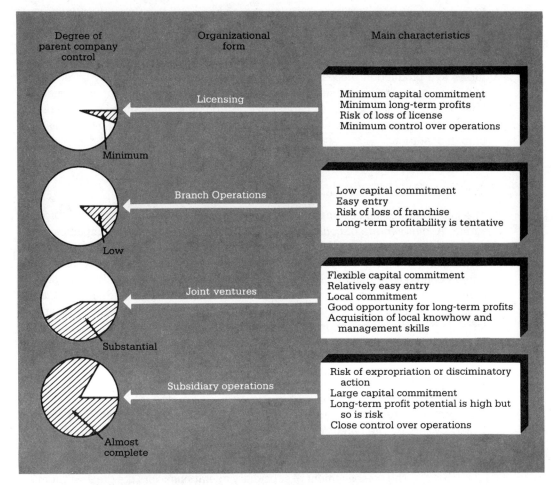

FIGURE 11.4
Basic Organizational Forms for Multinational Operations.

SOURCE: G. John Hutchinson, *Management Strategy and Tactics* (New York: Holt, Rinehart and Winston, 1971), p. 508.

LICENSING AGREEMENTS

Under licensing agreements, the exporting company grants the host country firm the right to handle specific lines, products or services in a given area. Licensing requires a minimum capital investment, of course, but also returns minimum long-term profits. However, it does gain entry to a foreign market and short-run returns may be good.

A disadvantage is that it may be relatively easy to displace a licensee through political maneuvers.

BRANCH OFFICES

Many companies begin by establishing branch offices in the overseas markets. The typical branch office operation also involves a relatively minimal level of commitment, compared to full-scale operations in the host country. In a branch operation, sales offices, warehouses, and distribution channels need to be established, but manufacturing and production processes are performed elsewhere. There may be problems of transportation costs, marketing, and pricing, but branch operation does offer relatively easy entry with limited capital risk. Automobile companies, because of the massive outlays required to achieve economies of scale, often begin by establishing branch operations.

JOINT VENTURE OR CONSORTIUM

The joint venture has become an increasingly popular form of multinational organization. A *joint venture* or *consortium* is formed when two or more companies unite to form a single business entity. Dow Chemical, for example, was involved in a joint venture in Japan with a Japanese firm, Asahi-Dow, because it was impossible for a foreign company to build its own plant. Similarly, Dow was involved in consortium agreements, usually with governments such as those of India and Saudi Arabia, in building chemical complexes. Although this is not necessarily the most desirable form of operation, there are times when it provides a means of operating when other methods are impractical.

SUBSIDIARY COMPANY

The most usual method of multinational operation is forming a subsidiary company, wholly owned by the parent corporation, such as Dow, but incorporated under the laws of the host country. Through the establishment of several subsidiaries, the company becomes a multinational corporation.

The establishment of subsidiary operations offers the greatest promise of long-term profits for the firm; but it also involves the highest degree of risk. Because of the enormous capital investment required in such operations, the political climate must be assessed very carefully, and even then, times can change, as many companies with operations in Iran found. The revolution in Iran exposed U.S. companies to potential losses totalling $1 billion. Many companies have found that as a result of political change industry has been nationalized and its assets appropriated. In many situations, the host country has seized subsidiaries without compensation, for example, the Anaconda and Kennecott Copper units in Chile and all subsidiary units in Cuba.

Dow Chemical, for example, has subsidiary operations in a number of countries, and has regional area managers to manage these various endeavors, such as Dow Europe, Dow Pacific, etc. From a strategic standpoint, these multinational operations involve more complex strategies because of the different conditions and competition, and because of the diverse environmental constraints.

THE PRODUCT/AREA MATRIX FORM

As we noted in the cases of Dow Chemical and Westinghouse, many firms are finding that the matrix form of organization helps with the problems of integration which multinational business entails. Where companies feel that an emphasis upon both product and market area is needed, then a matrix has advantages.

MULTINATIONAL STRATEGIC CHALLENGES

The multinational manager faces some significant new challenges in overseas operations. As we have noted, operating a multinational business introduces some different and more complex operational problems. There are a greater number of constraints tending to place limitations on managerial strategies from country to country. These include the legal, economic, political, and cultural constraints which impact the formulation and implementation of strategy on a worldwide basis.

LEGAL CONSTRAINTS

Multinational corporations have to be aware that each country has a unique set of laws and practices. There are also variations from country to country in terms of the degree to which laws are enforced or overlooked. As an example, in the United States bribery is illegal while in many countries around the world it is an unavoidable fact of life. In some countries tax laws are expected to be avoided, while in others exposed tax fraud brings legal action.

ECONOMIC CONSTRAINTS

Because of the size and scope of multinational operations, the economic system must be taken into account. Different countries exist in differing stages of development, and underdeveloped countries may offer low levels of income but also provide low labor costs. Also, the economy may be to a lesser or greater degree subject to governmental control and interference. Many countries are able to influence which companies are allowed access to certain markets, etc.

POLITICAL CONSTRAINTS

People who live in established governments such as the United States or Canada take political stability for granted. This is true because the transfer of power from one political party to another occurs in an orderly manner without political upheaval.

Unfortunately, in many countries, political instability is a constant way of life. MNCs doing business in politically unstable countries must be aware of these struggles for power. This is often a dificult task when several political parties are struggling for control of the government.

Political fortunes can shift quickly with dramatic impact in an unstable situation. For example, in 1966 the Christian Democratic government invited Dow Chemical Company to build a plastics plant in Chile. Yet in 1972, Allende's government seized the entire Dow operation outright and ordered its foreign managers to leave the country. And by 1974, Dow was back in Chile by invitation of yet another new government. According to James Weekly, expropriations have increased in both frequency and geographic dispersion since 1960.[20] The degree of political stability is an important factor, since the large investments required to build a manufacturing complex are not factors to be taken lightly. The political aspects often overshadow all other elements of multinational management. The degree to which the government is elected or dictatorial, and capitalist versus socialist or communist, also influences the way business is done. Generally, the more open the climate, the easier it is to operate; and the greater the restrictions, the more difficult it is to operate.

BROADER ISSUES

The top executives of multinational corporations often deal directly with top-level government officials and must consider the broader issues of public opinion and home government relations. However, the strategist faces greater turbulence abroad and operates from a position of less power than in the past.

According to Louis Kraar, writing in *Fortune*, "Since U.S. corporations face ever fiercer competition abroad, and their own power has diminished, the leaders of these enterprises have only one choice—to get smarter about the world."

"[Thus] . . . the top executives of major corporations are gradually acknowledging that they need both new skills and fresh insights to thrive overseas. The enjoyment of cordial personal relations with a head of state is no longer, if it ever was, a reliable way to appraise the prospects of their nation's market. Nor does the penchant of many CEO's for flying off to intriguing places, such as Islamabad or Peking, assure considered judgments back at their headquarters. Just as senior officers have long consulted their specialists on marketing and finance and law, they now sense the need for staff expertise to direct a more systematic approach to international affairs. Confronting the world these days cannot be a do-it-yourself job.

"This new political-risk game requires anticipating the currents of change abroad, then plotting how to move with them. To do this demands going beyond economic forecasting to gauge other forces, from religious movements to nationalistic passions. It also requires U.S. executives, who have learned the hard way, to refrain from plunging into foreign ventures merely on the strength of Washington's judgments.

"The potential for corporate disaster often lurks in seemingly stable places. A few years ago Aris Gloves, a division of Consolidated Foods, wanted to spread its risks beyond the Philippines, its only manufacturing base. In 1976, the company picked a spot that its vice president, James McDorry, says "everyone, including the U.S. embassy, described as a happy, sleepy country." This carelessly promised land was El Salvador. Within some two years, political turmoil hit the Aris plant, with leftist dissidents holding its president and about 120 local employees as hostages for nine days—until the company agreed to wage increases that it couldn't afford. In 1979, Aris fled from El Salvador."[21]

POLITICAL RISK ASSESSMENT

As *Business Week* recently reported, political risk assessment is rapidly becoming a fact of corporate life. Many firms are developing their own political assessment units to take a more accurate look at the risks inherent in operating overseas. Table 11.2 presents an assessment of the ten best and worst risk analyses by independent political risk consulting firms. Because MNCs are unable to dictate the political climate in a particular host country they must learn to assess the risk of doing business under a given political climate. As Vernon Terpstra has commented: "Most host

TABLE 11.2
Political Risk Assessment of Overseas Environments

Political analysts can't agree on . . .	
. . . the 10 best political risks . . .	
Frost & Sullivan	Business International
U.S.	Singapore
Denmark	Netherlands
Singapore	Norway
Finland	Kuwait
West Germany	Saudi Arabia
Austria	Switzerland
Canada	West Germany
Japan	Britain
Malaysia	Malaysia
Netherlands	Japan
. . . or the 10 worst	
El Salvador	Iran
Iran	Yugoslavia
Nicaragua	South Korea
Zaire	Algeria
Zambia	Brazil
Libya	Nicaragua
Bolivia	India
Turkey	China
Pakistan	Thailand
Philippines	Philippines

**Number of countries covered: Frost & Sullivan, 50;
Business International, 71**
Data: Frost & Sullivan, Business International
SOURCE: Business Week, December 1, 1980

governments accept the need for foreign investment. Many realize that they need the resources, technology, management skills, capital, and foreign exchange that foreign investment can bring. But governments increasingly want foreign investment on terms that maximize the contribution to national goals and minimize the threat to national sovereignty."[22]

In other words, both parties seek a mutual exchange of benefits.

CULTURAL CONSTRAINTS

Finally, the multinational firm must consider the cultural differences in multinational operations. Culture is the set of social norms and behaviors that are accepted, and cultural standards vary among nations. Thus, marketing a product may be very different in other cultures, and often TV advertisements which are directly translated are insulting to foreign cultures. An example might be marketing Chevy Novas in South America—in Brazil (Portugese) "no va" means "It doesn't go." The name had to be changed.

Products that are prized in one culture may have little appeal in another. Similarly, there are traditions and practices among labor groups, status symbols, etc., that must be recognized if the firm is to operate effectively in that cultural setting.

Multinational business is becoming increasingly important in a growing world economy. Yet because of the multiple challenges and constraints, the formulation and implementation of strategy is more complex and difficult.

THE REINDUSTRIALIZATION CRISIS

One of the major issues facing the United States in multinational markets is a growing inability to compete effectively. A local Spokane company, for example, used both Japanese and American steel in its products. Yet the production people preferred to use Japanese steel because it was a much higher quality material to work with, with lower levels of impurity, etc. This problem has been termed the issue of *"reindustrialization"* by Amitai Etzioni of Columbia University. His basic thesis is that America must choose between quality of life programs and reindustrialization, but we cannot afford both.

He suggests that the United States has let its industrial base decline relative to those of competing nations, and that rebuilding will require changes in both attitudes and policies. Our expenditures for plants and equipment ran slightly over 10 percent of GNP during the Seventies. This puts the United States last among the major industrial nations.

In general, the challenges to industry include the increasing price of energy and other problems: sharply declining productivity; relatively weak investment in capital goods; the leveling off of expenditures on research and development; the bloating of the public sector; growing government intervention and regulation of economic activities; the deterioration of the dollar; and the unwholesome combination of inflation and high unemployment.

The American industrial machine, with some important exceptions, is run, as it were, like the steel mills, with increases in labor settlements and divided pay-outs that vastly exceed increases in productivity. These factors, coupled with relatively low investment in new plants and equipment and in research and development, have resulted in an aging technology and an inability to compete with Japan and West Germany, which rebuilt their plants after World War II. (There are additional reasons for the inability to compete that need not concern us here.) A downtrend for most American industries has been recorded since 1966, a high peak, with a "worsened" trend as of 1973.[23]

In summary, then, Etzioni proposes that we face two options: either to invest in rebuilding our industrial strength, or to settle for a lower standard of living (and probably a lower impact on world affairs).

MANAGERIAL IMPLICATIONS

Multinational operations have been increasing in size and complexity for the past two decades, with emerging problems and opportunities. Organizaitons seek multinational expansion in order to broaden the scope of the options which are open to them, to obtain additional resources or labor and to operate on a more effective competitive level.

The expansion of operations raises new legal, cultural, political, and economic problems as well. Because of these constraints, managerial strategies must vary from country to country, thus bringing increased problems of integration for the strategist. The effective manager must be aware of both the similarities and the difficulties offered by overseas operations, and be sensitive to political and cultural norms and values associated with each locale.

Strategic management in multinational corporations is a highly complex, risky process.

The strategic manager of today must manage within constraints. Organizations do not exist in isolation. Many external systems exert influence on strategy: governments, society, customers, special interest groups, etc. As a result, strategy must be examined from an open system perspective, based on the assumption that the firm exists in a complex and dynamic environment.

SOCIALLY RESPONSIVE MANAGEMENT

While market, profit, and efficiency goals have been the major concern of managers, social responsibility goals are now becoming increasingly important.

The result is increasing complexity in the strategic manager's job. Because of these rapidly changing values, a dilemma is created for the manager: Where does the manager's real responsibility lie?

THE SOCIAL AUDIT

As the need for socially responsive management grows, the social audit has been developed as a means for reporting on such activities. While many managers are keenly aware of these responsibilities, they realize they cannot relegate the bottom line or economic success to any lesser importance. The strategic manager must view the environment as a set of interacting systems each of which has a different level of importance and an impact on the organization.

PROBLEMS AND CONSTRAINTS

The expansion of operations raises new legal, cultural, political, and economic problems. Because of these constraints, managerial strategies must vary from country to country, thus bringing increased problems of integration for the strategist. The effective manager must be aware of both the similarities and the difficulties offered by overseas operations and be sensitive to political and cultural norms and values associated with each locale.

The managerial process in international operations, however, is made even more complicated by a number of additional factors. These include the geographic distances, diversity of cultural settings, ownership forms, and host country political climate. These factors increase the time, expense, and margin for error in strategic decisions in multinational corporations.

Strategic management in multinational corporations is a highly complex, risky process.

REVIEW QUESTIONS

1   What is social responsibility? Describe the two different views, and tell which view you would support and why.

2   As an example of social systems, consider your electric power utility company. Examine the pollution, consumer service, employment, and other aspects in determining an approach. What do you feel is the primary responsibility of management?

3   How does the systems model help in diagnosing the interrelationships involved in external forces?

4   One of the arguments involving environmental issues is that the company passes along anti-pollution costs to the consumer in higher prices. Is this socially responsible? Why or why not?

5   What are the reasons for the growth of multinational corporations?

6   What advantages and disadvantages would you see in working as a multinational manager? Suppose you were offered an overseas job by a major chemical company. What factors would you consider? Would you accept it? Why?

ENDNOTES

1   Thomas Griffith, *"Weyerhaeuser Gets Set for the 21st Century,"* Fortune, April 1977, 75.

2   Ibid, 85.

3   D. Mileti and D. Gillespie, "An Integrated Formalization of Organization-Environment Interdependencies," *Human Relations* 29 (1976), 85–100.

4   V. Buehler and Y. Shetty, "Managerial Response to Social Responsibility Challenge," *Academy of Management Journal* 19 (1976), 66–78.

5   Keith Davis and Robert L. Blomstrom, *Business Society: Environment and Responsibility* (New York: McGraw-Hill, 1975), p. 39.

6   M. Friedman, *Capitalism and Freedom* (Chicago: University of Chicago Press, 1962), p. 135.

7   F. Byrom, *Koppers Foundation* (Pittsburgh, Pa.: Koppers Company, n.d.), p. 2.

8   Kenneth R. Andrews, *The Concept of Corporate Strategy* (Homewood, Ill.: Dow-Jones Irwin, 1971), p. 133.

9   Neil H. Jacoby, *Corporate Power and Social Responsibility* (New York: MacMillan, 1973), p. 196.

10 See "Giving Land to Save It," *Business Week,* September 13, 1976, 53–54; see also "Social Service Leave: Five Years Old and Looking Good," *Xerox World* 24 (April 1976).

11 "Corporate Clout for Consumers," *Business Week,* September 12, 1977, 44.

12 Robert Leone, "Heavy Hands on the Pollution Controls," *The Wharton Magazine* Fall 1976, 16.

13 "3M Gains by Averting Pollution," *Business Week,* November 22, 1976, 72.

14 John J. Corson and George A. Steiner, *Measuring Business Social Performance: The Corporate Social Audit* (New York: Committee for Economic Development, 1974, p. 24.

15 W. Hagerty, J. Aplin, and R. Cosier, "Achieving Corporate Success in External Affairs: A Management Challenge," *Business Horizons,* in press.

16 Suggested from S. Modic, "Maier," *Industry Week,* October 29, 1979), 56–58.

17 Aimeé L. Morner, "Dow's Strategy for an Unfriendly New Era," *Fortune,* May 1977, p. 312–15, 318, 320, 322, 324.

18 Susie Nazem, "Occidental Petroleum's Odd Couple," *Fortune,* November 19, 1979, 82.

19 See J. Daniels, E. Orgram, and L. Radebaugh, *International Business: Environments and Operations* (Reading, Mass.: Addison-Wesley, 1976).

20 See James K. Weekly, "Expropriation of U.S. Multinational Investments," *MSU Business Topics* Winter 1977, 27–36.

21 Louis Kraar, "The Multinationals Get Smarter About Political Risks," *Fortune,* March 24, 1980, 87.

22 Vern Terpstra, *The Cultural Environment of International business* (Cincinnati, Ohio: South-Western, 1978), pp. 240–41.

23 Amitai Etzioni, "Choose America Must," *Across the Board,* October 1980, 42.

CHAPTER

12

If I had to criticize A & P for one thing, it is that we still need to improve our systems of controls. Ninety-nine percent of my effort will be spent on the supermarkets.

James Wood, chairman, A & P, quoted in Peter W. Bernstein, "A & P calls in a Reliever," *Fortune*, June 2, 1980, 67.

Strategic Evaluation: The Review and Control Process

CHAPTER OBJECTIVES

When you have completed this chapter, you will be able to:

- [ ] *Identify the relationship between strategic planning, decision-making, and the evaluation process.*

- [ ] *Describe some of the intended and unintended consequences of review systems.*

- [ ] *Improve your conceptual and technical skills in using and designing review systems and techniques.*

- [ ] *Apply the concepts in this chapter in the analysis of a complex case.*

STREAMLINING

Jonathan Scott

"When Jonathan Scott took over as chairman and chief executive of A & P in 1974 the company was in desperate straits. It still is," judged *Fortune* in late 1978. Even Scott's proven record for effective leadership in this field was insufficient preparation for the colossal task of reversing A & P's profit slide.

"It's not that Scott hasn't *done* anything—he's done a lot. Among other things, he closed down almost half of the company's 3,468 stores, replaced almost all of top management, and spent hundreds of millions of dollars on new facilities. But all this has not translated into decent operating results. There have been serious errors of judgment or perception. The five-year recovery plan Scott announced in 1975 is a shambles and the company went back into the red. It lost $9.9 million in the first quarter of 1978 and $6.9 million in the second, and certainly finished with a large loss for the year. Most of the company's twenty-three operating divisions were unprofitable. Even a good many of the newer stores opened since 1970 were losing money. Operating expenses were out of line with those of competitors. Labor costs, which represent over 60 percent of total operating costs, ran to 12.4 percent of sales, 2.3 percentage points above the industry average. An A & P executive said the company's administrative costs amounted to approximately 2 percent, compared with an industry average of 1.25 percent. Stymied and overwhelmed by these problems, A & P was forced to call in high-priced management consultants for the second time in five years. Conceded one A & P executive: 'The company is in the same position today that it was in 1971.'

"Jonathan Scott . . . seemed to possess both the business ability and the personal qualities that would be needed to turn A & P around. He was recruited by Booz, Allen & Hamilton, the management-consulting firm that the A & P board turned to in 1974 when it decided to go outside for help. At the time he was the chief executive of Idaho-based Albertson's, the country's tenth largest supermarket chain, where he had started as a management trainee in 1953.

312

"In the process, Scott won a reputation as a hardheaded and innovative retailer who pioneered Albertson's geographic expansion as well as its development of large combination food-and-drug stores. Along with his business acumen, Scott has other commendable attributes. His quiet informality—almost everybody calls him Scotty—and an open, forthright manner make it hard not to like him. In fact, there are those who think that Scott's biggest problem in managing A & P has been that he was too nice. Says one man who has come to know him pretty well: 'He was not heartless enough to do it.'

"For whatever reason, the approach Scott took to the store-closing program, which he embarked upon immediately after he took over in February 1975, was fundamentally flawed. With the company's condition deteriorating rapidly, there was no question that Scott had to act quickly. The immediate problem was deciding which stores to close and which to save, a matter of considerable complexity. The shutting of a single store can have significant ramifications on a marketing area's distribution costs, its warehousing operations, its advertising expenses, and its labor situation, as well as on the A & P manufacturing facilities that are deprived of an outlet for their products."

Scott confronted a choice between two strategies. One was to close down the company's worst operating units, store by store, warehouse by warehouse, plant by plant. A more radical course of action was to shut down entire operating divisions. Scott opted for the first alternative. "We made a conscious decision to close down on a store-by-store basis," he recalls. "We decided to weed out the very worst and try to turn around the rest. We wanted to save as much as we could."[1]

STRATEGIC CONTROLS

The world in which strategic managers operate is continually changing—politically, socially, and technologically—and the rate of change seems to have accelerated in recent years. Because of this, it is impossible to develop strategic plans with complete certainty. There are too many forces in the external environment, and too many unknowns to do so. If strategic management is to be effective in an ever-changing world, it must be able to review the results of strategic decisions and make changes if necessary.

NO REVIEW SYSTEM

At A & P Jonathan Scott implemented a retrenchment strategy by closing unprofitable stores. Unfortunately, the strategy did not work as planned. But apparently A & P failed to have a review system which would enable it to take corrective actions. Strategic evaluation is the process in which managers, like Scott, compare the actual outcomes of a strategy with planned objectives. The test of a strategy is not the formulation of the strategic plan. The true test is whether management's commitment of resources brings about results.

If this is not being accomplished, as was the case at A & P, then the strategy is ineffective. When properly formulated, strategic plans and controls are inseparable elements, because the first relates directly to the second. As Harold Koontz (UCLA) has commented, "The two functions of planning and control are so closely interconnected as to be singularly inseparable . . . certainly, no manager can control who has not planned, for the very concept of control incorporates the task of keeping the operation of subordinates on course by correcting deviations from plans."[2]

MAKING CHANGES

If actual results do not track with planned results, then changes must be made. Harold Geneen and his top managers at ITT were continually reviewing the progress of strategic moves, so they could take corrective actions or countermoves if the original strategy had failed or if conditions had changed.

Richard Rumelt (UCLA) has suggested that, "Strategy can neither be formulated nor adjusted to changing circumstances without a process of strategy evaluation. Whether performed by an individual or as part of an organizational review procedure, strategy evaluation forms an essential step in the process of guiding an enterprise."[3]

The development and formulation of strategies and plans is of little value if the strategy is not implemented or carried out to achieve company goals. Any strategy is only as effective as management's ability to put it into action: the plan is not the end result. If strategies are to be effective, the manager must also be able to measure performance, to determine where deviations from the plan are occurring (as was the case at A & P), and be able to make corrective moves where necessary.

THE FINAL STAGE

The final stage (Stage 10) in the strategic process, then, is the review and evaluation of the results of the strategic plans and decisions. This stage is critical for any plan or strategy because an ineffective or losing strategy should not be followed blindly or a company may end up like the W. T. Grant stores, going out of business because of uncontrolled expansion. Determining how effectively the strategy is being implemented is essential to accomplishing strategic objectives. Therefore, strategic evaluation and control is an important element in the strategic process.

THE STRATEGIC CONTROL PROCESS

The strategic control process involves the interlocking elements of strategic objectives, planning, decision-making and control. The focus of control is on results. *Control* may be defined as the task of ensuring that activities are producing the desired results. The strategic goals and plans remain only if the plans are well executed to achieve results. At A & P for example, Jonathan Scott set forth a strategic plan to improve its ailing financial position. His strategy was to close out losing operations, thus restoring a smaller but healthier system. However, A & P apparently lacked an adequate information and control system and as a result the strategy failed to achieve the planned goals.

THE BASIC STAGES

The basic stages of the strategic control process are presented in Figure 12.1. To be effective, top management must be able to measure actual performance, compare to plan, recognize when deviations from the plan are occurring, and be able to take corrective action.

The strategic objectives evolve into detailed plans during the implementation stage. The strategic control process begins with the measuring of performance to determine if it conforms to planned expectations. The review and control process generates information for decisions: decisions to continue a strategy, decisions to increase or decrease the allocation of resources to specific elements, or decisions to change strategic directions if something has gone wrong.

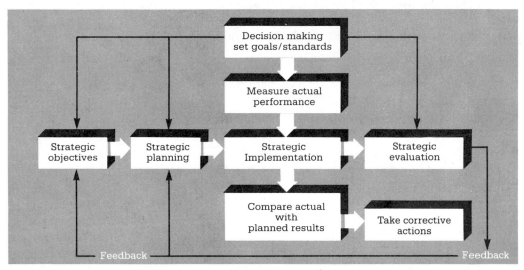

FIGURE 12.1
The Strategic Control Process

The basic purpose of control is aimed at the achievement of strategic goals. The best type of control process is anticipative in nature; that is, it predicts possible deviations from plan by anticipating their potential occurrence.

ELEMENTS OF CONTROL

Each manager has his own philosophy of control, which not only guides his behavior but influences the behavior of those around him. Take the style of Harry Gray, for example, the hard driving chairman of United Technologies. In the words of *Business Week:*

"Gray considers himself a prototype of the corporate generalist. He is as interested in financial management as he is in marketing, and he has introduced exceptionally tight-fisted financial controls on both operating expenses and capital investment. To generate more cash flow, he has reduced 'days outstanding' on accounts by as much as 40 percent and has increased turnover of inventories significantly. . . .

"Gray is also a very tough taskmaster. There has been a steady exodus of managers who have failed to meet his profit targets and controls. 'Harry is a helluva driver who demands constant attention to detail,' says a man who once worked for him. 'Although he delegated responsibility, he wanted to be part of the process. He wanted to know what every one of his people was doing every minute of the day. Some people wouldn't go to the bathroom without calling Harry.'"[4]

THE BASIC ELEMENTS

The basic elements of the control process are:

1 Setting predetermined standards of performance.

2 Measuring actual performance results.

3 Comparing planned to actual performance.

4 Taking corrective action, if necessary.

In the following sections the strategic control process will be discussed.

SETTING STANDARDS

One of the most important aspects of the control process is to determine beforehand what results, or standards, are expected from a given strategic action. Standards are the units of measurement or criteria against which actual performance can be compared. Without some standard or plan against which actual performance can be evaluated, control is impossible.

The strategy needs to be evaluated to be certain that it is working as planned. One question arises over what the appropriate criteria to be measured are. Many retail stores, J. C. Penney for example, set objectives for store and department managers in terms of sales per square foot of store space, or per labor hour. The stores use computerized cash registers to provide store and department managers with daily, detailed reports on sales, volume, etc., so that managers can immediately determine how well they are doing.

QUALITATIVE MEASURES

Seymour Tilles has suggested several criteria to evaluate strategy early after the implementation phase is completed.

1. Internal consistency. Does each policy implementation of the strategy fit an integrated pattern?

2. Consistency with the environment. Does each policy fit the current demands of the environment?

3. Appropriateness, given the enterprise's resources. Was the strategy implemented in a way which uses the critical resources most effectively?

4. Acceptability of degree of risk. Given the values of the management toward risk, does the strategy fit its preferences?

5. Appropriateness of time horizon. Does the strategic implementation include appropriate time goals?

6. Workability. Does it achieve the enterprise objectives?[5]

QUANTITATIVE MEASURES

These criteria present qualitative measures of how well the strategy is being implemented. The standards are often expressed in quantitative terms including such factors as:

> Net profit
> Stock price
> Dividend rates
> Earnings per share
> Return on capital
> Return on equity
> Market share
> Growth in sales
> Production costs and efficiency
> Employee turnover, absenteeism, and satisfaction indexes.

These quantitative criteria provide measures of how well the strategy is being implemented.

CRITERIA AT EMERSON ELECTRIC

At Emerson Electric, the criteria are growth and profits.

Here is a company with a relentless, almost heartless devotion to the true bottom line: return on investment. Wallace R. "Buck" Persons, former CEO, has been compared to the late Vince Lombardi (Green Bay Packers' Coach). Emerson's motto, to paraphrase Lombardi, might well be: Efficiency isn't everything; it is the only thing. Here is a company that does not hesitate to throttle back sales growth in the interests of a higher return on capital. Control, discipline, tough-minded decision making are hallmarks of Emerson. And the payoff is a five-year average return on capital of 17.7 percent that placed Emerson well up in the ranks of large manufacturing companies in *Forbes'* Annual Report on American Industry.

Emerson's planning sessions are among the most sophisticated in U.S. industry. The planning is done within a broad strategic framework that calls for doubling earnings every six years, which is an average of 12.5% earnings gain every year; no more than 10% of revenues from defense; no more than 20% to 25% from international; and $200-million worth of new products to be developed through corporate research and development by some target date.[6]

Many different criteria may be used, but they should provide a means to measure strategic performance.

MEASURING PERFORMANCE

Controls generate information for decisions. Harold Geneen had an impressive ability to ferret out the true "unshakeable facts" about a company or a product, uncovering layers of false factors before he reached the truth. However, performance cannot be reviewed unless there is a means of determining what performance has actually been. This may seem to be a very basic element, but unless there is a reporting system and a basis for measurement, confusion can develop. At A & P the cutting of stores left A & P spread thin in certain regions, thereby sacrificing economies of scale that had been gained by geographic concentration. Here the reporting system did not provide adequate information.

The basic purpose of strategic evaluation is to assess the achievement of organizational goals. In this sense evaluation is a positive process, since problems are anticipated before they emerge. The ITT meetings were aimed at bringing out potential problems before they occurred, so that they could be anticipated and corrective actions taken. The process also, of course, points out problems after they occur. This is where the negative connotations are often associated with the evaluation process: finding out where something has gone wrong.

However, the emphasis of strategic review is not so much on blaming someone for faults as it is on generating information. Consequently, this requires an effective management information system which provides timely data on operating results for review by top management. There are several issues which arise around the design of strategic review systems in the evaluation of performance data.

THE FEEDBACK PROCESS

Feedback refers to information from the output which is fed back to the input as an error correcting signal. Feedback is an integral part of the review process, because without feedback managers would be managing without information. Mike Miller, a young MBA, is a department manager for J. C. Penney. Each morning he receives a computer printout on the previous day's sales activities. This information, or feedback, allows Mike to compare actual with intended results, and use these up-to-the-minute data to decide whether more fast-moving products should be ordered, if slow-moving merchandise should be replaced, or if personnel changes are needed.

There is considerable evidence that objective feedback about performance, or knowledge of results can improve performance. A number of studies have focused on the way feedback affects performance. Latham and Yukl, for example, have indicated that feedback along with participation in goal setting was associated with improved performance.[7]

WHO RECEIVES FEEDBACK

Another consideration in the use of feedback is to whom the information should go, for example:

1 Top management.
2 Corporate staff units.
3 The department manager.
4 The individual member.

Management by objectives (as discussed in Chapter 9) emphasizes that not only planning but *control* ought to be accomplished to a substantial degree by those responsible. Consequently, feedback directly to the individual or to the department provides those closest to the decision with data they can use to take action. Information regarding strategic outcomes should be directed to higher levels of management, those responsible for the total performance of the organization.

AT A & P

At A & P, for example, the store closing operation became a hit or miss program, because of a lack of adequate information. A & P strategists could not be sure whether an individual store was really profitable or not. Says one close observer of the company, "When they wanted to close a store, they had to wing it. They could not make a rational decision, because they did not have a fact basis."[8]

The degree of accuracy of feedback depends upon the management level. At lower levels such as at the department manager level, detailed information is necessary, while at higher levels too much detail can obscure more important strategic problems and "muddy the water" rather than contribute to greater precision.

THE MOTIVATION TO EVALUATE

Another issue is the motivation of managers to evaluate performance. Using controls as a club to criticize performance can act as a negative motivational factor. Continued unfavorable feedback may lead to members creating ways to short circuit the system; that is, to appear favorable in the reporting sessions or to hide potential problems.

Another factor in measuring performance concerns whether managers are rewarded directly for good performance. Former ITT president Harold S. Geneen provided his managers with enough incentives to help them tolerate the system.

Salaries all the way through ITT are higher than average—Geneen reckons 10 percent higher—so that few people can leave without taking a drop . . . having bound his men to him with chains of gold, Geneen can induce the tension that drives the machine. "The key to the system," one of his men explained, "is the profit forecast; once the forecast has been gone over, revised and agreed, the managing director has a personal commitment to Geneen to carry it out; that's how he produces the tension on which the success depends." The tension goes through the company, inducing ambition, perhaps exhilaration, but always with some sense of fear: What happens if the target is missed?"[9]

ITT's motivation system is directed by the budgetary-control process and apparently used in a way that ignores the personal human needs of many managers by relying basically upon money, tension and fear for motivation.

On the one hand, to the extent that managers are rewarded by superior performance, control and review systems will be a more positive force, and will provide motivating forces toward the accomplishment of objectives. On the other hand, the control process often creates a situation where people attempt to subvert the system.

COMPARING ACTUAL WITH PLANNED PERFORMANCE

The next step in the control process involves the comparison of results against predetermined standards. The purpose of the comparison is to detect deviations—variances from the standard in time to make corrections. Since all performance has some degree of variation, it is important to determine the limits of regular performance variation. The manager must be able to distinguish the important variations, the potential problems or bottlenecks, from unimportant variances.

UNITED AIRLINES CONTROL SYSTEM

One example is United Airlines computerized system of reporting and controls.

"An intrinsic part of United's reporting system is what company executives like to call 'the room with the 14,000-mile view.' This is an information and planning center at Denver which is the business world's equivalent of the military briefing room. Facts funneled daily into this center present a clear picture of operations throughout United's 80-city system.

"In keeping with the idea of expansive vision, the room has glass walls on one side. Modern white plastic chairs are grouped before a map of the United States, 8 feet high and 20 feet wide, on which United's routes are outlined. Colored lights (red for weather, green for maintenance, and white for passengers) at major terminals show current operating conditions. If the red light glows steadily, for example, it means adverse weather; if it is flashing, the weather is marginal. Electric clocks above the map show the time in each zone through which United operates.

"The room is designed to provide management with operational facts in the most convenient form. Data, such as mileage flown, delays at terminals by type of plane and total number of departures, are posted on lucite panels, flanking the map. Dozens of supplementary charts deal with payload volumes and load factors, weather, actual performance as compared with schedule and related information."[10]

THE LACK OF CENTRAL SYSTEMS

The lack of control systems was one of the major causes of the dismal failure of W. T. Grant Company when it went bankrupt in 1975. According to reports, Grant's buyers often had to ask their suppliers for figures on Grant's inventories because the firm had no data; vendors were requested by some officials to underbill Grant and pay purchasers on the side; and store managers were not given authority to control the stock in their own stores. Perhaps worst of all, about 20 percent of all credit purchasers never paid their bills but the delinquencies were never detected.[11]

ANTICIPATING PROBLEMS

The purpose of comparing performance with standards is not only to spot errors in strategy, but also to enable the manager to anticipate future problems. A good control system will allow top managers to make fast, accurate comparisons and identify future strategic problems—as Harold Geneen said, "No surprises." The graphing of actual performance versus planned overtime will often reveal significant trends, suggesting possible danger signals before the problems have ever emerged.

As an example, Chrysler's chairman Lee A. Iacocca set strategic plans for the 1980–81 model year that did not actually come about: "Iacocca boasted of 'great product,' 'fuel-economy leadership,' 'leadership in front-wheel drive,' 'six of the most modern plants in the world.' He also forecast Chrysler would enjoy a 35% increase in unit auto sales in 1981, with its market share rising to 12% of a U.S. car market of 10 million.

"Introduced in September 1980 with great fanfare, the K car was a painful disappointment," says *Fortune* (February 1981).

"Not as a car. It is a stylish front-wheel-drive compact, slightly roomier and a bit more fuel efficient than GM's X car, with which it is always compared. That is the rub. Once again, Chrsyler was the laggard with a new product. Introduced 18 months before, the X car was a sellout for nearly a year. Chrysler apparently expected the K car to do almost as well. It projected sales of around 70,000 cars in the introductory months of October and November, and for all of 1981 the September operating plan forecast a volume of 492,000—41,000 cars a month and 85% of capacity.

"Instead, the car had a miserable debut. Sales came to a mere 34,273 units in the first two months—a 50% shortfall. At his December 4, 1980, press conference, Iacocca largely blamed steep interest rates ("this latest crippling action by the Fed will have its desired effect on Chrysler's financial results"). But interest rates began their surge on November 6, by which time the K car had already lagged badly. By the end of November, 1980, dealers had a 98-day supply of K cars, as compared with a 54-day supply of X cars."[12]

For Chrysler Corp., the comparison of actual to planned results means that drastic strategic action must be taken, if the firm is to survive.

TAKING CORRECTIVE ACTION

The final step in the control process is correcting significant deviations from plan. The purpose of the control process is to allow the manager to identify problems and take needed corrective actions. The decisions that are made at this point, then, are the culmination of the process. The manager must decide if corrective action is warranted, and if so what actions should be taken.

The manager must assess the various possible actions. The manager must avoid taking corrective action where no action is needed; yet he must not fail to take action when a problem has emerged. If corrective action is called for, then he must also decide what type of action is best, given the specific situation.

CHANGING CONDITIONS

As conditions change, plans and programs must also change. However, when there is a discrepancy between plan and results, the strategist will want to determine why. If the premises and assumptions underlying a given strategy are still sound the strategist may wish to continue the strategy but with some modification. If, however, some major factors have changed, then a major realignment of strategy may be called for.

General Electric, for example, made a strategic decision to enter the computer market in the 1960's in what was obviously a high-growth market. The strategic plan proposed early losses, than anticipated profits. However, as GE management reviewed the plan, it discovered losses of some $162.7 million. Consequently, it had to review this strategic move and determine what action to take. Its decision: to get out of the computer business.

AT ITT

In the past under Harold Geneen, ITT pursued an aggressive strategy of acquisition and growth. However, Geneen's successor, Lyman C. Hamilton, Jr., viewed the company as stretched too thin and shifted the emphasis to divestitures and controlled growth. As a result, ITT's profits fell below the industry average (see Figure 12.2) causing management to sell off some 33 of the operations that Geneen had acquired.

Two factors were driving these sell-offs. Sluggish profits for the past five years have pushed ITT to rid itself mainly of poor performers. But a second, less recognized factor weighs equally heavily. The future of ITT's main business, telecommunications equipment, was fraught with some awesome risks, partly because the company had been losing ground in a technological revolution. Both problems mean that ITT needed to trim itself to fight for improvement. How to wage that fight after

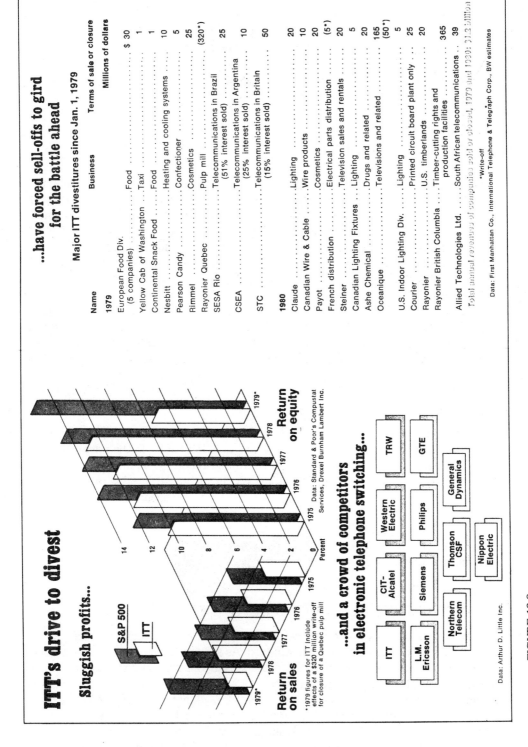

FIGURE 12.2
ITT Shifts to Divestitures and Controlled Growth.
SOURCE: *Business Week*, December 15, 1980, 66.

the pruning process was over was the primary strategic question facing it. The answer determined the viability of its conglomerate concept.[13]

The strategic control process at ITT indicated that either conditions were changing or the previous strategy was no longer working. As a result, ITT was developing new strategies to meet the changing conditions.

CONTROL SYSTEMS PROBLEMS

There are number of problems associated with the measurement of performance in control systems. The fact that a control system is well designed and sophisticated, like the one used at ITT, may cause it to be opposed by lower levels of management. Even an efficient and reasonable system may be ineffective if members feel that irrelevant data are collected or that the standards are unfair or unreasonable. Often this stems from "top down" planning where lower levels have not participated in the standard setting. No matter how technically sound the system may be, it will not work well unless it is accepted by organization members.

Similarly, there is a problem over what criteria of effectiveness are to be used. As Bruce Kirchoff has noted, "There is no ultimate criterion of effectiveness. Complex organizations pursue multiple goals. Real effectiveness can only be measured relative to a particular set of derived or prescribed goals.[14]

INVALID DATA REPORTING

Many time the reporting data are invalid, or includes data not under the manager's control. An unrealistic budget is an example of invalid data. In the past some companies went with a fixed budget and continued reporting against it even though conditions had changed. Economic recession or increased interest rates may have caused previous standards to no longer be meaningful measures of performance.

There are also instances where a manager is evaluated on performance even though he may not have total control of all factors. A manager may be measured as a profit center, for example, yet be forced to sell products to other divisions at unrealistic prices, and thus be penalized.

CONTRADICTORY DATA REPORTING

Often performance standards are set so that there are contradicting factors: as one element is maximized, another is minimized. As a result, no matter what the manager does, he is wrong. For example, the manager may be expected to increase market share and profits, yet lower expenditures. Or educators may be required to increase enrollments and maintain quality (class size, etc.), yet not add any new faculty members. Production people may be asked for increased production and fewer rejects yet be given no overtime nor allowed to hire new workers. *Business Week* reports:

"At Texas Instruments, for example, sales grew at a 32 percent rate, but profits fell from $24 million in 1978 to $2 million in 1979." The company blamed its profit problems squarely on the digital watch business, citing 'cost problems and competitive pricing pressure.' But as TI's major consumer electronics markets matured, there were increasing signals that the company's vaunted management systems were too burdensome a process for the volatile consumer marketplace. The watch business, in fact, was the poorest performer in a product portfolio whose 1979 performance was stalled by TI's inability to produce."[15]

As you can see, at TI there were many factors which could be measured, but which should not be used for evaluation. Organizational effectiveness is a complex concept, and it is not easy to decide which measures of performance actually relate to a successful strategy.

RESISTANCE TO CONTROLS

As noted earlier, one must consider the influence of control systems on human behavior. Given a good, fair system, employees may be motivated to increase performance: on the other hand, an unfair system may produce resistance in the form of "game playing" or "beating the system." As an example, the government requires universities receiving research funding to provide a detailed accounting of the way Ph.Ds spend their time in 20-minute blocks, how much time is spent on teaching, research, etc. The intent is to motivate people to manage time, and generate valid data about time allocation. The result, however, has been a great deal of resistance among highly skilled and competent professionals, who feel that such accounting is a waste of good time. The outcome involves either falsified reports with meaningless data, or an unwillingness to fill out such forms. Many universities are complaining about such systems.

Cortlandt Cammann and David A. Nadler summarize the effects of control sytems as shown in Figure 12.3. The existence of measures has an effect on subordinate behavior, but is not the only factor. These measures have to be perceived as being reasonably accurate, and they have to be used skillfully by the managers.[16]

THE NUMBERS GAME AT CBS

How the control information is used is of vital importance. If measures are used to play "numbers" games or to unfairly evaluate performance, then the effectiveness of the control system is reduced. One example of such a problem occurred at CBS, Inc., where John D. Backe announced that he had "resigned" from his $500,000-a-year job as president and chief executive officer.

"For precisely three years—he was named chief executive in May 1977—the 47-year-old Backe worked to shape up CBS, first, for the short haul and, second, for the new era of communications that today's rapid technological developments promise in the 1980s," *Business Week* again writes.

"Precisely what happened is that Backe discovered that the other members of the executive committee—made up of the outside board members, along with Chairman William Paley and himself—received an O.K. from the chairman to conduct a secret assessment of the job he had done, was doing, and might do once Paley was

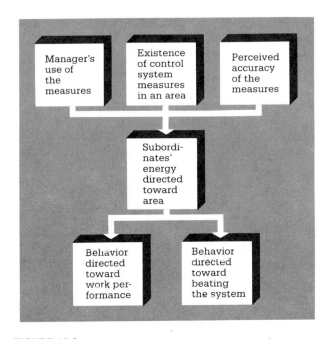

FIGURE 12.3

How Control Systems and Their Use Affect Behavior

SOURCE: Cortlandt Cammann and David A. Nadler, "Fit Control Systems to Your Managerial Style," Harvard Business Review, January–February 1976, 65. Copyright © 1976 by the President and Fellows of Harvard College; all rights reserved.

gone from the scene. Angry and startled, Backe 'brought about a showdown,' said Paley, who admitted that he initiated the study 'because of the factor of my age' and his concern about the future of CBS—not merely as a commercial enterprise but as an institution that he believes has the power to elevate the public welfare.

"Speaking forcefully, the white-haired executive said that he 'tried my damnedest to get Backe back on the track' after a confrontation over what the president obviously took as a loss of confidence in his leadership abilities. Paley insists that Backe's departure was not imminent 'because the assessment had not even been completed.' But he adds that it might have seemed 'we were certainly on our way to finding him disqualified, or not qualified, for the job ahead. He never gave us a chance to get there.' "[17]

As Cammann and Nadler suggest, control systems influence the way organization members direct their energies on the job. Managers are more likely to put time and effort into those areas covered by the control systems. Second, how members respond to control systems depends largely on the way managers use the systems. Third, different managers develop different strategies for using control systems. Finally, each control system has certain drawbacks and benefits.

TIME FRAME OF CRITERIA

Time is also a key factor in evaluating strategic performance. Do we evaluate in terms of short- or long-term criteria of effectiveness? In many situations, there is a tendency to overemphasize short-term performance at the expense of long-run goals, thus leading to longer-range problems. For example, a manager may optimize immediate profits by cutting R & D expenditures, but eventually this will result in an essential inability to compete technically at some future point.

RCA

Thornton Bradshaw

One example of this emphasis on short-term performance is at RCA Corp. where Thornton Bradshaw, has been named as the new chairman. He is a former Harvard Business School professor who has been given credit for bringing more sophisticated management and increased social awareness to Atlantic Richfield Co. during his 16 years as president. A leading periodical puts it this way:

"The events that led to the retirement of Edgar H. Griffiths, 59, and the appointment of Thornton F. Bradshaw, the 63-year-old president of Atlantic Richfield Co., as RCA Corp.'s chairman and chief executive, provide a rare view into the inner workings of a board when it is dissatisfied with its chairman's performance. That performance has been marked by internal wrangling and bitter public dismissals, all of which obstructed long-range planning. Such an atmosphere has long been troublesome to the board, which has wrestled with ways of altering it for nearly five years.

"With the appointment of Bradshaw, RCA's board may have found the solution. But the problems that faced Bradshaw were clear: He needed to establish long-range plans for each of the company's businesses, he needed to provide stable leadership and develop potential successors, and he needed to redirect the culture of the company from one based on intense politicking to one that rewards performance. Bradshaw himself agreed that the last problem was the most important.

"Almost since Griffiths took over as chief executive in 1976, the board sought long-range plans from Griffiths for each of RCA's operations. Instead it got an emphasis on short-term earnings. Says one source close to the board: Long-range planning at RCA meant, 'What are we going to do after lunch?' "[18]

YARDSTICK OF MANAGERIAL PERFORMANCE

One way to measure performance is by comparing the firm's results against those of other firms in the same or similar industries. There are two major published evaluations of large firms which provide objective comparisons on a range of criteria by *Fortune* and *Forbes*. *Fortune* publishes its Top 500 and second 500 largest manufacturing firms each year and ranks the best and worst performers on various financial criteria, including sales, profits, growth, price-earnings, return on investment, etc. *Forbes* also presents an overall evaluation of the largest firms in its Annual Report on

American Industry, ranking firms by industry on several key operating factors. *Forbes* also provides its "Yardsticks of Managerial Performance," in which rankings are made rating the firms on their comparative performance against similar companies.

The late William Glueck has noted that, "It is easier to measure performance when a company shows consistent results on most of these measures in most years. In fact, research indicates that there is a high intercorrelation among organizational variables. If a firm is a "winner" on three measures, chances are it is a winner on all measures. The most critical problem is the trade-off among measures."[19]

Both objective and subjective approaches to measurement become more difficult when using more than one criterion to rate success. For example, taking only two measures of success, efficiency and production effectiveness, four firms could be rated as shown in Figure 12.4.

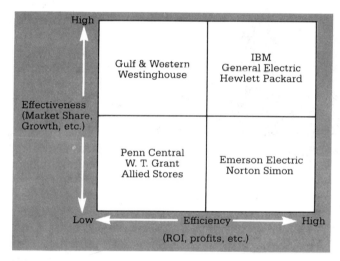

FIGURE 12.4

Company Efficiency to Effectiveness in Evaluation

SOURCE: Adapted from William Glueck, *Business Policy and Strategic Management* (New York: McGraw-Hill, 1980), p. 353.

The evaluation of multiple factors is important. Rensis Likert and others have found that it is possible for a company to make short-run results look better by firing or laying off employees (thus cutting direct labor costs). This strategy may achieve immediate financial improvement, but at the expense of deteriorating morale and performance in future periods.

MANAGERIAL IMPLICATIONS

The last stage of the strategic management process is evaluation and review of performance. The strategic control system is intended to allow managers to evaluate the results of their strategic decisions and plans. The control process is based on the measuring and reporting of actual performance, and a comparison of actual to plan to see whether the plan is, in fact, being carried out.

STRATEGIC CONTROL

Strategic control is the managerial function that ensures that actual organizational actions correspond to planned actions. Two aspects are important: First, control and review should take place at many stages of the implementation process; and second, control is closely related to other managerial functions—goal-setting, planning, and decision making. It is an interrelated function, rather than a separate activity.

An effective strategist is aware that formulating strategies, implementing action, and controlling to evaluate results are essential elements of strategic management. The manager must be able to correct faulty moves, and be able to adjust to meet changing situations. The manager should understand the characteristics and use of an effective control and reporting system, and must constantly be reviewing control systems and methods to be sure they are appropriate and realistic.

THE A & P STRATEGY

The control function is one of the most important and detailed stages in the strategic process. One of the keys to successful control is developing a positive and participative feedback and control system. Therefore, managers not only have a greater knowledge of the controlling operations; but since they are responsible for performance goals, they will likely be more highly motivated to work within the system.

In the case of Jonathan Scott and the A & P strategy, despite his efforts the strategy was a mistake, and Scott left the company.

"The only surprising thing about Jonathan Scott's resignation as chairman of A & P is that it did not come sooner. Ever since the Tengelmann Group, Germany's largest supermarket company, bought a controlling interest in A & P early last year, rumors had circulated that Scott would step aside. In April, he ended the suspense: he was leaving to form an investment company. The big news was that James Wood, fifty, a British citizen who had been running Grand Union, the eighth largest U.S. grocery chain, would take over.

"Tengelmann thought A & P could be returned to profitability in a year, but Rosemarie Baumeister, an A & P director and Tengelmann vice president, says, 'Things are worse than we anticipated. The mistakes of twenty to twenty-five years ago are still having an effect. In fiscal 1979, which ended in February, the company posted a $3.8-million deficit, the third loss in five years. It does not expect to be profitable in 1980, and Wood is not promising a quick fix.' 'It will certainly take me all of my five years,' he said after a few days on the job. 'We have a lot of work to do just to make A & P viable.'

"One thing Wood says he won't do is follow his predecessor's policy of shutting down a lot of stores. In 1975, guided by recommendations from Booz, Allen & Hamilton, the management consultants, Scott began closing units store by store. Even though the company also closed thirty-six food-processing plants and warehouses, it was left with huge manufacturing and distribution facilities serving fewer stores, an uneconomical way to do business. Then Scott called in McKinsey & Co., which recommended that A & P ax entire operating divisions.

"But the retrenchment strategy was abandoned soon after the Tengelmann Group appeared on the scene. 'Haub does not believe in closing stores,' explains Baumeister. 'Closing stores means giving away market share.' Not surprisingly, Wood concurs, 'It causes an imbalance in your company,' he says, 'I'm not excluding store closings, but it will only be a small ingredient in what I do.' "[20]

The intent behind management controls is to generate information about performance. Where something is going wrong, where there are deviations from plan, then corrective actions must be taken. Perhaps if Jonathan Scott had a better control and reporting system at A & P, he would have been able to detect problems earlier, made strategic alterations and possibly still be the CEO.

MANAGERIAL SKILLS

Control systems must be flexible enough to adapt to changes in the external and internal environments. The best controls are anticipative in nature; that is, they allow the strategist to anticipate problems before they occur. Therefore, the control system is not only used to examine the current state of the organization but, more importantly, to predict any important, developing trends.

The control system analyzes the entire management process—from goals and plans to implementation—and helps to pinpoint potential advantages and problems. The managerial skills necessary for the control and evaluation stage are as important as those skills necessary for the earlier stages. Managerial skills are crucial for designing and analyzing control procedures, for the interpersonal exchanges involved in presenting data, for integrating control systems with the strategic plan, and for determining the future impact of strategic countermoves.

The major key to success in the control process lies in integrating the controls into the total organization system and in adopting a broad-based, long-range approach to measuring performance.

SUMMARY

In walnut-paneled board rooms high above the major cities of the world, strategic decisions are being hammered out. Strategic decisions that will lead to success or failure, to profitability or losses, and to survival or bankruptcy. Strategic management is the key concept underlying a new systematic approach to the management of the total enterprise. Strategic management is the keystone, critical management function, yet it is only recently that strategy has been recognized as the central element in business success.

The central aim of the strategy/policy course is to learn about how to deal with all of the complexities and constraints involved in making strategic decisions. In this section, we will review some of the major points of strategic management.

THE BUSINESS CLIMATE OF THE EIGHTIES

The business climate of the 1980s will introduce dramatic changes. The rules of the business strategy game are changing and so is the game itself. Strategic management is redefining the way this game will be played. Major changes will be occurring in the environment, changes that will require an explicit identification and understanding of strategic concepts.

"FUTURE SHOCK"

The first of the changes involves a significant increase in the rate of change. This is the factor that Alvin Toffler termed "future shock," the enormous, exponential changes in technological, political, economic and social forces.

Because of these massive changes, managers will also be forced to implement strategic changes at an unprecedented rate.

INCREASING SIZE AND COMPLEXITY

The second significant change, as has been well documented by research, involves the increasing size and complexity of organizations. These changes will undoubtedly continue and result in new challenges to the integrating role of the manager. How managers will coordinate and integrate these complex and diverse structures is a continuing problem of strategic management.

GREATER INTERDEPENDENCE BETWEEN SYSTEMS

A third change is the greater interdependence between systems: everything is connected to everything else. As the size and complexity of our organizations increase and as external systems become directly related to the operation of the firm, the strategic manager must be more aware of socially responsible management.

MANAGING IN A WORLD OF SCARCITY AND CONSTRAINTS

Finally, managers of the eighties will be managing in a world of scarcity and constraints: making strategic decisions in an uncertain environment and with scarce resources.

Although experts may argue over exactly how long it will take to exhaust our various nonrenewable resources, the fact remains that in the eighties we will be faced with a growing world population and diminishing resources. This means that we will be managing with constraints, with new variables, more unknowns and greater unpredictability than ever before. How can the manager best use his limited human, technical, financial, and material resources to accomplish objectives in a constantly changing environment?

THE STRATEGIC MANAGEMENT PROCESS

This text has presented the stages of the strategic management process. Each stage has been examined separately; however in reality the stages are not so distinct, but rather overlap and are interrelated in the real world of management. Here they have been treated separately for purposes of explanation as a means to clarify the process. For our purposes, a strategy is that set of objectives, plans, and actions that taken together define the approach of the organization to its environment.

The strategic process begins with the basic purpose of the organization, and is aimed at allocating the resources of the organization through a complex set of plans, procedures and programs toward long-term goals. This process includes the formation of a strategy incorporating an analysis of all relevant factors, both internal and external forces, the development and evaluation of alternatives, strategic choice, the implementation of the strategy, and finally, the evaluation and review of the strategy to determine how effectively the strategic plan has worked.

THE STRATEGIC MANAGEMENT MODEL

The strategic management model includes an interrelated set of stages as follows:

Stage 1: Identifying the basic mission of the organization.

Stage 2: The impact of the strategic decision makers.

Stage 3: Determining strategic goals and objectives.

Stage 4: Identifying organizational strengths and weaknesses.

Stage 5: Analyzing the environment.

Stage 6: Identifying strategic alternatives.

Stage 7: Comparing strategic alternatives.

Stage 8: The strategic decision.

Stage 9: Strategic implementation—carrying out the plan.

Stage 10: Strategic evaluation and control.

SYSTEM OF MANAGEMENT

This process forms a system of management which relates strategic decisions to the long-range planning process and develops a systematic control over the organizations' complex operations. It is a process that begins with goals and objectives and then designs strategies, policies and controls to ensure that they will be achieved.

THE ART OF STRATEGIC MANAGEMENT

However, strategic management is not simply a process of analysis, evaluation and choice. It is the art of matching resources to opportunities, of calculating risks, deciding among alternatives, and then taking action. Strategy means overcoming barriers and constraints, developing and deploying sometimes limited resources, and implementing innovative strategies in resistant corporate cultures.

INCREASINGLY DIFFICULT DECISIONS

In an era of change, all strategies become ineffective or obsolete. Strategy, then, is a form of solution to a problem. The problems emerge as a result of the changing environment, as a mismatch between product, technology, and demand emerges in newly turbulent marketplaces. Strategic management offers a way to calculate the variables and risks in such problem situations. Strategic management allows the consideration of critical trade-offs and the deployment of resources for maximum returns. It focuses on exploiting new opportunities, counteracting threats, and out-manuevering the competition. Strategic management provides a direction and sense of urgency for the organization, and combines a calculated purpose with bold risk taking.

STRATEGIC MANAGEMENT: THE STATE OF THE ART

Effective strategic management requires a multidimensional thrust. Strategy is a general plan of action with an implied commitment of resources to achieve some basic goal. Broadly speaking, there are a number of dimensions to be considered.

First, effective strategies determine the overall direction and action focus of the organization: what business are we in, what do we want to do?

Second, effective strategies are formed around a few key businesses or thrusts, so that resources are not scattered throughout ineffective endeavors.

Third, effective strategy deals with the future. This means making decisions involving unpredictable and unknown variables. As a strategist, you can never know precisely how all the complex forces will interact and consequently, you must base your strategy on a carefully calculated assessment of a probable future.

Finally, an effective strategy aims at long-term goals, at developing a cohesive and comprehensive approach, and tying together in a systematic way many differing elements.

MORE EFFECTIVE

There is research evidence to suggest that firms that use the strategic process are more effective than those that do not, and that the process itself is changing, becoming ever more sophisticated and anticipative in nature. The emphasis on strategic management reflects the increasing complexity of the outside world and its impact upon the strategic manager.

Perhaps the most significant changes in the strategy field, however, concern the widespread adoption of advanced corporate planning and organization development techniques, so that the resource allocation and implementation processes are increasingly being emphasized. These recent techniques, including contingency theory and portfolio models, are the first major advances in systematically identifying the central, underlying strategic variables of large multibusiness firms.

CONCLUSION

There is one inescapable conclusion regarding strategic management. The real choice is not whether to use strategic management or not, but between management and nonmanagement. The degree to which a firm is effective in its strategy will largely determine whether the company will survive and be profitable, or decline and eventually fail.

In this text, you have learned about a new and challenging field: strategic management. The material, cases and real world examples have been presented to provide you with the current state of the art in this dynamic field. If the process of strategic management is used effectively, then the chances are that you will be a successful manager.

This text does not provide a panacea for managers. Instead, it seeks to provide you with a better understanding of how large organizations actually do derive their strategies, to bring you some new insights and ideas to blend with your existing approaches, and perhaps, to offer some new techniques and models which may be useful to strategists and students of strategic management.

The purpose of this book has been to assist you in understanding how and why strategic management can be used in the central, "big picture" decisions of managers in making those crucial decisions which can mean the difference between winning or losing. The text has been aimed at helping you make the transition from the classroom to the "real world" of organizations by allowing you an opportunity to practice your own managerial skills.

At some point in the future, you may well be in a boardroom making a presentation to the executive committee of a major firm. It is our hope that what you have learned here will help you get there, and to make the most of the opportunity when it arrives.

REVIEW QUESTIONS

1   What are the relationships between objectives, planning, and controlling?

2   What are the steps in the strategic control process? In what ways do they form a feedback process?

3   Jim Tillman is a project manager for plant construction projects. Each project manager is measured on how his performance meets subcontract provisions. How might Jim get better control of his subcontractors and total operations?

4   What are some of the intended and unintended consequences of the use of control systems?

5 How are effective or ineffective control systems related to motivation?

6 Suppose the MBA program in your university was overcrowded and wanted better quality control of its student population. What control would you recommend?

7 A small distribution company owns several local restaurants and college type bars and seeks a growth goal of 16 percent per year. The firm is considering the purchase of a small regional brewery. Do you feel that this would tie in with its overall strategy? Why?

ENDNOTES

1 See Peter W. Bernstein, "Jonathan Scott's Suprising Failure at A & P," *Fortune,* November 6, 1978, 35–36.

2 Harold Koontz, "A Preliminary Statement of Principles of Planning and Control," *Journal of the Academy of Management,* April 1958, 48.

3 Richard Rumelt, "The Evaluation of Business Strategy," from William Glueck, *Business Policy and Strategic Management* (New York: McGraw-Hill, 1980), p. 359.

4 "What Makes Harry Gray Run?" *Business Week,* December 10, 1979, 80.

5 Seymour Tilles, "How to Evaluate Corporate Strategy," *Harvard Business Reviews,* July-August, 1963, 111–21.

6 "Emerson Electric: Efficiency Isn't a Goal; It's a Religion," *Forbes,* March 20, 1978, 41.

7 G. P. Latham and G. A. Yukl, "A Review of Research on the Application of Goal Setting in Organizations," *Academy of Management Journal,* 23 (1970), 824–45.

8 Bernstein, "A & P Calls in a Reliever," 67.

9 Anthony Sampson, *The Sovereign State: The Secret History of ITT* (London: Coronet Books, 1974), p. 119.

10 Philip Gustafson "Business Reports: How To Get Facts You Need," *Nation's Business,* August, 1956, 78–82.

11 S. H. Slom, "Grant Testimony Shows It Lacked Curbs on Budget, Credit and Internal Woes," *The Wall Street Journal,* February 4, 1977.

12 Irwin Ross, "Chrysler on the Brink," *Fortune,* February 9, 1981, 38.

13 "ITT: Groping for a New Strategy," *Business Week,* December 15, 1980, 66.

14 Bruce A. Kirchoff, "Organization Effectiveness Measurement and Policy Research," *Academy of Management Review,* July 1977, 352.

15 "Why Consumer Products Lag at Texas Instruments," *Business Week,* May 5, 1980, 94.

16 Cortlandt Cammann and David A. Nadler, "Fit Control Systems to Your Managerial Style," *Harvard Business Review,* January-February 1976, 65-72.

17 "CBS: When Being No. 1 Isn't Enough," *Business Week,* May 26, 1980, 128.

18 "Why Griffiths is Out as RCA Chairman," *Business Week,* February 9, 1981, 72.

19 William Glueck, *Business Policy and Strategic Management.*

20 Peter W. Bernstein, "A & P Calls in a Reliever," *Fortune,* June 2, 1980, 67.

```
┌─────────────────────────────────────────────────────┐
│                                                       │
│                                          CASES        │
│            STRATEGIC IMPLEMENTATION                   │
│                    AND EVALUATION                     │
│                                                       │
│                                                       │
│                                                       │
│                                                       │
│                                                       │
└─────────────────────────────────────────────────────┘
```

CASE ANALYSIS

The Business Policy/Strategic Management course may be approached in many different ways, but, in general, the classroom becomes the board room. That is to say, you become involved in making strategic decisions. At ITT and other major corporations, managers are presenting plans, proposals and projects to the Executive Committee. They usually use slides, charts, transparencies and other visual aids to present complex problems and analyses. At ITT, Harold Geneen was famous for his probing questions and his search for "unshakeable facts." In the classroom, your classmates and the instructor fill this role. In academic programs, then, you are practicing and developing your managerial skills in the case analysis sessions.

WHAT IS A CASE?

A case provides a written description of actual managerial problems, situations and events. It provides factual information about an industry, an organization and its products and markets, its competitive position, and whatever financial, structural and economic data may be pertinent. In essence, the cases provide a simulation of the organizational problems facing managers on a daily basis.

Your role is to analyze, diagnose and evaluate the problem situation, and present recommendations about what should be done. You have the responsibility of being prepared, and of sharing your own ideas and solutions with the class.

WHY USE CASES?

Cases provide you with an opportunity to simulate actual experience by analyzing problems and making decisions. To learn strategic management, the student needs both knowledge of management techniques and experience at actually putting theory into practice. This method is known as *experiential learning*, or learning by doing. The experiential approach is different from traditional learning, because the major responsibility for learning is placed upon you.

Rather than looking for a "right answer" to memorize, you should be more concerned with identifying key problems, analyzing data, evaluating alternatives, examining the credibility of various strategies and making and defending your own decisions.

In experiential learning a four-step process is involved as shown in Exhibit 1.

1 *Analysis.* You will be doing pre-class preparation and analysis of the case. This often includes library research, determining financial ratios, etc.

2 *Case Presentation and Discussion.* You will be involved, either as a presenter or discussant, in the case presentation and your ideas will be subject to open debate and criticism.

3 *Critique.* You will be able to compare your analysis with others, evaluate your own approaches and decisions with others, and compare the results of different strategies.

4 *Generalization.* From each encounter, your own analytical and communication skills should be improving, and you should be able to find common elements and approaches to problem solving on a broader scale.

In experiential learning, the analysis and interchange that takes place in the class discussion is more important than finding a "right answer." There is an opportunity for you to sharpen your skills and develop your ability to apply your knowledge in "real world" situations.

The purpose, then, of the experiential approach is to become skilled in the process of thinking for yourself, of making managerial assessments, and defending your plan of action.

HOW TO PREPARE A CASE

There are a number of approaches to preparing a case but it is helpful to develop a systematic procedure for case preparation. First, the case analysis requires time and

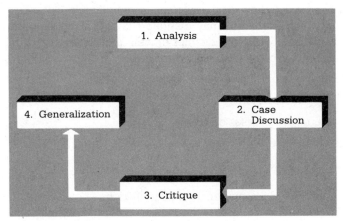

EXHIBIT 1.
Schematic Diagram of Experiential Learning Cycle.

effort for a conscientious preparation. Your main objective is not only to skim the case, but to comprehend its major points as efficiently as possible.

Most cases need to be read through at least twice; therefore you should try to schedule blocks of time such as 2-4 hours for case preparation.

Preparing cases involves two basic skills:

1 *Analysis.* Preparing cases requires sharpening your analytical skills. You will need to immerse yourself in the facts and behaviors presented in this segment of reality. Out of the confusing array of data, you must determine the critical issues, and develop a plan of action.

2 *Presentation.* Second, you must organize your analysis in a form that will allow you to discuss it clearly in class.

As you analyze the case, you should be asking questions:

What is the organization's current strategy?
What is the real problem facing this manager?
What factors have contibuted most to past success or lack of success?

Your general approach to case preparation may proceed as follows:

1 Read the case through, underlining or making notes in the margin on important facts. Try to get a feel for the overall content of the case, the industry, the management, etc.

2 Examine all exhibits carefully. These typically include operating statements, balance sheets, organization charts, etc. It is safe to assume that these items have been included for a purpose.

3 Prepare any necessary financial analysis, ratios or comparisons.

4 Read the text again, this time forming your analysis into a logical outline, collecting commen elements and examining in detail goals, policies, symptoms of problems, unresolved issues, managerial roles, etc.

5   Effective analysis is based on a systematic framework. One such approach is the systems approach. You may diagram the overall system and subsystems involved and specify the relationships of their interaction. Try to define precisely the interactions and the role of key characters.

6   Identification of problems and key issues.

7   Analyze the causes.

8   Identify alternative courses of action.

9   Evaluate alternatives according to some criteria.

10   Presentation of a plan of action.

You should remember, your plan of action should flow from your identification of problems, and that this is the "socko" part of your case. Regardless of the "rightness or wrongness" or your decision, you should have a solid, logical supporting analysis to defend your choice.

CLASS DISCUSSION

It is helpful to have your ideas arranged in organized logical form, so they will be clearly understood. If you need to present them in class, then visual aids are appropriate, including graphs, diagrams, etc., on flip charts, overhead transparencies, or on the blackboard. As the saying goes, "A picture is worth a thousand words," plus the visual aid gives you something to refer to as you talk.

Try to sharpen your analyses to a few key points, don't try to use overkill on your audience.

In the following section, a review of important financial analysis techniques is presented. You should enjoy the case analyses and discussion sessions, if you are well prepared. Remember, the cases are used to help you learn about managing. One of the primary advantages of the case method is the opportunity to exchange views from a diversity of experiences. Only by taking positions and making your point can you test yourself against your fellow class members and your instructors. *Good luck!*

HOW TO READ FINANCIAL STATEMENTS

While accountants must collect data in great detail, financial analysts are forced to group data (accounts) for analysis. Below is a brief guide to the balance sheet and income statement.

The balance sheet is a statement of financial position as of a specific date. With the usual caveat about the balance sheet's presenting historical rather than market values, here are the important account groupings:

Cash and securities	Current liabilities
Receivables	Long term debt
Inventories	Preferred stock
Other current assets	Common equity
Current Assets	
Fixed Assets — net of depreciation	
Total Assets	Total Claims

Note that the only detail, below the first level, is within the current assets. This is done because there is a vast difference in the liquidity (ease of conversion into cash) between the various current assets; and, current assets are held primarily for liquidity. (See the section on liquidity ratios.)

On the income statement, the expense accounts must be grouped into significant analytical categories. The result is as follows:

Net sales (revenues)
minus cost of goods sold
equals gross profit
minus selling and administrative operating expenses
  (net of depreciation)
minus depreciation
equals operating profit
minus interest charges
equals earnings before taxes
minus taxes
equals net income

Note that we separate depreciation from other operating expenses. This is because depreciation (and amortization, depletion, etc.) is not a cash expense. Therefore, the analyst may wish to separate this account, especially if liquidity is a matter for concern.

A particularly troublesome account which is appearing more commonly is lease expense. Leasing capital equipment is a popular alternative to borrowing and buying. With a lease, the firm incurs a fixed obligation, much like interest. Regardless of where it appears in the income statement, lease expense should be separated for analysis. (See the section on debt management ratios.)

ANALYZING FINANCIAL STATEMENTS

In many of the cases, you are given financial data, sometimes in summary form, sometimes in greater detail. You should make use of the financial data in your case analysis, even if the primary theme appears to be nonfinancial. Financial data, properly analyzed, can often confirm tentative conclusions and may provide clues that lead to other discoveries about the firm.

You may be provided with some or all of the following financial statements:

> income
> balance sheet
> retained earnings
> changes in financial position

Most commonly, you will have income statements and balance sheets, perhaps for the several most recent years. Financial ratios are used to analyze these two statements. Ratios are discussed below.

A Word on Precision Financial data may well be the only quantitative data provided. Numbers connote precision; but, remember that you are looking at numbers condensed from many detailed accounting reports. These summaries may, in fact, be designed to convey a certain impression of the firm, and vast differences in procedure are allowed under the aegis of "generally accepted accounting principles." So, a word to the wise: Look for confirmation to your conclusions. Confirmation can be found in the data itself—for instance, two or more financial ratios which support the conclusion. It is even better to find confirmation in the case text itself.

Using Ratios A ratio is simply a means of converting two numbers into one. Interpretation depends on comparison. If you are provided with several years of data, you may analyze trends. Better yet, you may use industry average ratios. Two financial service organizations provide these ratios. Each has a unique set, however, so you may have to match your ratios to theirs. These services are Dun & Bradstreet, Inc., and Robert Morris Associates' *Annual Statement Studies*. In addition, the Federal Trade Commission's *Quarterly Financial Report* provides manufacturing ratios.

You may have access to computerized financial statements for major firms, such as Standard & Poor's *Compustat* or *Value Line*. They often provide statements for ten years, and sometimes calculated ratios and even industry averages, firm trends and graphic displays. Securities brokerage firms are another source of (often voluminous) firm and industry data.

Keep in mind that "industries" are becoming increasingly difficult to identify. Diversification as a strategy, long practiced by such firms as General Electric, became popular in the 1960s. Using mergers, many firms were able to grow rapidly without arousing the ire of the U.S. Department of Justice. Through the 1970s, diversification has remained popular as a means of protection against an increasingly volatile business cycle.

Financial Ratios   The ratios that follow can be calculated from the income statement and balance sheet. Ratios are commonly divided into five categories. Within
each, several of the most useful ratios are presented. There is no one best set of ratios.
The skilled analyst uses those which he (she) needs, and, on occasion, devises his
(her) own to fill a specific need. The five categories are, liquidity, asset utilization,
debt management, profitability, and common stock.

   Liquidity is simply a measure of a firm's ability to generate sufficient
cash to meet its current obligations. Because liquidity is essential for survival, it
should take priority in the analysis. The two most common ratios are:

$$1. \quad \text{current ratio} = \frac{\text{current assets}}{\text{current liabilities}}$$

The higher the ratio, the greater the presumed ability of the firm to pay its current
debt.

$$2. \quad \text{quick (acid test) ratio} = \frac{\text{current assets} - \text{inventories}}{\text{current liabilities}}$$

Inventories are subtracted because they are the least liquid of current assets, and, in
fact, in a forced sale, may be worth very little. Substantial deviation below 1:1 may
indicate a cash crisis; a ratio of 3:1 or higher suggests a cash rich firm.

Asset Utilization   These are sometimes called "turnover" ratios. All relate an
asset to sales. Assets are acquired to produce sales. These ratios measure asset use
efficiency. Remember that holding any asset requires the use of increasingly high
cost resources. The first two ratios deal with current assets—receivables and inventories—and, therefore, are also liquidity measures.

$$\text{average collection period} = \frac{\text{receivables}}{\text{average daily sales}}$$

Average daily sales are total yearly sales divided by 360 (or 365) days. This is the
average number of days for which receivables remain uncollected. If this number is
high, it signifies either poor credit collection practices or a liberal credit policy.

$$\text{inventory turnover} = \frac{\text{sales}}{\text{inventories}}$$

This measures the average number of times per year that inventory is "turned over"—
purchased, processed and sold. The higher the number, the greater the efficiency.

$$\text{fixed asset turnover} = \frac{\text{sales}}{\text{fixed assets}}$$

Fixed assets are the "productive" assets—plant and equipment. High numbers are
generally desirable.

$$\text{total asset turnover} = \frac{\text{sales}}{\text{total assets}}$$

This is a gross measure. A low turnover can mean an excess of either current or fixed
assets.

Debt Management   Debt (and leasing) entails a fixed obligation. There is an opportunity to borrow at a low rate (interest is tax deductible), and invest this borrowed money at higher rates of return. This is called, "positive leveraging." It can greatly increase returns to the common stockholders and drive the firm's stock price up. The firm can also find itself in a negative leveraging position from a combination of high interest rates and declining return on investment. Nontheless, U.S. firms have become increasingly (some say dangerously) leveraged in the past two decades. The use of debt implies both opportunity and risk.

There are two categories of debt management ratios. One proportions debt to assets or capital. The other examines the ability of the firm to meet its debt obligations. The ratios in the first category are:

$$\text{debt to total assets} = \frac{\text{current} + \text{long term debt}}{\text{total assets}}$$

The higher the ratio, the greater the leveraging.

$$\text{long term debt to total capital} = \frac{\text{long term debt}}{\text{long term debt} + \text{preferred} + \text{common equity}}$$

This differs from the debt to total assets ratio in that current liabilities are deleted from both numerator and denominator. It may be more meaningful because current liabilities are transitory and do not represent permanent financing sources.

The second category of debt management ratios includes:

$$\text{times interest earned} = \frac{\text{operating profit}}{\text{interest charges}}$$

This is an important measure, since interest must be paid from operating profit. This ratio should be kept relatively high since operating profit can drop greatly under adversity, such as recession.

$$\text{fixed charge coverage} = \frac{\text{operating profit} + \text{lease payments}}{\text{interest} + \text{lease payments}}$$

This is a modification of times interest earned to cover lease payments. (See the discussion of leasing in the section "How to Read Financial Statements.") Lease payments must be added to the numerator because they are usually included as an operating expense, and, therefore, have already been deducted in calculating operating profit.

Profitability   There are two categories of profit ratios. One consists of "margin" ratios, proportioning profit to sales. These are derived from the income statement and measure cost control performance. They are usually considered less important than the second category, called "return" ratios. These measure profit against resources committed to the firm.

The primary margin ratio is

$$\text{profit margin} = \frac{\text{net profit}}{\text{sales}}$$

Other margin ratios, using gross, operating or before tax profit, can also be calculated. Return ratios include:

$$\text{return on investment} = \frac{\text{net profit}}{\text{total assets}}$$

This is the "ultimate" profit measure, since assets represent the total of the resources committed to the firm.

$$\text{return on equity} = \frac{\text{net profit}}{\text{common equity}}$$

This is of primary interest to the firm's stockholders. This is the ratio which will be most affected by positive or negative leveraging.

Common Stock   Three that are useful to investors are

$$\text{dividend payout ratio} = \frac{\text{dividends}}{\text{net profit}}$$

Dividends paid for the year are found in the statement of retained earnings (discussed below). It is important to know what proportion of earnings is paid and what is retained, for two reasons: First, dividends constitute a significant portion of the total yield on some stocks. Second, this ratio provides an indication of future prospects for the firm. A low payout, from a generally healthy firm, indicates that earnings are being reinvested for growth.

To calculate the next two ratios, the number of common stock shares outstanding must be given:

$$\text{dividend yield} = \frac{\text{dividends per share}}{\text{stock price}}$$

This is the measure of current yield to the stockholders.

$$\text{price earnings ratio} = \frac{\text{stock price}}{\text{earnings per share}}$$

This is a measure of the degree of acceptance of the firm's stock in the market. A high ratio connotes great acceptance. It may also mean that the stock is "overvalued." Some securities analysts look for "low P/E" stocks, which may mean undervaluation in the market.

Another common and simple analytical technique is to "common size" the balance sheet and income statement. This allows for easy comparisons, since size is abstracted and relationships are easily seen. All balance sheet items are percentaged to total assets and all income statement items percentaged to net sales.

Statement of Retained Earnings   This simple statement connects balance sheet common equity and net profit. Profit can be paid in dividends or added to common equity via retained earnings. The usual format follows:

retained earnings balance (previous year)
plus current year net income

minus dividends paid
equals retained earnings balance (current year)

Statement of Changes in Financial Position   This is also more descriptively called the source and application of funds statement. Funds are defined as net working capital—current assets minus current liabilities. This represents a net liquidity position of the firm. This statement examines the change in net working capital (in dollars) from one year to the next and changes in those noncurrent accounts which contributed to the change. Those noncurrent balance sheet accounts include fixed assets, long term debt and equity.

Sources of funds:	net profit
	depreciation
	sale of long term debt
	sale of stock
	sale of fixed assets
Application of funds:	net loss
	purchase of fixed assets
	decrease in long term debt
	stock repurchase
	dividends

THE MINI-STORAGE BUSINESS: ENTREPRENEURIAL DECISION MAKING

Marjorie G. Prentice

Dick and Judy LaVergne early in 1979 acknowledged that they have long wanted to expand their opportunities beyond full-time employment to include part-time management of a small business venture. The thrill of private entrepreneurship and the opportunity to make a substantial return on investment are key elements in their long term goals.

After much preliminary investigation into a variety of possible business ventures such as racquetball courts, fast food franchises and self-serve car washes, Dick and Judy have narrowed their consideration to an investment in the rapidly growing mini-storage industry. The decision to consider investing in this industry was made in response to their desire to find a business which (1) did not require a high level of technical expertise, (2) would have a high year-round customer demand, and (3) would be relatively easy to enter and operate.

At last they have reached the point of decision. Should they build in a mini-storage business? If they decide to build a mini-storage facility, where should it be located and what should be the mix of unit sizes? Can they handle the operations of a mini-storage business on a part-time basis? All of these questions, and many more, pass through Dick's mind as he and his wife review the information they have gathered over the past year.

GENERAL BACKGROUND

The LaVergnes live in Sacramento, the capital of California. Sacramento is surrounded by a number of "bedroom" communities, some relatively stable, and others growing rapidly. As the center of the state, county and city government, Sacramento has a large percentage of its labor force in service occupations. Within the extended metropolitan area there are two major Air Force Bases, Mather and McClellan, each with a relatively transient military population.

Beyond the immediate metropolitan area, there are still large expanses of undeveloped land which are of increasing interest to major industries wishing to expand or relocate in California. Such industries need space, not only for plant, facilities, but for a major influx of production workers if a local labor supply is not already available. Hewlett Packard is

This case was prepared by Associate Professor Marjorie G. Prentice of Drake University as a basis for class discussion rather than to illustrate either effective or ineffective handling of an entrepreneurial decision-making situation.

Copyright © 1980 by Marjorie G. Prentice

Distributed by the Intercollegiate Case Clearing House, Soldiers Field, Boston, Mass. 02163. All rights reserved to the contributors. Printed in U.S.A.

one such firm considering expansion in the Roseville area northeast of Sacramento. Should Hewlett Packard exercise their land option, it is estimated that they will need 4,500 employees by 1985.

The mild climate of the Sacramento area is particularly appealing to the American public in the face of increasing energy costs for home heating. This asset to home owners, coupled with the property tax relief resulting from California's 1979 "Proposition 13" is encouraging increased migration to the area. Outdoor recreational opportunities are an important feature of California living. Within two hours, Sacramentoans can have their R.V.s in the campgrounds of the Sierra Nevada mountains. Within less than one hour, most Sacramento sailers, boaters and water skiers can be at the highly developed facilities of Lake Folsom, just northeast of the city. These combined factors make Sacramento a very desirable place for a family to locate.

INDUSTRY BACKGROUND

The mini-storage business, often referred to as private storage rooms, or by such terms as "rent-a-space" facilities or "U-lock-it" units, provides private and secure individual storage units for such varied items as household goods, business records, retail-wholesale inventory, sports and out-of-season equipment, and recreational vehicles. Most present firms operating mini-sized self storage units tend to use a similar design known as modified warehouse units. Typically, each location has eight or more cinderblock buildings subdivided by wooden partitions into 350 to 800 units. These individual storge units vary in size from 4' × 6' closets to 10' by 30' indoor rooms. Many facilities also include outdoor parking areas for cars, campers, and boats. Each facility is surrounded by a chain link fence and has high intensity lighting and other extensive security precautions.

Customer Consideration.   Customer access to most individual units is from the outside of the building through individually keyed steel roll-up doors; however, some of the smaller units have only interior hallway access. The facilities are usually open daily, with entrance controlled through a key card or with a sign-in-out sheet in the manager's office. Units are rented on a monthly basis, with charges in relation to both unit square footage and demand.

Demand—As both residential and business construction costs have risen, architects and owners have tended to decrease the internal storage space of living and working accommodations. With storage space at a premium, mini-storage units have become increasingly popular. In addition to business storage needs for records and inventories, and apartment and residential dweller's needs for household and recreational storage, a currently expanding demand for storage exists for mobile home owners. The early 1980's recession appears not to have hurt the mobile home industry in California as it has conventional home construction.

According to managers of several operating mini-storage facilities, the demand for mini-storage units has resulted in a 90–92% average occupancy rate for all sizes of units during the late 1970's. They say the greatest demand is for the smaller units of 5' × 10' and under. Presently, mini-storage firms have larger numbers of these smaller units available, but there are still waiting lists for these small sized units. This is not to imply that the larger units are not needed, but only that the $10' \times 10'$ and larger sizes are less popular than the smaller units.

Competition—At the present time there is such a high demand for self-storage units from conventional and mobile home owners, small business managers and sports enthusiasts, that competition does not seem to present a problem. Two examples support this view. Three mini-storage facilities operate adjacent to the Folsom Boulevard and Sunrise Boulevard freeway interchange in Rancho Cordova, just east of Sacramento. The two older original facilities have 95–100% occupancy and the newest firm is reported to be filling quickly without causing any decrease in demand for the others. The second example is a storage facility currently being constructed in Roseville adjacent to an older established firm. The manager of the operating firm expects no decrease in her demand, and predicts sufficient demand for the new company to operate profitably. This apparently favorable climate may continue for the immediate future. However, in the long run, conditions may vary, depending upon the location selected.

Management Consideration.   There are several major advantages for the owner of a mini-storage business. Three of these are (1) low maintenance, requiring little in addition to trash removal; (2) relatively low original land costs, as facilities can be built close to freeways, on odd-shaped parcels of commercially zoned land, or other less desirable locations; and (3) below average construction costs, due to limited requirements for plumbing, interior finishing work and other items requiring high-cost skilled labor.

Two of the primary problems in the mini-storage business are day-by-day management and security. Most owners hire one or more resident managers to maintain a residence at the mini-storage facility on a 24-hour basis. However, the storage facilities are usually open to the customer only from 7:00 a.m. to 11:00 p.m., seven days a week. The restrictive life-style coupled with the heavy paper-work flow required by high turnover customers, especially those with seasonal or inventory related needs, are undoubtedly reasons for the high turnover rate of resident managers within the industry.

An effective security system requires a perimeter chain link fence and high intensity lighting. Of the dozens of variations of security systems available, there seem to be three main types which are appropriate for this industry:

1   An alarm, deactivated by a key, installed in each door of each unit. The security key is issued to the customer at the time the unit key is issued.

2   Zoning surveillance and electronic monitoring, which relies on a centralized system. Each door is monitored to signal the central office whenever that door is entered.

3   Guard dogs, usually German Shepherds or Doberman Pinschers, can be either owned or rented. The dogs are usually used in pairs, and are in addition to the resident manager. The rental, per dog, per month, in the Sacramento area is $195, including transportation and required care. Dogs are used by most of the companies in the Sacramento area, often in combination with one or more other security devices.

FINANCIAL INFORMATION

From banks, credit unions, building contractors, real estate firms, and government agencies, the LaVergnes have carefully gathered a great deal of financial information. They feel they now are in a position to make a decision on entering the mini-storage business. They have learned that a typical facility would need about 2.5 acres of land (a lot approximately 210 × 520 feet). The entire area must be enclosed by a high quality chain link fence and the entire surface within the fence must be asphalt covered, with the exception of the actual building footage.

Investigation has disclosed that, in this industry, the IRS expects the buildings to depreciate over a 30-year period, and fencing and asphalt to be depreciated over a 20-year period; accelerated depreciation is not permitted. A 65 percent occupancy rate is common for the first year, with a "conservative" 90 percent occupancy rate each year thereafter. Expenses and revenues should increase at the same rate over the foreseeable future.

Architectural considerations will influence the initial investment cost. For example, commercial building codes, maximizing fire and theft prevention while minimizing construction costs, and special code requirements for a live-in management unit must be considered in estimated cost projections.

Estimates of constrction costs and actual operating expenses are shown in Exhibits 1 and 2 respectively. Through the liquidation of several prior investments, Dick presently has the ability to raise $180,000 for the required 20 percent down payment on the $900,000 he will need for this new business. Thirty year loans are available at 14% interest through commercial outlets which will cover the remaining 80 percent needed for initial construction costs and first year working capital requirements.

SITE LOCATION INFORMATION

There seems to be a great deal of pricing consistency within the industry, at least in the Sacramento area. A comparison of unit sizes, numbers of units, and rental fees for three established firms are shown in Exhibit 4.

In order to maintain a high unit occupancy rate, location is a primary consideration. Land availability, land costs, zoning laws, freeway/thoroughfare access, high density population and ease of travel from LaVergne's home are all important. His preferences for location are in the area north-northeast of the metropolitan area, in either Sacramento or Placer counties. From this general area, he chose four sites to investigate; Folsom, Citrus Heights, Carmichael, and Roseville. (See Exhibit 3 for a map of the area and Exhibit 5 for population figures of the area.)

Folsom would be a high demand area because of the excellent recreational developments around Folsom Lake and the resulting need for storage of boats and other recreational equipment. Folsom has many parcels of available commercial land for building. The drawbacks, however, are in the strict zoning limitations to protect the natural environment, and the absence of good freeway access to the available land within the city.

Citrus Heights also seems to be a good site due to the fact that many new homes are being built in the area, most of which are smaller than in the past decade, and therefore, with limited built-in storage. There is also a present lack of competition from other storage firms in this area. The primary problems for a Citrus Heights location are (1) the limited availability of any easily accessible commercial land of sufficient size to handle this proposed development and (2) strict zoning regulations which would limit site and design options.

Carmichael is the nearest of the four cities to downtown Sacramento. It already has a high, relatively stable population. Many parts of the city are comprised primarily of older homes with an average larger amount of internal storage as well as basements and garages. Commercial land availability is limited due to the high residential population already established in the community.

Roseville's Chamber of Commerce reports that this city has a good growth potential, a wide variety of available commercial land near freeway access, and more new home construction under way than in the other three areas. In addition, a major firm has a land option for a proposed plant which will employ 4,500 persons within the next few years.

Recognition of site location is an important element in the mini-storage industry. Presently, the primary sources of advertising are: (1) multi-column space in the *Yellow Pages* of the telephone directory and (2) on-building signs painted or mounted on the freeway-adjacent storage units. As other companies enter the market, there will undoubtedly be the need for other forms of advertising. A location away from major freeway visibility would make additional promotional strategies necessary.

OPERATIONAL INFORMATION

Once a facility is in operation, maintenance is usually at a minimum, with trash control often being the most complicated task. If customer turnover is high, office records can be a problem.

Operating considerations are directly related to the number of buildings containing the individual units to be managed. In addition, excessive turnover rates for live-in managers pose a critical problem which must be solved if the operation is to function effectively and profitably.

Based on a series of interviews with present managers, the LaVergnes have decided that if they build, the facility should have no more than five sizes of units: 5×6, 5×10, 10×10, 10×20, and 10×30. The expected annual occupancy rate, after the first year, is 95% for the two smaller size units, 90% for the 10×10 size, and 85% for the two larger size units. Dick wants to spend no more than $660,000 for construction costs and expects a payback of his total investment within seven years.

EXHIBIT 1

ESTIMATED "START UP" COSTS

1979 cost estimates for a "typical" self-storage facility in the Sacramento area:

Land acquisition	75,000
Architect fees	16,400
Construction costs for storage units	660,000[1]
Additional construction costs for	
live-in management	20,000
Asphalting costs	70,000
Fencing costs	6,300
Security system	20,000
Legal fees (incorporation)	2,300
Working capital (1st year)	30,000
	$900,000

[1]The greater number of smaller units, the higher will be the total costs. For example, within a space of 10′ × 20′ you can build one storage unit at a cost of $2200, four 5′ × 10′ units at a cost of $2,400 or six 5′ × 6′ units at a cost of $2520. (Based on construction costs as follows:)

$$10 \times 30 \text{ units at } \$11.50/\text{sq. ft.}$$
$$10 \times 20 \text{ units at } \$11.00/\text{sq. ft.}$$
$$10 \times 10 \text{ units at } \$10.75/\text{sq. ft.}$$
$$5 \times 10 \text{ units at } \$12.00/\text{sq. ft.}$$
$$5 \times 6 \text{ units at } \$14.00/\text{sq. ft.}$$

EXHIBIT 2

ESTIMATED ANNUAL OPERATING COSTS

Expenses for a "typical" medium-sized faciity (575 units), include, but are not limited to, the following annual costs:

Insurance	$ 4,000
Security[1]	$ 5,000
Payroll—wages and fringes	$ 12,000
Advertising expenses	$ 5,000
Office supplies	$ 500
Property taxes	$ 14,000
Repairs and maintenance	$ 2,000
Depreciation[2]	$ 26,500
Utilities	$ 4,000
Loan repayment[3]	$102,800
Legal fees	$ 1,000
Accounting and auditing fees	$ 1,000
Corporate tax rate[4]	+

[1]Rental of two guard dogs for periods when the facility is not open.
[2]Actual Depreciation based on initial construction costs.
[3]Actual Loan payment based on size of loan; payment includes principal and interest (14%, 30 year loan on $720,000).
[4]Corporate form of structure is deemed advisable to minimize liability.

Corporate tax rates:		
	0–$ 25,000	17%
	$25,001–$ 50,000	20%
	$50,001–$ 75,000	30%
	$75,001–$100,000	40%
	over $100,000	46%

EXHIBIT 3
Map of the Area

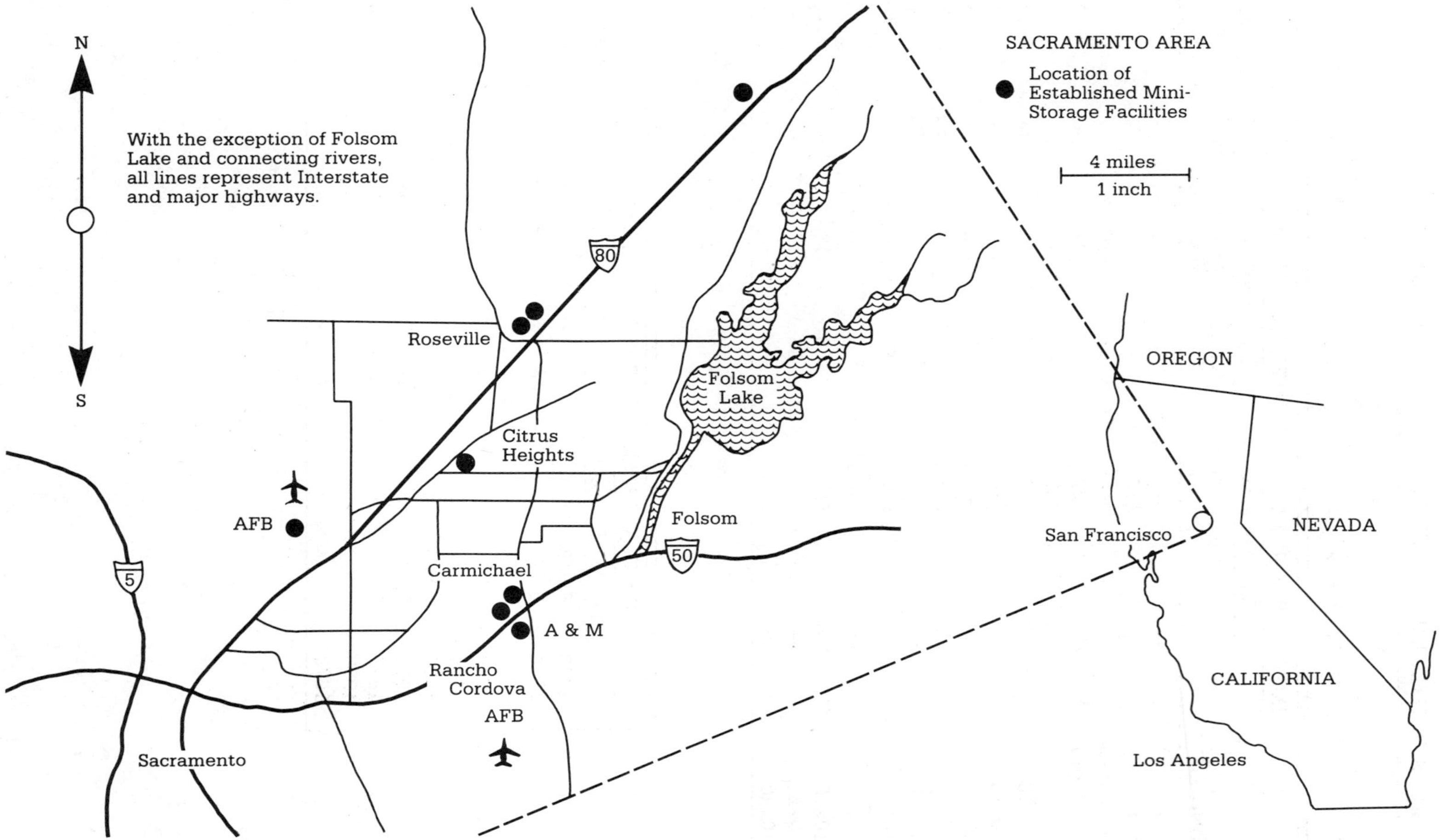

SACRAMENTO AREA

● Location of
Established Mini-
Storage Facilities

4 miles
1 inch

OREGON

NEVADA

CALIFORNIA

Los Angeles

San Francisco

Folsom Lake

Folsom

50

80

Citrus Heights

Roseville

A & M

Carmichael

Rancho Cordova AFB

AFB

Sacramento

5

N

S

With the exception of Folsom
Lake and connecting rivers,
all lines represent Interstate
and major highways.

EXHIBIT 4

	A & M Storage		Mini-Warehouse		Capital City Storage	
UNIT SIZE	No. of Units	Monthly Rental per unit	No. of Units	Rental per unit	No. of Units	Rental per unit
4x6	—	—	67	$15	—	—
5x6	15	$15	—	—	12	$15
5x10 (attic)	—	—	11	$10	—	—
5x10 (ground)	290	$22	299	$21	150	$21
6x10	76	$23	—	—	—	—
10x10	89	$36	69	$34	60	$34
10x12	—	—	28	$38	—	—
10x15	—	—	42	$42	50	$42
10x20	80	$54	85	$52	55	$52
10x25	—	—	34	$54	30	$64
10x30	36	$70	47	$74	25	$74
Parking Space for R.V. Units						
10x20	36	$15	60	$13	—	—
10x28	—	—	38	$18	—	—
10x30	24	$17	—	—	—	—

Title: PRICING AND SIZE OF TYPICAL COMPETITION IN SACRAMENTO AREA

EXHIBIT 5

	FOLSOM	CITRUS HEIGHTS	CARMICHAEL	ROSEVILLE
1970	6,618	45,324	37,608	18,139
1971	6,312	45,328	38,391	18,600
1972	7,102	47,052	39,914	19,100
1973	7,073	51,459	40,199	19,800
1974	7,037	54,459	40,773	20,500
1975	6,858	55,520	41,489	20,850
1976	7,837	57,301	41,780	20,500
1977	7,900	62,492	42,125	21,050
1978				
1979				

Title: POPULATION FIGURES FOR TARGET AREA LOCATIONS

ITTY BITTY MACHINE COMPANY

Charles F. Douds

THE IDEA

It all started one Friday night in February when Jim and his neighbor friend, Bob, went out drinking together. It was then that Bob told him about a new field that was suddenly exploding. Bob wanted to start a new business in this brand new industry of personal computing.

A year before, the first practical home computer system had been announced in *Popular Electronics,* an electronics hobbyist magazine. The company, MITS Inc., was suddenly deluged with orders for its Altair 8800—a computer kit costing just under $500. Within almost a matter of weeks, a number of other new companies jumped on board announcing products that could be used with the Altair. By fall there were several competing systems; a nationally distributed magazine, *Byte;* and one or two retail computer stores.

The sudden explosion of the market for computer kits and systems was unprecedented. For the same kind of money people spent on photography or hi-fi or other sports and hobbies, they could have their own computer for entertainment, education, or their profession. All kinds of people seemed to be getting involved for all kinds of reasons.

During their long evening at the bar, Bob, a systems analyst at a bank, explained all this and more to Jim. Bob proposed opening a retail computer store in the Chicago area.

At the time Jim, who already had his MBA and lived alone with his father, was working on a law degree and feeling disenchanted with his job in one of the nation's largest financial companies. He began to get excited about the prospects of computer systems that were practical for the individual at home or on the job.

Within a few weeks they had discovered a few more kindred souls. First there was Ted. Ted had written and published a book on computers. It was an imaginative and rather unusual production in typography and editorial style. It did an unusually good job of explaining many computer concepts in everyday language. It communicated a real sense of enthusiasm about what you could do with your own computer. This had been a favorite theme of Ted's for several years. When he lectured to an audience, as he frequently did, many would come away deeply intrigued with his ideas. Now it seemed that he was

This case was prepared by Professor Charles F. Douds of DePaul University, Chicago, Illinois, as a basis for class discussion rather than to illustrate either effective or ineffective organizational practices.

Copyright © 1978 by Charles F. Douds.

Presented at a Case Workshop and distributed by the Intercollegiate Case Clearing House, Soldiers Field, Boston, Mass. 02163. All rights reserved to the contributors. Printed in U.S.A.

a prophet—what he had been predicting had come to pass. The technology for the "hardware" was now in place and the electronic boards and boxes were being produced.

Ted's book, *Computer Lib/Dream Machines,* made clear to the reader what computer specialists already knew. A computer is no smarter than the programs within it. The programs—the "software"—had yet to be written that would make his visions come true.

Through Ted another member came to the group. Gerald was a professor in a university computer science department. He was very knowledgable in electronic engineering as well as programming. He had built computer circuits from the ground up and had practical experience as a consultant to companies designing and using such things. Ever since the invention of the transistor in 1955, the semiconductor industry had been characterized by extremely rapid technological advances. It was difficult for anyone to keep up with it, but Gerald had done so in computer applications.

It seemed like an ideal group to start the first computer store in the Chicago area. Jim with a MBA had an overall knowledge of business and law; Bob worked with computer information systems in a bank; Gerald was a technological expert; and Ted not only had a wide-ranging overview of the market, but had written a successful book that communicated effectively to laymen.

Their discussions became serious. A computer store had opened near a university less than 200 miles away in a neighboring state. Jim and Bob flew to California to visit the three computer stores in San Francisco and three in the Los Angeles area. They spent four hours talking with Dick Heisor, the founder of the very first retail computer store. From there they flew to Albuquerque to the Altair Computer Convention at the end of March. Of course, the only products on display were Altairs, but there were sessions for prospective store owners as well as the tutorial and technical sessions for the 1,000 hobbyists attending.

A store in Knoxville had been running big ads in *Byte* indicating a wide range of services, so Jim went on to see it. After considerable difficulty locating the front door, he found two young men crowded into two rooms hardly bigger than 12' x 12' each with equipment, boards, and boxes piled every which way. In this business with companies springing up overnight when a couple of electronic engineers decided to make the plunge, it was not surprising to find a manufacturing operation looking like this, but it was surprising for a retail store. Jim realized there was nothing you could take for granted in this fledgling industry.

SETTING UP THE CORPORATION

After the trips they really got serious. The major problem was capital. Money would be needed for rent, utilities, and salaries as well as stock. The store would need demonstration systems, computers in stock, circuit board kits, parts, books and magazines. Several expensive instruments would be needed for servicing equipment. It would be many months before they could expect to break even.

They decided to sell stock and convertible debentures with each of the principals subscribing to $15,000.

They incorporated as the ITTY BITTY MACHINE COMPANY and found a store in a good location in Evanston—one of the bedroom communities for executives and middle managers from the many corporations in Chicago. Twenty-nine investors subscribed, typically for $1000. For each $5.00 of stock, they received $95 in 6% convertible debentures. Most investors had a data processing background. A few were lawyers or relatives. Mr. Davis, the owner of the computer store in the next state, also became a stockholder. Their initial capitalization was $126,500.

They set up a board comprised of the major stockholders and counsel:

> Bob—president
> Ted—vice-president
> Jim—treasurer
> Their attorney—secretary

The other four board members were Gerald, Mr. Davis, another computer science professor, and a retired insurance agency owner.

They decided to work together as a group. Mutually they agreed each one would spend one day a week working in the store. While some of them were tied up with their regular jobs during normal working hours, the store would be open four evenings a week and Saturdays.

They also decided that the board would actively manage the corporation. There was a great deal of work to be done. Not only was there the store, but it was clear to them that "applications software" was needed. Ted had discussed that at length in his book and knew just the computer language that would be ideal for this purpose. Paul knew about a new microprocessor coming on the market that had very powerful capabilities. Equipment would be needed to exploit it and, of course, "operating systems" were needed for the computers. At that time there was much more available in the way of hardware than software. Systems sales would soon drop off if the programs needed to make microcomputers do useful or entertaining things were not available. It was clear that the Board had a great deal to do.

They met twice a month in long sessions that lasted from 6 P.M. until well after midnight. None of them were bashful; they all enjoyed a good argument. Each had his own point of view and was willing to express it. With each peson having strong views and interests of his own, they felt that it would be best to rotate the meeting chairmanship.

A SECOND PROJECT—THE NEW COMPUTER LANGUAGE

Almost from the start Ted was talking about the computer language, TRAC, he had discussed in his book. A computer language such as BASIC, COBOL, or FORTRAN is usually used to write the programs people or businesses actually use ("applications software"). The Board had discussed how programs for entertainment or practical use would be needed to help sustain future computer sales. Ted was enthusiastic, as always, about the power and versatility of TRAC for such applications.

The language could be licensed from its creator for $200 plus royalty. However, it would have to be rewritten and adapted to the small computer system. They would need a programmer and a computer for him to work with. This could not be a microcomputer system because for part of the work he needed capabilities only a larger computer could provide.

Ted had lots of ideas about how to do this. He wanted to get a LSI-11 minicomputer, a Diablo printer, and a video terminal—first class. Gerald immediately argued that this would be too expensive. While the LSI-11 itself started at $1500, by the time you got everything else needed, the cost would be nearly $10,000. Of course they realized that Gerald also wanted money to be available for the computer equipment projects he was talking about.

Among the many possibilities discussed, the Board eventually decided to rent time on a large computer through a timesharing service. As the various parts of the program were developed, they would be tested out on one of the store's systems. Ted said TRAC would be up and running by the end of August at a cost of $1,500. Dan, the programmer he had located, impressed them as being a very sharp fellow and a nice person.

STARTING THE STORE

Stock was needed for the store. MITS, Inc., makers of the Altair, was only accepting exclusive MITS dealerships. They decided not to get locked into one company so they ordered 100 computers from IMSAI, MITS' major competitor. There were two or three other companies advertising complete computers, but it was obvious that it would be some time before the products would be shipped—and then how good would they be? Computers, even microcomputers, are not simple devices. The delivery schedule from IMSAI was 25 in July, 25 in August, and 50 in September. Ted was sure that they would all be sold by the end of September.

There was another reason for ordering 100 computers with a retail price of $599 each. They knew a price increase of $100 would be announced soon so their markup would be appreciably better at the higher retail price.

Price to the dealer was a particularly troublesome issue. The industry had started on a direct mail order basis. The pricing structure did not include provision for dealer markups. As the business grew it was possible for the "well-established" manufacturers (those that had been in business for six months or longer) to buy their parts in quantity, and so to reduce their costs. However, few of these new companies knew much about manufacturing methods, and they did not have the capital to invest in efficient production techniques. It was difficult for them to adjust their retail prices upward to normal retail markups. They simply had little room in which to establish adequate dealer discounts.

The store needed many other items as well. Once a person bought a microcomputer he could tailor it to his particular needs by buying circuit boards to plug into it. As noted in Exhibit I, these items (only 5″ x 10″ in size) cost from $100 to $300 and had the same difficulty of narrow dealer margins. Discounts could be as low as 10%, with 20% being typical at the time. Shipments from these small, rapidly growing, cashtight companies who were dealing with newly established retail stores were invariably COD plus freight charges. Cash flow would become a major problem for many of the new stores.

They ordered a variety of these kits to test the water and see which ones would sell. This aspect of the business was pretty much an unknown to the old computer hands on the Board. As software types they had no background of experience with hardware. Gerald was the only one with appropriate experience, but he could not make judgments from advertisements alone. He needed a microcomputer and the equipment itself in order to test it adequately. But that would only provide part of the answer. Of course, it would be desirable—necessary, as he argued in the Board meetings—to test as many of the products as quickly as they became available.

As store manager, Jim did the actual ordering. The variety of equipment and advertising claims was a bit bewildering. However, Mr. Davis was getting practical experience with the equipment and the business practices of the manufacturers, so Jim was able to get a lot of good advice from him.

The ITTY BITTY MACHINE COMPANY opened on June 14 with little fanfare. But the word spread, helped along by an announcement at the local, 200-member computer club. A steady stream of people showed up with many coming back when new items arrived at the store.

Gerald built one of the IMSAI computers for the store, but it was several weeks after the store opened before it was available for demonstration. Jim found that there were more and more questions he could not answer adequately.

Gerald often called to find out if a new item had arrived. He would often borrow it for evaluation. His comments were helpful to Jim, but he could never be sure when the item would come back and it was rare that the manuals with their technical details ever returned. Gerald had several projects going on in his shop at home. These were sometimes discussed at the board meetings, but the Board members had difficulty following his technical discussion.

In their travels to the West Coast computer stores they had noted that many of the clerks were quite young. Bright high-school youths quickly learned the intracacies of computers and programming. They would work for low wages just to have the chance to be around the equipment. Ted felt and kept saying that the personal computers would sell themselves and he believed in youth, so they hired several sharp high-school students as part-time salesmen.

Jim wanted to learn more about the equipment and store operations. Mr. Davis was quite willing to have him spend time at his store so Jim began to spend days at a time there. To cover for him, the Board hired an assistant manager—a high school teacher familiar with computer programming. From June through October Jim spent about one-third of his time at Mr. Davis' store learning a great deal about the operations there.

Sales were slow during June and July, but by August they began to pick up a bit. A lot of people had been coming in to browse, but finally a few came back to buy. By the end of August they had sold 8 of the 50 IMSAI computers they had received. Jim was not drawing any salary—it was being deferred. Not only were there the clerks and the CODs, but Dan and the timesharing service had to be paid for the work on TRAC, the new computer language.

TRAC IN THE STORE

Dan was frequently in the store for long hours working on the TRAC project when he was not at his regular job. The Board had decided that the store should have three working demonstration systems of different types, but only one of these was suitable for Dan's work. Without it there was little else he could do; his time would be wasted. During the afternoons the system would sometimes be changed around as boards were removed or inserted to try something new or to test an item repaired for a customer. Of course, sometimes such activity would take its toll on the system itself. Occasionally, the system would not work properly. Naturally, Dan, devoted to his programming work, found it most irritating when this happened. The TRAC project was supposed to be finished by the end of August and it was becoming more and more obvious that it would not be. So when the system quit working it was upsetting to him and he wanted it fixed right away no matter what others were doing. His irritation did not make the best impression on customers.

But even when the system was working well—which actually was a high percentage of the time he was there—Dan's presence at the equipment created a difficulty for the store. There rarely were two other working systems. There was little space in the back of the store to do repair work. It usually wound up being done in the front and one system invariably would get involved in it.

For one reason or another the third system never seemed to actually exist. One time when it did, it was sold to an electronics laboratory of a major firm that wanted an assembled system. This nicely increased the store's margin on the sale. They had bought it at the dealers discount as a kit and it had been assembled by a person whose salary they had to pay anyway. (Even if they hired a person to assemble the kit, it still would cost them less and they would get it sooner than buying it assembled from the factory.)

The net result was that there was usually only one working system to be used in demonstrations to customers. It was right by the front window where it could be seen by passers-by, but during the times when there were the most customers in the store Dan was usually at it. Absorbed in his work, he was oblivious to the hubbub of the clientele—and to the salesmen—the "kids" as he called them. It was only with evident reluctance that he would relinquish the console when Jim wanted to demonstrate the system to a good prospect.

TED'S CATALOG AND A CONVENTION

Ted's imagination was very fertile and always at work. Even before they incorporated he was talking about franchising the operation. Never one to be concerned about details, he painted colorful and profit-filled work pictures of the variety of ways in which they could expand nationwide. Each of them on the Board had their own visions, and while not all of them were as facile with words as Ted, they were all eager to talk about their ideas and to seek ways to move closer to carrying them out. In the Board meetings the eight of them would attempt to deal with the nuts and bolts of running a business, and each had his own ideas on that, too, but it did make it rather difficult to arrive at specific decisions.

Jim, spending a great deal of time at Mr. Davis' store, saw the need for a catalog. Ted got quite excited when he saw Jim's draft. Yes, a catalog was a great idea—and he knew how to do it. He was the one that had the pulse of the marketplace. The draft, full of technical descriptions, was nearly complete. Jim decided to turn it over to Ted for his creative touch.

The catalog Ted turned out created a minor sensation. It was written up in a magazine distributed nationwide to computer professionals. Because of it, first one of the city newspapers and then another did major stories on the store. The newspaper stories led to TV coverage on the local news.

The catalog was in narrative form chatting about personal computing, the manufacturers and products, and the kind of people you would find in a computer store. It was warm, human, and responsive to many of the better values of the youth movement that characterized the 1968–72 period. A number of humorous and word-less cartoons graced its pages. The last page is shown in EXHIBIT 5.

The brief item on the last page headed "Ask About Our Franchise" says that the cost would be comparable to a small fast-food store. An information package was available for $3.00. It nicely and openly concluded: "We regret charging for what is scarcely more than a pamphlet, but we do not want to have to send it to the idly curious."

Even the physical form of the catalog was novel. It was printed on 22" x 34" glossy stock folded to 8½" x 11". To read it you unfolded it lengthwise in a convenient manner. There were eight pages of text which left the reverse side free for a full-size poster cartoon Ted had drawn.

The catalogs arrived from Ted printed at a cost of about $6000 for 10,000 of them. The items described in Jim's original version were mentioned in one-sentence descriptions that included the price, but absolutely no technical informa-tion.

The *Personal Computing Convention* had been announced for the end of August in Atlantic City. It seemed that all the manufacturers would attend and that it would draw a good crowd. Ted was to be one of the featured speakers. Sales on the exhibition hall floor would be allowed, so in June the Board had decided that the store should purchase a booth and take merchandise to sell.

The convention was a rousing success with over 10,000 people attend-ing. The catalogs seemed to be a big hit. Needless to say, working the store's booth was exhausting with such a crowd, but $6000 of the merchandise brought in a rented truck was sold. Of the eight IMSAI's sold by the end of August, three were sold here. They felt the trip had been worthwhile.

SEPTEMBER

Bob, president of the corporation, spent a week of his vacation in the store. Like other board members, he really had not lived up to the vow of working there one day a week. It was an illuminating experience. He really began to appreciate how much he did not know about the products and prices. He found that the youthful sales staff really did a pretty good job, but with high school getting started they were not available all the time to help him out.

The week of his family's out-of-town vacation gave him a chance to really think things over. He was particularly concerned about the diverse ways things seemed to be going. The TRAC project was still going full blast. It always seemed like he was getting different information about it. Ted never seemed to say the same thing about where it was going or how it was coming along. Gerald seemed to be generating useful information with his projects, but how did they all tie together? Here, too, he felt he was getting different stories. But maybe that was not it. Maybe the information was not really all that different. Perhaps he just did not understand the technical language and its implications well enough.

After he came back from vacation he began sharing these thoughts with Jim. Jim was quite concerned, also. The financial situation was not good even though sales were picking up. As Jim put it, these projects of Ted and Gerald "were beginning to take on a life of their own." Bob felt that he was making too many poor decisions because he was getting too many different stories. As he finally concluded, perhaps it was more that he did not know how to adequately interpret and weigh what he was being told.

OCTOBER

At the first Board meeting in October Bob announced that he was resigning as president. This took the Board by surprise. After a long discussion they elected Jim to the post.

Jim said it was only because he could quote all the prices and margins from memory. Actually, he had been doing a lot of the paperwork and had been becoming more and more specific with the figures in the September meetings. He was still the only one working full-time for the corporation; the rest had their regular jobs.

They never really had gotten a decent bookkeeping system set up because of all the work in getting the store started, the convention, and Ted's promises about what TRAC would be able to do.

The bills for the convention totalled $6000, the same amount they had grossed there. The margin on the items averaged 19%. They had lost $4860 on the trip, not counting the catalogs given away.

The catalog had cost $6000. They had yet to receive one mail or phone order from it even though about 5000 were in circulation. It had taken $126 in postage alone to answer all the franchise inquiries—just to say that the information package was not yet available. With no package in sight, despite Ted's enthusiasms, there would have to be another round of letters returning the $3.00 payments.

But the biggest things were Ted's TRAC project and Gerald's activities. Not only were these taking on a life of their own, as he had remarked to Bob, but they were expensive. As best he could figure out, Gerald had about $8,000 of the store's equipment at home—7% of their initial capitalization. The consulting fee for Dan and the timesharing service were running about $5000 per month, to say nothing of the aggravation and impact on sales it was causing in the store. So far the project had cost $15,000.

He got these figures with the supporting data into writing and had them ready for the second October Board meeting.

Sales were going up encouragingly (EXHIBIT 2), but their capital was being eaten up and their cash position was getting to be more and more of a problem. (EXHIBIT 4 shows the figures as of the end of October, but the situation was clear to Jim by the middle of the month.) He needed cash to pay for the goods coming in. It was becoming clear that their industrial customers would take 30 to 60 days to pay. At least sales to individuals were paid immediately.

He had been checking with the banks about loans. Sales growth was encouraging—but the bankers would not be convinced. They could not see how selling computers to individuals would be viable in the long run. None of the principals had any prior experience running a small business nor in retail sales. Etc., etc. No loan could be arranged.

Perhaps a merger? But with whom? It would take months to work out a deal even if an interested party could be found. They had to do something about the situation!

Shortly before the Board meeting he was at his desk—his desk??? He shared it with everyone!—when he heard Dan once again impatiently demanding that the system be fixed while a customer was in the store. As soon as the customer left he walked out firmly and said, "Dan, pack up all your things, get out, and don't come back. You and Ted figure out where you'll work!"

He knew the next Board meeting would be . . . perhaps "stimulating" was the word for it. He had better be really primed for it.

EXHIBIT 1

RETAIL PRICES OF REPRESENTATIVE MICROCOMPUTER BOARDS (MAY 1976)		
Dutronics 8K memory	$285 kit	
IMSAI 4K memory	$165 kit	$299 assembled
Processor technology 3P + S I/O	$135 kit	
Processor technology video display	$179 kit	
Polymorphic video display	$185 kit	$260 assembled

EXHIBIT 2

ITTY BITTY MACHINE CO. SALES, FIRST FOUR MONTHS	
July	$ 4,605.96
Aug.	$ 6,908.92
Sept.	$19,042.55
Oct.	$21,509.92

EXHIBIT 3

ITTY BITTY MACHINE COMPANY INCOME STATEMENTS			
	2 months 7-1-76 8-31-76	1 month 9-1-76 9-30-76	1 month 10-1-76 10-31-76
Revenues	$11,514.88	$19,042.55	$21,509.92
Less returns	(18.90)	(59.70)	(4.07)
Less discounts	(138.28)	-0-	(44.65)
	$11,357.70	$18,982.85	$21,461.20
Cost of Goods Sold			
Beginning inventory	$ -0-	$36,213.77	$36,213.77
Purchases	44,060.12	15,149.25	24,583.28
Ending inventory	(36,213.77)	36,213,77	(44,057.31)
	$ 7,846.35	$15,149.25	$16,739.74
Gross Profit on Sales	$ 3,511.35	$ 3,833.60	$ 4,721.46
Operating Expense			
Selling expense	$ 4,263.19	$ 4,338.59	$ 7,022.98
Gen. & admin.	4,601.27	4,659.11	5,742.11
	$ 8,864.46	$ 8,997.70	$12,765.09
Net Income	$(5,353.11)	$(5,164.10)	$(8,043.63)

EXHIBIT 4

ITTY BITTY MACHINE COMPANY
BALANCE SHEET
Oct. 31, 1976

ASSETS

Current Assets

Cash		17,572.72
Accounts Receivable		7,594.22
Inventory:		
Computers	24,434.20	
Boards	10,318.10	
Books	3,111.10	
Software	789.00	
Other	3,404.91	
		44,057.31
		$ 69,224.25

Fixed Assets

Organizational Costs	2,255.00	
Fixtures	5,007.65	
Test & Repair Equipment	1,579.75	
Demonstration Equipment	18,437.21	
Development	17,137.75	
		44,387.36
Other Assets		6,600.77
TOTAL ASSETS		**$120,212.38**

LIABILITIES

Current Liabilities

Accounts Payable	7,320.79	
Notes Payable	2,800.00	
Taxes Payable	1,290.00	
Unearned Income	862.43	
		12,273.22
Long Term Liabilities	------	------
		$ 12,273.22

STOCKHOLDERS EQUITY

Common Stock	6,325.00	
Convertible Debentures 6%	120,175.00	
Retained Earnings	(18,560.84)	
		107,939.16
TOTAL LIABILITIES AND STOCKHOLDERS EQUITY		**$120,212.38**

AND NOW SOME PREVIEWS...

Frankly, folks, the engineering hasn't been done yet, but we are holding deposits pending availability of...

HEAVEN-11™?

That, friends, is what we are calling our package of the LSI-11* with power supply and ALTAIR BUS.

That is why we are calling it the Heaven-11: it's the world's finest computer, effectively a PDP-11*, which few of us can afford, set up for the myriad weird and super accessories of the Altair world.

Our tentative price (kit, incl. LSI-11): FIFTEEN HUNDRED BUCKS.

Now some of you may want a computer that looks really zippy. We are considering styled packages for the Heaven-11 that include —

A JUKE BOX!
AN ART DECO SKYSCRAPER!
SWEPT-LINE RACER STYLING!

and for you who like vans, we hope to produce the

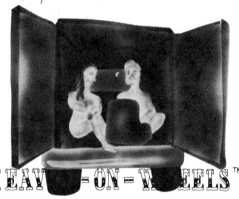

HEAV-ON-WHEELS™

which offers optional power brakes and steering, positraction, shag rug interior, terminal, and van. May be financed through local automotive dealer.

*A registered trademark of Digital Equipment Corporation.

"From the Dream to the Nitty Gritty –
TAKE THE TRIP
at Itty Bitty"

ABOUT MAIL ORDER:

You will not find an order blank. We're not dumb and neither are you, if you've gotten this far. Write a note. Or even **CALL COLLECT to order: 312/328-6800.** (We reserve the right to discontinue this policy.)

Prices, specifications and availability subject to change without notice. Customers will be notified when merchandise cannot be shipped immediately.

Shipping weight and charges are such a nuisance that we presently send freight-collect.

Illinois residents please add 5% sales tax.

EXHIBIT 5

366

Is it a book?
Or is it a way of life?

The answer is — YES!

THIS IS A TIME WHOSE BOOK HAS COME.

IT'S COMPUTER LIB
by Ted Nelson

$7 postpaid.
(For quantity discounts contact
Hugo's Book Service, Box 2622, Chicago IL 60690.)

"The best damned book on computer science I've ever seen."
— Carl M. Ellison, Professor of Computer Science, University of Utah

---

ASK ABOUT
OUR FRANCHISE

We think Ittybitty is going to go over big.

Can you get in on it?

Yes. If you qualify.

If you qualify, you can open a Second-Generation Computer Store in your city.

(In fact, guess who can come to your opening IN PERSON! Why, Itty and Bitty™ the Computer Clowns, Bill Juggler™ and Captain Computer™ *himself!*) #

The cost of opening an Ittybitty franchise depends on the location but is comparable to a small fast-food outlet store.

Our package of franchise information is $3 by mail. We regret charging for what is scarcely more than a pamphlet, but we do not want to have to send it to the idly curious.

Clowns and other personnel
subject to availability.

"From the Dream to the Nitty Gritty –
CARRY IT THROUGH
at Itty Bitty"

Thank you for looking at this catalog. Now we'd like to hear from you. We've told you our interests and ideas – how about yours?

Whether you are a hobbyist, a customer, or a passerby; whether you join our clubs and services or just look in now and then; or whether you actually join the Ittybitty family with an outlet of your own – we appreciate your interest, and we care about your problems.

CUMBER-LAND CRAFTS INC.

William W. McCartney
Phillip M. Van Auken
Harold D. Fletcher

Ann Stanfield, president of Cumberland Crafts Inc., comments "I have believed in this business from the very beginning, and I think the basis for any successful venture is believing in what you are doing." Cumberland Crafts Inc. is a wholesaler of craft supplies and accessories located in Santa Fe, New Mexico, a town of approximately 40,000 persons in the northern part of the state. Cumberland Crafts, as well as its retail counterpart Craft-Village, is owned and operated by Ann and Dick Stanfield. The Stanfields have been in the craft business since 1972, when Ann opened Craft-Village as a sole proprietorship.

Cumberland Crafts is one of only four craft wholesalers in the state of New Mexico, the others being located in Albuquerque, Tucumcari, and Hobbs. The Stanfields provide a wide variety of craft items (materials for decoupage, macrame, woodworking, plastic castings, etc.) to 350–400 retailers in a four state area.

BACKGROUND AND HISTORY OF CUMBERLAND CRAFTS AND CRAFT-VILLAGE

Craft-Village was begun in Ann Stanfield's garage as a part-time outlet for her interest in crafts as a hobby. In 1970, Ann decided to work towards the opening of a retail craft store by becoming as familiar as possible with crafts and craft accessories. She spent some two and a half years in this informal learning process. "I didn't really know how I was going to use all this I was learning, but I knew I wanted to become professionally involved with crafts because they were so interesting to me."

In 1972, Ann borrowed $5,000 (the maximum allowable) from a Santa Fe bank, withdrew the cash values from the family's life insurance policies and retirement pension plan, and opened Craft-Village in a small building that rented for $175 per month. The total investment in inventory and fixtures was approximately $8000–$9000. "We started out selling about $50 per day, and it gradually grew until it has now reached about $600 per day." Inventory was stored at home in the garage during the early months of operations.

This case was prepared by Professors William W. McCartney, Philip M. Van Auken, and Harold D. Fletcher of Western Kentucky University as a basis for class discussion rather than to illustrate either effective or ineffective handling of an administrative situation.

Copyright © 1977 by William W. McCartney

Presented at a Case Workshop and distributed by the Intercollegiate Case Clearing House, Soldiers Field, Boston, Mass. 02163. All rights reserved to the contributors. Printed in the U.S.A.

The Stanfields initially promoted Craft-Village by having Ann put on demonstrations for homemaker clubs, local high schools, and junior high schools. In 1974, due to increasing business, Craft-Village moved across the street in Sante Fe to a larger building, where it is now housed. "This was definitely a good move, because it helped us to increase our sales and our classroom space." Also in 1974, husband Dick quit his teaching job to join the growing business.

It was at this time that the Stanfields decided to expand into wholesaling in order to capitalize on what they perceived as a regional boom in craft retailing. "Nobody in the area was providing adequate wholesaling service in general. We saw the need for a generalist wholesaler and decided to step in."

The wholesaling operation was originally located in a series of adjacent offices in one building which rented for $500 per month. While in this temporary location, the Stanfields were able to open a line of credit at the local bank, where they eventually borrowed a total of $36,000. "At this time we were heavily in debt, but not to an excessive level for the kind of business we were doing," commented Ann.

In August of 1975, the Stanfields moved the wholesaling operation, which had been named Cumberland Crafts, into a central warehouse renting for $500 per month. For no additional cost, this new warehouse provided 7,500 square feet vs. 2,500 square feet in the previous location. By mid-1975, Cumberland Crafts had grown to the point where it employed four additional workers and was doing $20,000 per month in sales.

Also during the summer of 1975, both Craft-Village and Cumberland Crafts were incorporated, leading to financing problems with the local bank due to the changeover from personal liability to limited liability. As a result, a second mortgage was placed on the Stanfields' home, and their banker further recommended that they apply for a SBA loan. To the Stanfields' surprise, the SBA loan was not approved despite the backing of their local Congressman. Ann explained, "I was pregnant when we applied for the loan, and I guess the loan officer involved didn't take me very seriously. At this time we were really needing some financial backing, because we were in a tremendous growth period."

In January 1976, the Stanfields refinanced their patchwork loan arrangement with the local bank by agreeing to pay back the $36,000 on a monthly schedule over a five year period. In addition, the bank approved a $75,000 line of credit. "So finally, after all those years in operation, we had adequate financial backing. We were able to begin really growing without our hands being tied."

MANAGEMENT OF THE COMPANY

"I have been the main leader in the business simply because I was the one that started both of them and I had the most craft retailing experience," commented Ann in discussing the management of Cumberland Crafts and Craft-Village. Ann is president of both companies, with Dick Stanfield being Secretary-Treasurer for both firms. While Ann has responsibility for the overall administration of the company, Dick concentrates on sales to retail customers and on finance. The remaining management team consists of three department heads and an assistant manager at Craft-Village.

Kay Ridgeway heads up the accounting function, including invoicing. Kay is the product of a vocational school and several years of bookkeeping experience. Ann Stanfield feels "She's really been a fantastic employee for us. She was a lucky find."

Shipping and receiving is staffed by four shipping clerks, three warehouse people, and a supervisor. The shipping clerks pull orders from inventory, write and price invoices, weigh, and ship orders. The receiving crew checks arriving merchandise against purchase orders, prices merchandise and places it in inventory. Bill Cannon is warehouse supervisor, responsible for the performance of the other seven employees. Bill has had some previous plant-related experience. Dick comments that "Bill's a fairly good organizer. He'll take what we tell him and execute in logical manner."

Jerolyn Poe is the customer-relations coordinator for Cumberland Crafts, responsible for meeting and greeting customers at the warehouse and for explaining sales and purchasing policies. She is additionally responsible for coordinating customer seminars, workshops and other special customer services, such as the Cumberland Crafts catalog and newspaper. Jerolyn has a degree in agriculture, previous experience with the federal government, and with Craft-Village. According to Ann, "We created this position especially for Jerolyn because she's very bright and knows crafts inside and out. She's really done an outstanding job in laying out our fast-changing catalog."

The Stanfields estimate that they spend 95 percent of their time on the wholesaling operation and very little time retailing. Craft-Village is managed very much on a decentralized basis, with the assistant manager of Craft-Village carrying most of the work load. Ann comments that "My main job at Craft-Village is handling the promotions, which entails primarily running newspaper ads. Occasionally I go over there to help to solve employee problems and to help iron out other types of managerial problems."

The assistant manager for Craft-Village, Barbara Carnes, is also viewed in a very positive light by Ann. "Barbara is a fantastic type of person in that she has a great deal of loyalty, which is very important to me. She has faith in us as leaders. The fact that she believes in us and in the business makes her very conscious of doing what she thinks is right for Craft-Village. She may not always know what's right, but she'll always try to find out."

While the present employees are generally described in positive terms by Dick and Ann, this has not always been the case. Between February and May of 1976, just about all of the warehouse employees turned over as the company grew and changed performance expectations. Ann describes the morale of the present staff and warehouse employees as healthy. "For the most part, we have a beautiful working relationship among ourselves."

Ann feels employees in both organizations are satisfied with their compensation and benefits. "Just because an employee comes in for a pay raise doesn't mean he or she automatically gets one. We try to evaluate our people on the basis of their performance. We started our evaluation program recently and have already given several raises. From here on out, we intend to let the warehouse coordinator evaluate his employees twice a year, and then we will sit down with each employee and discuss raises."

Ann also feels that she and Dick are going to have to spend more time in personnel matters as the company continues to grow. "We really need to have more meetings with employees to better cement communications and instructions. Our personnel situation is tolerable but not as good as we would like it to be."

In discussing the couple's management style, Ann states "Our management style has always been very informal and loose. Lately we've grown to a point where we definitely need more formal structure and management. We're going to have to be more definite with our employees and less easy going."

As for future goals and plans, the Stanfields plan to stay in both retailing and wholesaling and even plan to move into manufacturing on a limited basis. "We don't anticipate for the future as much growth as we've had for the past couple of years. We hope to reach a plateau at some point so we will get things under better control."

Ann comments further on the future outlook: "The longest period I've been able to plan ahead for is about a year and a half to two years. I feel that the craft business is so fickle that we can't plan ahead any more than this. The popularity of different crafts changes from year to year, making it very difficult to base future predictions on past trends.

"For the short-range, over the next year or two, I've pretty well figured what I think the business will do dollar-wise. When we get into our small-scale manufacturing, things will probably go wild for awhile. For the next five years I have a general idea that we'll still have Craft-Village, although we'll probably switch locations, say to a shopping mall. I don't anticipate having a second retail store; we won't rule this out, but it's not a part of the plan simply because of the enormous effort required. Further retail growth would also depend on the availability of personnel. We'd have to come up with a strong assistant-manager type. For instance, Craft-Village has not done nearly as well as it could if I gave it my full attention. Running both a retailing and wholesaling business at the same time has presented some difficulties. In the future, however, our main emphasis will be in wholesaling."

In her assessment of future business problems and challenges, Ann states that "Our major problems at this point in time are those of employee productivity, employee evaluation and satisfaction, and inventory control, while our biggest challenge is keeping up with our growth. Another challenge we will face over the next year is getting together a complete staff and a good group of employees. I want our people to be compatible, to do as good a job as possible, and to be happy with what they're doing.

"We get behind on some problems because other larger problems arise. For instance, we've been intending to write up job descriptions for some time, but inventory problems have taken precedence. We probably know where most of our present problems are and between us should know how to solve them."

MARKETING

The Stanfields consider their primary market to consist of 350–400 retail outlets in New Mexico, Arizona, Utah, and Colorado which purchase products from Cumberland Crafts on a continuing basis. Ann feels that they do a good job with these customers:

"Cumberland Crafts is fairly close to being a full-line craft wholesaler. We distribute in most of the product lines wanted by our retail customers."

Elaborating on their product line, Ann says that "I can't even tell you how many different crafts you can do by going out in our warehouse." Also Ann could not give an accurate estimate of the number of different items stocked in the warehouse or displayed in the wholesaling catalog. "I can tell you in dollars, but I can't tell you by number of items."

In discussing market share, Ann states that "Cumberland's current market share of the wholesaling business in the four-state area is not a big concern of mine. This is because I'm so content with the amount of growth we've had here in New Mexico. For years, the state never had much in the way of crafts retailing, much less wholesaling. I think Craft-Village and Cumberland Crafts have done much in this regard. A lot of small craft stores are opening up all over this area, with most of them on a shoestring. No one really knows just how much demand is actually out there. I don't suffer from a great deal of greed and I think there's enough business out there for Cumberland Crafts and its competitors."

While the Stanfields do not worry much about market share, they have made an effort to learn something about their competitors. Ann comments, "Our competitors are not really very strong. The distributor in Tucumcari handles bicycles and parts and thus doesn't really specialize in crafts; the Alburquerque company greatly overprices its items; and the Hobbs wholesaler does little more than supply his own retail shop. Cumberland Crafts is definitely the largest crafts wholesaler in the state of New Mexico. We get at least 35 percent of the New Mexico retail business. The one thing I really strive to know is the strengths and weaknesses of my competitors.

"There are two or three things which separate us from our competitors and perhaps give us an advantage over them. One is the fact that we've had a designer—someone who creates new uses for a particular craft item. We try to find unique sources and then build the demand through our designers. Another competitive edge is our fast service. We try to give one to two day service on most orders. We added an extra shipping clerk just to provide for this capability.

"I would say that having unique sources is another competitive advantage; that is, having good selling items which most other major wholesalers have not been able to find a source of supply for. In the craft wholesaling business, sources of supply are a real competitive weapon; you have to know where to find the unusual craft items that are being produced. We've had pretty fair success with uncovering sources—so much so that I sometimes think I should be selling sources."

Dick is Cumberland Crafts' only salesman. He comments, "We've wanted someone else to travel for us but so far have not been able to make the right arrangements. It's hard to be real aggressive when you don't have a full-time salesman. However, I think we are the type of company that customers naturally come to because of our many competitive advantages."

The Stanfields do not plan to spend a great deal of effort developing new retail outlets. Ann states, "We would like to see most of our future growth come from existing customers, because we feel that our existing retailers already know how to do business with us. New customers have to be taught how to buy and sell. I would much rather keep an old customer who already knows these things and who is likely to purchase more because of the business already built up. However, I do anticipate adding four or five new customers per month.

"We are not really very aggressive in the area of seeking out new customers because they will seek us out. We feel we get a good number of new customers from yellow page ads and from the newsletters we send out. If Dick hears about a potential new account in an area, he certainly will call on them. Or if somebody gives me the name of a new store, I certainly will call on them.

"We have never carried out a formal market research program where we went out and tried to determine customer needs. Of course, we pay attention to market demand. When we go to a craft show, we always make a point to notice the best things at the show. Two years ago, the hottest item was macrame, and you could see it bloom all of a sudden. Five years ago, you couldn't give macrame away.

"Another way we do market research is by talking to salesmen and asking them about how business is in different regions. For example, What's going on in California will for sure be big here two years from now. Our area seems to be the very last to get all the new crafts. New Mexico has just lacked leadership in the craft industry. This is the leadership we've been trying to provide. Fortunately, after the start-up of a crafts business, you soon reach the point where you can make educated guesses about the market."

Cumberland's pricing policy follows the manufacturer's suggested retail price on most items, which normally involves about a 40 percent markup. For other items not having the manufacturer's suggested price, the Stanfields establish price on the basis of what the market will bear. The largest profit margins are on those items which are manufactured by Cumberland Crafts such as silk flowers, etc. Volume discounts are offered to retailers on the basis of a similar volume discount received by Cumberland Crafts from its suppliers. "We don't offer volume discounts on many items, because we don't purchase many things on this basis ourselves, and because it makes things pretty confusing for our shipping clerks."

The Stanfields feel that they could greatly benefit by spending more time in the areas of advertising and promotion. "We're already reaching a point where we're large enough to help mold demand. We can creatively push a certain item and, in effect, manufacture demand for it among our retailers. In this business it is so easy to create demand. If you know the right approach, you can create a demand for anything relating to crafts. It all starts with showing the customer how to be creative with something and then letting her interest catch hold."

Craft-Village has generated considerable customer interest by promoting craft classes. Ann explains that a $3.00 fee per class is charged "Because we found out that people won't come to class unless they pay for it." The store's normal procedure is to contract with free-lance instructors to conduct the classes. According to Ann the wholesale operation also promotes through classes for retailers, and instructions and demonstrations on new craft ideas. "Usually we bring in outsiders to conduct these seminars, because we don't yet have the trained people in Sante Fe to do it."

Cumberland Crafts advertises in the national trade publication, *Profitable Crafts Merchandising,* and carries yellow page ads in Denver, Salt Lake City, and Phoenix, as well as the several resort areas in New Mexico. The Stanfields state that their purpose for advertising in *PCM* magazine is to give Cumberland Crafts the image of a national-supplier. "This really helps our image and brings customers to our back door."

While the ads in *PCM* and the yellow pages are considered important by the Stanfields, the firm's chief means of promotion are its monthly newsletter (sent to over 500 retailers) and its merchandise catalogs. Currently the company has two catalogs with a third in the works. Customers can obtain catalogs for a small deposit, which is refundable upon first order.

The Stanfields are in the process of becoming small-scale manufacturers of selected craft items such as silk flowers. Ann estimates that the new manufacturing venture has the potential of generating $40,000 to $50,000 in additional sales per month. "Silk flowers have just gone like wildfire, We really based our initial wholesaling business around flowers, and we are becoming more interested everyday in flowers and related sources of supply. Getting our program for manufacturing and distributing silk flowers is going to be one of our major challenges over the next year. We are not really even sure who our distributors will be. This will open a whole other area for us to tackle."

The Stanfields have already applied for a trademark on the silk flowers and plan to market the product under a name other than Cumberland Crafts to keep their competitors (who are also potential customers) from knowing that Cumberland is the manufacturer. Ann feels that other wholesalers might also feel compelled to engage in manufacturing if they learned of Cumberlands' involvement.

Ann is not sure how much it will cost to manufacture silk flowers, but feels that it will be consideraly less than the ninety cents it currently costs to buy them. The silk flowers are wholesaled at a 30 percent mark-up and retailed for $2.25.

On the subject of long range plans for the new manufacturing side of the business, Ann states "I would very much like to always be manufacturing at least one hot craft item, because some of the most successful wholesalers I know operate this way. I think some manufacturing is a very healthy process."

FINANCE

The Stanfields employ a CPA firm to provide them with a monthly balance sheet and income statement. Ann feels that this information is a vital part of the company's daily operations. "I can't run this business by the seat of my pants. I've got to have figures to work with. In addition to reports prepared by our accountants, I take figures home with me and analyze them at night. Some of the figures on our financial statement may look a little out of line, but I would say that our company is in pretty good financial shape because our future potential is so strong."

Ann states that although both companies have been profitable from the very beginning, the couple has not yet drawn any salary from Cumberland Crafts. Instead, all profits have been plowed back into the business. In 1976, $18,000 was withdrawn in total salaries from Craft-Village, since Dick has resigned his teaching position.

Although Ann is certain that the firm is profitable, she states that profits are not her primary concern. "It's probably a mistake, but I don't spend as much time thinking about profit as I do sales. I do project sales figures and have been pretty accurate thus far. I know our sales are growing at a very rapid rate, and our before tax profit seems to be running at around 10 percent."

Business during the first four months of 1977 was very good. In fact, Ann comments that "I've been very pleasantly surprised at how brisk our sales have been this year." Normally, the company's sales exhibit a seasonal trend, peaking in the period from September to December as retailers build up their inventories for the Christmas rush. Sales fall off from December 15th to the 1st of January and then basically stabilize during the remaining months.

In mid 1976, the firm installed a WATS telephone line for most states west of the Mississippi to assist Ann with her customer contacts during the period of her pregnancy. The couple anticipates using the telephone as a sales tool, but Ann comments, "We've never really used the WATS line to sell like it could be. It has not yet become the selling tool that I think it eventually will be."

During the early years of operation, profits have been used almost exclusively to build inventory. In fact, Ann states that "Most of our assets are tied up in inventory, which I feel is not about to go bad on us. I believe in having a good inventory in the warehouse whether you pay for it or not. Most of the people we work with will give us short extensions on our payables with no problems."

Cumberland Crafts extends credit terms of 2/10, net 30, and has had less than one percent uncollectable accounts receivable. Credit control is not a big problem for repeat purchases. "We watch new retailers very closely, however, because they are often starting on very shaky ground."

While the Stanfields extend prompt payment discounts to their customers, they have their own philosophy concerning the taking of such discounts. "We generally don't take advantage of early payment discounts because we like Cumberland Crafts to stay liquid. When we need cash in a hurry, as is frequently the case, I like to have it. Right now we view our liquidity to be more important than the discounts. Anyway most creditors really give us sixty days before complaining, so here is an additional reason not to take discounts. We've established a good reputation with creditors, so that they believe us when we say we can and will pay them back. We've had only one company to ever cut off our credit." The cost of capital for both of the operations is approximately 9 percent, which the Stanfields view as quite reasonable for their region.

Neither Craft-Village nor Cumberland Crafts operate on any type of budget system. The lack of budgetary controls are explained by Ann: "We have tried doing budgeting but haven't had much success. Dick and I complement one another, because he's very conservative with financing and I'm very liberal. It'll be hard for us to budget much for at least another year until we can get a better grip on our sales and be able to better predict our overall operational picture. We do have a very close budget for our advertising, however. I don't think budgeting has been a bad problem for us, because we haven't had a cancerous kind of overgrowth. We've been able to control things."

OPERATIONS

Cumberland Crafts now occupies 10,000 square feet in office and warehouse space with another 5,000 becoming available in the near future. However, Dick Stanfield estimates that "This additional room will provide us with adequate space for probably no more than another year—then we'll have to move again." He comments further that "Our present physical layout could be a lot better than it is. The facilities we have are adequate or just barely so. For instance, we need more office space and we could really use some additional classroom space. We're currently in the process of rearranging shelves and trying to make more efficient use of our warehousing space. We may soon reach the point where we'll have to quit buying some items due to inadequate space. We now have a lot of clutter in the aisles which we're slowly doing away with. Over the next five to eight years, Cumberland Crafts will need in the neighborhood of 25,000 square feet of space, and I don't really know how much manufacturing capability. Demand is so dynamic."

The new manufacturing project is also putting demand on the already critical floor space. Equipment for manufacturing silk flowers has been ordered, including one press and tools for six varieties of flowers. Dick explains that "The manufacturing process is relatively simple, involving a clicker and dye. We were very fortunate recently to find someone here in town who has a clicker for silk cutting and is willing to subcontract this phase of making silk flowers. To have purchased our own clicker would have cost us $6,000. We'll buy the dyes." He estimates the initial set-up cost for manufacturing to be in the neighborhood of $10,000. "We are essentially ready to set the equipment in today."

By the Stanfield's own admission, inventory control is one of the biggest problems that Cumberland faces. According to Dick, "Someone knows where certain items are kept, but not everyone knows where every item is. We sometimes waste time searching for inventory, hidden throughout the warehouses. We've got to control this better to prevent cancerous growth.

"One of our inventory difficulties stems from the fact that today a great number of craft retailers are specialists who purchase large amounts of just one or two big demand items. For example, there currently are numerous macrame shops who carry many macrame products, but nothing else. This means that we have to greatly overstock certain items."

Another problem pointed out by Dick is that "Many people in the craft industry are inclined to go in too many directions at the same time, ourselves included. Consequently, we currently are trying to get grips on what we have already started and to better control our inventory growth. We want to reach the point where we have a place to put every item in inventory and exert closer control over each item. Only in this way can we give our customers the kind of service they need with as few errors as possible.

"In the area of inventory control and sales, we have one big advantage over a clothing company or some other kind of business that caters to customers with changing taste. We can have our designer come up with a new use for each item.

"Weeding out items from our wholesaling inventory is no easy matter. We don't have a cut and dried method for this. The only way we've had to do it so far is to go out into the warehouse to see if something has obviously been sitting too long. We're in the process of working up some data cards on inventoried items to help with control. However, 35–45 percent of our inventory items are staples always in strong demand, such as glues, spray paint, instruction books, felt, chenille, etc.

"My answer to our ever-growing inventory control problem is to go to a small computer. We're slowly getting our inventory system on a special by-card set up designed to help us keep track of the inventory. We would like to take our control system to the point where someone could be hired to fulfill this function on a full-time basis."

EXHIBIT 1

CUMBERLAND CRAFTS, INC.
MONTHLY INCOME STATEMENTS
FOR PERIOD ENDING OCT. 1977

	Nov.	Dec.	Jan.	Feb.	Mar.	April	May	June	July	Aug.	Sept.	Oct.
Total Sales	$75915	$39606	$33542	$51787	$82730	$61402	$77577	$70259	$54002	$73375	$97186	$99872
Less: Cost of Sales												
Beginning Inventory	176473	184556	195781	196510	192415	189472	194604	172729	179118	185863	169789	153571
Purchases	50115	41717	25079	36295	59122	51338	78384	62346	47659	38548	54568	69043
Ending Inventory	184556	195781	196510	192415	189472	194604	172729	179118	185863	169789	153571	146420
Total Cost of Sales	42032	30492	24350	40390	62065	46206	100259	55957	40914	54622	70786	76194
Gross Profit	$33833	$ 9114	$ 9192	$11397	$20665	$15196	$(22682)	$14302	$13088	$18753	$26400	$23678
Less: Operating Expense												
Salaries	$ 7272	$ 5087	$ 4659	$ 5854	$ 6502	$ 6838	$ 9827	$ 7159	$ 7635	$ 7180	$ 8283	$ 8122
Advertising	127	424	68	161	983	99	541	810	46	861	172	90
Rent	600	600	600	600	600	600	600	600	600	600	600	600
Telephone Expense	212	351	151	391	480	821	908	889	974	802	1006	934
Licenses and Taxes	10	17	0	0	5	0	0	30	0	242	0	2336
Insurance Expense	274	274	274	274	274	274	19	925	0	634	1289	519
Depreciation Expense	23	23	23	23	18	23	452	130	119	119	119	119
Office Expenses	315	393	839	471	547	209	534	553	387	664	407	227
Other Operating Expense	1352	1659	1259	1432	3792	2768	5310	1046	3980	2486	1689	2722
Total (Operating Expense)	$10185	$ 8828	$ 7873	$ 9206	$13201	$11632	$ 18191	$12142	$13741	$13588	$13565	$15669
Other Income or Expense	635	83	94	102	211	26	67	139	223	296	586	576
Net Profit Before Taxes	$24333	$ 369	$ 1413	$ 2293	$ 7675	$ 3590	$(40806)	$ 2296	$ (430)	$ 5461	$13421	$ 8585

EXHIBIT 2

CUMBERLAND CRAFTS, INC.
MONTHLY BALANCE SHEETS
FOR NOV. 1976 TO OCT. 1977

	Nov.	Dec.	Jan.	Feb.	Mar.	April	May	June	July	Aug.	Sept.	Oct.
ASSETS												
Current Assets:												
Cash	$ 2991	$ 378	$ 1401	$ 1243	$ 1525	$ 1334	$ 5175	$ 864	$ 1721	$ 3220	$ (118)	$ 285
Accounts Receivable	44323	19526	23536	39233	51000	52774	69226	61302	46949	54748	62059	72053
Inventory	184556	195781	196510	192415	189472	194604	172729	179118	185863	169789	153571	146420
Total Current Assets	$321870	$215685	$221447	$232891	$241997	$248712	$247130	$241284	$234533	$227757	$215512	$218758
Fixed Assets:												
Furn., Fix. and Equip.	$ 9463	$ 9463	$ 9463	$ 9463	$ 9390	$ 11136	$ 16319	$ 15438	$ 16340	$ 16808	$ 16869	$ 16869
Accum. Depreciation	(370)	(393)	(416)	(440)	(463)	(486)	(927)	(976)	(1095)	(1214)	1334	1453
Net Fixed Assets	$ 9093	$ 9070	$ 9047	$ 9023	$ 8927	$ 10650	$ 15392	$ 14462	$ 15245	$ 15594	$ 15535	$ 15416
OTHER ASSETS	100	100	100	100	100	7600	10100	10100	4096	4096	4096	4016
TOTAL ASSETS	$241063	$224855	$230594	$241732	$251024	$266962	$272622	$265846	$253874	$247447	$235063	$238190

LIABILITIES AND STOCKHOLDERS' EQUITY

Current Liab.												
Accounts Payable	$ 69600	$ 52384	$ 41847	$ 26903	$ 52539	$ 59352	$103972	$ 87933	$ 83973	$ 85554	$ 66709	$ 64707
Other Current Liab.	12978	13934	12668	14206	10889	16424	17960	17717	19357	4506	2054	3943
Total Current Liab.	$ 82578	$ 66318	$ 54515	$ 41109	$ 63428	$ 75776	$121932	$105650	$103330	$ 90060	$ 68763	$ 68650
Long-term Liab.												
Loans from Stockholders	$ 37428	$ 37409	$ 37409	$ 37409	$ 53050	$ 53050	$ 52710	$ 67375	$ 67375	$ 66698	$ 66355	$ 66010
Stockholders' Equity:												
Common Stock	$ 5000	$ 5000	$ 5000	$ 5000	$ 5000	$ 5000	$ 5000	$ 5000	$ 5000	$ 5000	$ 5000	$ 5000
Premium on Common Stock	14600	14600	14600	14600	14600	14600	14600	14600	14600	14600	14600	14600
Retained Earnings	101457	101528	119070	143896	114946	118536	78380	73221	63569	71089	80345	83930
Total Stockholders' Equity	$121057	$121128	$138670	$163496	$134546	$138136	$ 97980	$ 92821	$ 83169	$ 90689	$ 99945	$103530
TOTAL LIABILITIES AND STOCKHOLDERS' EQUITY	$241063	$224855	$230594	$242014	$251024	$266962	$272622	$265846	$253874	$247447	$235063	$238190

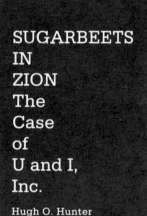

SUGARBEETS IN ZION The Case of U and I, Inc.

Hugh O. Hunter
Shane Sorey
Lynne McClure

Early fall of 1980 was not a happy time for the officers and directors of U and I, Inc. The United States had been through a sharp second quarter recession, interest rates had once more begun to rise, and the intensely contested presidential election was being fought over the issue of what many perceived to be a failed economic policy. In less than two years, U and I itself had undergone a series of dramatic changes born of desperation. They had foresaken the business which they had been in for ninety years. They had moved their corporate headquarters out of the region which had been their focus for those ninety years. They had reorganized, shuffling vice presidents here and there as if by some random process. Within the previous five years U and I had had a bitter fight with the State which was now their new home; and in the last three years they had suffered losses, the first since the great depression. There was internal dissention. The management abilities of the chairman, N. Eldon Tanner, and president, Rowland M. Cannon, were being questioned. It was impossible not to reflect on these seemingly cataclysmic events and ponder the circumstances which had led to them.

A BRIEF COMPANY HISTORY

The U and I story begins with Arthur Staynor, a Mormon horticulturalist from England, living in Utah in the 1880s. Staynor had experimented with various methods of producing sugar from cane and sugarbeets. He became convinced that sugarbeets could be grown in Utah, and processed into granulated sugar which could be sold to an expanding population in the intermountain states. Sugarbeet production was already under way in the Midwest and California using technology which had been developed in Napoleonic France. Some years earlier Mormon missionaries visiting France first saw beet processing plants in operation and were the first to alert the Church to the potential of this industry.

In 1889, the Utah Sugar Company was incorporated in Salt Lake City. Among the stockholders and officers were Staynor, George M. Cannon, John W. Young (son of Brigham Young), George Q. Cannon of the First Presidency of the Church of Jesus Christ of Latter-day Saints, and James Jack, financial secretary of the Church.

Copyrighted by Hugh O. Hunter

Much of the history of U and I, Inc. presented in this case is documented in Leonard J. Arrington. *Beet Sugar in the West: A History of the Utah-Idaho Sugar Company, 1891–1966.* Seattle: University of Washington Press, 1966.

In 1891, the first granulated sugar from Utah Sugar's Lehi, Utah, plant was produced. The history of the Company is one of association with the Church, and cooperation with State and local goverments of Utah. The officers and directors through the years have included a who's who in the Church and State. Generations of the same family have served the Company. The current president is Rowland M. Cannon. David O. McKay was president before he ascended to the leadership of the Mormon Church. The grandson of Utah Senator Reed Smoot, famous for imposing a tariff on imported Cuban sugar, is Executive Vice President and a director.

The Company represented a marriage of entrepreneurship to the work of the Lord. At the laying of the cornerstone of the Lehi factory in 1890, President Wilford Woodruff of the Mormon Church said:

> I want to say to all Israel that we believe it right to dedicate everything we engage in to the Lord. We have assembled today to lay this cornerstone, as is our custom in establishing all our temples. I will call on President George Q. Cannon to offer the dedicatory prayer. . . . I want you all to unite on the subject of sugar. There is not a question of public improvement which is of more value or has better prospects than sugar (Arrington, p. 10).

In the early years, Utah Sugar had difficulty in recovering the investment which had been made. The Mormon Church tried but failed to solicit donations from its congregation. Finally, the Church itself decided to lend financial support to the fledgling company. The reason was explained by President Joseph F. Smith in 1893:

> We started the sugar works here a few years ago. Why? Because when we came to reflect about it we saw that we had reached a point in our history where there was not a single enterprise of a public character that was calculated to give employment to our people. The railroads had gone into the hands of the outsiders, as we term them, and instead of their pursuing a wise policy, they abandoned the course that had been pursued by their predecessors, and discharged the Mormon people from their service, brought strangers from the east and west and gave them employment. . . . The government of the city has also been turned over. Every man that was suspected of having the least color of Mormonism about him was discharged from the service of the city, and strangers were imported and given work. There was not a thing being done of a public character calculated to give employment to the Latter Day Saints in any direction; and we began to feel that there was a responsibility resting upon us which required something to be done, in a small way at least, in the direction of giving employment to our people. So we started the sugar works, although few people had confidence in the success of the undertaking. . . . Men of means were very chary about it, and did not feel to take any very active part in attempting to start it (Arrington, pp. 12–13).

Production at the Lehi and other plants grew rapidly so that by 1906 sugar production exceeded one million bags, from a beginning of ten-thousand in

1891. The Company operated essentially in the way that Joseph Smith envisioned—that is, for the Mormon people. It sought to follow Mormon settlement of new lands in Utah and Idaho by building plants and growing beets. It acquired much needed capital by selling half the Company's stock to a giant from the East—The American Sugar Refining Company. Shortly thereafter, the Idaho Sugar Company, a subsidiary, was formed, followed shortly by other regional subsidiaries.

In 1914, following a generally prosperous period for the Company, and investigations of American Sugar for antitrust violations, the Mormon Church was able to repurchase the stock orignially sold to American Sugar. To this day, the Church retains control with 53% of the stock. Charles W. Nibley, Presiding Bishop of the Mormon Church and a director of the Utah-Idaho Sugar Company, explained the motive behind the stock repurchase:

> **Not the making of money, but with the desire to save the industry, when it was threatened and plainly threatened, from absolute destruction; to try to keep it going for the benefit of our farmers, for the benefit of the community more than with any view or special desire of benefiting the stockholders (Arrington, p. 82).**

Sugar production has never given the Company stability or long run profitability. It has survived relatively intact only through its association with the Mormon Church. In 1921, the Church saved the Company from failure by subscribing to a new issue of common stock. The Company suffered even through the relatively prosperous 1920s, losing money from 1925–29 because of low prices and over production. Once again, in 1931, the Company was in a crisis; and, as before, the Church came through with additional financing. Beginning with Roosevelt's New Deal and extending through World War II and beyond, the beet sugar industry became at least partially insulated from the vagaries of the market place by Government programs designed to control production, supply and price. To lessen its dependence on the unreliable sugar markets, U and I, in 1968, began a policy of diversification when it joined three dryland farmers in Pasco, Washington in developing a 21,000-acre block of land for pressure irrigation. The project was named K2H Farms, Incorporated, and became a subsidiary of U and I. In 1971, the company acquired 50,000 acres in south-central Washington and formed Prior Land Co., Inc. In 1974, another 50,000 acres adjacent to Prior Land Co. was acquired; this was named Horse Heaven Farms. U and I further diversified in 1975 when it bought 51% interest in Gourmet Food Products, Inc., a potato processing firm in Oregon. By 1980, U and I had expanded its interest in Gourmet Foods to 93%.

THE SUGARBEET BUSINESS

U and I contracted annually with indepedent growers to purchase specific quantities of beets at a price based on the sugar content of the beets and the net proceeds from the sugar sold. Under the participatory contract, sugar beet payments were related to the price of sugar and approximately 2/3 of the net proceeds from the sugar was paid to the growers. The Company manufactured sugar from beets and distributed sugar and sugar by-products, including dried beet pulp and beet molasses, both of which are used for livestock feed. Sugar was also sold through brokers in the western and midwestern states.

U and I, in the 1970s, owned four sugar factories, two in Washington, one in Idaho, and one in Utah; three sugar storage warehouses; one beet seed processing plant in Utah; and eight distribution terminals in Missouri, Wisconsin, Minnesota, Nebraska, Washington, Oregon, Illinois, and Utah.

THE SUGARBEET MARKET IN THE 1970s

The refined sugar market has been on a decline since late 1974. In this year, the U.S. Sugar Act, which had protected domestic sugar producers from the fluctuations inherent in the world sugar market, was discontinued. In the past, the government subsidized sugar growers for not overplanting, and the rest of the U.S market was allocated among some 30 foreign producers. The demise of the Sugar Act tied domestic sugar prices to the world sugar market. This market is volatile because it is mainly a residual market for sugar not committed through international trade agreements. The immediate effect on the sugar market was an increased price. High sugar prices acted as an incentive for sugar producers to increase their output and for the entrance of sugar substitutes into the market. Corn sweeteners began to be substituted for sugar by many beverage companies.

By 1976, there was an oversupply of sugar. Prices began to plummet downward and U and I found itself once again whip-sawed by the market. The price of sugar fell below the cost of production. In response to the market slump, U and I instituted drastic cost cutting programs in all areas. Costs were cut as much as possible without impairing future production capacity. High fructose corn sweeteners continued to increase their proportion of the sugar market. To meet customer demands and the increased competition, U and I began blending high fructose syrups with liquid sugars. In addition to product changes, U and I continued an aggressive advertising and merchandising campaign to protect and strengthen its brand distribution. Also, a new packaging line was introduced which utilized a polyethylene shrink wrap as a binder (outside wrapper) in place of the traditional binder. The new wrap reduced both packaging cost and breakage.

In 1977, the price of sugar continued to hover below production costs and U and I ended the year with a $2 million dollar net loss; the first loss since 1933. In addition to the low sugar prices, the entire sugar industry was plagued with a controversy concerning the nutritional aspects of sugar. The Federal Trade Commission proposed regulations limiting the advertising of sugary foods on television directed at children, and a Senate Select Committee recommended a 45% reduction in sugar use in diets.

This same year, Company sugar operations were restructured into a new Sugar Division, "to concentrate on a wider range of possible activity,"[1]

Again in 1978, the Company showed a net operating loss; this time over $8 million. Because of the long-depressed sugar market, the rising costs of production and uncertainties concerning any legislative solutions to industry problems, the Board of Directors announced on November 20, 1978, that the Company would terminate sugar-beet operations and concentrate on farming and potato processing. The four sugar production facilities were closed early in 1979 (after the 1978 sugar beet crop was processed) and the plants put up for sale. By early 1980, none of the facilities had been sold, although some equipment sales had been made.

OTHER EVENTS OF THE 1970s

Horse Heaven Farms   This 50,000 acre farm was acquired by U and I in 1974. It lies near other Company owned farms in arid south-central Washington. For high-yield crop production, irrigation is needed. In the years after the acquisition, U and I sought and was denied irrigation permits by the State of Washington. The State was trying to limit large scale corporate farming by denying rights to water. After a bitter struggle, U and I decided in March 1977 to sell Horse Heaven Farms. No buyers were found and the property was taken off the market in 1978 and used for dry-land farming of wheat and rangeland. In 1979, Horse Heaven Farms was organizationally merged into U and I, along with the other farm operations, and plans were made to partially irrigate.

Headquarters Move   In 1976, U and I was notified that the office building in Salt Lake City, where the Company had long maintained its corporate headquarters, was to be demolished. In May of that year, construction was begun on a new headquarters building in Salt Lake. The building was occupied in July 1977. In 1979, after the decision to terminate sugar beet operations, the Company decided to move its headquarters to Kennewick in south-central Washington. This relocation was completed in 1980.

Personnel   The period 1977–80 was one of a number of personnel changes. In the year following announcement of a phase out of the sugar beet operations, two of the twelve Board members resigned. Four others retired in the period 1977–80. There was also a considerable shifting of vice presidents:

—The V.P., Corporate Relations added the title, V.P., Sugar Division in 1979, after the decision to terminate operations.

—The V.P., Finance was made V.P., Sugar Division in 1978, then relinquished this duty in 1979 to become V.P., Farm Operations. In 1980, he added the duties of Corporate Treasurer.

—A new V.P., Finance, was named in 1978, but was gone by 1980.

—A new V.P., Farm Processing, was named in 1979.

Ownership and Dividends   Throughout this period of loss and re-direction, Mr. N. Eldon Tanner, First Counselor of the First Presidency of the Church of Jesus Christ of Latter-day Saints, remained as Chairman of the Board. The Mormon Church routinely places two of the twelve (later eleven) directly, and others indirectly through Church owned companies.

DIVIDEND POLICY (1973–1980)		
	earnings per share	dividends per share
1973	.77	.80
1974	2.25	.35
1975	2.39	.80
1976	4.60	1.65
1977	2.36	1.35
1978	(1.02)	.30
1979	(3.71)	.10
1980	(.41)	0

Organization   In 1979, a major organizational change was made when former subsidiary farming and food processing operations were integrated with the other Company operations. The present structure is presented in Exhibit 1.

Now in the fall of 1980, facing an uncertain future, those responsible for directing the company through these next crucial years contemplated not only the cure but the nature of the illness itself. Had U and I been a victim of circumstance? Had its management failed? Was its relationship with the Mormon Church a help or hindrance? How could they ensure a brighter future?

ENDNOTES

1   U and I 1978 Annual Report, p. 3

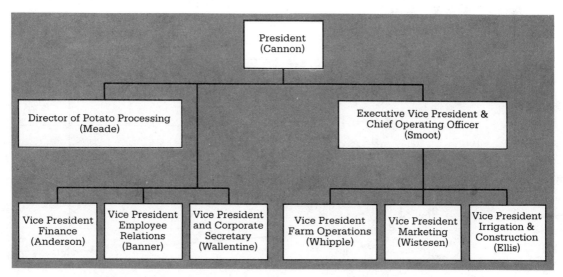

EXHIBIT 1
Organization Chart

Sugar Update: U.S. and World

U.S. Sugar Supplies
IN MILLION SHORT TONS

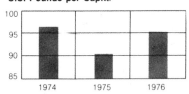

Percent of 1976 total

U.S. Pounds per Capita

World Production and Consumption
IN MILLION SHORT TONS

■ Production
■ Consumption

World and U.S. Raw Sugar Prices: Annual Average 1967-1976
CENTS PER POUND

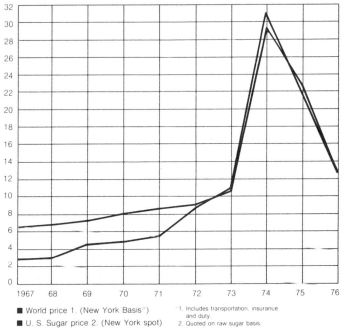

■ World price 1. (New York Basis°)
■ U. S. Sugar price 2. (New York spot)

1. Includes transportation, insurance and duty.
2. Quoted on raw sugar basis.

World and U.S. Raw Sugar Prices: Monthly Average 1976-1977
CENTS PER POUND

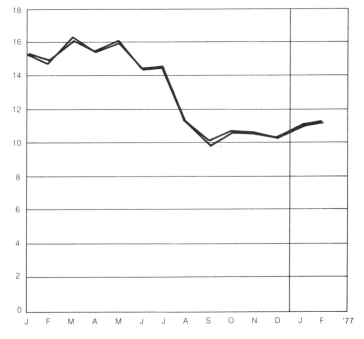

EXHIBIT 2
Sugar Update: U.S. and World

386

Summary of Operations
U AND I INCORPORATED AND SUBSIDIARIES

	Year Ended February 28 or 29				
	1980	1979	1978	1977	1976
From continuing operations:					
Sales of products	$64,332,898	$58,544,921	$45,992,709	$41,084,905	$25,516,222
Cost of sales	63,450,270	52,998,433	43,592,223	38,856,796	27,651,935
Interest expense	2,336,300	1,920,519	1,888,856	1,951,744	1,501,924
Provision for depreciation	3,778,624	3,313,796	3,319,337	3,359,822	2,901,494
Federal and state income taxes (credits), including deferred	(2,900,000)	700,000	(1,200,000)	(1,000,000)	(2,324,759)
Earnings (loss) from continuing operations	(658,000)	816,772	(746,486)	(314,517)	(1,773,562)
Earnings (loss) from discontinued operations	-0-	(8,851,766)	(1,278,091)	5,856,835	12,448,584
Net earnings (loss)	(658,000)	(8,034,994)	(2,024,577)	5,542,318	10,675,022
Dividends on Preferred Stock	249,009	249,009	249,009	249,009	249,009
Dividends on Common Stock	-0-	223,633	670,900	3,027,764	3,746,987
Per share amounts:					
Non-diluted earnings (loss):					
From continuing operations	(.41)	.25	(.45)	(.25)	(.89)
From discontinued operations	-0-	(3.96)	(.57)	2.61	5.49
Net earnings (loss)	(.41)	(3.71)	(1.02)	2.36	4.60
Fully diluted earnings (loss):					
From continuing operations	(.41)	.25	(.45)	(.13)	(.72)
From discontinued operations	-0-	(3.96)	(.57)	2.40	5.06
Net earnings (loss)	(.41)	(3.71)	(1.02)	2.27	4.34
Dividends — Class A Preferred Stock	1.265	1.265	1.265	1.265	1.265
Dividends — Class B Preferred Stock	1.265	1.265	1.265	1.265	1.265
Dividends — Common Stock	-0-	.10	.30	1.35	1.65
Industry Segments (Percent of total)					
Revenues:					
Farming and related processing	71%	76%	72%	92%	99%
Warehousing and distribution	29	24	28	8	1
Earnings (loss) before income taxes:					
Farming and related processing	(79)	97	(821)	172	(105)
Warehousing and distribution	(21)	3	721	(72)	5

EXHIBIT 3
Summary of Operations
U AND I INCORPORATED AND SUBSIDIARIES

Consolidated Statements of Operations and Retained Earnings
U and I INCORPORATED AND SUBSIDIARIES

	Year Ended February 28	
	1978	1977
REVENUES		
Sales of refined sugar and other products	**$162,096,870**	$183,460,383
Refund from revision of Company's		
insurance program	**481,278**	
Interest and other revenues	**151,469**	172,694
TOTAL REVENUES	162,729,617	183,633,077
COSTS AND EXPENSES		
Cost of sales	144,557,834	151,996,069
Selling expenses	19,144,638	19,308,990
Interest — Note C	4,398,722	3,038,257
	168,101,194	174,343,316
EARNINGS (LOSS) BEFORE		
INCOME TAXES	(5,371,577)	9,289,761
INCOME TAXES		
Current federal and state income taxes (credit)	(3,630,000)	2,739,265
Deferred federal income taxes	283,000	1,008,178
	(3,347,000)	3,747,443
NET EARNINGS (LOSS)	(2,024,577)	5,542,318
RETAINED EARNINGS		
Dividends paid on Preferred Stock:		
Class A — $1.265 per share	124,501	124,501
Class B — $1.265 per share	124,508	124,508
EARNINGS (LOSS) RELATED TO		
COMMON STOCK	(2,273,586)	5,293,309
Amount at beginning of year	46,505,872	44,240,327
	44,232,286	49,533,636
Dividends paid on Common Stock — $.30 per		
share in 1978 and $1.35 per share in 1977 ..	670,900	3,027,764
RETAINED EARNINGS AT		
END OF YEAR	$ 43,561,386	$ 46,505,872
EARNINGS (LOSS) PER SHARE OF COMMON STOCK		
Assuming no dilution	$(1.02)	$2.36
Assuming full dilution	(1.02)	2.27

See notes to consolidated
financial statements

EXHIBIT 4
Consolidated Statements of Operations and Retained Earnings
U AND I INCORPORATED AND SUBSIDIARIES

Consolidated Statements of Operations and Retained Earnings
U AND I INCORPORATED AND SUBSIDIARIES

	Year Ended	
	February 29 **1980**	February 28 1979
REVENUES		
Net sales	**$64,332,898**	$58,544,921
Interest and other revenue	**689,009**	122,458
	65,021,907	58,667,379
COSTS AND EXPENSES		
Cost of sales	**63,450,270**	52,998,433
Selling expenses	**2,793,337**	2,231,655
Interest	**2,336,300**	1,920,519
	68,579,907	57,150,607
EARNINGS (LOSS) FROM CONTINUING OPERATIONS BEFORE INCOME TAXES (CREDITS)	**(3,558,000)**	1,516,772
INCOME TAXES (CREDITS) — Note A		
Current federal and state income taxes (credits)	**(3,000,000)**	200,000
Deferred federal income taxes	**100,000**	500,000
	(2,900,000)	700,000
EARNINGS (LOSS) FROM CONTINUING OPERATIONS	**(658,000)**	816,772
DISCONTINUED OPERATIONS — Notes B and H		
Loss from discontinued sugar processing operations, less applicable income tax credits		(8.851,766)
NET LOSS	**(658,000)**	(8,034,994)
RETAINED EARNINGS		
Dividends paid on Preferred Stock:		
Class A — $1.265 per share	**124,501**	124,501
Class B — $1.265 per share	**124,508**	124,508
LOSS RELATED TO COMMON STOCK	**(907,009)**	(8,284,003)
Amount at beginning of year	**35,053,750**	43,561,386
	34,146,741	35,277,383
Dividends paid on Common Stock —		
$.10 per share in 1979		223,633
RETAINED EARNINGS AT END OF YEAR	**$34,146,741**	$35,053,750
EARNINGS (LOSS) PER SHARE OF COMMON STOCK		
Continuing operations	**$ (.41)**	$ .25
Discontinued operations		(3.96)
NET LOSS	**$ (.41)**	$(3.71)

See notes to consolidated financial statements

EXHIBIT 4 (Continued)
Consolidated Statements of Operations and Retained Earnings
U AND I INCORPORATED AND SUBSIDIARIES

BERVEN CARPETS CORPORATION (A)

David M. Hauntz
Gaylord L. McCabe

Although carpet making may not be the worlds oldest profession, the weaving of various fibers into mats suitable for a number of purposes, only one of which was floor covering, predated a significant number of other human activities. The craft of weaving developed early in every culture, first as a means of producing something to provide protection from the elements and eventually as a form of art. The weaving of fiber into carpet for use as a floor covering is a fairly recent development, historically speaking. Even more recent is the availability and use of carpet as a floor covering by the general public. In numerous Medieval European cities, guilds grew up around the craft of weaving rugs, protecting the weavers and improving the weaving process. Some of the weaving techniques in use today are identified by the name of the European city in which they originated. These guilds were, in effect, factories and although production was primarily by manual labor, carpet making was elevated beyond something done for personal use or for artistic purposes into a profit making business enterprise. Productivity was low, the labor was skilled, and the prices were such that only the rich could afford them. But the guildsmen, when they emigrated to America, took with them an industry.

The carpet weaving industry came to America in the late Eighteenth Century. Numerous small family owned or managed textile factories concentrating on a single fiber and/or process sprang up throughout the Colonies, but the actual weaving of carpet on a commercial basis was centered around the Philadelphia area.[1] "The early carpet manufacturers developed a production organization that has been described as a 'putting-out' system. Under this arrangement individual weavers appear to have owned and operated their looms while the 'employer' supplied the raw materials, paid the weavers a piece rate, and had complete control over the finished products."[2] The Industrial Revolution resulted in the application of power to the weaving process, causing woman to supplant men in the labor force as the need for skill and strength was reduced. The various machines developed were, of course, improved upon over the years, but these improvements were on existing machinery. From the granting of the patent for the Axminster Loom in 1874 until the 1950s, no revolutionary new technology appeared in the industry.[3]

Economic events, however, had a profound effect on the carpet industry. A world war, the advent of the automobile, and the Great Depression served to create intense competition, high prices, and low profit margins. Carpets were an expensive commodity beyond the reach of most middle class consumers. The traditional fabric of carpets, wool, became

Copyright © David M. Hauntz

scarce during World War II, and necessity sent the carpet makers in search of alternative fibers. First cotton, which proved unacceptable, then the synthetic fibers. Rayon was in use by 1940 and nylon appeared in the 1950s. A technological innovation in itself, the use of synthetic fiber eliminated some costly steps in the weaving process, causing prices to drop and putting carpets within the reach of·many more consumers. The dominant process, however, remained weaving.

All the way back in 1895 a lady by the name of Catherine Evans of Dalton, Georgia, duplicated a family heirloom bedspread using a process known as tufting. Five years later she sold that work, the news spread rapidly throughout the Dalton area, and "By 1930, the demand was such that local entrepreneurs had 'haulers' taking yarn and spread sized sheeting stamped with designs to some 10,000 persons who were hand tufting them into bedspreads in their homes."[4] The minimum wage laws of the 1930s made such cabin craft production too expensive to be profitable, however. Innovation in tufting machinery again made tufted carpets profitable by increasing productivity. "The area around Dalton, Georgia, became the center of the developing tufted carpet industry because of the technology and facilities that had grown up there to support earlier tufting enterprises."[5] It is notable that the tufted carpets were not made by a single manufacturer, but by small scale operators who specialized in one or two phases of the process. This had the effect of minimizing the capital investment required and removed the necessity for manufacturers to develop an expansive, and expensive, salesforce. Barriers to entry in the Dalton area were minimal and profits were high. So many people took advantage of these conditions that prices fell drastically and markets opened for the product throughout the United States. Weaving, still done by what was essentially a 19th Century technology, ceased to be a market force in the carpet industry. "What caused the revolution was simple economics. Tufting machines turn out broadloom eight to ten times faster than Axminster or Wilton looms, and reduced labor's component in the total cost of rug making from nearly one third to an average of 12%. Such savings are so important that, in the brief span since 1951, tufted broadloom has beaten the dust off all other carpeting. Tufting today accounts for almost 90% of total U.S. production."[6] The tufting process is illustrated in Appendix A.

The framework for today's carpet industry was formed in Dalton, Georgia, but several trends also developed which had significant effects on the industry. The textile industry in general, of which carpet making is a part, experienced horizontal and vertical integration. "The causes of these combinations appeared to be threefold: the shrinking of mill margins due to increased competition, the desire to control more closely the marketing of finished products, and the urge to control the source of fabric supplies."[7] At the same time, technological innovation and the absence of barriers to entry served to generate a huge manufacturing capacity. A large number of carpeting firms developed, none able to gain a dominant market share, all saddling the industry in general with excess capacity. Appendix B is a list of some of the companies engaged ·in carpet making today. Another factor is illustrated in Exhibit 1. In no other industry in the United States is the cost of material such a large percentage of the total cost of production. Inventories of finished goods, unless quickly sold, can dramatically affect a firm's profitability. In an industry suffering from overcapacity, carpet making firms are dependent upon high volume to make their production profitable. It is clearly evident that the carpet industry, producing a product for a market that is highly sensitive to demand from both a taste and price standpoint, is extremely vulnerable to the down side of the business cycle.

EXHIBIT 1

SUMMARY OF COST FACTORS IN THE PRODUCTION OF PIECE-DYED NYLON SHAG CARPET		
Item	Cost Per Square Yard	Percent of Total Cost
Materials		
Yarn		
Primary backing		
Dyes and chemicals	$3.333	76.0
Latex		
Secondary backing		
Packing		
Direct Labor		
Receiving		
Tufting		
Dyeing and drying	.148	3.4
Coating		
Shearing		
Final inspection		
Factory overhead	.231	5.3
Allowance for returns	.148	3.4
Other expenses		
Selling and marketing	.392	8.9
General administrative	.078	1.7
Product development	.026	0.6
Warehousing and shipping	.030	0.6
Total	$4.386	100.0

Enter Berven Carpets Corporation. Philip Berven founded the company in 1938 as a distributor of custom carpet catering to the needs of interior designers in the San Francisco area. Berven's strategy then, as it is now, was to concentrate on a more highly styled, better quality goods. During and after World War II California experienced rapid growth and Berven chose to grow with that market. That period of time was characterized by material shortages and a supply of goods insufficient to keep up with the growing demand. As a distributor, Berven needed a dependable supply of goods so they sought additional resources, entering into agreements for the importing of oriental rugs and, in 1945, by buying a small carpet mill located in Fresno, California. At that point Berven's internally supplied goods were still a minor portion of their total business, and Berven concentrated on expanding their distributorships geographically. Berven took note of the revolutionary developments occuring in Dalton, Georgia, and in keeping with their desire to be a leader in the carpet industry, began producing tufted carpets in their Fresno mill in 1951. In 1955 they purchased additional manufacturing facilities in Dalton, but logistical considerations soon forced them to consolidate their tufting operations in Fresno. Berven's commitment to market leadership led to their developing in the Fresno facility three separate operations: a dyeing operation to color their yarn, a broadloom tufting operation to produce quality carpet on a large scale, and a specialty mill to custom create carpet using a combination of techniques. Berven has since continued to expand their Fresno facility and to modernize it as technology improved. Their dyeing operation, called Veridye, supplies their own yarn needs. It also produces dyed yarn for other manufacturers. In 1974, Berven again sought additional capacity by purchasing Chandelle Carpets of Dalton, Georgia. Berven has expanded their distribution to their current 17 field offices located throughout the United States.

      Berven is thus a vertically integrated company, omitting from their operation only the very endpoints of the industry: yarn and dye synthesis from basic raw materials—mostly petrochemicals—and retail outlets. They market their products at the wholesale level through their own distributors and they also seek large commercial and governmental agency contracts. Berven's organizational structure, as shown in Exhibit 2, is actually quite simple, which is understandable given the fact that their total nationwide employment is less than 700 people and their net assets are less than $30 million. Their Fresno operation employs approximately 80% of their total workforce. The organization as it exists currently has evolved out of what were once three distinct business operations: the dyeing mill, the custom carpet mill, and the distribution operation. These were represented by a tier structure of parent and wholly owned subsidiary corportions. Changes in the tax laws and increased

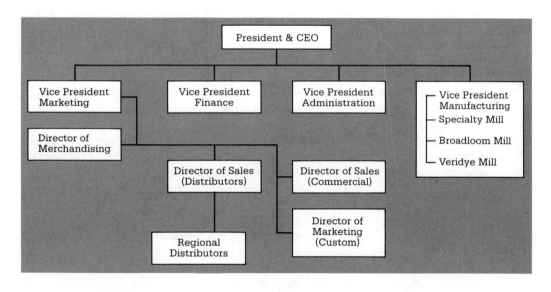

EXHIBIT 2
BERVEN CARPETS CORPORATION ORGANIZATION

pressure for cost efficiency led to a statutory merger by 1978, producing the outline of their current structure. Marketing is the major, if not dominant, part of Berven's business, and Berven has frequently altered the focus and structure of this part of their organization over the past decade in their search for profitability. At the present time, the marketing vice president has the responsibility for product and market research, product and market development, sales, and distribution, the manufacturing vice president handles production scheduling and quality control, the administrative vice president does the purchasing and production planning, inventory control and warehousing, and the financial vice president does the budgeting and cash and credit management.

The president and chief executive officer, Robert Hendy, who was elevated to that post in March 1979, actively manages all of Berven's activities. As in most small companies, he is the dominant force in the organization. Over the past ten years Berven has experienced considerable difficulty as shown in the summary of operations in Appendix C. "I hesitate to dwell on our past errors," Hendy reflected upon taking over, "but problems our firm encountered essentially encompassed the ills in our industry that arose from overcapacity and a lack of adequate market concentration. We're not implying that our problems were completely inevitable, but we literally grew into them along with a large percentage of other manufacturers that are aggressively growth oriented."[9] Hendy has taken a series of actions which are a shift away from previous management efforts to restore profitability and which also reflect the seriousness of their situation. "The pursuit of growth at Berven followed the conventional wisdom of the carpet industry, which tended to equate automatically the ability to produce with a commensurate ability to market or sell. The beginning months under my leadership were largely a period of gearing up equally important changes made in production procedures and controls. The net result has been to reduce costs materially in both areas through greater efficiencies."[10] Berven's goal is still growth, but the emphasis is survival. By cutting costs, reducing capacity to better fit forecasted sales, and increasing the marketing effort, Hendy believes ". . . we're alive and well, thank you, with solid programs to restore profitability."[11]

At least one industry observer has doubts about this, however, based upon his knowledge of the carpet industry and of Berven's financial condition. Until 1978 the growth rate of Berven's sales has been in line with that of the industry as a whole. Achieving renewed growth in sales will, of course, help, but there are economic factors which prevent this from being the total solution. Innovation in machinery and materials over the past 3 decades have exerted a downward pressure on manufacturer's prices. In 1950 the average manufacturer's factory price was $6.26 per yard and in 1974 it was $3.76. Inflation, and stagflation, has dramatically increased the price of raw materials and has, in varying degrees of intensity over time, affected the cost of financing production and the ability of consumers to finance the purchase of the final product. The current slowdown in the residential construction industry hardly represents the ideal market for carpeting. These are external problems however, and everyone has to deal with them. The way Berven has chosen to cope with them, according to an industry observer, has put Berven into a deep hole, so deep that they may not be able to get out. For example:

—Berven's ratio of cost of goods sold to total sales has increased from 79% in 1973 to nearly 87% in 1977. The industry average cost of goods sold ratio in 1977 was 80%.

—Interest expense, both long term and short term, and operating expenses in general have been increasing and are far too high. Berven's operating expenses are close to 15% of sales whereas profitable companies in the industry are down around 12%.

—Berven's average collection period for receivables has been around 66 days whereas the industry average is between 50 and 55 days. This represents approximately $1.5 million in cash flow lost annually which could be used to finance additional production or at least reduce the impact of financing production at present levels.

—Inventory levels are entirely too high as indicated by the often repeated practice of selling large amounts of carpet as discontinued styles at discount prices. Berven's average inventory turnover has been around 3.5 whereas the industry average is in excess of 5.

—Restrictive covenants and compensating balance agreements in their lines of credit give Berven's banks entirely too much control over Berven's operations.

—Continuous losses of increasing magnitude since 1975 severely reduce Berven's ability to generate capital, both externally and internally.

—Berven has been operating at around 40% of its manufacturing capacity whereas the profitable companies in the industry are up around 70% or more.

Hendy's response has been to seek additional market penetration in their present market by putting their product into the showrooms of independent full line carpet distributors and to seek an additional market with a lower priced product. The "growth" strategy of increased market penetration certainly offers hope because it is far less expensive than increasing the number of Berven's showrooms across the nation. The industry observer states "They produce a good product, maybe the best on the market," he states, "and the increased visibility should produce a lot of new sales." That Berven's product is good is not just idle boasting as evidenced by the fact that, in 1976, Berven produced and installed the carpet in the residence of the sister of the Shah of Iran. The new product line, however, is not a significant departure from their existing lines, and is not down into the mainstream of carpet prices nationally.

The indicated strategy at this point in Berven's game is retrenchment. Continued production of slow-moving carpet while using less than half of their capacity is a formula for, at worst, bankruptcy or, at best, merger. A re-evaluation of their market is also in order. One would not normally expect a problem in the collection of receivables when the company is selling in a market of affluent customers. By far the greatest percentage of carpet sold nationally is substantially lower in price than Berven's products so, if Berven is to survive, they may have to enter that market. Whatever the secret is, Berven is running out of time fast. The not too confident industry observer says, "They've got probably less than two years."

ENDNOTES

1   Steven S. Plice, *Manpower and Merger: The Impact of Merger Upon Personnel Policies in the Carpet and Furniture Industries.* Industrial Research Unit, The Wharton School, University of Pennsylvania, Philadelphia, Penn. 1976, pp. 84–85.

2   Ibid., p. 85.

3   Ibid., pp. 86–87.

4   Robert Coram, "Dalton, Georgia . . . Genesis of an Industry," *Textile World,* April 1968, 357.

5   Plice, 92.

6   David A. Lochwing, "Flying Carpets," *Barrons,* February 21, 1966, 16.

7   David C. D. Rogers "Management: The Pace of Change 1860 to 2068," *Textile World,* April 1968, 113.

8   Plice, 102.

9   Arthur S. Green, "Developing Programs to Restore Profitability," *Carpet and Rug Industry,* November 1979, 16.

10 Ibid., p. 16.

11 Ibid., p. 16.

APPENDIX A

Diagram Showing Sequence of Short Loop Tufting and Cut Pile Tufting

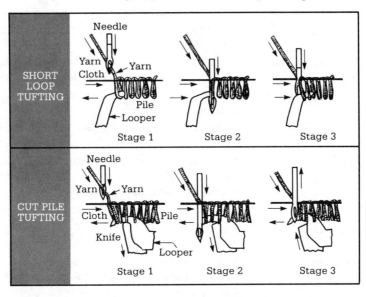

SOURCE: D. T. Ward, *Tufting: An Introduction,* 2nd Edit. (Manchester, England: Texpress, 1975). Used with permission of Hoover Worldwide Corporation.

APPENDIX B

Selected Textile Companies With Carpet Manufacturing Capabilities, 1976

Parent Company	Carpet Mills
Burlington Industries, Inc.	Monticello Carpet Mills Lees Carpets Burlington House Carpets
Collins & Aikman	Tennessee Tufting Corporation Collins & Aikman Carpet Division
Crown Crafts, Inc.	Crown Chenille Manufacturing Company Crown Crafts, Inc.
Dan River, Inc.	Wanda Weave (Dan River Floor Covering Division)
Deering Milliken	Floor Covering Business (Calloway Mills)
Fieldcrest Mills, Inc.	Karastan Rug Mills Laurel Crest Carpets
General Felt Industries, Inc.	GFI Carpet Division
J. P. Stevens & Co., Inc.	Gulistan Carpet Division

SOURCE: The Carpet and Rug Institute, *Directory and Report, 1973, 1974–75* (Dalton, Georgia: CRI, 1973, 1974–75, pp. 191–222.

Diversified Companies with Interests in Carpet Manufacturing 1976

Parent Company	Carpet Mills	Primary Line of Business
Champion International	Trend Mills	Plywood and Paper Furniture
Lehigh Portland Cement	Trinity Rugs Crusader Carpets	Cement
Sperry & Hutchinson Co.	Bigelow-Sanford	Home Furnishings Trading Stamps
Congoleum Industries, Inc.	Congoleum Industries Carpet Division (Lewis Carpet Mills)	Resilient Flooring Home Furnishings Ship Building
RCA	Coronet Carpets	Diversified
Armstrong Cork	E & B Mills	Resilient Flooring Home Furnishings
Jim Walter Corporation	Majestic Carpet Mills Meridon Carpets Crown-Tuft	Home Building Building Materials
Delta Diversified	Modulon Carpets	Diversified
Mohasco Industries	Alexander Smith Firth Carpets Mohawk	Home Furnishings
Burke Industries	Burke Carpet Mills	Molded Rubber Products
Ludlow Corporation	Walter Carpet Mills	Gummed, Coated, and Specialty Papers, Barrier and Flexible Packaging Materials

SOURCE: The Carpet and Rug Institute, *Directory and Report, 1973, 1974–75* (Dalton, Georgia: CRI, 1973, 1974–75), pp. 191–222; *Thomas Register of American Manufacturers and Thomas Register Catalog File, 1976* (New York: Thomas Publishing Co., 1976); Industry Source, May 1976.

EXHIBIT 1

Consolidated Balance Sheets

Consolidated Financial Statements   Berven Carpets Corporation and Subsidiary

ASSETS	December 31 1979	December 31 1978
CURRENT ASSETS		
Cash	$ 62,797	$ 379,716
Trade receivables, less allowances (1979—$408,000; 1978—$355,544)—Note C	7,463,630	6,986,297
Inventories—Notes B and C:		
Finished products	4,710,562	5,683,958
Work-in-process	1,023,488	1,288,153
Raw materials	3,049,031	2,256,202
	8,783,081	9,228,313
Prepaid expenses	228,849	254,190
TOTAL CURRENT ASSETS	16,538,357	16,848,516
PROPERTY, PLANT AND EQUIPMENT—Note C:		
Land	370,578	370,766
Buildings and improvements	6,770,140	6,302,338
Machinery and equipment	7,733,679	9,252,148
Furniture and fixtures	387,964	354,158
Leasehold improvements	370,428	358,340
	15,632,789	16,637,750
Less allowances for depreciation and amortization	5,837,940	6,133,706
	9,794,849	10,504,044
Excess land held for sale	—0—	233,000
	9,794,849	10,737,044
OTHER ASSETS	41,879	53,653
	$26,375,085	$27,639,213

LIABILITIES AND SHAREHOLDERS' EQUITY	December 31 1979	December 31 1978
CURRENT LIABILITIES		
Notes payable to bank—Note C	$ 3,835,435	$ 1,688,772
Trade accounts payable	3,480,515	3,069,071
Employee compensation	219,358	298,331
Other accrued expenses	553,593	359,004
Portion of long-term debt due within one year	106,167	97,080
TOTAL CURRENT LIABILITIES	8,195,068	5,512,258
LONG-TERM DEBT, less amount due within one year—Note C	5,935,139	6,041,306
DEFERRED INCOME TAXES—Note E	870,358	1,108,358
SHAREHOLDERS' EQUITY—Notes C and F		
Capital Stock:		
Preferred Stock, par value $10 a share —authorized 200,000 shares, issued and outstanding—none		
Common Stock, par value $.10 per share—authorized 10,000,000 shares, issued and outstanding 3,671,172 shares in 1979 and 3,669,528 shares in 1978	371,934	371,769
Additional paid-in capital	2,336,126	2,332,828
Retained earnings	8,666,460	12,272,694
	11,374,520	14,977,291
COMMITMENTS — Note G		
	$26,375,085	$27,639,213

See notes to consolidated financial statements

5

EXHIBIT 2

Consolidated Statements of Operations

Consolidated Financial Statements   Berven Carpets Corporation and Subsidiary

	Year Ended December 31	
	1979	1978
Net sales	**$ 39,261,752**	$ 47,032,195
Other income	**118,100**	175,564
Gain on sale of assets—Note H	**463,819**	1,328,798
	39,843,671	48,536,557
Costs and expenses:		
Cost of products sold	**34,532,978**	40,477,371
Selling, general and administrative	**7,229,826**	8,199,314
Interest:		
On long-term debt	**584,139**	757,352
Other	**281,569**	499,947
Other charges—Note I	**1,058,993**	—0—
	43,687,505	49,933,984
LOSS BEFORE INCOME TAX CREDIT	**(3,843,834)**	(1,397,427)
Income tax credit—Note E	**(237,600)**	(175,600)
NET LOSS	**$ (3,606,234)**	$ (1,221,827)
Loss per share	**$(.98)**	$(.33)

See notes to consolidated financial statements

EXHIBIT 3

Consolidated Statements of Shareholders' Equity

	Common Stock		Additional Paid-in Capital	Retained Earnings	Total
	Shares Issued	Amount			
Balance at January 1, 1978	3,668,977	$371,714	$2,331,910	$ 13,494,521	$ 16,198,145
Stock sold to employees	551	55	918		973
Net loss for the year				(1,221,827)	(1,221,827)
BALANCE AT DECEMBER 31, 1978	3,669,528	371,769	2,332,828	12,272,694	14,977,291
Stock sold to employees	1,644	165	3,298		3,463
Net loss for the year				(3,606,234)	(3,606,234)
BALANCE AT DECEMBER 31, 1979	3,671,172	$371,934	$2,336,126	$ 8,666,460	$ 11,374,520

See notes to consolidated financial statements

Desert Point, fashioned from Antron® III mid-luster nylon, features a dense, plush cut pile texture. Subtle shade variations of the ground color are accompanied with flecked random accents.

6

EXHIBIT 4

Consolidated Statements of Changes in Financial Position

Consolidated Financial Statements   Berven Carpets Corporation and Subsidiary

	Year Ended December 31	
	1979	1978
SOURCE OF FUNDS		
Net loss	**$(3,606,234)**	$(1,221,827)
Items recognized in net loss which did not affect working capital in the current period:		
Provision for depreciation and amortization	**773,743**	906,439
Decrease in deferred income taxes	**(238,000)**	(160,000)
Write-down of fixed assets	**903,993**	52,574
TOTAL APPLIED TO OPERATIONS	**(2,166,498)**	(422,814)
Book value of property, plant and equipment sold	**285,012**	1,312,083
Decrease in other assets	**11,774**	55,311
Common Stock sold to employees	**3,463**	973
	(1,866,249)	945,553
APPLICATION OF FUNDS		
Repayment and current maturities of long-term debt	**106,167**	1,821,797
Additions to property, plant and equipment	**1,020,553**	489,645
	1,126,720	2,311,442
DECREASE IN WORKING CAPITAL	**$(2,992,969)**	$(1,365,889)
CHANGES IN COMPONENTS OF WORKING CAPITAL		
Increase (decrease) in current assets:		
Cash	**$ (316,919)**	$ (700,453)
Trade receivables	**477,333**	(1,589,512)
Inventories	**(445,232)**	(5,051,514)
Refundable income taxes	**—0—**	(565,584)
Prepaid expenses	**(25,341)**	(116,147)
	(310,159)	(8,023,210)
Increase (decrease) in current liabilities:		
Notes payable to bank	**2,146,663**	(3,311,228)
Trade accounts payable	**411,444**	(2,630,682)
Employee compensation	**(78,973)**	5,904
Other accrued expenses	**194,589**	(105,158)
Portion of long-term debt due within one year	**9,087**	(616,157)
	2,682,810	(6,657,321)
DECREASE IN WORKING CAPITAL	**$(2,992,969)**	$(1,365,889)

See notes to consolidated financial statements

EXHIBIT 5

Auditors' Report

Report of Ernst & Whinney, Independent Auditors.

To the Shareholders
Berven Carpets Corporation
Fresno, California

We have examined the consolidated balance sheets of Berven Carpets Corporation and subsidiary as of December 31, 1979 and 1978, and the related consolidated statements of operations, shareholders' equity and changes in financial position for the years then ended. Our examinations were made in accordance with generally accepted auditing standards and, accordingly, included such tests of the accounting records and such other auditing procedures as we considered necessary in the circumstances.

In our opinion, the financial statements referred to above present fairly the consolidated financial position of Berven Carpets Corporation and subsidiary at December 31, 1979 and 1978, and the consolidated results of their operations and changes in their financial position for the years then ended, in conformity with generally accepted accounting principles applied on a consistent basis.

Fresno, California
February 18, 1980   *Ernst & Whinney*

7

401

EXHIBIT 6

Notes to Consolidated Financial Statements

Consolidated Financial Statements   Berven Carpets Corporation and Subsidiary

NOTE A—Significant Accounting Policies and Industry Information

Principles of Consolidation
The financial statements include the accounts of the Company and its wholly-owned subsidiary. During 1978 the Company liquidated and merged into the Company its other wholly-owned domestic subsidiaries.

Inventories
Inventories are stated at the lower of cost or market. Cost is generally determined on the last-in, first-out method (LIFO) except for certain inventories, which are valued on the first-in, first-out (FIFO) method.

Properties and Depreciation
Property, plant and equipment are stated at cost except for certain machinery and equipment, as discussed in Note I, which has been written down to estimated realizable value. Depreciation and amortization are computed on the straight-line method over the estimated useful lives of the assets.

Income Taxes
Investment tax credits are accounted for on the "flow-through" method. Accelerated depreciation methods are used for income tax purposes for qualifying property.

Retirement and Profit Sharing Plans
The Company has pension and profit sharing plans covering substantially all full-time employees. Pension costs are funded as incurred.

Loss per Share
Loss per share is based upon the weighted average number of shares of Common Stock outstanding during the year (1979—3,670,368; 1978—3,669,361). The assumed exercise of options was not utilized in the computation as the effect would be antidilutive.

Industry Information
The Company and its subsidiary manufacture and market a diverse line of tufted carpeting and dyed yarn for sale principally in the United States for both residential and commercial use.

NOTE B—Inventories

The LIFO method of determining cost was used for 93% and 71% of the inventories at December 31, 1979 and 1978, respectively. If the FIFO method of inventory accounting had been used by the Company for all its inventories, inventories would have been $1,017,000 and $477,000 higher than reported at December 31, 1979 and 1978, respectively.

NOTE C—Loan Agreement and Notes Payable

At December 31, 1979 and 1978, long-term debt consisted of the following:

	1979	1978
Note payable to an insurance company, due in monthly installments of $53,468 to 2001 including interest at 9¾%; collateralized by land and buildings having a cost of $5,900,000	**$5,764,949**	$5,840,440
Note payable to an unrelated individual, due in monthly installments of $3,300 including interest at 6¼%, with final payment in 1989	**276,357**	297,946
	6,041,306	6,138,386
Less amounts due within one year	**106,167**	97,080
	$5,935,139	$6,041,306

Aggregate maturities during the succeeding five years are $106,167 in 1980; $116,129 in 1981; $127,050 in 1982; $139,026 in 1983 and $152,161 in 1984.

The Company has available a bank line of credit providing for borrowings up to $7,000,000. Borrowings under the line bear interest at the prime rate plus 1%. Borrowings under the line are collateralized by accounts receivable, work-in-process and finished goods inventories, manufacturing equipment and certain land and buildings. This credit arrangement, which is reviewed and renegotiated annually, is currently due to expire on April 30, 1980.

The bank line of credit agreement includes restrictive covenants which, among other things, prohibits the Company (without the written consent of the bank) from purchasing any of its Common Stock and declaring or paying any dividends except from net income earned after December 31, 1978. Also the Company agrees not to incur future indebtedness in excess of $200,000, and will not obligate any of the assets collateralized by the line of credit with new debt in excess of $250,000. The agreement also requires the Company to maintain certain working capital and net worth requirements.

Average interest rates on short-term bank borrowings at December 31, 1979 and 1978, approximated 16.25% and 12.97%, respectively.

8

EXHIBIT 6 (Continued)

Notes to Consolidated Financial Statements

Consolidated Financial Statements   Berven Carpets Corporation and Subsidiary

The following information relates to short-term debt to banks for the years ended December 31, 1979 and 1978:

	1979	1978
Maximum amount outstanding at any month-end	**$3,835,435**	$5,336,460
Average daily amount outstanding	**$1,819,547**	$4,534,431
Weighted average interest rate (actual short-term interest expense divided by average short-term debt)	**14.20%**	10.50%

NOTE D—Pension and Profit Sharing Plans

The Company has a defined contribution pension plan and a profit sharing plan. Substantially all employees are eligible to participate in these plans. Pension plan costs for 1979 and 1978 amounted to $166,804 and $171,419, respectively. There were no contributions to the profit sharing plan in 1979 or 1978.

NOTE E—Income Taxes

The credit for federal and state income taxes includes the following:

	December 31 1979	December 31 1978
Federal:		
Adjustment of prior year tax provision	**$ —0—**	$ (16,000)
	—0—	(16,000)
State:		
Current provision	**400**	400
	400	(15,600)
Deferred credit	**(238,000)**	(160,000)
	$(237,600)	$(175,600)

Depreciation is computed using an accelerated method for tax purposes and the straight-line method for book purposes. Deferred taxes have been provided in the Company's financial statements in earlier years to account for this timing difference. During 1979 and 1978, deferred income taxes were reduced by $238,000 and $160,000, respectively, to reflect the tax effects of the depreciation timing differences that are expected to reverse in the tax loss carryforward periods. If the Company realizes a tax benefit from utilization of the net operating loss carryforward, the first $1,058,000 of such benefit realized will be reinstated to the deferred tax account.

The 1979 and 1978 income tax credit is limited to the reduction of deferred taxes and adjustment of the prior year tax provision.

The Company's net operating loss carryforward approximates $5,360,000 and, if not used, will expire as follows:

December 31, 1984	$2,065,000
December 31, 1985	800,000
December 31, 1986	2,495,000
	$5,360,000

At December 31, 1979, the Company's unused investment credits and new jobs credits amounted to approximately $93,000 and $82,000, respectively.

NOTE F—Employee Stock Option and Stock Purchase Plans

The Company had stock purchase plans that expired on February 1, 1977. Options granted under the plans may still be exercised until such options expire. During 1979, 144 shares were sold at a price of $1.91 per share. During 1978, 551 shares were sold at prices ranging from $1.59 to $1.91 per share. Options to acquire 3,368 shares at prices ranging from $2.66 to $5.31 were outstanding at December 31, 1979. At December 31, 1979, all outstanding options were exercisable.

In addition to the employee stock purchase plans, the Company had a qualified stock option plan that expired on March 6, 1979. Options granted to key employees to acquire shares of Common Stock at fair market value at the date of grant may still be exercised until such options expire. At December 31, 1979, options for 40,600 shares were exercisable and reserved for issuance under the plan. Options are exercisable one year from the date of grant and expire at the end of five years. The following table summarizes the transactions of the plan for the two years ended December 31, 1979:

	Shares Under Option	Option Price Per Share	Aggregate
Outstanding at Jan. 1, 1978	100,200	$2.125 to $3.625	$296,250
Granted	20,000	$1.875 to $2.125	38,750
Expired	(59,600)	$2.125 to $3.625	(188,124)
Outstanding at Dec. 31, 1978	60,600	$1.875 to $3.125	146,876
Exercised	(1,500)	$2.125	(3,188)
Expired	(18,500)	$2.125 to $3.125	(40,563)
Outstanding at Dec. 31, 1979	40,600	$1.875 to $3.125	$103,125

9

403

EXHIBIT 6
(Continued)

During 1979, a stock option and appreciation plan was approved by the shareholders to replace the qualified stock option plan. The plan provides for granting of options to key employees including officers and certain directors to acquire shares of Common Stock at the fair market value at the date of grant. The options are granted by a Committee appointed by the Board of Directors. Options may become exercisable six months after date of grant and expire ten years after date of grant. In connection with the granting of options, the optionee may be granted the right to exchange the option for an appreciation distribution. The appreciation distribution will be made in cash and Common Stock. The appreciation distribution amount will be calculated as the difference between the fair market value of the Company's Common Stock (on the date the option is exchanged for the appreciation distribution) and the option price for the Common Stock. At December 31, 1979, 180,000 shares were reserved for issuance under the plan and options for 15,000 shares were granted at option prices ranging from $1.87 to $2.75. No options were exercisable at December 31, 1979.

In addition to the above plans, an option was granted in 1978 to an officer of the Company to purchase 25,000 shares of Common Stock at $2.75 per share. The option expires in 1985.

Shares reserved for issuance under the plans aggregate 248,968 shares at December 31, 1979.

NOTE G—Lease Commitments

The Company and its subsidiary occupy certain facilities and rent equipment under various leases. The total rent expense net of sublease revenue (1979—$115,006; 1978—$105,583) for all leases, including contingent rentals based upon usage of equipment in excess of specified minimums, is summarized as follows:

	1979	1978
Minimum rentals	$372,772	$ 532,491
Contingent rentals	511,214	594,080
	$883,986	$1,126,571

The future rental commitments net of subleases as of December 31, 1979, for all non-cancellable leases are as follows:

1980	$198,597
1981	159,628
1982	148,659
1983	83,739
1984	53,534
Thereafter	231,409
	$875,566

The future minimum rental commitments are primarily for showroom facilities and have been reduced by sublease contracts amounting to $104,475 in 1980 and declining amounts thereafter. Certain leases contain renewal options.

NOTE H—Gain on Sales of Assets

During 1979, the Company sold land held for sale and other property which had a carrying value of $233,000. The sale, after deducting expenses related to the sale, resulted in a gain of $463,819.

During 1978, the Company sold its Dalton, Georgia, mill and a small, obsolete building in Fresno which had a combined carrying value of $1,088,905. The sales, after deducting expenses related to the sales (approximately $103,000), resulted in a gain of $1,328,798.

NOTE I—Other Charges

During 1979, management initiated a plan to restructure and consolidate certain administration and manufacturing facilities to provide more efficient operations and eliminate unproductive facilities.

In 1979 certain marketing and administrative activities were moved from the administration building to offices in the Broadloom manufacturing building, and the administration building was listed for sale. The remaining administrative activities will be moved to the manufacturing site in 1980.

The plan to restructure and consolidate operations includes relocating in 1980 certain Varidye space dye manufacturing equipment and operations and certain Custom mill manufacturing equipment and operations from their respective buildings to the Broadloom manufacturing building. The relocation and consolidation of these operations will eliminate the need for certain excess machinery and equipment (primarily from the Varidye operations). This machinery and equipment has been written down to estimated realizable value. The amount of the machinery and equipment write-down of $903,993 and the estimated costs of $155,000 to be incurred in 1980 to move the various facilities from their present respective locations to the Broadloom manufacturing building are included in other charges in the accompanying consolidated statement of operations.

10

EXHIBIT 7

Management's Discussion and Analysis of the Summary of Operations

This Commentary Should Be Read In Conjunction With The Content Of The Letter To Shareholders And Other Related Data Contained In The Annual Report

Fiscal 1979 vs. Fiscal 1978

Net Sales decreased $7,770,443 or 16.5% compared to 1978. More than $7 million of the reduction occurred in the Chandelle subsidiary. The Company's Chandelle mill, located in Dalton, Georgia, was sold in December, 1978. During 1979, sales through this subsidiary were intentionally reduced. The distribution network, which the subsidiary serviced, was reorganized with the discontinuance of certain accounts and the addition of others.

Other Income (including gain on sales of assets), as compared to 1978, decreased $922,443. Certain fixed assets (land, buildings and equipment) sold during 1978, increased other income by $1,328,798. During 1979, the Company realized profit from a land sale of $463,819. The difference between the above major transactions account for the majority of this year-to-year reduction.

Cost of Products Sold, as a percentage to net sales, increased 1.9% compared to 1978. This increase principally was caused by an aggressive program during the fourth quarter to dispose of discontinued and non-first quality product inventories and the reduction to market value of inventory in these categories remaining at year end. As commented on in prior years, a major factor contributing to the abnormally high cost of sales percentage is the substantial under utilization of existing manufacturing facilities. A partial solution to this problem will be the recently announced consolidation of manufacturing facilities into the main

600,000-square foot Fresno mill. This program will make available 200,000 square feet of prime manufacturing/warehouse buildings for lease or sale. The Corporation will retain modern manufacturing facilities capable of producing at a net sales level in excess of $100,000,000. With the completion of the manufacturing consolidation and the reorganization of the sales division, which is now well under way, the Company will be positioned to better match sales achievement with manufacturing capacity.

Interest on long term debt decreased $173,213 as compared to 1978. The majority of the decrease resulted from the liquidation of a term loan during the fall of 1978.

Other Interest Costs decreased $218,378 as compared to 1978. Proceeds from late 1978 and early 1979 sales of certain land, buildings and equipment reduced 1979 current borrowings to an average level well below the comparable 1978 figure.

Income Tax Credit for 1979 was $237,600 as compared to the 1978 credit of $175,600. Credits in both years resulted from a reduction of the deferred tax account.

Taxes Other Than Income Taxes declined $313,068 as measured against 1978. Payroll taxes decreased $121,541 reflecting the discontinuance of Chandelle operations and a decrease of personnel at Fresno. Year to year, other taxes declined $191,527. During 1979 Chandelle personal property tax was reduced and the California operations received the first full year of Proposition 13 benefits.

EXHIBIT 8

Summary of Operations

	1979	1978	1977
Sales	$ 39,261,752	$ 47,032,195	$ 48,984,315*
Other income	581,919	1,504,362	304,109
Total income	39,843,671	48,536,557	49,288,424
Cost of products sold	34,532,978	40,477,371	42,308,225*
Interest	865,708	1,257,299	1,188,790
State and federal income taxes (credit)	(237,600)	(175,600)	(1,239,600)
Income (loss) before extraordinary item	(3,606,234)	(1,221,827)	(2,022,296)
Extraordinary item			
Net income (loss)	$(3,606,234)	$(1,221,827)	$(2,022,296)
Per share data: Average number of shares outstanding	3,670,368	3,669,361	3,668,841
Income (loss) before extraordinary item	$(.98)	$(.33)	$(.55)
Extraordinary item			
Net income (loss)	$(.98)	$(.33)	$(.55)
Cash dividends per share			

The extraordinary item in 1970 represented a gain on the sale or abandonment of manufacturing facilities in National City, California, net of applicable income taxes.

*Amounts for freight billed to customers have been reclassified as a reduction of net sales to conform to 1978 and 1979 presentations.

11

EXHIBIT 8
(Continued)

Depreciation and Amortization decreased $132,696 as measured against last year. More than half of the reduction resulted from the December, 1978 disposal of Chandelle Dalton, Georgia fixed assets. The balance of this decrease resulted from an adjustment in depreciation expense.

Net Losses in 1979 increased $2,384,407 as compared to 1978. The 1978 loss was reduced by a gain on the sale of assets, $1,328,798. The comparable 1979 amount was $463,819, a reduction of $864,979. The restructuring and consolidation of manufacturing facilities resulted in a $1,058,993 charge to the 1979 statement of operations. This charge consisted of machinery and equipment write-downs (primarily from the Varidye operations) and estimated costs for relocation. A fourth quarter program to dispose of non-first quality and discontinued inventories together with a reduction in value of inventories in these categories remaining at year end contributed to the 1979 loss. In addition, a significant amount of trade receivables considered doubtful or uncollectible were reserved for or written-off during 1979. The continued under utilization of production capacities contributed, as in prior years, to the losses.

Fiscal 1978 vs. Fiscal 1977

Net Sales decreased $1,952,120, or 4% compared to 1977. This volume decrease is partially attributable to a decision early in the year to phase out and discontinue marketing programs involving products manufactured by other mills. This change allowed the sales and marketing divisions to concentrate efforts on the Company's own products; thus, improving

utilization of the production facilities. It was recognized that during the short term sales volume would be adversely affected.

A second contributing factor to the year to year sales decline was the lack of current styling in the Berven product line. A major new style development program was introduced in the second half of the year with initial product introductions appearing in June and July. This program matured with the introduction of five new products at the January, 1979 floorcovering markets.

Other Income as compared to 1977, increased $1,200,253. The higher 1978 figure was derived from profitable sales of certain fixed assets. Land, buildings and certain machinery, formerly owned by the Company, and located in Dalton, Georgia were sold in December and a small building located in Fresno was sold last October. The combined income from both sales totaled $1,328,798.

If the 1978 asset sales are excluded from other income, the year to year comparison shows a reduction of $128,545. The lower figure reflects reduced material scrap sales resulting from production efficiency improvements.

Cost of Products Sold, as a percentage to net sales, held constant compared to 1977. The percentage for both years is above normal and caused by two factors: A substantial under utilization of existing manufacturing facilities and the sale of higher than normal quantities of phase-out and discontinued inventory (this merchandise is sold at discounted prices).

Continued on page 13.

1976	1975	1974	1973	1972	1971	1970
$47,873,934*	$41,782,547*	$42,984,525*	$45,294,683*	$43,086,025	$38,891,023	$34,406,530
241,523	130,836	178,361	172,787	104,147	44,744	52,187
48,115,457	41,913,383	43,162,886	45,467,470	43,190,172	38,935,767	34,458,717
39,162,030*	34,465,590*	33,691,652*	33,953,726*	31,311,474	28,542,104	25,453,406
851,134	656,082	746,772	444,631	130,755	202,700	302,042
(155,028)	(517,435)	979,000	2,200,000	2,757,000	2,368,529	1,668,612
(54,080)	(419,711)	1,093,642	2,426,478	2,874,094	2,286,330	1,637,869
						106,051
$ (54,080)	$ (419,711)	$ 1,093,642	$ 2,426,478	$ 2,874,094	$ 2,286,330	$ 1,743,920
3,667,347	3,658,096	3,678,916	3,693,585	3,684,084	3,679,200	3,679,200
$(.01)	$(.11)	$ .30	$ .66	$ .78	$ .62	$ .44
						.03
$(.01)	$(.11)	$ .30	$ .66	$ .78	$ .62	$ .47
$ .06	$ .12	$ .11	$ .09	$ .075	$ .03	

12

APPENDIX C

B E R V E N   C A R P E T S   C O R P O R A T I O N
2626 S. Maple, P.O. Box 1792 • Fresno, CA 93717 • (209) 268-0771

—Press Release—

FOR RELEASE UPON RECEIPT

BERVEN CARPETS ANNOUNCES SECOND QUARTER
OPERATING RESULTS

FRESNO, CA., Aug. 1, 1980 -- Berven Carpets Corporation (ASE/PSE) manufacturer of broadloom, specialty carpeting and predyed yarns, today announced
operating results for the second quarter ended June 30, 1980.

Net sales of $8,892,000 were reported, compared to $10,357,000 for the
same quarter a year ago.

An after tax loss of $843,000, or 23 cents per share was recorded. This
compares with a loss of $78,000, or 2 cents per share, for the second quarter
of 1979.

Commenting on the results, Robert Hendy, Berven's president and chief
executive officer noted that, "Our industry, traditionally, has enjoyed strong
spring selling seasons. This year sales actually declined. With little warning
the full impact of the recession hit our industry in early April. Together with
our competitors we suffered a severe second quarter sales slump. Recently, sales
have improved. We judge that the worst is behind us and expect to see improved
second half sales".

In addition to its broadloom (distributed under Berven Of California
and WestWeave Of California tradestyles) and custom carpeting operations, Berven
predyes yarn for internal use and for resale throughout the carpet industry
and imports handmade rugs.

--end--

Berven Carpets Corporation is headquartered at:

2600 Ventura Avenue
Fresno, CA 93717
Tel: (209) 268-0771

EXHIBIT 9

BERVEN CARPETS CORPORATION SUMMARY OF OPERATIONS (Unaudited)

	3 Months Ended June 30, 1980	3 Months Ended June 30, 1979	6 Months Ended June 30, 1980	6 Months Ended June 30, 1979
Net Sales	$8,892,000	$10,357,000	$18,865,000	$19,291,000
Income (Loss) Before Income Taxes	(1,000,000)	(140,000)	(1,780,000)	(29,000)
State and Federal Income Taxes (Credit)	(157,000)	(62,000)	(157,000)	(12,000)
Net Income (Loss)	(843,000)	(78,000)	(1,623,000)	(17,000)
Net Income (Loss) Per Share	($0.23)	($0.02)	($0.44)	$0.00
Average Number of Shares Outstanding	3,671,172	3,670,835	3,671,172	3,670,835

Computation of loss per share is based on the average number of shares outstanding during the respective periods. Berven is listed on the American Stock Exchange and the Pacific Stock Exchange, symbol BVN.

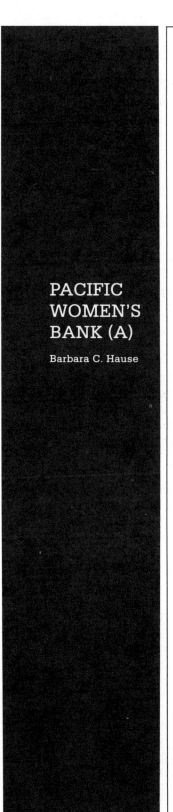

PACIFIC WOMEN'S BANK (A)

Barbara C. Hause

In March 1977, after over five months of operation, the board of the Pacific Women's Bank of San Francisco (PWB) unanimously asked its president to prepare a presentation of corporate objectives and strategies for the June meeting of the board. Historical information on the bank and the president's plan for the June meeting are discussed below.

In 1974 Helen Finch and Elaine Hendricks were the leaders in establishing the Pacific Women's Bank of San Francisco. Both women had had unsatisfactory personal experiences with local banks. After inheriting a small import business several years before 1974, Helen, inexperienced in finance, sought financial advice from several banks in San Francisco. She was insulted by their patronizing attitude toward her as a female. Helen had innate marketing accumen and did develop a very successful business. She also learned more about finance from study and subsequent experience. Helen was active in local politics and became acquainted with Elaine Hendricks, who was treasurer of a major political party.

Helen suggested the idea of a women's bank to Elaine. Elaine recalled an incident several years before when she tried to establish reserve credit on her checking account. The bank gave her the application and instructed her to have her husband sign it. She told the bank vice president that she would not ask for his signature. Since this incident she believed banks had an old-fashioned attitude towards women. Now something could be done about it by starting a women's bank in San Francisco.

In 1974 Elaine and Helen assembled a board of directors with Helen as chairman and Elaine as vice chairman. Twelve of the fourteen members were women. Among the board members were: Mary Nathan, president of a ski apparel manufacturer, Stella Walker, an associate publisher, Kay Reading, a former city supervisor, and Henry Benett, president and executive director of the Council on Economic Priorities.

There were several obstacles for the board to overcome before PWB was ready for operation. First, it had to submit an application to the Superintendent of Banking demonstrating a need for a bank that would have the financial needs of women as one of its principal objectives. Second, it had to obtain initial capital. Third, it had to find a qualified president. Fourth, it had

This case was prepared by Barbara C. Hause under the direction of Stephen T. McLin, Instructor, Golden Gate University, as the basis for class discussion, rather than to illustrate either effective or ineffective handling of an administrative situation.

Copyright © 1978 by Golden Gate University.

Distributed by the Intercollegiate Case Clearing House, Soldiers Field, Boston, Massachusetts, 02163. All rights reserved to the contributors. Printed in U.S.A.

to find a suitable location for the bank. The organizers were aware of the prolonged problems of First Women's Bank in New York on such matters. They endeavored to take these into account in plans for Pacific Women's Bank.

CAPITALIZATION

PWB planned to sell 100,000 shares of stock for $20 a share in minimum blocks of 20 shares ($400). In August 1975 PWB received permission from the State Superintendent of Banking to begin selling stock, but the $2 million goal had not been reached by May 1976. Since PWB did not intend to engage heavily in commercial or industrial banking and planned to be a retail oriented bank, the State agreed to lower the initial capitalization to $1.7 million and the minimum share requirement to ten shares ($200). Sponsors believed that the average working woman would be extremely interested at this lower level. The PWB opened for business in September 1976.

CHOICE OF PRESIDENT

The board preferred a woman president with a banking background, provided she was the most qualified applicant. The president had to meet the approval of the State Banking Department; it required a candidate to have at least 15 years of experience as a bank manager. Historically and traditionally, commercial banks have had very few women in their executive ranks. After a long search the board selected Roberta Smith as president and chief executive officer.

Roberta Smith was 44 yers old and had almost 20 years of banking experience. She was a graduate of Oklahoma University and had earned a M.B.A. from U.C. Berkeley. Roberta's studies had centered on the areas of finance and marketing. During her banking career, Roberta had worked at three different California banks and had accumulated 15 years of branch management experience. Prior to joining PWB, she was vice president of the business development department of a medium-sized San Francisco-based bank with 80 branches. Roberta was quite active in local affairs and had gained a wide acquaintance and recognition within the San Francisco business community. The board members at PWB were impressed by the combination of her management experience and expertise in business development and felt she possessed excellent qualities for a new bank president. Roberta was pleased to receive the appointment as president and chief executive and was looking forward to the challenge of starting and running a new bank. Roberta's responsibilities included investment advisory services, investment portfolio administration, new business development, financial planning, money position and lending.

OTHER OFFICERS

The task of selecting other officers at PWB was not nearly as difficult as finding a president. In fact, the board had numerous qualified applicants to choose from.

Linden McVey, Vice President in charge of administration and operations for PWB, was 32 years old. She had been in banking for nearly 14 years and had worked her way up from part-time teller while attending college to loan officer at one of the larger California banks. She recently had received her M.B.A. degree in Banking and Finance from Golden Gate University. Although Linden had been satisfied with her progress with her previous employer, she felt the bank was slow to recognize her capabilities for an executive level position. Therefore, she decided to seek a job with additional responsibility and accepted the position at PWB. In addition to her operational duties, Linden took part in the lending function and private counseling for loan applicants.

Rita Barrett, Assistant Vice President, had responsibility for the loan department. Prior to coming to PWB, Rita worked for a credit union for five years. She was 28 years old and had recently enrolled in courses at the American Institute of Banking to learn about bank operations. Rita has been responsible for setting up the financial seminars at PWB during the noon hour and evenings and has made most of the presentations herself.

Sheila Holder was an Assistant Vice President—Operations Officer. She was 31 years old and had a degree in art history. She acquired her expertise in bank operations while going to school and working part-time at the main office of a medium-sized California bank. After completing her college education she decided to stay with the bank and was then promoted to assistant operations officer. At PWB she supervised seven tellers. Three of the tellers were part-time employees. The rest were full-time, two of whom were men.

LOCATION OF PWB

The organizers decided to locate the bank close to the financial district in San Francisco since the bank's marketing strategy was to appeal to working men and women. Their selection of premises was to be initially modest in order to avoid a drain on capital similar to the one experienced by First Women's Bank in New York. The New York bank was located in a high rent district of Manhattan, and due to the delays in opening the bank depleted much of its capital. (See Exhibits 1 and 2)

The site selected for PWB was on Jackson Street in the financial district near the Embarcadero Center where many small new businesses were opening—especially retail and service businesses. The first floor was to be used for banking functions and the second floor was available for other purposes.

THE WOMEN'S MARKET

During the planning stage of PWB, the organizers researched the women's market. Most of their findings included information which was obtained from the U.S. Department of Labor, Bureau of Labor Statistics. Part of this information is illustrated in Exhibits Nos. 3 through 7. It demonstrates the continuous rise of women in the labor force.

Market research indicated that of all retail buying by households, more than 60 percent of the decisions were made by women. Women also conducted the bulk of the day-to-day family financial transactions and were highly influential in family decisions as to where to maintain checking and savings accounts and obtain installment loans. In addition, women controlled nearly 47 percent of the wealth in the United States.

Other research disclosed that women are not only entering and remaining in the labor force, but are becoming owners of businesses. They are doing so rather than risk a long wait for advancement in the corporate world. These new women business owners seek small business loans and many need technical assistance from banks.

From this information, the organizers concluded the women's market offered great potential. These women should patronize banks that take a personal interest in their financial development. PWB's planned marketing campaign, however, was to emphasize a nondiscriminatory approach. Male customers were to be as welcome as women customers, as of course is required by law.

GENERAL PHILOSOPHY OF PWB

PWB was interested in two market segments: (1) the personal accounts of Bay Area residents and (2) the accounts of small businesses. The board agreed that the bank would be able to provide many services to these groups without overtaxing the bank's resources.

PWB also hoped to appeal to young people who were new in the area and needed information about how to establish credit.

PWB did not want to go overboard with a "smorgasboard" of services like First Women's Bank in New York. PWB's planned services included regular checking accounts, overdraft protection (for qualified credit applicants), savings accounts, travelers checks, banking by mail, certificates of deposit, correspondent services and acceptance of Mastercharge and BankAmericard (VISA) drafts from merchants. PWB did not plan to issue its own credit card.

To meet the requirements of its customers, the bank was to offer three types of loans: (1) the installment loans primarily for personal use, travel or consumer durable purchases, (2) residential real estate mortgage loans, and (3) short term to medium term (90 days to five years) loans for local business. PWB was particularly interested in helping women who had been operating businesses from their homes and needed small business loans to establish storefront operations.

Credit criteria for women borrowers were to be the same as for men. Loan officers were qualified to give special financial consultation to customers who requested it. Loan officers had a private office available when customers preferred private and confidential discussions of their personal financial problems.

PWB planned to use its second floor space to offer free seminars to men and women on a wide range of financial topics. These seminars would be held during the lunch hour. People attending the seminars would be welcome to "brown bag" their lunch while listening to speakers.

The second floor space would be made available for meetings of different organizations and businesses in the area. Eventually, PWB intended to install a financial library for the use of its employees and customers.

Competitive Environment   In recent years most commercial banks and other lending institutions had been under pressure from women's rights groups regarding both personnel and lending policies. Consequently, their marketing campaigns were geared toward obtaining female as well as male customers.

United California Bank was one of the first banks in the San Francisco area to take a more aggressive and positive stance in campaigning for women customers. UCB embarked on an intensive one-month campaign designed to carry the basic message of the bank's interest in attracting women customers. Although it did not devote its entire advertising budget to this attempt to reach women, the program represented a major commitment on the bank's part.

Wells Fargo Bank offered seminars on personal financial management for women called "Financial Forums." Security Pacific targeted upper-income women for investments in municipal bonds. Other banks, in their promotion and advertising, were taking steps to minimize the use of stereotypic images of women and men. These banks emphasized their willingness to talk with customers, help them understand and evaluate their financial needs and recommend solutions with the individual's best interest in mind.

Not only was the women's market becoming more competitive because larger banks were starting to recognize the market's potential, but credit unions were being organized for a similar purpose. The Bay Area Feminist Federal Credit Union, almost two years old, had been very successful. It sometimes made loans to women who had lost their credit standing through separation or divorce. These women generally were unable to obtain credit and came to the Bay Area Feminist Federal Credit Union to establish an initial credit rating. A representative of the credit union said it made it possible for women to borrow even if they were penniless. Such prospective borrowers sometimes were granted loans with one or even several cosigners. Other times loans were given with the understanding that the women would come to the credit union for financial counseling.

Bank Policy Formulation   In March 1977 a major topic at the PWB board meeting was the bank's future goals and strategies. The board had not been surprised by a loss of $120,000 during the first quarter of its operations in 1976. President Roberta Smith by unanimous vote was requested to prepare a list of corporate objectives and strategies for presentation to the board at its June 1977 meeting.

Roberta Smith had recently been giving serious consideration to her assignment of formulating PWB's corporate objectives and strategies. Initially, she had been preoccupied with setting up the premises, obtaining the stock subscription, and dealing with other operational issues. She realized it was now time to concentrate on achieving better results, as measured by increased earnings per share and return on stockholders' investment. This required her to be continuously informed about changing circumstances and competition and to prepare a plan for the future. Up to this time, no one had really thought out some of the deeper issues involved with the women's bank movement and the new threats to be considered. Not only were large commercial banks recognizing women's market and the legal requirement of ECOA, but the near catastrophic problems that had been suffered by the New York women's bank had caused Roberta to take a hard look at some of these policy questions that might have an impact on PWB.

Equal Credit Opportunity in 1977   The ECOA was passed in 1974 shortly after the plans for First Women's Bank in New York and other women's banks had been initiated. Exhibit No. 8 sumarizes the Equal Credit Opportunity Act. Since the passage of ECOA, there had been much controversy as to its effectiveness. Much of the controversy had been instigated by various women's groups. Many felt the old stereotypes about women as credit prospects still existed; thus, too many bank officers denied credit to qualified women.

Rita Barrett, Assistant Vice President, had held a seminar for the purpose of discussing ECOA and its latest revisions. There were approximately 25 people at the seminar, including six men. During the discussions period several women raised arguments against ECOA.

One woman said her biggest complaint against ECOA was that the burden of major enforcement was left to the individual who chooses to bring suit. She felt it was not fair "to expect a woman who holds a full-time job, runs a household and is raising a couple of children to find the time, money and effort to bring suit against a major corporation."

Several other women complained that the "penalties for discrimination in the ECOA aren't big enough to strike terror into the hearts of major lenders." In court action, individuals may win actual damages, plus punitive damages up to one percent of net worth, or $500,000, whichever is higher.

Rita was aware of these arguments prior to this meeting. She remembered reading in the Wall Street Journal that 2000 women had complained to the Federal Trade Commission about credit discrimination in 1976 because they felt the law was not being enforced.

Roberta was not the only officer aware of the recent developments affecting the women's market; for instance, she had received a memorandum from Linden McVey which raised numerous questions about the general philosophy of women's banking. While Linden did not purport to have the answers to these questions, her memorandum to Roberta raised these questions as issues that the bank needed to examine now that some of the operational hurdles were behind it.

Some of Linden's questions were as follows:

1   The women's movement has been prominent in the 70s as it was in the teens and 20s. Will this movement continue with real momentum, or is it conceivably just a fad?

2   Is there really a role in the financial markets for "specialized" banking institutions, or are the economies of scale such that a specialized institution can't really survive?

3   What unique advantages or disadvantages can a women's bank be expected to offer?

4   What is the real market to be served by women's banks? Is it younger, professional women without much capital, or perhaps wealthier, older women? What about the economically disadvantaged women? Do they receive sufficient services from state programs or is there a need for a specific service? What about student loans for women? Are they discriminated against?

5   Has the Equal Credit Opportunity Act eliminated the need for women's banks?

6   Women's banks may be tempted to relax credit standards and grant loans to women that have been rejected by other banks for realistic, rather than prejudicial reasons. Is this likely to have an impact on our credit experience?

7   Given the general scarcity of executive level women and the emphasis to promote women in other companies, can women's banks be expected to compete with other institutions for women officers?

8   Is the emphasis on women's banking likely to discourage male customers who are probably necessary for the success of women's banks?

9   Is the future success of women's banks threatened by the fact that other commercial banks have started to recognize the women's market and have undertaken various programs to take advantage of this market?

Roberta felt that Linden's memorandum was an attempt to get involved in some of the policy making decisions of PWB. Consequently, Roberta decided to turn these questions right around on Linden by asking her to draft a report for the Board of Directors on the corporate objectives and strategies of PWB.

After her meeting with Roberta, Linden was both pleased and apprehensive about her new responsibility to draft a statement of corporate objectives and strategies for PWB. Although Linden had been through similar exercises and case studies at Golden Gate University, she suddenly realized that her work on these strategies would have a real impact on the future operations of PWB. As she returned to her office, she realized that she really had very little information to use in answering some of the questions that she had posed to Roberta, and yet she would have to develop answers to these and other questions before she could begin to formulate the objectives and strategies of PWB.

Financial Trouble for Feminists

When the First Women's Bank opened a year ago on Manhattan's 57th Street, it was heralded as the answer to a feminist prayer. Founded by a small group of activists, among them Author Betty Friedan and Dress Designer Pauline Trigère, the new bank was supposed to be run as well as owned primarily by women and to give "special attention to the needs" of female depositors and borrowers who felt unwelcome at big, established banks. If such a venture can be a commercial success, the first year has hardly proved the point.

Since the opening, the bank has run up an operating deficit of $400,000. That is not unusual for a new bank of First Women's small size (capital: less than $4 million). But the bank has also been beset by management problems that officers are reluctant to discuss publicly. Employees grumble that the troubles start with frequent policy disputes that divide the 12-member board of directors, which is headed by a Manhattan lawyer, Evelyn Lehman, and includes four men. Some directors got into the venture for idealistic reasons but soon discovered that the job of guiding a new commercial enterprise can be unexpectedly demanding. One of First Women's women, Betty Friedan, left the bank in March, citing as a reason her writing schedule. Says she: "They gave me hell for missing too many board meetings."

The board has discovered a scarcity of experienced women banking executives. When the directors went shopping for a woman to be president, they found barely 20 whom they considered qualified. They finally picked Madeline McWhinney, 54, an economist who had been an assistant vice president of the New York Federal Reserve Bank but had no experience in commercial banking. Then, in September, she resigned from her $37,500-a-year job, complaining, insiders say, that she had grown weary of dealing with a board whose main devotion seemed not to banking but to a cause. The bank is now headed —temporarily—by a man: Executive Vice President Robert Benedict, 35, who last January was hired away from a branch manager's job with Manufacturers Hanover Trust Co.

High Turnover. Of 57 staffers hired since the bank's incorporation, only ten remain. Such high turnover, quips Eileen Preiss, the only one of the original three executive officers remaining, is the way "we solved the problem of a staff without enough experience." The bank lost many accounts early this year when the inexperienced staff was slow to deal with computer foul-ups. Even more embarrassing, the bank has actually been accused of sex discrimination by a former teller, Susan Salvia, 23, who claims she was fired because she was pregnant. The bank says Salvia refused to take a new job assignment.

Many women still go out of their way to bank at First Women's. Some 75% of its more than 6,000 checking-account customers are women, although many of the accounts are small and inactive. Lourdes Rosa, 30, an office manager, frequently makes a long subway trip from her Bronx home to First Women's because the bank gave her a furniture loan and she finds its atmosphere "much friendlier than other banks."

Some 95% of the bank's personal loans have been made to women, although the bulk of commercial loan dollars has gone to "prime accounts" like Gulf & Western Industries—not primarily too small, female-run enterprises, as might have been expected. Says Benedict: "Our loan policy is no different from other banks." As a new institution, he adds, First Women's must be extra cautious in lending money because otherwise "every deadbeat in town will beat a path to our door."

Despite the New York institution's troubles, two other women's banks have opened in the past year: the San Diego Women's Bank and Western Women's Bank in San Francisco. Several similar banks have been incorporated but are not yet in business. Curiously, though, the whole idea sparks audible animosity among women who have succeeded in conventional banking. Says Patricia Weninger, vice president of Fidelity Mutual Savings Bank in Spokane, Wash.: "We don't need a 'women's' bank."

Too Little. One reason for thinking so is that, just as First Women's was opening in New York a year ago, the Federal Reserve Board spelled out rules that all banks must follow to comply with the Equal Credit Opportunity Act. If those rules are vigorously enforced, no bank will be able to discriminate against—or in favor of—women. In that case, many women may prefer the efficiency and wide range of services provided by the big established banks. Whether or not they are too little, the women's banks may be too late.

EXHIBIT NO. 1

SOURCE: *Time*, November 8, 1976, p. 99

Women Alone Not Enough Of a Customer Base, Says 1st Women's Pres.

By GORDON MATTHEWS

NEW YORK. — The new president of the First Women's Bank here, who begins her duties on Thursday, plans to widen the bank's scope beyond one major customer group and emphasizes the importance of striking the right balance between being a symbol for a cause and using proven, traditional business methods.

"I think most minority banks were organized with the idea of serving one constituency," said Lynn D. Salvage. "We certainly intend to give women a fair deal, but the banking market is made up of many segments and we plan a new marketing stategy with that in mind."

The $8.1 million-deposit institution she will be heading has been buffeted by a number of difficulties since it opened in October, 1975. Within its initial year of operation, the bank lost its first president, Madeline H. McWhinney.

Ms. Salvage plans a number of changes. Among them will be a stronger role for the board of directors, an advisory committee pared to workable size and infused with members having banking experience, a closer relationship with other New York banks and an increase in the bank's capital position.

In an interview Wednesday, she said she hopes to make greater use of directors' expertise in their specific areas to broaden the range of the bank's activity. Ms. Salvage would also like to bring the bank's board up to its authorized strength of 20 members from the present 13 directors and plans a first move toward this goal at the bank's annual meeting on March 22.

The bank's advisory committee now numbers over 80 members, including many who have been active in the feminist movement. While she hopes to retain some of the flavor of the current body, Ms. Salvage plans to reduce its size and obtain the services of officers at other city banks.

That task should be easier because of her former position as a vice president at the $16.9 billion-deposit Bankers Trust Co., New York, where she was manager of the international investment division. Prior to accepting the presidency at First Women's Bank, she had been on leave from Bankers Trust to serve as special assistant for international affairs at the United States Treasury Department.

Besides utilizing the advice and counsel of fellow bankers, Ms. Salvage, who is 30 years old, is already making efforts to forge stronger links with the banks themselves. She said Wednesday that pledges of cooperation have already been received and they extend to such important specific areas as consideration of loan participations.

The new president said she does not yet have a target number in mind for increased capital at First Women's Bank, but she emphasized that this is a high priority. In its organizational stage, the bank failed to meet its goal of $4 million and opened with $3 million in capital and $500,000 for start-up costs and other expenses.

Heavy start-up costs have been a major factor in the bank's losses since it opened. As of last June 30, the bank had reported a $400,000 deficit and has not yet issued a report on its financial status at yearend.

State banking regulators here have said, however, that losses can be expected during the first three years of a bank's operations. Ms. Salvage said she hopes to turn around the bank's financial situation as soon as possible, but could set no date as a goal at this time.

In addition to pursuing the full range of traditional banking customers, including major corporate customers, Ms. Salvage also plans to have First Women's Bank here take full advantage of its minority bank status. She said she hopes to talk with officers of other minority banks and participate to the maximum extent in the Treasury's minority bank deposit program.

The program is designed to aid minority financial institutions through placement of public funds as deposits. To qualify, a women's bank must have more than 50% of its stock owned by women, a majority of directors must be women and women must occupy a significant number of senior management positions.

Currently, there are 80 minority banks in the program and over $100 million in funds are involved.

EXHIBIT NO. 2

SOURCE: *American Banker*, February 3, 1977, p. 1

Women's Bank, NY, Has $938,627 Loss in First Full Year; Loan Drain Cut

NEW YORK — The First Women's Bank here announced its loss before and after securities transactions in 1976 was $938,621, compared with a loss of $565,813 between April 10, 1975, when the bank was incorporated, and Dec. 31, 1975.

"In June of last year the bank upgraded the criteria used in evaluating instalment loan applications and the loss rate in this portfolio subsequently fell to a percentage considered to be below the industry average for these types of loans," Lynn D. Salvage, president, said.

Miss Salvage also said that she expects improved earnings to result from "a well organized and aggressive marketing plan now being implemented by the bank.

"While I can't predict when the bank will break even, I feel our efforts to increase our business with all segments of the market will produce an improvement in income," she said.

In addition, Miss Salvage said controllable expenses were reduced in the second half of 1976 and efforts to hold down expenses have continued effectively into 1977, when expenses attributable to the bank's start-up phase are expected to be sharply reduced.

Deposits at the end of the year were $14,056,356, up from $8,086,602 a year earlier. Loans totaled $8,123,971, an increase from $1,531,591. Assets totaled $15,407,045, up 47.7% from $10,434,243 at the end of 1975.

EXHIBIT NO. 2 (continued)

SOURCE: *American Banker,* February 17, 1977, p.2

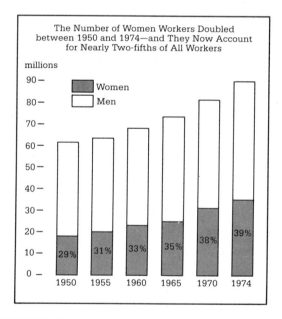

The Number of Women Workers Doubled between 1950 and 1974—and They Now Account for Nearly Two-fifths of All Workers

EXHIBIT NO. 3

Number and proportion of women workers in the civilian labor force April 1950–1974

SOURCE: U.S. Department of Labor, Bureau of Labor Statistics

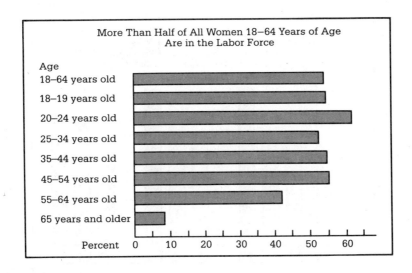

EXHIBIT NO. 4

Women's civilian labor force participation rates by age—April 1974

SOURCE: U.S. Department of Labor, Bureau of Labor Statistics

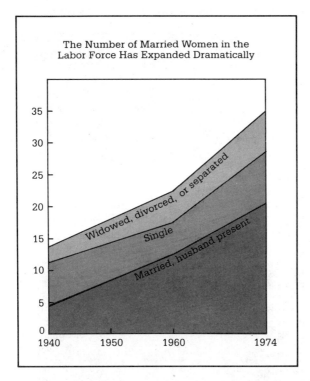

EXHIBIT NO. 5

Women in the labor force, by marital status selected years, 1940–1974

SOURCE: U.S. Department of Labor Bureau of Labor Statistics

419

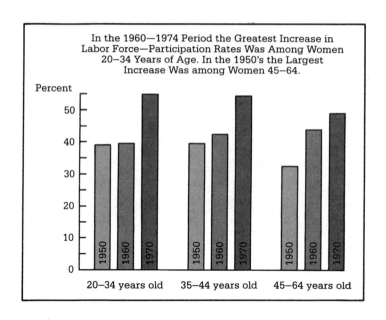

In the 1960—1974 Period the Greatest Increase in Labor Force—Participation Rates Was Among Women 20—34 Years of Age. In the 1950's the Largest Increase Was among Women 45—64.

EXHIBIT NO. 6

Civilian labor force participation rates of women in selected age groups 1950, 1960, and April 1974

SOURCE: U.S. Department of Labor, Bureau of Labor Statistics

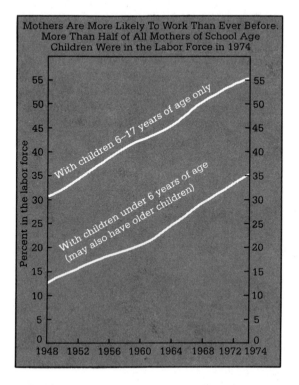

Mothers Are More Likely To Work Than Ever Before. More Than Half of All Mothers of School Age Children Were in the Labor Force in 1974

EXHIBIT NO. 7

Civilian labor force participation rates of ever-married women, by age of children, selected years 1948—1974

SOURCE: U.S. Department of Labor Bureau of Labor Statistics

420

"*Women and Credit.* The Federal Reserve Board has just issued regulations stemming from the Equal Credit Opportunity Act, passed by Congress last year. That act, effective October 28, makes it unlawful for banks, *department stores, finance companies and credit-card firms to deny credit on the basis of sex or marital status.* Aimed mainly at ending bias against all women, the rules will help many married couples, too. Here is a summary of the main points:

"*A wife will be able to get credit cards and unsecured loans in her own name,* if she is creditworthy in her own right and takes sole responsibility for paying bills. Generally, a creditor is allowed to ask about her marital status—married, unmarried or separated.

"When a husband and wife apply for a loan together, the lender must take into account all the income of the wife, even if it is from a part-time job. Questions cannot be asked about the couples' intentions on having children or about birth-control practices. The creditor cannot make assumptions, based on the wife's age, that she will have a child and stop working.

"A creditor must count income a divorcee receives from alimony and child support payments in determining her eligibility for an account or loan. She does not have to disclose information about alimony unless she is including it as part of her income in the credit application. Generally, in case of divorce or separation, a women's charge account cannot be closed out without evidence she is unable or unwilling to pay bills.

"Beginning a year from now, information given to credit rating agencies on joint accounts that both husband and wife use will have to be reported in both their names. That is designed to provide a credit history for women seeking credit on their own because of a divorce or widowhood. Now such information is often listed only under the husband's name.

"In any denial of credit, an explanation of the reasons must be furnished to the applicant. An individual who feels credit has been withheld because of sex or marital status can file in federal court for damages."

EXHIBIT NO. 8
SOURCE: *U.S. News,* 79:89 October 27, 1975

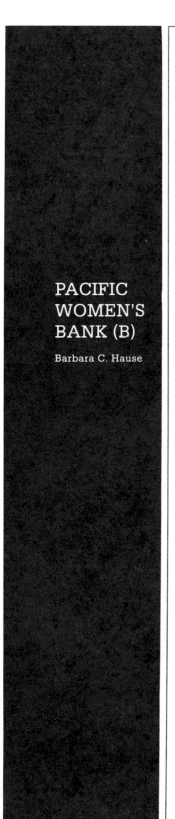

PACIFIC WOMEN'S BANK (B)

Barbara C. Hause

I n June 1977 Linden McVey, Vice President in charge of administration and operations for PWB, had completed her draft of objectives and strategies for the bank and was ready to discuss her recommendations with the President, Roberta Smith. In drafting the objectives and strategies, Linden decided not to let the changes the new president was implementing at First Women's Bank in New York influence her. (See Exhibit No. 1) She felt PWB had taken a more conservative approach in the beginning and was not bogged down with the same organizational problems; therefore, PWB's objectives could be future-oriented and not designed to remedy past problems.

Before writing the draft report, Linden was primarily concerned with an overall assessment of PWB's environment and consideration of the questions she had posed in her memorandum to Roberta. (See Pacific Women's Bank (A).) Also, she had recently received some selected findings on women's attitudes towards banks from the marketing consulting firm, Hartman & Davidson, Inc., which she felt were supportive of the approach PWB was taking towards the women's market.

ISSUES AFFECTING WOMEN'S BANKS

First, Linden considered the "women's movement." After researching the issue, she concluded that it was here to stay without the radical overtones that came with it in the past. Women in the Seventies were more independent, had higher paying jobs, ran their own businesses and had careers and families. Consequently, these women would always be seeking services from a bank that recognized and understood their needs.

Second, Linden projected the role "specialized" institutions might play in the financial market. For the first half of 1977, banks in California were reporting record high profits in retail banking. This was supportive of Linden's feelings that there would always be a need for smaller, personal loans. While other banks were becoming increasingly impersonal and bureaucratic, PWB intended to maintain a good share of the retail market by being flexible and responsive to people's needs.

This case was prepared by Barbara C. Hause under the direction of Stephen T. McLin, Instructor, Golden Gate University, as the basis for class discussion rather than to illustrate either effective or ineffective handling of an administrative situation.

Copyright © 1978 by Golden Gate University

Distributed by the Intercollegiate Case Clearing House, Soldiers Field, Boston, Massachusetts, 02163. All rights reserved to the contributors. Printed in U.S.A.

Third, Linden felt PWB should not feel threatened by the competition. The fact that the larger financial institutions had undertaken various programs to promote the women's market proved that the need existed and was being recognized. She believed the organization of women's banks helped get the change started.

Fourth, although the Equal Credit Opportunity Act was implemented several years ago, its effect had been gradual. The ECOA was frequently publicized in the media with controversy as to its overall effectiveness and enforcement. Linden was appalled by the attitudes displayed by some of the men at a recent banker's convention she attended in San Francisco. Many of these men were from smaller banks located throughout the country, and they still had biases against extending credit to women.

With respect to PWB's loan policy, the bank established strict credit guidelines for all loan applicants which were not relaxed for women customers. PWB's purpose was to help women establish good credit standings and not to lead them into default.

Finally, Linden thought one of the primary disadvantages of being a women's bank was the fact that men felt excluded. Sixty-eight percent of PWB's customers were women. Linden felt this percentage was high and not truly representative of PWB's philosophy—to maintain a totally nondiscriminatory approach to banking. PWB offered special financial services that could be beneficial to men as well as women and the bank needed to convey this message to the public.

Women's Attitudes   Hartman & Davidson, Inc. was a well-known marketing consulting firm located in San Francisco. The officers at PWB employed its services in late 1976 to learn more about the local women's market. Linden had just received a copy of the recently completed study from Roberta for her review and comment. Linden expected the results of the study to be helpful in planning PWB's future. Of particular interest to Linden were the selected findings from the focus group study of a number of women in the Bay Area who were asked for opinions on what they expected from a bank. Their attitudes are summarized below:

Women feel banks give preferential treatment to the wealthy, those with good employment records, and those who are financially experienced, sophisticated, and assertive. They feel banks place women in second class status.

Women with individual accounts feel they have an independent financial identity and value it. Women with joint accounts, even if employed, feel like financial nonentities and resent it.

Women value convenience, practicality and economy in banks and bank services.

Women view credit conservatively and do not feel credit standards should be relaxed.

Women feel it is important to have an established personal relationship with a financial institution and want to feel that that institution puts the customer's best interest first. This is especially important in a decision about where to apply for a loan.

Women want to feel accepted, approved, and valued in their banking relationship.

"Women feel banks have a responsibility to counsel and educate the young, the dependent (unemployed) woman, the poorly educated, and the financially inexperienced."

THE DRAFT REPORT

I. Introduction   This draft report outlines the corporate objectives and strategies which are necessary for PWB to follow in becoming a viable financial institution principally serving the special needs of women, without excluding men. In order to accomplish these objectives and strategies PWB must set priorities, establish goals and assign responsibilities. Board members and bank officers must acknowledge that PWB is a small independent bank and the best way to meet the competition is to offer a unique, personalized approach to banking, and that the interests of the shareholders cannot be compromised.

II Objectives

1   PWB's principal short-range objective is to make operations profitable by the third calendar year of operation.

2   PWB's principal long-range objective is to maintain a long-term return on shareholders equity of at least 10%.

3   PWB's objective is to serve 'the financial needs of all small business owners and all individuals desirous of credit in its marketing area.

4   PWB is not to undertake any type of banking relationship which does not meet PWB's established rate of return on investment, nor are service charges and other fees to be waived except under extraordinary circumstances.

5   PWB's objective is to place particular emphasis on the special financial needs of women, while promoting a good image among men as well as women in its marketing area.

6   With regard to size, PWB's objective is to continue operating as a small independent bank which will be first in quality and service, and not to emphasize growth for growth's sake.

III. Strategies

1   PWB will develop a long-term financial plan outlining the means to establish and maintain a 10% return on equity within five years, and profitability within three years.

2   PWB will limit services offered to those which can be demonstrated to provide a 10% rate of return, or be a *necessary* complement to other services such that the 10% overall return is not compromised.

3   PWB will set a dollar limit on its involvement in offering specialized services (such as seminar, resource library, student account program). If it is determined

these programs are unprofitable then their continuance must be based on a *demonstrated* long-range benefit to the bank.

4   All financing of small business is to have a maximum loan maturity of five years. PWB is to consider small credits refused by larger banks; however, these credits are to be in keeping with PWB's risk and return on capital criteria.

5   PWB will develop correspondent relationships to assist the bank in handling commercial customers. These relationships will be beneficial to PWB in the future when additional resources permit the bank to take a more active role in the commercial market and as existing customers "outgrow" PWB.

6   PWB will keep abreast of the changing trends in the environment and competition. This will be done by monitoring strategies which other financial institutions are directing towards the women's market and by hiring a reputable marketing consulting firm annually to analyze the women's market.

7   PWB will identify and utilize all available media to reach potential customers. Through these media PWB will try to promote:
a. PWB's good image with men as well as women;
b. PWB's policy of equal credit opportunity;
c. PWB's willingness to offer financial guidance to those in need.

8   PWB will seek student customers and will develop a student account program in keeping with PWB's financial objectives. PWB will encourage students to come to the bank for help in establishing credit and to take advantage of the seminars. The purpose of this program is to establish a good image among young people so they will continue to maintain their accounts with PWB in the future.

9   PWB will improve organization structure, policies, procedures and controls allowing for better bank service to existing customers. This will include such areas as:
a. Faster teller lines;
b. Monthly statements to be mailed out to depositors promptly;
c. Personal loans made available at competitive rates.

10   PWB will keep all employees informed of the objectives and strategies of the bank so acting responsibly will become the "shared goal" of the entire staff. Employees will be kept informed through staff meetings which will be held on a regular basis.

As she reviewed the objectives and strategies developed by Linden, Roberta realized that her job of executing the strategies and achieving the objectives was not going to be an easy one.

1st Women's Bank Cuts Loss by More Than Half

By LAURA GROSS

NEW YORK. — The two-year-old First Women's Bank here, which lost money at the rate of $70,000 to $80,000 per month last year, has cut its operating losses to $20,000-$30,000 in the past six months. It also has arranged for an increase of $2 million in capital and has put into motion plans for obtaining operating assistance from officers of some of the city's major banks.

Lynn D. Salvage, president of First Women's, disclosed this in a status report on the bank at a luncheon meeting of the Financial Women's Association of New York here Thursday.

Goldman Sachs has agreed to act without fee as investment advisor to the bank and to arrange for what will probably be a private placement to raise the bank's capital by $2 million before the end of the summer, Ms. Salvage noted. And Citibank and Chemical Bank have agreed, pending New York State Banking Department approval to lend First Women's expert officers to assist them, she added.

Other progress has been made through the implementation of an aggressive marketing plan aimed at increasing corporate as well as retail business, and the program is having dramatic results, she said.

She pointed out that it is possible that the bank will break even by the end of this year. She emphasized that critics often lose sight of the fact that the bank is new and that new banks usually take about three to four years to become profitable.

Ms. Salvage noted errors made by the bank in its first full year of operation were "the classic errors of any new business." Net operating loss for 1976 was $938,621, about $320,000 of which was covered by reserves for individual loan losses, she explained.

Contrary to some reports, Ms. Salvage emphasized, the largest losses were not on loans to women or women-owned businesses. Forty-five per cent of the bank's commercial loans outstanding at the end of the year were to these businesses, she commented, and there was not one write-off among them during 1976.

Coupled with the historic problems of beginning a new business, she added, was a philosophy at the start that the bank had to be innovative, but some of the innovations which were implemented failed and the bank lost money as a result. Ms. Salvage noted "the expense of this kind of innovation is behind us now and we are trying to be a topflight, personal-service neighborhood bank." She mentioned a 24-hour teller machine on the outside of the bank and a no-return check with carbon copy kept by consumers as programs which have been discontinued.

The bank's advertising budget of $110,000 for last year was cut to zero for 1977. Ms. Salvage said, but the new marketing plan is producing positive results in the form of increased business from corporations which had previously merely maintained what she called "token or dormant" accounts.

She emphasized, as she has since taking office in February, that the bank is a women's institution because it is primarily managed by women and not because its philosophy or goal is to lend only to women. It is most definitely in total banking. Ms. Salvage said, and that includes forming working relationships with corporate and retail accounts.

The new marketing program has brought from dormant to working status such accounts as those of Avon Products. Philip Morris and Saks Fifth Avenue, she noted — and these clients are urging other corporations to do business with First Women's, she noted. The bank, she added, is managing financing for the Saks credit union, and is now organized so that officers are actively soliciting, by market segment, account relationships with Fortune 1,000 companies, government, unions, insurance companies, retail businesses and women-owned businesses.

First Women's has also embarked on a reduced-rate installment loan program for qualified employees of certain corporations whose loan payments can be automatically deducted from payrolls each month. "This is a way to sell corporate and retail business at the same time," Ms. Salvage emphasized — something which the bank needs to do, since it has no advertising budget for this year.

The staff has been cut to 23 from 47 to 50, she said, and although the bank cannot afford full-time financial advisors for its retail customers now, it is continuing this service by participating in seminars presented in conjunction with the Commerce Department and other banks

Ms. Salvage stated the bank's capital is down from its initial $3 million to about $1 million, about $800,000 of which is invested in its offices on East 57th St., so the management is extremely grateful for the assistance from Goldman Sachs, Chemical and Citibank, she added.

Another program, she noted, is under way to secure top-level people of corporate stature and with good business contacts for the bank's board of directors. She said that indications are the Banking Department would probably welcome the kind of expertise which commercial bankers from some of the city's larger institutions could bring to the First Women's board, and that First Women's is seeking this kind of director.

When she took office, Ms. Salvage said, she found an advisory council of about 85 members which she did not think could operate as an effective working group. So management has now organized an active and effective 12-member advisory council which includes some former bank presidents and some financial experts, Ms. Salvage said.

She said the bank is interested in greater participation in syndicated loans and noted that there are about 80 minority banks across the country which, if they pooled resources to their legal lending limits could muster about $10 million for this purpose. First Women's will be looking into this, she added.

First Women's is interested in serving as a community leader and getting business at the same time, she said, explaining why the bank is sponsoring "Meet the Mayoral Candidates Evening" at its office next Tuesday.

The bank currently has about 3,500 demand deposit accounts, 4,800 savings accounts and loans of about $8 million, including approximately $3.5 million in loans to businesses. It is continuing its 1976 trend of increasing relationships with about 500 corporations both in and outside New York City.

EXHIBIT 1

Source: *American Banker*, June 10, 1977, p. 1.

THE BOISE CASCADE CORPORATION 1970s–1980s

Donald F. Harvey

I. INTRODUCTION

John B. Fery, Chairman and Chief Executive Officer of Boise Cascade looked out the window of his plush, carpeted and paneled office at Boise Headquarters. His company had posted a 4% gain in earnings for the 1st quarter of 1981, and sales had climbed 7% from the previous year.

Fery noted that the firm's paper and paper related businesses performed well, but the building-materials businesses continued to suffer. Looking ahead, John Fery said, "We expect healthy long term demand for our paper products," but added that, "a housing industry rebound is still some distance ahead of us."

As he surveyed the future prospects for the firm, Fery reviewed the history of the firm during the past years. The current plan's "tilt toward paper," as Fery puts it, is part of a reordering of Boise's investment priorities to put more emphasis and money into businesses with better growth prospects. Yet, Boise's quest for growth is not strong enough to cause it to stray beyond the forest products industry.

That is precisely where Fery's approach is a far cry from that of his predecessor, Robert V. Hansberger. In the late 1960s, Hansberger, then Boise's chairman, set about making Boise a freewheeling conglomerate. Hansberger acquired new and sometimes exotic properties with abandon, ranging from recreational vehicles and real estate to Latin American bonds and utilities.

For a while, Hansberger seemed to possess the Midas touch, as Boise became one of the glamour companies of the 1960s. By 1972, however, when Hansberger resigned and the board chose Fery, a veteran operations man who had been with Boise since its founding in 1957, the company was in desperate shape.

Under Fery, the change in Boise's strategic course and management style could hardly be more striking. In sell-offs that garnered $300 million within a few years, Fery jettisoned several of the company's nonforest-product businesses, which in 1971 accounted for $800 million or 44% of revenues.

Detailed planning, strict financial discipline, and "hands-on" management have been the pillars of Fery's regime. Fery, a Stanford University MBA, has schooled his corporate staff in the methodology of sophisticated planning. Five-year and 10-year blueprints, "comprehensive business reviews," "key budgets," and elaborate income and expense projections are the starting point for the strategic discussions at Boise headquarters.

II. BOISE UNDER HANSBERGER

In the twelve years since Robert Vail Hansberger became chief executive of Boise Cascade Corp., he had quietly built a record of growth in sales and profits that is worthy of the envy of the most flamboyant conglomerators. A "congeneric" rather than sheer conglomerate expansionist, he had extended a business that began with the log in the forest into tangibly related areas. When he took over at the beginning of 1957, Boise Cascade's sales were $35 million. In 1967 sales passed $1 billion and in the first half of 1968 they were still climbing. This represented a twelve-year annual growth rate compounded of 33 percent.

If Hansberger had sought this growth only for growth's sake, his performance would be one of the foremost among modern empire builders. But in the contemporary style, Hansberger professed to disdain mere growth in sales, regarding it only as an instrument for reaching his primary goal of increased earnings per share. On this score, he had moved Boise Cascade from 34 cents a share in 1956 to $2.00 in 1968, a sevenfold increase.

This record had been beautiful for both shareholders and executives of Boise Cascade. Some forty of the company's executives had each made more than a quarter of a million dollars in stock options, and a few of them became millionaires. Hansberger himself went into debt to buy Boise Cascade stock in 1957, and he also received his first stock options then. Those shares, taking into account splits since then, cost $3. At their market price in 1968, around $70, his total present personal holdings, including subsequent stock options, were worth about $20 million, which is quite a bit above par for present-day chief executives.

Hansberger had put an intellectual stamp on his company. A star graduate in a celebrated class at Harvard Business School (1947), he had been a recruiter of MBAs and a believer in trying new tools of analysis and decision. He and his top executives made an annual three-day pilgrimage to Stanford where they submitted to the scrutiny of MBA candidates in seminars.

III. CHANGES AT BOISE (AFTER HANSBERGER)

The following table summarizes the operation of Boise Cascade in the period 1971–1973:

	1970	1971	1972	1973
Sales (millions)	$ 836	979	1131	1324
Net Income (millions)	34	(85)	(171)	142
E.P.S.	$1.08	(2.74)	(5.48)	4.55

Following are memoranda written by the President of Boise Cascade between 1972 and 1974, as the management struggled to dig out of the worst financial crisis in the history of the 64 year old company.

August 12, 1972

TO: All Boise Cascade Employees
SUBJECT: Boise Cascade Progress Report

You have stuck by Boise Cascade through a mighty rough period, but today I can report that there's light at the end of the tunnel.

Several weeks ago, Bob Hansberger (formerly the President, now Chairman) wrote you that we were considering a decision which would have a major impact on the company's future. We made that decision at the end of July, and I'd like to take this opportunity to explain its significance. I also believe you should be aware of the progress that has been made on the rest of our program to restore the company's profitability.

The decision reached last month was to subtract $200 million from any profits we might earn this year. This amount would cover the costs of completing our withdrawal from the realty business and would increase the amount already set aside for potential losses from Latin American investments.

This is a major decision in the company's history because it is aimed at eliminating, not merely reducing, the biggest drain on our profitability.

In accounting circles, this charge is called "extraordinary," not because of its size, but because of the unusual events and circumstances which caused the action to be taken. The entire charge has been entered in our records, but the money doesn't have to be spent until the losses actually occur, and they may be spread over the next several years. I'm sure this sounds like a strange bookkeeping practice, but accounting rules state that if we foresee losing money down the road, we must record the potential loss now. The charge has had virtually no effect on the money needed to operate daily.

The speeded-up exit from our realty operations and the extraordinary charge make it necessary to revise our major loan agreements. We are now working with our principal lenders toward a revision, and, in the meantime, have been granted temporary waivers of certain provisions of these agreements.

I said earlier in this letter that the $200 million charge will be deducted from profits we might earn this year. The effect on our financial results for the first six months of 1972 is obvious. During this period we earned $3,900,000 from operations, but, after subtracting the $200 million, we actually lost $196,070,000.

It is important to note that our profit from operations for the first six months of this year would have been $20,630,000 if it had not been offset by losses of $16,700,000 from businesses which we are discontinuing.

Despite this sizable loss, you should know that most of our operations are performing very well. Our timber and building materials business, for example, is having an outstanding year. Residential housing starts, which reached record levels in the first six months of 1972, have created an exceptionally strong demand for lumber, plywood, and other building products. This same factor also contributed to excellent performances by our building materials distribution centers and kitchen cabinet operations.

The results of our manufactured housing (Kingsberry) business are also good. In fact, to keep pace with growing demand, we are expanding our panelized housing plant in Ft. Payne, Alabama and opening a new homebuilding facility in Muncy, Pennsylvania.

Profits from our paper, packaging, and composite can operations also continue to improve. Strong markets and firmer prices exist for newsprint, linerboard, and corrugated containers. In addition, our new $45 million pulp mill in Fort Frances, Ontario, has started up in time to take advantage of the increased demand for pulp. The results of our composite can business are excellent, and the improvement in our office supply operation can be traced to recently modernized facilities and a successful new nationwide sales program, as well as a more robust economy.

Our engineering and construction operation has recovered from the serious losses it suffered in 1971 and is now moderately profitable. The turnaround was helped by closing down Power Line Erectors and Tyee Construction Company, which had heavy losses last year. The brightest spot continues to be the performance of Ebasco Services, which has a growing backlog of orders for electrical power generating facilities. Chemical Construction Corporation is showing significant improvement over last year, and its backlog of orders for pollution control and chemical processing equipment is growing. Although recently increased backlogs may signal the beginning of better times for Walter Kidde Constructors, it is still losing money.

The extraordinary charge climaxed a series of decisions made during the past 13 months to write off our investment in an unprofitable urban construction company; discontinue our on-site homebuilding operation; withdraw from the recreation communities business; increase our reserve for Latin American investments; and sell certain nonreality assets, using the money to reduce debt. Here is a report on the progress we have made in carrying out these decisions.

Burnett-Boise Corporation: Last year, we wrote off our entire investment in this urban construction company. The firm, in which we had a minority ownership, has been dissolved.

On-Site Homebuilding: This business was historically profitable, but it failed to earn an acceptable amount on the money we had invested in it. We have succeeded in selling most of our active on-site housing projects, including those in California, New Jersey, and the Washington, D.C., and Chicago areas.

Recreation Communities: The recent decision to discontinue our recreation communities business is just now being put into motion, so it's too early for a meaningful progress report. However, you might be interested to learn why this once highly profitable operation fell on hard times.

We entered the recreation communities field in 1966 and shortly became one of the leading developers, particularly in California. This business performed well during the next several years, but, in 1970, our size and visibility had made us a target for those who claimed that recreation communities damage the natural environment. Although the environmental standards at most of our projects were high, we responded positively to the rising concern for ecology by upgrading them even further. Unfortunately, this resulted in construction delays and much higher development costs.

The environmental movement continued to gain strength in 1970, causing bad publicity for the land development industry in general and for our projects in particular. In addition, California's economy was suffering from the nationwide recession and greatly reduced employment in the aerospace industry. These conditions caused sales to drop which, together with higher development costs, plunged recreation communities into the red in the fourth quarter of 1970.

This condition continued in 1971, and in October the State of California filed a suit alleging that misrepresentations were made in connection with sales at some of our earlier projects. A class action with similar charges was filed at about the same time. These suits and other class actions that were subsequently brought created such a cloud that sales declined further. As a result, this operation recorded a large loss for 1971.

Sales were slow during the first quarter of 1972, which is not too unusual because of the winter weather. But, when sales failed to recover sufficiently in the second quarter, and because we could find no basis for expecting future improvement, we decided that we'd have to stop our involvement in this business.

Although we're getting out of the recreation communities business and halting retail land sales in California immediately, you're likely to continue seeing our advertisements. That's because we're selling vacation homes and condominiums at these projects. We're also going to fulfill our obligations to those who own property at our projects.

Latin American Investments: Since the beginning of the year, three significant developments have occurred in Latin America.

The leftist Government of Chile has failed to remain current on its financial obligation to the company. It has not paid the principal installment, nor one-half of the interest payment due in February on notes totaling approximately $75 million. Chile has expressed its intent to pay us, and we are discussing a revised payment schedule.

In Guatemala, we sold our utility at a loss to the Government for $18 million cash.

Our utility in Panama was seized by the Panamanian government in an unexpected move on June 1, during negotiations which we had hoped would lead to a new operating agreement that would assure the utility's economic well-being. The Government has now declared its intention to purchase the utility, and negotiations are currently being held concerning the sale. The Government has stated that it will nationalize the utility if we fail to reach agreement by September 1, 1972. The book value of our investment in this subsidiary is $30,000,000.

Sales of Nonreality Assets: The purpose of this program is to reduce our debt. A reduction in debt will lower the amount of interest we pay, thereby improving the company's profitability. Since the first of the year, we have sold some smaller operations. These are businesses which we do not consider essential to the company's future development.

At present, we also plan to make a public offering of a minority stock interest in our mobile housing and recreational vehicle business. We hope to accomplish this before the end of the year, subject to market and other conditions. I should add that this operation is continuing to perform very well.

As you know, the company has expanded its executive leadership and has taken steps to provide more depth in top management. To help better share the workload of Bob Hansberger, our Chairman and Chief Executive Officer, the board of directors elected Steve Moser to the position of Vice Chairman and named me as President. Just two weeks ago, the board elected John Clute as a senior vice president. John, as you know, is general counsel and is responsible for certain of our international operations and administrative functions. The board also named seven new vice presidents, including: Bill Bridenbaugh—packaging; Dick Maley—paper manufacturing; Peter Norrie—paper sales; John Scopetta—Latin American investments; Bob Smith—manufactured housing; Will Storey—controller; and Vern Veron—wood products sales.

In closing, I want to emphasize that the company's future is more clearly defined today that at any time since our troubles began. I believe this was made possible by the decisions made during the past 13 months to write off our investment in Burnett-Boise; discontinue our on-site homebuilding operation; withdraw from the recreation communities business; increase our reserve for Latin American investments; and reduce debt by selling certain non-reality assets. Our problems will not disappear overnight, of course, but we have a plan to solve them, and that plan is working.

I hope this report has brought you up to date on the status of your company. If you have any further questions, I encourage you to contact your group, division, or location management, or write directly to us here in Boise.

John B. Fery
President

October 20, 1972

To: All Boise Cascade Employees

When I wrote to you in August, it was to describe how a major financial decision would influence Boise Cascade. I write today to explain the significance of a major decision involving people.

Prompted by personal reasons, Bob Hansberger this week resigned as our company's Chairman and Chief Executive Officer. The Board of Directors has since elected Steve Moser as Chairman, and I have been elected to succeed Bob as Chief Executive Officer.

In my new capacity, I want to take this opportunity to restate and reinforce our corporate objective of 15 years—"to consistently increase shareholder value." In the future, however, I will emphasize the following three things as most important in attaining this objective:

1 *Profitability.* Profitability and return on investment go hand in hand. Consistent with responsible business practices, we must maximize both. You can help our company maximize the return

on its investment, as well as its profitability, by providing superior products and services at the lowest possible cost.

2 *Financial Strength.* We must reduce our debt. In the future, we will rely less on borrowed money to operate and expand, and more on money we earn from the products we manufacture and the services we sell.

3 *Planned Growth.* A company must grow purposefully. Our future growth will occur mainly in our existing and closely related businesses.

Pursuing our corporate objective by emphasizing these specific characteristics will put us well on the road toward establishing Boise Cascade as a financially strong and profitable company—one of which we can all be increasingly proud. I believe we have a solid foundation on which to accomplish this. Our success depends largely on your continued support.

I am also committed to creating within Boise Cascade a continually improving environment in which our employees can build a career. This, like profitability, financial strength, and planned growth, is essential to our company's future success.

Here's to better years ahead, for all of us.

John B. Fery
President

BOISE CASCADE IN THE 1980s

John B. Fery States: "We see 1981 as a year of continuing challenge for Boise Cascade. The sluggishness which characterized the forest products industry in 1980 probably will carry through at least the first half of 1981. Because of high interest rates at the end of the year, there is little hope for immediate improvement in the climate for housing. Additionally, a further deterioration of economic conditions may cause some softening in our paper-related businesses early in the year."

Boise Cascade's balance sheet, income statements (selected items), and funds flow statements for 1976 through 1980 appear in Exhibit 1. Exhibit 2 is a statement of sales income for each of Boise Cascade's major operating divisions and a profile of each division—production statistics, sales volumes, distribution, and market—as of 1980.

Boise Cascade's five-year, $1.1 billion capital spending program sought to achieve both operational and psychological goals. According to John Fery, the primary goal was to promote "balanced growth" among Boise Cascade's basic businesses. In addition, he said, "We had to demonstrate to Boise's employees, shareholders, and prospective shareholders that this company was going to grow.

Five-year Comparison of Selected Supplementary Financial Data Adjusted for the Effects of Inflation
Boise Cascade Corporation and Subsidiaries

	1980	1979	1978	1977	1976
		(dollars in thousands, except per share amounts)			
Net sales and other income					
As reported	$3,033,190	$2,948,440	$2,595,960	$2,324,310	$1,961,810
In constant dollars	$3,158,942	$3,496,603	$3,432,330	$3,304,498	$2,968,594
Income from operations					
As reported	$ 136,270	$ 174,920	$ 135,700	$ 115,610	$ 97,330
In constant dollars	$ 12,009	$ 73,933	$ 77,148	$ 61,905	$ 64,101
In current cost dollars	$ 42,988	$ 111,449	—	—	—
In constant dollars, including purchasing power gain	$ 135,044	$ 184,058	$ 142,792	$ 102,835	$ 85,335
Purchasing power gain from holding					
net monetary liabilities	$ 123,035	$ 110,125	$ 65,644	$ 40,930	$ 21,234
Income per share from operations					
As reported	$ 5.11	$ 6.52	$ 5.02	$ 4.00	$ 3.30
In constant dollars	$ .44	$ 2.75	$ 2.85	$ 2.13	$ 2.17
In current cost dollars	$ 1.61	$ 4.15	—	—	—
In constant dollars, including purchasing power gain	$ 5.06	$ 6.85	$ 5.28	$ 3.55	$ 2.89
Effective income tax rate					
As reported	16.0%	21.5%	37.1%	41.1%	36.0%
In constant dollars	69.4%	43.5%	57.9%	65.1%	56.5%
In current cost dollars	37.6%	32.6%	—	—	—
In constant dollars, including purchasing power gain	16.8%	23.7%	42.6%	52.8%	49.3%
Dividends declared per common share					
As reported	$ 1.75	$ 1.50	$ 1.25	$ 1.10	$ .76
In constant dollars	$ 1.83	$ 1.79	$ 1.66	$ 1.57	$ 1.16
Shareholders' equity					
As reported	$1,280,978	$1,178,400	$1,058,397	$ 959,088	$ 945,371
In constant dollars	$2,164,110	$2,065,737	$1,949,601	$1,855,532	$1,897,047
In current cost dollars	$2,262,762	$2,207,037	—	—	—
Shareholders' equity per common share					
As reported	$47.90	$44.09	$38.99	$35.34	$31.90
In constant dollars	$81.07	$77.42	$71.93	$68.47	$64.12
In current cost dollars	$84.78	$82.73	—	—	—
Market price per common share at year-end					
As reported	$34.13	$33.88	$26.75	$25.38	$33.63
In constant dollars	$34.13	$38.14	$34.12	$35.29	$49.93
Excess of increase in general price level over increase in current cost of inventories, property, plant and equipment and timber and timberlands	$ 50,425	$ 86,053	—	—	—
Year-end Consumer Price Index for All Urban Consumers (CPI-U)	258.4	229.9	202.9	186.1	174.3
Percent of increase in CPI-U	12.4%	13.3%	9.0%	6.8%	4.8%

Constant dollar amounts have been determined based on a comprehensive restatement of historical financial statements utilizing the end-of-year level of the Consumer Price Index for All Urban Consumers (CPI-U). Current cost amounts are based on a selective restatement of certain accounts. Accordingly, the constant dollar and current cost restatements are not directly comparable.

EXHIBIT 1

"However," he continued, "the rather hurried process by which the capital plan was formulated was not something that Boise Cascade wanted to repeat. That first five-year program was vital, but it should not be regarded as a model for our next five-year program," he said.

EXHIBIT 2

IV. **Product Segment Information**

A. *Timber and Wood Products*

Statement of Operating Income	Year Ended December 31		
	1980	1979	1978
Revenues (total sales)	$685,810,000	$697,244,000	$698,716,000
Income	30,058,000	61,142,000	100,613,000
Sales Volumes	1980	1979	1978
	(millions)		
Plywood (square feet)	1,205	1,387	1,528
Lumber (board feet)	653	796	799
Fiberboard (square feet)	347	427	484
Particleboard (square feet)	108	142	149

Wood Products

Sales (millions of dollars)		Operating Income (millions of dollars)	
74	402	74	25
75	389	75	7
76	554	76	56
77	638	77	73
78	699	78	101
79	697	79	61
80	686	80	30

B. *Building Materials*

Statement of Operating Income	Year Ended December 31		
	1980	1979	1978
Revenues (total sales)	$654,452,000	$794,468,000	$749,550,000
Income	(17,893,000)	22,926,000	40,988,000
Sales Volumes	1980	1979	1978
	(millions)		
Living units	6,183	8,199	9,822
Cabinets (thousands of cabinets)	240	942	831
Building materials distribution (sales dollars in millions)	$552	$621	$565

Building Materials

Sales (millions of dollars)		Operating Income (millions of dollars)	
74	324	74	7
75	337	75	2
76	462	76	16
77	609	77	36
78	750	78	41
79	794	79	23
80	654	80	(-18)

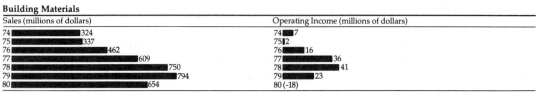

C. Paper

Statement of Operating Income	Year Ended December 31		
	1980	1979	1978
Revenues (total sales)	$1,069,915,000	$887,817,000	$695,057,000
Income	165,771,000	143,269,000	695,057,000
Sales Volumes	1980	1979	1978
	Thousands of tons		
Printing and publishing papers	1,223	1,129	1,004
Newsprint	418	379	329
Packaging papers & paperboard	139	205	145
Specialty paperboard	67	77	78
Market pulp	209	176	174
Total	2,056	1,966	1,730

Paper

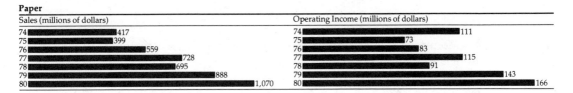

Sales (millions of dollars)
74 — 417
75 — 399
76 — 559
77 — 728
78 — 695
79 — 888
80 — 1,070

Operating Income (millions of dollars)
74 — 111
75 — 73
76 — 83
77 — 115
78 — 91
79 — 143
80 — 166

D. Packaging and Office Products

Statement of Operating Income	Year Ended December 31		
	1980	1979	1978
Revenues (total sales)	$853,406,000	$763,726,000	$656,016,000
Income	59,950,000	51,565,000	36,323,000
Sales Volumes	1980	1979	1978
	(millions)		
Corrugated containers (square feet)	5,855	6,075	5,577
Composite cans (equivalent units)	2,338	2,370	2,331
Envelope	5,576	5,611	5,228
Office products distribution (sales dollars)	$346	$306	$260

Packaging and Office Products

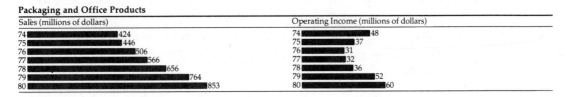

Sales (millions of dollars)
74 — 424
75 — 446
76 — 506
77 — 566
78 — 656
79 — 764
80 — 853

Operating Income (millions of dollars)
74 — 48
75 — 37
76 — 31
77 — 32
78 — 36
79 — 52
80 — 60

In late 1973 and 1974, with the worst of the financial crisis over and the new capital spending program under way, Boise Cascade management began devoting more time and attention to the process by which the company's newly stated goals would be achieved. Boise Cascade had not had a formal corporate planning process since 1971. At that time there was a small council of senior executives which considered longer-range capital expenditure, financial, strategic, and human resources matters. This process lasted until late 1971, when it was dropped along with a goal which had been in effect for all operating divisions, a 20 percent annual increase in net income.

Exhibit 3 contains an organization chart of Boise Cascade in 1974. The corporate planning function reported to the chief financial officer of the company. Late that year, a management decision was made to hire from the outside someone to take charge of the corporate planning effort. John Fery felt that the right person would give longer-range planning the boost it needed throughout the company and ensure that Boise upgraded its proven, firefighting management skills to deal with the increasingly competitive world in which the company was operating.

V. CONCLUSION

Cliff Morton, Vice President of Corporate Planning for the corporation, described the strategic planning approach as follows:

Each division manager was asked to look at, describe, and analyze the past performance of his division and to draw comparisons with the divisions's principal competitors, giving reasons for any differences. "We wanted to develop a point of view about the fundamental markets served by each of our businesses, the capability of the particular industry, and Boise Cascade's position within each industry." No additional corporate staff was hired to prepare or evaluate the lengthy analysis work, but individual division managers could and did engage outside consultants to assist them in the broad review assigned. It was anticipated at that time that such a thorough, internal, strategic audit would only be done once every ten years.

While the reviews were under way, Boise President, John B. Fery, issued a restatement of the corporate goals in his message to shareholders. The overall goal was expressed as follows: "To optimize the company's long-term value to its shareholders and to society." Six strategic objectives were listed as steps toward achieving that goal:

1 Be the most effective operator in each of our businesses.

2 Expand those businesses, optimizing the relationship between them and between our primary manufacturing and converting/distributing operations.

3 Maintain a strong financial structure, which gives the company latitude for planned growth.

4 Provide products and services which meet basic needs and offer fair value.

5 Provide an environment which encourages and rewards employee effectiveness at all levels.

6 Be capable of anticipating, constructively influencing, and adapting to the changing needs of society.

In line with the objectives and using the results of the division-by-division reviews, the President then asked each division to prepare a statement of strategy for the coming five years. The strategies were intended to be a direct outgrowth of the reviews, which inevitably produced a variety of alternatives for each division. Cliff Morton explained the strategy formation process with the following example:

"The review might reveal two major strategic options facing a business—Option X and Option Y. Under Option X, there is a high-growth opportunity with medium risk, for ten years, if you move in the next 24 months. Option Y is a low growth, no-risk scenario for the next 10 years, but you end up with a different sized business. Which do you want to do? That decision is a function of how we collectively feel about that business. The burden, though, is on the division manager. What part does he or she think the division plays in the Boise Cascade portfolio? How big a risk does the manager want to take? Does he or she want to put capital into it?"

Morton continued: "We have a business where what I told you earlier is exactly true. It has a capability in the next 10 years—if management does something in the next two years—to be the leader in the industry. It is medium-risk with big dollars involved. It could become a significant part of Boise's portfolio. The division also has a perfectly viable, low-growth scenario that would keep it at a pleasant level—cash-throwing, high-ROI-generating—with no investment and medium risk. Right now that manager doesn't know what he wants to do. He'll have a senior vice president and an executive vice president helping him decide, but that guy is running the business. John Fery will not tell him at this point which of the options to choose. Fery may veto his decision, but he won't dictate a choice in advance."

But Boise Cascade had become a commodity business again, and—as Fery put it—"the most important thing in a commodity business is efficiency. How do we put that product out at the lowest cost?" He did not restrict the company's goals to efficiency alone, however. In his address before the security analysts, he said: "You may take for granted that each operating division's plans specify an improved return on investment. This involves improving market share in most components of each of our businesses, improving productivity, improving margins to the extent we can affect them, making an extra effort to minimize or reduce overhead expenses, improving our safety performance (that is a real cost), and meeting or exceeding our EEO affirmative action plans." Mr. Fery also emphasized the role of planning: "Boise Cascade's improved performance in the years ahead rests on detailed business planning scenarios."

Boise Cascade Corporation Organization Chart

showing corporate officers, staff and divisional responsibilities

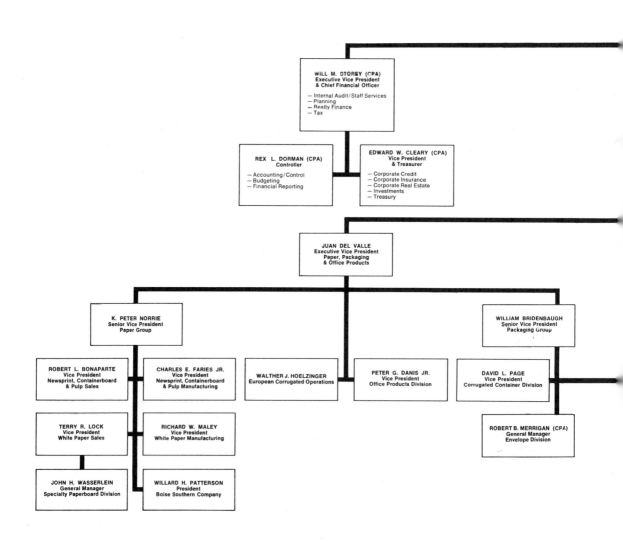

EXHIBIT 3

440

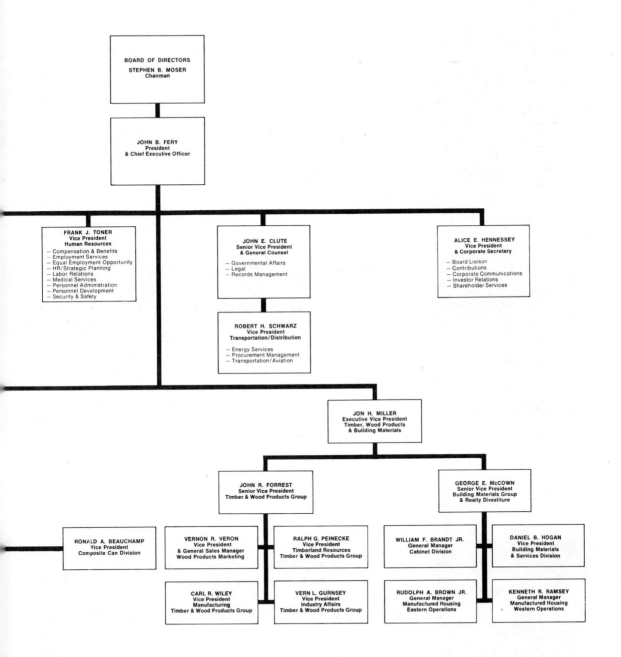

BOARD OF DIRECTORS
STEPHEN B. MOSER
Chairman

JOHN B. FERY
President
& Chief Executive Officer

FRANK J. TONER
Vice President
Human Resources

- Compensation & Benefits
- Employment Services
- Equal Employment Opportunity
- HR/Strategic Planning
- Labor Relations
- Medical Services
- Personnel Administration
- Personnel Development
- Security & Safety

JOHN E. CLUTE
Senior Vice President
& General Counsel

- Governmental Affairs
- Legal
- Records Management

ALICE E. HENNESSEY
Vice President
& Corporate Secretary

- Board Liaison
- Contributions
- Corporate Communications
- Investor Relations
- Shareholder Services

ROBERT H. SCHWARZ
Vice President
Transportation/Distribution

- Energy Services
- Procurement Management
- Transportation/Aviation

JON H. MILLER
Executive Vice President
Timber, Wood Products
& Building Materials

JOHN R. FORREST
Senior Vice President
Timber & Wood Products Group

GEORGE E. McCOWN
Senior Vice President
Building Materials Group
& Realty Divestiture

RONALD A. BEAUCHAMP
Vice President
Composite Can Division

VERNON R. VERON
Vice President
& General Sales Manager
Wood Products Marketing

RALPH G. PEINECKE
Vice President
Timberland Resources
Timber & Wood Products Group

WILLIAM F. BRANDT JR.
General Manager
Cabinet Division

DANIEL B. HOGAN
Vice President
Building Materials
& Services Division

CARL R. WILEY
Vice President
Manufacturing
Timber & Wood Products Group

VERN L. GURNSEY
Vice President
Industry Affairs
Timber & Wood Products Group

RUDOLPH A. BROWN JR.
General Manager
Manufactured Housing
Eastern Operations

KENNETH R. RAMSEY
General Manager
Manufactured Housing
Western Operations

441

CITY HARDWARE, INC. (A)

Paul Miesing
McIntire School of
Commerce
University of Virginia

City Hardware, Inc., is a closely held firm, its Board of Directors consisting of all six of the company's stockholders. Three families control the business: two father-son families and two cousins. All are prominent business and professional men and women and live in major cities throughout the state. The business has been in these three families since its incorporation and participation has been limited to two members from each family. Control has been maintained even as the new, younger owners have moved away to pursue their own professions.

In February 1973, the Board met to discuss the future direction of the firm. Current operations included both a retail hardware store in the downtown central city area and a wholesale plumbing supply division three blocks away in a railroad-siding warehouse. Considerable sentiment existed on the Board for a shift of the firm toward becoming exclusively a retail hardware store. Specific items on the agenda included the determination of the firm's future type of operation, possible locations available, and financing necessary for any such changes.

The General Manager attended the meeting and presented board members with his evaluation of the firm in a written memo dated February 4, 1973. The following excerpts from that memo present his viewpoint:

This case was prepared by Assistant Professor Paul Miesing with the aid of M. Anderson, W. Anderson, C. Klemstine, and W. Pankey as a basis for class discussion and is not intended to illustrate either effective or ineffective handling of an administrative situation.

Distributed by the Intercollegiate Case Clearing House, Soldiers Field, Boston, MA 02163. All rights reserved to the contributors. Printed in the U.S.A.

We draw our trade from a large area encompassing several counties, partly because of the wholesale business we have, partly because of the diversified inventory we carry, partly because we deliver, and partly because of our consumer credit program. It has been expressed by some of our customers that we are high priced, but we usually have what no other business carries. Also, we generally have had personnel who know the entire hardware line, although this is fading fast as our old-time employees retire.

Our Wholesale Plumbing Division is presently the most profitable segment of our business, but the firm has not been able to meet its goals of increased profitability from the retail end. As you have suggested, this Division should be the main thrust of the business. There is a real opportunity in the area known as "home-center" operation, catering to the "do-it-yourselfer." If we go to this type of operation we could capture a large share of the market because our existing strength in the hardware business would make us a one-stop center.

While we have shown a 43% increase in sales for the past year, the figures show that there was not a significant increase in any area except the sporting goods field, and most of that was at the wholesale level and at low margin. Our success in generating new sales has leveled off, partly because of inadequate physical space. We know that a new, modern facility would increase sales again.

One of the major obstacles we would have to overcome should we go into a new, more modern operation would be our pricing structure. I would suggest going to a one-price system with a lower margin. I believe we could improve our net profit figure with new homeowners' business that we presently do not have. A real education program would have to be done on our contractor and industrial accounts. But I believe we could convince them to stay with us despite the loss of their "wholesale customer" status. A couple former contracting customers have told us that they now purchase their hardware elsewhere. They are paying more for their merchandise, but they don't have parking problems to contend with. They figure they come out just as well, taking the cost of the men's time into account. Several contractors make us their first stop in the morning on their way to the job. Our best bet is to move right out where all the building is going on.

As a result of the aforementioned facts and given the goal of increased retail sales and profits, I see no alternative but to make immediate plans to relocate the main base of our hardware operation. The wholesale plumbing business could remain where it is for a few years, but it would simplify operations if we construct a combination facility to house both divisions. The general direction indicated by growth of present customers and potential new customers would be in the northern area of the suburban belt around the city. As previously reported, land costs are high where frontage on the highway is available. However, further inquiry has revealed that land which is a block from the highway can be purchased for around $20,000 per acre. This is considerably under our previous figures. Also, land east on Route 62 costs about 30% less than that out north on Route 53. With a building cost of $10 per square foot, a 20,000 square foot building plus land would run approximately $260,00. Add to this $50–75,000 for fixtures and equipment and $20–30,000 for parking lot paving and we come up with a figure of around $350–375,000 total cost. This would give us the large, high-ceilinged, modern design we've been dreaming about and allow us to go ahead with the full-line "home-center" retail hardware store in a good location. We would keep most of our contractor business with this plan and increase retail sales as well.

We could finance this move one of several ways: (1) raise capital through additional stock sales; (2) raise capital through debentures; (3) sell the present properties and lease the new property; or (4) establish a separate real estate holding operation, so the business can lease the property from the real estate operation. I have had informal discussion with real estate people who feel we could sell the two downtown properties for around $125,000.

BACKGROUND

Located in a mid-Atlantic state, City Hardware has been a respected local name in hardware for nearly a century. The charming store occupies its orignial high-ceiling building, complete with small bin storages up and along the walls and serviced by aged clerks sliding floating ladders to and fro as they picked items from memory. It was fun just to go in and see this quaint store out of the past.

The firm has shown total wholesale and retail sales of over $1,000,000 annually since 1947 and prides itself on its nickname "the dependable hardware store." The town in which it is located centers around the major state university and hospital complex, with light and medium manufacturing also providing jobs. Growth in the area has been steady since 1940 and the city-county population totals nearly 75,000. Surrounding counties provide approximately another 75,000 potential customers, most of whom come into town on Saturday to do their shopping. (Census data are shown in Exhibits 1 and 2.)

Residential migration has been along the major traffic arteries, as is characteristic of many cities experiencing growth. Residences along the northern Route 53 area have increased dramatically, and one shopping center and an additional large department store opened to satisfy the growing needs of the area. A second shopping center, featuring a large national chain department store, is rumored for the near future further north on Route 53. Growth to the east of the city along Route 62 has been slower, characterized by an increase in commercial businesses (almost all local car dealers, plus two building supply companies) with very little increase in residential dwellings. The interstate highway south of the city and the hilly terrain and high land prices to the west have kept growth slow in those directions. (A map of the area is included as Exhibit 3.)

The retail hardware industry has enjoyed steady growth in the past five years, according to a survey by the Retail Hardware Association. (Exhibit 4 shows relative sales and net income trends for the hardware industry.) Growth has been due primarily to increases in residential housing and leisure time. Home improvement items have experienced the greatest growth, as more homeowners make minor improvements and repairs themselves, citing self-satisfaction and lower costs as their major reasons.

BUSINESS ORGANIZATION

Two separate entities come under the title of City Hardware. The first, the Wholesale Plumbing Division located on Wood Street, specializes in plumbing supplies and sells primarily to contractors and builders. The personnel are considered extremely knowledgeable and personal service is highly stressed. Their large variety of supplies and accessories has made City Hardware the major supplier of wholesale plumbing in the area with thirty-five percent of the market, but space limitation has begun to present a possible constraint to growth. The present facility has 5,200 square feet of space. It is owned by the company, but current building codes prevent any additions to the building. Also, the building is old, preventing the installation of modern inventory handling equipment (such as conveyor belts and freight elevators) and necessitating costly manual inventory handling. Their primary competitor, C. J. Lilly Co., is located eight blocks away in a modern one story building.

The Retail Hardware Division is located in the city's downtown area, on the main street. It deals primarily in hardware and repair items, including paint, hand tools, and power tools. It also provides a large sporting goods selection and a china department. Seventy percent of its sales are on a wholesale basis to builders and to small "General Store" outlets throughout the state. The remaining thirty percent is in retail sales. The retail and wholesale departments are run by the same personnel out of the same store: each sales clerk decides whether a sale is "wholesale" or "retail." The store has the reputation of being high in price, but offering personal service and a complete selection. The Retail Hardware facility, also owned by the company, is a three story brick building. Total store area is 15,000 square feet; the first floor of the building serves as the main sales floor and the upper floors serve as storage areas. Most of the basement is also a sales area, housing such departments as sporting goods and china. Because of lack of space, only about fifteen percent of the merchandise inventory can be displayed in the sales area. At present, the clerk takes the customer's order and searches the storage area for the desired item. The average search time is five minutes.

Just as in the Wholesale Plumbing Division Warehouse, the hardware facility has become cramped, and the multistory building cannot be modified for mechanical inventory handling. Under present conditions, merchandise is handled an average of six times by company personnel between the railroad car and the final sales. (Financial statements are included as Exhibits 5 and 6.)

EXHIBIT 1

Selected Area Housing Characteristics, 1970			
	County	City	Total
Household population	34,361	37,957	72,318
Year round dwelling units	11,715	14,288	26,003
Season units	23	3	26
Occupied units	10,541	13,647	24,188
One unit structure	9,093	8,141	17,234
Multi-unit and mobile	2,622	6,147	8,769
Owner occupied units	6,758	6,583	13,341
Median value	$21,100	$20,200	$20,650
Lacking one or more plumbing facilities	1,299	137	1,436
Renter occupied units	3,783	7,064	10,847
Median rent	$122	$102	$109
Lacking one or more plumbing facilities	732	401	1,133
Crowded units	842	745	1,587
Lacking one or more plumbing facilities	440	66	506
Persons per unit	2.93	2.66	2.78
Persons per occupied unit	3.26	2.78	2.99

EXHIBIT 2

Selected City and County Demographics			
Effective Buying Power	1970	1960	% Change
City	$120,587,000	$53,251,000	126.4
County	108,198,000	41,641,000	159.9
Retail Sales			
City	$118,014,000	$72,443,000	61.5
County	21,650,000	13,415,000	61.4
Car Registrations			
City	13,854	7,479	85.1
County	12,817	7,373	73.8
Telephones	October 1971	October 1961	
	45,375	23,250	95.2
Water (gallons sent out)	July 1972	July 1962	
	224,539,000	147,290,000	52.4
Electric Meters	December 1971		
City	15,746	n.a.	—
County	11,086	n.a.	—
	26,832		
City Land Value	1971	1961	
Assessed Value	$ 21,736,970	$11,804,130	84.1
Taxes	77,667,180	40,576,670	91.4
Tax Rate	3,720,265	1,420,183	162.0
	4.70	3.30	42.4
County Land Value	n.a.	$ 5,342,470	—
Assessed Value	$ 52,191,130	18,692,060	179.2
Taxes	3,079,276	725,263	324.6
Tax Rate	5.90	3.81	54.9

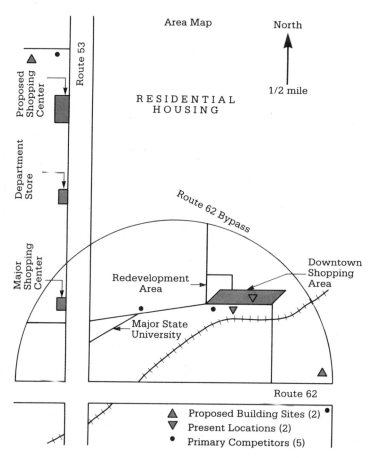

EXHIBIT 3
Area Map

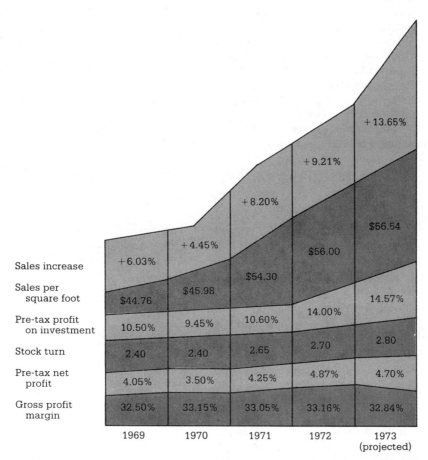

	1969	1970	1971	1972	1973 (projected)
Sales increase	+6.03%	+4.45%	+8.20%	+9.21%	+13.65%
Sales per square foot	$44.76	$45.98	$54.30	$56.00	$56.54
Pre-tax profit on investment	10.50%	9.45%	10.60%	14.00%	14.57%
Stock turn	2.40	2.40	2.65	2.70	2.80
Pre-tax net profit	4.05%	3.50%	4.25%	4.87%	4.70%
Gross profit margin	32.50%	33.15%	33.05%	33.16%	32.84%

EXHIBIT 4
Trends for the Hardware Industry

EXHIBIT 5

	City Hardware, Inc. Balance Sheets			
	1969	1970	1971	1972
Current Assets				
Cash	$ 39,000	$ 33,000	$ 16,000	$ 12,000
Accounts receivable—				
trade	169,000	154,000	162,00	244,000
Other receivables	7,000	9,000	18,000	4,000
Less allowance	6,000	9,000	10,000	15,000
Net receivables	170,000	154,00	170,00	233,00
Inventories	466,000	405,000	462,000	562,000
Other current assets	2,000	2,000	1,000	1,000
Total current assets	667,000	594,000	649,000	808,000
Property, Plant & Equipment				
Land	19,000	19,000	19,000	19,000
Building & improvements	98,000	101,000	128,000	128,000
Furniture, fixtures & equipment	26,000	30,000	37,000	38,000
Automobiles & trucks	14,000	15,000	16,000	18,000
Total cost	157,000	165,000	200,000	203,000
Less accum. deprec.	121,000	123,000	127,000	133,000
Net property, plant & equipment	36,000	42,000	73,000	70,000
Other Assets	3,000	12,000	12,000	4,000
Total Assets	$716,000	$648,000	$734,000	$882,000
Current Liabilities				
Notes payable to bank	$239,000	$ 40,000	$ 70,000	$ 65,000
Accounts payable	44,000	47,000	66,000	245,000
Long-term debt due	—	11,000	12,000	12,00
Other payables	61,000	23,000	26,000	11,000
Total current liabilities	344,000	121,000	174,000	133,000
Long-Term Liabilities—				
Bldg.	—	134,000	123,000	110,000
Total Liabilities	344,000	255,000	297,000	443,000
Capital				
Capital stock	80,000	80,000	80,000	80,000
Retained earnings	301,000	322,000	367,000	386,000
Total	381,000	403,000	447,000	466,000
Less treasury stock	8,000	10,000	10,000	27,000
Net capital	373,000	393,000	437,000	439,000
Total Liabilities & Capital	$717,000	$684,000	$734,000	$882,000

EXHIBIT 6

City Hardware, Inc.
Income Statements
Years Ended June 30, 1969 through 1972

	1969	1970 Hardware	1970 Supply	1970 Total
Net Sales	$1,136,000	$636,000	$520,000	$1,156,000
Less: Cost of Sales	823,000	485,000	390,000	875,000
Gross Profit	313,000	151,000	130,000	281,000
Operating Expenses				
Advertising	$ 8,000	$ 9,000	$ 1,000	$ 10,000
Auto & truck	5,000	2,000	2,000	4,000
Bad debts	10,000	9,000	3,000	12,000
Data processing	—	—	—	—
Depreciation	5,000	2,000	2,000	4,000
Interest	8,000	11,000	8,000	19,000
Repairs	1,000	—	—	—
Salaries	210,000	134,000	33,000	167,000
Supplies & office supplies	5,000	5,000	3,000	8,000
Taxes & licenses	15,000	9,000	7,000	16,000
Utilities (light & telephone)	6,000	5,000	2,000	7,000
Other	26,000	21,000	12,000	33,000
Total Operating Expenses	229,000	$207,000	$ 73,000	$ 280,000
Pre-tax Income from Operation	$ 14,000	$ (56,000)	$ 57,000	$ 1,000

EXHIBIT 6 (continued)

	1971			1972		
	Hardware	Supply	Total	Hardware	Supply	Total
Net Sales	$633,000	$474,000	$1,107,000	$985,000	$601,000	$1,586,000
Less: Cost of Sales	428,000	346,000	774,000	774,000	455,000	1,229,000
Gross Profit	205,000	128,000	333,000	211,000	146,000	357,000
Operating Expenses						
Advertising	$ 10,000	$ 1,000	$ 11,000	$ 11,000	$ 1,000	$ 12,000
Auto & truck	3,000	2,000	5,000	4,000	1,000	5,000
Bad debts	4,000	3,000	7,000	3,000	11,000	14,000
Data processing	—	—	4,000	5,000	—	5,000
Depreciation	3,000	2,000	5,000	4,000	3,000	7,000
Interest	8,000	6,000	14,000	10,000	7,000	17,000
Repairs	1,000	1,000	2,000	—	—	—
Salaries	138,000	53,000	191,00	149,000	55,000	204,000
Supplies & office supplies	6,000	3,000	9,000	8,000	2,000	10,000
Taxes & licenses	9,000	6,000	15,000	10,000	7,000	17,000
Utilities (light & telephone)	6,000	2,000	8,000	6,000	2,000	8,000
Other	19,000	12,000	31,000	19,000	18,000	37,000
Total Operating Expenses	$211,000	$ 91,000	302,000	$229,000	$107,000	336,000
Pre-tax Income from Operation	$ (6,000)	$ 37,000	$ 31,000	$ (18,000)	$ 39,000	$ 21,000

452

JOHNSON ENTERPRISES, INC.

David P. Gustafson

In early 1971 Johnson Enterprises, Inc., a medium-sized eastern manufacturing firm, was faced with the decision of whether or not to acquire The Norton Company. The Norton Company manufactured a motorized all-terrain recreational vehicle (ATV) that was sold under the trade name of GO-ROV. The Norton Company had been founded in 1966 by J. C. Norton, an engineer and inventor, and had grown in size until in 1970 it earned over $1,200,000 on sales of about $14,000,000. This potential acquisition represented a new field to Johnson Enterprises (JEI) and JEI's president, Mr. Roper, was considering the implications of this acquisition.

HISTORY OF THE ATV INDUSTRY

An ATV is an off-the-road vehicle powered by a 2-cycle engine. This vehicle allows two individuals to travel over a variety of terrains. The ATV was invented by Andrew Schmidt, who founded the Schmidt Company in 1959. (The Norton Company, which will be discussed later in the case, was started by an engineer who left Schmidt.)

Though the growth of ATV sales was slow during the early 1960s, sales grew rapidly during the late 1960s, as product reliability and customer acceptance increased. (See Exhibit 1) At the end of 1970 there were more than 50 manufacturers in the business selling about 70 brands. Five companies controlled about 71% of the market. Schmidt Company, which had recently purchased an engine manufacturer, had about 38% of the market. Schmidt had been very profitable in recent years making a 13% return on sales and a 45% return on assets. The second place company, possessing 13% of the market, had also been very profitable in recent years.

EXHIBIT 1

ATV Industry Sales	
Year	Retail Sales of ATVs (Units)
1965	26,000
1966	58,000
1967	112,000
1968	222,000
1969	360,000
1970	520,000

This case was prepared by Professor David P. Gustafson of the University of Missouri—St. Louis as a basis for class discussion rather than to illustrate either effective or ineffective handling of an administrative situation.

Presented at a Case Workshop and distributed by the Intercollegiate Case Clearing House, Soldiers Field, Boston, Massachusetts, 02163. All rights reserved to the contributors. Printed in the U.S.A.

All company names, names of individuals, and facts and figures have been disguised to assure anonymity.

Three of the top ten firms in the industry had been acquired by conglomerates in the last two years. These mergers had concerned many industry observers as to whether the financial strengths of the large companies would make it difficult for the independents to survive.

Even though there were nonrecreational uses, especially in forest management, the main use for the ATVs was for recreational purposes with approximately 90% purchased for this reason. Many ATV clubs had been formed by the recreation-minded users of these vehicles (there were over 1500 clubs in 1970) and approximately 900 ATV races were held in 1970. Some families owned two or more of these vehicles. The geographical markets for the vehicles were limited as access to land and appropriate environmental conditions where the vehicles could be used were necessary for their sale. Therefore, they tended to be sold in rural areas and small towns primarily in Canada and northern parts of the United States.

Though some spot television and radio advertising was used by the large manufacturers, much of the advertising for these ATVs was in specialty magazines such as *Argosy, True, Field and Stream, Sports Afield, Outdoor Life, Outdoor Field, Popular Mechanics* and *Popular Science*. Several manufacturers promoted their vehicles by sponsoring ATV races and/or ATV racers.

These ATVs sold for between $400 to $2000 with an average price of $1000. The vehicles had two cycle engines that ranged from 7 hp to 75 hp and could move at speeds up to 65 mph. Many of the sales were financed by banks in the same manner as automobiles. Normally, the terms were one-third down and 24 monthly installments but some banks offered as low as 10% down and as long as 36 months to repay the balance. It was encouraging to the industry to learn that most banks reported lower defaults with ATV customers than with other customers.

Some financial analysts predicted a potential market of more than 4.5 million vehicles. These analysts expected the market to grow about 30% in both 1971 and 1972, and 20% in 1973.

There were a number of factors that were of concern to other financial analysts which could have a potentially negative effect on ATV sales. Conservationists were concerned over the damage that these vehicles could do the environment. ATVs opened up wilderness areas that were previously only accessible to hikers. Some ATV riders used the vehicles to chase animals and to tear up the landscape. Other problems were associated with concerns about the high noise level and safety of the vehicles. The recent safety records of these recreational vehicles was poor; a recent survey had shown that one out of twenty-five drivers of the ATVs had been injured and over fifty people had died in accidents involving these vehicles in 1970. As a result several states had passed or were considering legislation on the permissible noise level and safety features of the ATVs, and several states were considering licensing ATVs.

Even members of the ATV industry felt that improvements needed to be made in:

1   Noise suppression

2   Braking

3   Lighting

4 Protective covering over the torque converters and other components that are likely to cause injury during failure

HISTORY OF JOHNSON ENTERPRISES

Johnson Enterprises was founded in the early 1900s to manufacture home appliances. By 1960, it had reached the $30,000,000 level in sales, but because of union difficulties, administrative problems, and decreased sales in several product lines, Johnson Enterprises lost money for the first time in its history in 1960. The present chief executive, Mr. Roper, became president of the firm in 1960 when he was given responsibility for turning the firm around.

Mr. Roper had been with JEI since 1945. He had held many administrative positions at JEI. His most recent position was vice president of manufacturing. Recognizing that the present functional organization could not cope with the diverse markets in which the firm competed Mr. Roper reorganized the firm along divisional lines. Three divisions were formed, household products, home appliances, and recreational products; each division had its own marketing, production and product development facilities. In implementing this structural change, he emphasized and encouraged product innovation and growth.

Mr. Roper set as his chief objectives: (1) to increase profits 14% per year, (2) to maintain an attractive financial balance sheet, and (3) to meet customers' needs in the home and recreational markets with quality products under the Johnson brand name.

During the 1960s, over 25 new products were introduced by Johnson Enterprises. Most of these products were developed internally, but several new products were obtained through acquisition. JEI's acquisition strategy was to acquire small firms with product lines which JEI did not manufacture but products that complemented those produced by Johnson Enterprises. After acquisition, they staffed these firms with several "JEI experts" and, "piggybacking" on the knowledge of the acquired firms, used their engineering and design skills to upgrade the products. Placing the acquired firm in the appropriate division on the basis of markets, the products were then marketed through the existing JEI distribution channels. Generally though, most of JEI's growth in the 1960s was internally generated rather than through acquisition.

Johnson Enterprises distributed approximately 65% of their products through regional distributors to over 25,000 retail outlets. About 30% of their sales were made directly to manufacturers who incorporated these products into their end product. For example, they manufactured sinks and hot water heaters that were then installed in mobile homes. In addition, Johnson Enterprises did about 5% of its business under private brands, primarily recreational products such as sporting goods and camping gear. Overall, Johnson Enterprises had a 30% or greater share of the markets in which it competed.

During the 1960s, the markets for Johnson Enterprises' products expanded rapidly. The financial data shown in Exhibit 2 indicate that, except for one year during the middle 1960s, the firm was able to achieve a growth rate of more than

EXHIBIT 2

Johnson Enterprises, Inc.
Financial Data (in thousands of dollars)

	Years Ending December 31										
	1970	1969	1968	1967	1966	1965	1964	1963	1962	1961	1960
Net Sales	$84,621	$73,318	$63,250	$55,461	$49,525	$51,742	$46,325	$43,159	$38,355	$35,172	$30,183
Net Income	4,060	3,380	2,820	2,390	1,863	2,060	1,725	1,463	857	425	(235)
Percent Return on Sales	4.8%	4.6%	4.5%	4.3%	3.7%	4.0%	3.7%	3.4%	2.2%	1.2%	—
Percent Return on Invested Capital	12.9%	11.6%	10.5%	9.4%	7.7%	8.8%	7.7%	6.8%	4.2%	2.1%	—
Working Capital	25,147	23,864	22,128	19,600	14,733	18,773	17,350	15,945	14,621	10,231	12,111
Current Ratio	3.5–1	3.4–1	3.6–1	3.2–1	2.6–1	3.7–1	3.8–1	3.6–1	4.2–1	3.0–1	3.8–1
Net Worth	31,531	29,111	26,961	25,371	24,211	23,373	22,338	21,638	20,585	20,138	20,123
Earnings per Share	.99	.82	.69	.58	.45	.50	.42	.36	.21	.10	—
Dividends per Share	.40	.30	.30	.30	.25	.25	.25	.10	.10	.10	.10
Book Value per Share	7.69	7.10	6.58	6.19	5.91	5.71	5.45	5.28	5.02	4.91	4.91
Price Range—High	35½	27⅜	23½	18½	12¼	17	14	17⅛	12½	10⅛	8½
Low	25¼	20⅛	17	10¾	10⅛	12	11	8¼	10¼	8¼	6¼

14% and maintain a respectable financial condition. Though Mr. Roper had reaffirmed the company's growth strategy for the 1970s, he was concerned with how he might achieve a growth rate of 14% in profits during the 1970s. Johnson Enterprises had been actively looking for additional acquisitions during the past year to help them achieve these goals. To allow for future stock splits and acquisitions via stock he had recently requested and received stockholder approval to increase the authorized common stock from 4.5 million shares to 15 million shares.

In early 1971 Mr. Roper stated that the chief strengths of Johnson Enterprises were:

1 a solid conservative financial balance sheet

2 product engineering strengths

3 quality brand image

4 five modern manufacturing facilities located in small towns in the east and southeast with good labor relations

5 an excellent distribution system

With his company's strengths and objectives in mind, Mr. Roper considered the opportunity to acquire The Norton Company in early 1971.

THE NORTON COMPANY'S HISTORY

In 1966 an engineer, J. C. Norton, left the Schmidt Company to form with two other investors a firm to manufacture a motorized all-terrain recreational vehicle. Mr. Norton had been dissatisfied with the opportunities for financial reward at the Schmidt Company and felt he could design an even more reliable and attractive ATV than the "Schmidt." He started the Norton Company in a 25 year old manufacturing plant in a small town in the midwest. The plant was a two story building with approximately 25,000 sq. ft. of usable space. Relying on the purchase of the engine and most of the key components from independent suppliers, Norton developed an ATV that had several features not found on the Schmidt models. Norton named his ATV the GO-ROV and marketed it primarily through independent distributors. The company achieved acceptance of its product and experienced a rapid growth in sales. By 1969, the Norton Company had its first profitable year as shown in Exhibit 3. In 1970, the Norton Company had about 5% of the market for ATVs.

Because Mr. Norton believed it was more profitable to make than buy and wanted control over the components in the GO-ROV, the Norton Company had turned from mostly an assembly operation to one where many of the components were manufactured in their own facilities. The second floor of the plant contained a number of special machines for manufacturing ATV components while the first floor included a conveyerized assembly line, office space and storage areas. They still purchased the engine (from a foreign supplier), the transmission, and some other components such as electrical components from outside sources as did many other ATV manufacturers. Recently several large conglomerates had bought out companies in the industry, and Mr. Norton was concerned that his company's lack of financial resources might make it difficult to compete. Like many rapidly growing companies, the Norton Company did not have sufficient internal resources to finance their expansion.

EXHIBIT 3

Financial Data for the Norton Company		
Year (Ending Sept.)	Sales	Profits
1966	$ 352,000	(425,000)
1967	929,000	(218,000)
1968	3,756,000	(113,000)
1969	7,425,000	384,000
1970	14,293,000	1,205,000

Balance Sheet
September 31, 1970
(thousands of dollars)*

Current Assets		Current Liabilities	
Cash	$ 283	Accounts Payable	$1598
Accounts Receivable—net	2725	Federal & State Tax	352
Inventories—lower cost	2957	Payable	
or market		Other	216
Miscellaneous			
	186		
Total Current Assets	$6151	Total Current Liabilities	$2166
Fixed Assets		Long Term Debt	$1512
Plant & Equipment—net	2516	Stockholders Equity	$5207
Other	218		
	$2734		
	$8885		$8885

*Unaudited

The demand for ATVs is highly seasonal. In order to reduce employment fluctuations and maintain good labor relations, production was spread out over the entire year. This increased the company's needs for working capital to finance the inventory between selling seasons. An additional need for working capital arose as Mr. Norton sought to manufacture more of the components in the GO-ROV and expand production. Recognizing that either the factory would need to be enlarged or new facilities would need to be acquired to allow for this expansion, Mr. Norton had begun to look for additional capital.

Mr. Norton recognized that changes were occurring in the marketing and distribution of ATVs. Originally, ATVs were sold through many different sources such as hobbyists interested in the vehicles, service stations, automobile dealers, small recreational vehicle dealers and marine product outlets. Gradually strong dealerships were being developed that could sell, finance, and service the vehicles. Though the GO-ROV was recognized by some industry observers as a quality product, Mr. Norton, whose experience was primarily design engineering, had never been able to develop a solid marketing organization to market the GO-ROV. Some observers felt that the GO-ROV dealerships were not as strong as Schmidt's and those of the other leading ATV manufacturers. Because of his concern over these issues, Mr. Norton explored various means of raising capital and acquiring marketing expertise. During his inquiries he had discovered through a merger broker that Johnson Enterprises was interested in moving into the ATV field.

In recent months the other two investors in Norton, Inc., had indicated a desire to sell out. These investors had suggested to Mr. Norton the desirability of merging with a firm that was listed on one of the major stock exchanges and was a good "growth" stock. Since Johnson Enterprises was listed on the New York Stock Exchange, was considered a growth stock by many financial analysts and had strong marketing and financial resources, Mr. Norton began negotiating a merger with JEI through the merger broker. During these negotiations a second firm made an offer of over $20 million in cash and stock. Unfortunately, this firm's stock was only traded over-the-counter and the firm did not have as good a reputation as JEI. Mr. Norton and the other two investors decided that they would merge with JEI if JEI's offer was approximately $18 million in stock. During the negotiations with JEI, Mr. Norton expressed his willingness to stay on and manage the firm as a division within Johnson Enterprises.

MR. ROPER'S DECISION

Mr. Roper was faced with the decision whether to acquire the Norton Company. He felt that acquiring this firm would allow entry into a new and rapidly growing field. The product was also counterseasonal to a number of other products sold by Johnson. Although JEI's engineers had not been able to adequately test out the GO-ROV because of the short time available for considering the acquisition, Mr. Roper, an avid outdoorsman, and several other executives had driven several of the GO-ROV models and had enjoyed the experience. They had felt that the GO-ROV was technically a good product, though some improvements in styling and manufacturability could be made. Johnson engineers had had very little experience with transmissions and two cycle engines; however, they felt that many of their skills could be applied to the other vehicle components.

The manufacturing facilities were adequate but old; they would need expansion for increased production. The present marketing and distribution channels were not adequate; a better sales force would be needed along with more and stronger dealers exclusively selling and servicing the GO-ROV. The GO-ROV probably could be marketed and distributed through the same channels and in the same manner as the Johnson Camper, one of the recreational products of Johnson Enterprises. Also, Mr. Roper felt that if JEI purchased the Norton Company, they would need to determine whether to call it the Johnson GO-ROV or stay with just the GO-ROV name. The Johnson name had wide consumer acceptance, but it might not be transferable to this product. On the other hand, the GO-ROV name would need to be more widely promoted and would need to gain acceptance if the company was to increase its market share.

The last issue that was important to Mr. Roper was the organizational implications of the merger. The Norton Company acquisition would be the largest one they had made to date.

WOODWARD AND LOTHROP, INC.

Odette Assiouty
Ulrich Wesche

Strategic Planning Means
Looking Beyond Current Success

Throughout the spring of 1977, Mr. Edwin K. Hoffman, the president and chief executive officer of Woodward & Lothrop, Inc., a Washington, D.C., area department store retailer, was debating whether or not he should initiate a comprehensive review of company plans and policies.

On the one hand, 1976 operating results had been the best ever, continuing record performances of the previous five years. On the other hand, he also knew that the 1976 growth in earnings and sales were largely attributable to the opening of a new store in affluent suburban Montgomery County, Maryland; and the next new store would not open until 1978. Beyond the short term, Mr. Hoffman was aware that several national department store chains had targetted Metro Washington for major marketing thrusts of their own, although government predictions clearly indicated that the local population would grow only sluggishly over the next fifteen years. He realized that this would heat up retail competition severely. He was concerned that the plans and policies which had been so successful in the past might not be adequate to assure Woodward & Lothrop's success in the 1980s.

By the end of May 1977, Mr. Hoffman had decided that it would be prudent to reassess company plans and policies and to change them as necessary before the radically different market had time to affect performance adversely.

BACKGROUND

Woodward & Lothrop, Inc., owns and operates department stores in the Washington, D.C., Metropolitan area. The main store is situated in downtown Washington, and there are also branch stores at suburban Maryland and Virginia locations (see Exhibit 1 for exact locations). To employees and customers alike, it is affectionately referred to as "Woodies."

It will celebrate its centennial birthday. The principal lines of merchandise carried in its stores are: womens, misses, childrens, infants, mens and boys apparel, and acces-

This case was prepared by Odette Assiouty and Ulrich Wesche, Assistant Professors, Howard University.

Copyright 1977 by O. Assiouty and U. Wesche.

Presented at a Case Workshop and distributed by the Intercollegiate Case Clearing House, Soldiers Field, Boston, Mass. 02163. All rights reserved to the contributors. Printed in the U.S.A.

sories, home furnishings, and other merchandise generally carried in a larger department store. It caters to the tastes of middle and upper class shoppers, but also carries some lower-priced merchandise. Woodies services its stores and customers from larger warehouses in Washington, D.C., and Fairfax County, Virginia. Woodies also maintains certain service units, such as in-store restaurants, repair and storage facilities, as well as an engraving and a dry cleaning plant. Woodies is a member of AMC, which enables it to compete more equitably with national chains.

In the spring of 1977, Woodies had slightly over 8,000 employees. Of these, 917 were supervisory personnel. Management consisted of 377 executives. The executive ranks include 97 buyers, 32 assistant store managers, 15 divisional merchandising managers, 13 store managers and 25 vice presidents and above, with the other 195 executives holding various corporate positions. Woodies is the largest department store operation in the Washington metropolitan area, and second only to the Sears chain. Sales grew from $121 million in 1967 to $241 million for 1976, while net earnings increased from $4.3 million to $11.7 million (see Exhibit 2 for a ten-year summary of operations).

Woodies' organization was based at the top on a functional delineation of responsibilities, but the management of the retail stores was organized geographically, and merchandising was managed by product line. The organization chart of Woodies' corporate officers as of the spring of 1977 is shown in Exhibit 3.

MARKET FACTORS WITH POTENTIAL IMPACT ON WOODIES' LONG-TERM PERFORMANCE

During June of 1977, Woodies' management discussed the scope of a review of plans and policies. Senior executives suggested that several factors other than competition could also affect performance adversely. It soon became apparent to Mr. Hoffman that a full-scale strategic planning exercise was called for, in which no aspect or assumption of operations would be exempt from review or, if necessary, from change.

It was the consensus of opinion among corporate officers that five trends would be particularly relevant to Woodies' long-term performance, as follows:

1 *The retail market of Metropolitan Washington is likely to grow at a lower rate than the national market.* This trend was distilled from the data in Exhibits 4, 5, and 6.

Relative to the country, Washington would decline in population, in effective buying income, and purchasing power. This trend would be particularly pronounced for the core city of the District of Columbia. The overriding cause of this slowdown was found in sharply reduced population growth rates. Given the dominance of the federal government as the major employer, in the face of a major national apprehension about a growing government and vocal local opposition to any major expansion of the infrastructure necessary to continue past population growth rates, Woodies management felt that this trend had a high probability of materializing.

2 *Specialty stores will take away a growing number of traditional department store customers.* This trend was identified using confidential Wash-

ington area market data and from customer comments on their shopping habits and store preferences.

Growing affluence has made many shoppers acutely fashion conscious. Such shoppers feel that boutique-style stores and limited-line merchandisers are more inclined to offer personal advice and service than traditional full-line retailers. Prices in such small establishments can be kept competitive with those of larger retailers, as the growing number of buying cooperatives formed by small retailers are quite capable of buying in bulk directly from manufacturers for their members.

In addition, the growth of smaller households and the greater dispersion of consumer units (see Exhibit 5) increase the number of permanently single adult shoppers. These individuals with significant purchasing power tend to frequent "life style" shops stocking short-lived "in" merchandise. These shops are small and flexible enough to spot and to capitalize on "trendy" merchandise long before full-line stores decide to compete.

Other inroads were coming from discount chains. Zayre, Kresge, and K-Mart were increasing their market penetration, and even supermarket chains like Giant were adding discount merchandise in separate facilities to attract the lower spectrum of traditional department store customers.

3   *National department store chains are expanding their Metro Washington operations.* This trend can be seen from the data in Exhibit 7.

Bloomingdale's opened its first area store in 1976, and experienced sales beyond expectations. In 1977, it opened a second store. Both stores are located in shopping centers directly competing with established Woodies' stores.

Neiman-Marcus opened its first area store in 1977, directly across from Woodies' store in wealthy Chevy Chase. Its patronage experience was also acknowledged to have been "quite satisfactory."

Lord & Taylor opened its third area store in the shopping center where Bloomingdale's second store was located. Again, an established Woodies store will be affected in its envisioned customer intake radius.

Three other national chains, Sears, Hecht and Garfinkle were face-lifting their existing stores, modernizing layouts and appearances. And management would be surprised if Montgomery Ward and J. C. Penney would be far behind in the effort to increase store attractiveness to shoppers.

Saks Fifth Avenue is known to actively look for a second store location in the area.

In summary, it is abundantly clear to management that the national chain competitors are stepping up their local operations. Given the limited growth of the market, much of the additional business expected must come from existing competitors. Management thus anticipates a serious fight for market share.

4   *Local department store chains are declining in importance*

Management is quite aware of the facts that Rich of Atlanta had been forced to sell out in 1976; that Highbee of Cleveland reported sharply reduced earnings for 1976; and that Marshall Fields of Chicago has still not recovered from the last recession, and is engaged in a very costly gamble to regain at least a part of its former glory.

The opinion of management is that local department stores are threatened in particular by the greater depth of national chain management, their intensive promotion and imaginative merchandising techniques, as well as by spillover effects of a national reputation into the local markets for the large mobile and transient segments of Washington's shopping public.

5 *Department store management will increase in complexity and risk*

On the cost side, management expects increases and additional complexities from the use of nonstore credit cards, the liberalization and higher ratio of credit sales, and the introduction of electronic equipment at the checkout counter and in the warehouses. Costs for additional and better educated professional managers should also increase. In general, there were a number of overhead items which would grow more for local retailers than national ones, as the latter had more volume to spread the increases over.

On the revenue side, customers would be more difficult to keep as additional competitive outlets opened their doors. Customer buying behavior would become more knowledgeable, reversible, and impulsive, requiring more sophisticated and intensive research as well as virtually immediate countermeasures.

Overall, operating and investment decisions were becoming more expensive. For instance, in the near future, a single poor decision on store location could threaten the viability of a company of Woodies' size, as a write-off of $20–25 million thus invested would distort the balance sheet beyond investor tolerances.

Finally, chains with their offsetting presence in several local markets could reduce their gross margins in any one location very sharply to gain market share by means of a temporary low-profit strategy.

WOODIES' CURRENT PRACTICES

After Mr. Hoffman had finalized the list of trends with impact on long-term performance, he requested inputs on Woodies' present policies. He called a meeting of corporate officers for the second week of July 1977, during which the executives in charge of marketing, merchandising, finance, and personnel outlined Woodies' position in their functional areas.

Summaries of their presentations are given below.

The Senior Vice President and General Merchandising Manager   I feel, as far as merchandising is concerned, Woodies is doing real well. The key to our success has been our willingness to accommodate changes in customer preferences and lifestyles. Let me give some telling examples of this flexibility.

While we are dropping the budget stores where we had them, we don't drop budget merchandise. As customers become more affluent and sophisticated, we eliminate inexpensive merchandise as a distinct department, but add to the medium-priced lines. This way, we avoid the undesirable "cheap" image, but still offer low-priced items for the bargain hunters.

We are now moving towards updated and advanced lines instead of traditional merchandise. We are enlarging all apparel lines into moderate and high-priced/value merchandise. We are definitely more interested in the fashion side of apparel. In the home store, we are phasing out the gardening equipment, and cutting back on paints, but we are increasing the gourmet department.

We can make these far reaching changes and seasonal changes in specific merchandise items in full confidence because we have a real good grass-roots purchasing program. Our buyers are the key here. They buy what is really in demand. The floor people are encouraged to spot trends and hot items and to tell the buyers. The merchandising managers help out by identifying merchandise categories that move fast or that are slowing down. In our organization, where we still know each other, we can get together quickly and make a purchase decision to capitalize on a trend long before the national chains can get a decision to go ahead.

Our prices reflect what we feel the customer will pay. Retail price maintenance by manufacturers is irrelevant; we mark up or down as we see fit.

I know that our prices are in line with the marketplace, considering our quality merchandise and competitors' prices. Mark-ups can be as low as 18 percent in brand-name TV sets or as high as 52 percent on women's dresses.

As a rule, we try to buy solely from the manufacturer. We are doing that for 90 percent of our volume. I feel that we get the same deal as the chains. Our volume is not that small and the federal antitrust people are real sharp on Robinson-Patman Act pricing violations. I would really raise hell if I found out the chains paid less than us.

With our great coverage in Metropolitan Washington, thirteen stores now, and one more in '78, we can offer a differentiated merchandise mix in the stores. Except for downtown, where we have everything, the stores in the less affluent areas don't feature as much expensive high-fashion lines as those in the affluent areas, which in turn have less low- and medium-priced items. But we don't vary price by location at all. We are trying hard that the different product mixes in the stores do not lead to a contradictory image of Woodies by only varying the ratio of products in the stores.

For the future we are improving our two strongest assets: superior execution of the fundamentals of merchandising, and total honesty in dealing with customers. The trust of customers is the key to our continued success. We must keep that even if it hurts us occasionally in the short-run.

The Vice President Marketing   In 1976, our customers consist of 65 percent women and 35 percent men. In terms of race, we have 70 percent white customers and 30 percent black, but in downtown D.C., the ratio is 50–50. There are two target categories of customers: heavy shoppers and fashion shoppers. Both groups have an income of over $25,000 per year.

- *Heavy Shoppers* tend to be housewives without jobs, at least college educated, aged between 35 and 49 years. They are 25 percent of all women shoppers, but account for 53 percent of department store volume.

- *Fashion Shoppers* tend to be women with jobs, married but no children, college educated, aged 18 to 34 years. They are 27 percent of all shoppers, but account for 35 percent of all department store volume.

At this time, we get satisfactory patronage from our target customers, but I feel they shop us more as a result of access convenience than of a specific intuition on their part. To increase customer loyalty, we are trying to improve customer perception on what Woodies stands for in three areas, as follows:

- *Repositioning of Merchandise:* Integration of budget store lines to medium priced lines; competitive price for superior merchandise.

- *Creative Advertising:* New slogans and media usage; stress on value; Woodies association with quality merchandise.

- *Improved Stores:* A new store in Gaithersberg in late 1978; redecoration of all stores to reflect the look and lifestyles of the late 1970s.

Stores are placed in a shopping mall at the center of a trading area. A trading area is delineated by three criteria:

- Number of credit cards issued, aggregated by zip code.

- Consumer sample of 500 persons, correlating place of shopping to place of residence.

- Driving time from residential areas to potential store locations.

- A trading area has a core: 10 car minutes away; a primary: 20 car minutes away; and a periphery: 30 car minutes away.

Woodies is committed to maintain a flag ship store in downtown D.C. This provides one location where all merchandise is offered; it allows office workers to shop during the work day; it serves as the focal point for corporate identity; and it has new drawing power due to the direct access from the new Metro subway system.

Woodies net advertising is about 2 percent of sales. The media distribution in 1976 was as follows: Newspaper, 60%; TV, 10%; Radio, 10%; Direct Mail, 15%; and Magazines, 5%. Print is handled in-house, while an agency is used for broadcasting advertisements. Whenever possible, Woodies engages in cooperative advertising with manufacturers.

While the merchandise is central to any ad, and we are thus stressing the informational purpose of advertising, we are also stressing our corporate image. We are trying to create loyalty and advantageous mental associations with the name "Woodies."

The Senior Vice President, Finance and Treasurer   I would like to highlight our 1976 record performance in a historical context.

Sales for 1976 increased 10.5 percent to $241.4 million compared with $218.5 million the previous year. The Company's sales were positively affected by the opening in March 1976, of a 155,000 square foot store at Montgomery Mall, in Montgomery County, Maryland. In the five years ended 29 January 1977, sales have increased at the compound annual rate of 9.5 percent.

Net earnings for the year increased 19.7 percent to $11.7 million compared with $9.8 million in the previous year. Improved gross margin levels and effective expense controls contributed significantly to the results of the year. In the last five years, net earnings have increased at the compound annual rate of 15.5 percent. Return on shareholders' equity was 16.5 percent in 1976, up from 15.4 percent in 1975.

Earnings per common share were $4.89, up 79 cents from $4.10. In the last five years, net earnings per common share have increased at the compound annual rate of 15.9 percent.

Credit sales in 1976 rose to $132.0 million, up 5.1 percent from 1975. In the first quarter of 1976, the Company began honoring third party credit cards in all of its stores, in addition to offering its own credit facilities. Credit sales, inclusive of third party credit cards, were 62.3 percent of total sales in 1976 and 57.5 percent in 1975. Receivables at year end were as follows (in thousands):

	1976	1975
Option payment plan	$44,314	$38,493
Time payment plan	8,524	7,801
Other	1,059	3,557
Totals	$53,897	$49,851
Less allowance for doubtful accounts	1,790	1,600
Receivables	$52,107	$48,251

Merchandise inventories at year end were $34.4 million, compared to $29.2 million at 31 January 1976. They are determined primarily by the retail method and are stated at cost, on the last-in, first-out basis, which is lower than market. If the first-in, first-out method of inventory accounting had been used, inventories would have been $7.2 million and $6.4 million higher than reported at 29 January 1977, and 31 January 1976, respectively.

Property and equipment at year end were as follows (in thousands):

	1976	1975
Land	$ 8,136	$ 8,082
Buildings	36,587	30,541
Fixtures and equipment	46,510	38,382
Construction in progress	2,378	7,497
Subtotal	$93,611	$84,502
Accumulated depreciation and amortization	26,215	22,563
Net property and equipment	$67,346	$61,939

Short-term borrowings averaged $5.8 million in 1976, and $10.1 million in 1975. The weighted average interest rates on these borrowings were 6.57 percent in 1976, and 7.58 in 1975. At January 29, 1977, the Company had unused lines of credit under informal arrangements with various banks totaling $17.4 million. During 1976 and 1975, maximum borrowings at any month end under these lines of credit were $10.1 million and $20.6 million, respectively. Each of the lines can be withdrawn at the option of the bank. In 1975, the Company entered into a loan agreement to borrow $20.0 million; $12.0 million of such loan was advanced in December 1975. The remaining $8.0 million was advanced to the Company in December 1976.

Long-term debt outstanding at year end amounted to $37,197 in 1975, and to $43,157 million in 1976. The aggregate payments required on long-term debt are: $4.1 mill in 1977; $4.1 mill in 1978; $3.9 mill in 1979; $4.0 mill in 1980; and $3.6 mill in 1981. The note agreements require minimum working capital, as defined, of $35.0 million. Working capital at 29 January 1977 was $60.1 million. Under these agreements, $32.8 million of retained earnings at 29 Janury 1977 is also restricted as to payment of cash dividends.

Capital expenditures for the year were $9.9 million compared with $9.4 million last year. Expenditures were made primarily for the construction of the Montgomery Mall store, the partial renovation of the Wheaton Plaza and Seven Corners stores, and for the purchase of electronic point of sale registers. Capital expenditures are expected to approximate $12 million in 1977. Funds will be used to renovate existing stores and to begin construction of a new store.

The table below shows the sources and applications of funds for 1975 and 1976:

	1976	1975
Source of Funds		
From Operations—		
Net earnings	$11,736	$ 9,801
Depreciation and amortization	4,436	4,002
Deferred compensation and deferred income taxes	730	728
Total funds provided from operations	$16,902	$14,521
Increase in long-term debt	10,445	12,000
Proceeds from stock options exercised	140	281
Other	20	23
	$27,507	$26,835

	1976	1975
Application of Funds		
Expenditures for property and equipment, net	$ 9,893	$ 9,445
Decrease in long-term debt	4,485	2,286
Dividends	3,415	3,338
Purchase and retirement of stock	2	19
Increase in working capital	9,712	11,747
	$27,507	$26,835

The major applications have been working capital and the new store. More than one-third of our applications have come from an increase in long-term debt. But the Company is in fine financial health.

The Vice President Personnel   At this time, we have a very fine staff, at the senior levels as well as lower down in the supervisory ranks. Woodies' top management is a good mix of people who started as trainees and those who started their careers in other department stores. We prefer to promote from within, but are not dogmatic about it.

Management trainees are recruited from college and from our own non-supervisory staff. From college we get BAs, some juniors, and even an MBA or two. Our internal trainee promotion program is very effective. Last year, fifteen of sixteen managerial entry positions were filled by our own people whom we promoted.

We train our lower level managers in a six-month program which combines floor experience and classroom instruction. As a first position, new managers become assistant buyers to a corporate buyer. Here they learn one way of merchandising. After a year or so, we promote them to be a department head in a suburban store where they can apply what they have learned and where they supervise sales people. Then we keep them as department heads for a number of years, but move them around: different stores, different departments, and more staff supervisory responsibility. During this time, my staff assess their progress and goals.

When we think a person is ready, we put him or her on a formal promotion list from which we fill vacancies at the level of buyer or equivalent. I am afraid we lose a few good people who get tired of waiting for an opening. Only growth will give us enough vacancies to keep our high potential junior managers.

We organize our own workshops to upgrade executive skills and merchandise know-how. But we also send people to outside seminars, particularly people slated to become store managers and vice presidents.

In terms of compensation, we pay competitive wages and give adequate fringe benefits. Promotion depends on turnover of staff and also on corporate growth, particularly new stores. Our management turnover is 12 percent, which is okay. But many executives are married women who stay in town for the jobs of their husbands. So this is no real indication of job satisfaction. I don't know what will happen when women's growing freedom and mobility, as reflected in our young female managers, begin to reach our middle management ranks. We may not have enough ready opportunities for our brightest people. They may quit rather than wait around for an eventual opening.

THE APPOINTMENT OF A STRATEGIC PLAN TASK FORCE

At the end of July 1977, Mr. Hoffman and the two executive vice presidents agreed among themselves that the strategic planning exercise should move to implementation. They decided to assemble a task force to develop a strategic plan which they would review, before it was communicated to the Board of Directors for adoption.

The following executives were appointed to the task force:

Chairman, vice president marketing
Vice president store
Vice president GMM
Vice president GMM
Vice president GMM
Vice president personnel
Senior vice president finance, treasurer
Vice president store planning

They provided the task force with the following objectives:

- To delineate the impact of important trends on Woodies' retail department store operations;

- To outline the areas where Woodies' plans and policies were inadequate; and

- To formulate plans and policies suitable for guiding Woodies' operations for the next ten to fifteen years.

They also decided not to restrict the task force in the scope of its work, and provided the task force only with a general criterion:

- To assure that the Company would continue to generate earnings attractive to creditors and stockholders.

They finally established the following schedule of reviews:

- First week of September: Results of trend analysis
- Last week of September: Identification of inadequacies
- Last week of October: First draft of revised plans and policies
- Last week of November: First draft of strategic plan

After agreement had been reached on these questions, the three senior executives briefed the task force on what was expected of them. When they had dismissed the task force, they were confident that they would receive a workable strategic plan by the end of 1977.

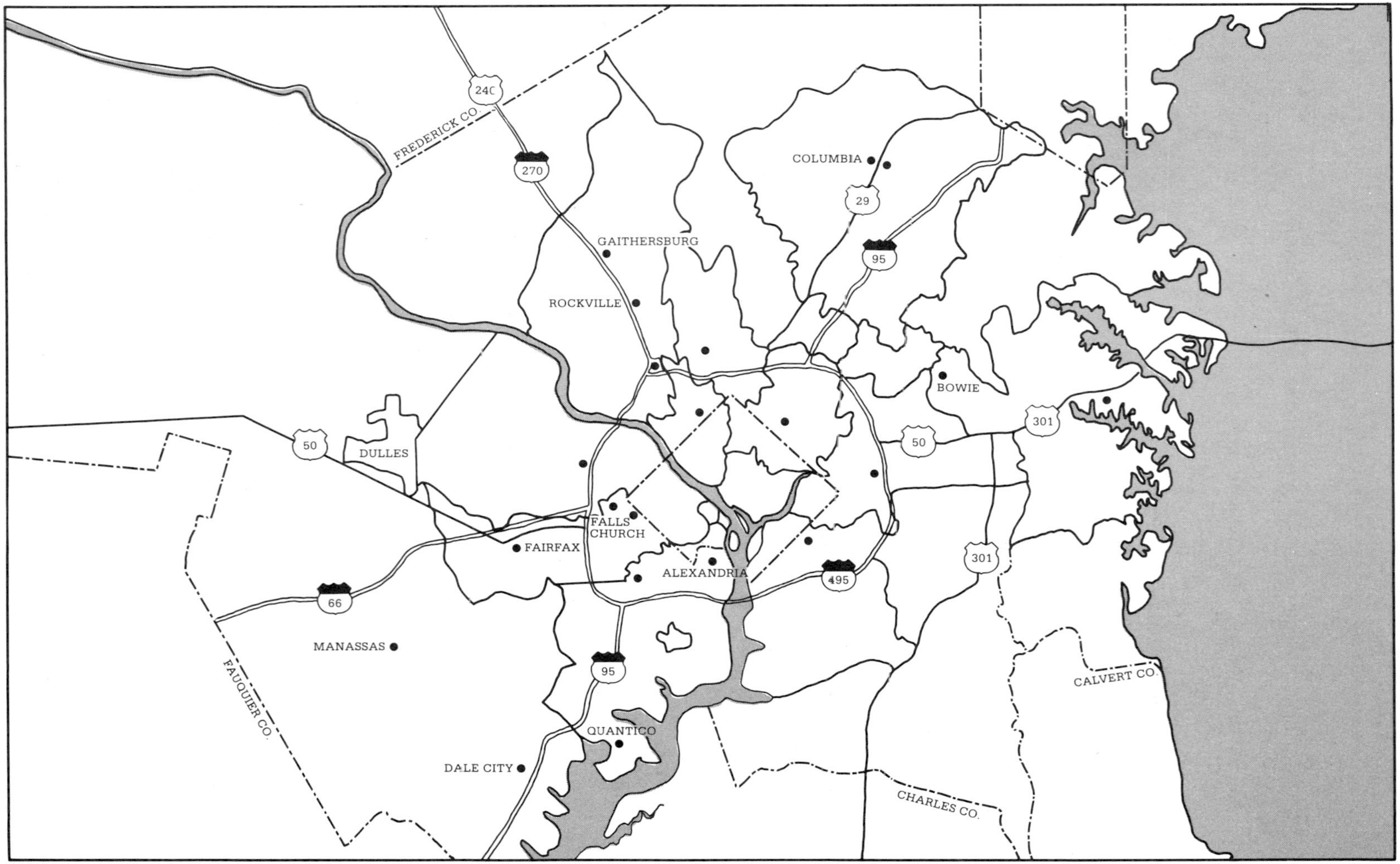

EXHIBIT 1

WOODWARD & LOTHROP TRADE AREA MAP

EXHIBIT 1 (continued)
WOODWARD & LOTHROP STORES

Washington District of Columbia 744,400 sq. ft. Opened 1887[1]	Prince Georges Plaza Prince Georges County, Maryland 149,000 sq. ft. Opened 1966
Pentagon Arlington County, Virginia 9,000 sq. ft. Opened 1946	Iverson Mall Prince Georges County, Maryland 173,800 sq. ft. Opened 1967
Chevy Chase Montgomery County, Maryland 178,200 sq. ft. Opened 1950	Tysons Corner Fairfax County, Virginia 229,200 sq. ft. Opened 1968
Seven Corners Fairfax County, Virginia 161,600 sq. ft. Opened 1956 Home Store added 1964	Columbia Howard County, Maryland 170,600 sq. ft. Opened 1971
Wheaton Plaza Montgomery County, Maryland 218,800 sq. ft. Opened 1960	Landover Mall Prince Georges County, Maryland 156,300 sq. ft. Opened 1972
Annapolis Anne Arundel County, Maryland 140,000 sq. ft. Opened 1964 Expanded 1974	Montgomery Mall Montgomery County, Maryland 150,000 sq. ft. Opened 1976
Landmark Alexandria, Virginia 158,900 sq. ft. Opened 1965	

[1]Between 1880 and 1887 Woodies operated a store at a different location.

EXHIBIT 2

Ten Year Financial & Operating Summary—Woodward & Lothrop, Inc.

(in thousands except per share data)	January 29, 1977	January 31, 1976	February 1, 1975	February 2, 1974	February 3, 1973[2]	January 29, 1972	January 30, 1971	January 31, 1970	August 1, 1970	August 2, 1969	August 3, 1968[2]
Summary of Operations											
Net sales	$241,389	$218,468	$187,451	$175,239	$169,005	$153,110	$136,384	$127,594	$130,527	$126,074	$121,881
Cost of merchandise sold including buying and occupancy costs	166,229	152,939	132,440	125,437	121,130	109,334	98,341	91,809	94,346	91,665	88,032
Selling, general and administrative expenses	48,897	42,498	40,012	37,657	35,435	30,305	26,617	25,485	26,114	24,587	24,094
Interest expense	3,627	2,910	2,548	2,612	2,210	1,713	1,850	1,740	1,839	1,801	1,654
	218,753	198,347	175,000	165,706	158,775	141,357	126,808	119,034	122,299	118,053	113,780
Earnings before income taxes	22,639	20,121	12,451	9,533	10,230	11,753	9,576	8,560	8,228	8,021	8,101
Percent of sales	9.4	9.2	6.6	5.4	6.1	7.7	7.0	6.7	6.3	6.4	6.6
Federal and state income taxes	10,900	10,320	5,900	4,700	4,446	6,045	4,970	4,565	4,367	4,252	3,850
Net earnings	$ 11,736	$ 9,801	$ 6,551	$ 4,833	$ 5,784	$ 5,708	$ 4,606	$ 3,995	$ 3,861	$ 3,769	$ 4,251
Percent of sales	4.9	4.5	3.5	2.8	3.4	3.7	3.4	3.1	3.0	3.0	3.5
Net earnings per common share	$ 4.89	$ 4.10	$ 2.69	$ 1.95	$ 2.35	$ 2.34	$ 1.87	$ 1.65	$ 1.58	$ 1.57	$ 1.77
Common dividends per share	$ 1.40	$ 1.37	$ 1.07	$ 1.07	$ 1.03	$ 1.00	$ .91	$ 1.14[3]	$ 1.14[3]	$ .91	$ .91

Operating Statistics	$	$	$	$	$	$	$	$	$	$	$
Preferred dividends	75	77	79	83	84	84	86	111[3]	110[3]	89	91
Earnings available to common shareholders	11,661	9,724	6,472	4,750	5,700	5,624	4,520[4]	3,884	3,751	3,680	4,160
Common dividends	3,340	3,261	2,568	2,624	2,516	2,424	2,192	2,695[3]	2,726[3]	2,130	2,130
Earnings retained	8,321	6,463	3,904	2,126	3,182	3,200	2,833	1,189	1,025	1,550	2,030
Depreciation	4,436	4,002	3,775	3,683	3,633	3,297	3,068	2,829	2,953	2,856	2,550
Real estate rent	2,615	2,529	2,214	2,060	2,209	2,146	1,890	1,825	1,913	1,815	1,701
Taxes other than income taxes	5,718	4,917	4,494	4,197	3,611	3,130	2,882	2,702	2,882	2,575	2,488
Capital expenditures	9,895	9,769	11,641	2,653	9,933	7,876	3,997	2,367	3,429	1,644	5,840
Year End Financial Position											
Accounts receivable	52,107	48,251	37,477	33,236	33,765	27,082	27,566	27,423	21,955	22,795	22,066
Merchandise inventories at LIFO cost	34,402	29,151	23,112	23,121	25,667	24,123	20,296	19,577	20,105	19,036	19,981
Working capital	56,512	46,800	35,053	41,587	39,799	34,078	37,100	36,597	34,523	24,615	22,730
Current ratio	2.47	2.45	2.29	3.04	2.71	2.43	3.22	3.08	3.48	2.17	1.96
Property and equipment, net	67,396	61,939	56,496	48,937	50,119	44,026	39,520	38,903	39,422	38,955	40,176
Long-term debt (noncurrent)	43,157	37,197	27,483	29,769	32,056	23,841	25,604	27,368	25,871	17,635	18,913
Preferred stock	1,502	1,506	1,540	1,613	1,678	1,699	1,716	1,746	1,738	1,761	1,809
Common shareholders' equity	73,832	65,369	58,610	55,640	53,477	49,609	46,058	43,106	42,849	41,095	39,529
Per common share	30.86	27.44	24.76	22.75	21.83	20.47	19.08	17.84	17.75	17.50	16.54
Number of common shares outstanding	2,392	2,382	2,367	2,445	2,447	2,419	2,409	2,412	2,409	2,343	2,343

[1] Per share data has been restated to reflect the effect of the 10% stock dividend in 1975.

[2] 53 weeks; all other years have 52 weeks.

[3] Due to change in dividend dates, an additional dividend was accrued in 1970. The common dividend was at the annual rate of 91¢.

[4] Excluding net earnings of $505 or 21¢ per share related to an extraordinary item.

SOURCE: Woodward & Lothrop, Inc.: 1977 Annual Report

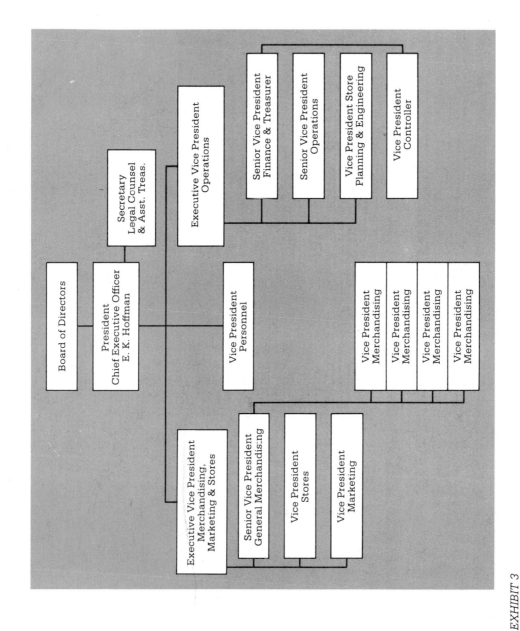

EXHIBIT 3
WOODIES' TOP MANAGEMENT ORGANIZATION, 1977

EXHIBIT 4

The Metropolitan Washington Retail Market of the Seventies
(Population, Income, Retail Sales, 12/31/72, 74, 76)

	Units	Metro Washington			District of Columbia		
		1972	1974	1976	1972	1974	1976
I. POPULATION							
Total Population	(000's)	3,037	3,082	3,057	746	718	705
Percent of U.S.	(%)	1.45	1.45	1.42	.36	.34	.33
Median Age	(yrs)	N.A.	28.4	27.9	N.A.	30.5	29.2
Total Households[1]	(000's)	986	1,042	1,057	270	287	285
II. EFFECTIVE BUYING INCOME[2]							
Total EBI	($ Mil)	15,585	19,073	22,361	4,013	4,503	4,980
Median Household EBI	($)	11,194	16,024	18,548	10,139	12,193	13,601
Percent of Households with EBI							
$ 0- 7,999	(%)	29.9	18.1	15.1	36.3	29.4	25.7
$ 8-14,999	(%)	39.5	27.5	22.6	35.1	31.8	29.9
$15-24,999	(%)	21.5	32.9	31.9	19.1	24.5	25.8
$25 or over	(%)	9.1	21.5	30.4	9.5	14.3	18.6
Buying Power Index[3]		1.81	1.75	1.70	.48	.40	.37
III. RETAIL SALES[4]							
Total Retail Sales	($ Mil)	7,847	9,067	10,374	2,317	1,887	1,994
Food	($ Mil)	1,569	1,682	1,978	356	332	353
General Merchandise	($ Mil)	1,475	1,403	1,565	281	213	208
Furniture, Furnishings, Appliances	($ Mil)	400	552	601	156	98	90

NOTES: [1] Households are units made up of families or unrelated individuals occupying a house, apartment, or a room regarded as a housing unit under the rules of the 1970 Census of Population.
[2] Effective Buying Income (EBI), a classification that removes from Disposable Personal Income compensation to government personnel stationed overseas.
[3] Buying Power Index is a weighted index of population, EBI, and retail sales, measuring a market's purchasing ability expressed as a % of the U.S. potential, where the weights are 2, 5, and 3, respectively.
[4] Total Retail Sales are sales revenues of retail establishments minus refunds and allowances for returns plus sales taxes.

SOURCE: Sales and Marketing Management, July 1973, 1975, and 1977.

EXHIBIT 5

The Metropolitan Washington, D.C., Retail Market in 1981
(Population, Income, Retail Sales by County as of 12/31/81)

COUNTY	POPULATION		INCOME		RETAIL SALES		
	Total Population (1,000s)	Total Households (1,000s)	Total Effective Buying Income (Mil $)	Average EBI per Household ($)	Total Retail Sales (Mil $)	Retail Sales per Household ($)	Buying Power Index (100.0 = Total U.S.)
Washington Area	3,109.0	1,144.7	35,146.8	30,704	15,498.6	13,540	1.66
District of Columbia	694.9	301.5	7,057.4	23,408	2,267.1	7,520	.31
Charles, Md.	65.0	19.5	622.5	31,925	370.8	19,020	.03
Montgomery, Md.	607.2	215.8	7,283.4	33,751	2,887.9	13,382	.33
Prince Georges, Md.	676.6	235.3	6,522.0	27,718	4,295.5	18,256	.35
Alexandria, Va.	106.8	47.9	1,339.9	27,974	790.6	16,506	.06
Arlington, Va.	144.8	66.7	2,362.2	35,416	945.2	14,172	.10
Fairfax, Va.	541.1	178.1	6,905.03	38,771	2,574.6	14,456	.30
Fairfax City, Va.	21.9	7.2	303.9	42,219	395.2	54,896	.02
Falls Church, Va.	11.6	4.9	165.4	33,768	213.1	43,497	.01
Loudoun, Va.	64.6	21.4	591.0	27,619	187.1	8,744	.02
Manassas, Va.	11.5	3.6	144.7	40,205	145.6	40,471	.01
Manassas Park, Va.	11.6	2.7	92.2	34,167	13.6	5,040	.01
Prince William, Va.	151.4	40.1	1,756.7	43,809	411.7	10,269	.07

NOTE: These data are projections.

SOURCE: *Sales and Marketing Management*, Oct. 24, 1977, p. 72.

EXHIBIT 6

Long Term Changes in Metropolitan Washington Retail Market (Population and Personal Consumption Expenditures, 1970–1990)					
	1970	1975	1980	1985	1990
I. POPULATION			(In thousands)		
a. Changes in Population					
Total Resident Population	2,920	3,036	3,135	3,241	3,327
Natural Increase	186	140	126	143	127
Net Migration	234	−24	−27	−37	−41
Net Change (prior 5 yrs.)	420	116	99	106	86
b. Age Distribution (year end)					
00–04 yrs.	261	203	212	240	235
05–14 yrs.	589	615	554	503	538
15–24 yrs.	537	593	647	670	606
25–44 yrs.	802	817	863	929	1,035
45–64 yrs.	549	584	593	586	555
65 up yrs.	175	224	268	313	357
c. Sex by Race Distribution					
Male, White	1,059	1,093	1,119	1,150	1,174
Non-white	355	373	389	401	414
Total Male	1,414	1,466	1,508	1,551	1,588
Female, White	1,115	1,156	1,191	1,230	1,263
Nonwhite	391	414	437	458	476
Total Female	1,506	1,570	1,628	1,688	1,739
d. Composition of Households					
+ Total Families	703	762	822	884	921
of which Husband/Wife Families	598	628	674	719	742
+ Unrelated Individuals	293	362	403	445	473
of which Female Unrelated Individual	167	197	215	233	244
= Total Consumer Units	996	1,124	1,225	1,329	1,394
− of which Secondary Individuals	81	96	94	90	76
= Total Households (year end)	915	1,028	1,131	1,239	1,318
II. PERSONAL CONSUMPTION EXPENDITURES			Millions, 1972 dollars		
Total Consumption (Annual)	11,595	13,668	17,026	20,379	N.A.
Food & Tobacco	2,512	2,779	3,016	3,164	N.A.
Clothing & Accessories	1,037	1,195	1,397	1,572	N.A.
Personal Care	183	203	222	236	N.A.
Housing Operation	1,748	2,128	2,808	3,524	N.A.
Recreation	740	914	1,204	1,510	N.A.
Foreign Travel	38	33	93	140	N.A.

NOTE: Sums are adjusted to rounding errors; data for 1980–1990 are projections.

SOURCE: Bureau of the Census: Series P-20, No. 305, Table 41, p. 130f, January 1977.

EXHIBIT 7

Retail Sales of Major Department Stores in Metropolitan Washington, D.C., 1971–76 (Millions of Dollars)						
	1971	1972	1973	1974	1975	1976
Total Department Store Retail Sales	888	976	1087	1161	1231	1330
Woodward & Lothrop	153	169	175	187	218	241
Sears Roebuck & Company	165	175	185	200	250	260
Hecht Company	140	155	155	170	200	220
Montgomery Ward	60	90	10	125	150	175
J.C. Penney Company	33	55	60	75	80	120
Lord and Taylor	25	23	24	25	35	37
Garfinkel's	39	45	45	47	50	55
Saks Fifth Avenue	7	8	10	12	18	21
Landsburgh's	30 +	30 +	closed	—	—	—
Zayre	N.A.	45	54	65	60	N.A.
Giant Food Inc.	N.A.	60	65	74	74	N.A.
Bloomingdale's	—	—	—	—	—	30
Neiman Marcus	—	—	—	—	—	12

SOURCE: *Women's Wear Daily:* 6/12/72, 7/9/73, 7/1/74, 7/14/75, 6/21/76, 6/13/77.

JOHNS-MANVILLE CORPORATION

Colleen Emry

INTRODUCTION

Johns-Manville, a large, multinational corporation located on the Ken-Caryl Ranch 18 miles southwest of Denver, Colorado, is one of the world's largest manufacturers and sellers of insulation products. The company is the largest producer of asbestos[1] outside the Soviet Union via ownership of the Jeffrey Mine in Canada, and mines more diatomite[2] than any other firm in the world. Eighteen hundred different products marketed in the United States, Canada, and 15 other countries contribute to annual sales in excess of $2 billion. Major product categories include: fiber glass products, wood and paper products, nonfiber glass insulation, asbestos fiber, and industrial and specialty products and services.

Gross sales from operations in 1979 were $2.28 billion earning the company a net profit margin of five percent. Percentages of sales and net profit by business segment at June 30, 1979 are listed below:

EXHIBIT 1
**Percentage of Net Sales and Income
by Business Segment
(June 30, 1979)**

Business Segment	Net Sales	Income
Fiber glass products	22%	28%
Wood & paper products	23%	21%
Pipe products & systems	14%	7%
Roofing products	11%	3%
Nonfiberglass insulations	11%	5%
Asbestos fiber	6%	21%
Industrial & specialty products & services	13%	15%

SOURCE: Johns-Manville Investor Reference Book, 1979

Johns-Manville products supply five major markets: residential building (23%), nonresidential building (19%), other construction (21%), industrial production of components, materials, and supplies used in connection with current production (31%), and paper and packaging (6%).[3] Even though sales of these products are dependent on current demand levels within the construction industry, their appeal to diverse markets (residential, municipal, industrial, sewage and water systems) somewhat evens out the impact of cyclical and economic variations.

The peak sales period for residential fiber glass insulation, remodeling and repair, and retrofit products is generally between the months of August and November. Federal and state tax incentives, higher governmental thermal efficiency requirements, and increasing residential fuel prices should increase demand for this product line in the future. The reroofing market is relatively stable, while new roofing construction fluctuates more closely with housing starts. Pipe products and systems sales vary seasonally with building activity, and with municipal and government spending. However, the cost and availability of raw material (PVC resin for polyvinyl chloride) can be and has been a problem in this production area, cutting into profit margins. Asbestos fiber is sold to both new and replacement markets and is supplied primarily from the Jeffrey Mine. Current monetary exchange rates, mining costs, and local (Canadian) taxes do affect profit margins but don't curtail marketing of the fiber. The mine now has enough ore reserves to last until 1990.

Johns-Manville management currently predicts that major growth in company sales will come from proprietary products where less competition exists than in current markets. Also, because of the current economic slump, about one-fourth of total sales are generated from remodeling and repair construction in lieu of new building starts.[4]

HISTORY

Henry Ward Johns began his roofing felt business in 1858. In 1901, Henry Johns and the Manville Covering Company merged their respective companies to form the H. W. Johns-Manville Company. The Jeffrey Mine and Asbestos and Asbestic Company, Ltd., of Quebec, Canada, were acquired in 1916 enabling them to expand their line of roof coatings, pipe coverings, woods, metals and fabric business. Stock was issued and JM became a public corporation on the New York Stock Exchange in 1927. The company continued to expand and diversify making several acquisitions of related businesses during the next 50 years, including the largest, purest source of diatomaceous earth properties in the world located in California. Capital expenditures of $3.4 million were made in 1936 to expand manufacturing facilities resulting in increased production of rock wool, asbestos cement, and better mining equipment.

By 1942, JM had shifted 80% of its production to wartime purposes. Products manufactured included battleship insulation, packing and gaskets for airplanes, marine sheathing for troop and supply ships, switchboards for destroyers, brake linings, packing for submarines, and camouflage. Sales of these products generated sufficient profits for the company to open new manufacturing plants and increase production facilities in others at a cost approximating $60 million. A fiberglass insulations company was purchased in 1958 which grew to become the company's largest business segment.

By 1970, annual sales totalled $578.2 million. However, these sales figures reflected an annual growth rate, during the last 20 years, of four percent lower than growth in the Gross National Product. Virtually no debt had been utilized in financing operations or capital expenditures. In fact, in 1970, long-term debt was virtually zero.

An old-line style of management of JM was reflected in the conservative company image and methods of operation. Though the management team was production-oriented, little time was devoted to the planning processes, long- or short-range. Advertising expenditures had been minimal and there existed no formal strategies for developing and marketing products. Inside executives and outside observers often referred to the executive atmosphere in the 1960s as "stodgy, starchy, and sleepy." One Wall Street analyst, Carmine Muratore, commented on the dreary JM offices, "Desks were always clean, guys had nothing in their out-boxes. There were no signs of life. It was like somebody had just died up there."[5]

By 1969, high level corporate directors recognized that their company was prime for corporate merger or acquisition by another company and decided they needed to strengthen internally in order to secure ownership. The key to doing this lay in the development and implementation of long-range planning policies and strategies. As an initial step, Richard Goodwin, a private consultant who taught "A Systems Approach to Business," at the university level was hired to develop a planning system in one of JM's divisions. His work impressed the management of JM so much that they offered him a permanent position with the company in April 1969, as vice-president for corporate planning.

Goodwin earned his Ph.D. in experimental psychology from Stanford University writing his dissertation on perception and learning. He spent 10 years at Rand Corporation and its spin-off, Systems Development Corporation, managing the development of the design and software for the Strategic Air Command's computer-based command and control system.[6] Later he became an independent consultant and teacher. Goodwin presented himself in a low key, personal manner but displayed an exceptional business sense. His personal and professional attributes exemplified the man Johns-Manville management felt could bring their company into a more progressive mode.

THE GROWING YEARS

In December 1970, after being with the company only 18 months, Dick Goodwin was named president and chief executive of Johns-Manville. He had demonstrated, in a short period of time, his ability to get along with the other executives as well as other capabilities they were looking for in selecting a new individual to lead the company forward. To many, this promotion implied the beginning of a reawakening process for the stagnant company.

Goodwin was a more progressive individual than previous JM presidents and immediately took steps to enhance the company's public visibility. He made many personal contacts, expanded advertising programs, and promoted corporate involvement in community and civic functions. Goodwin's internal reorganization activities included the creation of a position of senior vice president for corporate marketing and growth planning. The company began to make plans and develop long-range strategies for planned product success and improved profitability. The 12 corporate divisions were reduced to six, centralizing several administrative functions in anticipation of more control and greater cost efficiencies. Studies were undertaken to identify the company's most profitable products and those which had the greatest potential to increase market share. These profitable areas, including the building insulation business, were expanded through acquisitions of other firms and allocated capital expenditures.

The recession and new construction slump in 1974 resulted in a substantial decline in the demand for general building and pipe products. Nationwide cutbacks in housing, industrial, and municipal construction resulted in underutilization of plant capacity at JM. Sales in the insulation market, though, were not as badly affected because of the reinsulation demand. The roofing replacement market also remained fairly stable. However, a landslide occurred at the Jeffrey Mine resulting in many extraordinary expenses and delayed product shipments.

During this period JM began utilizing debt as a financial tool in their efforts to broaden markets and diversify product lines. Before the end of the year (1974), long-term company debt reached an all time high of $141.9 million accounting for about 25 percent of total capitalization.[7] However, as debt grew, inflation also brought increased interest rates and operational costs.

By 1975, JM was involved in six major business[8]:

Thermal insulation	26 (% of sales)
Pipe products & systems	18
General building products	16
Roofing products	16
Industrial products (packings, gaskets, oil seals, brake shoes)	12
Mining (asbestos, diatomite, perline, & talc)	12

The company was the nation's leading producer of asbestos, cement pipe, polyvinyl-chloride plastic pipe and one of the world's major suppliers of asbestos fiber. In addition, they were the second largest producer of fiberglass insulation products. JM employees totalled 26,600 and the company operated 106 plants, 13 mines, and 38 sales offices.[9]

Goodwin continued to emphasize both expansion and image. Further diversification was made into real estate land development, golf cart manufacturing, irrigation sprinklers, and industrial lighting systems. These new business segments represented a change in the company's past strategies of producing and mining only those products basic to the insulation and building markets. Goodwin's influence not only brought about internal reorganization and management changes but seemed to signify an expanded view of the company's mission. Instead of continuing to operate as a conservative, small product-line, vertically integrated firm, plans were being put into motion to diversify into a multinational conglomerate, manufacturing products that bore no relationship to existing product lines, and which went beyond existing management expertise.

THE MOVE TO COLORADO

It was during these growth years that JM executives began seriously to consider relocation from the New York area. Senior executives were presently scattered in many locations throughout the country making meetings difficult. The New York general headquarters were overcrowded and additional space would be needed if facilities were to remain in a single location. Feasibility studies indicated that it would be just as costly to move across town as across country. Goodwin also realized that a long distance move would provide the ideal opportunity for him to eliminate personnel which he felt were no longer needed or were a hindrance to JM's attainment of newly formed goals and objectives. An attractive setting for corporate headquarters would also help in the recruitment of new managers.

After reviewing several sites, the 10,000 acre (15.6 square mile) Ken-Caryl Ranch located 18 miles southwest of Denver, Colorado, was chosen for JM's new home. This seemingly ideal location boasted a good climate, excellent educational institutions nearby in the city, and plenty of of leisure time activities. Goodwin was an avid skier and the mountain slopes were within driving distance. This geographically central location would also allow more efficient travel and communication networking.

The people of Denver wanted JM to locate in their community. In addition to the company's adding to the economic development of the region, Colorado businessmen liked Goodwin, thinking of him as a personable and sensitive psychologist. They also respected his willingness to stand up and be counted on controversial public issues.

After finalizing the new location site, Goodwin made the following statement, "The ranch will be developed slowly and with painstaking care to ensure that the architectural quality is as high as possible and that the environment is protected. We have every reason to believe that we can carry it out as an economically sound project and show that taste and profit can go hand in hand."[10] Statements of this type made him popular with the local environmentalist groups as well as the business leaders.

The master relocation plan called for the development of an entire $182.2 million Ken-Caryl community on 1,500 acres which would include homes, recreational facilities, and a shopping center.[11] The entire project was expected to take 10 years to build. Care was taken to conserve nearby forests and wildlife.

To promote community interest a design contest was held for the new world headquarters building (760,000 square feet) which was completed in 1976. It is a seven level structure located on a 200-acre site. Facilities, in addition to office space, include a corporate library, employee cafeteria, training center, employee relations center and fitness center. The latter consists of a pool, exercise stations, sauna, locker room and multipurpose room.

The research and development facility built nearby was started in 1971 and completed in 1973. It has already been expanded beyond the original 281,000 square feet and employs more than 400 people.

The process of relocating from New York to Colorado occurred on a gradual basis. Families were given paid trips to Denver to find new homes and orientations of the surrounding area were given by local Denver Chamber of Commerce members. The company made every effort to ease the transition process and even helped employees with their relocation financing. As a result, very few JM employees became disenchanted and subsequently moved back to the east. Those managers whom Goodwin felt were no longer beneficial to the company, were simply not asked to make the move. Total company relocation costs approximated $70 million.[12]

The new Denver setting gave the company a whole new image and, along with the change in location, came more changes in corporate life-style. Visiting customers were brought by helicopter to the ranch and given a tour of the acreage by jeep. The mansion's chef prepared gourmet meals and good liquor flowed freely. The atmosphere presented an ideal setting in which to close the big deals.

Corporate management was more outgoing and the general internal atmosphere appeared relaxed and communicative. Francis May, a top executive, commented, "It isn't just that the company is so different. It's that we've changed so much, or at least it seems that way. We're more outgoing, and we talk more with one another. Our productivity is much higher out here too."[13] Goodwin's casual style of dress (sports jacket instead of three-piece suits) and longish hair exemplified corporate life-style. Many thought of him as having an uncommon flair for corporate sportsmanship. "The old bosses used to be very autocratic," explained Everett Truax, a general manager in the building materials division. "That meant everybody down the line was autocratic, including me. Things don't work that way anymore. It's more relaxed, and so am I. People speak up more often out here because they know everybody else is more willing to listen to them."[14]

Between 1970 and 1975, Goodwin had facilitated 11 acquisitions and 12 divestitures. JM's capital spending increased from $45 million to $119 million[15]; long-term debt from near zero to $186 million. Because 30 percent of the New York employees had not relocated to Denver, many new people came to the company during this period. Sales had nearly doubled to $1.1 billion. As one vice president commented on Goodwin, "The best thing he ever did was to get us out of New York. He put us into a totally different atmosphere."[16]

Financial data for the years 1972–1975 are presented on the following pages.

GOODWIN'S DEPARTURE

Unfortunately, Dick Goodwin never had the opportunity to work as Johns-Manville's chief executive in the new Denver facility. In September 1976, Goodwin was contacted by William F. May, director of JM, on the eve of the company's next board meeting, who asked him to resign from his $108,000 yearly salaried position. When Goodwin inquired about the reason for the request, he was told, "Under the bylaws of this corporation, we don't have to give you a reason."[17] Observers, however, have since speculated that JM's longstanding conservative board disapproved of Goodwin's apparent liberal use of authority as the chief executive. Many drastic changes had occurred over the last six years including the incorporation of styles and philosophies into the company which were 180 degrees from those which had been perpetrated by JM's founders. For a company once typified as stodgy, these changes had occurred very quickly. In addition, during the six years Goodwin was CEO sales had almost doubled while earnings remained flat.

Shortly before his resignation Goodwin decided, against board consensus, to break longstanding exclusive financial ties with their investment banker,

RESULTS BY MAJOR BUSINESS SEGMENTS	1975	1974	1973	1972
NET SALES				
Thermal Insulations	$ 323,134	$ 294,445	$244,616	$195,795
Pipe Products and Systems	192,416	231,794	164,106	147,194
Mining and Minerals	140,860	117,682	97,492	89,561
Roofing Products	169,928	168,122	134,855	115,113
General Building Products	166,462	172,773	167,073	162,777
Industrial and Other Products	114,212	120,692	97,275	88,266
Total	$1,107,012	$1,105,508	$905,417	$798,706
EARNINGS BEFORE INCOME TAXES, EXTRAORDINARY ITEM AND UNUSUAL NONOPERATING CHARGES*				
Thermal Insulations	$ 22,984	$ 15,273	$ 24,827	$ 23,092
Pipe Products and Systems	(3,665)	23,439	5,795	13,898
Mining and Minerals	20,838	22,446	17,369	18,102
Roofing Products	17,981	18,127	15,854	14,240
General Building Products	2,762	7,407	13,320	10,969
Industrial and Other Products	9,473	7,215	4,514	2,668
Non-Product Related Expenses	(1,367)	(1,117)	(1,699)	(251)
Total	$ 69,006	$ 92,790	$ 79,980	$ 82,718
EARNINGS BEFORE INCOME TAXES AND EXTRAORDINARY ITEM				
Thermal Insulations	$ 23,098	$ 15,273	$ 24,827	$ 23,092
Pipe Products and Systems	(3,817)	23,423	5,795	13,898
Mining and Minerals	20,882	21,872	17,369	18,102
Roofing Products	17,367	18,127	15,854	14,240
General Building Products	2,534	2,725	19,230	10,969
Industrial and Other Products	10,883	6,859	4,895	2,668
Non-Product Related Expenses	(1,209)	(1,117)	(1,699)	(251)
Total	$ 69,738	$ 87,162	$ 86,271	$ 82,718

*The unusual nonoperating charges consisted of asset dispositions, reduction of intangible assets and the provision for Flextran claims.

EXHIBIT 2
JOHNS-MANVILLE CORPORATION
Sales and Earnings
SOURCE: Johns-Manville 1971 Annual Report

	(Thousands of Dollars)	
	December 31	
ASSETS	**1976**	**1975**
CURRENT ASSETS		
Cash (including time deposits of $9,580,000 in 1976, $2,565,000 in 1975)............................	$ 25,064	$ 23,981
Marketable securities, at cost (approximates market).	66,132	391
Accounts receivable (net of allowances of $4,909,000 in 1976, $4,995,000 in 1975)....................	239,318	205,784
Inventories......................................	144,379	145,463
Prepaid expenses (principally deferred income taxes)	26,084	20,604
Total Current Assets......................	500,977	396,223
INVESTMENTS IN AND ADVANCES TO ASSOCIATED COMPANIES (principally outside U.S.).............	28,794	37,295
INVESTMENT IN AND ADVANCES TO REAL ESTATE SUBSIDIARY....................................	34,088	21,577
PROPERTY, PLANT AND EQUIPMENT, at cost		
Land and land improvements....................	63,918	64,966
Buildings.......................................	259,157	237,567
Machinery and equipment.......................	597,816	594,340
	920,891	896,873
Less, Accumulated depreciation and depletion	326,887	316,148
	594,004	580,725
DEFERRED CHARGES AND OTHER ASSETS..........	30,337	41,560
	$1,188,200	$1,077,380

EXHIBIT 3
JOHNS-MANVILLE CORPORATION
Consolidated Balance Sheet
SOURCE: Johns-Manville 1976 Annual Report.

Morgan Stanley, by hiring another firm to handle a stock offering. Many friendships and loyalties had developed between these two companies who had worked so closely for so many years. Goodwin had also taken steps to increase board membership. This latter action may have been construed by the existing board as a move to weaken individual board members' power and bring some people to the governing body whose views were more in line with Goodwin's

While Goodwin recognized that there had been some problems in his relationship with the board, i.e., personality conflicts and disapproval of some of his flamboyant methods, the request for resignation took him totally by surprise. He attributes the board's decision to the older, conservative element and, as part of his

	(Thousands of Dollars)	
	December 31	
LIABILITIES	**1976**	**1975**
CURRENT LIABILITIES		
Commercial paper..............................		$ 43,075
Other short-term debt...........................	$ 20,380	27,252
Accounts payable..............................	57,954	53,277
Wages and compensation........................	31,582	31,274
Income taxes...................................	31,506	21,750
Other taxes....................................	10,747	9,111
Other accrued liabilities........................	36,999	23,299
Total Current Liabilities...................	189,168	209,038
LONG-TERM DEBT..............................	208,161	186,322
OTHER NON-CURRENT LIABILITIES...............	10,731	9,227
DEFERRED INCOME TAXES.......................	108,125	92,281
	516,185	496,868
SHAREHOLDERS' EQUITY		
COMMON STOCK, $2.50 par, 50,000,000 shares authorized, 21,703,235 and 19,203,235 shares issued at December 31, 1976 and 1975, respectively.......	188,493	124,635
EARNINGS REINVESTED..........................	492,153	466,916
	680,646	591,551
Less, Cost of treasury stock, 1976—282,127 shares, 1975—360,841 shares...........................	8,631	11,039
	672,015	580,512
	$1,188,200	$1,077,380

EXHIBIT 3 continued

settlement agreement, has made himself unavailable for comment on the subject. Currently, Goodwin is in Denver trying to build his own insulation business.

A NEW PRESIDENT

John A. McKinney, then 52 and a senior vice president and top legal advisor, became president of Johns-Manville. No chief executive officer was appointed and, instead, a six-man committee was formed, reporting to McKinney who in turn reported directly to the board. McKinney is a U.S. Naval Academy graduate who joined Johns-Manville in 1951 as a patent lawyer.

With McKinney in the top position, several changes in company modus operandi occurred almost immediately, i.e., reversion to banker gray suits among the

(Thousands of Dollars, except Per Share Amounts)

EARNINGS	1976	1975
REVENUES		
Net sales...................................	$1,308,771	$1,107,012
Royalties and fees.............................	5,113	5,220
Equity in earnings of associated companies........	2,721	2,270
Dividends from associated companies carried at cost	1,312	1,827
Other income, net.............................	3,242	688
Total..................................	1,321,159	1,117,017
COSTS AND EXPENSES		
Cost of sales.................................	983,431	852,786
Selling, general and administrative................	166,159	151,842
Research, development and engineering...........	25,236	24,393
Total..................................	1,174,826	1,029,021
INCOME FROM OPERATIONS................	146,333	87,996
GAIN (LOSS) ON DISPOSITIONS OF ASSETS........	(19,735)	732
REDUCTION OF INTANGIBLE ASSETS..............	(6,124)	
PROVISION FOR FLEXTRAN CLAIMS...............	(4,100)	
INTEREST EXPENSE.............................	(15,153)	(18,990)
EARNINGS BEFORE INCOME TAXES.........	101,221	69,738
INCOME TAXES		
Current......................................	38,589	25,727
Deferred.....................................	9,215	5,598
Total..................................	47,804	31,325
NET EARNINGS...........................	$ 53,417	$ 38,413
NET EARNINGS PER SHARE......................	$2.64	$2.04

EARNINGS REINVESTED		
EARNINGS REINVESTED AT BEGINNING OF YEAR..	$ 466,916	$ 452,393
NET EARNINGS..................................	53,417	38,413
	520,333	490,806
DIVIDENDS ($1.35 per share in 1976 and $1.20 per share in 1975).............................	(27,251)	(22,589)
LOSS ON DISPOSITIONS OF TREASURY STOCK....	(929)	(1,301)
EARNINGS REINVESTED AT END OF YEAR........	$ 492,153	$ 466,916

EXHIBIT 4
JOHNS-MANVILLE CORPORATION
Consolidated Earnings and Earnings Reinvested
SOURCE: Johns-Manville 1976 Annual Report.

executives, no more first class airfares, and abstinence from liquor in the executive dining room until after 5:00 P.M. (liquor has subsequently been banned altogether). McKinney announced that he would continue to follow the major outlines of Goodwin's five-year profit plan but would place more emphasis on the bottom line (profit) and JM's basic business (building products: chiefly insulation, roofing, pipe, and asbestos fiber). While sales had risen substantially over the last six years, $578.2 million to $1.1 billion (91%), net profits were only up 15 percent.

McKinney cut product lines and divested business segments which showed little promise of earning satisfactory profits. Facilities shut down included a pipe production plant, a sprinkler maker, an airline, an asbestos mine, and a gypsum mine. A resort community development in Idaho was completed and sold. Price increases were implemented and greater attention was given to controlling costs in all areas with special emphasis in marketing and sales. He sought to widen communication channels throughout the company and get employees at every level to think in terms of bottom line results. The fiberglass and asbestos business segments were expanded and expenditures made to update facilities and increase output at the Jeffrey Mine. Production of other products predicted to have the greatest growth potential were emphasized: nonfiberglass insulations, fiberglass mat, and polyvinyl chloride pipe. The position of vice president of operations was established (formerly abolished by Goodwin) as a means to monitor daily activity more closely and determine if performance remained congruent with the firm's overall objectives.

Goodwin had diversified into areas that never significantly contributed to profits (10% of total products and services); McKinney's strategy, on the other hand, was to expand production for those items which were already generating the best profits for the company, i.e., thermal insulation and mining.

Near the end of 1978, JM purchased Olinkraft, a wood and paper products company. This wholly owned subsidiary headquartered in Louisiana employs 7,100 persons and is vertically integrated. It owns 600,000 acres of prime southern timber land and specializes in the production of packaging products and systems.[18] As JM's largest acquisition to date, Olinkraft's products are expected to complement the existing product lines.

In February, 1979, John A. McKinney was elected chairman of the board and chief executive officer of Johns-Manville. Fred L. Pundsack became president.

While sales of asbestos fiber overseas was strong in 1979, other factors affecting the company resulted in a disappointing overall performance. Price increases hadn't occurred quickly enough to cover cost inflation. Startup costs in new facilities were high and demand for building insulation in the first half of the year was low. In an attempt to get rid of the unprofitable sprinkler irrigation business, JM suffered a loss of $4.4 million. Currency devaluation and retroactive income taxes cost the Olinkraft Brazilian operation an additional $4.5 million.[19]

Johns-Manville presently employs 31,000 people at 130 plants, mines, and sales and administrative offices throughout the world. Sales, in 1979, were divided between five major markets: residential construction 24%, nonresidential building 19%, other construction (including electric utilities, highways, water, sewer, and other public works projects) 21%, industrial production 20%, and paper and packaging markets 16%. Seventy-seven percent of sales were generated from the domestic market, 9% from Canadian markets, and the remaining 14% from other foreign markets, especially Western Europe, Latin American, and the Far East. Foreign markets, including Canada, contributed 40 percent of JM's total operating earnings.[20]

THE NEXT FIVE YEARS

Johns-Manville predicts external factors having a negative influence on forthcoming sales will include energy inflation, a combination of high inflation rates and slow economic growth (stagflation), a decline in domestic housing, commercial, and industrial construction, and some negative carryovers of the current U.S. economic slump to overseas markets.[21]

The Johns-Manville 1979 Annual Report summarizes company goals and objectives for the next five years designed to strengthen their competitive position and improve financial strengths.

1 Increase selling prices on products sufficient to cover cost increases and bring operating margins in line.

2 Implement productivity improvements in an effort to reduce overall costs.

3 Optimally utilize new production capacities.

4 Capitalize on the need for individuals and businesses to conserve energy.

5 Renew emphasis on research and development to improve manufacturing methods and enhance competitive strengths of present products and development of new product lines.[22]

These goals are further amplified in the 1979 Johns-Manville Investor Reference book which states: "Johns-Manville's immediate short-term goal is to operate all its businesses in such a way as to improve financial strength. Most expansion programs have been completed or soon will be complete and this allows management once again to turn attention to programs which will improve productivity and achieve greater cost efficiencies in current product lines. These efforts will enable Johns-Manville to increase capacity—in actual physical volume—with minimal capital investment. Positive operating leverage thus will be gained and substantial amounts of cash flow will be generated. This cash throw-off, in turn, will permit paydown on the company's debt and reduction of its interest load. Further, in 1984, JM may refinance or retire its preferred stock to once again be in a good position to take a look at opportunities for greater growth."[23]

Moody's Investor Service writes, "In the near term, earnings will come under pressure due to a weaker economy and reduced housing construction. Also, a cost-price squeeze could continue to restrain earnings. However, continued growth of remodeling and repair markets (3% of sales) could help. Over the long term, price increases, productivity improvements, and new production capacity should provide benefits. The acquisition of Olinkraft resulted in a broader operating base and should reduce the dependence upon construction activity and asbestos."[24]

And, in conclusion, Johns-Manville says, "We are confident of our abilities to succeed. We have the people, products, natural resources, assets and strong market positions essential for success. Finally, our commitment will help us succeed."[25]

Financial results for 1979 follow in Exhibit 5.

EXHIBIT 5

Percentages Allocated to Business Segments		
Business Line	Revenue	Income
Fiberglass products	25.0%	34.1%
Forest products	21.7%	18.0%
Pipe products & systems	13.4%	6.4%
Roofing products	11.9%	5.1%
Nonfiberglass insulation	11.7%	9.7%
Other	16.4%	26.7%
Capitalization	$(000)	(%)
Long term debt	532,377	27.7
Deferred income taxes	194,642	10.1
Preferred	299,451	15.6
Common & surplus	896,421	46.6
	1,922,891	

SOURCE: Moody's Investor Service, March 9, 1981.

THE ASBESTOS ISSUE

Asbestos, mined in various locations throughout the world, is a fibrous mineral, highly impervious to heat, which possesses the unique quality of being the only mineral which can be woven into cloth. Eight-hundred thousand tons of asbestos are used every year in 3,000 products for which no substitutes exist.[26]

Within this century, worldwide use of asbestos has increased annually from 500 tons to more than four million tons.[27] An estimated five million people, who are employed in asbestos-related jobs, or who are using the products, breathe significant amounts of asbestos fibers daily.[28] Today, researchers are discovering a larger than anticipated number of people who show signs of inhalation and retention of asbestos fiber in their lung tissues. The multiple threats of asbestos contamination in the air, water, and our food, indicate the serious implications asbestos has on the environment in which we live.[29] While the worst exposures are found in the workplace, the hazard is widespread because asbestos is contained in such a wide range of products including ceiling materials, hairdryers, fire-retardant clothing, and automobile brake linings.

Johns-Manville is the free world's largest asbestos fiber producer and has been plagued over the last year by lawsuits from individuals who have contracted asbestos-related diseases. JM employees are covered by workers' compensation benefits but many workers have come in contact with the product when handling it in final form. These include a large number of government employees who handled asbestos while working in World War II naval shipyards. The U.S. remains the primary

The following tables summarize financial information
relating to the Company's operations within different industries:

| | Years Ended December 31 | | | |
	1979	1978	1977	1976
Revenues:				
Fiber Glass Products	$ 573,198	$ 514,287	$ 407,242	$ 357,823
Forest Products (e)	497,398			
Pipe Products and Systems	304,856	303,334	273,512	217,526
Roofing Products	272,677	253,807	203,612	171,197
Non-Fiber Glass Insulations	267,862	231,190	195,223	158,721
Asbestos Fiber	168,199	157,291	160,682	154,625
Industrial and Specialty Products and Services	308,390	290,845	301,173	309,450
Corporate revenues, net (f)	11,020	19,894	12,447	(22,574)
Elimination of intersegment sales (a)	(106,238)	(94,059)	(74,096)	(55,568)
	$2,297,362	$1,676,589	$1,479,795	$1,291,200
Income From Operations:				
Fiber Glass Products	$ 95,650	$ 107,279	$ 81,661	$ 59,823
Forest Products (e)	50,320			
Pipe Products and Systems	17,983	25,861	23,552	(2,688)
Roofing Products	14,360	23,219	13,754	8,363
Non-Fiber Glass Insulations	27,190	35,484	28,237	18,457
Asbestos Fiber	56,477	54,592	59,815	60,237
Industrial and Specialty Products and Services	43,474	35,911	25,431	18,741
Corporate expense, net (f)	(23,436)	(22,971)	(24,290)	(48,556)
Eliminations and adjustments (c)	(1,751)	944	3,492	1,997
	$ 280,267	$ 260,319	$ 211,652	$ 116,374
Depreciation and Depletion:				
Fiber Glass Products	$ 21,474	$ 17,995	$ 13,716	$ 10,598
Forest Products (e)	26,921			
Pipe Products and Systems	5,996	5,629	5,698	5,795
Roofing Products	2,343	1,964	1,818	1,688
Non-Fiber Glass Insulations	5,548	4,554	4,175	4,149
Asbestos Fiber	5,891	5,856	5,674	4,743
Industrial and Specialty Products and Services	4,872	4,343	5,198	5,274
Corporate	1,798	2,060	2,296	2,156
	$ 74,843	$ 42,401	$ 38,575	$ 34,403
Additions to Property, Plant and Equipment:				
Fiber Glass Products	$ 84,740	$ 109,554	$ 57,791	$ 20,224
Forest Products (e)	35,793			
Pipe Products and Systems	14,280	8,515	6,624	8,685
Roofing Products	11,497	5,065	3,707	4,034
Non Fiber Glass Insulations	23,313	19,923	6,974	5,579
Asbestos Fiber	5,440	10,761	10,232	9,419
Industrial and Specialty Products and Services	9,264	12,416	9,389	10,693
Corporate	4,994	7,773	5,436	14,433
	$ 189,321	$ 174,007	$ 100,153	$ 73,067

| | December 31 | | | |
	1979	1978	1977	1976
Assets:				
Fiber Glass Products	$ 561,625	$ 474,575	$ 361,545	$ 308,043
Forest Products (e)	826,447	805,798		
Pipe Products and Systems	193,303	204,440	197,138	188,772
Roofing Products	112,111	92,288	83,404	72,838
Non-Fiber Glass Insulations	190,612	156,990	130,868	122,265
Asbestos Fiber	146,045	137,232	141,034	129,582
Industrial and Specialty Products and Services	190,419	188,863	177,199	194,078.
Corporate (d)	208,688	245,630	321,494	245,326
Eliminations and adjustments (c)	(104,870)	(88,861)	(78,882)	(72,704)
	$2,324,380	$2,216,955	$1,333,800	$1,188,200

EXHIBIT 6

SOURCE: Johns-Manville 1979 Annual Report

The following tables set forth the Company's operations by geographic area:

| | | | Years Ended December 31 | |
	1979	1978	1977	1976
Revenues:				
United States	$1,802,860	$1,315,728	$1,147,680	$ 997,131
Canada	289,117	267,007	270,510	267,623
Overseas	308,751	195,400	152,436	148,312
Corporate revenues, net (f)	11,020	19,894	12,447	(22,574)
Elimination of intergeographic sales (b)	(114,386)	(121,440)	(103,278)	(99,292)
	$2,297,362	$1,676,589	$1,479,795	$1,291,200
Income From Operations:				
United States	$ 192,540	$ 185,227	$ 157,902	$ 84,723
Canada	57,366	61,456	54,571	53,987
Overseas	55,845	35,668	19,978	24,254
Corporate expense, net (f)	(23,436)	(22,971)	(24,290)	(48,556)
Eliminations and adjustments (c)	(2,048)	939	3,491	1,966
	$ 280,267	$ 260,319	$ 211,652	$ 116,374

| | | | | December 31 |
	1979	1978	1977	1976
Assets:				
United States	$1,661,749	$1,538,673	$ 722,479	$ 676,011
Canada	229,598	210,174	216,162	206,850
Overseas	328,998	311,238	152,734	132,935
Corporate (d)	208,688	245,630	321,494	245,326
Eliminations and adjustments (c)	(104,653)	(88,760)	(79,069)	(72,922)
	$2,324,380	$2,216,955	$1,333,800	$1,188,200

Notes:

| a/ Intersegment sales were as follows | | | Years Ended December 31 | |
(at prices approximating market):	1979	1978	1977	1976
Fiber Glass Products	$ 46,725	$ 32,666	$ 20,626	$13,304
Roofing Products	539	504	530	255
Asbestos Fiber	36,565	41,109	35,308	29,186
Industrial and Specialty Products and Services	22,409	19,780	17,632	12,823
	$106,238	$ 94,059	$ 74,096	$55,568

| b/ Intergeographic sales were as follows | | | | |
(at prices approximating market):				
United States	$ 34,649	$ 28,679	$ 28,751	$33,363
Canada	77,459	85,339	72,477	65,601
Overseas	2,278	7,422	2,050	328
	$114,386	$121,440	$103,278	$99,292

c/ Includes the elimination of intersegment and intergeographic inventory profits and the adjustment of business segment and geographic inventories, which are carried at standard costs, to the historical inventory bases used in consolidation.

d/ Corporate assets are principally cash, marketable securities, prepaid income taxes, investments in and advances to associated companies, and the assets of the real estate subsidiary.

e/ The "Forest Products" segment was acquired in a purchase acquisition of Olinkraft, Inc. and has been included in the consolidated balance sheet at December 31, 1978. The results of the Olinkraft operations have been consolidated in the statement of consolidated earnings beginning January 1, 1979.

f/ Includes a $30 million charge in 1976 for asset dispositions, reduction of intangibles and Flextran pipe claims.

EXHIBIT 6 (continued)

493

| | December 31 | |
Assets	1979	1978
Current Assets		
Cash (including time deposits of $11,112 in 1979, $25,187 in 1978)	$ 18,692	$ 28,161
Marketable securities, at cost (approximates market)	10,023	37,868
Accounts receivable (net of allowances of $8,939 in 1979, $6,507 in 1978)	361,635	327,621
Inventories (Notes 1b and 3)	228,988	219,249
Prepaid expenses (principally deferred income taxes)	30,786	31,871
Total Current Assets	650,124	644,770
Property, Plant and Equipment, at cost (Note 1c)		
Land and land improvements	114,413	98,512
Buildings	352,185	320,665
Machinery and equipment	1,160,697	1,042,715
	1,627,295	1,461,892
Less, Accumulated depreciation and depletion	430,448	373,926
	1,196,847	1,087,966
Timber and timberlands, less cost of timber harvested	367,771	371,662
Property, plant and equipment, net	1,564,618	1,459,628
Investments, Deferred Charges and Other Assets (Note 1a)	109,638	112,557
	$2,324,380	$2,216,955

EXHIBIT 7
SOURCE: Johns-Manville 1979 Annual Report

494

	December 31	
Liabilities	1979	1978
Current Liabilities		
Commercial paper and other short-term debt	$ 32,408	$ 23,367
Accounts payable	142,575	113,710
Wages and compensation	53,537	44,678
Income and other taxes	50,598	84,147
Other accrued liabilities	49,727	63,390
Total Current Liabilities	328,845	329,292
Long-Term Debt *(Note 4)*	532,377	543,244
Other Non-Current Liabilities	72,644	60,497
Deferred Income Taxes *(Note 1e)*	194,642	150,274
	1,128,508	1,083,307
Contingencies and Commitments *(Notes 5 and 6)*		
Preferred Stock		
Cumulative Preferred Stock, $1.00 par, authorized 10,000,000 shares		
Redeemable $5.40 series, at stated value of $65 per share; issued and outstanding: 1979—4,606,946 shares, 1978—4,598,327 shares *(Note 7)*	299,451	298,891
Common Shareholders' Equity		
Common Stock, $2.50 par, authorized 50,000,000 shares; issued: 1979—22,456,693 shares, 1978—22,008,466 shares *(Note 8)*	208,370	197,413
Earnings Reinvested	692,420	643,317
	900,790	840,730
Less, Cost of treasury stock, 1979—142,879 shares, 1978—195,329 shares *(Note 8)*	4,369	5,973
	896,421	834,757
	$2,324,380	$2,216,955

EXHIBIT 7 (continued)

Earnings	1979	1978
		(Note 2)
Revenues		
Net sales	$2,276,429	$1,648,599
Other income, net	20,933	27,990
Total	2,297,362	1,676,589
Costs and Expenses		
Cost of sales	1,747,031	1,190,318
Selling, general and administrative	238,964	193,401
Research, development and engineering	31,100	32,551
Total	2,017,095	1,416,270
Income From Operations	280,267	260,319
Interest Expense	62,441	22,255
Earnings Before Income Taxes	217,826	238,064
Income Taxes *(Notes 1e and 11)*		
Current	67,261	98,423
Deferred	35,959	18,039
Total	103,220	116,462
Net Earnings *(before preferred dividends)*	114,606	121,602
Dividends on Preferred Stock	23,553	
Net Earnings Available for Common Stock	$ 91,053	$ 121,602
Net Earnings Per Common Share *(Notes 1f and 8)*	$4.13	$5.62

Earnings Reinvested		
Earnings Reinvested at Beginning of Year	$ 643,317	$ 561,019
Net Earnings Available for Common Stock	91,053	121,602
Dividends on Common Stock *($1.89 per share in 1979 and*		
$1.80 per share in 1978)	(41,692)	(38,972)
Loss on Dispositions of Treasury Stock *(Note 8)*	(258)	(332)
Earnings Reinvested at End of Year	$ 692,420	$ 643,317

EXHIBIT 8

SOURCE: Johns-Manville 1979 Annual Report.

	1979	1978
Revenues		
Net sales	$2,276,429	$1,648,599
Other income, net	20,933	27,990
Total	$2,297,362	$1,676,589
Earnings Before Income Taxes	$ 217,826	$ 238,064
Net Earnings Available for Common Stock	$ 91,053	$ 121,602
Net Earnings Per Common Share	$ 4.13	$ 5.62
Average Common Shares Outstanding *(000 omitted)*	22,044	21,642
Average Preferred Shares Outstanding *(000 omitted)*	4,603	
Cash Dividends on Common Stock	$ 41,692	$ 38,972
Dividends Per Common Share	$ 1.89	$ 1.80
Cash Dividends on Preferred Stock	$ 23,553	
Dividends Per Preferred Share	$ 5.115	
Capital Expenditures	$ 181,923	$ 170,255
Working Capital	$ 321,279	$ 315,478
Common Shareholders' Equity	$ 896,421	$ 834,757
Number of Common Shareholders	27,600	27,500
Number of Preferred Shareholders	24,100	
Number of Employees	32,500	25,800

Market Prices Per Common Share	1979 High	1979 Low	1978 High	1978 Low
For the Quarters Ended				
March 31	25¼	22½	32¼	28⅛
June 30	25¾	23¼	34⅜	28¾
September 30	27¾	24	34¾	28⅛
December 31	26½	21⅞	32¾	22⅛

Market Prices Per Preferred Share	1979 High	1979 Low
For the Quarters Ended		
March 31	62½	61¼
June 30	64⅝	61⅝
September 30	64	58¾
December 31	59	54⅛

Results by Major Business Segments	Revenues		Income From Operations	
	1979	1978	1979	1978
Fiber Glass Products	$ 573,198	$ 514,287	$ 95,650	$107,279
Forest Products	497,398		50,320	
Pipe Products and Systems	304,856	303,334	17,983	25,861
Roofing Products	272,677	253,807	14,360	23,219
Non-Fiber Glass Insulations	267,862	231,190	27,190	35,484
Asbestos Fiber	168,199	157,291	56,477	54,592
Industrial and Specialty Products and Services	308,390	290,845	43,474	35,911
Corporate, net	11,020	19,894	(23,436)	(22,971)
Eliminations and Adjustments	(106,238)	(94,059)	(1,751)	944
Total	$2,297,362	$1,676,589	$280,267	$260,319

EXHIBIT 9

SOURCE: Johns-Manville 1979 Annual Report

497

EXHIBIT 10

1980 Financial Information		
I. Working Capital (actual) at September 30, 1980.		
Cash assets	$	36.6 (in millions)
Receivables		389.3
Inventory (LIFO)		219.6
Other		31.3
Current assets	$	676.8
Accounts payable	$	101.1
Debt due		99.3
Other		177.6
Current liabilities	$	378.0
Debt structure:		
Total debt	$	624.3 million
Due in 5 years		195.0 million
Long-term debt		525.0 million
Long-term interest		51.5 million
II. Calendar year, 1980, figures (approximate).		
Sales	$2,285	million
Depreciation	80	million
Net profit		76.5 million
Income tax rate	49%	
Net profit margin	3.3%	
Long-term debt	515	million
Net worth	1,205	million

SOURCE: Value Line Investment Survey, February 6, 1981.

customer of asbestos with increasingly expanding overseas markets. JM has profited from its $1.59 billion asbestos manufacturing business. The corporation operates 55 asbestos product plants in the U.S. and various subsidiaries in the international market. It now dominates the industry by producing 35 to 40 percent of the nation's fiber.[30] Other industry members such as Owens-Corning, Raybestos-Manhattan, Keene, etc., also are listed as defendents in pending litigation.[31]

As of the end of 1980 there have been 5,087 asbestos-related lawsuits against Johns-Manville with a probability of many more to come in the future. Two-hundred fifty suits have been settled out of court and, of the 28 court cases, 10 have been ruled in favor of the claimants. In the losses, the courts have contended that JM breached its duty to warn, and warning labels failed to communicate the seriousness of the risk. The high cost of defending these suits and unfavorable media attention are beginning to have a negative economic and social impact on the company. Of the total $5.3 million awards through 1977, JM has had to pay $1.4 million.[32]

Human asbestos-related diseases include several types of illnesses and are tied to intensity and exposure levels. Asbestosis is a severe scarring of the lungs caused by inhaling asbestos fibers over a long period of time. It adversely affects the lungs' function by creating a shortness of breath and, eventually, paralysis of other body movements, leading to breathing failure and other respiratory diseases.[33] One-third of the workers employed more than 17 years in asbestos-related occupations have x-ray evidence of this disease.[34] A second and rarer disease is mesothelioma, a swiftly developing cancer which normally proves to be fatal six months to one year after diagnosis. It usually takes the form of a malignant tumor on the membrane which lines the abdominal cavity[35] and is associated exclusively with asbestos occurring in approximately seven percent of asbestos workers.[36] Although not exclusively associated with asbestos, smoking increases the chance of lung cancer with asbestos inhalation by more than 90 times. According to the U.S. National Cancer Institute, 18 percent of all future cancer deaths (more than two million people in the next 30 years) will be attributable to asbestos which ranks only second to cigarette smoking in known causes of cancer. Lung cancer accounts for 20 percent of the deaths among asbestos workers.[37] Common to these diseases is that they can take a long period of time to develop, sometimes 20 to 40 years, and a cure is virtually unknown.

The increased awareness of medical implications to the workers affected plus the involvement by concerned pluralistic groups (other workers, consumers, lawyers, etc.) has resulted in substantial media attention and some government intervention regarding this issue. A Congressional hearing was held to discuss the past and potential asbestos product hazards to determine if JM and other asbestos and tobacco companies had failed to meet certain societal responsibilities. Politicization of the issue has contributed to an unfavorable public image for JM, has led to demands that the company account for previous actions, has caused a strain with company/employee relations, and has exposed the possibility of the hazard not only to those affected but to those potentially affected consumers.

As far back as 1949 asbestosis was found in the lungs of some workers via company medical diagnosis. Johns-Manville refrained from releasing this information to the workers about their condition believing that, as long as they could work and "felt" good, there was no reason to do so. Cautionary labels were placed on materials in 1964 but claimants state that those warning labels did not come soon enough and did not sufficiently disclose the seriousness of exposure. JM states that, at the time, they lacked adequate evidence that those not working directly with asbestos materials were in any danger.

A 1978 study predicted that asbestos-related deaths in the next 30–35 years will account for 13 to 18 percent of all cancer deaths.[38] The National Cancer Institute believes that "the major public health impact of asbestos-related cancer is just beginning to be reflected in overall cancer statistics."[39] Johns-Manville has issued several statements citing inaccurate and exploitive coverage by the press. Company management has also expressed the view that many of the published statistics, including those stated above, are not realistic.

The Company Position   Johns-Manville states that it has carried on continuing research to determine potential asbestos-related hazards since 1930 and has always complied with exposure limits of the U.S. Public Health Service. Ongoing physical examinations for employees have been routine and results released to employees in an attempt to eliminate work hazards. Over the last 30 years, measures have been taken to control dust through better ventilation systems, development of respirator-use programs, warning labels on insulation products, and a ban on smoking in the manufacturing facilities. Opponents to the company's position state that most of these actions were stimulated by federal standards which set exposure levels in 1970. JM has stated that it is company policy to discontinue operations rather than endanger life and that, even now, it is making efforts to find substitute products.

Johns-Manville has both economically and socially felt the brunt of this issue. Its public image has suffered causing loss of sales and a 20 percent decline in stock price during the congressional hearings.[40] Legal expenses have been costly and, since product liability insurance was not renewed by the insurance company in 1977, the company now must use its own resources in an attempt to self-insure against claims arising beyond that date. All punitive damages must be paid by the company and there is really no way to estimate future costs.

Johns-Manville states that because asbestos is "sealed in" consumer products and additional care is taken in the handling and preparation of material, exposure levels are not significant. Chief executive officer McKinney has stated, "There's no reason we can't use asbestos just as we use nitroglycerin," JM plans to produce more than 700,000 tons of asbestos fiber through at least 1990 from proven reserves. "Unless the courts start to hold us liable for punitive damages, we will survive."[41]

Union Reaction Union workers are very concerned about asbestos-related hazards and what they have interpreted as irresponsibility on JM's part to disclose the potential medical complications. In a recent contract negotiation proceeding, workers fought for and won the right to have company medical records released to employees. They also asked that generic names of chemicals be made available to workers and demanded that workers removed from positions because of product-related health issues lose no pay or seniority status. Ironically, the union also wants to eliminate the company's no-smoking policy. JM's policy of dismissing employees who do smoke in restricted areas is based on evidence that their chances of contracting asbestosis increase by 60 times or more.[42] These concerns by workers indicate a greater need for information and personal involvement in the future regarding occupational health hazards.

Unfortunately, the asbestos fallout has created a situation where no one wins in the short run. In some instances, employees and others who handle the product have been medically marred for life and many of those who die leave behind families with no means of support. On the other hand, JM is losing profits which can translate into lost jobs, lower dividends to stockholders, higher prices to consumers, and less capital for product investment and research and development. Also, sales are suffering because of the current general economic recession and media headlines which have scared consumers away from some JM products.

The government is currently considering raising the asbestos standard to a level which Johns-Manville says is impossible to meet because it can't be measured. The U.S. Department of Social and Health Services (formerly HEW) has established a study group on asbestos to:

1   estimate the risk of low level exposure,
2   estimate the cost of asbestos controls,
3   see if there are other fine fibers which might cause problems similar to those of asbestos.[43]

There seems to be a difference of opinion among JM workers and consumers as to how harmful asbestos really is, which may account for inaction by the company to recognize and deal with this issue in the past. The company still claims that the risk to workers was not identified until 1964 and that, while it was a known hazard for direct workers, it was not for indirect workers or consumers.

The question now seems to be how much government intervention is needed to protect the parties involved. If the asbestos and tobacco companies have to pay lawsuit damages from their own purses, they may go out of business. But, is it the responsibility of society and government to intervene and compensate individual members of society for their losses?

During World War II, the U.S. government employed some 4.5 million workers in the naval shipbuilding industry. A significant portion of the legal suits brought against JM today are from employees who were exposed to asbestos during that time. Evidence shows that the U.S. Navy disregarded policy directives and failed to provide a safe workplace. The Navy Department and the U.S. Maritime Commission had recognized the risk to insulation workers from high dust levels. In a booklet published in 1943, "Minimum Requirements for Safety and Industrial Health in Contract Shipyards," it noted that asbestosis was a disease that could arise from "any job in which asbestos is breathed," listing such tasks as sawing, cutting, or handling asbestos or asbestos mixtures.[44] The government specifications that required asbestos products to be utilized in the construction of its ships brought about this danger of exposure. It was fully responsible for shipyard practices and its employees' well being. Even though the government was aware of the hazards found in asbestos workplaces, it failed to begin controlling exposure levels and warning society of the dangers until the early 1970s. Asbestos substitutes were available to the government but it continued to use asbestos products even after 1975. Naval operations continually failed to meet government mandated standards established to prevent prolonged exposure.[45]

Johns-Manville has support legislation introduced by Representative Fenwick (N.J.) which proposes a "white lung" asbestos compensation program administrered by the U.S. Department of Labor and supported by the taxpayers, similar to the "black lung" program provided for U.S. coal miners.

The program would bar new court actions by prospective claimants and would offer the choice of continued court actions or applications to the "white lung" program by claimants of pending suits.

Funding for the program initially would be the responsibility of the U.S. Treasury and costs would subsequently be allocated one-half to the Treasury and one-half to the asbestos and tobacco industries. Any excess claims payable, due to inadequacy of the original award, would be the responsibility of the Treasury.

The white lung program would ease the financial burden of future and pending claims against Johns-Manville and other asbestos companies, construction companies, insulation companies, steel pipe plants, etc., as well as provide an efficient vehicle by which payments could be made to injured parties in this controversy. Johns-Manville arguments supporting the legislation are as follows:

> It would provide the means for prompt and fair settlement of needy cases versus years of delay dragging through the courts.

> It would give our own Manville employees a way to participate in fair compensation. (They are now only covered by workers' compensation and are excluded from the third party legislation route).

> It would make more money available for the injured parties avoiding the high non-compensatory costs of court administration and attorney fees.

> And, while not reducing our total costs, it would allow us to better predict our outlays, paying compensation over many years instead of in lump sums to the few who are awarded judgments.[46]

ENDNOTES

1   as-bes-tos (as bes' tes) n. 1. Mineral: a fibrous amphimole, used in making fireproof articles 2. a fabric woven from asbestos fibers, used for theatre curtains, fireman's gloves, etc. *The Random House College Dictionary,* 1975 revised edition, published by Random House, New York, N.Y., p. 78.

2   di-at-o-mite (di at' o mit') n. a fine siliceous earth; used in filtrations, as an abrasive, etc. *The Random House Dictionary,* 1978 revised edition published by Random House, New York, N.Y., p. 252.

3   Johns-Manville 1979 Annual Report.

4   Steven S. Anreder, "Johns-Manville Operations Firmly Back on the Upbeat," *Barrons* 55 (Nov. 24, 1975), 61.

5   Herbert E. Meyer, "Shootout at the Johns-Manville Corral," *Fortune* (October 1976) 146, 154.

6   Ibid.

7   Value Line (December 26, 1980), Co. No. 879.

8   Steven Anreder, Ibid.

9   Ibid.

10 "Ken-Caryl: A Study in Corporate Environmental Concern," *Industrial Development* 144 (July/August 1975), 6–7.

11 Ibid.

12 Wheeler, Dale D., "Have World Headquarters Will Travel," *Industrial Development* (March/April 1978), 14–17.

13 Meyer, op. cit.

14 Ibid.

15 Ibid.

16 "At JM It's Back to Basics," *Business Week* (October 31, 1977), 76–80.

17 Herbert Meyer, op. cit.

18 Johns-Manville 1978 Annual Report.

19 Johns-Manville 1979 Annual Report.

20 Ibid.

21 Ibid.

22 Ibid.

23 Johns-Manville 1979 Investor Reference Book.

24 Moody's Investor Service vol. 3, No. 47, see 54 (June 12, 1980) File N4465.

25 Johns-Manville 1979 Annual Report.

26 Shirley Hobbs Scheibla, "Heat on Asbestos," *Barrons* 59 (March 5, 1979), 4–5.

27 "An Asbestos Town Struggles With a Killer," *Saturday Review of the Society* 1 (March 1973), 28.

28 Ibid., 27.

29 "Asbestos," *Consumer's Research* 57 (January 1974), 17.

30 Ibid, 28.

31 Stephen Solomon, "The Asbestos Fallout at Johns-Manville," *Fortune* (May 7, 1979), 106.

32 Scheibla, op. cit.

33 "An Asbestos Town Struggles With a Killer," 29.

34 Solomon, ibid.

35 "An Asbestos Town Struggles With a Killer," 29.

36 Solomon, ibid.

37 Ibid.

38 Neil Maxwell, "How Johns-Manville Mounts Counterattack in Asbestos Dispute," *Wall Street Journal* (June 30, 1980).

39 Solomon, ibid.

40 Ibid.

41 Scheibla, ibid.

42 Solomon, ibid.

43 Scheibla, ibid.

44 Solomon, ibid.

45 Johns-Manville, 1980 First Quarter Report.

46 "The Asbestos Issue, Boston Security Analyst Presentation," F. H. May, vice chairman of the board of Johns-Manville Corporation (September 5, 1979), p. 5.

WEYER-HAEUSER IN THE 1980s

Stephen E. Barndt
Pacific Lutheran
University

In 1979, the Weyerhaeuser Company, a forest products company with sales in excess of $4,000,000,000 a year, qualified as the largest lumber manufacturer in the United States and one of the top 100 in *Fortune Magazine's* list of the 500 leading industrial corporations. Further, Weyerhaeuser is the only U.S. forest products company that produces, on the balance, more raw materials from its own timberlands than it uses. As of June 1980, the company listed owned timberlands comprised of 1,716,000 acres in Washington state; 1,154,000 acres in Oregon; and a total of 3,089,000 acres in Mississippi, Alabama, Arkansas, Oklahoma, and North Carolina. The company also has harvesting rights on 9,102,000 acres in Canada and 1,495,000 acres in Indonesia and Malaysia. The combination of such forest resources plus a heavy research commitment to better ways of growing and processing forest products and an orientation toward the future have helped to propel Weyerhaeuser to a position of strength and industry leadership in both forest practices and international operations in the 1970s.

Although engaged primarily in the ownership and management of timberlands, the processing of timber, and the marketing of those resources, the company is not limited solely to such activities. Weyerhaeuser has interests in real estate development and construction, financial services, chemicals, and ornamental nursery supplies in addition to the manufacture, distribution, and sale of lumber, plywood, pulp, paper, newsprint, paperboard, corrugated shipping containers, milk cartons, hardboard, particleboard, disposable diapers, laminated and other structural wood products, as well as assorted other wood and wood fiber products.

HISTORY

The company was started in 1900 when Frederick Weyerhaeuser and a group of midwest investors purchased 900,000 acres from Northern Pacific Railroad, incorporated in the state of Washington, and opened an office in Tacoma, Washington.

The Weyerhaeuser Company purchased its first sawmill, located in Everett, Washington, in 1902. More sawmills were added through the teens and twenties by acquisition, new site construction, and expansion. At the same time, timberland holdings were also growing, more than doubling to 2,013,404 acres by 1916.

This case was prepared by Professor Stephen E. Barndt of Pacific Lutheran University with the assistance of Michael Staudinger. The case was written for class discussion purposes and is not intended to illustrate either effective or ineffective administration.

Copyright © by Stephen E. Barndt

During the early years Frederick Weyerhaeuser set the tone for the company's view toward forest management practices. In 1905 he told a national forestry conference that "only by tremendous effort can the lumberman himself, the legislator, and the voter be made to realize the importance of forestry on timberlands and its possibilities."[1] Then in 1913, he testified before a Congressional committee to seek action concerning fire prevention and regulation of logging activities in the hopes that such legislation would help prevent soil erosion and preserve seed sources. During this period, he also pointed out that the then current property tax laws encouraged "cut and run," the practice of buying timberland, clearing cutting, and then leaving the area. In 1929, partly as a result of Weyerhaeuser-sponsored lobbying, Oregon became the first state to declare that reforestation not deforestation was to be a prime objective of property tax laws.

Company expansion through the thirties, forties, and most of the fifties was relatively slow. Weyerhaeuser expanded into the pulp industry in 1931, acquiring its first pulp mill in Longview, Washingtion. Then the company moved into the plywood industry in 1947, containerboard in 1949, composition board in 1954, packaging in 1957, and paper in 1961. Through the mid-fifties all plants remained in the Pacific Northwest.

A particularly significant move on behalf of Weyerhaeuser came in 1934. J. P. Weyerhaeuser, Jr., then president, implemented the first full scale reforestation policy of the company and began using the slogan "timber is a crop." Seven years later, *Operation Rehab* began in Montesano, Washington. This land rehabilitation plan covered 130,000 acres of burned land, which under the guidance of Weyerhaeuser's intensive forest management policies, became the nation's first large scale tree farm.

A second significant advance by Weyerhaeuser came in 1952 when J. P. Weyerhaeuser, Jr., began implementation of a new advertising policy. According to *Nation's Business* magazine, Weyerhaeuser was quoted as saying that "unless an institution merits goodwill and understanding, it cannot maintain a position as part of our American industrial structure."[2] This marked the beginning of a nationwide advertising attempt aimed not at selling products, but instead at selling ideas and information. One resulting advertising effort, Weyerhaeuser's "Wildlife Series," was one of the longest continuous advertising compaigns ever to run in the United States, running for fifteen years.

A third major change of direction began in the mid 1950s when the company geographically expanded outside the Northwest. Significant timberland acquisitions took place in the southern pine regions of the southeast and south central United States, giving Weyerhaeuser sources of materials closer to eastern markets.

A fourth important advance by Weyerhaeuser came in 1958 when the company entered the foreign market, with the formation of Weyerhaeuser International. Today Weyerhaeuser continues to emphasize the foreign market. By June 1980, the company reported that overseas markets regularly consumed about one-third of its total production.

The four cornerstones of (1) forest research and management, (2) advertising the company, (3) geographic expansion, and (4) international marketing have been associated with rapid company growth from the late 1950s into the 1970s. This growth, both internationally and domestically, is reflected in a current employment of nearly 50,000, in excess of 30 U.S. and 12 foreign major operating locations, and well in excess of 100 locations with smaller scale activities.

OPERATING ENVIRONMENT

Timber products have two major uses: (1) construction or manufacturing and (2) pulp products. The former use provides a substantial market for dimension lumber, logs, and plywood, primarily cut from softwood forests. Demand for such products is highly dependent on the demand for housing and commercial construction. High rates of family formation or high rates of economic growth, coupled with availability of capital, spur demand while high mortgage and construction loan rates, reduced availability of loans, and reduced levels of earnings available for investment reduce demand. In addition to the cyclical demand resulting form expansionary and recessionary movements in the general economy, demand for construction lumber tends to have seasonal peaks and valleys in the cooler climates where construction activities are curtailed in the winter. Pulp (and paper) products, although somewhat affected by the ups and downs of the economy, in general enjoy a more stable demand than construction building materials. Demand for shipping containers follows closely the demand for the products they are designed to protect and thus is subject to seasonal and cyclical ups and downs. On the other hand, trends in the demand for many paper products, e.g., newsprint, writing paper, and disposable diapers, tend to be much less affected by swings in the economy. Products that are traded internationally, e.g., logs, lumber, containerboard, newsprint, and pulp are affected both by patterns in world economic growth and world currency relationships. Besides the major uses of timber, a lesser amount is produced for use in furniture and miscellaneous manufactured products, e.g., skis, broom handles, boats, etc. Demand for wood used in making such products (except broom handles) tends to be sensitive to the state of the economy and spendable income.

Demand for timber products in the domestic (U.S. and Canada) market has, notwithstanding cyclical variations, continued to grow, generally mirroring the growth in population and standard of living. However, several foreign markets are growing at even faster rates. For example, Weyerhaeuser estimates that by the year 2000 European wood requirements will increase at a rate 50% greater than U.S. requirements.[3] Demand from the industrialized and growing Asian nations, notably Japan, Korea, and Taiwan, has grown and is expected to continue growing significantly. Recently, sales of U.S.-produced forest products in European and Asian markets has been favored by devaluation of the dollar relative to other currencies.

There are two basic categories of timber and wood producing trees: softwoods and hardwoods. Softwood trees are favored for production of dimension lumber, poles, and construction plywood. Hardwoods are preferred for paneling, furniture, cabinets, some crating, veneers, and other uses. Both hardwoods and softwoods are used in the production of pulp and paper products although softwoods are preferred in uses where strength is required. The major growing areas for softwoods are northern and western United States and Canada, southeastern United States, far eastern USSR, and northern Europe. The U.S., Canada, and Scandinavia are the largest exporters of softwoods to meet worldwide demand. Although Russia has a vast softwood resource, to date they have not been a significant factor in the world market (except in Japan) because of technological and economic disadvantages associated with an inhospitable climate and long distances to transportation terminals. Major hardwood forest areas are found in Southeast Asia, equatorial South America, northeastern North America, eastern Europe, and equatorial Africa.

Trees are unique as a resource in that they are renewable. Given the chance, nature replaces trees lost to insects, fire, natural death, and cutting. Further, nature can be helped and the renewal process speeded up by the careful selection, propogation, and nurturing of replacement trees. Such tree "farming" can not only replenish forests sooner than unaided nature but can also produce higher yields. For these reasons, in some area, tree farming becomes an economically viable course of action where nature cannot replenish soon enough or where harvest of more distant or rugged native forests would involve more difficult and costly harvesting operations.

Whether reforestation results from natural processes or tree farming, economic implications result for logging operations. Second growth forests are harvested at the earliest feasible regular intervals and since the trees are of the same age, they are both smaller and more uniform. Logging and sawmill machinery needed to handle a variety of sizes of logs, including those that are very large, becomes unnecessary and inefficient for processing the smaller logs. With a more uniform smaller log, more automation and technology-intensive practices can replace the old labor-intensive, but more versatile practices. And yet, as long as some of the old growth forests are being logged, some of the sawmills capable of handling larger logs must be retained. As a case in point, Weyerhaeuser estimates that by 1990, the mix of the timber it harvests in Western Washington will be 95% second growth and 5% old growth.[4] A problem for Weyerhaeuser and other forest products companies then is to determine the extent to which new small log processing operations will replace the older sawmills and where.

Transportation costs play an important role in determining locations of production facilities and the markets served by them. The bulky physical characteristics of logs, low value per log, and consequent high per unit transportation cost coupled with price competition in timber products sales dictate that sawmills and raw materials processing facilities be located close to timber stands. Transportation costs also determine those markets that can profitably be served. In the past, inexpensive transportation allowed a concentration of forest product processing facilities in the Western United States close to vast softwood forests. Two occurrences have effectively removed this nationwide marketing option and have fostered regional market specialization. First, the Jones Act required that intercoastal shipping be via U.S. flag vessels. Because U.S. flag vessels have higher costs (e.g., labor) and higher rates than foreign flag vessels, West Coast lumber mills cannot compete in Eastern U.S. markets with Western Canada mills that use non-U.S. vessels. Second, increases in rail and truck transportation costs spurred by the rapid rise in petroleum prices between 1973 and 1980 have made it all but impossible for distant mills to compete in areas that can be and are served by mills that are closer. As a result, Western U.S. plants ship principally to West Coast and export markets. South central plants serve the south central and midwest areas and southeastern plants serve the southeast, east coast, and export markets. Canadian mills serve much of the northeast and midwest. High transportation costs also impact the location of container plants.

However, in this case, the fact that in addition to being designed for specific customer needs, the finished product takes on added bulk, dictates that such container manufacturing plants be located near their markets.

Several economies of scale are potentially available to large forest products firms. Individual sawmills and processing plants offer little in the way of continuing economies of scale once volume is sufficient to warrant sophisticated automated sawing, converting, and materials handling equipment because added capacity generally means merely adding an additional economic sized production "unit." In addition, transportation diseconomies from shipping in raw materials (logs) discourages building capacity greater than needed for the local forest production. However, economies of scale can be achieved in marketing and distribution, e.g., consolidation of orders, break bulk at distant warehouses where individual order assortments can be built; transportation, e.g., use of owned or leased rolling stock, trucks, and shops; research and development, e.g., a useful development can be used in a number of different facilities or operations; and engineering, e.g., a lesson learned in one application can save time and dollars in other applications.

The forest products industry in the United States is, at the same time, dominated by a few large firms and yet shared by more than 8,000 companies. The large firms include International Paper, Georgia Pacific, Crown Zellerbach, St. Regis, Boise Cascade, Champion International, Mead, and Kimberly Clark, as well as Weyerhaeuser. Of these, Georgia Pacific leads in volume of business (gross revenue) with International Paper second, and Weyerhaeuser third. However, Weyerhaeuser generated the greatest after tax net income in the industry in 1979. In terms of product-market standings, Weyerhaeuser leads in lumber production with about 10 percent of the market; is fourth in plywood; and produces a significant volume of pulp, paper, paperboard products, containers, and building materials.

COMPANY OBJECTIVES

A company general policy statement formalized in 1971 stated the objective and means toward its accomplishment as:

The basic objective of Weyerhaeuser Company is to operate a vigorous, growing, diversified, and profitable business in the balanced best interest of its customers, shareholders, employees, suppliers, and the economy at large by generating earnings and profits at levels which will assure payment to shareholders of dividends sufficient to warrant their continued investment in the Company and at the same time sufficient for retention of funds in the business to assure growth and improvement.

To this end, the Company shall:

1 Energetically seek and develop opportunities for accelerating profitable growth both at home and abroad, with particular emphasis in fields where the Company may occupy an advantageous position because of raw materials, facilities, or management skills.

2 Seek constantly to devote Company land to those uses which will produce optimum long-term economic returns, and . . . maintaining ownership of strategically located forest lands. . . .

3 Constantly seek optimum profitability by adopting timber harvesting schedules in accordance with broad sustained yield principles . . . and by providing plants with the most favorable supplies of raw material, both as to volume and log mix. . . .

4 Produce and market customer-oriented products of appropriate quality and price under a policy which recognizes the integrated nature of the Company's operations and places at appropriate operating levels (a) responsibility for the establishment of goals relating to volume, productivity, and profitability, supported by programs to meet these goals, and (b) accountability for results achieved.

5 Be the most efficient operator, producer, distributor, and merchandiser in the industry by continually introducing modern cost-reducing processes, methods and equipment, and by making the most effective use of facilities, capital, personnel, and management skills.

6 Pursue intensively, research and related programs that will establish and assure continuing leadership in . . . products and services . . . efficient processes and methods . . . and improve the growth, quality, and utilization of forest resources.

7 Build and maintain an organization able to meet present and future needs by attracting competent personnel with growth potential. . . .

8 Build and maintain a favorable employee attitude that will encourage maximum contribution. . . .

9 Build and maintain, in customers, employees, shareholders, and the public, a reputation for honesty, fairness, and good corporate citizenship. . . .

10 . . . exercising the highest level of responsible stewardship of natural and environmental resources, practicing wise use of all resources throughout its activities, responding positively to opportunities for environmental, ecological and social problem-solving, and encouraging others toward the same commitments.[5]

Subsequently, growth, productivity and efficiency, and energy independence have been singled out as major topics for more definitive objectives.

The objectives of growth are to build a new and significantly larger earnings base, to upgrade the mix of products and markets, and to become a more balanced and international company. In the effort to reach these objectives, Weyerhaeuser has engaged in numerous activities to acquire forest lands and production operations as well as to build new production facilities. In addition, emphasis has been placed on expanding the company's export market to include pulp, newsprint, containerboard, dimension lumber, and plywood as well as logs. Further, the company has entered product lines that, although forest-product related, are much further removed than in the past, e.g., disposable diapers; lines that are only indirectly related through the land base, e.g., home building and salmon and shrimp growing; and lines that are not related, e.g., mortgage lending and restoration of buildings.

The objectives of increased productivity and efficiency and, hence, greater profit margins have resulted in efforts to gain economies of scale; develop new technologies, modernize capacity, obtain higher harvest utilization, and realize greater product yields; strengthen market coverage, sales, and distribution efforts; keep abreast of developments that could impact the industry and the company, anticipate them, and influence them in the way most favorable to the company; and increase energy self sufficiency.

Energy self sufficiency has been singled out as a special area for company efforts. Weyerhaeuser aims to be completely free from the direct use of petroleum fuels for plant production by the end of the 1980s and, in addition, wants to maximize co-generation of electrical power. The company expects to accomplish these objectives through a heavy commitment to research and development, increased use of wood wastes, and partial conversion to coal.

OPERATIONS

Major domestic U.S. Weyerhaeuser operations are concentrated in the states of Alabama, Arkansas, Mississippi, North Carolina, Oklahoma, Oregon, and Washington with Washington accounting for the greatest employment by far (see exhibit 1). As also shown in exhibit 1, the most important foreign operations are found in Canada, Indonesia, Malaysia, and, to a much lesser extent, France. The relatively more minor production and service operations are scattered over a significantly larger number of states and countries (see exhibit 2). The geographical spread of operating locations and facilities is a function of access to raw materials, costs of transporting them versus the converted intermediate or final products, need for customer responsiveness, and, in the case of acquired companies, their original locations. Production facilities for lumber, paper, plywood, and other bulky end products plus intermediate products tend to be located in close proximity to the company's large timber holdings. On the other hand, production facilities for some specialized end products such as milk cartons and shipping containers tend to be located closer to their markets. Warehouses (wood products customer service centers), nurseries, and residential or commercial building construction operations likewise locate close to markets for reasons of transportation economy and customer service.

Growth through acquisition and internal expansion since 1975 has placed greater relative emphasis on increasing output of wood fiber end products, manufactured construction materials, and new initiatives in less closely related product lines. Shifts in the company's emphasis on various products are reflected in the relative changes in production volume among the various types of wood products shown in exhibit 3. Even though production of the two largest revenue earners, logs and lumber, have shown a general increase between 1975 and 1979, the growth rates for plywood, particleboard, hardboard, paperboard, paper, and containers have been much greater. Further, recent expansion in the real estate construction, nursery supply, aquaculture, and soft disposables product lines provide additional evidence of change in product line emphasis.

Weyerhaeuser's major kinds of product or service producing operations are sufficiently varied that they can be thought of as different kinds of businesses.

EXHIBIT 1

Principal Timberlands and Manufacturing Facilities

Area	# of locations	Timber holdings	Employment	Products
Washington	8	1,716,000 acres	15,000	softwood lumber, plywood, cedar shakes, paperboard, pulp, paper, newsprint
Oregon	5	1,154,000 acres	7,400	softwood lumber, plywood, laminated products, hardboard siding, particleboard, linerboard
Oklahoma and Arkansas	9	1,841,000 acres	5,400	gypsum board, fiberboard, hardboard siding, insulating board, treated lumber and timbers, softwood lumber, softwood veneer, plywood, bag paper, linerboard, corrugating medium, pulp
North Carolina	5	586,000 acres	4,200	softwood plywood, softwood lumber, fiberboard, pulp, bleached paperboard, corrugating medium, linerboard, paper
Mississippi and Alabama	6	662,000 acres	2,000	softwood lumber, softwood plywood
North Central	11		2,400	hardwood lumber, hardwood plywood, particleboard, laminated products, paper, hardwood veneer, hardwood doors
Canada	9	9,102,000 acres	2,200	softwood lumber, hardwood lumber, pulp, hardwood veneer
Other Foreign: Malaysia, Indonesia, France	3	1,495,000 acres (harvesting rights)	3,500	hardwood lumber, paperboard, shipping containers

SOURCE: *Weyerhaeuser Handy Facts*, June 1980.

EXHIBIT 2

Other Weyerhaeuser Operations		
Product/Service	Geopolitical Areas	Number of Locations
Panel products	VA, CA	3
Milk cartons	WA, CA	2
Chemicals	WA, NC, AR, OK	6
Fireplace logs	WA, OR, NC	4
Research and Development	WA, MS, FL, CA, AR, OR, NC, OK	12
Secondary fiber	NC, WA, OR, MD, OK, CA	8
Shipping containers	CA, Spain, GA, MN, NJ, IL, Canary Islands, OR, IA, Greece, MI, France, NC, Belgium, HI, VA, TX, AL, KY, OH, NE, NY, ME, WA, WI	41
Environmental resources	WA, MS, AR, NC, OR, WI, Canada	7
Shelter group (real estate)	WA, FL, TX, CA, NJ, NC, MD, AZ, CO, NV, OR, SC	25
Aquaculture	OR, FL	2
Nursery supply	CT, FL, TX, CA, Washington, D.C.	7
Soft disposables	IL, PA, CA, GA	4
Energy and environmental equipment	CA	1
Wood products	CA, GA, NC, MD, OR, AL, NY, IA, OH, TX, MI, CO, MH, IN, PA, ND, IL, NJ, WI, CT, WA, KY, MO, TN, FL, LA, KS, AR, OK, AZ, RI, UT, SC, SD, MA, Canada, Australia	75

SOURCE: *Weyerhaeuser Handy Facts,* June 1980

Thus, even though there are sometimes materials, process, or locational interdependencies, the products and operations of the company can be categorized as falling in either the construction materials (solid wood products), fiber products, international, real estate, or special business segment operations.

The construction materials business is Weyerhaeuser's largest and involves the harvesting of timber; production of logs, lumber, plywood, panels, hardboard, particleboard, veneers, and other solid wood products; and their distribution directly to the buyers or through the company's 75 wood products customer service centers. Recent expansion and improvement has been through acquisition and modernization as well as new plant construction. Because large tracts of timber are not readily available, the company has been effectively restricted to acquisitions of smaller tracts, more intensive use of its present timber resource, and to the acquisition of small firms that contribute to product line and regional market expansion. The recent availability and stiff bidding for Bodcaw Company and its extensive forest lands in Louisiana highlights the scarcity of desirable large tracts. Weyerhaeuser actively bid for Bodcaw but withdrew when International Paper's offer exceeded the value Weyerhaeuser had placed on the assets. The failure to acquire Bodcaw leaves the 1969 acquisition of Dierks Forestry, Inc., and its 1.8 million acres of forestland, as

EXHIBIT 3

Production of Wood Products						
Product	Basis	1979	1978	1977	1976	1975
Solid wood						
logs	1000 cunits*	8713	9253	9162	9015	8771
lumber	million board ft.	2914	3068	2898	2701	2530
softwood plywood & veneer	million sq. ft. (3/8")	1454	1406	1207	1070	1033
hardwood plywood & veneer	million sq. ft.	887	995	963	857	277
particle board	million sq. ft. (3/8")	41 0	44 2	386	325	301
hardboard	million sq. ft. (1/8")	416	420	374	304	21 2
Fiber products						
market pulp	1000 air dry metric tons	912	917	858	923	818
newsprint	1000 tons	63	—	—	—	—
paper	1000 tons	521	527	471	358	319
paperboard & containerboard	1000 tons	1973	1999	1797	1758	1438
shipping containers	1000 tons	1241	1178	1046	1010	866
cartons	1000 tons	144	144	150	145	145

*cunit = 100 ft^3
SOURCE: 1979 10K Report

the company's last large acquisition. The current use of small company acquisitions in attempting to increase product and market competitiveness is evident in exhibit 4. Major modernization improvements involve introducing more efficient and productive small log production processes, introducing new processes and control technology to increase yield of the product mix, and converting from petroleum fuel as the primary energy source.

The fiber products business is involved with the production of pulp, bleached paper boards, paper, newsprint, milk cartons, shipping containers and containerboard, and recycling fiber products. This fast growing business has seen major expansion. A multiphase plant construction project at Columbus, Mississippi, planned to provide a light weight coated paper and wood pulp mill in 1982, will be followed later by another lightweight coated paper mill, a kraft pulp mill, and an uncoated free sheet paper machine. Other major expansion projects include an increase in the linerboard capacity at the Valliant, Oklahoma, mill and a second newsprint machine at the company's Longview, Washington, facility.

Weyerhaeuser's international business includes both the international marketing of forest products produced in the United States and the foreign production of forest products for marketing within the producing nation or internationally. The exporting of U.S. produced products, primarily pulp, linerboard, lumber, and plywood to Europe, and pulp, logs, wood chips, and newsprint to the Far East (principally Japan) accounted for approximately 20 percent of Weyerhaeuser's gross sales (see

EXHIBIT 4

Planned and Completed Acquisitions 1979–1980		
Company	Location	Benefit
Dixieland Lumber Co.	Southern California (San Diego)	market expansion
Delta Industries	Mississippi-Alabama	plywood production
Northwood Mills	British Columbia	lumber production
Travers Lumber	Alabama (Mobile)	export marketing of southern lumber
Eclipse Timber Co.	Washington (Port Angeles)	market expansion
Menasha Corp. (West coast operations only)	West Coast (North Bend, Ore.; Anaheim, Cal.; Portland and Eugene, Ore.)	corrugating medium, waste paper collection, and containerboard operations
Everitt Lumber Co. and Union Manufacturing & Supply Co.	Colorado (Fort Collins)	distribution
Northwest Hardwood, Inc.	Washington (Chehalis and Arlington)	alder lumber mills

exhibit 5). In 1980, approximately 60 to 65 percent of such exports were solid wood (e.g., logs) and 35 to 40 percent were pulp products. However, this mix is expected to change as more finished or semifinished products are exported, particularly in fiber form. For instance, in mid-1979, the North Pacific Paper Corporation, a new joint venture of Weyerhaeuser and a Japanese paper company, started producing newsprint at Longview, Washington, for sale in the United States and Japan on a 50–50 basis. At the same time, Weyerhaeuser has not shown any evidence that it wishes to relinquish its position as the largest U.S. log exporter. Weyerhaeuser's planned marshalling yard and port at Dupont, Washington, will allow cutting exporting costs by $10 per ton from the $20 to $70 per ton otherwise required. This facility, if completed, is expected to allow Weyerhaeuser to compete more effectively.

EXHIBIT 5

Volume of International Business			
Year	Total Sales of Products Exported from U.S.	Total Net Sales from Operations Outside the U.S.	Total Net Sales from All Operations, domestic & international
1979	$978,000,000	$482,000,000	$4,423,000,000
1978	729,000,000	370,000,000	3,799,000,000
1977	658,000,000	325,000,000	3,283,000,000

SOURCE: 1979 10K Report

The other aspects of international operations include the harvesting of timber, processing of timber into lumber, and the production of intermediate and finished products, principally shipping containers, in other nations. Canadian lumber and pulp are used domestically in Canada and, in addition, are marketed in the eastern United States, Europe, and Japan. Southeast Asian timber and lumber are principally marketed in Japan and a joint venture company in which Weyerhaeuser is a partner is planning to construct up to five processing plants in Indonesia in addition to the one in operation. Each plant is expected to be able to produce 4.2 million cubic feet per year. Besides the timber processing plants in Southeast Asia, Weyerhaeuser has a paperboard plant in France, situated to supply the company's European container plants which also supply European markets.

The real estate business, centered around the Weyerhaeuser Real Estate Company and its subsidiaries, makes Weyerhaeuser the seventh largest home builder and the seventh largest mortgage lender in the United States. The Weyerhaeuser Real Estate Company employs approximately 2,000 of the company's 48,000 employees and builds, sells, and finances single and multifamily dwelling units. Recent initiatives include plans to build a 800 housing unit and resort development in Oregon, consideration of entering the savings and loan field, and the formation of Cornerstone Development Corporation, a joint venture in which Weyerhaeuser holds the majority interest. Cornerstone was formed both as a profit making venture and to serve a social purpose through rehabilitating and redeveloping run down urban areas. The first project, planned for completion in the mid-1980s, is the renovation of a five block area of the Seattle waterfront into housing, retail, and parking facilities.

Special products businesses include aquaculture and the production of energy and environmental equipment, paper disposable diapers, nursery supplies, and chemicals. Two of these diversification efforts, i.e., production of energy and environmental equipment by Combustion Power Company and production of chemicals, provide Weyerhaeuser control over products for its internal use as well as profit. Chemical production capitalizes on some by-products, e.g., turpentine, and tall oil but is involved primarily with production of chlorine and caustics used in pulping, and with urea fertilizers used in forestry. Weyerhaeuser's entry into the disposable diaper field has left them the largest private label supplier (to Sears, Roebuck and other chains) with approximately 8 to 9 percent of the total domestic market. Recent company interest in aquaculture operations in Florida, Oregon and Brazil offers long range potential to capitalize on the company's waterfront properties, provide a social benefit, and profit as population pressures on the food supply make commercial shrimp growing and salmon ocean ranching feasible. In the latter line, Weyerhaeuser estimates that if even only one percent of the salmon released to the sea eventually reach harvestable size and return to be harvested, the company will break even.

An important aspect of Weyerhaeuser's operations is the management of its resource base. With 2.8 million acres of forest lands concentrated in the Douglas fir region of Western Washington and Oregon and the Ponderosa pine region of Eastern Oregon; 3.1 million acres in the Southern pine region of North Carolina, Mississippi, Alabama, Arkansas, and Oklahoma; plus 10.5 million acres of harvest rights in interior British Columbia, Eastern Ontario, Malaysia, and Indonesia, Weyerhaeuser alone among major companies has enough trees on a net basis to supply its own needs. This resource allows Weyerhaeuser to sell logs for export. Not only does the company export logs but it also produces more logs than it needs for its own manufacturing and converting and thus sells to its competitors. However, Weyerhaeuser at the same time, buys timber from others because of qualities needed for specific products or where it is more economical to do so from a logistics cost standpoint, even at locations where the company has an excess supply.

The company's basic policy is to manage lands to provide the highest yield on its investment consistent with a continuous supply of wood in the future. An early leader in tree farming, Weyerhaeuser now does about 16 percent of U.S. forest regeneration. Weyerhaeuser has, over time, improved its techniques so that its High Yield Forestry program can double production in a given replanted area over what nature unassisted can do. Forests selected for the High Yield Forestry program are now planted with genetically improved trees within one year of harvest, fertilized, and thinned as necessary. As a result of this program, Weyerhaeuser forecasts a dramatic increase in the Southern wood supply in the 1990 to 2010 period. However, improved forestry practices are not without cost—Weyerhaeuser estimates that it will spend approximately $140 million per year on forestry through the 1980s.

Weyerhaeuser's size has scale implications not only for forestry management but also for logistics and movement into new areas. A high volume of export shipments combined with capital make the logistics-cost-saving Dupont export facility possible. Similarly, volume and capital make operation of its own transportation systems possible. For example, Weyerhaeuser has been able to develop a network of 32,000 miles of internal roads on its lands, own and operate six short line common carrier railroads with 3,600 owned and leased rail cars, and charter eighteen ocean-going ships. Eight of the ships, two 660-foot Japanese-built and Norwegian-owned-and-operated ships used to carry newsprint, pulp, and other products from the West Coast to Japan and six similar ships that operate between the West Coast and Europe, are specially configured for efficient loading and are scheduled to serve Weyerhaeuser. Similarly, its railroads are dedicated to Weyerhaeuser, with both schedules and rail cars tailored to the company's needs.

RESEARCH AND DEVELOPMENT

Research and development at Weyerhaeuser is conducted by a work force of some 145 doctoral degree holders in 40 disciplines plus 338 other degree holders in 60 disciplines plus 376 technicians working on approximately 500 projects. These efforts are supported by an annual budget of approximately $50 million.

In the late 1970s, the company consolidated major research activities in a new 450,000 square foot technology center colocated with corporate headquarters at Tacoma, Washington. Here researchers work on exploratory research projects that may produce usable results in three to ten years or on applied research that has been advanced from the exploratory stage because of its high potential and lower risk. Such applied research is expected to have actual payoff in one to three years.

Two major thrusts dominate research—forest production and production plant technology. In the former direction, much effort has been aimed at genetically improving trees and techniques used in cultivating replanted forests. For example, research has developed a technique for planting new seedling trees that requires only 160 days of growth in a greenhouse before planting and results in fast growth after replanting. This is contrasted with the next best technology that requires two years of growth in a nursery before replanting and then produces a medium rate of growth. Production plant technology research and development is aimed at improving efficiency. A major area has been improving machinery to improve yield from logs in sawmills. Largely with the development of computer scanning equipment that permits saws and edgers to be positioned to maximize recovery, Weyerhaeuser's research and development effort has, in eight years, provided the means to double the volume of usuable wood obtained from logs. Weyerhaeuser's scale of operations allows the company to capitalize on this advancement not at just a single plant but at 20 or more sawmills. Another major area of research and development interest has been the development of technology specifically aimed at maximizing the recovery from small logs. As a result a number of small log sawmills have been constructed, the latest of which was slated to replace an older inefficient mill at Raymond, Washington, in 1980.

MARKETING

Strong competition from other forest products companies and producers of wood products substitutes is reflected in a marketing approach oriented toward flexibility and service. Flexibility is evident in several ways. First, marketing decision making is decentralized to the various business and product groups. Each uses its choice of a channel or channels of distribution tailored to the nature of the product and user. Construction materials are sold through wholesalers and directly to retailers and industrial users. Pulp, newsprint, and paper board are sold directly to industrial users, processors, and converters, while paper is sold through wholesalers or jobbers. Containers and packaging products are usually sold directly to industrial or agricultural users. Second, marketing is operating in an adaptive mode, focusing on matching the products that can be economically produced at each of its operating regions with the markets that can be economically served by each. This adapting has particularly taken the direction of shifting to the most profitable geographical markets as transportation economics effectively close out long standing markets such as the midwest and east coast for western timber products. Third, the company's marketing efforts are aimed at anticipating and adapting to changes in user tastes and locations. This has involved changing the product mix as consumer preferences and technology have shifted demand from lumber and plywood to hardboards and particleboards, for example. A major change that Weyerhaeuser sees is a growing Asian market, particularly Japan, Korea, and Taiwan now and, later, China. This change has shaped the company's emphasis on international operations, organization, export facilities, and sales.

Customer service as a marketing strategy shows itself in the company's plant location practices and its commitment to special facilities. For example, container and milk carton plants are located near their markets. This closeness coupled with technical advice and service provides customers with a higher level of service than otherwise. Similarly, the operation of more than seventy distribution centers in high growth or high volume areas, each carrying a full line of produced and purchased products, provides retailers and industrial users better service. Use of its own ships,

EXHIBIT 6

Consolidated Balance Sheet
End of Calendar Year
($ millions)

	1979	1978	1977	1976	1975	1974	1973	1972	1971	1970
Assets										
Current assets										
cash	176.1	141.1								
short term investments	186.8	105.6								
receivables	429.5	392.5								
inventories	465.4	407.1								
prepaid expenses	33.9	29.8								
Total current assets	1291.7	1076.1	1009.5	981.4	782.8	657.6	476.9	404.3	412.7	385.7
Investments and other assets										
Weyerhaeuser Real Estate Co.	201.7	182.4								
other	49.5	41.6								
	251.1	224.0	212.6	206.8	220.2	210.9	195.6	197.2	195.1	161.6
Property and equipment, at cost, less depreciation	2485.2	2199.1	2044.4	1848.4	1579.7	1238.8	1111.8	1101.3	765.6	679.0
Construction in progress	170.8	252.3	238.9	167.2	204.7	291.0	102.9	33.0	291.1	153.7
Leased property, under capital leases, principally ships, less amortization	150.6	166.1	181.1	—	—	—	—	—	—	—
Timber and timberlands	608.3	545.9	532.6	477.9	458.9	452.8	422.5	405.2	417.2	416.7
	4957.9	4463.6	4219.1	3631.7	3246.3	2851.0	2309.6	2141.0	2081.8	1796.7

Liabilities and Shareholder's Interest										
Current liabilities	645.9	589.5	488.4	469.4	395.2	378.0	349.2	210.2	338.5	233.4
Long term debt	1185.0	1187.1	1211.9	1093.4	929.4	915.6	526.4	780.5	531.6	519.0
Deferred income taxes	57.5	55.0								
Deferred pension and other liabilities	155.7	127.5								
Capital lease obligations	157.6	167.6								
Minority interest in subsidiaries	20.4	19.0								
Shareholders' interest										
preferred shares	4.0	4.0								
preference shares	.3									
common shares	241.2	241.1								
other capital	251.1	249.9								
retained earnings	2347.5	1980.5								
	2844.0	2475.5								
Treasury shares	108.1	157.7								
Total shareholders' interest	2735.9	2317.9	2177.1	1981.9	1784.5	1491.2	1390.5	1127.0	1189.0	1020.3
	4957.9	4463.6								

SOURCE: 1979 Annual and 10K Reports

EXHIBIT 7

Consolidated Earnings
(millions except per share figures)

	1979	1978	1977	1976	1975	1974	1973	1972	1971	1970
Net sales	4422.6	3799.4	3282.8	3868.4	2421.3	2529.0	2301.7	1675.9	1299.5	1233.4
Weyerhaeuser Real Estate Company earnings	57.1	51.8	47.1	16.9	5.1					
Other income, net	37.0	19.9	14.6	12.5	(10.5)					
	4516.7	2872.1	3344.6	2897.8	2416.0					
Operating costs	3325.7	3869.6	2543.9	2181.5	1842.5					
Selling, general and administrative expenses	302.5	255.1	228.6	207.5	182.9					
Research and development expenses	45.0	51.0	46.3	30.3	22.9					
Interest expense	113.3	113.0	103.4	78.8	82.5					
Less interest capitalized	8.7	9.2	8.0	13.1	15.2					
Earnings before income taxes and extraordinary charge	738.9	592.6	430.4	412.8	299.4					
Income taxes	226.7	180.0	128.9	106.8	110.6					
Earnings before extraordinary charge	512.2	412.6	301.5	206.0	188.8					
Extraordinary charge	—	41.5	—	—	—					
Net earnings	512.2	371.1	301.5	206.0	188.8	277.0	348.4	158.9	114.8	124.6
Average common shares outstanding	124.8	126.1	127.4	127.2	126.9	127.5	126.6	125.7	125.5	123.7
Net earnings per common share	4.02	2.85	2.28	2.32	1.48	2.17	2.72	1.17	.82	.93
Dividends paid	1.07½	.85	.80	.80	.80	.80	.47	.41½	.40	.40

SOURCE: 1979 Annual Report and 10K Report

under charter, is yet another means of providing increased speed and reliability of service, this time for foreign customers.

FINANCIAL PERFORMANCE

Weyerhaeuser experienced a general growth trend in assets, net sales, net earnings, and earnings per share during the decade of the 1970s. Assets were nearly tripled while long term debt was doubled (exhibit 6). As indicated in exhibit 7, earnings, although erratic, increased severalfold. After tax return on equity was characterized by a slight increasing trend and considerable variability with rates of 12.2, 9.7, 14.1, 25, 18.5, 10.6, 15.4, 13.8, 16, and 18.7 percent in 1970, 1971, 1972, 1973, 1974, 1975, 1976, 1977, 1978, and 1979, respectively.

Part of the realized rate of return is related to the long term holding of trees purchased in the past at very low prices (relative to today). Any positive difference between the value for tax purposes (based on current bids for future harvests of similar stands of government owned timber) and the value of the timber at the time it was acquired, plus growing and harvesting expenses, is treated as a long term capital gain subject to the lower rate capital gains tax.

Although growing, the rate of growth in total revenues has been at a decreasing rate recently, without even considering the undervaluation of assets associated with inflation and the generally increased price levels. Had materials and resources been costed at current values rather than historical costs, net earnings and return on equity would have been less. For example, had assets been valued at current cost, net owners equity would have been $4,775,164,000, rather than the $2,735,867,000 reflected in the 1979 balance sheet (exhibit 6). 1979 net earnings of $512,200,000 represent a 10.7 percent return on equity when adjusted for specific prices while the rate of return unadjusted for price changes was 18.7 percent.

The greatest rate of growth (in sales and contributions to earnings) is attributable to other, nonbuilding materials and fiber products sales. Based on data from exhibit 8, between 1977 and 1979 alone, this class of products increased its contributions 130 percent while increasing identifiable assets only 43 percent.

The company's commitments to growth and modernization of its asset base are reflected in its capital expenditure outlays that have exceeded after tax earnings in nine out of ten years in the 1970s. Operations has been the primary source of funds for capital expenditure and other corporate requirements with new debt and new equity providing only 21 percent of the needed funds during 1975–1979.

CORPORATE CITIZENSHIP

Once termed "the best of the SOBs,"[6] Weyerhaeuser evidences corporate citizenship in a number of ways beyond providing jobs, products, and profits. Responsible and complete use of forest resources, forest regeneration, resource development, energy conservation, protection of the environment, active involvement in the public policy making process, and corporate giving are all means by which the company may be considered by some to contribute to the well being of society.

EXHIBIT 8

Major Product Class Performance ($ millions)					
Net Sales:	1979	1978	1977	1976	1975
Building materials	2710	2346	1950	1627	1318
Pulp, newsprint, paper and paperboard products	888	753	715	680	621
Container and packaging products	685	590	539	514	454
Other	140	110	79	47	28
	4423	3799	3283	2866	2421
Approximate Contribution to Earnings*:					
Building materials	726	671	515	418	307
Pulp, newsprint, paper and paperboard products	181	87	69	152	157
Container and packaging products	26	13	18	18	25
Other	23	20	10	7	8
	956	791	612	592	497
Identifiable Assets:					
Building materials	2293	2094	1919		
Pulp, newsprint, paper and paperboard products	1435	1351	1321		
Container and packaging products	295	254	240		
Other	173	141	121		
	4196	3840	3601		

*excludes: general, administrative, certain research and other expenses; interest expense; income taxes; earnings of unconsolidated real estate and finance subsidiaries; and other unallocatable income such as dividends, interest, and royalties

SOURCE: 1979 10K Report

Forest use practices point toward full use of its forest land resources—from efficient conversion of timber into wood products, use of by-products, reduction of waste and scrap, to the regeneration of logged-off lands for greater yields in the future. A major thrust of the company's research and development effort has been in these directions. The scientific tree farming that began in the 1930s and that evolved into the High Yield Forestry program has been expanded to include commitments to nonsilviculture activities such as design of more efficient processes and new product developments, both forest products based and others, e.g., aquaculture.

Energy conservation has been another subject of company policy and expenditure. Substantial research, development, and engineering modification efforts have been directed toward the use of waste products as sources of energy. As a result of these efforts, Weyerhaeuser was rated most energy efficient of eighteen paper and forest products companies surveyed by Kidder, Peabody and Company, in 1978.[7] Concern with energy conservation has also been manifested in a company sponsored carpooling program. Under its van pooling program, Weyerhaeuser buys and provides vans for groups of employees wishing to share rides. Members pay only a periodic fee calculated to pay the costs of the van, over time. The van pool driver-sponsor in return for organizing, collecting, and driving, has limited use of the van for personal travel in off work hours.

With an early start in pollution abatement and expenditures on environmental costs that amount to between 10 and 15 percent of its capital expenditures budget, Weyerhaeuser has been a leader in regulatory compliance among the large companies in its industry. Such pollution control efforts have sometimes been combined with those aimed at other objectives such as the recovery and reuse of chemicals used in pulp making.

The company's approach to solving problems concerning conflicts between profitable company operations and protection of the ecology and the environment has been both proactive and accommodating. The company policy statement concerning use of resources is to ". . . perform in concert and harmony with nature and the public interest by: exercising the highest level of responsible stewardship of natural and environmental resources, practicing wise use of all resources throughout its activities, responding positively to opportunities for environmental, ecological and social problem solving, and encouraging others toward the same commitments."[8] Carrying out this policy has involved attempting to anticipate environmentalists' concerns, using their input in planning, and then actively championing the resultant plan. The proposed Dupont export facility is a case in point. Arguments against the facility have been based on two issues. The first and most emotional issue was whether or not the port facilities and activity would have an adverse effect on the fish and wildlife of the nearby Nisqually River delta and wildlife refuge. Second, opponents argued that exporting logs from the facility meant exporting jobs and forest resources that are needed in the U.S. Weyerhaeuser's response was to study the economic and environmental consequences of operations, solicit inputs from concerned governmental bodies, private groups, and the public, and then attempt to present facts and arguments on both sides of the issue to the public and government officials. Basically, the company has stressed that the facility should not be expected to have any significant impact on the surrounding environment and that adequate precautions will be taken to prevent any unforeseen impacts that are humanly controllable. With respect to the arguments against exporting logs, Weyerhaeuser has taken every opportunity to explain that the facility is designed for manufactured product exports and that any logs shipped from Dupont will be in lieu of exporting them from other ports, that logs exported are from trees, surplus to manufacturing needs, that jobs are actually created because people are employed in the export business over those needed for meeting domestic demand, that employment is stabilized because foreign demand and sales do not follow U.S. seasonal patterns, and that the nation is better off because of the net benefit to the U.S. trade balance. Despite the company's efforts, it has not yet won approval of the port.

The proactive approach to public policy making is visible in George Weyerhaeuser, Chief Executive Officer of the company, who has been outspoken as a supporter of U.S. national interest, such as log exporting, and a critic of federal government economic policy. However, the company does not rely solely on personal opinion leadership. Organizationally, Weyerhaeuser operates a liasion office in Washington, D.C., employs the services of lobbyists, belongs to and supports national and state general business interest and industry interest groups, and sponsors a political action committee. The political action committee typically channels its campaign contributions to candidates who are believed to consider information from multiple sources, and who are from states where the company has sizable operations.

The Weyerhaeuser Company Foundation is the primary vehicle through which the company supports selected social goals. The foundation has two missions: to improve the quality of life in employees' living environments and to provide leadership, information, and understanding of significant issues impacting both industry and society, specifically as they relate to forest land use. Toward these purposes, grants totalling over $32 million have been made since 1948 to social, health, educational, cultural and civic organizations, primarily in communities where the company has a high level of employment. In 1979 alone, the Foundation distributed over $4 million to organizations. The Foundation is currently administering two ongoing programs, the quality of life program and general education grants, and a third, the forest land use grants program, is in the planning stage. The quality of life program is aimed at improving basic services and amenities in communities where Weyerhaeuser operates. Grants are selectively made in these communities to support social service, health, recreation, culture, the arts, civic causes, employment, training, and supplemental educational projects; based on priorities and guidelines approved by local employee review committees. General education grants cover three traditional programs: scholarships, fellowships, and matching gifts to private colleges and universities.

Although Weyerhaeuser has been long recognized as a leader in the responsible use of resources, it has at the same time been the subject of criticism. Among the criticisms in addition to those associated with the export of logs and the building of a port at Dupont, Weyerhaeuser has been accused of:

1 Genetically tampering with salmon and thus possibly weakening them in their natural environment.

2 Growing uniform forests of a single species of trees, thus creating a monotonous landscape and tampering with the balance of plant life.

3 Establishing tree farms only where they can be seen, leaving other forest lands in nature's hands after the timber is cut.

4 Continuing to pollute. For example, notwithstanding expenditures on pollution control, the company was cited for failure to meet standards at its Longview, Washington, plant in a suit by the Environmental Protection Agency.

5 Unethical or illegal behavior. In the late 1970s, the company was the subject of several criminal and civil actions for alleged price fixing practices and was fined $632,000 by a federal judge after pleading "no contest" to one charge. Despite failure to obtain indictments, an acquittal in federal court, and the settlement of most civil suits out of court, the company's name was associated with the price fixing scandal.

In the effort to preclude further evidences of unethical behavior by employees, George Weyerhaeuser has expressed his and the company's concern, to employees, about the company's image and has been adamant concerning adherence to the letter and intent of the law. As an aid to employees faced with doubtful decision situations, the company developed a Business Conduct Committee that can be contacted for advice, guidance, and clarification, before the fact; disseminated written policies concerning employee behavior; and developed criteria by which employees can self certify their compliance with the policies.

ORGANIZATION AND MANAGEMENT

Growth, primarily since the 1950s, into new products, new geographical areas, and international operations, often through acquisition, has spawned structural changes. The added complexities associated with centralized management and coordination of multiple materials sources, production plants, and markets for several different kinds of products caused Weyerhaeuser to decentralize operations decision making to regions and to assign each of its various products to a business grouping of similar product lines. This reorganization, initially effected in 1972 with the formation of five business groups and eleven geographical regions has evolved into a structure that involves four major kinds of organizational units, each with its distinct role. These four organizational groupings or units are senior management, businesses, operating regions, and corporate staff.

Senior management includes the president and chief executive officer and seven senior vice presidents who assist the president in overseeing the corporation and providing general direction. Each member of this top management group is charged with co-ordinating the efforts and needs, evaluating the performance, and assisting in establishing appropriate policy and plans for those assigned businesses or staff functions. Exhibit 9 shows the assignment of major staff functions, businesses, and operating regions among the president and senior vice presidents.

Currently, twelve major business or resource groups report to senior management. The vice presidents of *pulp, paper, newsprint,* and *paperboard packaging* report to the senior vice president for pulp, paper, and paperboard. The vice presidents of *land and timber; raw materials; lumber; panels, hardwood, and consumer products; plywood;* and *wood products sales and distribution* report to the senior vice president, timberlands, wood products, and international. The vice presidents for *shelter and special businesses* (aquaculture, chemicals, nursery supply, soft disposables, and Combustion Power Company) report to the president and the senior vice president, finance and planning, respectively.

The businesses are the primary units for strategic planning and marketing. Each is a profit center responsible for business planning including the formulation of objectives, strategies, and policies. They are held accountable for developing marketing strategy; developing supporting financial plans; selling, distributing, and secondary manufacturing of products; and planning new manufacturing facilities, processes, and product developments. In addition to the responsibility for log, timber, and chip marketing and planning, the raw materials business provides functional guidance to operating regions for maximizing raw materials values. The land and timber resources group is responsible for management and analysis of the timber asset, including directing the high-yield forestry program; nursery-and-seed orchard management; timber and seedling sales; land classification; recreation de-

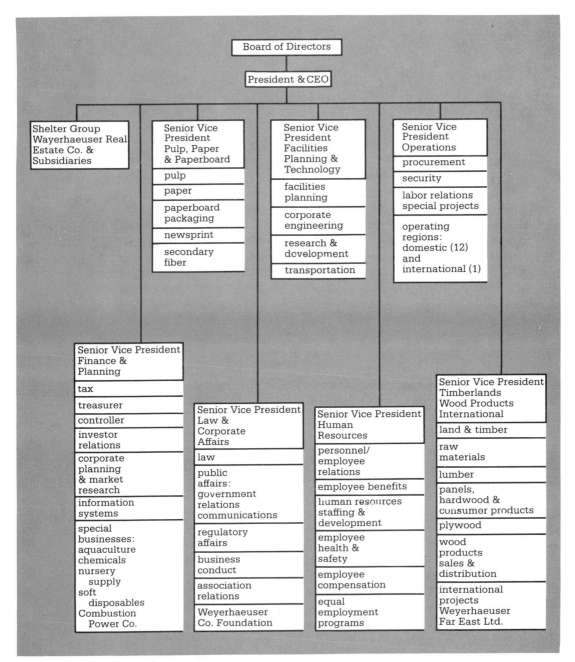

EXHIBIT 9

Organizational Relationships

SOURCE: Weyerhaeuser Company Profile July 1979, Management Bulletin No. 861, and Weyerhaeuser Handy Facts, June 1980.

velopment; mineral and agricultural development; road-use agreements; and land acquisition, sales, or transfers.

Although the major business strategy is formulated and effected from the business groups at corporate headquarters, decision making with respect to operations is decentralized, resting with the twelve domestic and two international regions. As the primary unit for operations, the regions are responsible for maximizing production efficiency of timber and primary manufacturing operations and achieving optimum value from the raw materials available. Within regions, this profit responsibility and decision making is further delegated to local plant managers. The vice presidents for the eastern Oregon; Willamette (Oregon); southwest Oregon; northern Washington; Twin Harbors (Washington); southwest Washington; central Arkansas; Mississippi/Alabama; North Carolina; north central Oklahoma; southwest Arkansas regions and the president of Weyerhaeuser Canada, Ltd., report to the senior vice president of operations. The only other operating region, Weyerhaeuser Far East Ltd., reports to the senior vice president, timberlands, wood products, and international.

Corporate staff units, under vice presidents or directors, are clustered for reporting purposes by functional groupings. Generally, the staff serves to perform three functions:

1 Assist in the planning process through fact gathering, analytical, and counseling service.

2 Support the chief executive officer, operating units, and the corporation as a whole by providing advice and expert services in specialized areas.

3 Assist management in setting objectives, policies, and budgets; developing procedures; and evaluating performance.

Management of foreign-based businesses and resources follows two forms. In the case of Canadian and European operations, management is usually accomplished through subsidiaries (e.g., Weyerhaeuser Canada, Ltd., and Cartonpack S.A.) which function as units in the operating region or business structure. The other case applies to the management of Far Eastern enterprises where joint ventures represent a significant portion of Weyerhaeuser's activity. In this case, the president of Weyerhaeuser Far East, Ltd., represents Weyerhaeuser's interests in its joint ventures in the role of Weyerhaeuser's shareholder representative. In addition, Weyerhaeuser Far East, Ltd., performs as the operating and administrative reporting unit for all Weyerhaeuser subsidiaries and offices in that part of the world.

Acquired and newly formed subsidiaries have played an increasingly noticeable role in Weyerhaeuser's production, manufacturing, and marketing efforts. Even before the latest round of acquisitions shown in exhibit 4, the company had integrated a substantial number of subsidiaries into the existing business, regional operations, and the international organization. As listed in exhibit 10, the majority of these subsidiaries are wholly owned.

With nearly 50,000 employees working in more than 100 locations in and outside the United States under twelve business/resource groups, fourteen geographical regions, or other staff and operational units, capable managers and executives are needed to effect decisions and coordination. Accomplishing this task involves the efforts of a large number of executives and senior managers. This team includes, in addition to the various plant and operations managers, forty-five executives of vice president or similar status, and a top management group of the president and seven senior vice presidents. The top eight executives, identified in exhibit 11, represent a total of 166 years of experience in the company. All of the top executives except two, Ben Borne and William Ruckelshaus, were appointed to their present positions from within the company.

ENDNOTES

1   "The Tree Farm and How It Grew," *Nation's Business,* January 1971, 94–95.
2   Ibid., p. 95.
3   Weyerhaeuser Corporation, *A Long History and A Sense of Corporate Responsibility* (undated).
4   Ibid.
5   Weyerhaeuser Corporation, *Policy-General: Company Objective* (August 16, 1971).
6   John G. Mitchell, "The Best of the SOB's," *Audubon,* September 1974, 48–59.
7   Pamela G. Hollie, "Slow Growth for a Giant," *New York Times,* Sunday, April 20, 1979, p. 9.
8   Company draft statement concerning intentions and use of the Dupont site, June 8, 1979.

EXHIBIT 10

Subsidiaries		
Name	State Country of Incorporation	Percentage Ownership of Immediate Parent
Camad Veneer, Inc.	Oregon	50%
Chehalis Western Railroad Company	Washington	100
Columbia & Cowlitz Railway Company	Washington	100
Combustion Power Company, Inc.	Delaware	100
Curtis, Milburn and Eastern Railroad Company	Washington	100
De Queen and Eastern Railroad Company	Arkansas	100
Erickson Hardwoods, Inc.	Wisconsin	100
Miss/Ala Plywood Company	Mississippi	100
Sumter Plywood Corporation	Alabama	100
Mississippi & Skuna Valley Railroad Company	Mississippi	100
Mountain Tree Farm Company	Washington	50
North Pacific Paper Corporation	Delaware	90
Oregon Aqua-Foods, Inc.	Oregon	100
Oregon, California & Eastern Railway Company	Nevada	100
Shemin Nurseries, Inc.	Delaware	80
Texas, Oklahoma & Eastern Railroad Company	Oklahoma	100
Weyerhaeuser Export, Inc.	Delaware	100
Weyerhaeuser Miquon, Inc.	Delaware	100

Weyerhaeuser International, Inc.*		
(domestic parent)	Washington	100
The Capricorn Corporation	Philippines	100
Cartonpack, S.A.	Greece	100
Cargal Hallas L.L.C.	Greece	100
de Bes' Insurance Ltd.	Bermuda	100
Iberoamericana del Embalaje, S.A.	Spain	100
Iberoamericana de Catalunya, S.A.	Spain	100
Kennedy Bay Timber Sendirian Berhad	Malaysia	100
Timber Trading (International), S.A.	Panama	65
Weyerhaeuser (Aust.) Pty. Ltd.	Australia	100
Weyerhaeuser Belgium, S.A.	Belgium	100
N.A. Weyerhaeuser Packaging	Belgium	100
Weyerhaeuser Canada Ltd.	Canada	100
Weyerhaeuser Deutschland Gmbh	Germany	100
Weyerhaeuser Europe, S.A.	France	99.5
Cartonneries du Forez	France	100
Dropsy Carton	France	100
Societe Novelle des Paperteries de La Haye Descartes S.A.R.L.	France	100
Weyerhaeuser (Far East) Limited	Hong Kong	100
P.T. International Timber Corporation Indonesia	Indonesia	65
Weyerhaeuser Italia, S.r.l.	Italy	100
Weyerhaeuser, S.A.	Panama	100
Weyerhaeuser Overseas Finance Company	Delaware	100
Weyerhaeuser Townsite Company	Arkansas	100
Weyerhaeuser Real Estate Company*	Washington	100
The Babcock Company	Florida	100
Centennial Homes, Inc.	Texas	100
Cornerstone Development Company	Washington	80
Par-West Financial	California	100
Marmont Realty Company	California	100
Pardee Construction Company	California	100
Pardee Construction Company of Nevada	Nevada	100
Parvada, Inc.	Nevada	100
Westwood Associates	California	100
Westwood Insurance Agency	California	100
Weyerhaeuser Mortgage Company	California	100
Weyerhaeuser Venture Company	Nevada	100
The Quadrant Corporation	Washington	100
Quadrant Development Limited	Canada	100
Scarborough Corporation	Delaware	100
Bob Scarborough, Inc.	New Jersey	100
Scarborough Constructors, Inc.	Florida	100
The Scarborough Company	New Jersey	100
Quill Corporation	New Jersey	100
Westminster Company	North Carolina	100
Weyerhaeuser Real Estate Company of Nevada	Nevada	100
Winchester Homes, Inc.	Delaware	100

*George H. Weyerhaeuser is president of this subsidiary

SOURCE: 1979 10K Report

EXHIBIT 11

Name and Position	Age	Years with Weyerhaeuser	Background (Weyerhaeuser unless other noted)
Senior Management			
George H. Weyerhaeuser President & Chief Executive Officer	54	31	Yale (B.S., Ind Adm); manager, V.P.: exec. V.P., wood products; exec. V.P. operations, President and CEO since 1966.
Charles W. Bingham, Senior Vice President, timberlands, wood products & international	47	20	Harvard (LL.B): law dept.; wood chip supply manager; corp. raw materials manager; area manager; V.P., wood products.
Ben W. Borne, Senior Vice President, human resources	56	2	Spring Hill College (B.A.), Loyola Univ. (J.D.); FBI; industrial relations V.P., Litton Industries division; V.P. & director human resources, Motorola.
Alexander M. Fisken, Senior Vice President, facilities planning and technology	57	35	Yale (B.S., Engineering); engineering development, new business; manager in several products divisions; engineering director; V.P., facilities planning and engineering.
Harry E. Morgan, Jr. Senior Vice President, operations	58	34	Stanford (A.B.); wood & plant operations; asst. logging superintendent; admin. asst.; branch manager; manufacturing manager; V.P. timberlands division, Corp. V.P.
William D. Ruckelshaus, Senior Vice President law and corporate affairs	48	4	Princeton (B.A.); Harvard (LL.B.); attorney in private practice; deputy attorney general & chief counsel, State of Indiana; minority attorney, Indiana Senate; member Indiana House of Representatives; asst. attorney general, U.S. Dept. of Justice; Federal Administrator, EPA: acting director, FBI; Deputy Attorney General, U.S.; senior partner in private practice.
Robert L. Schuyler, Senior Vice President, finance and planning	44	14	Nebraska (B.S. in B.A.), Harvard (M.B.A.); manager, financial analysis; manager, investment evaluation; V.P., finance & planning.
John Shethar, Senior Vice President, fiber business	53	26	Yale (B.S. in econ); sales representative; manager, pulp sales; pulp division manager; pulp & paper division V.P.; V.P., pulp, paper, & consumer packaging.

530

THE CHRYSLER CORPORA- TION LOAN GUARANTEE ACT OF 1979

Paul Miesing

**"What's good for Chrysler
is good for the country."**

As the 1980 automobile year began, one issue emerged that brought together Chrysler's management, the United Auto Workers, Michigan Congressmen, former President Gerald R. Ford, and President Jimmy Carter long enough to successfully defeat a combined force which included the likes of consumer activist Ralph Nader and free-marketeer Milton Friedman. These unlikely sides were formed as Chrysler—the nation's tenth largest industrial company—found itself in a grave situation. A marginal manufacturer in a traditionally cyclical business, Chrysler has historically had erratic profits due in part to its relatively high costs and weak financial structure. But when the market share of the third largest U.S. car maker plummetted from 16.1 percent in 1970 to 9.6 percent for 1979, the beleaguered company was near bankruptcy. Its losses of over one billion dollars in 1979 were the largest in U.S. corporate history, and were expected to be followed with a half-billion dollar loss in 1980. (See Exhibits 1 and 2 for industry sales and profits.) Spending from thirty to fifty million dollars a day on cars that would not be available for two years, the company could not generate enough cash to meet its daily operating costs. Only by raising massive amounts of new capital could Chrysler hope to survive. But bankers are reluctant to extend funds to a firm facing such an uncertain future unless the loans are guaranteed by the federal government. Such a proposal was initiated by the Carter Administration, but remained an extremely emotional and controversial issue throughout its subsequent Congressional hearings.

Many of Chrysler's problems were blamed on the skyrocketing costs for meeting tight (and some believed unreasonable) government legislation, costing consumers around ten percent of the price of an automobile. With a billion dollars budgeted for 1979 and 1980 just to meet regulatory requirements, Chrysler claimed that the situation it faced was merely a symptom of excessive government intervention into the affairs of U.S. industry. Their argument continued that, if the company was failing as a result of public policy which required corporations

The research and written case information were presented at a Case Research Symposium and were evaluated by the Case Research Association's Editorial Board. This case was prepared by Professor Paul Miesing of the State University of New York at Albany based on published accounts and public documents, and it is intended as a basis for classroom discussion rather than to illustrate either effective or ineffective handling of an administrative situation.

Distributed by the Case Research Association. All rights reserved to the author and the Case Research Association. Permission to use the case should be obtained from the Case Research Association.

to meet social demands, then federal assistance was justified. Besides, the government had already amply demonstrated its willingness to support the economy through its numerous assistance programs, subsidies, grants, and other policies that aided businesses.

EXHIBIT 1

| | Total Units (000s) | Market Share (%) | | | | U.S. Cars (000s) | Imports | |
		GM	Ford	Chrysler	AMC		Total (000s)	Market Share (%)
New Automobile Sales in the U.S.								
1975	8,700	43.4	23.0	11.5	3.8	7,100	1,600	18.4
1976	10,100	47.5	22.3	12.9	2.5	8,600	1,500	14.8
1977	11,200	46.1	22.8	10.9	1.6	9,100	2,100	18.7
1978	11,300	47.7	22.8	10.1	1.5	9,300*	2,000	17.7
1979 (est.)	10,600	45.9	20.1	9.6	1.5	8,300*	2,300	21.6

*Excludes imports produced by foreign manufacturers for U.S. firms, and Volkswagens manufactured in the United States.

EXHIBIT 2

Comparative Sales and Profits for U.S. Automobile Manufacturers

| | Sales ($ billion) | | | | Profits ($ million) | | | |
	GM	Ford	Chrysler	AMC	GM	Ford	Chrysler	AMC
1975	35.7	24.0	11.6	2.3	1151	323	(260)	(28)
1976	47.2	28.8	15.5	2.3	2903	983	423	(46)
1977	55.0	37.8	16.7	2.2	3338	1673	163	8
1978	63.2	42.8	13.6	2.2	3508	1589	(205)	42
1979	66.3	43.5	12.0	3.1	2893	1169	(1097)	68

Taking his case to the public by writing in the December 3, 1979, issue of the *Wall Street Journal,* Chrysler chairman Lee A. Iacocca stated that "the unequal effects of government regulation" were unfairly hurting Chrysler. (Exhibits 3 and 4 demonstrate the results of Chrysler's disadvantage.) Citing 1965 emission standards as the predecessors for automobile mandates, he claimed that the industry had already reduced pollutant levels by ninety percent and it would cost $250 per car to reach the additional five percent required by 1981. Another example of inane involvement in industry affairs were the safety standards established in 1967, which eventually evolved into forty-four separate and confusing rules. The final imposition of Washington wisdom was 1975's fuel economy standards that demanded doubling the average miles per gallon for the 1985 fleet. Since "regulations amount to a regressive sales tax that hits the smallest company the hardest," Iacocca suggested that "helping Chrysler get through a financial crunch resulting from these regulations is itself a socially desirable thing to do." Insisting that the company's problem arises from its "need to raise massive amounts of new capital to meet federal law," he made a passionate argument for seeing Chrysler through its temporary crisis:

The issue we have raised by going to the government is not free enterprise. We really don't think a loan guarantee to Chrysler is in any sense a reward for failure, nor would it lead to a breakdown in market discipline.

Nor is the immediate issue the need for regulatory reform—even though certain reforms are necessary.

Rather, the central and critical issue at stake in Chrysler's survival is people and jobs. If government wants to do something about unemployment, if it wants to keep the nation's urban areas and cities alive, if it wants to prevent increased welfare dependency and government spending, if it wants to offset an $8 billion imbalance of automotive trade with Japan, let it approve Chrysler's legitimate and amply precedented request for temporary assistance.

Iacocca's position was at odds with that of such business leaders as General Motors' Thomas Murphy, Eastern Airlines' Frank Borman, General Electric's Reginald Jones, and Citicorp's Walter Wriston, among others, who stated that government support on such a huge scale would be inimical to a free enterprise system. They shared the "free enterprise" view that corporate managers are responsible to operate their businesses efficiently within environmental constraints and that their performance should ultimately be judged and rewarded by the market place. The government's responsibility to protect the public's interest does not extend to awarding windfalls to owners, managers, creditors, and others merely because they have a large stake in a corporation's outcome. Indeed, any forced distortion of investment flows would lead to lower productivity and fewer jobs over the long-run.

EXHIBIT 3

Comparative Expense Structures for Major U.S. Automobile Manufacturers (1974–78 Average Ratios)				
	GM	Ford	Chrysler	AMC
Net sales	100.0%	100.0%	100.0%	100.0%
Less: cost of goods sold	85.0	89.3	93.8	90.0
Gross profit	15.0	10.7	6.2	10.0
Less: depreciation	2.1	1.9	1.1	.9
selling, general & administrative	3.7	3.8	4.0	9.0
Operating profit	9.2	5.0	1.1	.1
Add: other net income	1.0	1.1	.1	.8
Less: interest	.6	.7	1.0	.7
Pretax income	9.6	5.4	0	.2
Less: income tax/ extraordinary	4.5	2.2	.1	.2
Net income	5.1	3.2	(.1)	0

EXHIBIT 4

Selected Financial Statistics for Major U.S. Automobile Manufacturers (1979 Year-End)				
	GM	Ford	Chrysler	AMC
Total assets (millions)	$32,023	$23,510	$6,653	$1,123
Total debt (millions)	$ 2,094	$ 2,082	$ 4.8B	$ 162
Debt/equity ratio	0.1	0.1	0.4	0.2
Current ratio	1.7	1.3	1.3	1.5
5-year average return on equity	19.8%	15.4%	deficit	1.5
5-year average return on capital	18.0%	12.7%	deficit	2.3
5-year average sales growth	13.2%	12.7%	8.2%	10.9%
5-year cash flow/growth needs	94.9%	90.5%	59.6%	59.5%
Outstanding shares (millions)	289.4	120.2	66.7	31.9
Stock price	$50	$32	$6¾	$6⅞
Dividend	$5.30	$3.90	$.20	$.08
Quality rating (S & P)	AAA	AAA	B	B

In a Darwinian system where only the fittest are worthy of survival, Chrysler may conceivably wind up as only one of the many thousands of annual casualities of free enterprise, which already include such major corporations as Arlen's Department Store, Equity Funding, Food Fair Stores, Franklin National Bank, W. T. Grant, and Robert Hall. Companies that go bankrupt merely pay the price for its prior management's poor decisions and miscalculations. This would also be true for Chrysler which was out of step when it re-designed big cars for 1974 and 1979, both times caught by surprise with a fuel crisis. Although no one could have predicted the energy crisis, Chrysler insisted on remaining a full-line producer even after American consumers shifted to fuel-efficient cars, only to find later it did not have enough small cars on hand to satisfy the surge in demand. Moreover, periodic economic downturns in no way helped sales.

While some viewed the bailout debates as a test case for future business-government relations, others saw labor unions exerting political pressure to save jobs in an upcoming election year. As evidence of this, an intense lobbying effort was mounted by Chrysler's allies who were attempting to convince the Congress that the aid it was seeking would give the corporation a profitable future and the U.S. economy a valuable manufacturer. Therefore, a one-year reprieve would be worthwhile to the nation.

The bill to approve federal assistance was placed on the U.S. Senate's calendar to follow their year-end debates on the oil companies' windfall profits tax. But for any loan guarantees to be meaningful, legislation had to be enacted before Congress adjourned. If aid were not forthcoming, the company claimed it would go bankrupt by February 14, 1980—St. Valentine's Day. As the long recess rapidly approached, there were fears that a compromise bill would not be agreed upon before the holidays. But Chrysler got its Christmas gift on Friday, December 21, 1979—the last day of the sessions—when Congress passed a multibillion dollar rescue package, just minutes before a majority of representatives went home. For the last week of the year, Chrysler's share of the market jumped to 12.4 percent.

The "Chrysler Corporation Loan Guarantee Act of 1979" created an independent, Cabinet-level loan board chaired by the Secretary of the Treasury and including the chairman of the Federal Reserve Board, the Comptroller General, and two other Cabinet officers who are nonvoting members. The board was authorized to grant $1.5 billion of loan guarantees at a charge of one percent per year which must be repaid by the end of 1983. But the company had to allow the government to monitor its operations in detail, audit its books, and even shuffle around top executives if deemed necessary. In addition, Chrysler had to come up with another $2.1 billion on its own while maintaining existing loans owed to current creditors. Of this amount, domestic banks, financial institutions, and other creditors would have to grant $500 million in new loans. Suppliers and dealers were obliged to give Chrysler $180 million in loans and/or stock purchases and states and cities where facilities are located were required to offer $250 million. Chrysler, on the other hand, was mandated to dispose of $300 million assets beyond the $400 million already liquidated and sell $50 million of additional stock. And its nonunion, white-collar employees were compelled to sacrifice $125 million by freezing their wages and benefits for three years and cutting the salaries of top officers.

Perhaps the most sensitive requirement was demanded of the United Automobile Workers. The House version of the bill called for $400 million in extra wage cuts whereas the Senate's bill called for $525 million. The final compromise of $462.5 million—including previously agreed-upon contributions totalling $203 million in wages and benefits—would require new contract negotiations and ratifications by the union members. In turn, the white-collar employees and blue-collar workers would receive $162.5 million in Chrysler stock. The union voted in favor of the proposal on January 5, 1980, and President Carter signed the bill into law two days later.

Immediately afterward, Iacocca announced plans to introduce cars ranging from subcompacts to a new down-sized Imperial. Since Chrysler needs only two good years to survive as a full-line carmaker, the eighteen months immediately following passage of the Act are crucial. But, since the loan guarantees will not be extended again, some feel that Chrysler's inevitable demise had only been postponed.

BRIEF HISTORY OF THE AUTOMOBILE INDUSTRY

The early part of this century saw 181 different automobile manufacturers come— but mostly go. Through consolidation and failure, the industry eventually became dominated by three firms. The evolvement into a concentrated oligopoly began when Henry Ford first revolutionized the then-fragmented industry in 1908 by using an assembly line to bring out an inexpensive car for the masses. His Model-"T" was an instant success with its high reliability and low maintenance cost. That same year, the lesser-known William C. Durant, using a business philosophy of organization and finance, turned the Buick Motor Company into the nation's leading automobile producer by selling eight thousand cars compared to Ford Motor Company's six thousand Model-"T"s. A year later, Durant's Wall Street backers rejected his proposal to buy Ford for eight million dollars. But continued success allowed Durant's holding company to evolve into the General Motors executive offices. Ford was able to maintain half the market with its low-priced, high-volume Model-"T" and low-volume, high-priced Lincoln. General Motors only had twelve percent of the market, but decided to offer a greater variety of automobiles in order to avoid direct head-on competition with Ford.

General Motors added numerous divisions as it grew over the next decade, but Durant insisted on making decisions about Buick without consulting its new president and general manager, Walter P. Chrysler. During the 1920 depression, after Durant and Chrysler had another of their frequent, stormy confrontations, Chrysler left the company to supervise the reorganization of the failing Maxwell Motor Corporation which had gone into receivership. The company was rescued and Chrysler had his name on an automobile by 1924. When the Chrysler Corporation was incorporated on June 6, 1925, it was the last successful entrant into the industry. But its real opportunity opened when Ford, losing market share to General Motors, ceased production in 1927 to design and produce the Model-"A". Chrysler had already pioneered such innovations as high-compression engines and four-wheel brakes, and now its Plymouth was able to take advantage of Ford's absence. The following year, Chrysler purchased the larger Dodge Bros., Inc., although the former Ford supplier had managed to escape a General Motors acquisition bid in 1926. Combined into Chrysler, the new company had one of the largest and most complete car plants in the world. DeSoto was added to Chrysler, and by 1929 the company joined General Motors and Ford as a member of the "Big Three." Thereafter, smaller firms would be unable to compete in the high volume market for the average car buyer.

Automobiles became the largest U.S. business by 1930 and General Motors became its leader for good in 1931, forcing Ford and Chrysler to follow its shift to a marketing orientation which differentiated products and emphasized annual model changes. After Chrysler made costly miscalculations in the mid-thirties as to how much change in appearance the public would accept in one year, the company finally managed to nudge out Ford for the number two spot for 1937 by once again deciding to emphasize research and development. Chrysler eliminated the debt it had acquired for its prior expansions, and in 1946 its reputation for engineering allowed it to repeat its second place finish behind General Motors by capturing a quarter of the automobile market. But Henry Ford II had taken over his grandfather's company after the second World War and immediately recruited the so-called "whiz kids," who reorganized the company and brought professional management techniques to it. Ford's first post-war automobile was introduced in 1949. After the United Automobile Workers struck Chrysler in 1950, the company permanently fell into third place.

The rapid economic growth of the fifties allowed automobiles to become shining examples of free enterprise and the pursuit of happiness. Detroit's chariots typified the "bigger is better" mentality as they continued to grow larger, more comfortable, and conspicuous and came to symbolize mobility, freedom, status, and self-expression. America's romance with the automobile was reflected in billions of dollars in gasoline taxes collected by the Federal Highway Trust Fund. But there were setbacks for the industry as well. Ford's Edsel became a legend in marketing fiascos, and Chrysler's DeSoto was finally dropped. The smaller firms—Kaiser, Willys, Nash-Kelvinator, and Hudson—found it difficult to compete, and so consolidated into the American Motors Corporation. Chrysler then decided to borrow funds to revamp the 1954 model, which was "smaller on the outside and bigger on the inside." Unfortunately, the public preferred General Motors' and Ford's larger cars, and the company's market share dropped to thirteen percent. Only after Chrysler bounced back with its own large car in 1957 did it capture nineteen percent of the market—which has not been reached since.

While Ford responded to a shift in consumer sentiment toward smaller cars by bringing out its highly successful Falcon and Mustang in the early and mid-sixties, Chrysler decided to stay with its higher-priced large cars by continuing to innovate in design, styling, and interior comfort, even introducing high-performance cars into its lineup. It was during this decade of social sensitivity to the quality of life and a struggle to become a "great society" that automobiles fell victim to industry regulations. The "Clean Air Act of 1963" (amended in 1970 and 1977) mandated the amount of pollutants that cars could emit. "Re-tuning" engines to accept emission control devices required an additional ten percent of gasoline consumption. Then, partly as the result of a forty percent increase in motor vehicle-related deaths from 1961 to 1966, and partly the result of a young, obscure Washington lawyer by the name of Ralph Nader writing *Unsafe at any Speed,* the U.S. Congress passed the "National Traffic and Motor Vehicle Safety Act of 1966." Adding the necessary five-hundred pounds of weight to meet these safety and emission requirements reduced mileage another ten percent. America's honeymoon with the automobile was coming to an end.

Although the automobile industry would continue to grow buoyed by the booming economy of the sixties, the coming collision between energy and the environment would emphasize the shift of corporate decision making from the market to the political arena. The end of the sixties saw an increasingly unpredictable economy with money and materials in short supply. But at the time, few could have realized how the transformation of the industry during the next decade would end in an uncertain future for automobiles and, in the process, force a re-examination of government intervention in the free enterprise system.

TURMOIL IN THE SEVENTIES

On several occasions in the early seventies the government was called upon to decide when a company had become too important to fail. The first of these decisions was in June 1970, when the Penn Central Railroad was denied the two hundred million dollars it claimed it needed to survive. Congress chose instead to let the regulated company go bankrupt and thus become the largest in U.S. history to do so. During the debates, former Senate Majority Leader Mike Mansfield had declared: "I do not believe it is the function of a democratic government to pick up the tab for the failure of [a] private enterprise." Protected from creditors' claims, the profitable segments of Penn Central were able to survive while the government disposed of the remainder. This was done by establishing the "National Railroad Passenger Corporation," or AmTrak, in 1971, to run intercity rail service for passengers.

Chrysler's financial subsidiary found it difficult to re-finance its short-term I.O.U.s after the Penn Central failure caused a softening of the financial markets. Having overproduced and overpriced its restyled intermediate models as a result of misjudging the automobile market which was now swinging back toward big cars,

Chrysler went to Washington, D.C., for help. Although Congress rejected the Federal Reserve Board's suggestion to establish special lines of credit that would make it easier for consumers to buy new cars, an internal study had concluded that the Federal Reserve Board had legal authority to directly loan or guarantee such loans to an industrial concern if it felt that failure of the company would imperil the national financial system. As a result, Chrysler's banks were told to loan the company whatever it needed and that the government would cover any losses. Escaping financial difficulties, Chrysler decided to avoid head-on competition with General Motors' Vega and Ford's Pinto subcompacts by instead going after the big-car buyers.

Although Congress had rejected requests for aid by Penn Central and Chrysler, it suddenly reversed itself in 1971 when it narrowly approved $250 million in loan guarantees to the nation's largest defense contractor. Lockheed, with two-thirds of its production going to U.S. military weapons, had lost nearly one-half billion dollars while building the Air Force's C-5A carrier at the same time it was receiving too few orders for its unexpectedly costly L-1011 TriStar. In order to obtain government backing, the company had to come up with $245 million worth of credit on its own, pledge its assets and collateral, and open all of its dealings to public scrutiny. Lockheed became profitable and the U.S. Treasury had earned thirty-one million dollars in interest payments by the time their relationship was terminated in 1977.

These precedents became important as large automobiles were battered in the turmoil of the seventies. In 1970, subcompacts had accounted for only three percent of the U.S. automobile market and many of these were imports. By 1973, Chrysler had managed to capture forty percent of this unprofitable market segment with its best-selling Plymouth Valiant and Dodge Dart but had gambled $350 million to replace them the following year by re-styling its more profitable lines. Its timing could not have been worse. With Detroit's 1974 models guzzling a third more gasoline than their smaller and boxier predecessors had twenty years earlier, only General Motors had the foresight to recognize the government's inability—or disinterest—in dealing with the pending energy problem. It re-organized its top management structure to meet the future, and successfully took on new challenges while retaining its strategy of "a car for every purse and purpose": to capture a large share of the small-car market while dominating the bigger car segment.

The oil embargo by the Organization of Petroleum Exporting Countries which lasted from October 1973 to May 1974, vividly demonstrated that the nation's economy and its automobile industry had been operating under the very frail assumption of cheap and plentiful gasoline. The quadrupling of oil prices in three months contributed to the worst economic crisis since the Great Depression. Large numbers of Americans—upset by uncertain gas supplies and long lines at filling stations—began looking overseas to buy their cars. Traditionally capturing fifteen percent of the U.S. automobile market, all foreign cars by now had nearly twenty percent as American car sales had their sharpest slump since the thirties. Although large car sales picked up again shortly after, Ford and Chrysler could not recapture a good share of their markets lost to the imports. Chrysler, once again approaching financial difficulties, responded by firing numerous engineers, designers, and salespeople to cut its overhead costs and reduce its break-even point. This move would later make it difficult to react quickly to market demands and government commands.

Two Congressional debates held in 1974 were to have a bearing on Chrysler and the automobile industry. One was over the possible re-establishment of the Reconstruction Finance Corporation as a lender of last resort. Originated during the Depression to permit the government to act as trustee of ailing companies by eliminating the stockholders, the R.F.C. had made loans amounting to fifty billion dollars during its twelve-year life. Its revival was defeated. Among the proposal's opponents was Senator William Proxmire (D-Wis.), who was then preparing to assume the chair of the Senate Committee on Banking, Housing and Urban Affairs from which he would reign as self-appointed protector of free enterprise.

The other debate studied the feasibility of increasing the industry's "corporate average fuel economy" (CAFE) by forty-five percent. General Motors argued that such legislation was unnecessary since the market was already demanding more efficient automobiles. Although their entire fleet averaged an industry low of 12.2 miles per gallon, General Motors announced that they would be able to substantially increase the mileage on their 1978 cars if safety and emission standards were suspended. Congress refused to go along and passed the "Energy Policy and Conservation Act of 1975" which mandated an 18.7 mile per gallon fleet average by 1980. By 1985, all automobile fleets must obtain an average of 27.5 miles per gallon.

Confident that the public would begin to trade down, General Motors' president Elliott ("Pete") Estes took the risk of downsizing the largest cars for the 1977 model year. These new cars would have interior room, comfort, and driving quality comparable to larger cars, yet would allow General Motors to achieve an industry high of 17.8 miles per gallon. In order to blunt Ford's and Chrysler's introduction of small cars, General Motors also brought out America's first "sub-subcompact," the Chevette, in half the typical three to four years by having its foreign subsidiaries develop it: Opel designed the body in Germany and the engines were made in Brazil. Though the Chevette was not immediately successful as customers began returning to bigger cars, General Motors was poised to introduce its downsized cars. By the spring of 1979, the highly successful front-wheel-drive "X" cars were brought out after four years of development at a cost of $2.7 billion. The compacts were two feet shorter and a fifth lighter than the cars they replaced, allowing them to get twenty-five miles per gallon. By anticipating the market well and correctly responding to it, General Motors should leave the seventies stronger than when they entered it. It introduced a series of small sporty cars (designated the "J"-cars) in the spring of 1981; a year later will come out with a family of smaller intermediates; and by 1983 will have downsized full-size models available. In addition, General Motors has been increasing its capacity for diesel engines, four-cylinder engines, and front-wheel-drive components.

Ford Motor Company not only successfully passed the mid-seventies storm, but 1976 through 1978 were its best years in history. One reason was that then-President Lee A. Iacocca (known as "the Father of the Mustang") felt that he could take advantage of General Motors' downsizing program by staying with big cars in 1976, although this decision was contrary to the many dire predictions of big car sales at that time. Also recognizing that intermediaries and compacts would play a significant role in the future, Iacocca introduced the Fiesta to counter General Motors' Chevette. For his accomplishments, Iacocca was thought certain to become Ford's next chairman, succeeding Henry Ford II who by then had run the company for over thirty years. Instead, the strong-willed Ford ("My name is on the building") felt that Iacocca's talent for developing and selling small cars would not be sufficient to run his company. Ford wanted a successor that also possessed managerial and financial skills. For refusing to accept a secondary rung on the corporate ladder, Iacocca was fired in July 1978, becoming Ford's seventh presidential casualty in two decades. As Ford entered 1979 with over $3.5 billion in cash, it planned to retain its traditional strength in small cars by replacing the highly-successful Pinto in the fall of 1980 with the smaller Escort, its first front-wheel-drive and the first U.S.-built "world car" to be assembled in several countries from parts made in many countries and sold anywhere around the globe.

Chrysler had been pursuing a full-line strategy similar to Ford's but with far less success. Only its strong truck sales, not yet subject to federal fuel requirements, had prevented a cash crisis in 1975. Rather than meet new government standards, the company dropped its trucks in favor of vans and pickups. While General Motors was downsizing its cars, Chrysler—like Ford—stayed with its luxury cars in hopes that customers would rush out to buy the last of the big cars. Chrysler did manage to bring out the smaller and successful Volaré and Aspen in 1976, but buyers were then returning to full-size cars. In attempting to turn the company around, Chrysler's board of directors replaced than-president and chairman Lynn A. Townsend with Eugene Cafiero as president and John J. Riccardo as chairman. One of their first announcements was a five-year plan to spend $7.5 billion to re-model the company's plants and product line by 1979. But delays prevented the redesigned New Yorker and St. Regis from being delivered until later that spring. Then the Shah of Iran was deposed in January 1979, and long gas lines developed by April and lasted until September. Chrysler's habit of shipping cars to dealers before they were ordered had caused its inventory of large cars to swell to eighty-eight thousand cars valued at seven hundred million dollars. Added to the 355,000 cars that dealers already had on hand, the company found itself with a supply good for one to two hundred days out of the three-hundred day sales year. This glut of cars not only cost two million dollars per week in handling and interest charges, but also interfered with the new model introductions.

Buyers by now were demanding fuel-efficient cars. But sales of the immensely popular Omni-Horizons, the first small four-wheel-drive cars made in the U.S. when introduced in 1977, were limited to the 300,000 engines a year that Chrysler had earlier decided to purchase from Volkswagenwerk AG rather than investing one-hundred million dollars to refit an existing Chrysler plant. Although these cars helped Chrysler get the best fleet mileage of the "Big Three" with 20.2 miles per gallon, low-priced small cars continued to remain money losers. Complicating matters, organized labor was lobbying for legislation requiring American manufacturers to include in their fleet average only those cars having at least a seventy-five percent "American content." If passed, this law would effectively exclude from future fleet average Chrysler's high mileage captive imports, such as the Arrow, Challenger, Colt, and Sapporo, manufactured by Japan's Mitsubishi Motors Corp. which is fifteen percent owned by Chrysler.

During the sixties, Chrysler had followed General Motors and Ford overseas by acquiring the failing French Simca and British Rootes Motors, Ltd. Beginning to turn into cash drains at the time large investments were needed, those European operations were finally sold in August 1978, to France's Peugeot-Citroen for three hundred million dollars in cash and fifteen percent in equity for a total value of some $430 million, making the European automaker the fourth largest in the world behind Chrysler. In addition, Peugeot had agreed to assume responsibility for the four hundred million dollars that these operations owed to European creditors. Chrysler holdings in Australia, Latin America, South Africa, and Turkey were also sold shortly thereafter.

To help stem this tide of adversity, Chrysler gave Lee A. Iacocca a one million dollar bonus and a quarter million dollar annual salary to become its president in November, 1978. Given the long lead-time to introduce new cars, Iacocca could not make changes until the company's 1982 offerings. Not only did this challenge represent a fulfillment of Iacocca's aspirations to head a full-line auto company, but it also gave him an opportunity to demonstrate that he had substance to match his style. After bringing along several Ford executives, Iacocca cut inventory costs in half by offering rebates, automatic transmissions, and five-year warranties on large cars. Next, he got out of leasing operations that had cost the company eighty-one million dollars, and saved eighty-five million dollars in insurance premium costs by closing old plants. He also asked suppliers to absorb $150 million in inflationary costs that are conventionally passed along.

In June 1979, Volkswagen, already producing its Rabbits in a Pennsylvania assembly plant acquired from Chrysler, was reportedly looking into buying Chrysler for about fifteen dollars a share, or one billion dollars. This rumor was never verified by any source and was vigorously denied by both firms, who further stated that they would be opposed to any merger or acquisition. Chrysler then began its lobbying campaign in Washington, D.C., for federal relief, relying heavily on Detroit mayor Coleman Young—also the vice chairman of the Democratic National Committee and a strong Carter election backer—to defend this cause. But in July, the government refused to offer Chrysler its billion dollar aid request.

CHRYSLER'S RESCUE PACKAGE

The upcoming 1980 model year was feared to be the worst in a long time for automobiles since the inevitable recession would hit the volatile industry first. (See Exhibits 5 and 6 for economic impacts and trends). Making matters worse, around twenty-two percent of the cars sold in 1979 had been imports and this figure was expected to rise as high as thirty percent in 1980. As a result, domestic automobile operations were twenty-five percent below their trend line. Such a drop hurts Chrysler because of its large debts. For instance, a total of $4.8 billion was owed to some two-hundred and fifty banks and other financial institutions, causing the company's net interest payments to jump to $128.9 million in 1978 compared to $74.9 million in 1977 and $52.5 million in 1974. In addition, its long-term debt of $1.2 billion was the industry's largest. Furthermore, the company will be in technical default if its working capital falls below six hundred million dollars. In 1980, $303 million in European loans and another $284 million in U.S. loans become due. As a result of these obligations during an economic downturn, the financial rating services lowered the quality ratings on Chrysler's securities, effectively preventing the company from selling any additional promissory notes.

On August 6, 1979, G. William Miller left as chairman of the Federal Reserve Board to become the Secretary of the Treasury. Three days later, although philosophically opposed to direct government intervention in the free enterprise system, his first public act was to announce that Administration support for Chrysler would be in the public interest. Although tax credits were rejected out of hand, loan guarantees would be considered if Chrysler submitted an acceptable overall financial operating "survival plan." The troubled company, by then losing around seven hundred dollars on every car it sold, submitted its "Proposal for Government Assistance" on September 15 and requested the U.S. Treasury Department to guarantee $1.2 billion of loans.

This request was rejected by the Treasury Department. Although the stated reason was that the amount requested nearly doubled the three-quarter billion dollars which the Administration had indicated it would accept, some believed that past management's continuing association with the company hindered approval while others felt that there was too much controversy for Congress to agree to any bill. The government responded that commitments of help would have to be made by workers, suppliers and dealers, banks, state and local governments, and any others having a large stake in the company. Chrysler was then sent home to reduce its aid request.

On September 20, 1979, Iacocca moved up to become Chrysler's chairman by replacing John Riccardo who had suddenly and unexpectedly decided to retire three months earlier than planned. Facing the toughest selling job of his career, Iacocca once again offered rebates and by the end of September, Chrysler's inventory of unsold 1979 cars had dropped by a quarter to near-normal level and was the lowest of the "Big Three"—but at a cost of ninety-two million dollars in lost profits. In addition, the planned capital expenditures for 1980–1985 had been reduced by $1.1 billion.

Concerned about White House delays in putting together a financial aid package, Chrysler took its argument to Congress in mid-October. Trying to force the Treasury Department's hand, Chrysler executives began testifying before the Senate and House Banking Committees in early October that federal automobile regulations, gasoline shortages, and an economic recession were the major factors contributing to the company's severe cash shortfall. A revised rescue package was presented to the Administration on October 17, 1979. (See Exhibits 7 and 8 for Chrysler's income statements and balance sheets.) In Chrysler's "modified survival plan," the company reduced its federal loan guarantee request to cover a third of the needed $2.1 billion, with the remainder coming from outside sources. In this plan, Chrysler detailed how it would remain viable by selling enough cars at prices that could pay for labor and capital—if there are no new gas shortages, the recession is mild and short, and its market share goes up from 10.2 percent to 12.4 percent. Also included were plans for reducing overhead costs by half-a-billion dollars to allow the company to break even with a market share of 10.5 percent. (Exhibits 9, 10, and 11 detail anticipated market demands and cost reduction programs). But the management consulting firm of Booz, Allen & Hamilton reported to Chrysler that this amount would be insufficient if sales turn down, there is a faster shift to small cars, or Chrysler's market share is less than planned. Any of these situations might necessitate another seven hundred million dollars in contingency funds.

On October 25, 1979, Chrysler and the United Automobile Workers— the country's second largest union with its one-and-a-half million members mostly urban bluecollar workers—agreed to a $1.3 billion wage pact over the next three years. Alfred Kahn, Chairman of the Council on Wage and Price Stability, immediately condemned the thirty percent wage hike (from $8.67 an hour to $11.32 an hour) and benefits over three years as violating the Administration's seven percent wage guideline. (Recommended changes to this guideline may be reviewed by the newly formed Pay Advisory Committee, of which U.A.W. president Douglas A. Fraser is a member.)

EXHIBIT 5

Changes in Gross National Product and Automobile Production and Employment			
Total U.S. Real GNP Growth (% Change)	Automobile Production		Automobile Employment (% Change)
	Industry (% Change)	Chrysler (% Change)	
1960 2.3	17	34	5
1961 2.5	−16	−34	−13
1962 5.8	23	14	9
1963 4.0	11	43	7
1964 5.3	2	19	2
1965 5.9	20	17	12
1966 5.9	−7	−1	2
1967 2.7	−13	−6	−5
1968 4.4	20	17	7
1969 2.6	−6	−12	4
1970 −0.3	−19	−7	−12
1971 3.0	29	5	6
1972 5.7	6	11	3
1973 5.5	12	14	12
1974 −1.4	−21	−20	−7
1975 −1.3	−10	−21	−13
1976 5.9	28	45	11
1977 5.3	11	−4	7
1978 4.4	2	−6	6

EXHIBIT 6

Selected Economic Forecasts					
	Real GNP Growth (% Change)			Real Spendable Income (% Change)	
	1979	1980	1981	1980	1981
Chase Econometrics, Inc.	−2.5	−1.4	2.7	0.4	3.3
Data Resources, Inc.	−2.3	−1.4	3.3	0.0	1.7
Wharton Econometrics	−2.4	0.0	3.4	0.1	1.8

EXHIBIT 7

Chrysler Corporation Balance Sheet
October 17, 1979
(Millions)

	Actual			Projections						
	1976	1977	1978	1979	1980	1981	1982	1983	1984	1985
Cash	$ 168	$ 208	$ 123	$ 150	$ 150	$ 150	$ 150	$ 150	$ 150	$ 150
Accounts Receivable	798	897	848	612	659	795	850	950	1,050	1,150
Inventories	2,354	2,623	1,981	1,815	1,613	1,722	1,814	2,016	2,225	2,462
Other	558	425	610	160	167	170	170	170	170	170
Total Current Assets	$3,878	$4,153	$3,562	$2,737	$2,589	$2,837	$2,984	$3,286	$3,595	$3,932
Investments, Property, Plant & Equipment	3,196	3,515	3,419	3,678	4,152	5,449	4,784	5,910	6,442	6,737
Total Assets	$7,074	$7,668	$6,981	$6,415	$6,741	$7,621	$8,433	$9,196	$10,037	$10,669

Accounts Payable	$1,351	$1,912	$1,301	$2,283	$1,978	$2,147	$2,308	$2,542	$2,822	$3,129
Short-Term Debt	172	250	49	16	10	10	10	10	10	10
Long-Term Debt Due Within One Year	69	91	12	123	145	168	184	194	186	152
Other	1,234	837	1,124	—	—	—	—	—	—	23
Total Current Liabilities	$2,826	$3,090	$2,486	$2,422	$2,133	$2,325	$2,502	$2,746	$3,018	$3,314
Other Noncurrent Liabilities	385	413	381	651	625	623	618	613	613	736
Long-Term Debt (Before New Financings)	1,048	1,240	1,188	1,166	1,096	1,020	928	828	734	666
Net Worth	2,815	2,925	2,926	1,842	1,333	1,738	2,269	2,896	3,775	4,786
Liabilities & Net Worth	$7,074	$7,668	$6,981	$6,081	$5,187	$5,706	$6,317	$7,083	$8,140	$9,502
Funds to be Obtained From New Financings: Current Year	—	—	—	334	**1,220**	361	201	(3)	(216)	(730)
Carried F'wd from Prior Years	—	—	—	—	334	1,554	1,915	**2,116**	2,113	1,897
Total	$7,074	$7,668	$6,981	$6,415	$6,741	$7,621	$8,433	$9,196	$10,037	$10,669

EXHIBIT 8

Chrysler Corporation Income and Financing Requirements
October 17, 1979
(Millions)

	Actual			Est.	Projections					
	1976	1977	1978	1979	1980	1981	1982	1983	1984	1985
Revenue	$12,240	$13,059	$13,618	$12,415	$13,586	$15,630	$17,811	$19,765	$21,812	$24,142
Costs	11,759	12,863	13,904	13,486	14,059	15,255	17,285	19,110	20,833	22,863
Earnings Before Taxes	481	197	(286)	(1,071)	(473)	375	526	655	979	1,279
Taxes on Income	153	34	(81)	2	9	(18)	10	10	112	283
Net Earnings	$ 328	$ 163	$ (205)	$(1,073)	$ (482)	$ 393	$ 516	$ 610	$ 867	$ 996
% Return on Sales	2.7%	1.2%	—	—	—	2.5%	2.9%	3.1%	4.0%	4.1%
Funds Applied				$ 143	$ 690	S 765	$ 714	$ 656	$ 645	$ 373
Funds Generated:										
Profits After Tax				(1,073)	(482)	393	516	610	867	996
Borrowing				(33)	(4)	2	2	2	2	2
Sale of Shares				29	—	40	42	45	47	50
Financing Arranged				510	24	—	—	—	—	—
Change in Deferred Taxes				3	(68)	(31)	(47)	2	(55)	55
Net Funds				$ (707)	$(1,220)	$ (361)	$ (201)	$ 3	$ 216	$ 730
Cumulative Shortfall				334	1,554	1,915	2,116	2,113	1,897	1,167
Typical Financing				1,493	1,536	1,540	1,590	1,627	1,690	1,740
Total Funds Required				$ 1,827	$ 3,090	$ 3,455	$ 3,706	$ 3,740	$ 3,587	$ 2,907
Cumulative Asset Disposition				101	496	728	928	1,058	1,091	1,155
Balance to be Financed From Other Sources				$ 233	$ 1,058	$ 1,187	$ 1,188	$ 1,055	$ 806	$ 12
U.S. Treasury Cumulative Shortfall*				—	$ 1,593	$ 1,994	$ 2,196	$ 2,309	—	—
at 95% Volume				—	$ 1,689	$ 2,258	$ 2,687	$ 3,037	—	—
at 90% Volume				—	$ 1,784	$ 2,522	$ 3,179	$ 3,837	—	—

*Revised October 17, 1979, and assumes reduced capital spending; savings of $6 billion over six years; and additional improvements in fixed costs and variable margins for Exhibits X and XI.

EXHIBIT 9

Projected Automobile Sales and Chrysler Corporation Market Share						
	1980	1981	1982	1983	1984	1985
U.S. Car Sales (millions of units):						
Chase Automobile	10.5	11.1	11.2	11.4	11.7	11.9
Data Resources, Inc.	10.3	11.0	10.8	11.1	12.9	12.2
Wharton Econometrics	10.6	11.5	12.5	13.0	13.2	12.9
Merrill Lynch	9.7	11.2	12.3	12.5	12.5	12.5
U.S. Treasury Low*	9.3	10.3	10.8	11.4	—	—
at 95% Volume	8.8	9.8	10.3	10.8	—	—
at 90% Volume	8.4	9.3	9.7	10.3	—	—
Chrysler Market Share (%):	10.2	11.1	11.6	11.9	12.1	12.4
Small	11.3	13.2	15.0	16.0	15.5	14.8
Medium	12.9	11.6	10.2	9.7	11.3	12.5
Large	4.6	5.6	4.7	3.6	3.5	4.9
U.S. Treasury Low*	10.5	11.1	11.6	11.9	—	—
at 95% Volume	10.0	10.5	11.0	11.3	—	—
at 90% Volume	9.5	10.0	10.4	10.7	—	—

*Revised October 17, 1979 and assumes reduced capital spending; savings of $6 billion over six years; and additional improvements in fixed costs and variable margins per Exhibits 10 and 11.

EXHIBIT 10

Annual Fixed Cost Reduction Program (Millions)				
	1980	1981	1982	1983
Personnel—reduced salaried employees by 8,500 people	$201.9	$204.2	$204.2	$204.2
Compensation—freeze salaries and benefits of nonunion employees and reduce senior executive salaries	22.2	12.2	12.2	12.2
Facility closings—shut down four plants	69.5	121.5	121.5	121.5
Operating expenses—launch, preproduction, supplies, and service costs	91.6	91.6	91.6	91.6
Marketing—reduce advertising and sales promotions, and sell rather than lease cars to major fleets	137.8	137.8	137.8	137.8
Other	(9.2)	(.5)	(.5)	(.5)
Total fixed cost savings	$513.8	$566.8	$566.8	$566.8
U.S. Department of Treasury adjustments:				
Personnel	$ (3.8)	$ (7.0)	$ (7.0)	$ (7.0)
Facility closings	(14.0)	(18.0)	(18.0)	(18.0)
Operating expenses	(21.0)	(51.0)	(27.0)	(20.0)
Marketing	(26.5)	(40.5)	(7.6)	(21.0)
New fixed cost savings	$448.5	$450.3	$507.2	$500.8

EXHIBIT 11

Variable Cost Reduction Program				
	1979–1982		1982–1986	
	per Car	per Truck	per Car	per Truck
Product improvements—new style, design, or performance elements to increase profitability	$174	$ 35	$ 59	$ (52)
New options & equipment changes—making new technology items available for comfort and convenience	55	69	45	40
Design cost reductions—material or component substitutions, parts simplifications, and changes in design to lower material or manufacturing costs	83	37	60	40
Manufacturing improvements—more efficient techniques, facilities, and equipment	82	47	66	65
Component insourcing—building own four-cylinder engines and power train	80	—	48	(10)
Warranty improvements—increased quality and reliability through component redesign, stronger quality control procedures, and additional inspectors	31	56	12	14
Purchasing programs—ensure purchases are made at the lowest cost available	54	52	77	80
Market demand changes—expect greater demand for fully equipped cars, and for luxury and specialty cars	34	34	40	45
Average variable cost savings	$593	$330	$407	$222

	1980	1981	1982	1983	Total
Cumulative variable margin improvements (millions)	$385.3	$759.5	$1008.9	$1223.7	$3377.4
U.S. Department of Treasury adjustments (millions)	(76.1)	(141.5)	(195.0)	(254.5)	(667.1)
	$309.2	$618.0	$ 813.9	$ 969.2	$2710.3

Kahn later retracted his controversial statement, and the U.A.W. was the first to make concessions to Chrysler by deferring two hundred million dollars of pension payments (the amount by which it was then overfunded) and delaying an additional $203 million in wage and benefit improvements over the next two years. The union imposed three stipulations. First, part of the pension contributions must be used by Chrysler to fund "socially desirable" projects, such as saving decaying urban areas in the industrial north or recommending investment sanctions against companies doing business in South Africa. Second, Chrysler's compensation package would have to increase by a third over the next three years so that its workers could reach General Motors' and Ford's already negotiated compensation package of twenty dollars an hour. Third, American workers will finally have a voice at the highest policy-making level of a major company when U.A.W. president Douglas A. Fraser is nominated at Chrysler's stockholders meeting in May 1980, to become one of Chrysler's twenty board directors. Fraser did not expect a conflict of interest to arise by having a labor official represent all Chrysler owners equally or by having a Chrysler director that will remain loyal to U.A.W. members at General Motors and Ford.

While Chrysler's supporters were busy arguing the level of support, there were those that felt that the impact of a Chrysler failure would be mitigated by the "Bankruptcy Reform Act of 1978" that took effect on October 1, 1979. Under the revised Chapter 11, debts would be frozen so that operations could continue. Instead of court-appointed trustees making decisions, existing corporate management would retain control while the company underwent reorganization, saving jobs for workers and paying back creditors quickly. Large creditors could not readily veto a reorganization plan, although it would be easier to force a business into bankruptcy. Chrysler would be able to stay in business, although the company may be forced to contract and make what the market wants by assembling cars from parts supplied by others. But Iacocca had steadfastly insisted that the nature of Chrysler's operational structure and dealer network would not permit downsizing over the short-run without causing severe disruptions. In addition, he felt that full-lines were needed in order for the company to remain profitable, considering the higher profit margins on large cars, scale economies of volume production, and the variety that dealers needed to effectively compete with General Motors and Ford. Besides, costly government regulations hindered Chrysler's ability to specialize.

Chrysler might be able to avoid re-organization by following American Motors Corporation's strategy of building good cars for specific markets, such as small or family-size cars. Or, by segmenting into high-price, low-volume "niches," Chrysler—always weak in functional business areas such as finance, marketing, manufacturing, and service—could finally capitalize on its traditional engineering strength. Furthermore, consolidation of its Chrysler-Plymouth and Dodge operations would simplify assembly and reduce its parts inventory. Chrysler might even pursue mergers or other types of business combinations or affiliations with another automobile manufacturer or large, financially sound company. Forced by re-organization or initiated on its own, Chrysler must choose a core of business to emphasize and then begin to liquidate its underutilized operations, perhaps selling these facilities to other automobile manufacturers.

Bankruptcy seemed near when Chrysler reported that for the entire first nine months of the year, sales had fallen seven percent from $9.6 billion to $8.9 billion, causing the company to lose $721.5 million so far for the year. On November 1, 1979, previously unsympathetic Secretary Miller surprised Chrysler's management and labor by announcing plans to support a $1.5 billion loan guarantee in Congress, stating that the Administration feared that Chrysler's problems were far greater than had originally appeared. It was made clear that such help would be available only until December 31, 1983.

There were several key considerations which led to this decision by the Administration. First was the fact that automobiles are an important industry, directly comprising five percent of the U.S. Gross National Product and doubling that figure when dependent industries are taken into account: Automobiles use over one-half of domestically produced lead, rubber, and iron; forty percent of all petroleum products and consumer installment credit; over a quarter of all zinc, steel, and glass; and large amounts of aluminium, copper, and plastic. In addition, automobiles also support many ancillary services, such as suppliers and repair shops. It has been estimated that as many as one job of five in the private sector is attributable to the auto industry.

Chrysler's domestic sales of $12.9 billion in 1978 was equivalent to 0.6 percent of the GNP, and $7.9 billion of this amount went to purchase parts, materials, and services from forty thousand domestic suppliers (many of which are small firms that rely on Chrysler's business) with another $2.9 billion spent for wages and salary. Although the extent to which a Chrysler failure would prolong or intensify a 1980 recession is debatable, there certainly would be serious local impacts and economic distress in the older industrial areas of the upper midwest which often bear the brunt of a national recession. For instance, in Detroit—where Chrysler is the largest private employer—a complete shutdown would double that city's already high unemployment rate of eight percent and devastate its economy. Widespread unemployment among Detroit's inner city blacks and other minorities could invariably lead to an increased rate of crime and incidence of violence.

A second justification for government support of a Chrysler bailout is that a bankruptcy could cost more. Neither a failing domestic company nor a profitable foreign corporation contribute to U.S. tax revenues. In addition, since more than a hundred thousand people work for Chrysler and several times that many work for its dealers and suppliers, the U.S. Department of Transportation's worst-case scenario estimates that a complete shutdown could directly add ninety-seven thousand Chrysler workers, 180,000 suppliers, one-hundred thousand dealers, and twelve thousand shippers to the currently six million jobless Americans. An identical number of indirect jobs could also be lost. It is not known how many of these would be permanently unemployed, unable to be absorbed by General Motors, Ford, or other sectors of the economy. According to some government estimates, the cost to taxpayers and to local, state, and federal governments in unemployment compensation, welfare payments, food stamps, other assistance, and the loss of tax revenues might be as high as sixteen billion dollars for 1980 and 1981.(See Exhibit 12.)

Included in the cost to the nation of a Chrysler bankruptcy is the impact on Chrysler's pension fund affecting fifty-two thousand beneficiaries and 120,000 employees. With assets of only $1.4 billion to cover $2.3 billion in liabilities, the unfunded pension liabilities greatly exceed the reserves of the Federal Pension Benefit Guarantee Corporation. Formed shortly after Studebaker's bankruptcy fifteen years

EXHIBIT 12

Impact of Chrysler Failure on U.S. Economy (millions)				
	1979	1980	1981	Total 1979–81
Loss in personal income tax revenues	$100	$2,400	$3,500	$ 6,000
Loss in corporate profits tax revenues	400	2,400	1,600	4,400
Loss in Chrysler property tax revenues	—	45	30	75
Loss in social security tax contribution	100	1,300	2,000	3,400
Increase in tax expenditures	200	1,300	300	1,800
Loss of government guaranteed pension fund	—	800	—	800
Total loss to government	$800	$8,245	$7,430	$16,475
Change in balance of payments	$500	$2,800	$3,900	$ 7,200

earlier left forty-five hundred employees with only fifteen percent of their pension benefits, the FPBGC insures employee pension funds and is entitled to use up to a third of Chrysler's book value after liquidation to cover these obligations. Should this amount be insufficient to meet future pension commitments, then the agency itself may be unable to continue its existence without further Congressional appropriations.

A third concern was the significant role that automobiles play in international trade and the U.S. balance of payments. Imports were already increasing their U.S. market penetration thanks to their fuel economy, low purchase price, and the unavailability of domestic small cars. If Chrysler were to go out of business, as much as seven billion dollars would go overseas if General Motors and Ford could not pick up the demand for small cars. Jobs would then follow, reducing the GNP by four billion dollars in 1980 and by six billion dollars in 1981 (or by 0.15 percent and 0.20 percent, respectively) and widening the federal budget deficit by one billion dollars and one-and-three-quarter billion dollars in those corresponding years.

The fourth and final argument for saving Chrysler was that vigorous national competition, and the corresponding benefits of lower prices, product innovation, and efficiency that come with it, requires three significant automobile makers. If the industry were to become even more concentrated in the future, then it would constantly be facing antitrust threats to prevent alleged noncompetitive effects. Such continuous harrassment would result in higher costs of litigation to both the companies and the government. Loan guarantees would help Chrysler remain as a third viable competitor in the future, operating on its own resources and being a contributing member to the nation's economic system.

A significant requirement of the bill was that all parties having an economic stake in Chrysler's outcome were to make enough sacrifices to match the government's $1.5 billion backing. At first, most were reluctant to extend themselves further. Even when Chrysler announced its plans on November 28, 1979, to offer $250 million of new preferred stock to these vested interests, no one was willing to accept an equity position. Several Congressmen had other conditions to justify the bailout: Senator Russell Long (D.-La.), Chairman of the Finance Committee, wanted Chrysler to establish an Employee Stock Ownership Plan; Henry S. Reuss (D.-Wis), Chairman of the House Committee on Banking, Finance and Urban Affairs, suggested that Chrysler produce only mass transit vehicles; and Congressman S. William Green (R.-N.Y.) thought that the government should take its own equity position in the company in exchange for a loan guarantee.

Chrysler's initiatives on Capitol Hill were beginning to pay off as the House of Representatives passed what was essentially the Administration's version of the bill. But as the bill moved to the Senate Committee on Banking, Housing and Urban Affairs, Chairman Proxmire came out firmly opposed to a federal bail-out that would prevent the failure of individual firms:

> We have a free enterprise economy and free enterprise means the freedom to fail as well as the freedom to profit. Last year, over 6,000 business firms went bankrupt and no one rushed to Washington with a bill to prevent their failure. If we bail out Chrysler, where do we draw the line? On what basis do we say that some firms but not others are worthy of a Federal bail-out?
>
> In the last analysis, the only reason we are bailing out Chrysler is that the sheer size of the corporation enables it to deploy enough lobbyists, pubic relations specialists, dealers and suppliers to bring its claims to the attention of the government ahead of the 6,000 other firms that routinely fail every year.

On November 29, 1979, the Senate Banking Committee approved a four-billion dollar package consisting of $1.25 billion in loan guarantees and $2.75 billion in outside financing—if the U.A.W. would agree to a three year wage freeze that would save the company $1.3 billion. Senators Richard Lugar (R.-Ind.) and Paul Tsongas (D.-Mass.), who had co-authored this version of the bill, simply felt that the workers were not making enough of a sacrifice. Treasury Secretary Miller retaliated by calling this new imposition unworkable since it would result in the loss of many of the best workers and the impairment of productivity.

The U.A.W.'s rejection of this legislative effort on December 3, 1979, threatened to destroy any rescue package for Chrysler. The workers claimed that tying government aid to a three-year wage freeze would reduce their standard of living by thirty to forty percent at the current rate of inflation. In addition, Fraser felt that re-opening contract negotiations and ratification would conflict with the union's constitution and pose major logistical problems. It would also be politically risky for the union leadership, especially for Fraser who had recommended acceptance of the contract based on his estimate of what it would take to convince Congress that labor was doing its fair share. Fraser had previously rejected the options of buying stock or loaning money to the company out of the union's strike fund.

The compromise that was reached by Congress on the last day it was in session implied that Chrysler was unique among U.S. corporations and, therefore, was entitled to special government treatment. Its long-term ability to compete had come into question since it was the weakest major competitor in an industry undergoing radical transition. Small fuel-efficient automobiles would double their market share by 1985—perhaps eventually capturing forty-five percent—if they could first get through 1980's tight money, high interest rates, anticipated gasoline shortages, high fuel prices, and overall economic decline.

In order to make the kind of automobiles that Americans will want in the future, the industry needs to undergo a complete transformation at a cost of eighty billion dollars through 1985, over half of which would go to meet federal fuel, emission, and safety requirements. General Motors alone will invest fifty billion dollars. Although Chrysler now has the government's backing, it will still have to cut back on its planned $13.6 billion investment plans through 1985. (See Exhibit 13.) Re-tooling will allow Chrysler to replace the Volaré and Aspen in the 1981 model year with 500,000 small, fuel-efficient, four-cylinder, front-wheel-drive automobiles getting twenty-five to thirty miles per gallon. The government rescue should give the company enough time to bring out these new cars (designated as "K"-cars and called the Plymouth Reliant and Dodge Aries) to compete directly with General Motors' current "X"-bodies and Ford's planned Escort by offering 2.2 liter engine with diesel or turbocharge engines as options. Chrysler will be building its own four-cylinder engines by 1980. Such investments will require losing one billion dollars in 1979 and half-a-billion dollars the following year, but Chrysler hopes to earn a billion dollars by 1985.

Around the time that Congress was debating Chrysler's loan guarantees, General Motors reported third quarter operating losses of a hundred million dollars while Ford's domestic car business was on its way to losing a billion dollars for the year, offset only by its financial operations, overseas operations, a large tax credit, and profits from internal sales. By year-end, the automobile industry had temporarily closed thirteen of its forty-three U.S. car plants, indefinitely putting 129,000 employees out of work. Such economic declines make future government policies toward business even more imminent. During the Congressional hearings, several members of the House Committee on Banking, Finance and Urban Affairs offered this dissenting view:

> Where do we draw the line? What criteria do we use to determine who gets what, when, how much and why, and for what reasons? These questions have not been answered in either a specific or broader context. If we start today with the Chrysler Corporation, who will we see tomorrow? . . . Before we legislate blindly, we must be aware that other companies may be supplicants for the Federal dollar in the future.

EXHIBIT 13

Planned Expenditures by Chrysler Corporation
(millions)

	1979	1980	1981	1982	1983	1984	1985	Total
Type:								
Tools, facilities, and investments	$ 857	$ 959	$1,137	$1,253	$1,228	$1,334	$1,192	$ 7,960
Engineering research and development	346	367	375	456	465	455	511	2,975
Launch and preproduction	139	261	127	205	253	174	228	1,387
Project expense	104	171	173	188	222	228	214	1,300
Total	$1,446	$1,758	$1,812	$2,102	$2,168	$2,191	$2,145	$13,622
Program:								
Cars	$ 521	$ 655	$ 532	$ 712	$ 954	$ 827	$ 666	$ 4,867
Trucks	83	120	296	383	109	378	584	1,953
Powertrain	345	461	557	452	481	298	167	2,761
Other (e.g., manufacturing improvements)	497	522	427	555	624	688	728	4,041
Total	$1,446	$1,758	$1,812	$2,102	$2,168	$2,191	$2,145	$13,622

HIGH POINT PRODUCTS, INC. 1963–1970

K. K. Das
Afife N. Sayin

INTRODUCTION

High Point Products, Inc. (HPP), manufactured a quality line of naturally sweetened, noncarbonated apple juice, apple cider, and flavored fruit drinks. Located in Virginia, 50 miles west of Washington, D.C., it was organized in June 1963, by Benjamin Sloan, a retired executive. Sloan wanted to provide an outlet for apples grown in his High Point Orchard. He and his two friends, Thomas Hagler and Milton Jones, felt that a small well-run company with low overhead in a cheap labor area like Virginia could compete successfully, especially in the regional market, with the high overhead "bigs" in the juice business.

Sloan owned High Point Orchard which had been in operation for almost 25 years. His association with it began in 1942, when he, as an army officer, moved from the Midwest to the Washington, D.C., area. At that time, he and his wife bought an old farm house and a 40 acre apple orchard in High Point County with the idea of making the orchard a hobby and providing opportunities for his wife's talents.

By 1970, the Orchard had grown from a few acres of worn out trees to almost a thousand acres of young plantings of the newest and best varieties. HPP prided itself on selling an extra fine fresh fruit. (In the fruit business a high quailty of fresh apple pack means more fruit can go into the "canner's bin." This includes fruit that is completely edible but slightly off color, or has small bruises or a limb rub.) Traditionally, this "canner" tonnage went to the big processors who made apple sauce, apple slices, apple juice, etc., but paid little or nothing for the fruit itself. To get a better dollar return for this tonnage, Sloan decided to go into the processing business.

Sloan's decision was based on several other considerations including: (1) sharply rising national consumption of fruit juices, including apple juice (Exhibit 1); (2) small capital required for plant and equipment necessary for production; and (3) ready availability of reasonably priced juice grade apples in the area (in addition to what his own orchard was to yield).

This case was made possible by the cooperation of Inner City Investing, Inc. The project was funded by the Institute for Minority Business Education (Warren K. VanHook, director), School of Business and Public Administration, Howard University. It was prepared by Dr. K. K. Das, Professor of Management and Dr. Afife N. Sayin, Associate Professor of Management, both of the School of Business and Public Administration, Howard University. This case is designed to be used as a basis for class discussion rather than to illustrate either effective or ineffective handling of an administrative situation. Names of all parties have been disguised.

Copyright © 1976 by K. K. Das and Afife N. Sayin

Presented at a Case Workshop and distributed by the Intercollegiate Case Clearing House, Soldiers Field, Boston, Mass. 02163. All rights reserved to contributors. Printed in the U.S.A.

Sloan's decision was made easier because the president of a large food chain, XYZ, Inc., with 75 stores in the Washington-Baltimore area assured him of providing an outlet for HPP's production. The arrangement was informal, but Sloan's close friendship with the president of the food chain encouraged him to place heavy reliance on this outlet. In fact, Sloan, an engineer by profession, who had spent most of his career in large corporations, hardly considered setting up any planned marketing program for the juicery.

Sloan's decision was based on several other considerations including: (1) sharply rising national consumption of fruit juices, including apple juice (Exhibit 1); (2) small capital required for plant and equipment necessary for production, and; (3) ready availability of reasonably priced juice grade apples in the area (in addition to what his own orchard was to yield.) Sloan's decision was made easier because the president of a large food chain, XYZ, Inc., with 75 stores in the Washington-Baltimore area assured him of providing an outlet for HPP's production. The arrangement was informal, but Sloan's close friendship with the president of the food chain encouraged him to place heavy reliance on this outlet. In fact, Sloan, an engineer by profession, who had spent most of his career in large corporations, hardly considered setting up any planned marketing program for the juicery.

CAPITALIZATION

HPP was set up with an initial capitalization of 342 shares of common stock at par value of $100. Almost the entire stock was issued to Sloan in exchange for land, buildings, and other assets that the company secured from him. Interest was set at the rate of 6% semi-annually. The company took over about 3.5 acres of land from Sloan's orchard. Later, HPP issued further stock to Sloan, bringing Sloan's holding to 1,410 shares out of a total of 1,665 shares issued. At this time, Sloan held 85 percent of the stock, the remainder being held by others.

In 1964, the company obtained a loan of $79,000 from the Small Business Administration (SBA) at 5.5% interest, repayable in 8 years. The loan was used to set up the plant—capital expenditure on new, used, and rebuilt equipment in order to hold the fixed investment under control. About $49,000 was used for this. The balance was kept for working capital.

In 1966, there was another infusion of capital: $88,000 at 5.5% interest repayable in 8 years. The SBA granted this new loan and renewed the loan already outstanding, that is, $62,000 out of the first loan of $79,000. Sloan also made another loan of $10,000 to the company at this time. The SBA loan, now consolidated at $150,000, was secured by the assets of the company—land, building, and equipment totalling about $210,000 at cost, and $132,000 in book value.

The plant facilities consisted of warehouses, processing equipment and area, docks, platform, apple storage and other areas, representing an occupied area of about 30,000 sq. ft. The process area included a processing room with two presses, a tank room and two fill lines—one for glass and the other for cans. In 1966, the warehouse was extended by 6000 sq. ft.

ORGANIZATION

(The organization of HPP can be found in Exhibit 2.) Sloan was not only the principal investor but also the chairman of the board and president of the company. Sloan's son Joseph became the vice president, Milton Jones became secretary-treasurer on a part-time basis, and Thomas Hagler, the plant manager. Joseph Sloan received no compensation, but Milton Jones and Thomas Hagler received shares of stock in the company in return for professional services. Hagler was also given a weekly salary. Two salesmen, one plant maintenance man, one secretary-bookkeeper (the latter two on hourly basis), and about 30 production workers made up the total personnel of the company. Described by Sloan as a "cost conscious manager," hard worker, and a good planner, Hagler was the second most influential man in the organization.

PRODUCTION

Apple Juice and Cider[1]   The plant was set up for a one or a two shift operation, depending on need. On the two shift basis and maximum production capacity, 35 workers were considered adequate.

Production started with on-the-spot purchase of apples from nearby Virginia orchards, including the High Point Orchard. The manufacturing process was simple, as depicted in Exhibit 3. The apples were pressed by either hydraulic[2] or rotary presses, and the raw juice obtained was pumped into large storage tanks to be held for 24 hours to allow the juice to settle. Then came the filling, filtering, and pasteurizing, prior to bottling and canning.

Two parallel production lines were maintained: A glass line and a can line, though only one was operated at a time. The glass line packed gallons, half gallons, and quarts, and the can line packed 46-oz. cans.[3]

Flavored Fruit Drinks   Producing apple juice or apple cider is a fall and winter operation. To keep the plant busy during spring and summer months, HPP, in 1964, decided to make flavored fruit drinks and secondary products such as apple sauce, apple candy, and fruit syrup. While flavored drinks proved to be helpful in levelling the production process, effort in regard to secondary products was soon given up. Flavored drinks blended eaily with the main production process. The company concentrated on the three most-popular flavors—orange, grape, and fruit punch.

During 1964–66, the company developed an efficient operating schedule to streamline and improve the process steps and experimented in blending a variety of apple juice to produce an apple juice with superior flavor.

MARKETING

As already indicated, XYZ, Inc., a leading food chain in the region, was the major outlet for the company's products. The arrangement offered initial advantages for the company: (1) the trucking costs for its products were low thus giving it an advantage over competitors in reaching the regional market from long distance, and; (2) the company did not have to set up any elaborate marketing organization or strategy. The products were sold under house labels (manufacturer's labels) and private labels, including that of XYZ, Inc.

XYZ food chain purchased HPP brands of apple juice and cider and gave them shelf space along with other brands. XYZ's attitude was simply that "customer acceptance will soon tell you if your product is superior." When XYZ found out that the HPP brands were outselling all other brands in the Washington area, it gave the company its entire private-label business of apple juice, cider and flavored drinks.

Although XYZ, Inc., accounted for over 62% of the company's sales, other chain accounts were also developed. By 1969, HPP was sending solid trailer loads of apple juice to Cincinnati, Philadelphia, Jacksonville, Miami, and to warehouses in New Jersey. Most sales to food chains were made on a company-quoted case price, terms of payment being net 14 days after delivery, with no discounts.

The growth in sales, shown in Exhibit 4, created a kind of prosperity squeeze. Around 1969, the issue of financing inventory began to appear as a problem. This was particularly so because in the tight-money market condition, HPP was not able to borrow money on satisfactory terms to build up inventory from spring through fall when the new "pack year" would start. In fact, the company was obliged to schedule production on a day-to-day basis depending upon how orders came in. Frequent changes in production lines to match the flow of orders and delivery dates aggravated the situation. Moreover, the plant was frequently operating inefficiently as the cost of set up time began to mount when the process was changed from cans to bottling or from quarts to half-gallons and to gallons. Selling came almost from the production line and there was practically no cushion of inventory.

Pressed for inventory financing, Sloan turned to his principal customer, XYZ, Inc., which advanced money on a "bill and hold"[4] basis. However, this was no help for other potential accounts. As a result, an estimated order for 50,000 to 75,000 cases was lost during the year. The company had planned a second-shift operation during the fall, but was able to operate it for only a very short period. However, according to Sloan, the two-shift period was long enough to demonstrate:

1   That there was ample available labor for second shift and that management could handle it;

2   That there was plant capacity to support two shifts without more fixed capital investment;

3   That production from the second shift was more profitable, the total operating overhead being covered from the first shift. (The company estimated about 20 cents a case more profit in the second-shift output on that account.)

OPERATIONS: FINANCIAL DATA

Exhibit 6 gives the financial data for the periods 1967–70. It is interesting to note that during this four-year period, sales increased much faster than in the earlier four-year period. It would appear that the company reached a breakeven point by 1968 (around $400,000 in sales). But, by 1970, the company was again losing money. Exhibit 7 gives the balance sheets of these years. From 1967 to 1970, HPP's total gross investment almost doubled, only to be drained away by considerable losses from operations in the last year. The company came to depend more and more on trade credits while its long-term liabilities began to drop very drastically. This is particularly true of 1970. Interestingly enough, long-term notes showed a decline of over $100,000 in one year.

As HPP's volume increased during this period, it highlighted the problem of working capital shortage. Sloan was almost fully occupied with this problem of additional finance. The implication is reflected in the operating costs data shown in the income statements, difficulties in scheduling different orders optionally, and developing a level operating schedules. It may well be that there were problems in getting labor as required and the small management structure proved inadequate to solve the problem. However, the plant was experiencing a growing upward trend in prices of processing apples, more so because Sloan's own orchard could not obviously provide the necessary supplies. In the fall of 1969, operational experience revealed problems of many dimensions—working capital shortage, scheduling, scarcity and rising price trend, particularly in the region where HPP was located. Sloan decided to examine his situation carefully.

FIVE YEAR PLANNING[5]

He came up with a five-year plan. Within these five years, 1969–1974, he hoped to increase his sales from about one million to three million dollars, and estimated a net profit of 5 percent on its planned volume of sales.

1969–70 Pack Year—$900,000 to 1 Million in Sales **1970–71 Pack Year—$1.4 Million in Sales** **1971–72 Pack Year—$2.0 Million in Sales** **1972–73 Pack Year—$2.5 Million in Sales** **1973–74 Pack Year—$3.0 Million in Sales**

The five-year plan provided for a fixed capital investment on the order of $47,000. The plan was to install a large Wilmer press to ensure additional daily capacity of 10,000 gallons, to extend the fill rooms and improve various other equipment. The company also developed a year-round operating plan. The plan was to produce about 80,000 cases of flavored drinks both for sale and inventory in September—to be done by a two-shift operation. Approximately one-half of this was to be carried into inventory to be sold the end of December. From October to December, apple juice was to be the main production item, about 10,000 gallons a day. From January to April the company would build up a new inventory of apple juice to carry through the five summer months to October. A minimum inventory of 100,000 cases requiring about $200,000 investment was estimated. It was estimated that about $25,000 of additional working capital would be needed for other activities.

LATER DEVELOPMENT

In October 1969, Sloan was still holding on to his assessment of the total situation, that HPP required a large infusion of capital to attain viability and growth.

About this time, Sloan's health was also failing and he was obliged to spend several months of the year in Florida. His wife also passed away, requiring him to face up to the problem of his orchard business. Thus, Sloan decided to sell the business and advertised it in the *Wall Street Journal* and the *New York Times*. There were responses from large companies, according to Sloan, but the negotiations did not proceed very far.

Sloan's next move was to seek a venture capital group to join him. His effort led him to Dagmar French, the black president of Inner City Investing, Inc.[6] French became interested in HPP around November, 1969, hoping that such an enterprise could be an ideal investment for black investors. His interest was based on the prospect of claiming Small Business Administration (SBA) 8 (a) contracts under black ownership. So enthused by such consideration, French started to plan for an *ad hoc* black syndicate to invest in the company.[7]

In November, 1969, Sloan made a complicated and unusual offer to French. He offered to sell either his entire stock of 1,410 shares, or 859 shares, at $80 per share. Alternatively, he also offered to sell 275 shares at $100 flat per share. If the payment for the first two offers was to be stretched beyond 1969, the price was to be $90 per share and beyond 1970, $100 per share. Sloan assured French about the correctness of the financial statements and the prospects of the business. His further words to French were, "There is no question about our selling additional *quantities* and HPP operating on $10 per share profit."

Sloan's offer was flexible in nature, leaving French to determine how big an investment the black syndicate could make, in case he should be interested in the proposal. As it turned out, French asked a financial analyst to examine the financial statements (Exhibits 6 and 7).

ENDNOTES

1   For methods of processing apple juice, see Donald K. Tressler and Maynard A. Joslyn, *Fruit and Vegetable Juice Processing Technology,* the Avi Publishing Co., Westport, Conn., 1971, pp. 186–233.

2   Old fashioned method of pressing out apple juice.

3   Normally apple juice comes in quarts and gallons.

4   "Bill and hold" is a commercial arrangement in which a customer places an order for a product and pays in advance. Delivery is spread over a given period. In the meantime, the customer continues to order at his normal quantity and pays at the normal pace, less the hold arrangement.

5   This was prepared on the basis of available records of the company and interview with Sloan's associates.

6   Inner City Investing, Inc., is a venture capital company designed to invest and participate in the development of minority enterprises. It provides front money and expertise for minority investors to purchase controlling interest in businesses. Its basic criteria for investment are: (a) an ongoing business at least five years old; (b) annual sales of over half a million dollars; and (c) the potential for national distribution.

7   It is interesting to take note of Sloan's shopping for black investors to come to his rescue. Indeed as he represented to French that he was turning to black investment prospects out of his genuine concern to lead the black investors into the mainstream of American business.

EXHIBIT 1

Canned and Chilled Fruit Juices: Per Capita Civilian Consumption
1960–1970
(in pounds)

| | CANNED | | | | | | | | | | | | | | CHILLED | | |
| | CITRUS | | | | | | | | | | PINEAPPLE | | | | | | |
Year	Orange	Grapefruit	Blended orange and grapefruit	Lemon and lime	Tangerine	Citrus concentrate	Total	Apple	Fruit nectare	Grape	Single strength	Concentrate[2]	Prune	Total	Orange	Grapefruit	Total[1]
1960	2.12	1.51	.51	.13	.07	1.45	5.79	.89	1.06	.76	2.15	1.25	1.06	12.96	2.10	.02	2.12
1961	1.70	1.39	.45	.13	.06	1.52	5.25	.95	.52	.71	2.07	1.19	1.05	11.74	1.65	.03	1.68
1962	1.92	1.48	.47	.13	.06	1.05	5.11	1.05	.52	.65	2.09	1.18	1.06	11.66	2.19	.08	2.27
1963	1.69	1.30	.42	.13	.04	1.70	5.28	1.21	.36	.63	2.61	1.74	1.11	12.94	1.14	.03	1.17
1964	1.17	1.09	.30	.11	.04	1.61	4.32	1.49	.28	.65	1.97	1.64	1.11	11.46	1.29	.07	1.36
1965	1.24	1.39	.30	.10	.02	.97	4.02	1.53	.38	.74	1.84	1.19	1.16	10.86	1.90	.05	1.95
1966	1.53	1.73	.34	.10	.02	.99	4.71	1.17	.40	.63	1.92	1.73	1.10	11.66	3.04	.14	3.18
1967	1.57	2.33	.39	.10	.02	1.08	5.49	1.35	.39	.67	1.76	.96	1.09	11.71	4.15	.23	4.38
1968	1.19	2.22	.32	.10	.01	1.35	5.19	1.69	.37	.55	2.14	1.51	.75	12.20	3.96	.24	4.20
1969	1.30	2.94	.33	.10	.01	2.55	7.23	2.41	.41	.54	1.61	1.83	1.10	15.13	3.87	.30	4.17
1970	1.75	2.98	.33	.10	.01	1.45	6.62	2.67	.70	.58	1.60	1.37	1.11	14.65	4.35	.34	4.69

1. Excluding frozen juices.
2. Single strength equivalent

SOURCE: *Fruit Situation* (TFS–199), Economic Research Service, U.S. Department of Agriculture, Washington, D.C., June 1976

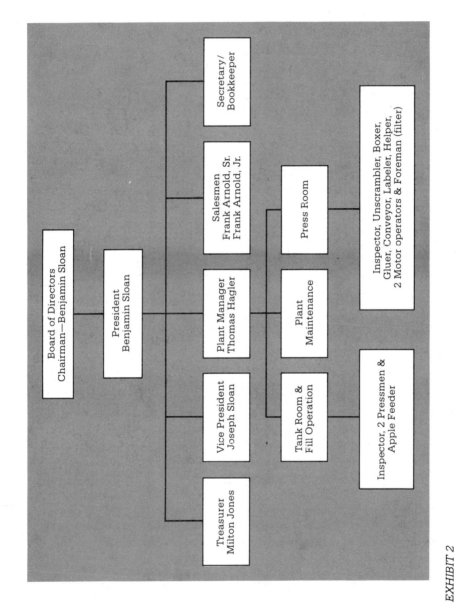

EXHIBIT 2
High Point Products, Inc. Organization Chart

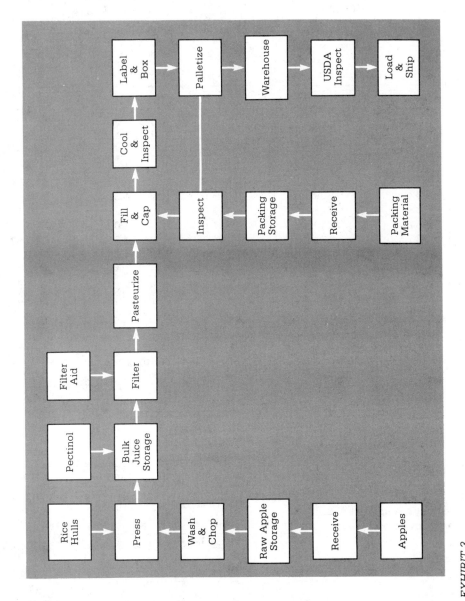

EXHIBIT 3
High Point Products, Inc. Process Flow Diagram: Apple Juice Manufacture

EXHIBIT 4

	High Point Products, Inc. Sales by Cases 1967–70		
Fiscal Year	Total Cases Apple Juice	Total Cases Fruit Drink	Grand Total
1967–1968	106,277	101,198	207,475
1968–1969	128,967	121,084	205,051
1969–1970	216,281	142,291	358,572

SOURCE: company files

EXHIBIT 5

	Apples, Commercial Crop[1]			
	Production (millions of pounds)		Price Per Pound (cents)	
Year	U.S.	Virginia	U.S.	Virginia
1960	4,917.5	473.0	4.84	4.29
1961	5,696.3	489.0	4.15	3.94
1962	5,689.1	456.0	4.32	4.18
1963	5,752.6	433.0	4.21	4.25
1964	6,319.4	461.0	4.00	3.36
1965	6,131.5	494.7	4.35	3.67
1966	5,756.2	212.0	4.64	4.34
1967	5,425.1	368.0	5.67	4.37
1968	5,453.8	417.0	6.27	4.82
1969	6,721.8	472.0	4.09	3.80
1970	6,222.5	463.0	4.48	3.75

1. Estimates of commercial crop refer to the total production of apples in the commercial orchards of 100 or more fruit bearing ages.

SOURCE: *Fruits—Noncitrus by States,* Statistical Reporting Service, U.S. Department of Agriculture. Statistical bulletins No. 407, FRNT 2–1(7, 67) (5–68) (5–69) (5–70)

EXHIBIT 6

	High Point Products, Inc. Income Statement *for the year ended June 30*			
	1967	1968	1969	1970
Net sales	$349,785.41	$488,409.41	$645,467.93	$935,626.84
Less: cost of goods sold (cost & expenses – inventory)	306,037.72	419,496.68	523,537.81	706,424.98
Gross profit	43,747.69	68,912.73	121,930.12	229,201.86
Sales, general and admin. expenses	50,031.28	70,445.26	99,118.14	241,332.22
Operating profit (loss)	(6,283.59)	(1,532.53)	2,281.98	(12,130.36)
Other income (expense)				
Interest	(4,607.65)	(7,220.55)	(10,230.17)	(12,887.24)
Miscellaneous	10,000.00	10,000.00	—	—
Income before taxes (deficit)	(891.24)	1,246.92	12,581.81	(25,017.60)

SOURCE: company files

564

EXHIBIT 7

	High Point Products, Inc. Balance Sheet *June 30*			
	1967	1968	1969	1970
Assets				
Current Assets				
Cash	$ 2,390.74	$ 4,964.74	$ 40,470.45	$ 3,048.28
Accounts receivable	9,482.00	25,612.69	60,427.90	23,694.87
Inventory	78,607.85	68,315.18	158,376.84	125,441.06
Other current assets	—	—	—	42,795.64
Total current assets	90,480.59	98,892.61	259,275.19	194,979.85
Fixed Assets				
Land & building	110,583.30	137,640.97	151,744.85	155,227.47
Machinery & equipment	113,137.32	145,556.61	157,462.60	168,781.03
Less: accumulated depreciation	39,594.75	53,983.33	66,617.72	89,514.77
Net fixed assets	184,125.87	229,214.25	242,589.74	234,493.73
Other assets	2,031.78	183.03	—	—
Total assets	276,620.24	328,289.89	501,964.93	429,473.58
Liabilities & Capital				
Current Liabilities				
Accounts payable	17,110.11	35,423.93	72,832.74	135,738.46
Accrued taxes	581.53	—	1,264.36	2,211.51
Customer inventory deposits	—	—	90,317.38	16,383.38
Notes payable	—	—	—	88,353.19
Accrued expenses	—	—	—	3,627.20
Total current liabilities	17,961.64	35,423.93	164,414.48	246,313.36
Long term notes	118,128.99	153,319.53	156,422.41	51,833.09
Total liabilities	135,820.63	188,743.46	320,836.89	298,146.45
Owner's Equity				
Common stock	139,000.00	136,500.00	165,500.00	166,500.00
Paid-in surplus	—	—	—	20,000.00
Retained earnings	1,799.61	3,046.43	15,627.24	55,172.87
Total owner's equity	140,799.61	139,546.43	181,127.24	131,327.13
Total liability & equity	276,620.24	328,289.89	501,964.13	429,473.58

SOURCE: company files

APPENDIX

INDUSTRY BACKGROUND

Virginia Apple Belt   HPP is located in the heart of one of the intensive apple producing regions of the country. The apple belt in Virginia supplies around 5 to 10% of the country's 120 to 145 million bushels of apples during the year. The Virginia growers maintain a good growing average of 500 bushels of apples per acre. However, an efficient operation entails a yield of about 600 to 1000 bushels per acre. In the High Point county, where HPP is located, the yield is relatively low, averaging around 350 bushels per acre.

Fresh Apples versus Bruised Apples   About 65% of the fruit from the orchards is processed into apple products each year (apple sauce, apple slices, apple juice, etc.) and about 30% enters the market as fresh fruit. The percentage of cull out of fresh packs which goes to canner's bin is variable. Of 100 apples, 15 to 25 may go into canner's bin. These are: (1) small apples, (2) off color apples or (3) apples with limb rub and other minor defects. The grower has very little control over these, weather playing an important part in the outcome. Canners, therefore, experience sudden changes in supplies and/or prices.

Some apples are used entirely for processing. The York Imperial variety, for example, is almost entirely utilized for processing, whereas the Red Delicious and Golden Delicious varieties are essentially for fresh pack. The Stayman variety is both for fresh pack and for processing, depending on which is the better alternative. Rome and Jonathan varieties are utilized about 50 percent for fresh pack and 50 percent for processing.

The demand and price of good sound apples versus bruised apples depends upon the supply and demand for apples. The quailty of apples is influenced by the weather, production and handling operations. There can be 50 to 100% difference in price between good and bruised apples. For example, if the crop harvested is of poor quality a greater percentage of apples goes for juicé processing.

The market for bruised apples depends upon supply and demand. In some years apples are shipped across the country for processing. An area may have a subnormal or even a normal supply of apples, but if another region has a bumper crop it may be advantageous for a processor to buy apples from this heavy supply area, provided the price plus transportation costs are more favorable than the local price offerings for apples.

Competition   In High Point County, there are a few small, seasonal cider plants which are and have been, for the most part, family owned for generations. Therefore, HPP, being a larger juice processing operation, did not encounter much competition within the county. However, within a 50- to 60-mile radius there is much competition both for juice apples and apples for other uses. There are 8 or 10 other manufacturers of apple juice who operate on a year-round, or nearly year-round basis. Moreover, their sales are multiregional. Some of the processors who were direct competitors included, McCutchin Apple Products in Maryland; Old Virginia, National Fruit Products Co., and Shenandoah Apple Cooperative in Virginia, Red Cheek Inc., Knouse Food Cooperative, Inc., and Musselman Fruit Products in Pennsylvania.

What is true of the Virginia region is true of other states. There are a large number of operators. Some of the larger apple processors are producer cooperatives; Red

---

*Background study was prepared by Tribhuwan Narain, a Graduate Assistant, with help from Fred P. Corey, Director of Market Development, International Apple Institute, Washington, D.C.

Cheek, Inc., Knouse Foods Cooperative, Inc., and Shenandoah Apple Cooperative, Inc., are the three major ones. They process apple juice and most other apple products. These producer's cooperatives have some credit advantages because they are able to borrow from cooperative farm credit sources. These sources are often managed by knowledgeable farm people who better understand farmer's needs and are organized to service farm credit needs better than most conventional credit sources. The grower-owned processing cooperatives have advantages over the non-grower owned processing facility stemming from their integrated operation, and cooperative credit facilities, etc.

Price and Utilization   Exhibit 5 shows the production and price trends of apples for the United States and Virginia. Within a ten year period (1960–1970) the annual production of apples varied from about 4,917 to 6,222 million pounds for the U.S. and from about 212 to 494 million pounds for Virginia. The annual price of apples varied from 4.00 to 6.27 cents per pound for U.S. and from 3.36 to 4.82 cents per pound for Virginia.

Procurement   The raw apples procurement procedure involves announcement of a price or prices offered by the processor (usually published) subsequent to its involvement in the processing activities; and announcement of grade, variety, size, kind of apples desired, and usage (i.e., apple sauce, apple juice, etc.). Quotations such as "$5,000 f.o.b. orchard/delivered, U.S. number one canner grade, 2¾ and larger per c.w.t. (hundred pounds) for York" are standard terminology. Apples for juice and cider are generally the smaller size apples in orchard run (all apples) procurement schedules; and the "cull-out" (for reason of size, color, minor defects, etc.) from fresh apple packing operations. These are priced well below the more premium size and quality fruit desired for apple sauce, sliced apples, etc.

Size and diversification of product line by processors greatly influence their procurement practices, prices offered, etc. HPP, being a comparatively small, one-product (juice) processor, did not have the purchasing flexibility and power of the nearby and more diversified processors.

CONAGRA INCORPORATED

onAgra, a company committed to growth in the basic foods business, foresees excellent opportunities from the ever increasing worldwide demand for food. The company today is a major factor in the processing and marketing of a broad range of food products. In ConAgra's business three broad basic food groupings account for 90% of sales and profits. They are: grain milling, agri-products, and poultry products. In addition ConAgra has a commitment in the consumer area consisting of pet accessories, dog food, private label flour and corn meal, farm raised catfish and Mexican fast food restaurants.

HISTORY OF CONAGRA

ConAgra was founded in 1919 as Nebraska Consolidated Mills when four flour millers joined together. Today ConAgra is the second largest U.S. grain miller and the tenth largest producer of broiler chickens. The majority of the company's products are sold at the distribution level so the Con Agra name is still relatively unknown to the average housewife.

From 1955 to the early 1970s, ConAgra experienced rapid growth; sales increased from $35 million to $633 million. The chief architect of this growth was J. Allan Mactier who developed an aggressive acquisition program. Mr. Mactier began his career with ConAgra in 1946 as a family flour salesman. He served as advertising manager and vice president, and was elected president and chief executive officer in 1954 at the age of 32. For twenty years he made the key strategic operating decisions.

Following a substantial loss in 1974, ConAgra initiated major organizational changes that returned the company to profitability in 1975. Earnings per share increased from a loss of $3.69 in 1974 to a profit of $3.57 in 1977 lifting the company from the brink of bankruptcy to a sound financial position. In comparison to other companies in the food processing industry, ConAgra's 1977 earnings were the highest; however, their P/E ratio of 5 is one of the lowest. C. M. Harper, President and Chief Executive Officer, in reviewing his company's position in March 1978 forecasts a very profitable future for each of the company's four major product groups.

This case was prepared by Dwayne Dvorak, Mike Merrick, Leo Peterson, Ed Splittgerber and Regina Worthington, graduate students at the University of Nebraska at Omaha under the direction of Professor Bruce A. Kirchhoff. It is designed to be a basis for class discussion rather than to illustrate either effective or ineffective handling of an administrative situation.

Distributed by the Intercollegiate Case Clearing House, Soldiers Field, Boston, MA 02163. All rights reserved to the contributors. Printed in the U.S.A.

Grain Milled Products   ConAgra's grain-milled product operations include: 1) *wheat flour* and *mill by-products,* primarily for sale to commercial bakers, but also to industrial food and feed markets and the government; 2) *distribution of flour and other supplies to bakers,* and 3) the *merchandising of grain.* Flour milling was the foundation of ConAgra business; and for the company's first 22 years, ConAgra expanded the flour business, serving markets in many states from mills located in Nebraska. Following this period the expansion thrust moved to the southeastern part of the United States through acquiring flour mills and diversifying into fomula feeds and poultry products. In 1959 the expansion included establishing a flour milling operation on the island of Puerto Rico. Today flour milling is still ConAgra's single most important line of business accounting for 42% of operating profits in the FY 1973–1977 period.

     ConAgra operates 16 flour mills (15 in U.S. and one in Puerto Rico) producing 9% of the total U.S. wheat flour. They are the second largest supplier of wheat flour to the commercial baking industry which uses over 55% of all flour milled.

     The industry is becoming increasingly concentrated. A recent congressional study shows the 12 largest flour millers controlling 70% of the market, up from 50% in 1965.

     ConAgra's success in flour milling is credited to its being one of the first in the industry to locate its mills near the consumer rather than near the producer. This strategy is based on lower transportation costs for raw grain from using "unit trains." Milled products, on the other hand, must be shipped by truck at considerably higher cost. This location strategy also allows ConAgra to provide better service to its major customers, the commercial bakeries.

     Total U.S. flour milling capacity has stablized at approximately 100,000 hundred weights (CWT) per day for the last five years (Exhibit 1). ConAgra's strategy is to increase capacities of existing mills where the economics of specific local or regional markets indicate there are profit opportunities. ConAgra estimates the cost of capacity increases to existing mills at $400–600 per daily hundredweight while a complete new mill costs from $1500 to $2000 per daily hundredweight. Capacity expansion in fiscal year 1978 is expected to be 8% with acquisition of an existing mill at York, Pennsylvania and expansion of two mills in the southeast. For the following three years, expansion at 4% per year is expected.

     Market prices of grain products, the raw material for the flour milling operations, are influenced by supply/demand factors typical of agriculture products. As is normal in the industry, ConAgra has an inventory management policy which requires "hedging" of all wheat inventories to minimize risk of loss from price changes.

     The extension into domestic grain merchandising was made in May, 1977. This area of business involves the storage, handling and transportation of grains from the upper midwest to point of use. ConAgra has acquired 5.7 million bushels of grain elevator capacity and is in the process of negotiating for an additional 4.7 million bushels.

Agri-Products   Agri-Products is the second largest segment of ConAgra's business. This consists primarily of Formax formula feeds for dairy, poultry, beef, and swine; Red Hat feeds in Puerto Rico; plus a fertilizer operation in Montana.

EXHIBIT 1

		Flour Production (millions of CWT)[3]	
Year	Industry Daily Capacity[2] 1000 CWTs	Total U.S. (calendar year)	ConAgra (fiscal year)
1967	1128		
1968	1006		
1969	1005		
1970	1006	253.1	
1971	995	249.8	
1972	1000	250.4	
1973	1013	249.3	20.2
1974	991	242.1	20.9
1975	979	247.1	20.7
1976	994	259.5	22.9
1977	971	259.3	24.0
1978[1]			26.0

U.S. Flour Milling Capacity and Production

(1) ConAgra Plans
(2) Bureau of Census Data
(3) ConAgra Data

EXHIBIT 2

Top Ten Domestic Milling Companies		
	Mills	Capacity in CWTs
Pillsbury	8	108,000
Peavey	9	98,900
ADM Milling	11	96,000
ConAgra	16	91,700
Seaboard Allied	10	83,290
Intl. Multifoods	10	70,200
General Mills	8	55,100
Nabisco	3	42,500
Cargill	4	42,060
Dixie-Portland	4	41,500

SOURCE: *Milling & Baking News*, December 9, 1977.

ConAgra diversified into this business as an outlet for the byproducts from flour milling. This diversification started in 1942 and operations were greatly expanded in the 1960s with the acquisition of several mills in the midwest, southeast and in Puerto Rico. These operations in 1977 accounted for 25% of sales and 26% of profits.

The majority of the Agri-Products group's sales consist of fully mixed feed sold in bulk and delivered in company trucks. Various grades of concentrated feed are sold in bags directly to large producers of dairy cattle, beef cattle, and poultry permitting bulk deliveries in larger quantitites. Efforts are being made to reduce or close distribution channels for the bagged feeds in certain areas.

Agri-Products' feed mills are located in southeastern U.S. (10 mills), Puerto Rico (3 mills) and Montana (2 mills). Of this group, 40% of sales are for dairy cattle and poultry feed in the southeast, 30% of sales are for dairy cattle and poultry feed in Puerto Rico; and the remainder is other feeds, plus fertilizer sales in the Montana area.

The Formax formula feed operation is now located primarily in four states in the southeast and in the state of Montana. The company enjoys a number-one and number-two share of the markets in which they operate. Because of over-capacity in the formula feed industry and unfavorable economics in the cattle industry, ConAgra sold operations in Iowa, Kansas, Michigan, and Nebraska in 1977 which did not meet minimum return on investment objectives. The Formax operation is now comprised of three decentralized businesses, organized to serve the regional areas and needs of customers in these areas. The areas served are the southeast and the state of Montana.

Products made in Montana consist mostly of cattle feed and fertilizer sold to large bulk users. Sales of fertilizer are made directly to larger farmers with the company providing application of the fertilizer as part of the sale.

The feed business in the United States is a highly fragmented one; ConAgra is one of the top ten producers, which include Ralston Purina, Allied Mills (Continental Grain), Central Soya, Agway (a group of cooperatives), Cargill, Farmland Industries, The Federal Company, and Carnation. Despite ranking in the top ten, CAG's share of the total feed market is less than 1%. Because ConAgra's business is a regional one, the company is an important factor in many of its local markets and typically the top competitor.

The Puerto Rican operations produce and distribute feeds and grains in bulk and bags to large dairy, poultry, swine and egg producers. Packaged feed is also sold through super markets. Sales of both bagged and bulk feed will continue in Puerto Rico since the company supplies approximately one-half of the commercially sold animal feed in the market. ConAgra also conducts formula feed operations in Spain through a 50% interest in Saprogal, a Spanish firm.

Poultry Products   Poultry Products is the third largest segment of ConAgra's business. These operations involve production and distribution of both broiler chickens and table eggs and were 23% of sales and 18% of profits in 1977.

ConAgra diversified into this business in 1963 with the acquisition of Dalton Poultry Processing Company of Dalton, Georgia. Through additional acquisitions the company has become one of the top ten producers of broilers in the United States and accounts for 3% of the total industry production. ConAgra sells 87% of their broiler production in the U.S., 7% in Puerto Rico, and 6% in Spain. In Puerto Rico, ConAgra is the principal integrated producer of broilers and supplies over 90% of the USDA inspected broilers. The company's position in the U.S. egg industry is small and regional.

Broilers are produced in four integrated complexes in this country and one in Puerto Rico. Each complex is a complete operating entity with its own breeder flocks, hatcheries, feed manufacturing facilities, and processing plants. An interesting feature in the poultry operations is the participation of the independent growers who are typically family operations providing housing and feeding services for a commission based on the processed weight of the broilers. ConAgra supplies chicks and feed. Then eight weeks later, ConAgra's "catch and haul" men go out to pick up the broilers and take them to the packing plant. There they are slaughtered and packaged for shipment to the buyers.

ConAgra sells its broiler output to a broad spectrum of customers which include retailers, fast food operators, and distributors. ConAgra is trying to strengthen the brand recognition of their "Country Skillet" brand broilers to cushion themselves from the broiler cycle and to improve profitability. However, there is no evidence in the industry that U.S. producers can obtain a premium price for branded products. Most broilers produced in Puerto Rico are sold to retailers under the "To-Ricos" brand.

Broiler industry profit margins are highly cyclical with cycle durations ranging from 25 to 35 months. The cycle is regularly recurrent and average profit margins over the cycle tend to be consistent from one cycle to the next. The broiler cycle is influenced by delayed reaction of broiler supplies to changing broiler prices. Pork is usually the lowest cost red meat and is therefore a partial substitute for chicken. Despite the cyclical nature of this business, ConAgra has never reported a net loss in this area, and expects to average a 35% return on invested capital to this business.

Growth strategy in this line calls for major capacity additions through optimization of existing slaughtering facilities, of acquisitions during the down cycle, and the use of two-shift operations. Two-shift operations were implemented in Louisiana and North Georgia in 1977. Plans are to double the southern Alabama operation over the next two years. ConAgra expects to increase total production of broilers to around 400 million by mid-1979.

Sales to major buyers are usually made weekly for the quantities of broilers for delivery the following week. Prices are determined on a commodity exchange with offers-to-buy and sell at various prices resolved on a supply/demand basis.

ConAgra's table egg production capacity increased 35% in 1977 to 28 million dozen eggs yearly with the acquisition of a second facility. Sales of commercial eggs are predominantly made in the southeast and northeast; and these sales are handled primarily through food brokers, distributors, and large retailers. This business is also highly cyclical in nature so no additional expansion is planned for the immediate future.

Consumer Products   The consumer area provided 9% of sales and 8% of profits in 1977. This area of business includes private label family flour, corn meal and prepared mixes; pet products; fresh, farm-raised catfish; and Mexican fast-food restaurants.

A. Flour/Corn Meal Mixes

ConAgra's private label flour and corn meal mixes are sold to a number of retail grocery organizations and food service accounts throughout the southern parts of the country. The private label flour is marketed from mills in Decatur, Alabama, and Sherman, Texas. Corn products are distributed from the Decatur mill and oat products are distributed from the Fruen Mill in Minneapolis. Sales are made on a direct basis to major accounts and through food brokers. Some private label prepared

EXHIBIT 3

U.S. Broiler Production and Consumption

Year	Broiler Production	Average Price Received by Producers	Value of Production	Civilian Per Capita Consumption	Broiler[1] Production	ConAgra[1] Production
	(millions)	(¢ per pound)	($ millions)	(pounds)	(billions pounds)	(millions pounds)
1950	631	27.4¢	$ 533	8.7		
1955	1,092	25.2	844	13.8		
1960	1,795	16.9	1,014	23.4		
1965	2,334	15.0	1,218	29.6		
1970	2,987	13.6	1,475	36.9		
1971	2,945	13.7	1,487	36.7		
1972	3,075	14.1	1,623	38.4	7.82	205
1973	3,009	24.0	2,690	37.4	7.79	206
1974	2,993	21.5	2,436	37.5	7.92	210
1975	2,933	26.3	2,899	36.9	7.97	230
1976	3,280	23.6	2,951	40.4	8.99	230 (48 weeks)
1977 Prel.	3,360	24.2	N.A.	41.2	9.23	266

(1) ConAgra Memo: ConAgra Production-Fiscal Year; ConAgra Production includes Puerto Rico

SOURCE: U.S.D.A Poultry and Egg Situation Reports

EXHIBIT 4

Top Ten Domestic Broiler Producers, 1977	
	Weekly Slaughter*
	(millions of broilers)
Holly Farms	4.5
Gold Kist	4.5
Valmac	3.0
Lane Poultry	3.0
Central Soya	2.75
Perdue Foods	2.75
Tyson's Foods	2.75
Country Pride	2.50
Wayne Poultry	2.0
ConAgra	2.0

*SOURCE: *Broiler Industry,* December 1977

baking mixes are marketed in the southwest. In Puerto Rico, the "Amopola" brand of family flour has a major share of the retail grocery market.

B. Pet Products

ConAgra entered the pet supplies and accessories business with the acquisition of the Geisler Pet Products Company in 1973. They entered the distribution side of the industry with the acquisition of Norso Distributors in 1976, and Pet Dealers Supply Company in 1977. ConAgra plans an aggressive program to increase the size of this business. Geisler products began using the "Snoopy" cartoon character endorsement to their product line which includes some 600 pet products. These products range from bird seed to dog food and include hygiene supplies and pet care accessories, product lines that are currently dominated by one company, Hartz Mountain.

C. Catfish

ConAgra produces about 4 million pounds of farm raised catfish in the Delta regions of Mississippi. Sales of catfish are made primarily to retail stores under the "Country Skillet" brand and to institutions in southern regions.

D. Restaurants

In 1977 ConAgra entered the Mexican fast-food restaurant business by acquiring what is now known as Taco Plaza, a Texas-based operation of 53 fast-food restaurants. Twenty-seven of the 53 units offer Mexican food items and the remaining 26 are either to be converted to a Mexican fare or disposed of. The lack of maturity in this segment of the fast-food business is seen by management as an excellent growth opportunity. The profitability of Mexican food tends to be higher than other fast-foods and this business is important to ConAgra in attaining its long term goals.

Growth in the pet products along with restaurant business and private label flour and mix products will be the major thrust of ConAgra's involvement in the consumer goods and services business segment.

Management   ConAgra has undergone a fundamental change in management since 1974 which deeply altered the character of the company. In prior years, ConAgra businesses were operated very successfully under a highly centralized management style with few responsibilities decentralized. In 1974 when ConAgra's earnings declined, it was reported that the highly centralized management was under extreme pressure and ". . . (some) management decisions were made which, in retrospect, proved to be serious mistakes." This loss catalyzed a major change in ConAgra's management. On August 19, 1974, ConAgra's Board of Directors named Claude I. Carter, with 33 years of experience in ConAgra, president and chief executive officer. Also named to the top management team during this year were Charles M. Harper, executive vice president and chief operating officer, and Thomas E. Brady, executive vice president and chief financial officer. Charles M. Harper joined ConAgra in 1974 with 19 years of Agri-Business Management experience at Pillsbury and Thomas E. Brady joined in 1973 with 20 years of financial and general management experience at Josten's, Fabritek, and Peat, Marwick, Mitchell. C. M. Harper became president and chief executive officer in March 1976, replacing Carter who then became vice chairman of the board.

This new top management team adopted a mission of changing the character of ConAgra. A participative management style was initiated with responsibility and authority decentralized. Division managers were given expanded opportunities to manage their businesses within corporate guidelines. Initially, three priority objectives were established by this management team: 1) return the company to profitability; 2) restore a sound balance sheet; and 3) resume dividends.

By 1976, many changes had been instituted within ConAgra, far beyond the initial three priority objectives. The 1976 Annual Report emphasizes "a 'new' company—a revitalized 57-year-old company that is 'new' from many standpoints"—earning power, financial strength, professional management, marketing and growth plans. ConAgra's commitment to change the style of management is reflected in the mission statements for the Corporate Resource Group. This group's first priority is "to change the character of the company" to decentralized multidivision organizations operating with a minimum of corporate controls. The decentralized operations are controlled through the use of strategic plans, supported by management objectives and corresponding commitments from the management teams responsible for their attainment. An incentive compensation plan is tied to those commitments for management personnel.

ConAgra's "new" professional approach to management was described by Mr. Harper in the 1976 Annual Report as:

> A commitment to a higher level of professionalism in management requires that ConAgra be staffed by outstanding people at every level of the company. To help reach this objective we have put increased emphasis on the identification and development of our human resources. It is our objective that the future leadership of the company come from within our own organization. Even so we recognize that, from time to time, we have to search outside the Company for special talent and experience.

The "new" ConAgra also includes a stated goal of "openness." The "new" company is described in considerable detail in published material for distribution to employees, stockholders and the general public. This information explains the company's philosophy, mission, strategic plans, and objectives in a very open manner. ConAgra sees its basic responsibility is "to maximize the wealth of ConAgra's stockholders." To fulfill this responsibility, corporate mission statements are published in terms of service to three publics: 1) the stockholders, 2) the 4,400 ConAgra employees, and 3) the general public, consisting of ConAgra customers and the society in which they operate. Supporting these mission statements are objectives for each of these publics. Exhibit 11, taken from the 1977 Annual Report, compares the results achieved relative to stockholder related objectives.

In addition, each of ConAgra's major businesses publishes statements describing "Strategies for Growth." These statements combine to delineate management philosophy and operating strategy for the ConAgra businesses (Exhibit 12).

Financing   When new management was established, ConAgra formalized financial objectives as follows:

1   Return on Equity—earn in excess of a 15% return on common stockholders' equity.

2   Growth in Earnings per Share—increase trend line earnings per share, on average, in excess of 10% per year from the Fiscal 1973 base. (Adjusted upward to a 14% trend line growth rate in February 1978)

3   Dividends—dividend payments will be increased based on the achievement of the objective of increasing the growth in the trend line earnings power.

4   Return on Invested Capital—earn a minimum after tax return on invested capital of 20%.

5   Financing—maintain a conservative balance sheet:
    a) Long-term debt ratio—35% to 40%.
    b) Equity to noncurrent assets—100% to 120%.
    c) Short-term debt—paid off at each year end.

At the end of fiscal 1974 ConAgra's total debt was $136.1 million versus stockholders' equity of $34.4 million. Interest expense of $16 million in fiscal 1974 was up $10.5 million from the previous year. By selling off marginal properties, management reduced total debt to $41.5 million, from a 1974 peak of $158 million. Short-term borrowings, which in mid-1973 ran as high as $84 million, were reduced to zero at year end, and have been for the past two fiscal year-ends. Interest costs were also reduced, totaling $5.2 million in 1977.

In July 1976, ConAgra replaced a six year, fluctuating interest, term loan with a fifteen year 10 1/8% note. This improved ConAgra's financial structure by avoiding fluctuating interest rates and extending the repayment schedule from six to fifteen years. As of May 29, 1977, ConAgra had a bank line of credit of $38,753,000 available.

Capital Spending   Capital spending of $80 million over the next three years will be required to support ConAgra's strategic plans. About three-fourths of the $80 million will be in basic foods; the rest is earmarked for the balance of ConAgra's businesses. This capital spending will be funded from internal sources. These projected increases in stockholder equity will support some additional long-term borrowing, without exceeding the forty percent of total capitalization guideline.

Quality Control (R and D)   Quality control activities place primary emphasis on applied research and technical services directed at product development improvement and quality control. Principal research and development activities are conducted in the company's quality control and research laboratories in Omaha, Nebraska. Quality control laboratories are also located at all principal manufacturing plants. Expenditures in 1977 for quality control and research totaled approximately $622,000.

Patents, Trademarks, etc.   Generally, patents, trademarks, licenses, and franchises are not material to the Company's product lines. An exception is in grocery products and agri-foods where trade name identification is a factor in competition for sales. Some of the Company's significant trademarks are Formax, Red Hat, and Country Skillet. The Company has also acquired rights to use the characters of the Peanuts Comic Strip, including "Snoopy" in connection with dog food and pet accessories business.

ConAgra's Future   The president of ConAgra discussed the company's operations and future. Mr. Harper, a very personable individual, appeared to be extremely knowledgeable of every aspect of ConAgra's business. He displays great confidence in the firm's employees, particularly the staff and managers, and their ability to keep the "new" ConAgra strong and prosperous. Mr. Harper appears to be thoroughly convinced that he not only has the best people in the industry, but also the best company.

In 1978 ConAgra increased its growth expectations of earnings per share from 10% to 14% per year compound rate. "The strength of the Company is in basic foods, and that's where we intend to grow," according to Mr. Harper. He emphasized the goal of the company to earn a return of 20% on common equity, after taxes; "We can do it," he said. Also, "We aim to put a lot of our resources in the basic foods business . . . 75% of capital. . . ."

Using Geisler, Norso Distributors, and the Pet Dealer Supply as "building blocks" ConAgra plans a strategic thrust in the pet products business. The Company plans to gain a significant share of this industry which is dominated by Hartz Mountain.

A thrust is also planned in the private label area. "Private labels will become more and more important to the housewife over time," according to Mr. Harper.

The future appears bright for the Company in the Mexican fast-food restaurant business which is forecast to grow at a rate of 20% a year. ConAgra's analysts, and outside consultants, agree on this growth projection, but some outsiders believe it is too optimistic. ConAgra is planning to substantially expand their taco business on a regional basis, with both company-owned and franchised businesses.

EXHIBIT 5

	ConAgra Consolidated Balance Sheet ($ in thousands)				
	5/30/77	5/30/76 (1)	6/29/75	6/30/74	6/24/73
Current Assets					
Cash	5,985	17,605	3,685	19,909	16,254
Receivables	35,277	36,588	35,349	48,928	42,463
Inventories	52,036	37,505	36,338	61,387	73,322
Other	1,190	1,119	1,161	2,408	505
	94,488	92,817	76,533	132,632	132,544
Property, Plant, and Equipment	74,356	73,766	71,216	87,479	87,391
Less Accumulated Depreciation	31,096	30,591	28,680	29,046	28,311
Net Property, Plant Equipment	43,260	43,175	42,536	58,433	59,080
Other Assets	2,550	2,177	5,234	2,352	3,105
Goodwill	2,962	3,088	2,007	2,084	716
	143,260	141,257	126,310	195,501	195,445
Current Liabilities					
Notes payable	—	—	10,000	66,944	84,000
Current installments L-T debt	3,530	6,585	9,529	2,499	2,561
Accounts payable	26,444	34,501	19,246	23,108	24,080
Dividends payable	839	598	—	78	369
Income taxes	7,353	6,348	1,258	673	1,171
	38,166	48,024	40,033	93,302	112,181
Long Term Debt (2)	37,971	36,384	46,490	66,673	37,450
Other Liabilities	986	627	1,006	1,241	1,539
Total Liabilities	77,123	85,035	87,529	161,216	151,170
Stockholder Equity					
Preferred stock	5,875	6,816	6,833	6,833	4,613
Common stock	17,614	17,193	16,369	15,854	14,772
Add'l. paid-in capital	14,648	13,327	12,832	12,922	11,779
Retained earnings	28,689	18,886	2,748	(1,324)	13,112
Total Equity	66,137	56,222	38,781	34,285	44,275
	143,260	141,257	126,310	195,501	195,445

(1) Fiscal year-end changed to last Sunday in May
(2) Excludes present value of financing leases: 1977: $5,340,000; 1976: $7,118,000; 1975: $7,539,000; 1974: $7,959,000; 1973: $4,833,000.

EXHIBIT 6

ConAgra, Inc. Consolidated Statement of Earnings ($ in thousands, except per share)					
	May 29, 1977 (52 Weeks)	May 30, 1976 (48 Weeks)	June 29, 1975 (52 Weeks)	June 30, 1974 (53 Weeks)	June 24, 1973 (52 Weeks)
Revenues:					
Net sales	$532,218	$504,114	$573,544	$633,644	$422,125
Other income	1,634	1,256	1,210	1,060	984
	533,852	505,370	574,754	634,704	423,109
Costs and Expenses:					
Cost of goods sold ..	482,419	451,380	531,656	603,740	386,777
Selling, administrative and general expenses .	27,635	22,025	25,712	26,638	23,275
Interest expense	4,482	6,274	13,428	16,025	5,547
Sundry expense	459	821	184	247	97
	514,995	480,500	570,980	646,650	415,696
Operating income ...	18,857	24,870	3,774	(11,946)	7,413
Gain on disposal of assets	1,664	206	822	(1,427)	(157)
Income taxes (recoverable)	7,690	10,270	525	(1,520)	1,193
Earnings (loss) before special credit	12,831	14,806	4,071	(11,853)	6,063
Special tax credit ...	—	4,320	—	—	—
Net earnings (loss) ..	$ 12,831	$ 19,126	$ 4,071	$ (11,853)	$ 6,063
Primary Earnings (Loss) per Share:					
From operations before disposal of assets and tax credit	$ 3.28	$ 4.16	$ .85	$ (3.26)	$ 1.81
Disposal of assets ...	.29	.03	.24	(.43)	(.05)
Tax credit		1.26			
Net earnings	$ 3.57	$ 5.45	$ 1.09	$ (3.69)	$ 1.76
Dividends Declared per Share of Common Stock	$ .75	$ .25	$ —	$ .125	$ .495
Depreciation	3,957	3,852	4,383	4,692	3,710
Additions to Property, Plant and Equipment	5,471	2,797	1,858	9,364	15,857

EXHIBIT 7

ConAgra, Inc. Sales and Profit Contribution by Line of Business
($ in thousands, except per share)

	1977 (52 Weeks) Sales	Operating Profit	1976 (43 Weeks) Sales	Operating Profit	1975 (52 Weeks) Sales	Operating Profit	1974 (53 Weeks) Sales	Operating Profit	1973 (52 Weeks) Sales	Operating Profit
Flour Products	$226,012	$13,071	$219,135	$11,079	$256,719	$ 8,372	$258,534	$ 9,394	$149,267	$ 7,191
Agri Products	139,011	7,206	123,863	3,815	132,742	4,788	143,993	3,750	118,814	3,944
Poultry Products	120,939	4,964	114,254	17,790	115,164	4,512	121,974	2,891	83,420	7,429
Consumer Products	46,256	2,018	46,862	1,633	68,918	3,391	109,143	1,817	70,624	1,120
Total	$532,218	$27,257	$504,114	$34,317	$573,543	$21,063	$633,644	$17,852	$422,125	$19,684
Interest Expense		$ 4,482		$ 6,274		$13,428		$16,025		$ 5,547
Unhedged Grain Inventory Loss		—		—		—		7,890		—
Loss (Gains) for Disposition of Assets		—		—		(822)		1,575		—
Corporate Expense		2,256		2,967		3,861		5,735		6,881
Pretax Income (Loss)		20,521		25,076		4,596		(13,373)		7,256
Income Tax (Rate)		7,690 (37%)		10,270 (41.0%)		525 (NM)		(1,520)(NM)		1,193 (16.4%)
Net Income		$12,831		$14,806		$ 4,071		$(11,853)		$ 6,063
Earnings per Share		$ 3.57		$ 4.19		$ 1.09		$ (3.69)		$ 1.76
Diluted Earnings per Share[1]		$ 3.31		$ 3.83		$ 1.09		$ (3.69)		$ 1.76

(1) Adjusted for 5% stock dividend in fiscal 1976, 1974

EXHIBIT 8
ConAgra Operating Locations

GRAIN MILLED PRODUCTS		AGRI-PRODUCTS		POULTRY PRODUCTS		CONSUMER PRODUCTS & SERVICE	
Wheat Flour Mills		**Formula Feed Manufacturing**		**Poultry Processing**		**Flour/Corn Meal Mixes**	
Alabama	1	Alabama	1	Alabama	2	Alabama	1
California	1	Florida	2	Georgia	1	Puerto Rico	1
Florida	1	Georgia	3	Louisiana	1	Texas	1
Georgia	1	Montana	2	Puerto Rico	1	**Dog Food**	
Illinois	1	Tennessee	1	Spain	1	Missouri	1
Minnesota	1	Portugal	1	**Poultry Hatcheries**		Illinois	1
Montana	1	Puerto Rico	3	Alabama	4	**Pet Accessories**	
Nebraska	3	Spain	2	Georgia	1	Nebraska	1
Pennsylvania	4	**Swine Breeding**		Louisiana	1	New Jersey	1
Puerto Rico	1	Portugal	1	Puerto Rico	1	**Norso Distributors**	
Texas	1	Spain	5	Spain	1	California	2
Bakery Distribution Centers		**Feed Ingredient Merchandising**		**Table Egg Processing**		Illinois	1
Florida	1	Nebraska	1	Alabama	2	Texas	1
Pennsylvania	1	Puerto Rico	1	Spain	1	Virginia	1
Oat Milling		**Fertilizer Plants**		**Feed Production**		Washington	1
Minnesota	1	Montana	2	Alabama	1	**Fish Products**	
Corn Milling		**Feed & Fertilizer Retail Distribution Outlets**		Georgia	1	Mississippi	1
Alabama	1	Alabama	1	Louisiana	1	**Restaurants**	
Puerto Rico	1	Florida	1	Puerto Rico	1	Texas	53
Grain Merchandising		Montana	7				
Minnesota	1	**Commercial Hay Production**					
Wisconsin	1	Puerto Rico	1				

EXHIBIT 9

ConAgra, Inc. Stock Market Performance

Fiscal Year Ends Last Sunday in May (a)	Fully Diluted Earnings Per Share (b)	Dividends Per Share (b)	Price Range (b) (c)	Average Price (b) (c)	Average Price (c)/ Earnings	Yield (d)
1977	$3.57	$0.75	19¾–11¾	$15.750	4.4X	4.8%
1976	4.19	0.25	13 – 8½	10.750	2.6	2.3%
1975	1.09	—	9⅝– 3⅛	6.375	5.8	—
1974	(3.69)	0.12	10 – 2⅞	6.488	def	1.8%
1973	1.76	0.45	16¼– 6¾	11.500	6.5	3.9%

(a) Prior to 1976, last Sunday in June.
(b) Adjusted for 5% stock dividends in fiscal years 1974 and 1976.
(c) Calendar years.
(d) Based on average of high and low prices for calendar year.

EXHIBIT 10

ConAgra Executive Officers

Name	Title & Capacity	Age	Year Assumed Present Office	Year Joined ConAgra	Previous Association
C. M. Harper	President & Chief Financial Officer—Director	49	1976	1974	Pillsbury
Business Managers					
W. T. Adcox	Vice President & General Manager—Poultry Division	56	1966	1963	Acquired poultry co.
N. Allen	Vice President & General Manager—Agri-Products Div.	48	1975	1968	Formula Feed Industry
R. W. Hall	Vice President & General Manager, ConAgra-Europe	48	1976	1966	W. R. Grace International

Name	Title	Age			
R. B. Hill	Vice President & General Manager—Caribbean Division	43	1972	1970	Colgate-Palmolive
R. G. Holmes	President, Pet Accessories Division	46	1976	1976	Pet accessories
L. J. Kennedy	Vice President—Corporate Director of Marketing & General Manager, Consumer Products	49	1976	1976	Armour Foods
R. F. Morrison	Vice President & General Manager—Grain Milled	52	1969	1969	Acquired Montana flour mill
Corporate Resource Group					
T. E. Brady	Executive Vice President & Chief Financial Officer	53	1974	1973	Josten's; Fabritek; Peat, Marwick, Mitchell
C. C. Hansen	Vice President—Public Affairs	59	1976	1966	Walnut Grove Products
W. J. McCoy	Vice President—Public Relations	60	1977	1976	Pillsbury
D. T. Peters	Vice President & Corporate Controller	50	1975	1971	Peat, Marwick, Mitchell
H. F. Schuler	Vice President—Human Resources	53	1976	1975	Pillsbury
L. B. Thomas	Vice President—Finance and Treasurer	41	1974	1960	Started with ConAgra
R. J. White	Vice President—Planning and Development	49	1976	1976	General Mills

OBJECTIVES

1. RETURN ON EQUITY—
EARN IN EXCESS OF A 15% RETURN ON COMMON STOCKHOLDERS' EQUITY

We will consistently exceed a 15% return even though some of our businesses are cyclical in nature. We believe that we may be able to average a 20% return.

2. GROWTH IN EARNINGS PER SHARE—
INCREASE TREND LINE EARNINGS PER SHARE, ON AVERAGE, IN EXCESS OF 10% PER YEAR FROM FISCAL 1973 BASE.

Operations of basic food businesses do not always permit quarter to quarter or year to year increases in reported earnings; however, ConAgra will increase its "trend line" earnings power each year.

3. DIVIDENDS—
ConAgra's dividend will be increased based on the achievement of the objective of increasing growth in trend line earnings power.

4. RETURN ON INVESTED CAPITAL—
EARN A MINIMUM RETURN ON INVESTED CAPITAL OF 20%

ConAgra will invest in new capital projects which present an opportunity to earn in excess of 25%, before taxes, on the total permanent capital invested in the project.

FINANCING—
MAINTAIN A CONSERVATIVE BALANCE SHEET

We believe this is a prerequisite to earning a satisfactory return on stockholders' equity. The key balance sheet objectives are:

Long-term debt ratio maintained between 35% and 40%. (Long-term debt as a percent of long-term debt plus stockholders' equity).

Equity balance is equity as a percent of noncurrent assets. Our objective is to maintain equity at 100% to 120% of noncurrent assets.

Short-term debt will be used to finance only seasonal borrowing needs. Short-term debt will normally be paid off at each year end.

RESULTS

| | The "New" ConAgra | | | | |
	F1973	F1974	F1975	F1976	F1977
Return on Common Equity	16.5%	—	13.3%	58.7%	25.2%

Return on common equity is defined as net earnings, less dividends on preferred stock, divided by common stockholders' equity at the beginning of the year.

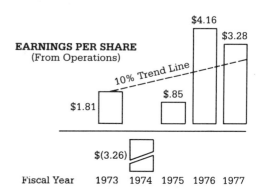

EARNINGS PER SHARE (From Operations)

$4.16 $3.28 $1.81 $.85 $(3.26) 10% Trend Line

| Fiscal Year | 1973 | 1974 | 1975 | 1976 | 1977 |

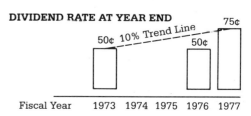

DIVIDEND RATE AT YEAR END

75¢ 50¢ 50¢ 10% Trend Line

| Fiscal Year | 1973 | 1974 | 1975 | 1976 | 1977 |

| | The "New" ConAgra | | | | |
	F1973	F1974	F1975	F1976	F1977
Return on Invested Capital	11.7%	—	9.0%	30.2%	22.4%

Return on invested capital is defined as earnings from operations before gain or loss on disposal of assets, long-term financing costs, and income taxes, divided by invested capital at the beginning of the year. Invested capital is the sum of working capital, fixed assets and other noncurrent assets, and the present value of noncapitalized leases.

| | The "New" ConAgra | | | | |
	F1973	F1974	F1975	F1976	F1977
Capitalization ratio	45.8%	66.0%	54.5%	39.3%	36.5%
Equity balance ratio	71%	55%	78%	116%	135%
Short-term debt (millions)	$84.0	$66.9	$10	0	0

EXHIBIT 11
ConAgra's Objectives And Results

EXHIBIT 12
ConAgra Strategies for Growth

The Corporation

ConAgra intends to continue to be a basic foods company, operating internationally as well as domestically. We will expand in our current lines of business; enter new industries engaged in the processing and marketing of basic foods; and bring more balance to our portfolio of businesses through entry into related fields. Our strategies are:

1 Diligently pursue our basic businesses by improving our quality of products and service to customers, and by becoming the most efficient producer in each of the industries in which we compete, with the objective of earning an increased return on stockholders' equity.

2 Expand our present basic food businesses, both through internal development and acquisition, consistent with the economies of their industries.

3 Develop internally major new businesses based on our strengths, supplemented where appropriate by acquisitions.

4 Seek more balance in our business through acquisition of appropriate new lines of business that can serve as earnings-growth vehicles.

Grain Milled Products

1 Add 2 million hundredweights of annual flour milling capacity by the end of fiscal 1978—an eight percent increase.

2 Become a significant regional factor in the domestic grain merchandising business by the end of fiscal 1979 through increased utilization of existing facilities and addition of new.

3 Reach a satisfactory return on invested capital in the bakery distribution business during fiscal 1978, and complete plans to expand this business.

Agri-Products

1 Marketing programs tailored to customer needs, in addition to our low-cost production program.

2 Develop a strong Formax feed business on a regional basis, better utilizing existing production capacity.

3 Expand fertilizer business in the northwest through additional blending plants and distribution facilities.

4 Maintain Red Hat share of market in Puerto Rico in the face of new competition.

Poultry Products

1 Increase broiler production to a rate of 320 million pounds per year by the beginning of fiscal 1979—a 23 percent increase over fiscal 1977 production.

2 Add broiler capacity, through internal development and acquisition, that will average a return on invested capital in excess of 35 percent.

3 Increase the volume of broilers marketed under the "Country Skillet" brand in supermarkets.

4 Increase commercial table egg production by 15 million dozen per year, over the next two years, by internal development and acquisition.

5 Continue to emphasize ConAgra's position as a low cost producer of broilers and table eggs.

SOURCE: ConAgra 1977 Annual Report

APPENDIX A

THE FLOUR MILLING INDUSTRY[1]

Historical Market Trends   U.S. flour consumption has not changed substantially over the last five decades. U.S. flour production reached a low of 190 million hundred weights (CWT) in the depression of the 1930s; a strong postwar export market swelled production to a high of 305 million CWT in 1947. Since 1947 production has generally trended slightly downwards as exports contracted, reaching 247 million CWT in 1975. Foreign countries are now largely self-sufficient in milling capacity and 1975 U.S. flour exports were only 5% of total U.S. production.

U.S. per capita flour consumption has declined from about 200 pounds annually at the turn of the century to 107 pounds in 1975, while population growth has offset the decline in per capita consumption. Rising real income and development of food processing and distribution has changed dietary patterns in favor of meats, fruits, vegetables, and processed foods. These trends have continued to the present day, but the rate of decline in per capita flour consumption appears to be diminishing. Domestic wheat flour consumption was 226 million CWT in 1975, up from 210 million in 1960.

An estimated 47% of 1975 industry production was hard wheat flour, 30% soft and 23% family. Over the past decade, industry sales of family flour have declined substantially, offset by an increase in bakery flour, particularly soft wheat bakery flour. An estimated 65% of flour sold to U.S. commercial bakers in 1975 was used in bread products, 17% in sweet goods, 10% in cookies, and 8% in crackers.

Future growth of the U.S. flour industry is expected to follow domestic consumption now that exports are insignificant. The recent domestic growth in consumption averaging approximately 0.5% appears to be a reasonable projection for U.S. industry production.

Types of Wheat and Flour   There are many types of flour, depending on the type of wheat from which the flour is ground and the degree of purity of the flour.

Wheat and flour are classified mainly by hardness. Hard wheat flour ("strong" flour) is milled from hard varieties of wheat and soft wheat flour ("weak" flour) from soft varieties of wheat. "Family" flour, i.e. flour sold at retail, is mostly general purpose flour blended from hard and soft wheat flours.

The Milling Process   The average wheat seed is comprised of 85% endosperm, the white interior part of the seed which serves as nutrient to the embryo if a seed germinates; 13% bran, the hull of the seed; and 2% germ, the embryo.

Flour is finely ground endosperm of the wheat seed. A modern efficient flour mill is capable of separating 85%–88% of the endosperm from the bran, achieving flour yield of 72%–75% of the weight of the wheat seed. Patent (low ash, high grade) flour is usually more than 90% of a mill's flour output. Unrecovered endosperm and bran constitutes a by-product known generally as "mill feed" used mainly as an animal feed ingredient. Flour prices and mill feed prices move indepedently because demand for flour is unrelated to demand for mill feed. Nevertheless, flour prices have averaged in the vicinity of two times mill feed prices over the longer term.

The flour milling industry converted from millstones to steel cylindrical rollers about a century ago and has since had no fundamental technical change. Processing refinements, such as better bolting (sifting) and purifying machinery, more breaking and reduction stages, and refinements in pneumatic handling, have permitted increased yields

SOURCE: Lehman Brothers, Inc.

586

of the more valuable patent (high grade) flour. Nevertheless, milling machinery as old as 50 years or more can still be utilized in modern, high-yield plants.

The industry has converted 60%–65% of production from bag to bulk shipment in the last two decades. Nearly all commercial bakeries now recieve flour pneumatically from large truck or railroad cars similar to tank cars.

Industry Capacity and Factors Affecting Return on Investment   The U.S. wheat flour milling industry had 270 mills in 1975; of these, 83 had capacity of 5,000 or more hundred weights per day and accounted for 77% of total industry capacity.

Industry capacity is presently balanced with demand despite some contraction in total production over the last several decades. General Mills closed a large portion of its flour mills in 1968, reducing industry capacity approximately 10% and substantially eliminating the industry overcapacity that had developed. Industry capacity has also been reduced by shut down of many small mills, but capacity of many larger mills has been increased.

Industry profitability has improved since 1968 and return on capital based on depreciated historical plant costs is now respectable. However, return on capital based on replacement costs, which are well over five times the depreciated value of the industry's plant, cannot justify new plant construction. Over the last decade, the industry has constructed only seven new mills accounting for less than 5% of industry capacity. Three of these new mills are ConAgra mills.

Incremental flour mill capacity can be achieved at substantially less cost than that of a new mill. Costs savings exceeding 50% of the cost of a new mill can result from use of existing buildings and second-hand machinery.

Flour millers avoid speculation on wheat price trends by fully hedging all cash wheat inventories and all contracts for future flour delivery. Consequently, profits achieved by flour millers are normally consistent, without fluctuations related to grain prices.

APPENDIX B

THE BROILER INDUSTRY[1]

Historical Market Trends   Broilers are an increasing portion of total U.S. meat consumption. Broilers accounted for 16% of total U.S. meat consumption in 1975, up from 5% in 1950. Per capita consumption of broilers has more than quadrupled since 1950. Total per capita chicken consumption including both broilers and mature chickens approximately doubled. Growth of the broiler industry has accompanied a sharp decline in mature chicken consumption to less than one-third the amount of per capita consumption in 1950. Broilers accounted for 91% of chicken consumption in 1975, up from 42% in 1950. Per capita turkey consumption approximately doubled since 1950, while per capita beef and veal consumption increased only 65% and per capita pork consumption actually declined slightly.

Broilers have increased their position in total meat consumption because they are much more efficient converters of grain into meat protein than hogs or cattle. Dry feed consumption per pound of live weight is approximately 2 pounds for broilers, 8 pounds for cattle and 4 pounds for hogs. Broiler meat is 18%–19% protein, beef approximately 15% and pork 10%. The higher protein content of broiler meat causes broilers to be even more efficient converters of feed into protein than live weight conversion figures suggest. An average of 20 to 25 pounds of dry feed is required to produce a pound of beef protein and 70 pounds for a pound of pork protein.

The relative cost advantage of broilers as a protein source has increased substantially under high grain prices. Retail prices of broilers averaged 82¢ per pound less than beef in 1975 compared with 47¢ in 1968; broilers were 69¢ less than pork in 1975 compared with 28¢ in 1968.

The broiler industry has also substantially outperformed other meat industries in efficiency improvements. The short growing cycle for broilers is a great benefit in developing improved genetic strains. Better feed formulations, genetic improvements and optimized environmental conditions have reduced average growing time to seven or eight weeks, approximately half that of three decades ago.

U.S. broiler consumption is expected to grow at an average rate of 3%–4% annually, a somewhat slower rate than in past decades. Displacement of mature chicken broilers will no longer be a significant growth factor for broilers. Broilers should, however, continue to increase relative to red meat.

Industry Structure and Method of Production   Large-scale production of broilers is a recent development. There was some large-scale broiler production prior to World War II, but most of the industry's development has occurred since then. Major integrated producers are increasingly important. The ten largest broiler producers now account for an estimated 40% of total industry production, up from an estimated 30% a decade ago.

An integrated broiler producer normally maintains and operates facilities for all aspects of broiler production except grow-out facilities. The producer is responsible for brood flocks, hatcheries, the processing plant, and usually formulates and produces all of the feed used in his operations. Other frequent facilities are an ice plant, a rendering plant, and waste treatment facilities for each processing plant.

Integrated poultry producers use independent contractors for grow-out. Newly hatched chicks are innoculated, debeaked and shipped to contract growers. A typical contractor is a small-to-medium-sized family farm which has several hundred feet of growing sheds, typically approximately forty feet wide. Contract growing is standard practice in the broiler industry because labor costs and overhead, such as employment taxes and real estate taxes, are lower for individual farmers than for large corporate growers. The

SOURCE: Lehman Brothers, Inc.

independent farmer contractor provides the growing shed, labor, and utilities. The integrated producer provides the chicks and feed, retaining title to the birds as they are grown. The farmer is paid 2¢–3¢ per pound of live weight, usually with incentives for efficient feed conversion. The compensation plus incentive allows an efficient contract grower to amortize his investment in facilities within four or five years.

The integrated broiler producer collects finished birds from contract growers and processes them in large processing plants. In the processing plants the birds are killed, picked, eviscerated, cut and packed. Broiler producers who ice pack normally produce all of their own ice on the plant premises. Viscera, legs, heads and feathers are taken to rendering plants, many of which are owned and operated by broiler producers. Rendering plants convert the waste chicken parts into protein meal for use in poultry feed. A poultry processing plant issues large quantities of waste water, which can either be purified in large ponds at the plant site or discharged into a municipal sewer system.

The broiler industry uses 3 methods to pack the product: ice pack, chill pack and frozen. Ice pack accounted for approximately 56% of 1975 industry shipments, chill pack 22% and frozen 22%. Chill pack is a relatively new technique where the product is maintained at a controlled temperature of 28°–30° F, a few degrees above the freezing point of broiler meat. Chill pack extends shelf life to 15–18 days, compared to about 14 days normal shelf life for ice pack. Chill pack also keeps the product relatively dry, an advantage for packaging less-than-whole-bird packages at the processing plant. Ice pack promoters claim ice pack chicken is tendered better than chill pack; chill pack promoters claim product uniformity and freshness. The shelf life of frozen product is indefinite and all poultry exported from the U.S. are shipped frozen. However, most consumers prefer fresh rather than frozen product, even though they usually freeze the product themselves after purchase.

The Broiler Cycle and Return on Investments   Broiler industry profit margins are highly cyclical with cycle durations ranging from 25 to 35 months. The cycle is regularly recurrent and average profit margins over the cycle tend to be consistent from one cycle to the next. The broiler cycle is influenced by delayed reaction of broiler supplies to changing broiler prices, and by the hog cycle. The hog cycle often determines timing of the broiler cycle with a lag period because pork prices affect broiler prices. Pork is the lowest cost red meat and is therefore a partial substitute for chicken.

The broiler industry is financially attractive despite its severe cyclicality. The best of the major broiler producers approximately break even when broiler prices are near cyclical lows. Over the entire cycle such producers are able to achieve average returns on capital significantly above average for all U.S. industry. The contract grower system permits integrated producers to minimize capital investment. Growers compensation formulae insulate the growers from any effect of the broiler cycle so that the full brunt of the cycle is absorbed by the integrated producer.

Major efficient broiler producers are able to achieve above average growth by expanding market share as the trend toward larger broiler producers continues. Large producers are able to achieve above average efficiency through their work in broiler genetics, feed formulation and procedures to maximize operating efficiency.

APPENDIX C

THE FORMULA FEED INDUSTRY[1]

The $5 billion U.S. formula feed industry is fragmented and regional with approximately two thousand participants. The largest U.S. participants, Ralston, Allied Mills (division of Continental Grain), Central Soya and Agway (a group of cooperatives), are estimated to account for less than 20% of U.S. industry volume.

Formula feed is ground and mixed from a variety of basic ingredients including corn, soya beans, soya bean meal, cotton seed meal, mill feed (wheat bran by-product from flour milling), oats, fish meal, animal by-product meal and roughage. Formula feeds use thousands of combinations of such ingredients and various additives such as vitamins, minerals, trace minerals and antibiotics.

Feed can be sold as: fully mixed; concentrate (200–600 pounds/ton); super concentrate (50–250 pounds/ton); or premix 10–25 pounds/ton). Concentrates, super concentrates and premixes include only the more specialized ingredients (in the case of premix, most additives). Most fully mixed and concentrate feed is sold in bulk, while super concentrates and premix are usually sold in bags.

The economic rationale for the feed industry is sound, particularly for relatively small customers, even though capital costs for a feed mill are low and entry barriers minimal. The feed industry provides convenience, ingredient buying power, and nutritional expertise to the farmer. A feed manufacturer is better able to purchase ingredients, match current market prices of ingredients to the desired nutritional qualities, and then grind and mix the feed to an optimum lowest cost formula for the stage of life and desired characteristics of the animal to be fed.

However, when animal feeding becomes a large scale commercial operation by specialized companies, the feed customer tends to integrate backwards with his own feed mill. Backward integration by customers first became important in poultry in the 1950s and early 1960s, then spread to beef cattle feeding in the 1960s and appears to be beginning in hog feeding. Backward integration has not, however, been significant in the dairy industry except with a few of the largest dairies. A large integrated animal grower may find it economical to purchase premix, super concentrate or other specialized ingredients from a feed supplier but is usually not a customer for bulk fully mixed feed.

The radical increase in ingredient costs in 1973 lowered the number of beef cattle and hogs on feed, and sharply increased feed industry overcapacity in major beef cattle and hog growing regions. Under these industry conditions, profits of most feed suppliers to beef and pork growers have suffered for several years.

Based on an outlook for some improvement in the number of cattle and hogs on feed over the next five years, these currently depressed sectors of the feed industry are expected to recover gradually. Overall formula feed industry growth is forecast at approximately 3% annually.

SOURCE: Lehman Brothers, Inc.

APPENDIX D

CONAGRA COMMENTS RELATIVE TO FISCAL 1974 LOSS

The loss of $11,853,000 that ConAgra reported for fiscal 1974 had little, if any, relation to the fact that some parts of ConAgra's business, particularly poultry products, are cyclical in nature, for fiscal 1974 was a relatively good year for ConAgra's operating division engaged in flour milling, poultry and formula feed. All of ConAgra's major competitors in its various lines of business reported increased earnings for their fiscal 1974.

There were two principal reasons for this loss:

1 The company's balance sheet was highly leveraged in a period of high and volatile commodity prices and high interest costs. At the end of fiscal 1974 ConAgra's total debt was $136.1 million versus stockholders' equity of $34.3 million. Interest expense of $16 million in fiscal 1974 was up $10.5 million from the previous year.

2 The company's inventory management program was not adequate in a time of high and volatile commodity costs, and the lack of proper hedging policies resulted in large losses as a result of speculative commodity positions.

Under the "New" ConAgra both of these problems have been corrected:

1 The company established objectives aimed at maintaining a conservative balance sheet, which includes having long-term debt maintained between 35 and 40 percent of total capitalization. This objective was accomplished in both fiscal 1976 and 1977. At the end of fiscal 1977 stockholders' equity was $66.1 million versus total debt of $41.5 million.

2 New inventory management policies are in place which emphasize that the company will make a profit from the processing of basic foods, and not from speculation. There are close limitations on the daily "open" market positions that may be taken, and positions in all commodities are monitored daily, reviewed by the chief financial officer, and reported to the Board of Directors on a regular basis.

SOURCE: ConAgra Memo.

APPENDIX E

LEGAL PROCEEDINGS

For the fiscal year ended May 29, 1977, ConAgra has a number of pending legal matters. The Company's counsel advised that collectively, the suits should not be materially important in relation to the current assets of the Company. Briefly, the substance of these legal proceedings is as follows:

1 In October 1974, the Company was joined, along with a number of other persons, with alleged violations of the Sherman Act in the production, marketing, and sale of broiler chickens and has agreed in principle to settle this litigation for $1,850,000. This amount has been provided for in prior fiscal years; the settlement is subject to approval by the District Court.

2 In October of 1975 a Federal Grand Jury investigation of exchange of feed product prices among manufacturers resulted in a subpoena for ConAgra to furnish documents to the court. ConAgra has complied.

3 Interstate Brands Corporation in January 1976, alleged violation of the Sherman Act by ConAgra through an attempt to monopolize the sale of bakery flour, restricting production, and utilizing uniform pricing formulas. The plaintiff seeks treble damages in an amount as yet unspecified.

4 The Company has also been served a subpoena requiring it to produce documents for a Grand Jury investigation of sales to the United States Department of Agriculture of Bulgor Fortified Foods. The Company has complied with the subpoena.

5 The Company and its subsidiary, ConAgra Montana Incorporated, were sued by Montana Hatcheries, Incorporated in a Montana District Court for allegedly watering feed. The complaint prays for $100,000 in actual damages; incidental consequential damages of $100,000; for loss of business reputation and goodwill $1,000,000 and punitive damages of $10,000,000.

6 The Company conducts its business in Puerto Rico under a consent decree with the Puerto Rican Government with respect to future acquisitions of poultry operations and with respect to its dealings with Puerto Rican chicken growers.

APPENDIX F

SECURITY ANALYST SUMMARY OF CONAGRA— MARCH 21, 1978[1]

Under new management, ConAgra has achieved a remarkable financial and operational recovery since 1974 when a loss of $3.45 per share was registered and the company teetered on the verge of bankruptcy. Last year ConAgra reported fully diluted earnings per share of $3.21 after a one-time credit of 29¢/share, and is grinding out another fine performance in the current year. Earnings per share are expected to exceed $3.60 this year and could possibly reach as high as $3.75. For next year, although it is impossible to forecast ConAgra's earnings with any degree of precision, we are tentatively projecting record fully diluted earnings in the $3.90–4.20/share range.

Clearly, CAG's turnround has been dramatic. As a consequence, management has dubbed the company the "New ConAgra" and has set out for itself extremely ambitious goals which, if attained, could result in a major price/earnings multiple expansion. At this juncture we see only a few tangible signs that give us confidence that management can reach its objectives, given the nature of its businesses.

Nonethless, we do feel present management has accomplished several things during the past few years that makes ConAgra common stock an interesting commitment. First, *the company's financial position has been strengthened materially* and a rigid discipline has been imposed to prevent any reversal of this trend. Asset management has been emphasized resulting in a significantly higher ROI. Second, *management has been broadened and deepened,* consistent with the quasi-autonomous operating philosophy of the company. Third, as a necessary by-product of this less centralized modus operandi, *inventory and operating controls have been imposed* to prevent a repetition of the 1974 fiasco that virtually became the company's undoing. Fourth, management reassessed the company's operations. As a consequence, *a major asset restructuring program was initiated to eliminate marginally profitable businesses* and those that did not fit into management's long range plans. Some $20 million of fixed assets were sold (most with a net gain to CAG), which is one of the major reasons why sales in the current fiscal year will fall $100 million-plus short of FY 1974's $638 million record, despite near-record earnings being recorded. Fifth, *strategic plans by management were established with ambitious growth objectives.* In our view, CAG's goal to grow 14% from 1973's base of $1.68 per share is clearly ambitious, despite the fact that it appears as though it will have been achieved for the five year period ending in May. By management's own admission, ConAgra is a basic foods company, which suggests inherent growth and profitability limitations. A more realistic expectation on the part of investors is a long-term growth rate of something less than 14%, perhaps 10–12%, although even that figure could well prove too optimistic, as well. Furthermore, it may be that some of management's other goals are set too high and are unattainable.

While the jury is still out on these issues, there is little question in our mind that ConAgra is well managed today with solid competitive positions in three commodity areas (flour milling, formula feed, and poultry products) and the potential to achieve additional growth in a couple of interesting consumer categories. With this in mind, we believe ConAgra's stock is attractive. Selling at a very low price/earnings multiple of five, yielding 6.8%, and only slightly above book value, we believe the risk-reward for investors is a favorable one.

ConAgra's stock has been an outstanding performer in the past few years. In 1975 it advanced 183%; in 1976 it was up 49%, and last year it rose another 51%. In fact, CAG's shares recently hit $20, an all-time high. Notwithstanding this performance Con-

[1] © 1978 by William Blair & Company. Reprinted with permission.

Agra's stock is still reasonably priced, in our opinion. Should near-to-intermediate term market weakness and/or the possibility of a disappointing quarter or two depress the company's common shares, we would be inclined to use the decline to establish new positions or add to existing holdings. In this connection, investors should be aware that it is possible for one and possibly two quarters in FY 1979 to show unfavorable earnings comparisons reflecting depressed broiler margins.

BERVEN CARPETS CORPORATION (B)

David M. Hauntz
Hugh O. Hunter

In July 1980, a group of people gathered after dinner in a Northwestern city to discuss the plight of Berven Carpets Corporation. The evening sun was still high in the sky when the meeting was convened. Assembled were two Berven stockholders, a manufacturer's representative, a professor who taught business policy at a local university, and two graduate business students.

The question before the group was, Where does Berven go from here? To form a basis for discussion, the professor presented a strategy model developed in 1975 by Charles W. Hofer.[1] The model attempts to relate appropriate strategies to stages in the life cycle of a business. The professor contended that Berven clearly exemplified a firm in the maturity stage of the life cycle. He then distributed to the group a brief explanation of Hofer's work on mature firms. These handouts are shown in exhibits 1, 2, and 3.

While the degree of product differentiation in the carpet industry is arguable (see exhibit 2), few would view the consumers' needs as being economic as opposed to non-economic. The appropriate strategies for categories N2 and N3 are presented in exhibit 3. There was discussion of the Hofer model. Most felt that it served as a reasonable baseline for the evening's topic. There was not complete agreement on whether the industry was characterized by high or low product differentiation, but the concensus formed around category N2 (low differentiation).

The manufacturer's representative was knowledgeable about the company. It was immediately clear to him that Berven was not complying with at least some of the strategies suggested in exhibit 3 for category N2. He cited Berven's policy of specializing in high-priced, high quality carpeting. "That's not all," he said, "The Company has a modern plant, but sales are lagging, keeping production down. There's a lot of excess capacity down there."

One of the stockholders, noting strategy d in exhibit 3, asked the representative whether the 20% market share rule applied to Berven. "I don't have the exact information, but I would be willing to bet that it does. There are some big boys in this business—Burlington, Stevens, plus some big conglomerates. These guys really advertise too. We have attempted to carve a segment out of the market and live with that. These bigger companies offer full lines, just as our model here suggests."

At this point, the stockholder broke in and in a rather derisive tone, said, "Mr. Hofer's conclusion is that we pack it in. If we believe that, we can leave early tonight."

Copyright © Hugh O. Hunter

"Dropping out is one option," replied the professor, "but there are some survival strategies open to Berven. It seems clear that they are going to have to make some changes. The question is, should they—that is, is survival in some form preferable to dropping out? If so, what are their survival options, and which one should they select? Which one has the greatest chance of success, given this Company's strengths and weaknesses, and the predilections of management?"

"And, just incidentally, what might be best for the stockholders," one of the two said abruptly. "Yes, we certainly don't want to forget you." replied the professor.

At this point, one of the graduate students, who had been studying exhibit 3, said, "As I see it, Berven has a couple of survival options. I guess the most obvious is to broaden their product line to keep their plant utilization high. The second is to decide whether they want to be a regional or a national distributor; and, whichever way they go, increase their presence in that market." The second student said, "Yes, and those two aren't mutually exclusive either." "Not necessarily," replied the manufacturer's representative, "but remember that national marketing campaigns are expensive, and Berven is pretty small and has a lot of debt." "And then the question is, can a regional distributor keep the plant busy," said the professor. There was silence as all pondered Berven's dilemma.

A stockholder broke the silence. "There's always another option. Acquisition. Allow Berven to be acquired at a fair price." "That's hardly a survival strategy," said the second stockholder. "Well," said the professor, "It means survival of the production facility, the marketing network, and the employees. If the stockholders get a fair price, they simply liquidate their holdings in Berven and find an alternative investment."

A student, in a quizzical tone, said, "Berven is not my idea of a terrific merger candidate. It has problems. Who would be willing to pay much for this company. Wouldn't it be better to get this company on its feet, and then seek a partner?"

"There's no question that the price would go up for a healthy company," replied the professor, "But, there's some risk involved. We have discussed the survival strategies. If we sell now, we are asking someone else to take the risk." "So there's a tradeoff," said the student. "The key, of course, is to find the right kind of merger partner, and to negotiate a fair price," continued the professor. "Negotiations can sometimes take months, and then end in failure."

The manufacturer's representative, who knew Berven better than anyone in the room, said, "Berven has a net operating loss carry-forward of over $5 million. I don't know whether that could be transferred to the acquiring company. If it could, it would make us more attractive. Also, our stock is selling way below book value. That makes us a likely target."

A stockholder asked, "Does anybody see Berven being acquired by a conglomerate or simply by one of the big textile companies?"

"I think it could go either way," replied the professor. "A conglomerate acquisition, let's say by a company seeking entry into the industry, would be picking up a weak company; but the parent could infuse new management and capital, and perhaps revive Berven fairly easily. Acquisition by a textile company, one in the carpet business, would be a horizontal merger. Here, the parent would expect to capitalize

Berven's strengths, strengths which would complement the parent's strengths. A proper fit is important."

Once again, silence prevailed. Questions had been raised. Options discussed. It was clear to all that no obvious solution had surfaced, only that Berven could not continue for long on its current course.

EXHIBIT 1
Maturity Stage of the Life Cycle

In the maturity stage of the life cycle, the major determinants of business strategy are the nature of buyer needs, the degree of product differentiation, the rate of technological change in process design, the degree of market segmentation, the ratio of distribution costs to manufacturing value added, and the frequency with which the product is purchased. This proposition should really be broken into two parts:

A. In the maturity stage of the life cycle, the two major determinants of business strategy are the degree of product differentiation and the nature of buyer needs.

B. The secondary determinants of business strategy during the maturity phase of the product life cycle vary depending on the degree of buyer's needs.

Degree of Product Differentiation

		High	Low
Nature of Buyer Needs	Primarily Economic	N4 —purchase frequency —absolute price paid —rate of technological change in process design —buyer concentration	N1 —rate of technological change in process design —ratio of distribution costs to manufacturing value added —purchase frequency —buyer concentration —degree of capacity utilization
	Primarily Non-Economic	N3 —market segmentation —product complexity —purchase frequency —nature of barriers to entry	N2 —market segmentation —degree of specialization within the industry —marketing intensity —manufacturing economies of scale —ratio of distribution costs to manufacturing value added

EXHIBIT 2
Matrix: Nature of Buyer Needs and Degree of Product Differentiation

EXHIBIT 3
Appropriate Strategies

HYPOTHESIS N2

a. Use universal rather than specialized marketing appeals.
b. Reduce geographic scope or increase their marketing expenditures sufficiently so that their per capita marketing expenditures within their geographic service areas are in excess of the industry average.
c. Attempt to keep their degree of capacity utilization high and their fixed assets relatively modern.
d. Withdraw from the industry if their market share falls to less than 20 percent of that held by the industry leader within their geographic service area.

HYPOTHESIS N3

a. Focus their R & D funds first on modifying and upgrading their existing product lines, second on developing new products, and last on process innovation.
b. Allocate substantial funds to the maintenance and enhancement of their distinct competencies, especially those in the marketing areas.
c. Develop a strong service capability in their distribution system.
d. Seek to expand the geographic scope of their operations if possible.

ENDNOTE

1 Hofer, Charles W., "Toward a Contingency Theory of Business Strategy," *Academy of Management Journal,* December 1975, 784–810.

CITY HARDWARE COMPANY, INC. (B)

Paul Miesing

TO: Board Members, City Hardware, Inc.

FROM: Chairman of the Board

RE: Future direction of the company

DATE: May 14, 1976

Due to the disappointing results of the past two years, I feel it is necessary for us to meet as soon as possible. Therefore, I am calling a meeting of the Board for Friday, May 21 at 10:00 a.m. The purpose of the meeting will be to determine feasible ways to reverse the current situation. Since the General Manager will not be present, please use discretion in discussing this matter.

Signed,

Mark Taylor, Jr.

BACKGROUND

In the Spring of 1973, the Board of Directors of City Hardware, Inc., acting on the recommendations of the General Manager, decided to move the company from its long-established downtown location to a new site in the northern suburbs of the city. This move involved relocating the company's downtown hardware store and a wholly owned plumbing supply company—with separate locations and store managers—to a single building. The company based its move decision on the expanding growth to the north.

The firm decided to concentrate on retail hardware sales. As the General Manager noted, most residential developments of the past few years occurred in the northern suburbs. He saw sales potential in contractors going to the job as well as home owners who continue working around their homes after construction is completed.

Summary financial information for the period preceding the move decision was as follows:

This case was prepared by Assistant Professor Paul Miesing with the aid of M. Anderson, W. Anderson, C. Klemstine, and W. Pankey as a basis for class discussion and is not intended to illustrate either effective or ineffective handling of an administrative situation.

Distributed by the Intercollegiate Case Clearing House, Soldiers Field, Boston, MA 01263. All rights reserved to the contributors. Printed in the U.S.A.

Year	Net Sales	Cost of Goods Sold	Gross Profit	Operating Expenses	Net Income
Hardware:					
1969	$660,000	$477,000	$183,000	$211,000	$(28,000)
1970	636,000	485,000	151,000	207,000	(56,000)
1971	633,000	428,000	205,000	211,000	(6,000)
1972	985,000	774,000	211,000	229,000	(18,000)
Supply:					
1969	$476,000	$346,000	$130,000	$ 88,000	$ 42,000
1970	520,000	390,000	130,000	73,000	57,000
1971	474,000	346,000	128,000	91,000	37,000
1972	606,000	455,000	146,000	107,000	39,000

The move took place just before the onset of the recession–inflation phenomenon which followed the end of the Vietnam War and extended through the Nixon–Watergate era. Although unemployment was high with the economic slow-down in full swing, inflation continued unabated. (See Exhibits 1 and 2.)

PERSONALITIES

Howard Martin began his career as General Manager of City Hardware in 1970. He had previously held the same position in a nearby city and was hired by City Hardware on the basis of his character references there. Howard managed the store with a loose administrative style, giving his employees free reign. Both Howard and his wife were much involved in local activities, maintaining a respected personal image within the community. In addition, Howard concentrated considerable time and energy toward qualifying for trips and other business-related benefits. As a result, the Martins were able to visit many places which they would never otherwise have seen.

Board members and stockholders comprise a very interesting group. None of them live in the immediate vicinity of the stores. The majority stockholders are two father-son teams. In addition, two cousins also serve on the Board.

The two fathers, most knowledgeable of the group, are no longer active in the organization. Their two sons have taken over leadership. Mark Taylor, Jr.—who together with his father controls 45% of the company's stock—is president of the company. An MIT graduate, he now owns his own high-technology corporation in the northern part of the state. Les Hill, III and his father own 25% of the stock. Like Mark, Les has been a corporate officer for a long time. Les, a graduate of a prestigious Eastern university, is now vice president of a major tool manufacturing corporation.

Primarily due to the physical distance between the stockholders and City Hardware, they interact only with Howard, and feel rapport with him in times of success. But in times of losses, misunderstandings and a lack of communication predominate, and their disagreements often become volatile.

Howard has employed older, "handy-man" types who are knowledge-able in hardware. Most consider their jobs long-term, although many had problems once they moved to the new modernized store. Traditionally, Howard wanted to be an ally to his employees, supporting their side in arguments with the Board. Much as Howard tries to remain on their good sides, the employees (as will most employees) still recognize his weak points and take advantage of them.

STORE OPERATIONS

City Hardware's pricing policy is largely set by department buyers (see Exhibit 3) who have overall responsibility for sales as well as buying all inventory items in their departments. Based on a 27% to 30% mark-up over cost, prices depend on the buyer's perception of what will move the inventory. A buyer might also adjust the price asked of an individual customer in order to make a particular sale.

The management of City Hardware seeks to compete with other local hardware stores, building supply, and plumbing supply houses on the bases of price, personal relationships between customers and employees, broad credit policies, wide product selection and delivery to retail customers. The company had a reputation of being somewhat high-priced, but also of being a place where you can get almost anything you want. The older salesmen have a reputation for knowing the hardware business so well that they are able to listen to your problem and help you solve it. Also, you can get parts for items which haven't been manufactured or offered for sale for some years. Past policies of buying in car-load lots, formerly facilitated by the railroad siding near the plumbing supply operation, assured this ready supply of parts.

With the new move to the new location, City Hardware management switched to a self-service retailing policy, with fewer salesmen on the floor and standard packaged items replacing the old-line bin operation. However, price markups of the downtown location were retained in the new store.

Accounting systems for the company primarily consist of multicolumn journals and a ledger, maintained by an accountant assisted by a bookkeeper. Since total sales maintain a stable dollar level, the management does not feel a need for complex financial or cost accounting systems.

Specifics of the Move   In the Spring of 1973, when the Board of Directors approved the decision to move all operations to a new site in the northern suburbs, it was estimated that a three acre tract of land would probably cost $60,000. Active negotiations began promptly, resulting in the April 1973 purchase of four and one-half acres at a total cost of $229,000. The acquired site is located next to a large building materials supply store, one block west of the main north-south highway into town. The land purchase was financed with a $45,000 addition to an existing mortgage from a local bank, $4,000 of internal funds, and the issuance of $180,000 in 8% bonds to the prior owners of the land.

Les Hill wanted to work with the General Manager in developing the design of the new building, especially the office area. Les felt that the offices—especially the General Manager's—should reflect the prestige locally associated with the company. Accordingly, he helped to contact a well-known local architect with a reputation based on the homes he had designed. The City Hardware building was his first venture into the commercial building field.

He designed a 22,00 square foot building (see Exhibit 4) characterized by open steel beams. The center of the sloping ceilings is sufficiently high to accommodate offices on the second floor. This design allows the Manager to look down from a gallery outside his office onto the housewares, china, and sporting goods selling area approximately the size of a grocery store. Mr. Martin could view the hardware selling floor, equivalent in size, from another gallery adjacent to the 1,000-square-foot conference room. The galleries are interconnected, providing access to the various offices and to the stairs. The basement is given over entirely to the plumbing supply operation.

Although Mr. Martin had originally estimated building costs of $20,000 based on an estimate of $10 per square foot, it became evident that costs would run somewhat higher as the actual construction time approached. Since the proceeds from the sale of the downtown store went to pay off a mortgage on the property, two of the Board members came forward and agreed to construct the building, which the company would then lease. This plan relieved the company of all obligations except a guarantee for a building construction loan in the amount of $775,000. As of June 30, 1976, however, the old supply company building had still not been sold.

The company ultimately negotiated lease agreements calling for annual rental payments of $109,000 over the next twenty-six years, the rental of furniture and fixtures adding $21,000 per year, to be renewed annually.

Operations began in the new building on August 11, 1975. (Financial statements are included as Exhibits 5 and 6.)

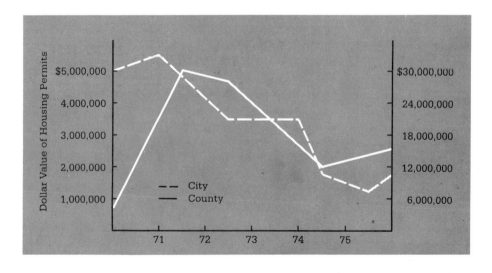

EXHIBIT 1
Area Housing Starts

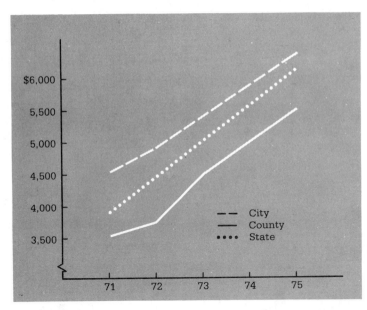

EXHIBIT 2
Per Capita Income

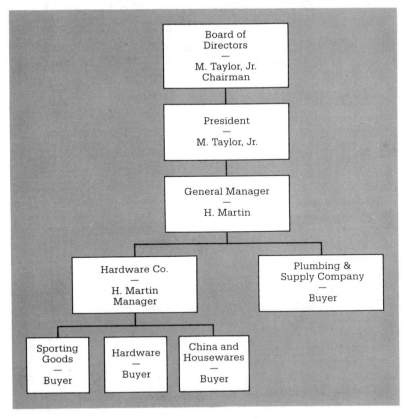

EXHIBIT 3
City Hardware, Inc. Organization Chart

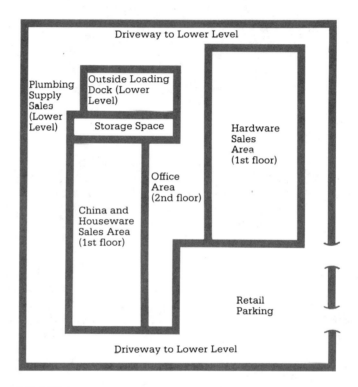

EXHIBIT 4
New Store Layout

EXHIBIT 5

City Hardware, Inc. Balance Sheets
June 30, 1972, through 1976

	1972	1973	1974	1975	1976
Current assets					
cash	$ 12,000	$ 16,000	$ 9,000	$ 15,000	$ 14,000
accounts receivable—trade	224,000	203,000	156,000	137,000	91,000
other receivables	6,000	6,000	5,000	3,000	55,000
less allowance	14,000	12,000	9,000	11,000	7,000
net receivables	236,000	197,000	152,000	129,000	139,000
inventories	560,000	510,000	606,000	690,000	471,000
other current assets	3,000	2,000	2,000	31,000	9,000
total current assets	811,000	725,000	769,000	765,000	633,000
Property, plant & equipment					
land	18,000	247,000	247,000	243,000	233,000
buildings & improvements	128,000	129,000	128,000	129,000	48,000
furniture, fixtures & equipment	38,000	46,000	47,000	48,000	62,000
autos & trucks	19,000	19,000	20,000	20,000	18,000
total cost	203,000	440,000	442,000	440,000	361,000
less: acc. dep.	133,000	138,000	141,000	149,000	81,000
net property, plant & equipment	70,000	302,000	301,000	291,000	280,000
Other assets	1,000	7,000	69,000	7,000	8,000
Total assets	$882,000	$1,034,000	$1,139,000	$1,063,000	$921,000
Current liabilities					
notes payable to bank	$ 65,000	$ 65,000	$ 90,000	$ 135,000	$180,000
accounts payable	245,000	154,000	191,000	146,000	223,000
L-T debt due	12,000	47,000	51,000	52,000	39,000
other payables	11,000	16,000	53,000	14,000	60,000
total current liabilities	333,000	282,000	385,000	347,000	502,000
L-T liabilities—bldg.	110,000	291,000	248,000	197,000	59,000
Total liabilities	443,000	573,000	633,000	544,000	561,000
Capital					
capital stock	80,000	80,000	80,000	80,000	80,000
retained earnings	386,000	405,000	450,000	463,000	304,000
total	466,000	485,000	530,000	543,000	384,000
less treasury stock	27,000	24,000	24,000	24,000	24,000
net capital	439,000	461,000	506,000	519,000	360,000
Total liabilities & capital	$882,000	$1,034,000	$1,139,000	$1,063,000	$921,000

EXHIBIT 6

City Hardware, Inc. Income Statements
Years Ended June 30, 1973, through 1976

	1973			1974		
	Hardware	Supply	Total	Hardware	Supply	Total
Net sales	$874,000	$602,000	$1,476,000	$822,000	$650,000	$1,472,000
Less: Cost of sales	676,000	439,000	1,115,000	537,000	467,000	1,004,000
Gross profit	198,000	163,000	361,000	285,000	183,000	468,000
Operating expenses						
advertising	$ 11,000	$ 2,000	$ 13,000	$ 11,000	$ 1,000	$ 12,000
auto & truck	3,000	1,000	4,000	3,000	1,000	4,000
bad debts	2,000	2,000	4,000	11,000	22,000	33,000
data processing	6,000	2,000	8,000	5,000	3,000	8,000
depreciation	5,000	3,000	8,000	5,000	3,000	8,000
interest	12,000	8,000	20,000	20,000	14,000	34,000
repairs	1,000	2,000	3,000	—	1,000	1,000
salaries	143,000	75,000	218,000	153,000	80,000	233,000
supplies & office supplies	7,000	2,000	9,000	7,000	2,000	9,000
taxes & licenses	11,000	8,000	19,000	13,000	9,000	22,000
utilities (light & telephone)	7,000	2,000	9,000	7,000	3,000	10,000
rent	—	—	—	—	—	—
other	21,000	14,000	35,000	20,000	11,000	31,000
Total operating expense	229,000	121,000	350,000	255,000	150,000	405,000
Pre-tax income from operation	$(31,000)	$ 42,000	$ 11,000	$ 30,000	$ 33,000	$ 63,000

EXHIBIT 6 (continued)

	1975			1976		
	Hardware	Supply	Total	Hardware	Supply	Total
Net sales	$669,000	$572,000	$1,241,000	$742,000	$373,000	$1,115,000
Less: Cost of sales	414,000	451,000	865,000	540,000	274,000	814,000
Gross profit	255,000	121,000	376,000	202,000	99,000	301,000
Operating expenses						
advertising	$ 12,000	$ 1,000	$ 13,000	$ 31,000	$ 7,000	$ 38,000
auto & truck	3,000	3,000	6,000	3,000	2,000	5,000
bad debts	3,000	14,000	17,000	6,000	11,000	17,000
data processing	8,000	2,000	10,000	10,000	2,000	12,000
depreciation	5,000	4,000	9,000	5,000	4,000	9,000
interest	20,000	13,000	33,000	17,000	12,000	29,000
repairs	—	—	—	3,000	2,000	5,000
salaries	164,000	65,000	229,000	185,000	71,000	256,000
supplies & office supplies	8,000	1,000	9,000	12,000	2,000	14,000
taxes & licenses	13,000	9,000	22,000	16,000	10,000	26,000
utilities (light & telephone)	8,000	3,000	11,000	24,000	5,000	29,000
rent	—	4,000	4,000	68,000	46,000	114,000
other	22,000	11,000	33,000	39,000	23,000	62,000
Total operation expense	266,000	130,000	396,000	419,000	197,000	616,000
Pre-tax income from operation	$(11,000)	$ (9,000)	$ (20,000)	$(217,000)	(98,000)	(315,000)

THE AMERICAN SIGN AND INDICATOR CORP.

Donald F. Harvey

INTRODUCTION

At American Sign and Indicator, management was reflecting on twenty-five years of consecutive growth. This was a rewarding example of opportunity and fulfillment, working within the framework of the American free enterprise system—an achievement that could only happen in America. Looking ahead, it was clear that a continued high level of activity would be required to meet the challenge of successfully expanding their marketing thrust into the dynamic electronic information industry. Changes that had been made within the company over the past year would help assure that success.

As Chief Executive Officer Luke G. Williams noted, "June 25, 1977 marked the 25th anniversary of the American Sign and Indicator Corporation. During this period of time, our company has grown from an embryonic beginning with $600 capital to the largest on-premise sign company in the world.

"We are naturally proud of this accomplishment and feel it is a tribute to the American free enterprise system—living proof that in a free society the opportunity still exists to invent a product and develop an organization that will provide real and valuable services to users. With these elements identified, capital and creative people can be attracted to chart the course and provide the energy to build a new industry.

"However, even with the past growth record of our company, we stand today on the threshold of future opportunities that pale our past accomplishments. We anticipate these opportunities with great enthusiasm and confidence."

Copyright 1981 by Donald F. Harvey

This case was prepared from published information. The company in no way participated in its preparation.

II. COMPANY BACKGROUND

The American Sign and Indicator story is one of American entrepreneurship. Luke Williams Jr. and his brother Chuck started the business in 1946 with $600 capital. They were inspired by their father who was a commercial sign painter and a pictorial artist.

Over the years the company experienced many ups and downs, hovering near bankruptcy at times. They have expanded their production facilities, hired more employees, and diversified into different kinds of signs.

Today, American Sign and Indicator remains the largest specialized sign leasing company in America and the only sign company that operates nationally. They believe their customer base will be expanding shortly with the new unisplay technology. Unisplay technology, marketed under the trade name "Unex", provides total flexibility and versatility in many aspects of signs. Letter sizes, letter styles, languages, and graphics of many varieties will be available.

The company is engaged in the electronic visual communications business. It designs, engineers, and manufactures a broad range of electronic visual-communications display products and systems. It also provides for the installation of such products and continuing maintenance. Two basic technologies are used in its products: the lamp-matrix technology, which uses individual incandescent lamps and the dot-matrix display, which is basic to the Unex technology and utilizes computer controlled electromagnets to open and close apertures to reveal light from a common light source. Its lamp-matrix products include alternating time and temperature displays, message centers, and indoor and outdoor sports scoreboards for university and professional stadiums. Its dot-matrix Unex display products are used for public service messages, advertising, internal corporate communications, flight information, and other applications. The company believes that it is the leading producer of lamp-matrix electronic display products and systems in the world and is the only manufacturer of Unex technology products in the world, excluding Japan. Although the company's customers consist primarily of banks and savings and loan associations, they also include an increasing number of industrial and commercial concerns. The company is presently serving over 7,200 customers on a worldwide basis.

As of October 31, 1980, the company employed 598 persons, of whom 187 were engaged in production activities (including supervisors, technicians and assembly personnel), 167 in sales and marketing, 132 in service and installation and 112 in executive, supervisory, clerical, administrative, and accounting positions. In October, 1979, the company employed 691 persons.

III. FINANCIAL OPERATIONS

The following consolidated statement of operation represents the consolidated operating results of American Sign and Indicator Corporation and Subsidiaries for the five years ended April 30, 1980.

	Year Ended April 30,					Six Months Ended October 31,	
	1976 (Unaudited)(b)	1977	1978	1979	1980	1979 (Unaudited)	1980 (Unaudited)
Net lease sales (c)	$ 7,610,734	$11,252,169	$13,151,962	$15,056,771	$15,702,444	$ 5,693,355	$ 5,318,922
Direct sales	4,334,609	4,907,797	9,163,820	9,729,547	9,639,584	3,588,925	5,781,724
Net sales of installed displays ..	11,945,343	16,159,966	22,315,782	24,786,318	25,342,028	9,282,280	11,100,646
Cost to build, ship and install displays (Note 4)	5,196,188	8,178,341	9,088,844	11,441,891	12,272,176	4,304,783	5,611,862
Gross profit	6,749,155	7,981,625	13,226,938	13,344,427	13,069,852	4,977,497	5,488,784
Finance revenue earned	8,066,301	8,928,080	9,306,083	9,726,552	11,220,340	5,641,177	5,625,729
Maintenance revenue earned ..	2,744,484	3,191,640	3,648,740	4,201,399	4,973,764	2,321,326	2,492,771
Net revenue on installed displays	17,559,940	20,101,345	26,181,761	27,272,378	29,263,956	12,940,000	13,607,284
Gain on sale of contracts (Note 11)	—	—	—	126,483	1,190,095	—	2,523,770
	17,559,940	20,101,345	26,181,761	27,398,861	30,454,051	12,940,000	16,131,054
Operating expenses: Interest (Note 11)	3,033,477	3,036,486	3,932,942	6,278,749	10,523,173	4,408,216	4,965,520
Maintenance	2,467,381	3,132,167	3,530,107	3,594,579	4,116,771	2,050,688	2,227,763
Selling, general and administrative	8,906,051	11,581,968	15,072,810	17,501,992	15,625,841	7,274,133	6,956,430
Total operating expenses	14,406,909	17,750,621	22,535,859	27,375,320	30,265,785	13,733,037	14,149,713
Operating income (loss)	3,153,031	2,350,724	3,645,902	23,541	188,266	(793,037)	1,981,341
Other income (deductions): Interest (Note 11)	—	661,298	179,987	159,836	153,007	50,410	85,173
Other, net	(120,969)	162,121	479,144	54,434	145,131	279,186	117,803
	(120,969)	823,419	659,131	214,270	298,138	329,596	202,976
Earnings (loss) before income taxes	3,032,062	3,174,143	4,305,033	237,811	486,404	(463,441)	2,184,317
Income tax provision (benefit) (Note 9)	1,316,524	1,324,823	1,738,739	(214,474)	59,160	(340,625)	950,851
Net earnings (loss) (Note 14)	$ 1,715,538	$ 1,849,320	$2,566,294	$ 452,285	S 427,244	S (122,816)	$ 1,233,466
Earnings (loss) per share	$ .75	$ .81	$1.13	$ .20	$ .19	$(.05)	$ .54
Ratio of earnings to fixed charges(d): Actual	1.96	1.99	2.05	1.04	1.05	.90	1.43
Pro forma (unaudited) ..					1.05		1.38
Average shares outstanding ...	2,272,500	2,272,500	2,272,500	2,272,500	2,272,500	2,272,500	2,272,929
Dividends per share	$ .14	$ .20	$ .20	$ .10	$ .05	$ .05	$ –0–

Numerical note references are to Notes to Consolidated Financial Statements.

NOTES TO CONSOLIDATED STATEMENTS OF OPERATIONS

(a) See Note 1 to Consolidated Financial Statements for a summary of significant accounting policies.

(b) Although the financial statements for the year ended April 30, 1976 were originally audited, they were not reaudited subsequent to being adjusted to conform with new lease accounting principles set forth in Statement of Financial Accounting Standards No. 13, "Accounting for Leases", which was issued in November 1976.

(c) The amount of net lease sales is derived as follows:

	Year Ended April 30,					Six Months Ended October 31,	
	1976 (Unaudited)	1977	1978	1979	1980	1979 (Unaudited)	1980 (Unaudited)
Gross lease sales..	$20,378,798	$28,122,539	$30,561,007	$35,333,282	$36,259,166	$15,199,856	$13,233,473
Less:							
Unearned finance revenue	10,034,169	12,997,420	12,676,925	15,406,420	19,191,260	8,507,367	6,710,047
Unearned maintenance revenue .	2,733,895	3,872,950	4,732,120	4,870,091	1,365,462	999,134	1,204,504
	12,768,064	16,870,370	17,409,045	20,276,511	20,556,722	9,506,501	7,914,551
Net lease sales	$ 7,610,734	$11,252,169	$13,151,962	$15,056,771	$15,702,444	$ 5,693,355	$ 5,318,922

(d) For the purpose of calculating the ratio of earnings to fixed charges: (1) earnings have been calculated by adding to net earnings (loss), interest expense, the amount of taxes on earnings and the interest component of rent expense, and (2) fixed charges comprise total interest and the interest component of rent expense. The pro forma ratios of earnings to fixed charges give effect to the issuance of the Debentures offered hereby, the elimination of interest expense on the bank borrowings to be repaid with the net proceeds of this offering and the reduction in the effective interest rate on bank borrowings resulting from the new term loan and revolving credit agreement. The Debentures will require initial annual interest payments of $3,750,000.

611

MANAGEMENT'S DISCUSSION AND ANALYSIS OF FINANCIAL CONDITION AND RESULTS OF OPERATIONS

NET SALES OF INSTALLED DISPLAYS	Year Ended April 30,					Six Months Ended October 31,	
	1976	1977	1978	1979	1980	1979	1980
	(in thousands of dollars)						
Net sales of installed displays	$11,945	$16,160	$22,316	$24,786	$25,342	$ 9,282	$11,101
Cost to build, ship and install displays	$ 5,196	$ 8,178	$ 9,089	$11,442	$12,272	$ 4,305	$ 5,612

Net sales of installed displays increased at an annual compounded rate of 36.7% over the three fiscal years ended April 30, 1978. This increase was attributable to the growth of the Company's customer base, expansion of its product line and renewals of existing leases during this period. Since 1978, the Company's net sales of installed displays increased at a lower rate due primarily to its emphasis on developing a market for the Unex system. Net sales increased by approximately $1,819,000 (20%) during the six months ended October 31, 1980 from the prior comparable period due to substantially higher sales of Unex displays and sports information systems. The Company's cost to build, ship and install displays as a percentage of net sales during the first six months of fiscal 1981 increased from approximately 46% to 51% over the prior comparable period as a result of a change in product mix and promotional markdowns primarily associated with Unex sales. See "BUSINESS." The Company historically experiences greater sales during the second half of its fiscal year. See "Interim Results" for a discussion of the decrease in net sales of installed displays during the two months ended December 31, 1980 as compared with the two months ended December 31, 1979.

NET FINANCE INCOME	Year Ended April 30,					Six Months Ended October 31,	
	1976	1977	1978	1979	1980	1979	1980
	(in thousands of dollars)						
Finance revenue earned ...	$ 8,066	$ 8,928	$ 9,306	$ 9,727	$11,220	$ 5,641	$ 5,626
Interest expense	3,033	3,036	3,933	6,279	10,523	4,408	4,966
Net finance income	$ 5,033	$ 5,892	$ 5,373	$ 3,448	$ 697	$ 1,233	$ 660
Effective average interest rate paid*	9.4%	9.2%	8.9%	12.8%	17.7%	15.4%	16.0%

* The effective average interest rate paid was determined by using the interest expense for the fiscal year divided by the weighted average monthly outstanding debt during the period.

Most of the Company's borrowings have been made pursuant to the Credit Agreement under which interest payments have been based upon a formula tied to the prevailing prime lending rate. Recent high interest rates have resulted in substantially increased interest expense. During fiscal 1979 and 1980, interest expense increased approximately $2,346,000 (60%) and $4,244,000 (68%), respectively, over the prior comparable periods. Interest expense increased by approximately $557,000 (13%) during the six months ended October 31, 1980 over the prior comparable period. Implicit interest rates in the Company's lease contracts have been raised to reflect the Company's increased costs of borrowing, but the income recognized on such contracts will be realized over a period of years as compared with the immediate recognition of the increase in interest expense. Similarly, increased payments to the Company under its lease contracts as a result of the provision for cost of living increases have not entirely offset increased interest expense. The Company's lease contracts provide for a maximum annual 4% increase under such cost of living provision. Finance revenue earned in fiscal 1980 increased approximately $1,493,000 (15%) in comparison to fiscal 1979 primarily due to a lower estimated maintenance reserve requirement. Excess maintenance reserves were transferred to, and earned as, finance reserves. Finance revenue earned remained relatively constant during the first six months of fiscal 1981 compared with the prior comparable period due to the sale of certain lease receivables and the resultant loss of the related finance revenues. See Note 11 to Consolidated Financial Statements.

NET MAINTENANCE INCOME	Year Ended April 30,					Six Months Ended October 31,	
	1976	1977	1978	1979	1980	1979	1980
	(in thousands of dollars)						
Maintenance revenue earned	$ 2,744	$ 3,192	$ 3,649	$ 4,201	$ 4,974	$ 2,321	$ 2,493
Maintenance expense	2,467	3,132	3,530	3,595	4,117	2,051	2,228
Net maintenance income ...	$ 277	$ 60	$ 119	$ 606	$ 857	$ 270	$ 265

Maintenance revenue earned increased during the past five fiscal years due to the Company's expanding customer base. Net maintenance income increased during the past three fiscal years as a result of the Company's control of its maintenance expenses. As a percentage of maintenance revenue earned, maintenance expense declined from a high of 98% in fiscal 1977 to 83% in fiscal 1980.

SELLING, GENERAL AND ADMINISTRATIVE EXPENSES	Year Ended April 30,					Six Months Ended October 31,	
	1976	1977	1978	1979	1980	1979	1980
	(in thousands of dollars)						
	$ 8,906	$11,582	$15,073	$17,502	$15,626	$ 7,274	$ 6,956

During fiscal 1980, the Company implemented an overhead reduction plan for its selling, general and administrative expenses ("SG&A") which had almost doubled from fiscal 1976 to fiscal 1979. Specific measures implemented included the closing of three regional sales offices, the reduction of the number of production and administrative personnel and the consolidation of certain departments at the Company's executive offices. During fiscal 1980, SG&A decreased by approximately $1,876,000 (11%) from the prior fiscal year. The Company's overhead reduction plan was implemented without significant adverse impact on sales or service. Additional budget reduction measures were taken during the six months ended October 31, 1980 which resulted in a decrease of approximately $318,000 (4%) in SG&A from the prior comparable period.

NET EARNINGS (LOSS)	Year Ended April 30,					Six Months Ended October 31,	
	1976	1977	1978	1979	1980	1979	1980
	(in thousands of dollars)						
Earnings (loss) before income taxes	$ 3,032	$ 3,174	$ 4,305	$ 238	$ 486	$ (463)	$ 2,184
Income tax provision (benefit)	1,317	1,325	1,739	(214)	59	(341)	951
Net earnings (loss)	$ 1,715	$ 1,849	$ 2,566	$ 452	$ 427	$ (122)	$ 1,233

Earnings (loss) before income taxes have been affected by the factors discussed above and, in addition, in fiscal 1980, benefited from a gain of approximately $1,190,000 recognized on the sale of certain lease receivables. Earnings (loss) before income taxes increased significantly during the six months ended October 31, 1980 from the prior comparable period as a result of a gain of approximately $2,524,000 on the sale of certain lease receivables and a $1,818,000 increase in net sales of installed displays. Net earnings (loss) in fiscal 1979 were benefited by a $214,000 net operating loss carryback for income tax purposes in 1979 and a significantly reduced effective tax rate in 1980.

LIQUIDITY	Year Ended April 30,					Six Months Ended October 31,	
	1976	1977	1978	1979	1980	1979	1980
	(in thousands of dollars)						
Total minimum lease payments to be received ..	$75,481	$81,627	$92,070	$103,128	$110,542	$107,425	$111,393
Net investment in sales type leases	$41,887	$46,805	$54,972	$ 62,865	$ 68,797	$ 69,176	$ 72,948
Debt	$36,663	$44,377	$44,278	$ 51,236	$ 60,907	$ 62,685	$ 63,587

Leasing operations have required the Company to raise capital in order to finance the costs associated with products under lease. Such capital has been provided primarily by bank borrowings under the Credit Agreement, cash generated from operations and sales of certain lease and installment sale receivables. The Company also offers a prepayment program which permits substantially all of its customers to prepay annually their lease obligations at a discount, which discount is less than the effective interest rate in their respective lease contracts. During 1980, approximately 55% of the Company's customers participated in this program through the prepayment of approximately $11,442,000. See Note 2 to Consolidated Financial Statements.

The Company believes that its greatest potential source of liquidity is its lease portfolio. As of October 31, 1980, the total minimum lease payments to be received by the Company were approximately $111,393,000, of which approximately $81,206,000 was expected to be collected over the next five years. See Note 3 to Consolidated Financial Statements. In 1979, the Company initiated a policy of selling from time to time certain of its lease and installment contract receivables for cash. See Note 11 to Consolidated Financial Statements. As described under "USE OF PROCEEDS AND FINANCING REQUIRE-MENTS," the Company has available to it various methods of financing, including borrowings under the new term loan and revolving credit agreement.

The Company has budgeted $323,000 in capital improvements during its current fiscal year which will be financed internally. No other material commitments have been planned.

IV. MARKETING

The company designs, engineers, manufactures, and provides installation and maintenance services for a broad range of electronic visual communications systems and display products. These consist of alternating time and temperature displays, lamp matrix message centers, indoor and outdoor sports scoreboards, and Unex display systems.

From the organization of the company in 1952 through approximately 1970, the company's principal source of revenues was derived from the sale and lease of alternating time and temperature displays to financial institutions. During the 1970s the company expanded the basic time and temperature display technology to include a variety of sequential message and sports information display systems and, in 1975, it purchased the rights to manufacture, sell, and exploit patented technology which is being marketed by the company under the name "Unex." Recognizing the appeal of certain of its products as an advertising medium, the company has begun to broaden its market to include commercial customers such as automobile dealerships and shopping centers. The company has also begun to market certain of its products to industrial customers seeking a medium through which to communicate with their employees.

PRINCIPAL PRODUCTS

Lamp Matrix Displays *Time and temperature displays.* Time and temperature displays consist of an incandescent lamp-matrix display that shows time and temperature alternately. The time and temperature display is typically installed outside a building and advertises the name, slogan and/or logo of the customer combined with the alternating time and temperature display. The time and temperature display was invented by Charles Williams, Senior Vice President and co-founder of the company, and is marketed under the name "Double TT"™ primarily to banks and savings and loan associations throughout the country. The time and temperature display can be programmed to show both fahrenheit and celsius readings. The company has installed in excess of 5,200 time and temperature display systems, with over 80% owned by the company and leased to customers. Sales prices for time and temperature display systems currently range from approximately $10,000 to $20,000.

Message centers. Electronic message-center displays ("Message Centers") consist of an incandescent lamp matrix that is capable of displaying sequential messages and a microprocessor data-base controller which is programmed to display such messages. The control system generally consists of a signaling and information storage device such as a computer. The signaling and storage device sends a message through data cable or telephone lines to a lamp-matrix controller in the vicinity of the display. The controller then sends an on–off signal to each lamp in the display resulting in a message. Message Centers can combine the features of a time and temperature service with a message; they are primarily used by financial and commercial customers to promote their services and products and to provide community service information. To date, the company has installed over 1,200 Message Centers, with more than 80% owned by the company and leased to customers. Sales prices for Message Centers currently range from approximately $12,000 to $120,000.

Other. The company also manufactures several products which utilize Message Center components, including displays showing the Dow Jones stock averages and highway displays indicating traffic patterns and warnings. The company designed a display system known as "Spectacolor", a multicolor lamp matrix capable of providing continuous messages with animation features. The company has granted a limited license for the sale of its multicolor animation system. Spectacolor is typically used by a customer to produce revenue from the sale of advertising time on the display. The most well-known Spectacolor system is located in New York City's Times Square.

Sports Information Systems   A sports information system is a display which consists of a combination of animation panels, Message Centers, Unex displays, and scoring formats for the various events held in sports complexes. Sports information systems can include large computer-memory storage capacities, four-color display capability, and grayscale capability, which is an enlarged simulation of black and white television. The company manufactures these systems for university and professional sports complexes. Recent installations include systems in the Rose Bowl, University of Oklahoma, University of Alabama, University of Notre Dame, Reunion Arena in Dallas, RFK Stadium in Washington D.C., and Balboa Stadium in San Diego. Other sports information systems manufactured by the company include those in Madison Square Garden in New York City, Riverfront Stadium in Cincinnati, and Pontiac Stadium in Detroit. The company is currently designing a mobile system for the Tournament Players Association, Inc., for use at golf courses on the PGA tour.

Sports information systems are generally sold, as opposed to leased, and payments are sometimes made on an installment basis over a period of up to ten years. In connection with the sale of a sports information system, the company often arranges for advertisers to purchase and donate the scoreboard to a university or professional stadium. To date, the company has installed in excess of 250 sports information systems in the United States.

Unex   Unex displays consist of fluorescent lights in an enclosure, the design of which is a matrix of apertures that may be selectively opened or closed magnetically by a computer-controlled head which sweeps the face of the enclosure changing the message displayed in a matter of seconds. The company has developed several computer controllers for the Unex system, which provide versatility in the letter sizes, letter styles, languages, colors, and graphics used in the display of messages. In addition, computer memory sources make it possible for numerous messages consisting of both text and graphics to be programmed for sequential display. Messages are displayed in light with an extremely high resolution which provides greater clarity with lower energy requirements than conventional incandescent lamp-matrix displays. Unex displays lend themselves to both interior and exterior use and are being used for transportation information systems in airports and train stations, as advertising displays for stores, shopping centers, automobile dealerships, and broadcast stations, and for marquees at arenas and public entertainment facilities. Recent Unex installations include transportation information systems at Miami International Airport and Taiwan's International Airport. The company has also recently begun to market Unex display systems for internal communications in industrial plants.

The company obtained the right to manufacture, sell, and exploit the Unex technology pursuant to a license agreement entered into in April 1975 with Unisplay S.A., a Swiss corporation that is the owner of the patent related to Unex. The license agreement granted to the company the exclusive right to sell in North and South America, excluding Canada, the West Indies, and the Republic of Guyana. The license agreement was amended in February, 1979, to give the company the exclusive right to manufacture, sell, and exploit such technology in Canada, and on a non-exclusive basis, to do so elsewhere in the world, except Japan. The company is required under the license agreement to pay presently a minimum royalty of $33,000 per quarter, subject to adjustment, to Unisplay until the applicable U S. patent expires in 1988. (See Note 13 to Consolidated Financial Statements for the aggregate royalty and consulting fees paid to Unisplay during the last five years.) The company spent an aggregate of approximately $3,500,000 on the development and improvement of the Unex display.

Through 1980, the company has installed in excess of 585 Unex units. The sales price for a single Unex display system, including a controller, currently ranges from approximately $5,000 to $70,000, while the sales prices for multiple unit Unex installations, such as a transportation information system, range up to $1,000,000.

MARKETING AND CUSTOMERS

The company markets its products from three regional offices located in Jacksonville, Florida, Dallas, Texas, and Spokane, Washington. The company has divided each region into a number of districts which are the exclusive territory of individual sales-persons. Regional offices provide administrative, art, and other support services for marketing and sales personnel. The company obtains customer leads through advertising programs, industry trade shows, referrals from customers, and unsolicited direct calls by company sales personnel.

At the beginning of fiscal 1980, the company shifted its marketing emphasis toward the sale or lease of newly manufactured products and away from rewriting contracts for existing installations. The company also changed its sales force compensation arrangements to provide for the payment of a substantially larger commission on new product sales or leases than on renewals, as well as for the payment of a bonus based upon designated quotas.

The company's products are sold abroad in over ten foreign countries through company personnel and independent sales representatives, including, in Mexico, sales through a 49% company-owned corporation. To date, foreign sales have not been material to the company's operations.

Historically, the company has sold or leased its products principally to banks and savings and loan associations. However, the company has more recently attempted to broaden its customer base to include commercial and industrial concerns. During the five fiscal years ended April 30, 1980, and six months ended October 31, 1980, no single customer of the company accounted for as much as 10% of net sales of installed displays in any period.

COMPETITION

Although there are no reliable statistics available, the company believes that it is the leading producer of lamp-matrix electronic display products and systems in the world. The company is one of the few manufacturers of electronic display systems which markets its products nationwide directly to end users. The company competes with numerous firms, most of whom operate regionally or locally. In certain instances, some of these competitors may realize cost advantages for particular displays. However, the company believes that its reputation for innovation, quality manufacture, and complete service, together with its ability to maintain leasing programs and to undertake large display commitments, can, in many cases, overcome competitor's price advantages.

The company competes, through the sales of its products, for customers' advertising dollars with numerous advertising media, including billboards, newspapers, radio, and television. The company believes that its products compete effectively for advertising expenditures on the basis of lower overall costs to reach the desired customer in a user's primary advertising market area.

Major U.S. competitors are

1   Everbrite Electric Signs, Inc., South Milwaukee, Wisconsin. 1978 Sales $29 million. 430 employees.

2   Cummings Incorporated International Sign SV, Nashville, Tennessee. 1978 Sales of $29 million. 666 employees.

Cummings makes, installs and maintains electrical signs which are sold or leased throughout the United States and Canada. Through a system of local sign firms (about 170 as of December 31, 1979) licensed by it, Cummings offers nationwide installation and maintenance service to its national customers. Financial Ratios of Cummings Incorporated are as follows:

	1978	1979	1980
Current ratio	2.43	2.10	2.15
Quick ratio	2.60	1.52	1.72
Sales/total assets	1.86	2.02	1.86
Long-term debt to total assets	38.25%	31.06%	37.41%
Net sales (millions)	$28.863	$30.595	$31.065

RESEARCH AND DEVELOPMENT

The company devotes a substantial portion of its operating budget to research and engineering of new products and improvements to its current product lines. During the fiscal year ended April 30, 1980, the company spent approximately $1,155,000 for redesign of the Unex display and engineering, an increase from approximately $673,000 during the preceding fiscal year. In October, 1980, 49 employees of the company, including approximately 15 engineers, were engaged in research and engineering activities.

The company is currently concentrating its research and engineering efforts upon improving and expanding the capabilities of its existing products and upon applying its technology to reduce the energy costs associated with the use of its products. The company expects to market in fiscal 1981 a new product line known as the "Solar Matrix." As part of the Solar Matrix line, the company has recently introduced a low-energy "7-Segment Time and Temperature Display" which utilizes light reflective modules.

V. MANAGEMENT

The succeeding exhibit outlines principal management personnel and their relationships:

MANAGEMENT

Directors and Executive Officers

The following table sets forth certain information regarding the directors and executive officers of the Company:

Name	Age	Position with the Company
Luke G. Williams*†	57	Chairman of the Board of Directors; Chief Executive Officer
Charles M. Williams*	59	Senior Vice President; Director
Paul Smyly†	45	President and Chief Operating Officer
Donald Sherwood*†	79	Treasurer; Chairman of the Finance Committee; Director
Cameron Sherwood	80	Director
Horton Herman*	69	Secretary; Director
Edward J. Leary	33	Vice President for Legal and Industry Affairs
William H. Justus	59	Senior Vice President for National Field Services
John E. Holcomb	56	Vice President of Plant Operations
David L. Gray	45	Vice President for Sales and Marketing
John C. Kersch	50	Vice President for Finance
Arnold Corbridge	41	Controller

* Member of Executive Committee.

† Member of Finance Committee.

Directors serve until the next annual meeting of stockholders and until their successors are elected and qualified. Under the by-laws of the Company, the date of the Annual Meeting of Stockholders is scheduled for the third Thursday in August of each year. Each executive officer of the Company is elected or appointed by the Board of Directors and holds office until his successor is elected and qualified. Paul Smyly has an employment contract with the Company which expires in August 1982. See "Other Transactions." The Chairman of the Board and Chief Executive Officer of the Company has the power to appoint additional officers to serve at his discretion in addition to those elected or appointed by the Board.

Luke G. Williams, a co-founder of the Company, has been Chairman of the Board and Chief Executive Officer since May 1980. Mr. Williams had previously served as President, Chief Executive Officer and a Director for more than the past five years. Mr. Williams also serves as a Director of Sea-First Corporation and the Seattle-First National Bank, one of the lenders to the Company under the Credit Agreement. Mr. Williams has been acting as Chief Financial Officer.

Charles M. Williams, a co-founder of the Company, has been Senior Vice President and a Director for more than the past five years. In addition, Mr. Williams is in charge of research and development for the Company. Luke G. Williams and Charles M. Williams are brothers.

Paul Smyly has been President and Chief Operating Officer of the Company since May 1980. Mr. Smyly joined the Company as Executive Vice President and Chief Operating Officer in August 1979. From 1975 to 1979, Mr. Smyly was President of Key Electro Sonic, Inc., a subsidiary of Applied Magnetics Corporation, which at the time was principally engaged in the manufacture of food processing equipment.

Donald Sherwood has been Treasurer and a Director for more than the past five years. From 1976 to May 1980, Mr. Sherwood was also Chairman of the Board of Directors of the Company. Mr. Sherwood owns Pioneer Investment Company, a personal holding company engaged in investments. See "Other Transactions."

Cameron Sherwood has been a Director for more than the past five years. Prior to 1976, Mr. Sherwood served as Secretary to the Company and was a member of the law firm of Sherwood, Tugman, Gose & Reser. Mr. Sherwood continues to practice law in the State of Washington. Donald Sherwood and Cameron Sherwood are brothers.

Horton Herman has been a Director since 1975, and since 1976, Secretary. Since January 1974, Mr. Herman has been of counsel to the law firm of Paine, Lowe, Coffin, Hamblen & Brooke, formerly Paine, Lowe, Coffin, Herman & O'Kelly. See "Other Transactions." Mr. Herman also serves as a Director of Hecla Mining Company.

Edward Leary has been Vice President for Legal and Industry Affairs since September 1979. From October 1978 to September 1979, he served as Director of Legal Affairs for the Company. Prior to joining the Company in 1976, he was District Supervisor in the Office of Support Enforcement for all departmental programs in Eastern Washington.

William Justus joined the Company in 1952 and has been Senior Vice President for National Field Services since 1978. From 1975 to 1978, he was Vice President for Transportation Information Systems.

John Holcomb, who joined the Company in 1962, has been Vice President of Plant Operations since May 1980. From 1979 to 1980, Mr. Holcomb served as Vice President of Manufacturing and from 1976 to 1979, he was Vice President of Williams Brothers Manufacturing Company, a wholly owned subsidiary of the Company. In 1975 and 1976, Mr. Holcomb was Manufacturing Manager of the Company.

David Gray, who joined the Company in 1972, has been Vice President for Marketing and Sales since April 1979. From May 1976 to April 1979, Mr. Gray was a Regional Sales Manager. Prior to that time, Mr. Gray was a District Sales Manager.

John C. Kersch has been Vice President for Finance since January 1981. From 1979 to 1981, Mr. Kersch was Treasurer for Enterprises Incorporated in Olympia, Washington, a publicly owned holding company primarily engaged in the manufacturing of material handling systems for the pulp and paper industry. Prior to 1979, Mr. Kersch was Vice President for Finance of Pullman Torkelson, a subsidiary of Pullman Incorporated, which at the time was involved in engineering, construction and manufacturing.

Arnold Corbridge joined the Company as Assistant Controller in 1974 and became Controller in September 1976.

James Moran, who joined the Company in 1969, has been Vice President of Sports Systems since May 1976. Prior to that time he was Regional Manager for Sports Systems. Management considers Mr. Moran's contribution to the sales of Sports Information Systems to be significant. Mr. Moran is 38 years old.

The organization chart of AS & I is as follows (as of October, 1980):

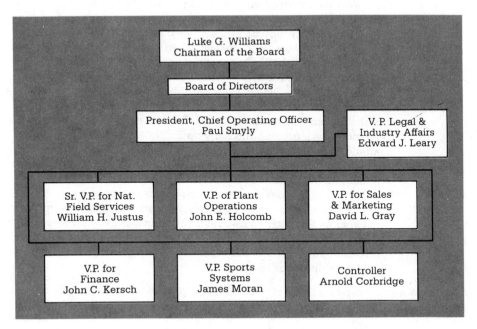

VI. CONCLUSION

In 1980, Luke G. Williams was looking ahead to the 1980s:

> In the 79–80 fiscal year ending April 30, American Sign and Indicator Corporation generated gross sales of $46,008,000, a four percent increase over the previous year, but short of our $51 million budgeted goal. The decline in our sales occurred during the first quarter of calendar year 1980 when interest rates soared creating a "wait and see" attitude by our market. Revenues from installations for the fiscal year were $42,900,000 as compared to our plan for the year of $42,539,000. Net earnings were $1,055,000 as compared to our fiscal year projections of $1,511,000. Earnings were materially impacted by higher than projected interest rates which, essentially, diluted our earnings from potentially record levels to the lowest in years.
>
> The 79–80 fiscal year was a difficult and uncertain period; however, necessities of the times precipitated certain changes and alterations in our organization which assures our continued confidence in the company's future.
>
> At the beginning of the 79–80 fiscal year, an overhead reduction plan was implemented. This plan was carried on through the year and resulted in more than $2 million in cost savings. The plan called for reduction of overhead in all areas in the company. One area dramatically affected by the overhead reduction plan was the sales and service organization, wherein we reduced our number

of regional offices from six to three. The three former regional offices were converted into sales and service facilities. These changes, while significant in cost reduction, have not affected our ability to sell our products and service our customers.

Another notable accomplishment during the year was the completion of the Unex development project. The initially designed product lacked a reliability factor associated with our other product lines. The greatly improved reliability factor as well as customer acceptance of this product during the past twelve months has indeed been gratifying. In each succeeding month sales have increased, proving the early optimism we had for this unique communications technology. We continue to find new applications and markets for the Unex technology and look to it as being a major product line in our future.

Our company is placing greater emphasis on professional management. Paul Smyly joined our company early last fiscal year as Executive Vice President and was elected President on May 1, 1980. We are planning other high-level additions in the future to support orderly management succession and to upgrade the leadership of our company.

As Luke Williams prepared to meet with his management committee, he wondered what direction American Sign and Indicator's future strategy for growth should take.

SEAFLITE
(Revised)

Jimmy D. Barnes
Viki Arbas

Revised by
Hugh O. Hunter

INTRODUCTION

SeaFlite jetfoil ships were introduced to Hawaii in June 1975, marking the first water transport system since 1948. For two and one-half years Pacific Sea Transportation, Ltd., operated the jetfoil service amid mounting losses. The losses, caused by technical problems and disappointing passenger revenues, resulted in a cessation of operations by the end of 1977. In spite of a continuing interest in the state in a water transport system, additional financing for SeaFlite did not materialize, and the three ships were sold to a Hong Kong company.

In mid-1979, the owner of a Waikiki hotel bought one Boeing jetfoil ship. He announced that the new ship would transport passengers between the islands of Oahu and Maui by mid-1981. The jetship cost $10.8 million and an additional $3 million was to be spent on accessories. The total capital investment was estimated to be $18 million by 1981. (See Exhibit 1, Projected Operating Expenses, 1980.)

The dimensions of the new jetfoil were to remain the same as its predecessors', but the propulsion features and design would be improved. The new ship would hold 270 passengers, compared to 190 in the earlier ships. It was estimated that the new ship would have to run at 47% capacity for the two trips per day to be profitable. Fares were to remain in line with airline fares. A new jetfoil would be purchased one year from the beginning of operations, if demand proved high enough.

It was estimated that 60 employees would be hired, including a crew of 13 for the ship.

The Public Utilities Commission of Hawaii transferred the operating licenses to the new owner. The State Department of Transportation signed over the leases for the existing harbors on Honolulu and Maalaea in Maui. It was a promise for a new, more modest beginning of private industry implementing a waterway system between the Hawaiian Islands. The question was whether the company could achieve long-range survival where the prior company could not.

Following is an overview of the history of operation of Pacific Sea Transportation, Ltd., which had run the SeaFlite system and had failed.

SeaFlite copyrighted by Jimmy D. Barnes and Viki Arbas

Revision copyrighted by Hugh O. Hunter

HISTORY

The major industry of the State of Hawaii is tourism. Visitors who stayed overnight or longer in Hawaii numbered:

> 1975—2,830,000
> 1976—3,220,000
> 1977—3,434,000

During this period, the major interisland airlines reported 15,754,000 total revenue passengers. Visitors made up about half of those traveling between islands. (See Exhibit 2.)

Oahu, home of the State Capitol of Honolulu and the famed resort of Waikiki, was the most heavily populated and traveled island. Traffic congestion was a problem in the higher density areas, particularly between the airport and Waikiki, as well as between the downtown business district and the residential suburb of Hawaii Kai.

Oahu's neighbor islands were basically agricultural, and population and per capita income were declining. The island of Maui had the fastest growing resort-destination traffic, and tourism contributed some revenues and jobs on the other islands.

Air traffic to and from Honolulu had increased dramatically over the years. Amid concern over congestion in the Honolulu area, there was also a strong desire by the state to encourage travel to and development of the neighboring islands. The results were creation of an Oahu General Aviation Master Plan to study air traffic dispersal, and creation of a state task force to study the feasibility of a marine highway.

Two types of marine service were studied. One was interisland passenger service; the other was a shuttle service between primary destination points on Oahu. The interisland service showed promise, but the shuttle concept seemed doomed for three reasons:

1 the harbor at Waikiki was dominated by pleasure yachts and boats which rendered it unusuable.

2 no way was seen to provide fast and efficient baggage handling.

3 a large number of vessels required to provide peak period service would lie idle the rest of the time.

Interest in interisland service had begun in the 1950s. A number of studies had resulted, most centering on some sort of ferry service for passengers, autos and cargo. While these studies had generated questionable demand and cost forecasts, they did provide some consistent and useful findings. Among them were:

1 The public indicated enthusiasm for water travel, but intentions to ride the ferry were more wishful thinking than a forecast of actual use.

2 There was some debate as to whether the ferry system could be handled by private enterprise without government subsidies.

3   Breakdowns could cancel the service altogether.

4   There was a strong preference among local residents for air travel.

5   Success hinged on low fares and fast, comfortable rides.

6   Although travel by air has the advantage of speed, high costs preclude it ever becoming the prime mover of people to the outer islands.

7   Demand for travel is price inelastic.

8   Patronage of a ferry system was dependent on sea conditions and was seasonal.

9   Passenger and cargo transport did not appear to be a good mix.

10   There was some opposition to the ferry by the public, because of the long travel time involved.

In the mid 1970's two companies were providing marine transport service on Oahu. The most ambitious was the Sea Transit which operated a commuter run between Pearl Harbor, Hickam and Iroquois Point. It charged 50¢ for the ride, and $1.00 each way for a trip between Kewalo Basin and Iroquois Point. Sea Transit also operated a Pearl Harbor cruise, but at $5.00 it was more expensive than some competing cruises. Sea Transit operated between 1972 and 1978.

The other company operated the Paradise Cruise which provided lavish and expensive excursions during the day. At night, it became a floating restaurant for a 2½ hour dinner cruise. On Saturdays, at 9 pm, the boat would leave Kewalo Basin for a "disco rock boogie party." The business was sold in March 1978.

THE COMPANIES

SeaFlite resulted from a partnership between two giants in the aerospace industry—Boeing Company and LTV Corporation. Each had a great deal to gain from the partnership, LTV through its existing operating subsidiary in Hawaii, and Boeing through the sale of its hydrofoil ships.

Boeing   By the early 1970s, with the war in Vietnam coming to a close, Boeing was seeking commercial applications for some of its military hardware. Once in a while the application of military technology to commercial use can be phenomenally successful, as in the case of the 707 jetliner.

Some years earlier, Boeing had produced a 60-ton hydrofoil gunboat for the Navy called the Tucumcari. This was being converted into a 110-ton, 90 by 31 ft jetfoil capable of speeds of 48 to 52 miles per hour (42–45 knots).

Surface piercing hydrofoils were in use in Florida, travelling between the Keys and the Bahamas. These, however, had a tendency to roll over in waves six feet or more high. A submerged hydrofoil was then developed which could take waves up to ten feet high. Waters around the Hawaiian Islands exceed ten feet no more than 10% of the time year-round.

These ships were propelled by an inboard system of gas turbines which does to water what the jet plane does to air. Thus it was named the Jetfoil. The forward speed caused the vessel to lift several feet above the suface, minimizing water resistance. The ships were able to turn in short distances like banking aircraft. The Jetfoil could hold up to 250 passengers, but a model seating 190 was selected for SeaFlite operations.

LTV   LTV was a formerly highly successful Dallas-based conglomerate, engaged in aerospace, steel and meat packing as its primary industries. As with many conglomerates, the end of the 1960s brought hard times, and in 1970, LTV nearly failed. As part of its survival strategy, the corporation began to expand into tourist-related activities, and by the mid 1970s, owned a Mexican hotel and a Colorado ski resort.

Kentron Hawaii, Ltd.   Kentron Hawaii was the catalyst bringing together these two corporate giants into the SeaFlite venture. Kentron is a subsidiary of LTV's Aerospace Division. It provides logistical and technical support to various government agencies on Hawaii, including the Department of Defense, NASA, and the Federal Aviation Agency. The company is also engaged in commercial tourist services in Hawaii.

Kentron had earlier participated in the Oahu General Aviation Master Plan. It had also produced a study for the State on an airport – Waikiki marine shuttle service. Kentron was hoping to be able to offer this service for an investment of $30 million. The planned fare was $4. The idea was shelved when no adequate harbor facility could be found on Waikiki.

With the shuttle service providing little promise, attention was shifted to interisland service. Kentron, through its participation in state marine transport studies, was aware that speed would be a primary factor in passenger acceptance. To provide the necessary speed, a high technology craft would have to be used. The British Hover-craft, which rides on a cushion of air, was considered, but it was deemed unsuited to the unpredictable Hawaiian currents, and it was excessively noisy.

Two U.S. companies, Grumman and Boeing, had been developing commercial models of hydrofoil ships which had originally been designed for military service. Versions of the hydrofoil models had been operating for some twenty years outside the U.S., including the route between Hong Kong and Macao and in the English Channel between London and Ostend, France. Some were also operating on inland waterways in the Soviet Union.

Safety was a key factor in these models. Not a single fatality had occured over some two billion passenger miles, and only very infrequent mishaps had occurred. However, Hawaii's rougher seas between islands, particularly through the Molokai channel, would prove to be a tougher test of the hydrofoil's technical capabilities.

Kentron's president became interested in Boeing's design of a passenger ship fashioned from a 60-ton hydrofoil gunboat, which had been used in Vietnam. Boeing had sold two of these to the Far East Hydrofoil Co. for the Hong Kong route, and was investigating further potential markets. Ultimately, Hawaii was to be a showcase for Boeing's jetfoils.

Pacific Sea Transportation, Ltd.   A decision by Boeing and Kentron to proceed with interisland jetfoil service resulted in the formation, in February 1973, of Pacific Sea Transportation, Ltd., owned 75% by Kentron and 25% by Boeing. The ships, purchased from Boeing at $4.8 million each, were named SeaFlite. The venture received the encouragement and support of the State administration and legislature.

From 1973 to June 1975, development of facilities was undertaken and SeaFlite was promoted. Because of the need to tailor the facilities to the ships themselves, PSTL elected to develop their own facilities. Terminals were built or upgraded on four islands: Pier 8 downtown Honolulu on Oahu, Nawiliwili on Kauai, Mallaea on Maui, and Kawaihae on Hawaii. The cost of facilities was $2.8 million.

Delivery of the new jetfoils to Hawaii was scheduled for November 1974, after testing in Puget Sound, Lake Washington, and the ocean. The delivery was first delayed until January 1975, and an accident at the Boeing plant caused further delay until May 1975.

On June 15, 1975, the first hydrofoil ship began service between islands, followed by the second in August and the third in October. By this time, an additional $6 million over the purchase price of the ships had been allocated to the program. (See Exhibit 3 for Interisland Transportation Routes.)

SeaFlite was totally financed by private capital. The only indirect support was by the Seventh Legislature, which excluded use tax on the import of the three hydrofoils, and by the use of Title xi Maritime Administration Insurance on bonds which were sold by Pacific Sea Transportation. The company's goals, at that time, were to:

1 appeal to half the current interisland air travel market;

2 develop greater demand for travel by promoting a mixed mode of travel: by surface and air, thus offsetting any passenger losses due to airlines;

3 show a profit by 1977;

4 service additional areas such as Molokai, Kahalui on Maui, Hilo on the Big Island of Hawaii, and Lanai, expanding the service to 18 ships by 1995;

5 develop waterways connecting Oahu destination points.

A plan developed in 1975 was to dredge near Hawaii Kai on Oahu to open a channel for SeaFlite, connecting with downtown. Since non-peak hours of interisland service were in the morning and late afternoon, a commuter service was planned for these hours. This plan called for the state to purchase the ships, then priced at $7 million each, and PSTL would lease them for operating the runs. Moonlight rides could also be added for additional revenues. Some 80% of the dredging costs could potentially have been financed by Federal Highway funds, in conjunction with the Marine Highway proposal. This plan, however, was never carried through.

Another plan developed to coordinate services with Young Brothers, a local interisland marine cargo transportation company. The plan centered around jointly transporting passengers and their autos. This idea also was dropped.

Other plans also died in their infancy; one for transporting sports fans to and from Aloha Stadium, and another to have the State take over SeaFlite facilities. SeaFlite contended that this latter transfer of facilities would simply put them on an equal footing with other marine transport companies and the airlines, all of whom used State facilities.

HYDROFOIL OPERATIONS IN HAWAII

Reliability   In the first year of operations, SeaFlite's vessels experienced 20–30% downtime, mostly due to mechanical failures. Only two weeks after the maiden voyage, on a busy Fourth of July weekend, the two large turbines of the only ship then in operation failed. As the ship skimmed over choppy water, it lifted six feet out of the water, causing air to hit a water intake vent. The interruption of the flow of water caused the engine to automatically shut down. The boat plopped in the water and tossed about in the waves.

This automatic shut down when air was ingested into the engine, and chronic gearbox problems caused SeaFlite's reliability to be below expectations. The gearboxes had an expected life of three years, but SeaFlite went through twenty in its first year, at a cost of $200,000 each. There was also incidental damage from high waves, and a fire aboard one of the ships. All of these meant that the third ship had to be retained for what was essentially a two-ship schedule.

Boeing flew technicians to Hawaii to redesign some of its most troublesome engine parts. Boeing honored all of its parts warranties, but some of the subcontractors did not, claiming that usage had been harder than originally specified. SeaFlite ships in drydock became a common sight for passing motorists on the main highway between the Airport and downtown Honolulu.

Costs   Total employment costs were higher than expected. In 1972, labor costs had been projected as:

On Oahu—69 full time, 12 part time, $750,000 per year

Other islands—2 full time, 3 part time $27,000 per year

By the second year of operations, actual employment figures were:

On Oahu—41 full time, 32 part time

Other islands—11 full time, 36 part time.

In 1978, after the close of operations, PSTL disclosed the following costs during its operating life:

$17,978,000 for materials, services and labor
252,918 paid to the State Department of Transportation for rent of State land and facilities.

In addition, the company had paid a Public Service Tax of 4% of revenues. Diesel oil consumption had been projected at 420 gallons per hour at $200 per hour. Actual consumption was 560 gallons per hour.

Operational losses were as follows:

1973—	$209,000
1974—	424,000
1975—	1,990,000
1976—	3,950,000
1977—	4,494,000
Total	$11,077,000

Schedule Performance   Because of the continuing mechanical problems, on-time performance of SeaFlite was poor. (See exhibit 6: The Schedule of Departure and Arrival Times.) SeaFlite had planned to operate ten trips daily. However, it seldom operated more than eight trips, and for a time, only six.

MARKETING AND COMPETITION

The Airlines   SeaFlite's primary competitors were the two major interisland airlines, Aloha and Hawaiian. The Airlines had been in service for twenty-five years, and, in the mid-1970's were operating without Federal subsidy. Hawaiian flew DC-9 jets, seating 138 passengers. Aloha flew 118-seat Boeing 737 jets. The Airlines served all the major islands. Each had 28 flights per day between Kauai and Honolulu, and 40 flights between Maui and Honolulu

Hawaiian and Aloha Airlines	1975	1976	1977
Total revenue passengers	4,787,000	5,263,000	5,724,000
Combined operating profits		$2,318,000	$2,193,000
Load factor	65.3%	64.3%	65.8%
Breakeven factor	65.1%	61.6%	65.6%

SeaFlite in the Interisland Passenger Market   The breakeven load factor for SeaFlite had been calculated at 54% for the ten scheduled trips per day. In 1977, the actual load factor was 38–40%. Passengers carried for the three years of operations were:

> 1975— 69,000
> 1976—195,000
> 1977—260,000

SeaFlite served two publics, visitors to Hawaii and local residents. In its last year of operation, SeaFlite's passenger mix was 70% tourist and 30% resident. The two interisland airlines by contrast had approximately a 50–50 mix. (See a profile of Hawaii's visitors, Appendix I.)

In 1975, the *Honolulu Star-Bulletin* conducted a survey of local interisland travelers. It found that 96% had used an airline for their most recent business trip, as had 94% for their most recent nonbusiness trip. Only 6.2% had traveled on SeaFlite.

In 1976, the Hawaii Chamber of Commerce found that about one-third of the local travelers travel on business, while 80% travel for pleasure. (Some, obviously, do both.)

Terminal Location   Only in Honolulu did SeaFlite enjoy a locational advantage over the airlines. While the airport was 15–20 minutes driving time from downtown, SeaFlite was within walking distance. Advertising was directed to Honolulu business people, but this market never developed.

On the island of Hawaii, the SeaFlite terminal at Kawaihae was thirty miles from the popular destination area of Kona, while Ke-ahole Airport is only seven miles. The area surrounding the SeaFlite terminal maintained only 4% of the island's population. Another airport at Hilo directly served that popular community.

On Maui, the SeaFlite terminal was at Maalaea, which is close to the popular resort of Lahaina. The airport at Kahalui serves a region which contains 92% of the island's population.

Pricing   Both SeaFlite and the airlines operated as common carriers, with fares regulated by the State Public Utilities Commission. Fares were set to provide a fair rate of return on investment.

Fares for the major airlines were regulated by the Civil Aeronautics Board. These airlines offered a common fare for travel between the neighboring islands and Oahu with purchase of a round-trip ticket between Hawaii and the Mainland. The Common Fare Plan applied only to interisland trips made by air. Under this plan, visitors could fly between islands for $13. SeaFlite's fare was $22. SeaFlite was not incorporated into the Common Fare Plan until early 1977.

During its brief life, SeaFlite experimented with a number of promotional fares. These included a $5 annual "membership" which entitled the passenger to a 15% discount. SeaFlite also offered military standby, youth and group fares.

Between the two airlines, there was no price competition. Both charged the same fare. They also used promotional fares extensively. In 1976, they introduced Travel Clubs, which, for a membership fee of $5, allowed residents the same fares as those in the Common Fare Plan. The Travel Clubs also allowed fare reductions of 20% to 50% for off-hours trips.

Advertising and Promotion   Both SeaFlite and the airlines used Mainland airline booking agents, tour operators and travel agents to book visitors' travel.

SeaFlite's advertising budget was set at 3% of revenue after an initial promotional campaign. Advertising was directed, in more or less equal proportions, to the resident and visitors markets.

Advertising in the local print and broadcast media began in July 1975 and stressed novelty and scenic rides. Tourist advertising featured the navigational history of Hawaii, as well as repeated references to "flying" on SeaFlite. Departures were called "take-offs" and journeys, "flights." Special "flights" were arranged for environmental groups, charities, and educational organizations. SeaFlite services were also provided to the *Hawaii 5-0* television series.

	1976	1977
Hawaiian Airlines		
Promotion and Sales Expense	$10,792,066	$12,185,998
Passenger Revenues	$57,243,393	$61,718,255
Aloha Airlines		
Promotion and Sales Expense	$ 8,388,827	$ 9,421,091
Passenger Revenues	$44,177,172	$47,851,442

PACIFIC SEA TRANSPORTATION, LTD. IN 1978

Late in 1977, in an effort to keep SeaFlite alive, the stockholders of PSTL sought a buyer for the Company. When none materialized, SeaFlite operations were suspended, and the three jetfoils sold to the Far East Hydrofoil Company for $5 million each. To date, these ships remain in service between Hong Kong and Macao.

The State Administration and the Governor's Advisor on Marine Affairs opposed the suspension of operations and sale of the ships, contending that such service was important to the State. The Public Utilities Commission, which granted permission for the suspension and sale, asked that PSTL continue to try to find a suitable operator. Through part of 1978, PSTL retained some key personnel, continued to search for a buyer, and made rental payments to the State for the terminal facilities.

Under terms of the facilities lease agreement with the State, PSTL was prohibited from subleasing the facilities. Finally, by August, 1978, PSTL's payments to the State were nearly half a million dollars in arrears, and the Company proposed State takeover of the facilities.

In 1978, the State, along with the major airlines flying to Hawaii, began to extensively advertise travel to Oahu's neighboring islands. Advertisements appeared in *National Geographic, People, Smithsonian, Time, Newsweek* and *Better Homes and Gardens.*

Thus, as the State continued to promote interisland travel, and encourage a sea transport system, a new operator came on the scene, and promised resumption of jetfoil service in 1981.

EXHIBIT 1

Projected Operating Expenses, 1980	
Parking lot rent	$ 39,600
Rent	45,700
Maintenance	14,000
Utilities	13,120
Guard service	1,415
Property manager	18,000
Salary—President	25,000
Professional services	20,000
Insurance	8,000
Auto expense	1,200
Taxes	1,890
Estimated general excise tax	7,880
Total projected operating expenses	$195,805

EXHIBIT 2

Statewide Airport System Interisland Passengers (Arrivals, Departures, Thru)		
Year	Passengers	Growth %
1967	4,235,114	
1968	4,695,898	10.8
1969	5,449,244	16.0
1970	5,985,554	9.8
1971	6,760,062	12.9
1972	8,186,676	21.1
1973	9,618,194	17.4
1974	10,349,828	7.6
1975	10,648,170	2.8
1976	11,746,276	10.3
1977	12,827,694	9.2
Interisland by Airport 1977		
	IN	OUT
Total	6,413,847	6,413,847
Honolulu	2,568,533	2,601,860
Hilo	585,382	540,260
Upolu	1,512	1,297
Waimea	13,381	12,189
Ke-ahole	545,990	560,267
Kahalui	1,400,385	1,420,339
Hana	10,685	10,945
Kaanapali	46,935	47,708
Molokai	99,016	96,268
Kalaupapa	4,163	4,449
Lanai	23,814	23,324
Lihue	1,095,060	1,093,606
Other	991	1,335

SOURCE: Hawaii Department of Transportation, Air Transportation Facilities Division, *State of Hawaii Airport Statistics,* Myra Tamanaha, research statistician, 1978, p. 3 and 47.

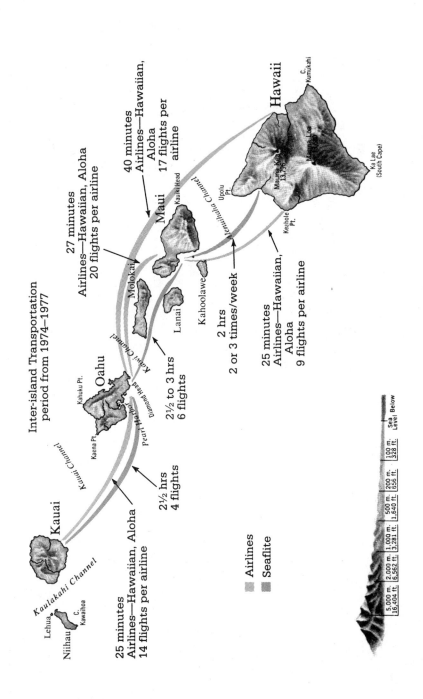

Inter-island Transportation
period from 1974–1977

Kauai

25 minutes
Airlines—Hawaiian, Aloha
14 flights per airline

2½ hrs
4 flights

Kaulakahi Channel

Lehua
Niihau
C.
Kawaihoa

Oahu

Kahuku Pt.
Kaena Pt.
Diamond Head
Pearl Harbor

Kauai Channel

Kaiwi Channel

2½ to 3 hrs
6 flights

27 minutes
Airlines—Hawaiian, Aloha
20 flights per airline

40 minutes
Airlines—Hawaiian,
Aloha
17 flights per
airline

Maui

Kauiki Head

Molokai

Lanai

Kahoolawe

Pailolo Channel

Alenuihaha Channel

Upolu
Pt.

2 hrs
2 or 3 times/week

25 minutes
Airlines—Hawaiian,
Aloha
9 flights per airline

Hawaii

C.
Kumukahi

Mauna Kea
13,796

Mauna Loa

Keahole
Pt.

Ka Lae
(South Cape)

Airlines
Seaflite

5,000 m. | 2,000 m. | 1,000 m. | 500 m. | 200 m. | 100 m. | Sea | Below
16,404 ft. | 6,562 ft. | 3,281 ft. | 1,640 ft. | 656 ft. | 328 ft. | Level

EXHIBIT 3
The Principal Hawaiian Islands

633

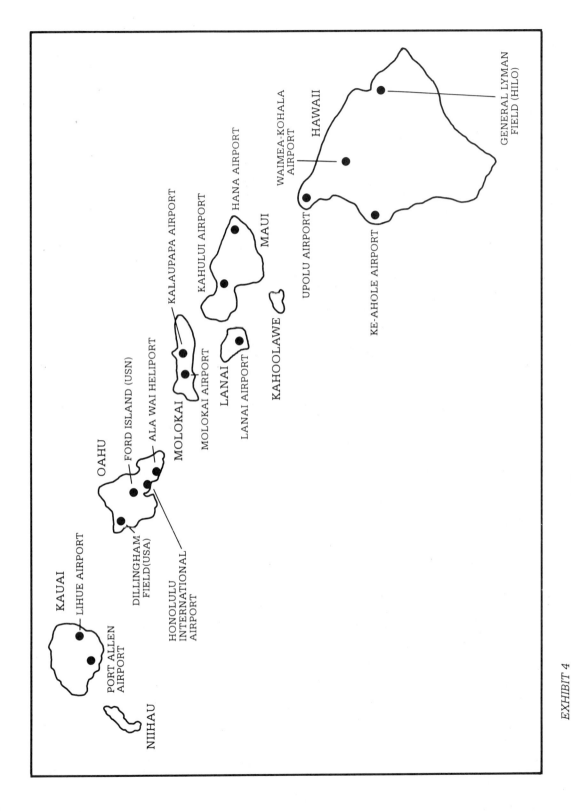

EXHIBIT 4

Map Showing Principal Islands of State of Hawaii and the Statewide System of Airports

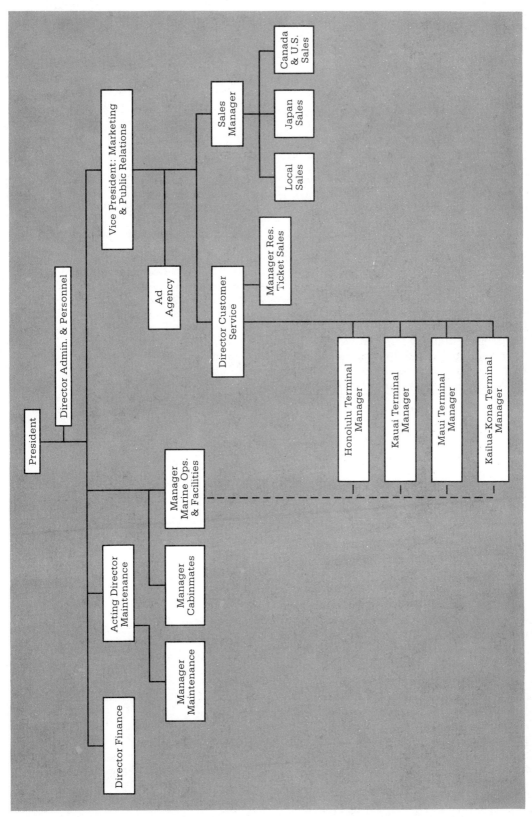

EXHIBIT 5
SeaFlite Organization Chart

EXHIBIT 6
SeaFlite Schedules

Schedule of One Way Fares

		Nawiliwili Kauai	Maalaea Maui	Kailua-Kona Hawaii
Honolulu Oahu	FF	22.00	22.00	28.00
	MF	19.00	19.00	25.00
	YGF	11.00	11.00	14.00
Maalaea Maui	FF			22.00
	MF			19.00
	YGF			11.00

Children two through eleven years old pay ½ adult fare
Roundtrip fare twice one way full fare
FF = Full fare adult
MF = Military standby fare (active duty)
YGF = Youth group fare (passengers under 20 yrs. of age
traveling as group of 10 or more accompanied by
an adult fare passenger over 20 yrs. of age).

Ask about our hourly charter
rates for special cruises,
either local or interisland.

Baggage

3 Normal Size Bags	
per Passenger	FREE
Additional Bags	$3.00
Surfboards	$4.00
Bicycles	$4.00

SeaFlite Schedule Commencing 5/28/76

Eastbound		Daily 215	Daily 225	Daily Ex. Sunday 245	Daily 142	Sunday Only 226
Nawiliwili, Kauai	LV				4:10 pm	
Honolulu	AR				6:50 pm	
Honolulu	LV	7:30 am	8:00 am	1:50 pm		
Maalaea, Maui	AR	10:00 am	10:30 am	4:20 pm		
Maalaea, Maui	LV					11:00 am
Kailua-Kona	AR					1:00 pm

Westbound		Daily 502	Daily Ex. Sunday 512	Daily 522	Daily 241	Sunday Only 622
Kailua-Kona	LV					2:00 pm
Maalaea, Maui	AR					4:00 pm
Maalaea, Maui	LV	10:20 am	10:55 am	4:40 pm		
Honolulu	AR	12:45 pm	1:20 pm	7:05 pm		
Honolulu	LV				1:10 pm	
Nawiliwili, Kauai	AR				3:50 pm	

APPENDIX A

Hawaii's Visitors:
Type of Westbound Traveler to the State

Year	Westbound Travelers	Visitors	Intended Residents	Returning Residents
1967	893,103	754,910	44,117	130,995
1968	1,015,844	869,116	42,236	140,592
1969	1,181,029	1,008,802	41,162	152,404
1970	1,326,135	1,127,950	40,073	173,252
1971	1,430,325	1,207,898	41,562	162,967
1972	1,782,737	1,540,268	44,288	171,772
1973	2,067,861	1,815,443	36,886	194,974
1974	2,184,620	1,899,632	37,007	154,154
1975	2,207,417	1,935,396	39,233	178,040
1976	2,551,601	2,245,252	40,690	186,684
1977	2,763,312	2,453,541	43,617	179,298

Type of Travel—Percentage Distribution

	1977	1976	1975	1974
Organized tour group/ incentive trip	42.1	46.2	45.1	47.2
Individual basis	57.5	53.4	54.6	52.3
Government-military	.4	.4	.3	.5

Westbound Visitor Profile by Percentage

Family income	1973	1974	1975	1976
Under $5,000	2.5	1.7	1.5	1.5
$5,000–$7,499	5.4	4.2	3.6	2.8
$7,500–$9,999	8.5	6.9	6.1	4.6
$10,000–$14,999	21.8	19.5	18.1	16.8
$15,000–$25,999	33.3	35.0	33.3	35.5
$25,000 and over	28.5	32.8	37.4	38.8
Median income (dollars)	($18,600)	($20,100)	($21,200)	($21,800)
College graduates	47.3	48.6	47.9	47.9
Using travel agent	73.0	76.8	77.9	82.9
Arrangements for Outer Island travel				
made before arrival	79.7	81.4	82.3	81.7
made after arrival	20.3	18.6	17.7	18.3

21% of all westbound visitors remained on the island of Oahu exclusively.

Number of Trips to Hawaii by Westbound Visitor Party Heads
By Percentage

	1977	1976	1975	1974
First trip	58.9	61.3	60.3	62.7
Second trip	17.5	16.9	17.1	16.2
Third trip	7.4	7.0	7.2	6.7
Fourth trip & over	16.2	14.8	15.4	14.4

Eastbound Visitor Profile

Year	Numbers		
1967	231,715	Intended length of stay:	
1968	298,727	1 to 6 days	90.7%
1969	345,988	7 to 12 days	7.2%
1970	420,835	13 days and over	2.0%
1971	388,619	Median stay: 5 days, 4 nights	
1972	461,640	Type of travel:	
1973	563,091	organized tour group	87.9%
1974	601,869	other	12.1%
1975	621,688		
1976	688,550	Neighbor Islands are usually visited in	
1977	670,355	one day. Few visitors remain overnight.	

Westbound Visitors to the Neighbor Islands

Year	Maui	% of State Total	Hawaii	% of State Total	Kauai	% of State Total
1967	304,437	34.1	286,590	32.1	275,461	30.8
1968	364,364	35.9	369,509	36.4	327,813	32.3
1969	396,145	33.5	410,967	34.8	363,759	30.8
1970	447,985	33.8	445,401	33.6	410,075	30.9
1971	554,799	38.8	522,166	36.5	472,663	33.0
1972	710,050	39.8	637,562	35.8	565,386	31.7
1973	766,791	37.1	694,170	33.6	590,575	28.6
1974	852,204	39.0	742,839	34.0	601,703	27.5
1975	931,863	42.2	769,779	34.9	632,821	28.7
1976	1,110,726	43.5	816,514	32.0	699,275	27.4
1977	1,257,142	45.5	839,008	30.4	740,501	26.8

Percentage of Westbound Visitors by Their Intended Length of Stay in the State Who Traveled to the Respective Islands

Length of Stay	1977		
	Maui	Hawaii	Kauai
1 to 6 days	3.6	4.2	2.8
7 to 12 days	56.1	51.8	51.4
13 to 18 days	33.9	38.3	39.6
19 to 24 days	4.3	3.8	4.3
25 to 30 days	1.2	1.1	1.1
31 to 60 days	0.7	0.6	0.6
60 days and over	0.1	**	**
Median (days)	(11.5)	(11.8)	(12.0)

** = less than .05%

Percentage of Westbound Visitors by Type of Travel Arrangements to the State

Travel Status	1977		
	Maui	Hawaii	Kauai
Organized tour group	42.2	49.6	46.5
Individually arranged	57.7	50.3	53.4
Military	0.1	0.1	0.1

Residence of Westbound Visitors by Percentage

Area of Residency	State	Maui	Hawaii	Kauai
Pacific Coast	37.6	38.2	33.9	39.4
Mountain	5.9	6.5	7.3	7.7
West North Central	6.6	6.5	6.7	6.5
West South Central	5.7	5.8	7.1	6.0
East North Central	15.7	17.3	18.1	17.1
East South Central	2.1	1.7	2.2	1.6
New England	3.3	2.9	2.9	2.7
Mid Atlantic	10.4	9.6	10.2	8.7
South Atlantic	6.6	5.7	7.4	6.2
Canada**	4.9	4.9	3.1	3.1
Other foreign	1.3	0.9	1.0	1.0

**Only Canadians included in this survey are those arriving from American ports or on American carriers. Percentages can be assumed a good approximation.

BENDIX CORPORATION

Donald F. Harvey
Jo Messex

INTRODUCTION

William M. Agee, 43 year old chairman of Bendix, climbed out of the helicopter at the corporate headquarters in Southfield, Michigan, ready to revitalize his company's strategic game plan. Like the company he heads, William M. Agee is self-assured. Bendix Corp., the Michigan-based manufacturer of automotive and aircraft parts, house-building materials, metalworking tools, and many other things, is a no-nonsense, tightly reined outfit. It made money throughout the recession and stacked up just under $3 billion in sales in 1980. Agee, who was named the company's chairman in December 1976, after Michael Blumenthal was selected to be Jimmy Carter's Treasury Secretary, is a tested and talented manager and financial man—as he tells anyone who asks. Practically the only thing he is touchy about is his age: businessmen, Wall Streeters and journalists often remark how unusual it is for a 43-year old to run a company so huge. "Look," said Agee, "there aren't a lot of people who have had—at whatever age—the top management responsibility and deep involvement that I have had."

In the 1979 annual report, Agee suggested, "This encouraging performance during the disquieting seventies is the result of a conscious strategy begun before the dawn of the decade. One strong element in the strategy was a policy of diversification aimed at insulating the company's total profitability from the cyclical troubles of any particular industry or business. Another was our careful effort to search out the high-return, high-growth segments of the markets we serve.

"The effectiveness of these strategies can be seen in the results of our industry segments in 1979 that are shown later in this report. The results are especially pleasing because they bolster our belief that we can manage Bendix resources in the most uncertain economic environment and still attain our goal of predictable earnings growth. A strategic approach to the special challenges of each market we serve has permitted us to anticipate and plan effectively. Yes, this diversity produces complexity. We must monitor conditions that affect hundreds of products across numerous markets. But from that same diversity, we draw strength, choice and continuity.

"A corporation is a legal entity. So far as the dry legal paper that describes its existence can tell us, a corporation is a fiction of the law, invisible and impersonal. The wonder and vitality of any company, including Bendix, spring from the people who breathe life into the corporate shell, and who give it behavior and expression drawn from their ideas, their ambi-

Copyright © 1981, by Donald F. Harvey. (This case is prepared from pubished information. The company in no way participated in its preparation.)

tions, their energy, and their excellent work contributed every day. It is important to celebrate the human side of corporate performance, and to say that without human effort, we would be nothing."

But changing this once sleepy automotive giant may not be as easy as Agee had imagined. Bendix, under former chairman Mike Blumenthal, had been rated by Dun's Review as one of the nations five best managed companies because of its impressive growth in profitability. But Blumenthal's approach was very tough, a bottom-line style that monitored each manager's performance through a detailed financial control and reporting system. Twice a month the managers had to submit reports showing the results of their operations, compared with their own annual forecasts. And by *results*, Blumenthal meant profits. The fact that Bendix was a technological leader in an industry or product line did not matter. "It would be wrong from the shareholders' point of view," he said. "Nothing works if you don't make money." Such an approach often works well in low-technology manufacturing operations, but may not be as effective for managing high technology businesses.

Following the first drop in profits in a decade, William Agee announced a sweeping reorganization plan and major changes in its future goals. At the same time the company initiated these extensive changes, the meteoric rise within the corporation of a 29-year-old woman and close friend of the company's chief executive attracted major publicity. Her promotions were the subject of considerable criticism from both inside and outside the corporation. After several weeks of adverse publicity and speculation, the board of directors reluctantly accepted the young woman's resignation.

COMPANY BACKGROUND

Bendix Corporation is an international organization which operates plants in the United States, Germany, France, and other Western European countries. Bendix is organized into four major industries. These industries are: (1) automotive; (2) aerospace-electronics; (3) forest products; and (4) industrial-energy.

The automotive segment of Bendix produces Fram automotive parts and brake and steering systems for transportation. The automotive segment contributed 52% to the company's total revenue in 1979 but contributed only 49% to operating profit. The automotive industry as a whole has been hit by lagging new car sales. This has resulted in a decline of new car production over last year. Bendix anticipated this decline and redefined their primary automotive strategy to concentrate on the consumer automotive parts industry (i.e., oil filters, spark plugs).

The aerospace-electronics segment of Bendix produces avionics packages consisting of weather-avoidance radar, communications, navigation, and identification equipment. They also produce hydraulic wheels and brakes for aircraft. In 1979, the aerospace-electronics segment added 28% to total revenue (a 5% increase over 1978 performance) and 34% to operating profits. Continued expansion of commercial and military aviation markets indicates considerable potential for development in the segment.

The forest products segment provides construction lumber, manufactured wood products, and other materials to the home-building and remodeling industry. In 1979, forest products contributed 12% to total revenue but only 9% to operating profit. The forest products industry is suffering from a decline in new home construction and increasing government constraints on the timber industry.

The industrial-energy products segment produces precision measuring equipment, automotive machine tools, assembly systems, piping systems for power generating and exploratory geophysical services. In 1979, this segment contributed 9% to total revenue and 9% to operating profit. The outlook for this segment appears strong.

The Bendix Corporation ranks 88th on Fortune's 500 list with total revenue at the $3.8 billion level, a 5.7% increase over 1978's financial results. As indicated in Exhibit 1, Bendix's revenue has steadily increased for the last 10 years. Their 1979 net income was over $162 million, a 24.4% increase over 1978 results. Total current assets are $1.4 billion with total current liabilities of $850 million.

The Bendix blue chip stock reflects its financial position. As shown in Exhibit 2, earnings per share have increased steadily. In 1979, Bendix stock shows

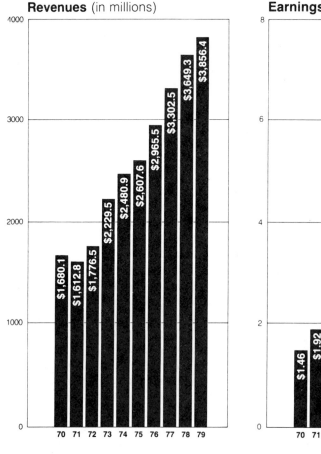

EXHIBIT 1
Bendix Revenues

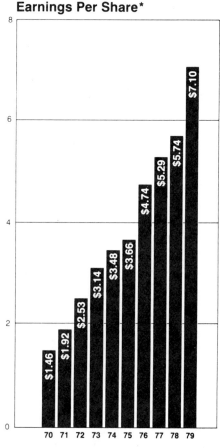

EXHIBIT 2
Bendix Earnings Per Share

EPS values of $7.10, a 23.7% increase over 1978 EPS values. Bendix common stock has been paying increased dividends for the past five years. In 1979, dividends were $2.56 per share, a 12.3% increase over 1978 dividends. The average return on stockholders' equity has increased from 14.5% in 1978 to 16.5% in 1979.

The 1979 Consolidated Statement of Income is shown as Exhibit 3, the 1979 Balance Sheet as Exhibit 4, and Statement of Changes in Financial Positions as Exhibit 5. *Forbes Magazine* ranked Bendix as number 169 in profits and 215 in market value in 1980.

1979 Performance Information by Business Segment is shown in Exhibit 6. As may be noted, the Automotive and Aerospace-Electronics provide almost 80% of total revenues.

WILLIAM M. AGEE

William M. Agee is the son of a Boise, Idaho, farmer. He started school at Stanford, married after his freshman year and transferred to Boise Jr. College. He graduated at the top of his class from the University of Idaho, earned a CPA and, in 1963, received his MBA from Harvard. He immediately went to work for Boise Cascade. At 29, he became their treasurer, and at 33, their senior vice president and chief financial officer. The third highest paid in the company, he was widely regarded as a financial genius.

Agee recognized that Boise Cascade top management had already chosen one of his associates, John B. Fery, as its next chief executive, and was, in effect, feeling stalemated when approached by Bendix in 1972. At that time, Michael Blumenthal, a 5-year veteran with the company and its chairman since 1971, had just established the "office of the chief executive" composed of himself and three executive vice presidents. He offered the job of executive vice president and chief financial officer to Agee. Agee, recognizing the potential for growth was over at Boise Cascade and was just beginning at Bendix, accepted the position.

In 1976, four years later, Blumenthal eliminated the other two vice presidents and appointed Agee president. Two weeks later, Blumenthal left Bendix to become President Carter's Secretary of the Treasury, and handpicked Agee, then 39, to take his place. Blumenthal's recommendations were snubbed by the Carter administration and he later resigned. Agee, his successor, did not make the customary gesture and name him to the Bendix Corporation Board. This move was only one indication of Agee's independence and lack of concern over tradition.

WILLIAM P. PANNY

William P. Panny, 55, was recruited by Agee from Rockwell Industries. He hired a strong operating man in Bill Panny, who had been executive vice president at Rockwell International. He set about the straightforward tasks of attacking the company's operating and managerial problems.

The Bendix Corporation and Consolidated Subsidiaries

Consolidated Statement of Income

For the Years Ended September 30	1979	1978	Comparative Information		
			1977	1976	1975
		(in millions, except share amounts)			
Income					
Net sales	**$3,828.7**	$3,625.5	$3,283.2	$2,947.0	$2,589.7
Royalties and other operating income	**27.7**	23.8	19.3	18.5	17.9
Miscellaneous income (deductions)—Net	**(1.7)**	4.7	21.5	.5	.8
Total	**3,854.7**	3,654.0	3,324.0	2,966.0	2,608.4
Deductions					
Cost of sales	**3,053.4**	2,909.4	2,653.3	2,353.9	2,097.6
Selling and administrative expenses	**500.5**	451.9	411.1	382.2	320.6
Interest expense	**57.5**	52.5	44.1	39.2	42.8
Unusual items		2.0			16.0
Minority interests	**6.5**	5.2	3.7	5.4	6.5
U.S. and foreign income taxes	**102.0**	106.1	95.5	82.2	48.3
Total	**3,719.9**	3,527.1	3,207.7	2,862.9	2,531.8
Income From Consolidated Operations	**134.8**	126.9	116.3	103.1	76.6
Equity in net earnings of nonconsolidated companies	**27.8**	2.7	1.8	1.6	3.2
Net Income	**$ 162.6**	$ 129.6	$ 118.1	$ 104.7	$ 79.8
Average Number of Common and Common Equivalent Shares Outstanding (in thousands)	**22,904**	22,591	22,316	22,097	21,772
Net Income Per Share	**$7.10**	$5.74	$5.29	$4.74	$3.66
Cash Dividends Per Share	**$2.56**	$2.28	$2.00	$1.66	$1.39

See Notes to Consolidated Financial Statements which constitute an integral part of this statement.

EXHIBIT 3
Consolidated Statement of Income

The Bendix Corporation and Consolidated Subsidiaries

Consolidated Balance Sheet

September 30	1979	1978
	(in millions)	

Assets

Current Assets

Cash and marketable securities	$ 46.3	$ 37.6
Trade receivables (less allowance for doubtful receivables)	534.8	472.2
Inventories and contracts in progress (less progress payments)	777.0	689.2
Prepaid expenses	42.9	38.2
Total Current Assets	1,401.0	1,237.2
Investments	171.8	137.4
Land, Buildings, and Equipment—Net	600.3	532.7
Timber and Timberlands (Less Depletion)	38.0	32.5
Goodwill and Other Intangibles (Less Amortization)	65.7	70.7
Miscellaneous Assets	34.2	26.9
Total	$2,311.0	$2,037.4

Liabilities and Stockholders' Equity

Current Liabilities

Notes payable	$ 117.3	$ 93.0
Accounts and drafts payable	352.1	323.5
U.S. and foreign income taxes	53.0	58.4
Other accrued liabilities	328.1	257.4
Total Current Liabilities	850.5	732.3
Long-Term Debt	390.3	343.2
Deferred Income Taxes	3.8	5.1
Minority Interests	30.8	25.4

Stockholders' Equity

Preferred Stock, no par (authorized, 7,000,000 shares, issuable in series)—Series A $3 Cumulative Convertible (authorized, 3,000,000 shares of $7.50 stated value each; issued, 293,502 and 329,739 shares, respectively; liquidation preference, $16.2 million)	2.2	2.5
Common Stock (authorized, 60,000,000 shares of $5 par value each; issued, 22,411,141 and 22,305,290 shares, respectively)	112.1	111.5
Additional capital	30.9	30.2
Retained earnings	894.2	791.0
Total	1,039.4	935.2
Less—Cost of treasury stock (22,769 shares of Preferred Stock and 83,487 shares of Common Stock)	3.8	3.8
Stockholders' Equity—Net	1,035.6	931.4
Total	$2,311.0	$2,037.4

EXHIBIT 4
Consolidated Balance Sheet

The Bendix Corporation and Consolidated Subsidiaries

Consolidated Statement of Changes in Financial Position

For the Years Ended September 30	1979	1978
	(in millions)	
Source (Use) of Funds		
Net income	**$162.6**	$129.6
Add (Deduct) items not affecting funds		
Depreciation, depletion, and amortization of tangible assets	**71.2**	69.0
Minority interests	**6.5**	5.2
Deferred income taxes	**(1.5)**	(14.8)
Equity in undistributed earnings of nonconsolidated companies	**(23.4)**	1.0
Other	**2.1**	5.4
Total	**217.5**	195.4
Working capital items†	**(73.5)**	(74.1)
Additions to land, buildings, and equipment	**(132.1)**	(135.2)
Disposals of fixed assets	**3.4**	7.3
Miscellaneous	**(9.6)**	(4.4)
Total Before Financing and Investment Activity	**5.7**	(11.0)
Financing and Investment Activity		
Increases in long-term debt	**119.4**	157.5
Decreases in long-term debt	**(72.3)**	(64.4)
Increases in notes payable	**24.3**	9.1
Cash dividends	**(57.9)**	(50.8)
Issuance of treasury shares for acquired businesses		11.4
Acquisitions of businesses, less funds provided	**(26.8)**	(24.8)
Investment in ASARCO Incorporated	**(7.7)**	(120.0)
Funds provided from dispositions	**24.7**	42.9
Stock options exercised	**.8**	1.9
Miscellaneous	**(1.5)**	1.3
Total	**3.0**	(35.9)
Net Increase (Decrease) in Cash and Marketable Securities	**$ 8.7**	$ (46.9)
Analysis of Working Capital Items†		
Trade receivables	**$ (77.7)**	$ (87.7)
Inventories and contracts in progress	**(88.5)**	(78.1)
Prepaid expenses	**(5.4)**	(4.8)
Accounts and drafts payable	**38.1**	56.3
U.S. and foreign income taxes	**(6.0)**	19.8
Other accrued liabilities	**66.0**	20.4
Total	**$ (73.5)**	$ (74.1)

EXHIBIT 5

Consolidated Statement of Changes in Financial Position

Segment Information

Segment Information by Industry The Corporation's operations are concentrated in the following industry segments: (1) automotive, consisting of components and systems for the original equipment and replacement markets; (2) aerospace-electronics, consisting of products and services for the aviation industry and space programs; (3) forest products, consisting of building materials; (4) industrial-energy, consisting of capital equipment and perishable tools for the metalworking industry and products and services supporting the exploration and development of energy resources; and (5) other operations, consisting primarily of the U.S. and Canadian operations of Bendix Home Systems, Inc. (for years prior to 1979) and sundry operations. A financial summary of operations by industry segment follows:

	1979	1978	1977	Unaudited 1976	1975
			(in millions)		
Revenues					
Automotive	$1,985.1	$1,881.8	$1,693.2	$1,501.6	$1,256.5
Aerospace-Electronics	1,089.4	875.5	810.6	724.5	715.2
Forest Products	446.0	429.8	353.0	281.3	225.1
Industrial-Energy	327.3	281.2	243.6	242.5	246.7
Other operations and intercompany eliminations	8.6	181.0	202.1	215.6	164.1
Total	$3,856.4	$3,649.3	$3,302.5	$2,965.5	$2,607.6
Operating Profits					
Automotive	$ 173.5	$ 171.9	$ 168.0	$ 154.6	$ 122.8
Aerospace-Electronics	118.5	89.1	79.6	60.3	58.7
Forest Products	32.4	36.5	26.0	16.9	9.1
Industrial-Energy	32.2	28.8	26.8	31.0	36.9
Other operations and intercompany eliminations	(6.3)	1.9	(3.8)	(1.2)	(6.2)
Total	350.3	328.2	296.6	261.6	221.3
Equity in earnings of Asarco	25.5				
Total	375.8	328.2	296.6	261.6	221.3
Deductions					
General corporate expenses—Net	47.2	32.8	35.2	30.1	27.9
Unusual items		2.0		*	16.0
Interest expense	57.5	52.5	44.1	39.2	42.8
Minority interests	6.5	5.2	3.7	5.4	6.5
U.S. and foreign income taxes	102.0	106.1	95.5	82.2	48.3
Total	213.2	198.6	178.5	156.9	141.5
Net Income	$ 162.6	$ 129.6	$ 118.1	$ 104.7	$ 79.8

EXHIBIT 6
Segment Information

647

MARY CUNNINGHAM

Mary Cunningham was working as a junior officer at chase Manhattan. She became disenchanted with what she saw as the lack of social concern at Chase Manhattan and realized that to change things she needed to be in a position to establish policy rather than follow it. This requires power, power that was available with more education. To this end, she enrolled in the Harvard Business School in 1977. She was one of 30 out of 800 students elected to Harvard's Century Club as leaders of tomorrow. Classmates regarded her as confident, calculating, and manipulative, the perfect teacher's pet. The Dean of Harvard projected her to become a chief executive officer in a Fortune 500 company within 10 years of her graduation. She graduated in 1979 with an impressive academic record and a MBA.

Agee and Cunningham first met in 1979 shortly after her graduation when he went from corporate headquarters in Southfield, Michigan, to New York for an interview. The scheduled one-hour interview turned into a 3 to 4 hour marathon, later described as a "meeting of minds." It was her only job interview.

During the meeting, Cunningham revealed her goal was to change business for the good of society. She was ambitious, intelligent, energetic, and committed to morality in business. After hours of interviewing, Agee offered her the position of his executive assistant.

At this time, Cunningham had four job offers in the $50,000 range from companies in the investment banking field. These companies (Goldman Sachs, Morgan Stanley, Baine and Co., and Braxton and McKenzie) were as impressed with her credentials and potential as Agee. She was a highly sought after MBA.

THE MANAGEMENT

Management policy at Bendix was largely established by the top management team of eight executives, termed by Agee the "brave band of eight." Agee also removed the table from the board room—the directors now sit in a big circle with nothing in front of them.

THE BOARD OF DIRECTORS

Bendix has a 19-member board, including 6 inside members, as follows:

William M. Agee: Chairman and Chief Executive Officer of the Corporation. Director of ASARCO Incorporated, Detroit Economic Growth Corporation, Detroit Renaissance, Inc., General Foods Corporation and The Equitable Life Assurance Society of the United States; Trustee of New Detroit, Inc.

Malcolm Baldrige: Chairman and Chief Executive Officer and Director of Scovill Inc., Waterbury, Connecticut, a diversified manufacturing company. Director of AMF, Incorporated, ASARCO Incorporated, Connecticut Mutual Life Insurance Company, Eastern Company and Uniroyal, Inc.; Trustee of Swiss Reinsurance Company.

Wilbur J. Cohen: Professor of Public Affairs, University of Texas, Austin, Texas, and Dean Emeritus of the School of Education, the University of Michigan, Ann Arbor, Michigan. Director of Esquire Corporation; Chairman of National Commission on Unemployment Compensation; member of Board of Governors of Haifa University and National Commission on Social Security.

Harry B. Cunningham: Director and Honorary Chairman, Kmart Corporation, Troy, Michigan, retail merchants. Director of Burroughs Corporation, Institute for Educational Affairs, National Detroit Corporation, National Steel Corporation and Weaver Exploration Company; Trustee of Citizens Research Council of Michigan and Institute of Economic Education, Inc.

Charles F. Donnelly: Vice Chairman of the Corporation. Trustee of Business/Economic Education Alliance and Merrill-Palmer Institute of Detroit; Director of Boysville of Michigan; member of Advisory Board and Chairman of Finance Committee of Providence Hospital.

Coy G. Eklund: President and Chief Executive Officer and Director of the Equitable Life Assurance Society of the United States, New York, New York. Director of Americans for Indian Opportunity, Grand Central Art Galleries, National Urban League, Salk Institute, U.S. International Council and Women's Action Alliance; Trustee of Columbia Presbyterian Hospital.

John C. Fontaine: Partner, Hughes Hubbard & Reed, New York, New York, attorneys. Trustee of Samuel H. Kress Foundation.

Paul F. Hartz: Vice President of the Corporation. Director of Friona Industries, Inc., Jamesbury Corporation, Outlet Company and Rhode Island Hospital Trust National Bank.

Charles E. Heitman: Former Vice Chairman and Chief Operating Officer of the Corporation. Director of Maccabees Mutual Life Insurance Co.

Jewel S. Lafontant: Partner, Lafontant, Wilkins & Butler, Chicago, Illinois, attorneys. Director of Continental Illinois Corporation. The Equitable Life Assurance Society of the United States, Food Fair, Inc., Foote, Cone & Belding Communications, Inc., and Trans-World Corporation.

Paul S. Mirabito: Chairman and Chief Executive Officer and Director of Burroughs Corporation, Detroit, Michigan, a manufacturer of data processing and office equipment. Director of Consumers Power Company, Warner-Lambert Company and Economic Club of Detroit.

William P. Panny: President and Chief Operating Officer of the Corporation. Director of Economic Club of Detroit, Engineering Society of Detroit and Highway User's Foundation; Trustee of Marygrove College and Rackham Engineering Foundation.

Robert W. Purcell: Former business consultant to Rockefeller Family and Associates, New York, New York. Director of Basic Resources International, S.A., C.I.T. Financial Corporation, International Basic Economy Corporation, International Minerals & Chemical Corporation, The Investors Group, Kmart Corporation, the Pittston Company and Seaboard World Airlines, Inc.

William C. Purple: Executive Vice President of the Corporation. Director of Aerospace Industries Association, American Defense Preparedness Association and Institute of Electrical and Electronic Engineers.

Donald H. Rumsfeld: President and Chief Executive Officer and Director of G. D. Searle & Co., Skokie, Illinois, a manufacturer of health care products. Director of Compagnie Geomines S.A. and Sears, Roebuck and Co.,; Trustee of Rand Corporation; member of Board of Governors of Atlantic Institute for International Affairs.

Alan E. Schwartz: Partner, Honigman Miller Schwartz & Cohn, Detroit, Michigan, attorneys. Director of Burroughs Corporation, Core Industries, Inc., Cunningham Drug Stores, Incorporated, Detroitbank Corporation, Detroit Edison Company, Handleman Company, Howell Industries, Inc., Michigan Bell Telephone Company and Pulte Home Corporation.

Jonathan L. Scott: Chairman and Chief Executive Officer and Director of The Great Atlantic & Pacific Tea Company, Inc., Montvale, New Jersey, a food retailing and processing company. Director of Morrison-Knudsen Company.

Hugo E. R. Unterhoeven: Timken Professor of Business Administration, Harvard Business School, Boston, Massachusetts. Director of Schroders Incorporated and The Stanley Works.

George R. Vila: Former Chairman and Chief Executive Officer of Uniroyal, Inc., New York, New York, a manufacturer of rubber and other products. Director of Church and Dwight Co., Inc.: Trustee Emeritus of Wesleyan University.

THE ORGANIZATION

The Bendix organization is structured into a corporate staff and division vice presidents, reporting to W. Panny—see Exhibit 7 (Organization chart).

THE REORGANIZATION

William Agee embarked on an ambitious and risky plan to transform Bendix from a nondescript automotive and aerospace supplier into a glamorous, high-flying, high-technology company. And the metamorphosis did not go smoothly. Since becoming the chief executive in 1977, Agee has exerted his own style of management which combines an easy going manner with a keen business sense and a penchant for the innovative. Anticipating a decline in the automotive industry, he reversed the company policy of expansion in automotive operations, heretofore the backbone of the

THE BENDIX CORPORATION

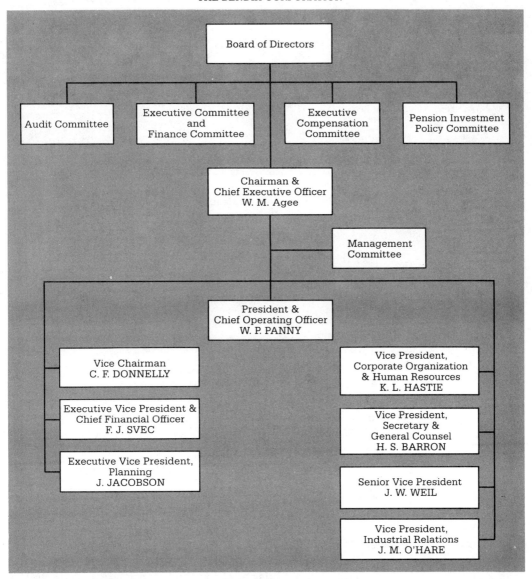

EXHIBIT 7
Organization Table   THE BENDIX CORPORATION

company. He revamped the organization chart, changing Bendix from a centralized organization to one with decentralized structure.

His unusual approach to management shows in the numerous changes he instituted in the company policies. These range from abolishing the parking lot pecking order and removing the table from the executive boardroom to allowing employees to use the executive dining room. This unorthodox management style was new to the staunchly conservative firm and alienated many of the traditionalists on his staff. Most threatened were the members of upper management trained in the

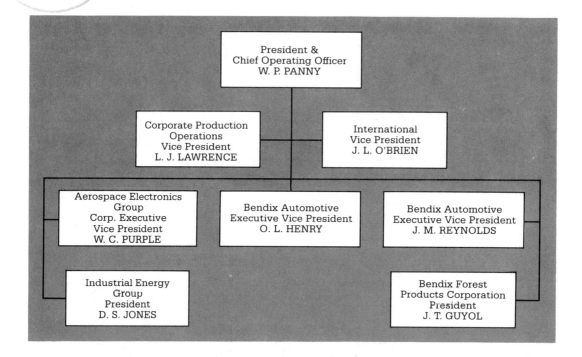

PRESIDENT & CHIEF OPERATING
OFFICER'S ORGANIZATION
SEE SECTION II

EXHIBIT 7 (Continued)
**Organization Table   PRESIDENT & CHIEF OPERATING OFFICER'S
ORGANIZATION**

old school of management thought (put in your time, don't rock the boat, and you'll
get your reward)

In business matters, he is conservative and uses a straightforward
method to deal with operational and management problems. His financial background
has made him bottom-line oriented—get rid of divisions which don't measure up to
corporate standards. He is credited with making decisions that have improved company business, reversed losses and made Bendix second in the nation's machine tool
industry. Critics applaud his keen business sense and decisions but question the
methods he has used to solve problems.

Agee is an unusually likeable man with a ready smile. Indeed, he often
plays a set of tennis before his 7 AM arrival at the company's Southfield, Michigan,
headquarters where he then works a 12-hour day.

"I think a person my age can be a more constructive agent of change
than somebody in his twilight years," says Agee. He believes Bendix has in it most
of the talent necessary to cope with the management losses. He intends to run the
company with a larger team, the "brave band of eight." It will operate in a manner
similar to the previous four-man executive committee. The number of members of
the new committee will be flexible, says Agee, who eschews bureaucracy and rigidity.

"The one thing we are not going to do is formalize our committee," he vows. He even avoids naming it. "It's just a group that gets together and talks," he says.

Recently, Agee proposed diversification to lessen corporate dependence on the declining auto industry and move the company into higher technology and more profitable activities. He planned widespread changes in corporate management and corporate goals and strategies. A major reorganization was announced. This reorganization would result in the transfer or termination of over one-fourth of the employees at corporate headquarters in Michigan. In addition, Agee's plan called for reversal of the policy of centralized organization established by his predecessor, Blumenthal, as well as disposal of two of the corporation's major subsidiaries, a forest products firm and a nonferrous metals producer. Elimination of these operations underscored the commitment by management to change the company emphasis from its automotive past to the high technology of the future.

While Agee cannot be faulted for scrutinizing the most troubled area of his business, he has not been politic in the way he has done it. In June, 1980, he asked Mary Cunningham to prepare an exhaustive report on Bendix's North American automotive operations. A team of seven was assigned to work with her; the task force was dubbed "Snow White and the Seven Dwarfs." Within 40 days, they produced a three-volume study.

Given Cunningham's limited experience in the automotive industry, her work was bound to be called into question no matter how solid it was. "It didn't show us much that we didn't know," said William Panny, though he conceded it did focus needed attention on some low-volume products. Added another insider: "The problems were all well understood. It didn't take a task force like this to bring them to light." Cunningham got the harshest criticism for the way she went about the job. "She created problems by going directly to the plant floor without coordinating with the management in place," complained the same insider. "That was disruptive, caused confusion, and undermined the management." One key member of top management, however, found the Cunningham report most impressive. His name: Bill Agee.

Agee has been tackling the company's organization chart as boldly as its balance sheet. Under Blumenthal, Bendix evolved into a highly centralized organization with a large corporate staff and strict financial controls. A financial man himself, Agee was comfortable with that style of administration, but he gradually became convinced that the company was too bureaucratic and had to be decentralized. His conviction was widely shared. "There is no question that Southfield was too involved in divisional affairs," admitted one former Bendix executive who was otherwise critical of Agee's decentralization plan.

To Agee, the most important business question was how dependent Bendix should be on the auto industry. In the past, the automotive group had driven Bendix. It is still its biggest operation, accounting for about half the company's sales and operating profits. But the group's profits have been flat since 1977 and in 1979 they were down substantially.

One way to lessen the company's dependence on the auto business is to redeploy other assets into faster-growing and more profitable endeavors—the strategy Agee began implementing. Another approach would be to revamp the auto operations. "All of our businesses are always under scrutiny," Agee recently told a meeting of security analysts in Boston. "If automotive doesn't measure up, then we will get rid of it, but it is too early to tell." Agee is hardly sanguine about the industry's prospects. Striking at the core of Bendix, he said, "Automobile brakes are in the winter of their life, and so is the entire automobile industry."

Bendix executives generally agreed that the automotive business had to be trimmed. Said one: "You can easily get over $100 million in assets out." Indeed, that process has already begun. The company closed its plant in Windsor, Ontario, earlier in 1980. The question now is how deep the cuts have to go, a determination that will decide the future of Bendix's two largest facilities, a brake-and-steering plant in South Bend and a hydraulics plant in St. Joseph, Michigan. According to Bill Panny, this was an issue on which "Agee and I did not have common agreement." Added Panny: "I say that you've got to trim them but you don't want to run away from these businesses. It is a tough row to hoe, but you know these businesses, unlike the ones you buy." Agee has not publicly taken any position on the fate of these two operations, except to tell a gathering of Bendix employees in late September, 1980, that these were "troubled operations" but "at the moment there are no plans to move them."

In mid-September 1980, Agee suddenly ousted Bendix's president and chief operating officer, William P. Panny. Simultaneously, Jerome Jacobson, executive vice president for strategic planning, resigned, opening the vacancy for Mary Cunningham. A week later the company announced two major decisions: it would sell its forest-products operations for $435 million and put up for grabs its 20% stake in ASARCO, the nonferrous-metals producer. Selling those shares brought another $300 million into the company's coffers and gave Agee more than $700 million for acquisitions. Later that same week, Bendix unveiled the details of a major reorganization that would trigger the termination or transfer of about 250 of the 800 employees working at company headquarters in Southfield, Michigan. Finally, in late September, 1980, Mary Cunningham resigned.

In important ways, the Agee-Cunningham association had a lot to do with the changes in Bendix's direction. While Agee was unquestionably the principal architect of the company's new strategy, Cunningham's role in devising it was critical. "She has been my right and left arm ever since she came into the company," said Agee not long before Cunningham quit. "She is the most vital and important person within the company and has played an important part in conceptualizing the strategy.

THE DYNAMIC DUO

Agee removed the chief operating officer, William P. Panny, 52, whom he had hired to help straighten out operating problems, because he decided Panny's "hands on" management style did not fit with his announced goals of decentralized management and a more participative style. This move caused the executive vice president for strategic planning, Jerome Jacobson, to also resign. Agee filled this vacancy with his protegée, Mary E. Cunningham. Cunningham had been with the company 15 months during which time she held a succession of jobs all of which reported directly to Agee. Her rapid rise in the company was unusual and controversial. She was credited with being instrumental in developing the new strategic plan.

In September 1980, at age 28, after one year with Bendix, Mary Cunningham became the most powerful woman executive in the company, the vice president for corporate and public affairs. The woman she surpassed, Nancy Reynolds, suggested Mary be more discrete in her dealings with Agee and in her demeanor in general. Mary had declined to accept the sexless role required of a successful executive woman and insisted on including her femininity as a part of her, showing that it made her no less intelligent or capable. She continued to wear her hair long and wore dresses when most executive women mirrored their male counterparts. Mary refused to heed these well intentioned warnings and did not cater to the preconceptions of others. Her rise in power meant the decline of others. The natural result was envy, jealousy, and resentment. Her appearance, youth, gender, and closeness to Agee were obvious targets.

Agee and Cunningham found they were very compatible. Mary's concern for morality in business struck a responsive chord in Agee, who was also concerned with social inequity. They were alike in many ways—both were young, successful, intelligent, ambitious. Both had strong financial backgrounds, and Harvard MBAs. Together they were visionaries, different from the conservative corporate officers who surrounded them. They did not fit the executive mold. They were not old school establishment but were innovative and progressive. The two of them meshed together like well made gears. They thought alike, got along, worked well together, and brought out the best in each other. They were a natural team and became close allies against the rest of the corporate management team.

One of the things the two shared was a lack of awareness about what other people thought. They were not sensitive to those who did not share their views nor were they concerned with image or conformance to standards. They believed in honesty, openness, and a forthright approach in a business where the language is tempered with subtle diplomacy and the very idea of business is image and conformance. Though their goals may have been commendable, this approach at Bendix created waves.

The dynamic duo, two of the youngest corporate executives in the country, traveled together to business meetings, shared adjacent hotel suites and were constantly seen in each other's company. Their corporate offices were even next door to each other. One was divorced, one separated. He was handsome, she was young and good looking. Both were successful and intelligent. Gossip was inevitable. They were seen together on various social occasions: at the Winter Olympics, "smiling fondly at each other" (*Time*, Oct. 27, 1980); at the Republican Convention; and again at a U.S. Open Tennis match. Rumors of an affair between the two were increasing and finally reached the board of directors in September of 1980.

Putting a stop to that speculation clearly required more than a hotline phone call. Thus Agee summoned a meeting of company staff to dispel the rumors that his new vice president had become a most favored employee. "I know it has been buzzing around that Mary Cunningham's rise in this company is very unusual and that it has something to do with a personal relationship we have," he said. "It is true that we are very close friends. But that has nothing to do with the way that I and others in this company evaluate her performance."

As publicity and speculation concerning the Agee-Cunningham relationship increased, Agee held private meetings with Bendix top management and the executive committee of the board to deny any affair between the two. He later called an employee assembly to publicly defend Cunningham's promotions in an effort to dispel rumors. The media were invited, but the effort failed and the possibility of scandal made national headlines.

The story was perfect, it combined the world of the international business jet set, youth, success, power, sex, and scandal. As publicity increased, Mary announced she would make a major statement the following day, and rumors of a marriage announcement grew. She cancelled her scheduled announcement and asked for a temporary leave of absence, a maneuver designed to force a vote of confidence. She received a unanimous vote of confidence from the board of directors who rejected her leave-of-absence request. Shortly afterwards, she resigned. The board accepted the resignation with regret saying publicity had impaired her effectiveness. Agee stated that he felt Bendix Corporation had lost a valuable asset and an essential part of the top management team.

CONCLUSIONS

As the Bendix company collects the cash from its divestitures, Agee intends to confront the job he has cut out for himself: the building of the new Bendix. So far, he has spoken only in the most general terms about what Bendix will become. He says it will remain a diversified company making three principal products (automotive parts, aerospace equipment, and machine tools) but will put greater emphasis on technological innovation. Beyond that the blueprints are sketchy. "I think we have some basic strategic decisions to make," said John Weil, a senior vice president and the company's chief technical officer. "You can't be a technology company and go in all directions at once."

According to *Value Line* (Jan. 23, 1981), "Bendix's housecleaning is nearly complete. These shares are likely to maintain their recent standout market performance in the year ahead."

Bill Agee and Mary Cunningham, two Harvard MBAs tried to create a "Camelot" out of an old line company. Only time will tell whether they have succeeded, or whether it will erode away. As King Arthur said, "Remember, that for one bright, shining hour, there was a place called Camelot."

REFERENCES

1   "Theres' a Girl in My Soup." *The Economist,* Oct. 4, 1980, 77.

2   "William M. Agee of Bendix: Careful Campaigner." *Forbes,* Feb. 15, 1977, 93.

3   "People of the Financial World." *Financial World,* Mar. 1, 1977, 18.

4   "Blumenthals' Balancing Act." *Duns Review,* Dec. 1976, 40.

5   "Upheaval at Bendix." *Fortune,* Nov. 3, 1980, 48.

6   "The Mary and Bill Story." *Time,* Oct. 27, 1980, 80.

7   "Bendix Abuzz." *Time,* Oct. 6, 1980, 83.

8   "Bendix Battle." *Time,* Oct. 20, 1980, 78.

9   "Cunningham: Goodbye to all that." *Newsweek,* Oct. 20, 1980.

10   "Executive Sweet at Bendix." *Newsweek,* Oct. 6, 1980.

11   "The Mary Cunningham Story." *Newsweek,* Oct. 27, 1980, 82.

12   "The Gail Sheehy Series" in *The San Francisco Chronicle,* Oct. 13–17, 1980.

13   "The Bendix Annual Report," 1979. Bendix Corporation.

CRISIS AT SOUTHERN UNIVERSITY

Robert A. Swanson
James Calvert Scott
Omar Belazi

At the general faculty meeting all members sat quietly as the tellers sorted the ballots and counted the votes. Finally the chief teller turned to the group and announced: "The motion expressing 'no confidence' in the administration of President Will B. Anderson and asking for his resignation has passed. Thirty-seven faculty members voted in favor of the motion, twelve faculty members voted against the motion, and one faculty member abstained."

INTRODUCTION

Southern University*, located in the American Southwest, is a small liberal arts school with a student population of approximately 1,600. It is located in the town of Poncho City, population 14,000, which serves as the hub for a large geographic area with a relatively low population density. The local population is approximately 50 percent Anglo-American and 50 percent Hispanic-American.

Because Southern University draws students primarily from the southwestern corner of the state in which it is located, the governor until recently has restricted his choice of regents for SU to those who live within a few miles of the campus. But as a result of recent pressures placed upon the governor to obtain wider geographic representation among regents some significant changes have taken place in the composition of the SU Board of Regents. A woman from Guadalupe, a town about 100 miles distant, and a Hispanic-American man from La Misa, a town about 175 miles distant, have been appointed as regents. The addition of these two regents has tended to change the role of the regents from one of essentially rubber stamping to one of studying and questioning the SU president's action.

Each member of the Board of Regents serves a term of six years and may be reappointed. Their responsibilities include: 1) determination of objectives and the setting of the policies of the university; 2) selection of the president; 3) determination of remuneration for the president; 4) overseeing the president's administrative activities; 5) review and approval or disapproval of presidential actions and/or recommendations concerning certain personnel and financial matters.

This case was prepared by Dr. Robert A. Swanson, Dr. James Calvert Scott and Dr. Omar Belazi, as a basis for class discussion rather than to illustrate either effective or ineffective handling of an administrative situation.

Copyright © 1980 by Dr. Robert A. Swanson

Distributed by the Intercollegiate Case Clearing House, Soldiers Field, Boston, MA 02163. All rights reserved to the contributors. Printed in the USA.

*Southern University is a fictitious name

The current president of Southern University, Will B. Anderson, D. Ed., was appointed in 1964. His orientation is primarily toward efficiency in financial and administrative matters, rather than toward increasing the quality of education. Several years ago, for example, he dropped the special accreditation of the Department of Education and Psychology, one of the two major departments on campus, explaining that such accreditation "isn't necessary."

Anderson's roles in the areas of public and university relations are accomplished with a minimum of contacts. So far as the local businessmen are concerned, none can recollect hearing Anderson speak before any business organization. Contacts with faculty members are infrequent and, almost invariably, formal and distant.

His behavior toward community groups is similar: he has played neither a leadership nor a subordinate role in civic or fund raising activities.

Currently, Anderson receives a salary in excess of $50,000, the highest salary paid any university president in the state—even higher than that of the presidents of the two major state-supported universities whose student bodies are approximately ten to fifteen times that of Southern University. During Anderson's incumbency of 15 years, university enrollment has remained essentially the same; however, a number of new buildings have been constructed and the grounds have been significantly improved.

The organization chart shows the administrative structure of the university and identifies the three positions shown on the chart currently filled by Hispanic-Americans.

CRITICAL INCIDENTS

1. The Appointment of a Regent   In 1978, Juan Escudero, an experienced Hispanic-American school administrator and a graduate of Southern University, was appointed to the university's Board of Regents. This appointment was significant, for Escudero became the first Hispanic-American to serve on the board. With his appointment, students, particularly Hispanic-American students, faculty, and lower-level administrative personnel recognized that they had a regent to whom they could bring intra-university problems of concern to themselves without fear of the consequences. He became so knowledgeable about university-related matters within a few months that during one regents' meeting after he had provided some detailed background information on a local faculty problem, another regent who had served for many years said that Escudero must have "divine insight" into the situation because he himself knew none of these details!

2. The Formation of the NEA Chapter   By the early 1970s, faculty members were becoming increasingly discontented with Anderson's administration. Efforts were made to use the American Association of University Professors (AAUP) organization to effect change, but these efforts proved fruitless. Subsequently, in an attempt to vent their increasing frustration with the university administration—and particularly with Anderson—a local chapter of the National Education Association

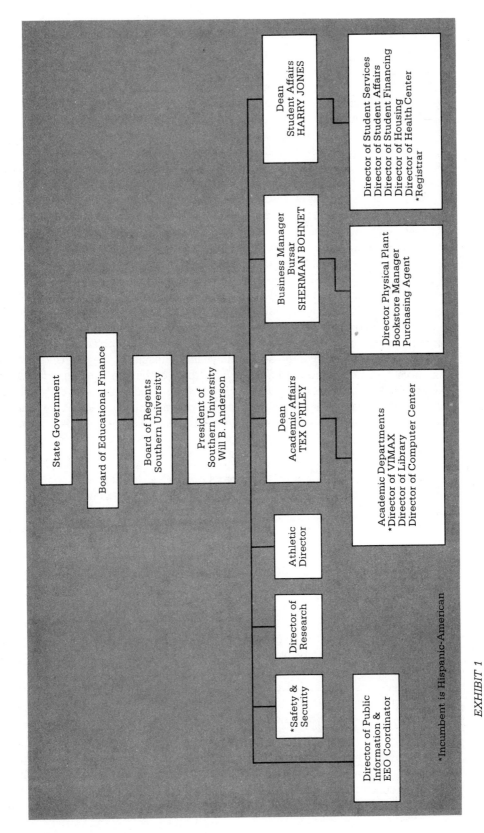

*Incumbent is Hispanic-American

EXHIBIT 1
Organization Chart of Southern University

(NEA) was organized by approximately 25 percent of the total university faculty during the fall of 1978. The primary objective of the chapter was to work toward replacement of Anderson with a president who would, among other things, establish better relations with the faculty and reduce the priority of capital expenditures for athletic facilities. Under the protection of NEA, faculty members increasingly expressed their ideas and dissented publicly. Within three months of its formation, the NEA chapter challenged the governor's reappointment of one regent on the grounds that he was overly concerned with expenditures for athletic facilities rather than with facilities for the university's academic departments and with faculty salaries. The NEA chapter also questioned the governor's selecting as a candidate for regent an attorney who had previously defended in court two of the university president's sons, who were working in the local police department, on charges of police brutality. After well-publicized hearings, however, both of the governor's selections were confirmed by members of the state legislature for six-year terms.

Following their defeat but encouraged by their growing membership, NEA members established contacts with local state legislators to apprise them fully of the SU situation as they saw it and to encourage whatever legislative support might be necessary in the future in order to rectify the SU problems.

By the end of the academic year, the results of the intensive membership drive became apparent: More than 50 percent of the total university faculty had become NEA members. As evidence of the widespread feelings of dissatisfaction among faculty at all levels, all but one of the departmental chairpersons became NEA members, and one of the departmental chairpersons became president of the local NEA chapter.

4. The Viewpoint of Hispanic-American Groups   In June 1979, spokespersons for several Hispanic-American groups including the SU student senate met with Anderson to discuss the low percentage—approximately ten percent—of Hispanic-Americans in university faculty and administrative positions. This is in contrast to the student and local ethnic mix of approximately 50 percent Hispanic-Americans. Perceiving discriminatory selection of administrators and faculty by the university administration, Hispanic-American groups had been pressing Anderson to hire more Hispanics.

During the confrontation, Anderson stated that he is committed to the EEOC objectives and that the university sought to hire those persons who are most quailfied for all existing vacancies; if Hispanic-Americans were the most qualified applicants, he would then be pleased to hire them. He pointed out that few Hispanic-Americans applied for vacant university positions, and that, of those applying, few were qualified, or more significantly, most qualified for the openings. The Hispanic-American representatives left the meeting unconvinced of Anderson's sincerity and sensitivity to the matter of minority hirings.

5. The Developments in the Department of Business   The Department of Business is the largest and fastest growing of the ten departments within the university and one of seven departments offering master's degrees. The department has been authorized six full-time faculty positions although it typically offers between 40 and 50 classes. Because of relatively low rates of pay, few opportunities to engage in consulting work, and relative geographic isolation of the university community, one or two full-time faculty positions have remained unfilled during each of the past several years. Part-time instructors have been recruited from the local business community and high schools to augment full-time departmental faculty. During the 1978–79 academic year when five full-time faculty members were employed, over 50 percent of the departmental courses were taught by these part-time instructors.

Immediately prior to the beginning of the 1978–79 academic year Dr. Marie Meyer was hired by Alan Eaton, department chairman, at the direction of Anderson without being brought to the campus for customary interviews with Tex O'Riley, the Dean of Academic Affairs, and Anderson. She was the lowest ranked applicant, according to a report prepared by the departmental search committee. She was hired, however, because of an urgent need as perceived by the administration to have the position filled immediately. She arrived on campus nearly two weeks after the fall semester began. Within a few weeks she alienated many students with her loud gruff manner, jumping to unwarranted conclusions, and distrustfulness of others. Some students in her classes were irate and complained individually and in groups to Eaton, to O'Riley, and to Anderson. In spite of the uproar, little was done to placate the students and resolve the problems although meetings were held with her on several occasions by Eaton, by O'Riley and/or by Anderson.

Early in the second semester of the 1978–79 academic year, Joe "Blacky" Black, one of the department's faculty members, talked with Eaton concerning the numerous student complaints regarding Meyer. He pointed out that he and other members of the department were becoming increasingly concerned about the serious negative impact which Meyer's behavior was having within the university and the community. As a direct result of her behavior, the reputation of the department and the university was being seriously jeopardized, "Blacky" told Eaton. "Blacky" concluded his remarks, "If something isn't done about this situation, the school will lose students, and some faculty members within the department may leave."

Within a few weeks the situation worsened. Miguel Flores, a senior at SU, filed a lawsuit against SU because it was "allowing an unqualified instructor, Marie Meyer, to teach a course entitled "Government and Business!" According to Flores, Meyer announced in class at the beginning of the semester that she was not qualified to teach the course. She did, however, continue to teach it for much of the semester before a replacement was brought in to finish the course. The matter has not yet been resolved.

During the late spring and early summer, the department tried unsuccessfully to fill its two faculty vacancies. In July 1979, Dr. George Riskin, who was the faculty member overseeing the recruitment efforts during the summer sessions, and Dr. David Mark, the departmental member selected to become chairman effective beginning fall semester, 1979, convinced O'Riley to prevail upon Anderson to amend the departmental vacancy announcements to read "salary and rank negotiable." Up to this time faculty members had been hired as assistant professors and at the low end of the pay range. Since no qualified candidates had previously applied for the vacancies and the fall semester was to begin in about six weeks, Anderson reluctantly accepted the change in wording. The two vacancies were then reannounced with salary and rank negotiable and a mid-August application deadline.

Shorty thereafter, "Blacky" advised Mark that he had received an offer from an AACSB approved business school at a higher salary and rank. Mark immediately advised O'Riley of "Blacky's" job offer. Because the offer which "Blacky" received had been made after the "salary and rank negotiable" change in the SU job announcement, O'Riley stated that perhaps "Blacky" was "hoodwinking the administration"; i.e., he had no bona fide offer but was merely taking advantage of the fact that there was a shortage of business professors and was attempting to capitalize on it to increase his salary and rank.

On the application deadline date for the announced vacancies, "Blacky" submitted an application for the advertised positions with "salary and rank negotiable." By applying for the advertised positions, "Blacky" was enabling Anderson to negotiate a new contract more consistent with the terms of the offer he had received, more consistent with his experience which included teaching at two universities, the American Institute of Banking and the U.S. Air Force and more consistent with his work experience which included twenty years of varied management experience.

The following week Riskin, Mark, and Eaton sent a letter to O'Riley which stated "Blacky's" strong qualifications in such areas as educational and work experience, teaching excellence, rapport with students and involvement with the business community. More significantly, the letter predicted some potentially adverse consequences if "Blacky" were not retained; i.e., departmental goals would become more difficult to achieve, standing with the North Central Association of Colleges and Schools may be adversely affected, departmental morale may drop, and students may decide to transfer to other schools. In closing, the writers strongly urged O'Riley and Anderson to negotiate a more realistic contract with "Blacky."

No response—orally or in writing—was made to the department members regarding their letter of concern about "Blacky's" possible resignation. Following receipt of the letter from Riskin, Mark, and Eaton, however, Anderson held a brief meeting with O'Riley and "Blacky." Anderson began the meeting by saying, "There is a rumor going around that you have accepted an offer from another school. . . ." "Blacky" asked him where he had first heard the "rumor." Anderson replied "From Dr. Mark." "Blacky" then asked, "Is information provided to you by departmental chairpersons to be considered as rumor?" Anderson did not respond. In that meeting he asked, "What do you want?" "Blacky" responded by reminding Anderson that he, Anderson, had called the meeting, that he, "Blacky," was present only because Anderson presumably wished to discuss some facet of the job offer which he had received. Anderson and O'Riley, however, discussed nothing of substance with "Blacky," and the meeting abruptly ended.

After a review of the eight persons who had applied for the vacant departmental positions, Drs. Riskin, Mark, and Eaton sent a letter to O'Riley indicating that five of the eight applicants were not qualified for the vacancies. Among the three qualified candidates, "Blacky" was ranked first. None of the applicants—including the three recommended individuals—was hired and only the second choice applicant was contacted and interviewed by Anderson and O'Riley. That applicant was later hired on a part-time basis only.

Then, just before the beginning of the fall semester, Dr. Mark, the designated departmental chairman resigned the chairmanship because of serious differences of opinion between himself and the SU administration regarding a number of departmental matters, including personnel. Further explanation of the circumstances leading up to his resignation was offered in a six-page letter to Anderson.

A few days later, after learning that the members of the department had received no feedback from either Anderson or O'Riley relating to their earlier letters, "Blacky" submitted his letter of resignation. In his letter, "Blacky" quoted the faculty handbook which allows for waiver of notice under certain conditions: "If he feels that observance (of timely notice) might deny him substantial professional advancement." The circumstances were such that Anderson could not deny that this criterion had been met. He, therefore, accepted "Blacky's" resignation in spite of the fact that classes were to begin two days later and that this would create a third unfilled full-time faculty vacancy in the Department of Business.

The following day, "Blacky" visited the building in which registration for the fall semester was taking place in order to say goodbye to faculty members and students he knew. As he turned to leave he was accosted by Dean Jones who stated that O'Riley had reported that "Blacky" was "creating a disturbance" and "should be kicked out of the gym." At that time, "Blacky" had not received any notice that his resignation from his academic position had been accepted. As a result, "Blacky" wrote in a letter to the regents that "O'Riley's fast reaction time in considering me a nonfaculty member (even before I received a letter honoring my resignation) is in sharp contrast to the university's slow reaction time in hiring business professors. Thus, SU seems more interested in severing people from the university than in hiring them!"

On the third day of fall semester, a group of concerned students met with Anderson to discuss the fact that 22 of the 47 courses offered by the Department of Business did not have instructors. They were further concerned because many of the instructorless courses were upper division and graduate courses which are required for graduation. In spite of the fact that Anderson had already received the letter from the members of the department expressing serious concern about the three unfilled full-time departmental positions, he said he was unaware of the problem because he had been out of town the latter part of the previous week. He blamed O'Riley for the problem. According to Anderson, O'Riley was in charge of reviewing and recommending hiring for all vacancies. He stated, "O'Riley is in charge of this and has obviously not done it." In its account of the meeting, the *Poncho City Daily Press* also reported that O'Riley was hospitalized with a potentially serious illness. Anderson told the students that since he was not aware of the situation, he would "personally take over the responsibility for this problem."

On the day after the student confrontation, Anderson, and Jones, who had assumed the duties of the ailing O'Riley, met with Drs. Riskin, Mark, and Eaton to discuss and to seek their approval for the persons whom the administration had identified as instructors for the courses. In a letter which was sent to the chairman of the Board of Regents of Southern University, Drs. Riskin, Mark, and Eaton described the meeting and their response to it.

> **"Dean of Student Affairs Jones and/or President
> Anderson in most cases identified the individual who would teach
> each course. In some cases, the qualifications and previous
> teaching performances of the individuals were known to us; in**

these specific situations, our tentative recommendations coincided with theirs. In a number of other cases, however, the educational and experiential qualifications were less well known or not known at all to us. In these cases, we were presented with a fait accompli: a list of names matched with courses needing instructors but without written documentation from the candidates that they had applied in response to the public announcements to teach these courses or in some cases that they have an interest in teaching a business course. In fact, some of these vacancies have not to our knowledge been publicly advertised in accordance with Equal Employment Opportunity (EEO) procedures. To the best of our knowledge, we do not know unequivocally that President Anderson and Dean Jones received and reviewed written applications and credentials from each of these persons. In addition, so far as we know from the minimal amount of information supplied to us, none of these candidates had earned a Ph.D. or D.B.A. degree; nor is it clear to us that all of these individuals would be considered sufficiently qualified by departmental personnel, by representatives of accreditation agencies, or by members of the Graduate Council of Southern University to teach undergraduate and/or graduate classes.

"In sharp contrast to the situation described above, we point out that an advertisement was placed in proper channels by the Southern University (EEO) Office to notify the academic community of the openings for Ph.D. and D.B.A. personnel to teach courses on a full-time basis for the Department of Business. Proper concern was given to (EEO) procedures. Educational and experiential data were obtained from the candidates, were provided to the departmental search committee for review to determine qualifications in terms of departmental courses needing to be taught, and were used as the basis for recommendations to the dean of Academic Affairs, O'Riley. A copy of these recommendations was also hand-delivered to President Anderson's office on the same day. As of this time, we are not aware that the administration of Southern University has contacted the applicant who in the judgment of the departmental search committee is considered most qualified and highest ranked among those responding to the advertised positions with salary and rank negotiable. The administration of Southern University, however, has talked with an applicant who in the judgment of the members of the departmental search committee is less qualified in terms of education and experience. Yet within a time period of approximately 24 hours after the student confrontation, candidates whose written applications we have not seen as a matter of written record and whose educational and experiential qualifications we have not seen as a matter of written record are being offered jobs!

"Based on the procedures adopted by the search committee as compared to the method used in conjunction with the above-described meeting, we wish this demurrer of the selection process of the administration of Southern University to be made a matter of record:

1 We do not approve or condone the selection of lesser qualified personnel when better qualified candidates in the judgment of the members of the departmental search committee have not been contacted.

2 We do not approve or condone the selection of candidates regardless of qualifications until written evidence is available for review in a thorough and timely manner.

3 We do not approve or condone the selection of candidates regardless of qualifications unless we are assured by Southern University's EEO consultant that all EEO procedures have been faithfully followed.

4 We do not approve or condone the administration of Southern University's apparent lack of consideration for the following stated departmental objective: 'Increase to 75 percent the percentage of courses taught by full-time faculty members with the remaining courses taught by qualified resource personnel in the community and/or by members of other departments.' "

The Developments in the Department of Education and Psychology   During the summer of 1979, staffing problems also developed in the Department of Education and Psychology, the university's second largest department. One faculty member retired at the end of the 1978–1979 academic year. In July 1979 two popular and highly competent faculty members accepted administrative positions elsewhere at substantially higher rates of pay than the university offered. Both professors preferred to remain at SU. Both attempted to negotiate a higher salary but Anderson refused to negotiate with either of them even though it appeared that they would seriously consider staying at SU if even a portion of the salary differential were offered. After resigning, one of the two professors, who essentially doubled his salary by accepting the offered position, wrote a letter to the members of the Board of Regents which explained the negative circumstances surrounding his decision to resign: Anderson's offering of noncompetitive salaries; Anderson's unwillingness to negotiate salaries; Anderson's unwillingness to consider previous academic experiences in promotion decisions.

In an effort to fill the three departmental vacancies prior to the beginning of the fall semester, the departmental chairman asked Anderson to negotiate salary and rank with prospective candidates. Anderson refused to do so. As a result, there were also three unfilled full-time faculty vacancies in the Department of Education and Psychology when the fall semester began.

The department chairman responded to the staffing crisis by asking that each member of the department take one or more of the instructorless classes until such time as instructors could be hired. By doing so, all departmental classes had instructors. By mid-semester, all three positions had been filled by newly hired faculty members.

The August Regents' Meeting   Because of widespread university and public interest regarding a number of university-related problems, the regents held their monthly meeting in a large SU auditorium rather than in the small regents room where such meetings usually were held. Immediately prior to the meeting, 25–40 students displaying placards stating concern for the administration's handling of student-centered problems had marched through the administration building and into the auditorium where the regents' meeting was to be held. The placards carried such messages as: "Quality Begins at the Top," and "SU Professors—Here Today, Gone Tomorrow." Emotions during the demonstration ran high; in fact, when Anderson entered the auditorium, he was booed by a number of attendees. Among the significant items discussed during the open session of the meeting were these: 1) Two mid-level administrative personnel had filed suit against the university and/or Anderson because they had not been paid according to the terms of their current contracts. At an earlier meeting, the regents had advised Anderson to honor the contracts; but he had not done so. Again the regents advised him to pay the administrators according to their current contracts; 2) Anderson was questioned regarding the flexibility he had to pay faculty members. He advised the regents that in the specific case of new faculty he was already authorized to pay them at least $5,000 more than the minimum for their grade on the current salary schedule if they were well qualified; 3) When asked about the meeting involving himself, Dean Jones and Drs. Riskin, Mark, and Eaton, Anderson informed the regents that Riskin, Mark, and Eaton had agreed "with a single exception" to the list of names of instructors that the administration had selected following the student confrontation. Regent Escudero, after reading a copy of the letter of Drs. Riskin, Mark, and Eaton to the regents (quoted earlier in this case) and hearing Anderson's discussion of the merits of each of the hastily selected part-time instructors succinctly stated the student and full-time faculty concern by publicly stating, "I strongly recommend that the chief executive follow the intent of the Board of Regents in hiring the best qualified faculty, not just covering a class for the sake of covering a class." He further indicated that he found it "regrettable" that the university had to scramble to fill instructional positions after school started and doubted that the situation contributed to "quality education." As a direct result of the staffing problems in the Department of Business, the regents dropped an effort to have an accrediting team from the American Assembly of Collegiate Schools of Business evaluate the business department during the current academic year.

The Governor's Investigation of Problems at SU In late August and early September, students, faculty, and interested community members wrote a number of letters to the regents, legislators, and the governor expressing concern about the quality of education at SU. According to one account headlined "SU Improvises a Fill-In Business Faculty" in a major newspaper with statewide circulation, "The Governor's Office and the State Board of Educational Finance will be probing the vacancy situation in the school's business department. The Governor's Office has received almost a dozen letters daily from faculty and students concerning Dr. Black's resignation and the possible harmful effect on student and faculty morale."

In mid-September an article headlined, "Governor to 'Monitor' Troubled SU," quoted the governor as saying, "SU has had a great deal of trouble. We just want to see how we can improve operations. We are not investigating them; we are just going to monitor them." The governor declined to link the university review directly to the recent controversy in the SU Department of Business saying, "Generally, we need a great deal more correspondence and closer communications," with the university. The governor indicated that his staff would proceed through the channels of the Board of Educational Finance, the SU Board of Regents, and the university in its probe. "I am sure that I will be talking to Anderson at some time," the governor indicated, "but I am not going to be working against anyone."

Within a few weeks, the governor's special representative spent a week on the SU campus gathering information about the expressed concerns of students, faculty, and members of the community.

The Appointment of an Acting Dean of Academic Affairs   In September, another newspaper article provided this information:

> An acting academic dean has been named in a surprise move by Southern University's Anderson during a continuing dispute involving students and faculty apparently dismayed by administrative operations. Dr. Bruce Dominguez, formerly Chairman of Language and Literature Department, was named Tuesday by Dr. Anderson to act in the position of Dean of Academic Affairs until Dean O'Riley has recovered from illness. Apparently the latest action by Anderson will ensure campus preparation for a series of visitations early next year by accreditation agencies, including a team expected this spring from the North Central Association of Colleges and Secondary Schools. The announcement by Anderson of the appointment came only as the besieged president was drawing attention from the governor during the governor's regular press conference. Also planning to visit the campus next year will be other accreditation teams, including the Education Standards Commission of the State Department of Education.

The September Regents' Meeting   The regents' meeting in late September was noteworthy for two events: 1) Rudy Herrera, president of the SU student body, told the regents, "We are accomplishing what every member of the community least wanted, the deterioration of our campus. We can't even get students to come to Southern University, much less stay, because of bad publicity." He then added, "With an accreditation team visiting in the spring, there is talk of probation. Is this possible?" 2) The regents again discussed the litigation regarding salary contracts of two mid-level administrative personnel. Regent Escudero stated, "What concerns me is that we are continuing to expend taxpayers' dollars needlessly in this particular litigation." A motion to honor the contracts of the two midlevel administrative personnel was again passed. The chairman of the Board of Regents said to Anderson, "I think you can be absolutely legally right on an issue but you can be dead wrong as far as overall administration is concerned and general climate might be concerned."

The Faculty Vote of No Confidence   In its October meeting, approximately 75% of the general faculty approved a resolution of "no confidence" in Anderson and asked for his resignation.

The Governor Personally Investigates Problems at SU   The day after the faculty vote of "no confidence," the governor visited with Poncho City businessmen, community leaders, faculty, and students to discuss the SU situation. When the governor met with representatives of a powerful local union, Ramon Montoya, president of the local, cited "alleged improper treatment of Chicanos by college officials." He summarized the union's position by saying, "It is our feeling that the only way to solve this problem is by having Dr. Anderson resign."

The Student Senate Vote of "No Confidence"   On the day following the governor's visit, the student senate debated a resolution stating in part that "students no longer have confidence in the leadership of Dr. Anderson." The resolution asked that Anderson resign because "the current situation at SU has caused extensive hardship on the student body and because the students see no constructive change for the student body under the present administration." The resolution passed the student senate by a vote of eleven to one.

The October Regents' Meeting   Two weeks after the governor's visit, the Board of Regents of Southern University held its October meeting. At that time, they held a four and one-half hour closed session in which they met individually with Student body President Rudy Herrera; Faculty Senate Chairman Dr. John Morrison; Dean of Student Affairs Harry Jones; Acting Dean of Academic Affairs Dr. Bruce Dominguez; and President Will B. Anderson. The board reconvened in open session only long enough to adjourn the regular monthly meeting. After the adjournment, the chairman of the board declined to comment on what was discussed in the closed meeting. He said only, "It will have to unfold as it unfolds."

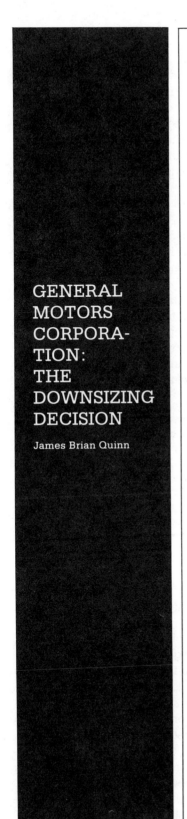

GENERAL MOTORS CORPORATION: THE DOWNSIZING DECISION

James Brian Quinn

In his book, *My Years with General Motors,*[1] Alfred P. Sloan, Jr., describes in detail the crucial policy shifts of the 1920s and 1930s that made General Motors Corporation the leading automobile manufacturer in the world. Emma Rothschild later summarized these shifts rather colorfully as follows:

> Ford in the early 1920s made about half of all cars sold in America, and General Motors about one quarter; by the middle of the 1930s the position was reversed. The transition from Ford leadership to GM leadership can stand for the transformation of the industry. Henry Ford wrote passionately about the 1920s, about industrial and engineering expansion, about the falling prices of his Model T's. . . . Alfred Sloan of GM wrote with similar rapture about his company's expansion in the 1930s, about the development and elaboration of the car market, about the rising quality and rising prices of GM cars, their bright colors and sculptured lines.[2]

GM had developed a complete spectrum of automobiles, consisting of five well-known lines. Each line had several models, occupied a specified price-quality niche, changed its styles annually, and competed not just with other manufacturers but also—at the margin—with other GM lines. This basic posture continued through the 1950s and well into the 1960s. Each line fulfilled a designated portion of GM's goal "to supply a car for every purse and every purpose." The late 1960s brought changes that would slowly alter the whole strategic posture of General Motors, then the largest industrial corporation in the world.

HIGHWAY SAFETY

In 1965, reportedly motivated by his outrage over a small girl's unnecessary death in an automobile accident, Ralph Nader wrote *Unsafe at Any Speed,* a scathing indictment of the whole automobile industry. One of the targets he picked out for special treatment was GM's first serious entry into the U.S. small car field, the Corvair. Although acclaimed by engineers for its innovative design, the Corvair's rear suspension system became a focal point of Nader's attack. With the Nader book and testimony as a catalyst—and with a televised furor over GM's lawyers' having detectives tail Nader—Congress passed the National Traffic and Motor Vehicle Safety Act of 1966.[3]

Copyright, 1978, James Brian Quinn, The Amos Tuck School of Business Administration, Dartmouth College, Hanover, New Hampshire. All rights reserved. Reprinted by permission. The point of view and arrangement of materials in this case study are the author's. Mrs. W. L. Baldwin was Research Associate on this case.

This Act led to the issuance of a number of initial safety standards, covering such items as seat belts, energy absorbing instrument panels, lights, energy absorbing steering columns, etc. for all automobiles sold in the U.S. General Motors and the industry had earlier subscribed to self-imposed Society of Automotive Engineers (SAE) standards on structural features affecting automobiles. Since these formed the basis of the 1967 mandatory standards, many had already been incorporated into U.S. automobile design. Later safety standards became more complex and reached into other areas of vehicle design and performance.

Automotive Safety Engineering   In 1965–66 the Automotive Safety Engineering Group was formed to act as a bridge between the Federal government and GM operating divisions. Under GM's decentralized philosophy the car divisions were still responsible for the design, sale, and profitability of their lines. Auto Safety Engineering made sure that the proper parties within GM: (1) understood the nature of the new safety requirements, (2) could meet the standards, and (3) integrated the standards into all aspects of their operation. At first a number of operating people felt confused, insulted, or genuinely hurt. They had spent their lives as professionals trying to design safe vehicles that customers would buy. Now they were being told by regulators with a lot less expertise how their cars must perform. Some were not too keen about the idea or too impressed with many of the regulatory proposals. But as one member of Auto Safety Engineering said:

> Despite resistance on both sides, we tried to walk the government regulators patiently through the details of what we could and could not do. At the beginning of the Safety Act the regulatory people were not always very technically expert in the automotive field. We tried to go through each proposed change slowly and carefully so they could understand the issues and how complex any change in this industry is. And we tried to explain the purpose of the regulations to our managers and designers. At first the government people were leery of this, and some of our design people were quite impatient. Now both are responding more and more.

Later, some of Nader's allegations about the 1960–63 Corvair were investigated by the National Highway Safety Bureau, which concluded that the Corvair's "handling and stability performance is at least as good as the performance of some contemporary vehicles both domestic and foreign."[4] Nevertheless, the production of Corvair ended in May 1969, partly because of the bad press the car had received from Nader's book and partly because of changed consumer preferences. At that time GM had not lost a single final court case on the Corvair.[5] Earlier the company's chairman, Mr. Roche, had made a public apology to Nader because of the "tailing incident." As one executive said, "Everyone around here was terribly embarrassed about the whole affair. Soon thereafter, a strong feeling emerged at the top that the standards were here to stay—that we had better believe them and accept them."

In early 1969, a safety engineer was put in Washington to act as liaison between GM and the regulatory groups. This liaison provided a single point of contact within GM for the safety regulators and helped establish Automotive Safety Engineering as the group that would coordinate all responses on safety issues for GM.

Responding to the new regulations required important attitude changes. The way these were implemented was, according to several different executives ". . . very individual and highly personalized" . . . "Various top executives took individuals aside and said to them 'We are in the public arena now whether we like it or not; and all our statements and actions must reflect this.' " . . . "A hard line, 'goddam-it-we-just-make-cars' attitude was no longer realistic. At meetings management started saying 'the standards are here to stay. Find out what the regulators are doing. Help them out. We have to learn to live with this.' . . . It all took time but the process was effective."

The Basic Dilemma   Over the years the Department of Transportation (DOT) and its National Highway Traffic Safety Administration (NHTSA)* have developed numerous safety standards and regulations, affecting many aspects of auto safety performance and design. By 1975 such standards had added 169 pounds to GM's (2,400 pound) compact car weight and 275 pounds to the (4,375 pound) standard Chevrolet.[6] One regulation—that requiring a seat belt interlock system—had proved so unpopular that it was eliminated by Congressional action. Congress also specifically retained the right to make the final decision on the controversial air bag safety device. The industry accepted many regulations as reasonable or inevitable. Others—like air bags and 5 mph shock resistant bumpers favored by individuals within DOT or NHTSA— were severely questioned as expensive, fuel consuming, experimental, or ineffective in meeting the needs of automotive safety. Nevertheless automobile companies were required to work on the development of such features. And GM volunteered to install production capacity to provide some 100,000 cars with air bags as optional equipment (but only some 10,000 cars so equipped were sold over a 3-year period).

It was theoretically possible to design a car that very few people would be killed in. But several GM spokesmen expressed the company's basic dilemma concerning product safety. "Such a car would be an elaborate and prohibitively expensive tank, and no one would buy it. We also know that eliminating potentially unsafe drivers, requiring people to use their safety belts, and more thorough driver training and law enforcement would save many more lives less expensively. But we feel very uncomfortable recommending mandatory actions in these areas. After all, such things impinge upon the personal freedom of our customers, their values, and their choices."

AIR QUALITY CONCERNS

By the late 1960s the public had begun to voice serious concerns about the impact of the automobile on air quality. The problem first emerged in the 1950s smogs of Los Angeles when studies began to indicate that sunlight broke down trapped automotive exhaust gases into eye-stinging ozone and nitrous oxide compounds. At first, top GM officials were skeptical that their product was to blame. At this stage GM contributed limited amounts of scientific talent, primarily to see whether the automobile was in fact a major contributor to smog. Once Dr. Arie J. Haagen-Smit of Cal. Tech. had

---

*NHTSA was created by the Highway Safety Act of 1970. It combined the National Traffic Safety Bureau and the National Highway Safety Bureau established by the DOT Act of 1966.

identified the composition of photochemical smog[7] and the mechanisms through which the automobile contributed to it, the company made a determined technical effort to reduce emissions drastically. By 1966 all new cars sold in California had crankcase (1961) and exhaust control (1966) devices which reduced emissions of some hydrocarbon and carbon monoxide pollutants by about 40%. Under the Clean Air Act Amendments of 1965 these became standard on all new U.S. cars in 1968. GM also test-marketed a kit to reduce older cars' pollution some 30–50%. But in the smog-prone Phoenix (Arizona) area—despite an intensive promotional campaign—only 528 of an estimated 334,000 potential customers were willing to pay the approximate $20 cost for such a retrofit.[8]

The 1970 Clean Air Act Amendments   In 1970 HEW proposed tighter exhaust standards for 1975 cars to reduce hydrocarbons 97%, carbon monoxide 91%, and nitrogen oxide effluents 85% below uncontrolled levels.[9] Then in a sudden move, led by Senator Muskie of Maine, Congress passed the Clean Air Act Amendments of 1970, cutting these permissible effluent levels essentially in half. Although no specific cost benefit studies suggested the new standards as optimum, the Senate passed the "Muskie Bill" with a close to unanimous vote. Mr. E. N. Cole, then GM's President, had earlier said the Muskie standards "simply aren't attainable . . . with existing technology" and had proposed an alternate set based upon GM's own calculations.[10]

Nevertheless, General Motors now had to meet the new standards. A variety of options existed including the stratified charge engine, catalytic converters, or entirely new engines—like the Wankel rotary design. All had their proponents and opponents inside and outside the company. Because of the importance of this and other similar decisions, GM formed a Research Policy Committee consisting of top level technical, operating, and financial people to weigh the alternatives. GM took a license on the Wankel engine, reportedly prepared to spend some $50 million on its development.[11] Many engineers preferred the stratified charge engine—which was satisfactorily demonstrated on small cars and later successfully scaled up by Honda for a demonstration 6-cylinder Chevrolet-sized engine. But GM's decision eventually favored the catalytic converter approach.

Although requiring use of completely nonleaded fuel, the catalytic converter: (1) provided the ability for better gasoline mileage than some alternative approaches; (2) allowed GM to use its existing engine manufacturing facilities; (3) could immediately be adapted to all engines regardless of size; (4) could be guaranteed to meet effluent standards for 50,000 miles (while radically redesigned engines might fail to meet standards if they wore differentially during this period); (5) avoided extensively retraining dealers, mechanics, customers, service stations, and the full infrastructure necessary to maintain redesigned engines. Even before Congress passed the Clean Air Amendments of 1970, GM was planning to install catalytic converters on all 1975 models,[12] and it was urging the oil companies to reconstitute fuels to eliminate lead and sulphur and reduce other toxic components.[13] But the 1970 standards required a crash program to get large scale catalytic converter production underway in the fall of 1974.

Damned If You Do or Don't   Many GM executives referred to the high risk of this decision. A $100-million plant had to be constructed and put into operation in 3 years. It had to produce an entirely new product to work continuously and safely on millions of vehicles for at least 50,000 miles. GM knew that the cost and availability of platinum for the catalyst could make the converter a difficult long-term solution. The new plant had to proceed into early construction stages while researchers were still trying to find a proper blend of sufficiently effective and available catalysts to make this solution realistic. Yet these catalysts would become the very heart of the product the plant was to make.

Similarly, decisions on the product's size, container shape, mechanics, catalyst form (pellet or solid), expected fuels chemistry, production volume, etc., had to be factored in as the plant was being built. Then there was the very real problem of testing sample devices adequately to guarantee 50,000 miles of service after release on a mass production basis. One GM executive later said, "Frankly we got lucky. The converters worked better than we ever expected. We actually improved on gas mileage. Then we found ourselves in the incongruous position of losing credibility by performing better than we thought we could. Our earlier statements about the difficulty or 'impossibility' of the standards were thrown in our faces. We were accused of lying or foot dragging. You are damned if you do and damned if you don't."

The company was frequently stumped in finding an effective way to present its case to the public. During the 1960s California smog crisis, it found that careful technical discussions about the unknowns of air chemistry provided no answer to emotional demagogues who used simplistic slogans like: "smog kills," "you're destroying the lungs of millions," or "GM is the worst polluter in the world." Complex arguments about economic trade-offs were useless against simple statistics comparing auto fatalities to war casualties or gory photographs of accident victims. As the largest auto company, GM bore the brunt of numerous attacks on the industry. These culminated in Earth Day's ritual burials of large American automobiles and in Ralph Nader's 1970 "Campaign GM" attack.

Nader's purpose was "to pursuade GM's nearly 1.5 million stockholders to demand stronger public interest efforts by GM. . . ."[14] At the May stockholders meeting a proposal was put forward "to add three representatives of the public" to GM's Board. Another would have set up a shareholders' "Committee of Corporate Responsibility." Both were overwhelmingly defeated at the meeting. But the company did appoint a "Public Policy Committee" of directors later that year. Soon thereafter it established a Science Advisory Committee of distinguished independent scientists to insure that GM responded properly to developing evidence about the impact of its products on the environment. And in February 1971, Ernest S. Starkman, a University of California (Berkeley) professor, well respected in engineering and environmental circles, became Vice President of Environmental Activities for GM.

SMALL CARS AND FUELS

About this same time two other major issues began to achieve prominence—the invasion of foreign car imports into the U.S. market and a projected rise in fuels costs. In March 1969 *Fortune* pointed out that foreign cars' share of the U.S. market had risen from below 5% in 1962 to more than 10% in 1968. And that share was expected to increase to 14% in 1970.[15] *Fortune* chided the industry noting that:

> **The perennial ability of the U.S. auto industry to sell**
> **by the millions a product so complex and expensive as the motorcar**

is one of the marvels of commerical history. But for the last dozen years the feat has been blemished by the industry's repeated failure to grasp the true nature of the minority market for small cars. . . . [In the early 1960s, American compacts had achieved] an initial stunning success. . . . By 1962 they had won a market of almost 1,800,000 cars a year . . . and had cut U.S. sales of imported cars to little more than half the 1959 level. But as the compacts grew in size and price, their sales declined and imports rebounded.[16]

GM spent about $100 million for design and manufacturing techniques to produce its new compact, Vega, in fall 1970. It assembled the Vega in an automated plant in Lordstown, Ohio. The plant was designed in part to eliminate some of the more onerous jobs on older assembly lines. Both the plant and the Vega later ran into significant problems. Emma Rothschild and the commercial press attacked the plant's automated features and played up the alienation of "the new generation" of workers. Company investigations indicated these were "press issues," that the "new work-force" was not radically different from that in other plants, and that in some cases workers were actually "putting on" the press visitors. After a 3-week strike at Lordstown in March 1972, the plant settled down and became an efficient operation. But Vega's higher than expected price and early quality problems—overheating aluminum engine block, body rust, and three safety recalls—held sales well below its expected 400,000 sales level in 1971. Meanwhile Volkswagen led in small car sales with 520,000 in units sold.[17]

Fuel Efficiency   In the early 1970s there was still a glut in world oil supplies. Nevertheless, analyses in the GM Chief Economist's Office began to project a developing U.S. dependency on foreign oil and the likelihood of higher future oil prices. These concerns led the board in 1972 to create an ad hoc energy task force headed by David C. Collier, then Treasurer, later head of GM of Canada and then the Buick Division. Collier's group included people from manufacturing, research, design, finance, industry-government relations, and the economics staff. After a half year's research, in May of 1973 the task force went to the board with three conclusions: (1) there was a developing energy problem, (2) the government had no particular plan to deal with it, (3) energy costs would have a profound effect on GM's business. Collier's report created a good deal of discussion around the company in the ensuing months. "We were trying to get other people to think about the issue," said Richard C. Gerstenberg, then chairman of GM.[18]

"There was not a good feel as to when all this would come to a head, and no complete strategy was worked out to cope with it," said one of the executives involved. Nevertheless GM initiated work on two fuel-efficient car designs in the U.S. and in Germany. These became known as the "K Body" (later Seville) and "T Body" (later Chevette). And the board asked Collier's group to report back in October 1973 with an analysis of the company's overall product program. GM also began to experiment with stack gas scrubbers and to convert some of its own internal power plants from oil to coal. Mr. Gerstenberg even got blistered by some of the utilities for suggesting that electric power be produced with coal, not oil. But no one expected the embargo and dramatic oil price increases that hit the U.S. in late 1973, when posted prices of oil rose from $2.59 to $11.56 per barrel between May and December, with some oil auctioned off at $17 per barrel.

Instead GM sales had reached highs in both 1972 and early 1973. Throughout the industry, mid-1973 production was near maximum capacity, slowed only by delays in parts deliveries.[19] But GM profits were lower than anticipated by some analysts. One speculated GM was being hurt by the buyers' interest in small economical cars at a time when GM's lines were focused on large cars and compacts.[20] Another stated, "The surge in imported car sales has stunned Detroit's top marketing executives, who believed that the [Nixon] devaluation triggered increases in car prices [and the elimination of the surtax on U.S. cars] would finally halt the steady rise in imports."[21]

The Embargo   The October 1973 oil embargo hit GM hard. The company closed 16 of its 24 assembly plants for a week in December 1973 and cut first quarter 1974 schedules 15–20%. A crash increase in capital spending for small car capacity came too late. GM's share of the new car market dropped from 45% in 1972–73 to 37.5% by March.[22] Early quarterly profits dropped 85% and 62% below the preceding year's[23] and annual earnings per share fell from $8.34 to $3.27.[24] The company stopped construction projects at one Oldsmobile and two Buick plants because of declining large car sales,[25] and a new goal was set to boost small car output to 40% of production by fall 1974.[26]

While GM moved to expand its small car production, it was not ready to abandon its traditional interest in larger lines. Some 75% of its late 1973 cars had V-8 engines. Still GM expanded its smaller engine plants in 1974 and bought back tooling for a V-6 line it had sold to AMC in 1968. After GM's annual meeting in May 1974, Chairman Gerstenberg announced, "In 1975 we will offer a new small car in every GM division."[27] The Chevrolet, Oldsmobile, Pontiac, and Buick small cars would be variations of the Vega. And Cadillac would offer its own special compact.[28] GM was also "speeding programs to first lighten—and eventually shrink—all its big cars."[29]

These were among the first public announcements of the most momentous shift in GM's product posture since Alfred Sloan's restructuring of the 1920s. They were made against a backdrop of great uncertainty about which direction customer preferences would take. Mr. Gerstenberg predicted "the family car will continue to command a major if somewhat lesser share of the market." Richard L. Terrell, then GM's executive Vice President, said, "Some see 50–60% small cars (in the near future) . . . but we see the possibility of it swinging the other way."[30]

Some Drastic Revisions   Mr. Elliott M. (Pete) Estes, later president of GM, described the way these corporate decisions were reached. "We had done a lot of talking and thinking about how to modify our line to meet developing fuel economy, environmental, and customer demands. In October 1973 the Middle East War broke out, the embargo came on the 22nd, and the curtain came down on auto sales. This led us to discuss our reactions in somewhat more of a 'panic mode' than we would have liked. We concluded: (1) we should have a car smaller than Vega, (2) we needed a smaller luxury car. The members of the executive committee essentially arrived at a consensus on these approaches during its regular daily work sessions at the lunch hour. GM had to introduce these cars faster than ever before. We had always operated with the GM committee system which was very slow. We knew we would have to bypass our usual procedures. The decisions on these two cars were basically made in October-December 1973."

It is difficult to pinpoint the precise time when these "decisions"—or many other major decisions—in General Motors were actually made. Well prior to the presentation of matters at formal sessions of GM's governing committees and policy groups, a broad consensus is generally obtained among members of senior management. Part of this occurs as members of the executive committee sit along with other key staff and operating executives on various policy groups—subcommittees of the executive committee—where important topics are discussed. In addition, all top executives receive continuing input on significant matters from varied levels of the organization outside of the formal setting of policy group meetings.

Fortunately the company had been designing smaller cars for years. The executive committee had agreed that the new subcompact car "had to be number one in fuel economy." None of the domestic designs would do this. The corporation therefore reached across the Atlantic to pick up its "T car"—a car that had originally been designed in Germany, introduced in Brazil, contained an engine produced in Brazil, and was being restyled in Britain. Britain had a "three-door design," larger than a standard small car, with a modern look, and more storage space because of the rear door. The executive committee wanted an available car which would do the best job and be flexible for future changes. On January 23, 1974, the decision was to go ahead and introduce the "T car"—soon-to-be Chevette—to the U.S. in an unprecedented eighteen months. As Estes later said, "The job had to be done in a hell of a hurry. We flew a team to Germany to pick up the drawings for the Chevette. We even stayed with the metric systems to simplify our problems in debugging the car over here."

The search for a fuel-efficient luxury car disclosed that GM had a design that was partially completed in engineering. But the vehicle had never been fully developed because people had perceived the car as having a marketing appeal primarily limited to the relatively few customers who traditionally bought Mercedes class cars. The clay models were finished, and many parts were already being made in the United States. Mr. Estes said, "We made the decision to kick off the [Cadillac] Seville on January 23, too. We wanted production on the Seville by March 27, 1975, and the Chevette by August 18, 1975. People said we'd have to do something exotic to meet the Mercedes quality challenge. We decided to introduce fuel injection into the car. The car had to have a formal look. It had to come out at the top of the line. Previously, big was good, and bigger was better. Now we had to put a smaller car, at a higher price, at the top of the line. Other than increasing the back seat room by two inches, we accepted the clay models. Essentially two or three of us agreed on what needed to be done and rammed it through . . . but all of us came out of the closet together."

DOWNSIZING THE LINE

By themselves, these two decisions would have been simply the introduction of two new models—common enough for an auto company. But they were made in the context of other events, which ultimately led to the downsizing of the total GM line.

A New Concept for GM?   How did this concept come into being? Mr. Gail Smith, General Director of GM Advertising and Merchandising, said, "Downsizing was a part of a recognition that fuel economy would be an important factor in the marketplace. Foreign cars were attracting a sizable share of the market in the early 1970s. Our market research showed many foreign car buyers made very different tradeoffs from big-car customers. They discounted comfort heavily in favor of maneuverability or gas mileage. We also recognized there were whole new social trends in the life styles of younger people, new family forms, and so on. But we had trouble competing with their favorite, Volkswagen, until the devaluation in 1973." Despite some compact entries, the Vega and Monza, GM did not have a strong presence in the extremely small car field.

One executive said, "In the early 1970s, there was a distinct awareness of a conservation—or economy—ethic. This contributed to the early 1971–72 concepts of what became the Cadillac Seville. But our conclusions were really at the conversational level: that the big car trend was nearing its end. At that time there was certainly no tendency to go whole hog in emphasizing economy-conservation factors. We were not at all sure sufficient numbers of large car buyers were ready to move to dramatically smaller-lighter cars. We were dreadfully aware of how Chrysler had been hurt by moving too soon to smaller cars in earlier years." The company was then thinking in terms of a relatively modest downsizing to be followed by successive and more drastic product changes in later years.

In April 1973, a 10-year product plan was presented to corporate top management. In each division there had traditionally been 5-year plans. These had to be extended and revised to reflect a 10-year horizon. Mr. Estes said, "This is the first such 10-year presentation I can remember. The intermediates [A body] designs were new in 1973. But the larger cars [B and C bodies] were up for redesign in 1977. Fuel costs were rising and fuel economy appeared saleable. So we set an initial target of reducing weight by 400 pounds. This figure had two merits: (1) we couldn't figure out how to get out more weight than that, (2) it would give us one more mile per gallon in fuel economy. But we needed to do this without decreasing the comfort level, baggage capability, or six-person capacity of the cars."

Informal Discussions   Another executive described the decision process as follows: "There were a lot of informal discussions going on among different people and small groups around the company. Even at the top level I don't think there was an attempt to get everybody together to analyze this as a momentous issue. At the Product Policy Group level a lot of discussion always occurs before a formal meeting. From this, perhaps 6–7 key people will convince themselves—for a variety of reasons—that something must be done. That is where the crucial decisions are really made. In an organization as big as this, it is very important that the major decision makers appear to be together when a big decision is reached. They don't even want too much difference in viewpoint within the meeting as to the sense of direction their comments may convey. Otherwise there could be a lot of confusion throughout the design process. The major conceptual decisions are really thoroughly discussed and reviewed before the formal meeting. In the meeting they make a number of small decisions which require the authority of the group. . . .

"The formal meeting is just to make sure everything gets looked at. One is forced to listen to a complete rationale. We get clear cost estimates and a thoroughly worked out plan for a given product line. Everybody feels much more comfortable about the decisions after they have been discussed in a forum like that. More importantly, the line people know how we are planning to get where we are going. The more they understand this, the more they know what to do on their own as the program progresses.

"At the product design level one doesn't hear much about the total structure of the company's line. Management doesn't issue precise instructions on how to position the B car, for example. Instead, the messgae would come as 'provide full space and function for the customer, but with much greater fuel economy.' Against that instruction, proposals come forward through a specified procedure. But there is a lot of moving out of channels in this organization. Product Planning knows in advance what is acceptable. People are involved in a lot of presentations at multiple levels. Everybody knows everyone. And the top decision makers have actually had a chance to meet and deal with a number of people on a person-to-person basis. We try to keep these key decision makers informed about the marketplace and whom to go to for detailed information. They have input from formal presentations, from continuous flow of informal information, and also bring to bear their own considerable experience garnered from a lifetime career in the transportation business."

The Project Center   An important change in the design process occurred in early 1973. Prior to this time, most major components of the car had been assigned to a specific division as "lead group" for its design; for example, air conditioning went to Pontiac, frames to Chevrolet, brakes to Buick, etc. This had been begun in 1964 to promote commonality in parts and resultant scale economies. Previously each car division had designed the entire car minus the Fisher Body. Slowly more and more parts and systems were brought under a lead division's control. The corporation tried to get as many common parts as possible to ensure efficiency without impairing marketability. But the car divisions maintained control over those aspects which lent individual difference—grilles, bumpers, trim, dashboards, ride, handling characteristics, etc.—and marketability to their lines.

As the conversation centered on eliminating 400 pounds from the B and C cars, even more coordination was needed. Mr. Estes said, "Rather than just turn this over to the divisions, we formed a Project Center to coordinate the task.[31] We wanted to get most of the advantages of a centralized engineering group without losing the advantages of divisionalization. Pontiac's assistant chief engineer, Bill Collins, was brought in to be project manager. The development engineers were on a loan basis from all divisions. Typically, we would take an engineering manager from the lead division on each major component involved. We wanted a new design that would give each section of the car as much compatibility as possible across the full GM line."

Collins had certain general guidelines for the cars. The car designers had "packaged" the external features of the car. And management had approved that package. Mr. R. L. Dorn, Chief Engineer, Corporate Car Programs, said, "The Project Center group had a feeling for the kind of car they wanted. The objective was basically a B/C (regular car) space interior with an A body (intermediate) exterior. It was to have an A car weight, but perform functionally for the same sized people, number of people, and use patterns as then current B/C cars. The project group was to optimize the efficiency of the design. At first we only assumed we were making a car for a B/C price. We knew there would still be A cars on the market. And in engineering we also had a feeling for the cost and volume figures. But we didn't work out these figures specifically. That is the province of the finance group. As we moved forward we understood more and more what the target economic specifications for the car would be."

In April 1973 the Project Center took over system interface negotiations that had previously occurred at the divisional level—i.e., when component, subsystem, or marketing-design conflicts affected two or more divisions. Generally, this gave much more rapid feedback for the whole design process, both for engineers and management. But a Project Manager could not force a car division to accept a standardized part. The general manger and chief engineer of each car division had to be satisfied with the change for it to be implemented. Enough time and discussions were essential to make sure these key people were comfortable with their final product offering. The Project Center concept augmented, rather than replaced, the lead division concept. Its success rested on the same delicate balance of persuasion and direction that underlay the rest of GM's complex system of coordinated decentralization. (For a more detailed amplification of GM's decision making style, see Appendix A.)

Downsizing Goals   Mr. Dorn said, "When I came to the Project Center in November 1973, the original goals for downsizing had not been modified very much. But the embargo had caused a major sales loss and a lot of rethinking of the approved program content for the redesign of the large car lines. We began to bring up and address other design alternatives with the result that the car sizes were cut a bit more. Shortly thereafter (December 1973), the Product Policy Committee posed a lot of 'what if' objectives. What if we gave you this—or that—weight objective? We pointed out that we could meet different objectives, but at a cost—of aluminum, tooling, structural materials, etc. As a result of these discussions some models had to reduce their wheel base further, and we had to take a lot of investment out of the B/C programs."

The Product Policy Committee soon decided that the 10-year plan had to be drastically revised. From a product policy viewpoint, the goal became "to get approximately 3 mpg improvement." This meant removing some 800—1000 pounds of vehicle weight for most cars. Estes again said, "We had found by then that taking weight out of one area had an additive effect. A pound out of the body lightened the chassis; both lightened the engine, which helped the chassis some more—and so on. The target of 3-miles-per-gallon (800–1000) improvement was intended as a challenge. . . . It was arrived at as a seat-of-the-pants judgment. But everyone agreed it *was* a challenge. . . . We wanted to accomplish this while maintaining six-passenger seating capacity, the same luggage space, and equal or greater comfort characteristics in the vehicle."

Key Thrusts and Increments   A marketing executive said, "Strategy formulation here tends to be pretty amorphous, but with a few key threads. For example, there was some discussion as to whether we should drop full-sized cars altogether. But this was not long or drawn out. There was substantial psychological commitment to total market coverage, hence little serious thought that we should serve only selected functions in the marketplace. . . . The strategy really evolved in a series of incremental steps. As one of my colleagues says: when I was younger I always conceived of a room where all these concepts were carefully worked out for the whole company. Later I didn't find any such room. . . .

"In this company there is a real competition of ideas. We thrive on the adversary process. Anyone with a good idea can get heard. The top people have been around a long time. They know each other and their way down in the organization very well. They have had many opportunities to appraise people's actions, their capabilities, their judgments. In this kind of organization, there are rarely single instants of decision. I frequently don't know precisely when a decision is made in General Motors. I don't remember being in a committee meeting when things came to a vote. Usually someone will simply summarize a developing position. Everyone else either nods or states his particular terms of consensus."

The December 23rd Meeting   A crucial meeting on product strategy occurred on December 23, 1973. The Executive Committee (GM's seven top officials) met in the Technical Center's design dome to review various proposals of the car divisions and the Product Policy Committee (the Engineering Policy Group at that time). Discussion was lively, intense, but not prolonged. Whenever there was a choice between a division's view and corporate's, Mr. Gerstenberg listened carefully to both viewpoints, and generally sided with the divisions. For example, there was some inclination within the executive committee not to have Buick and Oldsmobile in the small car field. Gerstenbarg backed the divisions' desire to have a full range of automobiles for their dealers. Mr. Cole preferred a larger (though scaled down) Cadillac. But the division had designed the Seville and preferred it. Again Gerstenberg chose the division's viewpoint.

One of the executives present said, "So much of the December 23 discussion was really instinct; there were strong feelings, rather than studies or data, that said every division should have a small car in its line. Some board members had been very vocal in pressing Gerstenberg for smaller cars. The Olds and Buick groups were influenced primarily by concern for the competitive positon of their dealers. The Cadillac Division staff saw they needed a smaller car. And Chevrolet felt it needed a car still smaller than its Vega to offer its dealers. The decision process was highly unstructured." But as a result of this meeting the executive committee instructed the engineers to make the final modifications on small cars for each line and to complete the pending plans for substantial reductions in the 1977 big cars.

How and When to Downsize   There had been much discussion as to when and how to downscale the various lines. How would downsized large cars affect the intermediates? Why not just put the Impala name on a modified Chevelle? How could the company maintain differences between the downsized line and the next smaller line? GM could not afford to downsize all its line at once. Yet it wanted to have the highest possible effect on fuel efficiency, while maintaining saleability and not developing any gaps in its total line. The final consensus—like the other decisions concerning target specifications—was largely achieved during the Executive Committee's lunch sessions in December 1973. GM would downsize the B and C cars first. This keyed in part to the fact that the A cars had just gone through a major redesign. But it also reflected a complex of other factors.

Mr. Estes said, "Our real job was to move our customers over to a fuel economic car without taking anything from them. It was very important for us to maintain our customers. One of the big problems was to get the dealers to realize the full potential of these newly designed cars. From the start, we emphasized that the downsized regular car would not sacrifice the interior space, comfort, or value of the 'regular' car, and was not a 'compact' or 'smaller' car. We knew that our prices had to be competitive. And there had to be an opportunity for our dealers to maintain profitability. Many reporters at first thought the resized line would be a disaster and said so. But when people actually saw the new cars standing by themselves they looked big enough. I said the only difference the customer would notice was that he had more room to walk around it in his garage."

Small Cars for Each Line   In February 1974—after Chevette and Seville were approved—GM management decided to let Buick, Oldsmobile, and Pontiac each have its own small car. The Chevrolet small car was the Nova, Pontiac's was the Ventura, Oldsmobile's the Omega, and Buick's the Skylark, Oldsmobile also offered the Starfire, and Pontiac got the Astra, a Vega size car. These were to support each division's dealer body in light of the plummeting 1973–74 sales of large cars.

In response to an early 1974 Federal Energy Administration (FEA) inquiry about what GM could do to improve fuel economy, a GM task force produced a report, *Comments by the General Motors Corporation to the Federal Energy Administration on Passenger Car Fuel Economy,* dated August 1974. Somewhat earlier Congress had asked the Ford Administration to study the feasibility of a 20% improvement by 1980 in fleet mpg performance. The Administration responded in what is euphemistically known as the "120 Day Report" with the statement that fuel economy could be improved 50% by 1980. The Energy Resources Council, headed by Rogers Morton, geared up what became the "voluntary fuel economy program." A series of meetings and letters with the auto industry followed. GM indicated that it "had committed itself to an all out effort" to meet or exceed the 18.7 mpg fleet goal (or 50% improvement) by 1980. GM pointed out in the letters that emission standards more stringent than the 1975 levels and weight added to meet future safety standards could adversely affect its ability to reach the goal. These letters became the "voluntary aggreement" with President Ford in early 1975.

Discipline and "Plastic Cars"   In mid-1974 the Environmental Protection Agency (EPA) came forth with its proposed methods for measuring the mileage and exhaust characteristics of automobiles. Cars would be tested according to weight classes, with all cars in a given class measured in terms of the midpoint of their weight class. For example, all cars in the 3750–4250 pound weight band would be tested with a 4000 pound dynamometer load. Mr. Dorn said, "As these standards became clear, the Product Policy Committee decided to put all the B cars into the 4000 pound EPA weight class. All C body cars would go into the 4500 pound class. Later, after the Project Center showed that this was feasible in the new sizes, the car divisions' Chief Engineers decided to move station wagons from the 5000 to 4500 pound weight class. This move was approved by top management. These became the real design objectives, not a specific weight reduction per se. They really dictated the move from the initial target weight reduction of 400 pounds to what became 700–1000 pound reductions for specific models.

"Oddly enough, the EPA classifications became the discipline to control the weight of a car. Previously, there was always a temptation to solve a problem by adding a little more weight. Each car's weight crept up—incremented by minor design changes. But if we didn't watch the EPA standards carefully we paid a great penalty both on emissions and on dynamometer mileage ratings. In our early planning, we built in a 3% reserve below our target weight to allow for errors in estimating and other miscellaneous contingencies. Then as the program got further along in its evolution, we might weed out some of the most costly weight reducing features and still not suffer heavy penalties in meeting the EPA weight category. Of course, the divisions had a real incentive to perform in this business-like manner.

"Initially, we proposed a program using a lot of aluminum and substitute materials to meet the new 'mass' targets. But this would have meant a very high cost, and would have strained the suppliers' aluminum capacity. However, when we presented this program to management, they said, 'Okay, if necessary, we'll do it.' They didn't back down. We began to understand then that they were dead serious. Feeling that the company would spend the money was critical to the success of the entire mass reduction effort.

"In addition, new computer techniques gave us a big boost. Because of computer design techniques we could get a much more thoroughly worked out design before we went to prototypes. This meant that the divisions could spend more on their prototypes and tooling. And the cars that went into production were much more thoroughly developed. Because of these several factors, I believe the new B/C cars perhaps represented the best car design strategy we had ever had.

"We were really under the gun for time and money. Fortunately, the divisions assigned topflight people to the Project Center. These people began searching for entirely new ways to do things. This was also the first real participation by the GM Assembly Division in a whole new car."

Set up in 1965 "to tighten and revamp assembly operations that GM believed had becme seriously deficient under car divisional direction," General Motors Assembly Division had taken over all but 4 of GM's 22 assembly plants by early 1972.[32] The shift was seen as a centralizing move to cut costs and eliminate duplication. John de Lorean, then General Manager of Chevrolet, had noted, "It became illogical to put a B Chevrolet, an A Chevrolet (Chevelle) and an F Chevrolet in the same plant because they weren't built the same way. . . . It became more logical to put a B Chevrolet, Pontiac, and Oldsmobile in the same plant. Then if the plant made more cars for other divisions than Chevrolet, why should Chevrolet control the plant?"[33]

Mr. Dorn added, "Having the manufacturing divisions involved simplified the transfer of the design to manufacturing. Getting the reliability people involved in early design stages, we think, will also improve the reliability of the car. The fact that the Project Center spoke for all the car divisions (to Fisher body and the

Design Staff, for example), in effect, increased the leverage of the car divisions to obtain the significant weight changes they needed.

"We had only about 20 people in the Project Center to coordinate this whole project. Consequently, the real credit belongs to the divisional people who did the design work and to the division managements that were willing to change some of their prior practices. The division general managers got on board as well as their design people. The project managers reported technically to the chief engineers of the car divisions and administratively to the engineering staff, rather than working for only one of the car division chief engineers. The fact that we had the support of the chief engineers and general managers of the car divisions provided an umbrella to give clout vis-à-vis other divisions when we needed it."

ORGANIZATION CHANGES

But these moves took a long time to implement. Fall 1974 was bleak. A combination of high interest rates, oil shortages, inflation, and Watergate had destroyed public confidence. And the automobile industry suffered most seriously. By December 1974 GM had 130,000 people laid off as it cut back large-car production and tried to gear up for its smaller cars. In October–November 1974 both GM's Chairman (Gerstenberg) and President (Cole) retired mandatorily at age 65. Thomas A. Murphy, who like Gerstenberg had a finance background, became Chairman and CEO. Elliot M. ("Pete") Estes, an operating man with substantial international experience, replaced engineer Cole as President and Chief Operating Officer.

Every summer GM's executive committee undertook "an inventory of people"—a review of its 6,000 or so top managers for promotion or replacement. In 1974 it had also been charged with recommending replacements for Gerstenberg and Cole and for making an inventory of GM's problems. In September 1974 the executive committee recommended to a newly created Organization Review Committee, consisting mainly of outside board members, a major reorganization. This expanded the top management group and brought four new and relatively young men into the higher echelons. All—future prospects for the top jobs—would serve on the executive committee and the board. It strengthened the roles of the new president (Estes) over all operations, the executive vice presidents in their specific fields, and the vice chairman (Terrell) under whom all technical and many nontechnical staff activities were consolidated.[34]

One of the Industry-Government Relations Staff described an event which took place just after the new management team took over: "In early December 1974, I was preparing a draft statement of a possible GM position on auto fuel economy for presentation at December 10, 1974, hearings by the Senate Commerce Committee. I had finished the first draft on about December 1st, the day Mr. Gerstenberg retired. In this draft, the position I was proposing was hinged on technical matters—what was technologically possible. But in mid-stream the decision was made that the emphasis in our position should be oriented not just to what was technologically feasible but more toward what was practicable from the standpoint of economics. Our Chief Economist, Henry Duncombe, made the presentation to the Commerce

Committee and became GM's principal spokesman on fuel economy issues. Now we were pointing out that fuel economy was essentially an economic issue. We questioned whether it was good public policy to require the production of vehicles that might not be acceptable to the public."

When asked how policy on such matters comes about, the same executive said: "For the most part the policy simply evolves. In meetings, people say things that do or don't hold up to argument. Slowly everyone begins to sort out a sensible position from all of this. . . . We may write this position into testimony or a speech writer will put it into a draft speech for one of our corporate officers. After an initial review by the principal, we will then circulate the draft to all the appropriate staffs for comment. . . . The top people are very open to critiques of this sort. The ideas tend to flush upward so the top level can adopt them as they see a consensus emerging. If there is a major policy question, the executive may take the statement to the Executive Committee for comment or approval. Mr. Murphy will nearly always comment on any important issue. Once a corporate officer has spoken publicly on an issue there is a tendency to give his statements weight and wide circulation."

The New Team   Although viewpoints on personalities might differ widely, various people used the following terms to describe the new management team which was to have such impact on GM's future. *Wall Street Journal* reported:

> **Known as a stern and sometimes demanding boss to insiders, Mr. Murphy swept past a number of other GM officials [in 1972] to become vice chairman and the clear front runner for the top job. A dyed-in-the wool finance man, he had spent all but four of his years at GM on the finance staff.[35]**

GM executives said: "Mr. Murphy is basically a finance guy." . . . "He always has a briefcase jammed full of papers. . . . He has to be the most prodigious reader of internal documents in the place. He has always done his homework, and any memorandum to him is likely to come back with questions or comments for its originators or any recipients." . . . "He always appears distinguished, formal, a bit distant in a group setting. But one-on-one he's very friendly, warm, perceptive. His door is always open to people here at headquarters." Mr. Murphy's own broad-ranging and thoughtful management philosophies have been expressed in a number of public statements. Some are included in Appendix B.

Of President "Pete" Estes, GM executives reported: "Estes is an engineer, a manufacturing guy. He's held in unbelievable awe by the organization. He is very effective as an operating man. He will be excellent and responsible in ensuring that the product meets all the requirements of the customer and the government." . . . "Estes has a kind of humble midwestern charm. People find him easy to talk to. He comes across as honest, straightforward, not flashy, but very competent."

Of other executives: "Roger Smith [chief financial officer] is similar in many ways to Mr. Murphy. He also represents the buck in GM. To him the name of the game is profit." . . . "Mr. F. J. McDonald runs 35 divisions. He's very competent, but with this responsibility it's hard to see how he could do much more than operations. Mr. H. H. Kehrl has to stay on top of the entire corporation's technology, and Mr. Jensen has his hands full with overseas operations. In essence, all these are very effective operating guys." . . . "Mr. Terrell [vice chairman] is the single strongest force for change in the organization. He came up through the nonautomotive groups of GM. He talks about the lack of longer range planning in the organization and likes to think about the major forces in the environment. He tends to use the organization structure as a way to get change."

Disappointment and Rebounding Morale   In early 1975, the new team had to announce, "For General Motors the first quarter of 1975 turned out to be the worst since 1946. . . . Earnings fell to $0.20 per share and net income was less than 1% of sales."[36] Faced with declining profits and determined to make changes in virtually all its cars, GM reduced its quarterly dividend and in March 1975 floated $600 million of new debt. This was the largest fixed income financing by an industrial company in history. In keeping with its voluntary agreement with President Gerald Ford to improve its fleet fuel consumption more than 50% by 1980, GM would spend some $2 billion by 1978 to reach that goal.[37]

Mr. Estes later commented, "By spring 1975 we knew our product program was very right. . . . We thought we could be two years ahead of anyone else with our strategy. In March or April, Tom Murphy and I began talking around the organization that things were getting better. At the same time people at Ford were saying 'things are in a hell of a mess.' But we went ahead with a 10-year plan for the downsizing of *intermediate* cars. In March 1975 we decided to remove 700 pounds from these to gain approximately 3 mpg for their introduction in 1977 (1978 models). Our financial forecasts still said we couldn't meet even reduced dividend targets. But Tom and I started boosting our idea that 1975 was not going to be a loss year. We needed to increase earnings $600 million to meet our reduced dividend targets. Instead, we got $960 million. This took a lot of postponing projects and not fixing windows. But we got the job done. By late 1975 you could feel the morale coming up."

A Two Pronged Attack   In mid-1975 the broad lines of GM's strategy became apparent to outsiders. *Forbes* trumpeted:

> On the one hand, [GM] plans to move into the market for VW-sized cars and grab a big chunk of it. On the other, it plans to remain dominant in the more expensive middle and high ends of the market by making six-passenger cars that are more in tune with today's gasoline prices and parking problems.[38]

Estes later said, "A lot of people inside and outside of GM were skeptical that downsizing was right. Our first job was to move our customers over to a fuel economic car without taking anything away from them. . . . But we may have to move them considerably further after two more design cycles." In December Congress passed the Energy Act of 1975 converting President Ford's voluntary agreements into law and further mandating each manufacturer to meet fleet fuel economy averages of 20 mpg by 1980 and 27-1/2 mpg by 1985.

The "World Car."   At the same time the multinational structure of the company was undergoing major changes. "Overseas used to be another GM," according to one top executive. "But we could no longer afford duplicate engineering and environmental certification costs in the various divisions. The energy situation was worldwide. U.S. fuel costs were becoming comparable to those in Europe and other advanced countries. Increasingly, we found we could design better, more compatible cars on a worldwide basis. We brought out the Chevette and a small car for Buick this way. Now whenever we do a new car, it will be a world car. For example, we have a worldwide manager for our 1980s car. He is in Germany."

Part of the 1974–1975 reorganization brought overseas operations together directly under Estes. It also began the consolidation of staff groups at the corporate level to help coordinate GM's far flung activities. Corporate planning, public relations, and the legal staff began to operate increasingly on a worldwide basis. By 1976 GM was consciously expanding its exchanges of top operating managers among various national units. As one top executive said, "We are increasingly realizing that we have very good people overseas—as good as we have in the U.S. We will see much more derivation of worldwide cars from Opel. They are already a design source for Vauxhall, and the new Brazilian and Australian cars could be engineered in Germany."

An important decision of this era was to take a joint ownership position in Isuzu. Historically GM had insisted on 100% ownership in overseas units. But the company began to realize that this policy might exclude it from major growth markets. The areas where it had positions would account for an increasingly small share of the world market. In 1972 GM ranked as only the 5th automaker overseas with only 9% of total sales outside North America. But total auto sales abroad were growing twice as fast as the United States.[39] If GM wanted to expand into many of these markets, it would have to accept the idea of joint ownership.

Mr. Thomas McDaniel said, "The proposed GM investment in Isuzu had been discussed with the Board for several months without any decision being reached. This was a difficult decision—the Corporation had no recent experience with this type of association with a foreign firm, and both top management and the Board were reluctant to reach a decision until all issues were fully aired. Meanwhile, competitive pressures in the Pacific area were intensifying and the need for GM to somehow establish a manufacturing base in Japan was growing more evident all the time. Finally, in the process of preparing a normal quarterly summary of GM Overseas operations for presentation to the Board at its March 1971 meeting, Mr. Estes instructed me to include a strongly positive management recommendation—along with rationale—regarding the proposed investment. After careful consideration, the Board Chairman, Mr. Roche, reviewed and approved the recommendation and the matter was—after months of discussion—formally presented to the Board for a decision. Approval of the proposed investment was granted shortly thereafter, leaving only formalities to be concluded prior to GM's purchase of 34% of Isuzu's outstanding stock on July 15, 1971."

GM's 1972 Annual Report noted austerely: "General Motors sees an important part of its future in the rapidly growing overseas market. . . . [But] the realization of these opportunities depends to an important degree on the ability of GM and other American business enterprises to trade and invest throughout the world without undue restrictions. Protectionist measures like the Burke-Hartke Bill . . . import quotas, limits on further investments overseas, and restrictions on the overseas use of patents and licenses could cause trade retaliation at a time when our national purpose is to draw the nations of the world closer together. . . ."[40]

Product Introductions   Then to the tune of "It's About Time," GM introduced the internationally designed, U.S. modified, Chevette in fall 1975. It was 16.7'' shorter and 629 pounds lighter than the Vega. Its automatic transmission was 35 pounds lighter than other GM models but—in keeping with GM's standardization program—could be mated to engines large enough for Buick Electra.[41] Another version of the Chevette "World Car" came into the Buick line as "Opel by Isuzu." The Isuzu car was similar to the (German GM) Opel Kadett. Versions of this car were being built in Britain, Brazil, and Australia.[42] But imports of the German car in the U.S. were stopped because of changing currency relationships, import duties, and a lackluster sales performance by Buick's own dealers.[43]

SUCCESSES AND FAILURES

By the 1977 model year approximately one fourth of GM's line—virtually all its full-sized models—would be scaled down in length and weight. In 1978 the intermediates were to be reduced in external dimensions and weight to that of compacts. And a year later the compacts would be compressed to Audi size. But a critical point of the strategy was as Estes said, "to make the big car the right size so people will buy it."[44]

One of the problems was to maintain distinction among the various car lines. Murphy said, "We want to make everything under the skin as close to identical as possible so the cars will be sound and solid functionally. At the same time we want to give customers variety and distinction in areas they think are important."[45] By the end of 1975 GM's share of American-made cars had rebounded to 54%, profitability had improved and reports said the company was aiming, unofficially at 60%.[46] The year 1976 saw record dollar sales ($47.2 billion) and earnings ($10.08 per share). The fickle public was shifting its taste in new cars. As gasoline supplies became more plentiful and less expensive, people moved up to larger cars more rapidly than expected. Less than a year after its highly successful introduction, Chevette's production plans had to be cut 50% below anticipated levels.[47] GM resumed expansion of its Lansing, Michigan, Oldsmobile plant—a project which it had halted in 1974.[48] Imports of the Isuzu-Opel, whose sales were "far below expectations," fell off. Then came intermittent shutdowns of the Lordstown plant for Vega and Astra. Finally, GM offered $200 rebates on all these small cars to cut inventories which had built to twice the 60-day supply the company wanted.[49]

In introducing its 1977 standard cars GM found itself countering advanced press comments about the "downsized" cars. It also had to hold off Ford's campaign for larger cars. "Welcome to the home of the Whopper," Bennett E. Bidwell, Ford's Vice President of Sales, boasted to a group of reporters, "Our big Mark V Lincolns and Fords are virtually unchanged."[50] For all its lines Ford's TV advertising blared forth, "Ford's better idea! We give you a choice!" For the first time Ford was making the biggest cars across its full line, but GM was betting that its new models would make its competition seem "over the hill, like men with middle-aged spread."[51] By mid-1977, both had gained at the expense of Chrysler and American Motors.

According to public sources: In the spring of 1979 GM planned to execute the third round of its automobile shrinkage. GM's compacts would be replaced by its X body design—a half ton lighter than 1977 compacts, with the same interior space, and powered by a transverse mounted front wheel drive engine. Further into the 1980's GM forecast a new "minicar," further shrinkage of its big cars and intermediates, and replacement of virtually all its V-8 engines with 4- to 6-cylinder engines.[52] Estes said that GM had "several scenarios" on how to meet the 27-1/2 mpg mandated targets of 1985. The problem was to choose the one the customer would like best and be willing to buy.

CHALLENGES OF THE TIMES

The costs of overhauling the product lines were enormous. Annual R and D expenditures were running over $1 billion on a net income of $2.9 billion in 1976. And by 1980 GM estimated it would have invested $25 billion in safety, emissions control, and downsizing. But in 1977 GM seemed to have successfully worked its way out of the crises of 1973–74. Not the least of these was, as *Fortune* said, "a revivified sense of purpose and a much sharper understanding of the outside world." John de Lorean, once considered one of GM's rising stars, had left in 1973 complaining that GM had "gotten to be totally isolated from the world." And Edward Cole retired from the presidency in 1974 with the gloomy remark that "the fun is gone . . . I wouldn't go into the automobile business again."[53] By late 1977 GM's Headquarters was confident and optimistic. Its new aggressive spirit was perhaps best exemplified in Mr. Murphy's statements that he would not be satisfied "until we sell every car that's made."[54] Still many important challenges remained.

Government Pressures   Perhaps the greatest concern to most managers was how to lead the company effectively in a climate of ever-increasing goverment regulations. On the one hand the pressure GM had from environmental and mileage standards had excited the engineers and stylists more than anything else had in years. On the other, the company still had a credibility problem as "nay sayers." As one executive said, "We didn't believe we could double our mileage without upheaval. Now that we have applied ourselves to the problem and really worked on the technologies, we think it can be done. But if we disclosed what we think we could do, we would give our competition a free ride. What can we do? We want to be as helpful as possible, but we don't want some arbitrary decision wrecking the entire industry or our particular business—or requiring things our customers really don't want."

There were several specific concerns about regulation. One was the government's mandating excessively costly or ineffective solutions to problems—like requiring passive restraints such as air bags in all cars when seat belts, if used, were cheaper and more effective. A second was conflicting standards like "5-mile-per-hour bumpers" or extremely tight No_x standards which foreclosed important technological alternatives—like diesel engines—for mileage improvement. Third were constant shifts in standards and their last minute promulgation—for example, Congress's not issuing final standards for 1978 autos until mid-summer 1977, by which time production preparation had to be nearly finished. Fourth was the habit of some agencies, notably OSHA, to promulgate so many detailed standards that it was virtually impossible to comply with all of them. Finally, many standards did not seem to be desired by those they were intended to benefit—usually customers or workers.

By 1978 government agencies were requiring vastly increased information about auto companies' internal activities, including more and more details about their future product plans. The companies were concerned that this material be kept confidential because of the very significant competitive damage disclosure could cause. The problem was magnified by widespread efforts to obtain companies' proprietary information through the Freedom of Information Act. Another grave concern was the danger of government bodies in courts "second-guessing" the industry's product planning decisions "after the fact" without really being able to take into account the full range of uncertainties, engineering judgments, economic and style preference trade-offs such decisions always involved. A case in point was the much (retrospectively) analyzed Ford Pinto gas tank decision.

Issues for the Future   Other challenges of enormous proportions also faced GM's management. These included: the uncertain potentials of the automotive business in the U.S. and the world; the relationship between the various car divisions' lines; the role of the small car in GM's line and the U.S. economy; the appropriateness of the company's organization and management style in light of its changing future problems; the relationship between its automotive and other transportation businesses; GM's function and posture as a multinational company; the legitimate demands of workers for a better "quality of work life" in its plants; and planning how to handle these issues in light of massive worldwide resources shortages and shifts, 3–10 year lead times in plant and design decisions, ever changing government regulations, fickle consumer tastes and changing social values.

These, and other issues of a constantly changing world, faced GM's new, but now aging top management in 1977. There were questions not just of what to do, but how to get the job done effectively in one of the largest organizations in the world. As Pete Estes said, "The day is gone when any one man can have all the right answers for this company or swing a two-by-four at anyone's head and get anything done. We need to provide confidence and leadership for people and persuade them what needs to be done. I think this is good for the organization, for our people, and for the country."

ENDNOTES

1   A. Sloan, Jr., *My Years with General Motors,* New York: Doubleday, 1972.
2   E. Rothschild, *Paradise Lost: The Decline of the Auto-Industrial Age,* New York, 1973, pp. 36–37.
3   *Wall Street Journal,* May 13, 1969, p. 2:2.
4   *Evaluation of the 1960–1963 Corvair Handling and Stability,* N.H.T.S.A., U.S. Department of Transportation, July 1972.
5   *Wall Street Journal,* May 13, 1969, p. 2.

6   *1974 General Motors Report on Programs of Public Interest,* Detroit, Michigan, April 1975.

7   Referenced in: *Environmental Quality: First Report of Council on Environmental Quality,* Washington, D.C.: GPO, 1970, p. 62.

8   *Wall Street Journal,* July 30, 1970, p. 2, April 8, 70, p. 7.

9   *Environmental Quality,* 1970, op. cit., p. 77.

10 *Wall Street Journal,* November 18, 1970, p. 8.

11 *Wall Street Journal,* November 19, 1970, p. 1.

12 *Wall Street Journal,* September 17, 1970, p. 2.

13 *Wall Street Journal,* November 18, 1970, p. 2.

14 *Wall Street Journal,* February 9, 1970, p. 9.

15 *Wall Street Journal,* September 10, 1970, p. 1.

16 "Detroit's Reluctant Ride to Smallsville," *Fortune,* March 1969, 113, 164.

17 *Ward's Automotive Yearbook,* 1972, pp. 26, 111, 119.

18 C. Burck, "How GM Turned Itself Around," *Fortune,* January 16, 1978, 87–96.

19 *Wall Street Journal,* May 29, 1973, p. 1.

20 *Wall Street Journal,* October 25, 1973, p. 3.

21 *Wall Street Journal,* September 6, 1973, p. 30.

22 *Business Week,* March 16, 1974, 76.

23 *Wall Street Journal,* July 29, 1974, p. 4.

24 General Motors Annual Report, 1975.

25 *Wall Street Journal,* February 1, 1974, p. 3.

26 *Business Week,* March 16, 1974.

27 *Wall Street Journal,* May 28, 1974, p. 7.

28 *Automotive Industries,* June 15, 1974.

29 *Wall Street Journal,* March 22, 1974, p. 1.

30 *Wall Street Journal,* June 25, 1974, p. 4.

31 Mr. Terrell is given credit for spotting the program management idea when he was head of the nonautomotive divisions, one of which (Delco) was a NASA supplier. NASA used the system extensively as did the aerospace industry as a whole. *Fortune,* January 16, 1978, op. cit., p. 92.

32 *Business Week,* March 25, 1972, 46.

33 *Automotive Industries,* January 15, 1972, 19.

34 C. B. Burck, "How GM Turned Itself Around," *Fortune,* January 16, 1978, 96–97.

35 *Wall Street Journal,* October 1, 1974.

36 *General Motors Annual Report,* 1975, p. 4.

37 *Wall Street Journal,* March 4, 1975, p. 3.

38 *Forbes,* August 15, 1975, 23.

39 P. Vanderwicken, "GM: The Price of Being Responsible," *Fortune,* January 1972.

40 *General Motors Annual Report to Stockholders,* 1972, p. 3.

41 *Industry Week,* September 29, 1975, 73.

42 *Wall Street Journal,* July 23, 1975, p. 34.

43 *Business Week,* July 28, 1975, p. 52.

44 *Dun's Review,* January, 1976, 32–34.

45 *Business Week,* July 28, 1975, 53.

46 *Wall Street Journal,* January 7, 1976, p. 1.

47 *Wall Street Journal,* April 21, 1976, p. 7.

48 *Wall Street Journal,* June 14, 1976, p. 7.

49 *Wall Street Journal,* November 11, 1976, p. 3.

50 *Wall Street Journal,* October 29, 1976.

51 *Fortune,* July 1976, 101.

52 *New York Times,* October 16, 1977, Section 12, p. 5.

53 C. Burck, "How GM Turned Itself Around," *Fortune,* January 16, 1978, 87–96.

54 Ibid.

APPENDIX A

THE GENERAL MOTORS STYLE

Several executives described GM's style in approaching complex strategy issues as follows:

Mr. Estes: "Everyday you have a problem at the top of this list. My approach is to discuss it with everyone. I also try to hang on and not make a decision until I have all possible inputs. Then I decide what *ought* to be. After that I go out and try to sell it. When you arrive at your conclusions, you hope it is a majority opinion, but it may not be. Mr. Murphy and I may have discussed a problem to the point where we understand that we really do disagree. But when the chips are down, we must put forward a unified front.

"Many decisions are crystal clear when you get all the facts together. That is why one seeks out all possible information on major issues first. The tough ones are when such clarity does not come about. Then all you can do is get the facts together, close the door, and kick it around. You may come out of the meeting with a whole list of questions to be answered. But ultimately after several sessions like that, you all come out of the door together.

"We do not try to tell people how to get there from this level of the organization. We try to give them the broad concepts we are trying to achieve. We operate through questioning and fact gathering. Strategy is a state of mind you go through. When you think about a little problem, your mind begins to think how it will affect all the different elements in the total situation. Once you have had all the jobs that you need to qualify for this position, you can see the problem from a variety of viewpoints. But you don't try to ram your conclusions down people's throats. We try to persuade people what has to be done and provide confidence and leadership for them. For example, yesterday, we had 130 people at the Technical Center, each division gave its plan through the 1980s. The only guidance we gave them was: 27-1/2 miles per gallon by 1985, 6-person capacity, luggage space comparable to the present, and comfort for the customer. Each product line could have a compact, subcompact, intermediate, and regular product in its line. And each of the supporting divisions (Fisher Body, etc.) had to have at least one major new product available each year. Now we have three or four possible strategies from each group. These provide somewhat different scenarios but they are not all over the lot. We have begun to bring together the highly varying ideas which are available deep in the organization. Now we begin to hone in on a few divisions and a few crucial decisions that these strategies pose."

Mr. J. N. Stewart, Director, Marketing Staff: "No one has written down strategic objectives, for example: 'to produce a product that will meet as wide an array of needs as possible.' But these are well understood throughout the organization. The decision process tends to work within these broad concepts. And the concept itself is molded by a series of incremental decisions made in response to particular opportunities or problems. The inputs and weightings used in these decisions vary widely. But the sum of these decisions and ideas represents the strategy. It is not a one-man, one-vote, system. Certain people with greater expertise will wield a heavier vote on an issue. And people will defer to the most persuasive person. The strategy of GM may not even exist in the mind of one man. I certainly don't know where it is written down. It is simply transmitted in the series of decisions made.

"Finally, we don't go on line with our goals. This would make for too much rigidity. Around here, if it is written down, it is out of date. We certainly don't want to stop thinking about options because we've written something down. The people who have a commitment to writing things down find themselves very frustrated as to how the company really does operate. Instead, things work up through a series of screens. A fundamental change is worked out long before it reaches the Finance Committee. Virtually nothing gets to the Finance Committee that is turned down. Sure, there may be changes in programs, amounts, or timing. But our management wouldn't put forward something the board wouldn't countenance. Individual board members are, of course, asked for their advice ahead of time. They are well informed. Few surprises would reach the board level."

Mr. James Morris, Industry-Government Relations Staff: "Sometimes the top executives lay out broad guidelines, but more often they will respond to a specific issue or item that has been brought to the surface by the various staffs and divisions. For example, once a month there is a meeting of the Emissions Review Board, which consists of Messrs. Estes, Terrell, McDonald, Kehrl and other vice presidents including my boss, Bob Magill. The ERB considers various matters dealing with fuel economy and vehicle emissions. Motions or votes are seldom taken, but usually we can discern a consensus and end up with a very good idea of the direction the management group wants to take.

"Occasionally there is a directive, but that is the exception. The first corporate-wide fuel economy conference in November 1976 was a notable exception. Several of our top executives participated and set the following theme: 'Although in the past we may have had a negative attitude toward the government's fuel economy and emission standards, it is apparent that the public supports them. Furthermore, if anyone can meet the standards, GM can, because our people are the best in the world. Therefore, at this conference we are not going to discuss whether we can do the job but how we are going to do it.' In essence, the standards were transformed into a challenge, not a problem. . . . To some extent the top brass acted as a Lombardi or a Rockne, stimulating the group. A good deal of enthusiasm was generated in the whole organization."

F. Alan Smith, Vice President-Finance: "Another major dimension of change has been our response to issues like equal employment and quality of work life movements in the U.S. We have developed a Quality of Work Life Program with the union. It is a joint exercise with employees—a bottom up sort of thing. We begin by brainstorming about what bothers the employees and what each manager can do. In white collar groups this is handled directly between employee-manager groups. Within the represented hourly group, a union representative is of course important and desirable. In the past we tried a number of 'Volvo operations.' They simply didn't work. We tried to move people around and expand their job scope. They said to heck with it, let me do a job I know how. Now we have a number of special task groups on environmental affairs. As an extension of our staff concept, they are available directly to the divisions on demand. . . .

"The data are rarely clear on which way to go in these or other major decisions. Each data set presented to management is persuasive, if you believe it. But at least some part of each major decision is intuitive. You have to judge the credibility of data sources and their basic assumptions. In addition there is no way you can say precisely what customers will want 3 years—and especially more—in the future. However, each division has its goals and forwards business programs and product plans five years ahead. . . . But there are no explicit fixed overall corporate goals in a formal sense. We use an iterative process to make a series of tentative decisions on the way we think the market will go. As we get more data we modify these continuously. It is often difficult to say who decided something, when—or even who—originated a decision."

APPENDIX B

SOME PHILOSOPHIES OF MR. THOMAS AQUINAS MURPHY, CHAIRMAN, GENERAL MOTORS CORPORATION

Several recent published accounts offer some lively insights into the philosophies of Mr. Thomas A. Murphy, Chairman of General Motors Corporation. Excerpts from some of these are quoted below.

"The biggest man in the largest manufacturing company in the world sits at a cluttered desk that is piled high with sales reports, production analyses, sheaves of magazines and a couple of dime-store signs that proclaim BLESS THIS MESS and PLEASE DON'T STRAIGHTEN THE MESS ON MY DESK! YOU'LL GOOF UP MY SYSTEM. . . . As he looks ahead, Mr. Thomas A. Murphy reckons that the United States is moving toward a conservation ethic, a society in which products will be smaller, more durable, with more built-in quality. That does not worry him a whit, but he is concerned about several other trends.

"One is what he views as unfair competition from Japan, Inc. 'The government and the business people and the bankers there move as one. The Japanese sell more than 1 million vehicles a year in the United States, but they import fewer than 50,000 vehicles from all countries. They have a way of operating to make sure that their markets are served by their own manufacturers. When I look at the value of the yen today compared with its value three years ago, I have to conclude that their autos are not fairly priced because the value of the yen has appreciated a heckuva lot more than they have raised their prices. In the U.S., we have to take a hard look to make sure that we are not victims of our own desire to continue on a free-trade course. Any alternative would be bad for the U.S. and bad for the world, but I don't think the game should be rigged against us."

"Murphy also worries about the rising impediments to productivity, which he thinks are threatening the U.S.'s ability to pay high wages. 'I like those high wages,' he contends. 'They make our people better customers.' He notes that the U.S. is rightly concerned about the environment, about health and safety in the workplace, yet many of the new regulations not only impede productivity gains but also put the U.S. at a competitive disadvantage against countries that are much less fastidious. If the U.S. continues to place restrictions on anything that might pollute or present any hazard to customers or workers, he argues, then its economy will become a service economy—'We will just shine each other's shoes'—and its standards of living will decline. Worse, its freedoms will suffer. Says Murphy: 'There's a desire today for more security and for a risk-free society. But that becomes a choiceless society, not a free society.' "[1]

"[He] does not believe that the great corporations of our economy possess vast power within the political democracy. To the contrary, he contends that consumers hold true life-or-death power over the corporations. . . . Mr. Murphy says: 'The ability of successful businesses to provide "goodies" like jobs and security does not mean they have the power to shape the attitudes of the public. It's the other way around; without public approval, businesses have no "goodies" to give.' Anyone who disagrees, Mr. Murphy suggests, should set up a company to try to sell the products that precisely satisfy his or her own appetites regardless of whether they appeal to anyone else—'and see how much employment and security you can provide.' "[2]

" 'There is not another economic system . . . that we in America could emulate in whole or in part which would not cause our quality of life and our standard of living to go down instead of up. . . . On purely humanitarian grounds, free enterprise proves superior to any other system for the simple reason that its greater productive efficiency produces more wealth for popular distribution . . .'

"A free society makes no guarantees, only the promise that effort will be rewarded and that the reward will belong to the individual. In Murphy's words: 'Guarantees demean achievement.' They also undermine and often prevent achievement."[3]

" 'America's business leaders have an abundance of information and expertise to offer in the public interest. But if American business wants to have its help accepted by government it will have to come to government with specific, constructive proposals—not as a partisan, not as an adversary—but as a concerned citizen who has done his homework and wants to be helpful by presenting perspectives on both sides of an issue,' GM Board Chairman Thomas A. Murphy told the National Press Club."[4]

" 'The only arguments and proposals business should advance are those that emphasize the factual, scientific and legal merits of its position. The whole point is that the objective of business, no less than that of government, must be the public's interest. If business leaders approach Washington in this way, I think we will be far more successful than we have been in the past. We will be listened to there, and perhaps equally important, through the media we will be heard by the country. For, make no mistake, it is what the country thinks that moves Washington. . . . '

"Describing the American economic system as 'a marvelous meld of private enterprise, individual initiative and public oversight,' Mr. Murphy advised that 'when we begin to doubt the system's continued effectiveness and to monkey around with its operation—often to meet purely imaginary threats—that's when we are most likely to get ourselves into trouble. . . . Many businessmen like myself believe that this is what's happening today,' he said. 'Everywhere, we see too much doubt and suspicion about the business establishment—about its operation and about the ability of the system to continue its remarkable record of progress. The result has been an overreaction by the overuse of the regulatory powers of government. . . . Many of us are not comfortable in the spotlight, or on television,' he said, 'but if we are to develop a healthier relationship of mutual respect and confidence with the government and public it is the individual executive—the flesh-and-blood person—who must personify the corporation and demonstrate the seriousness of its concerns.' "

ENDNOTES

1   "Murphy's Law: Things Will Go Right," *Time,* March 27, 1978, p. 70.
2   "Where the Power of Business Lies," *New York Times,* July 4, 1978, p. 24.
3   *The Monroe (Ala.) News,* February 21, 1978.
4   *GM News* Press Release, Detroit, Michigan, July 20, 1978.

B. J. GUNNESS CONSTRUC- TION COMPANY

Neil C. Churchill

"I would like to get off the hook to the bonding company but I don't know if I can do it," said Benjamin J. Gunness, President and founder of the B.J. Gunness Construction Company. "The bonding company insists that every officer of the construction company they bond put his personal financial statements behind the bond. If I pull out of the Company, it could cut our bonding capacity and our ability to bid for new work. If I stay, all that my wife and I have worked for can be wiped out by one or two really bad jobs. I like the business; it is at least half of what I own; and I don't want to jeopardize it since it is going to my boys, Frank and Charles. But while they do most of the work, I still like to be involved; and people in this town know me and like to do business with me. Besides, I really don't have any other interests. Yet at my age I would like to know that my wife and I have financial security."

HISTORY OF GUNNESS CONSTRUCTION

B. J. Gunness moved to Arizona in 1922. Although he came from a construction family, B.J. was interested in banking and worked in it in Tucson and then Phoenix, until the banks closed at the start of the depression. With jobs in banking essentially nonexistent, B.J. moved back to Tucson with his new wife "doing most anything I could, including repairing and remodeling repossessed houses using the skills I picked up working with my father. My wife also worked as a secretary/bookkeeper in a number of offices." When the economy turned up a bit, B. J. began to manage properties for mortgage and insurance companies which had repossessed the properties back "when their owners couldn't make the payment and simply walked away."

His property management work led B.J. to start a small house-building operation with his wife and one or two employees in the late 1930s. When the war came along, and building materials could be obtained only with government allocations, Gunness kept his business afloat by bidding on small government contracts and working in a Tucson aircraft factory. "My wife did the payroll and kept the books. I was out at the job early in the morning and at the plant from 4:00 P.M. until midnight. I kept this up during the war until 1945 when I finally got a medical discharge from the factory."

With the war over, B.J. began building houses and small commercial buildings one or two at a time. He increased his equity capital by buying old houses, fixing them up

This case was prepared by Professor Neil C. Churchill as a basis for class discussion rather than to illustrate either effective or ineffective handling of an administrative situation.

Copyright © 1977 by the President and Fellows of Harvard College.

and selling them on a contract basis. He then moved into school construction and "just grew with Tucson", becoming a city council member and then vice-mayor in the late 1950s. In addition to construction, he developed some desert land for cotton outside of Tucson and then in Mexico—flying back and forth between Tucson and Hermosillio, and in his words, "keeping pretty busy." By the late 1950s, Gunness Construction was doing between $2 million to $3 million a year and had moved out of housing into heavier construction, employing engineers and supervisors capable of building hospitals, schools, and industrial buildings.

In 1960, B. J.'s oldest son, Frank, entered the business—although he had worked in all its aspects part time and in summers during his school years. Frank left the company in 1963 to work for Rhyne & Murdoch, a large construction company in San Francisco. He returned in 1965 to become General Manager—the job he has held ever since.

During the 1960s Gunness Construction took on increasingly larger jobs—including a community college project for $3.5 million ("$8 million to $10 million at 1977 prices," remarked B. J. Gunness) and expanded the sphere of its operations to communities up to 150 miles from Tucson and developed the capability to do more complex engineering jobs. In 1968, B. J.'s other son, Charles, entered the company from college. At that time, Frank was 30 and B. J. was 64.

THE COMPANY AND ITS ENVIRONMENT

Gunness Construction, as a general contractor, has two main sources of business. In the first, it submits competitive bids to governmental organizations or private businesses for construction work usually against very detailed specifications. For the second type of work, it "negotiates" contracts with organizations in situations where Gunness helps develop the specifications as well as constructing the building. The profit margin on the negotiable contracts is usually higher than on competitively bid jobs. In either case, Gunness subcontracts some 80% of the job and performs the other 20% with its own employees. Gunness, however, guarantees the satisfactory completion of the building and if one of its subcontractors goes out of business or does the job poorly, Gunness has to finish the job—"A situation that can cost us a lot unless the subs are bonded."

To perform its work properly, Gunness has engineers and estimators evaluate what the job requires, develop a detailed plan to do the job, and "take off the costs of the specifications" to determine the bid price. Besides the bids themselves, a key factor in contract profitability are the job superintendents who manage the jobs and see that the subcontractors do their work properly. Gunness also tries to keep a nucleus of good carpenters and laborers employed all year long so they can be spread out among those hired from the union when new jobs come along.

To give a financial assurance for performance, all major contracts require that Gunness take out a construction bond for the value of the contract. The bonding company is then libel for the buildings being completed properly. It in turn has recourse against Gunness Construction and, as mentioned before, the personal assets of its owner/managers.

Bonding companies limit the extent of their liability by restricting the dollar amount they will go "on risk" to a construction company. This "bonding capacity" of the construction company is based on the perceived strength of the management, its track record, its financial strength, and its owners' financial assets. This bonding capacity is usually stated as a multiple of the construction company's "net surety allowed" which is defined as (1) current assets, not including prepaid expenses, deposits, inventory, and receivables from officers, less (2) current liabilities plus one years' interest on all debt. Gunness has nominally had a multiple of 20:1 of its net surety allowed but has had exceptions being regularly made on a contract-by-contract basis. Gunness has also found that it can plan to "sell" about 130% of its bonding capacity a year, since the amount of the bond required on each job is for the uncompleted construction which decreases as the job proceeds.

There is a third type of business which Gunness and the larger contractors are involved in called "construction management." In construction management, the contractor assumes the role similar to that of an agent for the organization which wants a building constructed. As such, Gunness works with the designers, architects and contractors "managing" the process and ensuring that what is constructed is what the owners want in design and quality and done at a relevant price. They do not, however, do any construction work. It is, in Frank Gunness' words, "a more technically and managerially challenging type of business with less risk. It also does not use up very much, if any, of our bonding capacity."

THE CURRENT SITUATION

During the late 1960s and early 1970s, Gunness Construction grew and prospered. It built a number of schools, hospitals and public and private buildings in and around Tucson. In 1975 it established a branch in Phoenix, acquiring an office building and incurring for the first time in the Company's history some long-term debt. As B. J. put it, "Perhaps because I worked in a bank or maybe because of what I saw during the depression, I have always tried to keep our debt down. All the equipment we bought was for cash; the Tucson building was paid for in cash; and, until the Phoenix acquisition, I hadn't borrowed a dime from the bank in 10 years."

Gunness Construction not only constructed buildings on its own, but also entered into joint venture arrangements with Rhyne & Murdoch on several larger projects in Arizona. Profits were good in the late 1960s and early 1970s and Gunness shared them with its employees through profit-sharing and pension fund plans that gave 25% of each years' profits to the employees. "The reason for this," said B. J. Gunness, "is that there is a very uneven profit cycle in the construction business. When the company makes money, the people who produced it should share in it; when it doesn't, you don't want these payments locked into high wages. The IRS challenged me for going over 15%, but they gave in, since we had been allocating 25% for so many years."

Besides substantial bonuses, Gunness Construction also provided transportation and entertainment allowances to its top employees and had entered into two or three tax saving ventures in the last few years. The result was a growth in sales, growth in profits, but little or no growth in working capital. To paraphrase a representative of the bonding company, "We could not tell if B. J.'s intent was to grow the company or gradually liquidate it."

In 1973 the economy in Tucson turned down and building contractors "started to hurt badly". Gunness, however, had several large jobs in process so that it did not feel the effects until late 1974—and its May 31, 1975 statements showed an operating loss—see Exhibits 1 and 2. The recession worsened and became, for the building industry in Tucson, "The worst since the depression of the 1930s. Competition grew very severe." In 1975 and 1976 Gunness increased its volume, due in part to $4 million in sales from its Phoenix office. The sales, however, produced little profit due to severe competitive pressures and to increased activity by open shop contractors and the increasing use of nonunion subcontractors by union shop construction firms. The summer and fall of 1976 found Gunness unable to successfully bid for any contract under $500,000 in size. "We would bid along with 20 others and be the lowest of all the union shop bidders and maybe four or five down from the top of the ten open shop people." said Frank Gunness. "We could never get as low as the others and we would lose the bid." Gunness, however, did obtain two or three negotiated contracts and a number of smaller jobs in the latter part of 1976. In early 1977, business began to pick up and Gary Thompson, the controller, estimated that Gunness Construction would end the 1977 fiscal year with a sales volume of $8 million and continue at that level through the first six months of fiscal '78. Profits, however, would probably reflect the extreme competitiveness in Tucson and an over $100,000 negative adjustment on two jobs in Phoenix. These jobs produced a $40,000 loss but Gunness Construction had, through its construction in-process accounting system, recognized profits of $60,000 on them in the 1976 statements.

THE UNION SITUATION

Gunness Construction is a closed shop. Every third year, it signs a contract with five craft unions,* as do most of the large contractors in Arizona. In recent years, quite a few contractors have moved to an "open shop" operation and several have begun to operate two companies, one open and one union shop. In addition, a number of other contractors have begun using nonunion subcontractors on their jobs. The advantage of a closed shop is the greater availability of trained people to take on large projects or those under time pressure. "On the airport facility we built last year, we had 35 electricians working at one time," said B. J. Gunness. "That was a six month, $2 million plus job and we couldn't do that any way except as a union shop." The disadvantages of a union shop are higher labor costs per hour and less flexibility in work rules and work assignments—one estimate has the effective cost some 60% higher.

"To meet competition, we used a non-union electrical subcontractor for the first time," said Charles Gunness. "We can only do that for the unions which are not signatories to our labor contracts, such as the electricians and plumbers, and we may get into trouble with union subcontractors on later bids. But we can only wait and see. Maybe we should try to have two companies, one union and one nonunion. Some contractors have done it successfully and some have had trouble. The law may

*Laborers, cement finishers, carpenters, operating engineers, and teamsters.

change on union picketing and make this all unworkable, but until then it is sure something we have to consider, otherwise I don't see how we can compete at least on the smaller jobs, in the competitive bid market."

BONDING

Gunness Construction Company had done business with one bonding company, a subsidiary of MMF, Inc., for many, many years. Then in 1974 MMF and a number of other bonding companies had experienced a series of losses nationwide. While most bonding companies cut back their exposure and their bonding limits, MMF closed down its bonding operations entirely and Gunness Construction moved to Acme Bonding.

Acme Bonding has a firm policy of having those responsible for activities of the construction companies they bond—"stand behind what they ask of the bonding company with their personal assets," said Woody Jones, Gunness' account representative from Acme. "This keeps them from walking away from any problem jobs. They work on them, save most of them, and we are all better off."

Besides requiring personal indemnification, Jones was concerned that Gunness demonstrate that it could make a profit. "We don't want Gunness Construction to be a well for B. J. to drop his money into; we want it to be a viable company." He stated that Acme's commitment to Gunness Construction had been reduced to $6 million in bonding capacity because of Gunness' financial trend, and that this limit was subject to:

1 Gunness making at least a $25,000 profit in the first six months of the 1978 fiscal year (June through November 1977) and showing a positive profit trend thereafter;

2 Increases or decreases in bonding capacity in subsequent periods based on 20 times the "net surety allowed" at the beginning of each six month period.

In discussing B. J.'s involvement on the bond, Woody Jones reemphasized Acme's policy of personal commitment of those involved in the business. When asked what would happen should B. J. have to suddenly leave the business because of ill health, he replied, "The bonding limit would depend on Frank's ability to manage the company when such an event occurs." He added, "If there were no problems with the financial position of the company due, say, to inheritance taxes, and there were profits and management continuity, I would see no problems in bonding Gunness." Jones then reminded Frank, Charles, and B. J. that a bonding capacity of $6 million would require a surety capital of $300,000 by November 30 and that he would like to see some money stay in or even enter the company "instead of being withdrawn."

FRANK GUNNESS

When asked to comment on his position in Gunness Construction and how he sees its current problems, Frank Gunness said: "My present role is general manager of operations and new business development (see the organization chart, Exhibit 5); I make the assignments as far as project management is concerned; I do the selection of the projects we want to bid, and I hire and fire personnel—although as far as the engineering personnel are concerned I don't get out into the field. The field superintendents do their own hiring and firing but I will hire and fire the superintendents and it is up to me in the final analysis to see that we maintain control.

"I think over the last couple of years I have had to assume more responsibility for financial control and planning: I had more or less left these up to my dad in the past—to set policy, collect money, and distribute funds—but in the past couple of years I have had to do more of this. That is why I went to the SCMP* program—to get a little more in-depth understanding of financial principles, accounting, and control, since I see myself getting more intensely involved in this in the next few years. This was why I hired a CPA with some experience early this year—to provide us the information we, as top managers, need to make the decisions in both the long run and the short run. Gary has been with us only a short time but he has been very helpful.

"What we need now is more negotiated contract work, design and build work, and construction management work. We have been fortunate, for our joint-venture experiences with Rhyne and Murdoch have given us the capability to handle the large jobs this work involves. We have the people and we have the in-house expertise to do projects up to $5 million in size—and we have the joint venture capability for larger projects, we could even be the sponsor on joint ventures up to $10 million. the competitive bid market is not so hot these days and these are the areas we should be looking at.

"Now one problem we have is that I don't really have enough time to do as much in sales as I would like. I think I should put more of my time in operations for we have had some cost overruns that we can't afford to repeat. We moved into Phoenix too rapidly without the necessary staff. The hardest thing in expanding into a new market is having the proper experienced and knowledgeable people behind the operation. We didn't and we paid for it. Phoenix is a good market but it will require some time to run it well and it will take some time of someone to build up a selling effort. When I was back at Harvard for the second SCMP Unit, I talked with an MBA who will be graduating this June, Zachary Roberts, who seemed interested in moving out to the southwest and getting involved with a small company. He doesn't know construction but he has been involved in real estate with a Boston bank. He is coming out to visit us next week and we can take a closer look at each other. I had thought about moving to Phoenix myself last year, but now with the bonding company problems I think I should stay here. We could move with a marketing man there; if we hire one it could really pay off. We have a good project manager in Phoenix now and they could be the team we need. That way I can stay in Tucson, for this is where our estimating will be done. We are selling our office building in Phoenix and will rent a smaller facility.

"Charles, my younger brother is still in the process of learning the management ropes. He knows field work and he is coming along with his new responsibilities, but he is not ready for a general management job just yet. If we grow larger—particularly if we develop the Phoenix market—there will be work for both of us and we will need, in addition, more and more professional people.

"Right now, however, the priority should be on getting more negotiated contracts and more contract management business. I think we need a well-thought-

*Smaller Company Management Program at Harvard Business School.

through marketing effort and that's what I am looking for in Zack Roberts. I also think that his background at Harvard will help all of us at Gunness. One of the things he can do is to help professionalize the firm. I hope I can figure out how to afford him if he is interested and if he fits.

"It is also clear to me that we will have to change our way of thinking about this corporation and get it out in front instead of thinking primarily about our own private interests. We are going to have to build up working capital and cut down on the distribution of earnings to the shareholders. If we want to grow, we will have fewer officer perks and maybe substitute stock options for cash bonuses. This is all going to take planning. This year we are getting, for the first time in the History of the company, an operating budget. Gary Thompson is preparing a budget for fiscal 1978 and we can compare costs against it on an item-by-item basis. I think Roberts could work with Gary in this area as well.

"With the market the way it is, we may have to get into nontraditional construction areas even beyond the negotiated contracts we are used to. There are other contractors doing 'design and build' projects, turnkey projects, real estate development, and the like. Here too, Zack Roberts could be of help. All this means working capital, however, and I think B. J., Charles, and I are going to have to look a little bit more at equity growth than cash payout. We also have to worry about Dad's financial commitment on our bonding contract and start phasing his exposure out and getting the company on its own two feet.

"As an alternative, we could cut back to $3–4 million a year, start over, and go back up. We have the experience, the record of successful projects, but we would have to let almost all our personnel go. Charles and I have talked about it but neither of us like it.

"We have a devil of a problem with this open shop competition but building trends are up. The bonding company has us between two edges of a scissors—we have to live with a reduced bond but we also have to turn a profit. We know we have to raise working capital so we are selling our Phoenix office building and taking out a bank loan on our construction equipment. You know, when Dad walked into the bank to borrow the $250,000, the bank manager asked him why he needed the money since we had $148,000 in our operating account and $140,000 in a savings account. All we are going to do is put the money in CDs through the bank—and that is pretty good business for them.

"We know we have to make profits so we've worked out a plan to reduce overhead. We let an engineer go last week; a payroll clerk will go by Friday; and we are letting an estimator go in Phoenix the end of the month. Gary worked up an operating budget with B. J., Charles and me—Exhibit 3—which cuts our overhead from $500,000 to $328,000. We cut the rent we pay Dad on the building by half; I'm going to sell the Maserati, and we all are cutting personal charges. It will take us April and May to get there but that is what we will live with next year. I hope it is enough."

GARY THOMPSON

Following his interview with Frank, the casewriter discussed the financial projections with Gary Thompson. Gary stated that his best estimate was that Gunness Construction would lose, after tax refunds, $55,000 in 1977 and have surety working capital on May 31, 1977, of approximately $120,000. The company had taken out a 5-year installment loan on its construction equipment and machinery with the bank for $250,000 at 1½% over prime. This would add about $180,000 to the net surety allowed—since the first year's principal payments of $50,000 and interest of about $20,000 would have to be subtracted from the proceeds. Gary also believed that the sale of the Phoenix property would yield $80,000, giving them $380,000 surety at the start of the fiscal year.

In looking toward 1978, Gary stated, "We are working at a rate of about $675,000 a month and that is 135% of a $6 million bonding capacity—130% is about what we have managed historically. Our gross profit figures have ranged between 3½% and 5%—and if I would project our current market mix, I would use 4% based on the recent past. We have enough contracts to give us a $25,000 to $30,000 operating profit by November and since we will put the borrowed money in CDs, our net interest expenses won't be very much.

"As I see it, we have to move faster to be competitive. We haven't moved with the times in bidding, in using nonunion subs, or moving into negotiated work. This means we have to have some type of marketing program. If it costs more we will just have to take the money from somewhere else. We need a strong marketing man, particularly in Phoenix, for the potential there for negotiated business is outstanding. Maybe this Zachery Roberts is our man and maybe he isn't, but we can't afford to wait too long. We have six months to mount a marketing effort that gets us the jobs we need to produce a profit in the six months following our November statements. These are the ones that are critical to the bonding company."

Gary and the casewriter discussed the financial projections beyond November 30, 1977. When Gary stated that the market beyond November was so unsettled that he was hesitant to make a forecast, the casewriter suggested, and Gary agreed, that it would be useful to have a forecast prepared using three different estimated rates of return on contract revenues—4%, 4½%, and 5%, with sales (contract revenues) calculated in each case at the maximum allowed under Gunness' bonding agreement. The 4% rate forecast represented a good level of profits that could be expected from business that was predominantly competitively bid. The 5% rate forecast represented a reasonable level of profits expected from negotiated contracts and the 4½% rate a level that would be the maximum Gunness could aspire to without a substantial change in market direction. It was also agreed to build into the costs an extra $50,000 a year needed to obtain a high percent of negotiated contracts, $25,000 a year for the 4½% forecast, and no extra expenses at the 4% profit level. Gary said he could have a three year forecast for the planning meeting scheduled the next morning.

THE PLANNING MEETING

The planning meeting, attended by B. J. Gunness, Frank Gunness, Gary Thompson, and the casewriter, began with Gary distributing his operating projection (Exhibit 4) and explaining what assumptions lay behind the numbers.

"The November 30, 1977 figures are pretty solid; we have almost all the contracts in the house and with enough progress on the bigger ones to estimate our six month profit. The bonding company will let us have $6 million capacity so with construction revenues 1.3 times bonding capacity, I estimate six month sales at $4,050,000 and a gross profit of $202,500. Our budgeted operating expenses are estimated to be $327,810 a year (Ehxibit 3). But I think we will be a bit slow getting there, so I estimated $175,000. This gives us a profit of $27,500. We will make $25,000 in installment payments to the bank so this leaves us with a $2,500 addition to working capital. If we begin with the $380,000 I told you about earlier, we will have a bonding capacity of $7,650,000 for use in the six months following November 30. I assume that this will take effect in the middle of the period, so I took an average and got a $6,825,000 average bonding capacity. At a 130% utilization for one half a year that is contract revenue of $4,436,000 for the last six months of our next fiscal year.

"Now in the six months ended 5/31/78, I assumed three different gross profit margins and three different levels of operating expenses. For operations that produce a 5% gross profit, I added one-half of $50,000 extra marketing expenditures a year to our budget operating expenses; at 4½%, one-half of $25,000; at 4%, I just took the budgeted figures. To cover a minimum level of inflation, I added $25,000 a year after 1978 in two $12,500 steps. Any questions?"

While the profit planning worksheet was being read and discussed with Gary, the casewriter drew up a graph of profits that Gary forecasted. This graph, Exhibit 6, was then shown to the group. "You will notice," said the casewriter, "that the bonding capacity holds you down on the one side so you can't spread high overhead over a lot of low-profit contracts. On the other hand, overhead, inflation and debt repayment holds down your working capital, and hence your bonding capacity. There is a phrase that comes to mind—'between a rock and a hard place!' "

B. J. Gunness: "Well I hear the numbers and I see the picture. What do we do, Gary?"

Gary: "If we could cut our operating expenses back to $250,000 a year we can survive handsomely at 4%. If we can't, then we better get the 5% business. If that is not possible, then we had better bite the bullet as soon as possible and shrink the company and its overhead."

B. J.: "Well, if we can get away from competitive bidding the 5% margin is no problem—but we can't get it if we have to bid—at least not as we are—and I don't know if we could do it successfully on an open shop basis.

"On the other hand, how can we, with these numbers and with our present overhead, afford to go out and spend another $50,000 to open up another market with the limited bonding capacity we have to work with? And how can someone who doesn't know contracting and doesn't know Tucson or Phoenix do it in time to help us? This is the thing in mind and I wish someone could answer it."

Frank Gunness: "We would have to gamble and take on the overhead before we would see any results—and there would be a learning period in front of that. I don't think that $50,000 is the right cost, however, I think that salary, fringes, automobile, and T&E wouldn't run over $35,000 a year."

Gary: "But how can we continue in the markets we are in and make the profits the analysis shows we need?"

Frank: "I don't think a 1% difference in price is going to really make that much difference as to whether we get a job or not. The difference between a low bidder and the second low bidder is greater than a 1% spread— usually 2% to 2 ½%."

B. J.: "I agree with that, Frank—and the economy is turning around now. This has been a really bad year in Tucson; all the architects in town have laid off people and that doesn't happen here very often. I think the picture is changing and I think next year will see a lot of jobs up for bid and we have always gotten our share. I really don't think we have to get excited and go out after new business—at least as long as our pipeline is full."

Gary: "Well whatever we decide it has to be done quickly. We have a month and a half to make a plan—April and May; four months to implement it— June through September; and two months to react one way or another before November 30 when the bonding company looks at our situation. We aren't really pressed; but we don't have that much breathing room either."

Frank: "One thing I learned at SCMP is that any plan we put together has to fit our interests and the realities of the business market and it has to be co-ordinated; all the pieces put together under the same assumptions."

Casewriter: "That's right, Frank. As I see it you have two simultaneous sets of de-cisions to make. The first is what should be the business strategy of Gunness Construction; what do you want the company to be and how do you plan to get it there—competitive bids, negotiable contracts, open shop, open subcontractors, marketing, Zack Roberts, or what?

"The second is what do you want your role in Gunness Construction to be, Frank; and yours, B. J.? What do you personally want from the company and what do you want to put into it—time, energy, money? And most importantly, how does the second set of factors fit in with the first? If you want to remain active in the company for personal reasons, B. J., and you have said that you would rather do that than play golf or gin, then that has an implication not only on your financial exposure but on the bond size and even on the way the bonding com-pany will view you, Frank, and the company. I think the idea of devel-oping a corporate plan is a good idea but it seems to me you have some personal planning to do at the same time."

Questions

1 What is the best strategy for the company? In answering this ignore the positions of the owners and think of the company as an entity. Should it stay with its traditional mix of business? Should it go towards negotiated contracts? If so, how?

2   What is the best strategy for the owners? How can the company be structured and managed to satisfy their idividual needs?

3   There is an old saying that "in a small company, some things are business, some things are family and you don't mix them up without some care." If Gunness was to hire its second professional, Zachary Roberts, and it grows and is successful what changes will the family have to make to accommodate this new professionalism?

EXHIBIT 1

B. J. GUNNESS CONSTRUCTION COMPANY
Statement of Income and Retained Earnings
For the Periods Ended 1974–1977
(thousands of dollars)

	Year ended May 31			6 months ended Nov. 30 1976	Projected year-ended 5-31-77
	1974	1975	1976		
Contract Income	7385.9	6186.0	13669.7	4924.9	8100
Cost of Contract Income	6849.4	5821.9	13154.8	4830.8	7800
Gross Profit	536.5	364.1	514.9	94.1	300
Cost of Contract Guarantee				(7.2)	
Joint Venture Income, Rentals, etc.	154.5	62.2	(11.9)	(3.8)	–0–
Gross Profit from Contracting Operations	691.0	426.3	503.0	83.1	300
Operating Expenses	400.3	512.2	497.6	249.1	500
Operating Income	290.7	(85.9)	5.4	(166.0)	(200)
Interest and Other Income (Expenses)	44.5	(36.0)	7.7	4.5	5
Profit (Loss) before Taxes	335.2	(121.9)	13.1	(161.5)	(195)
Taxes (Including Reduction in Deferred Amounts and Tax Carry-backs)	169.5	(92.3)	(12.3)	(140.0)	(140)
Net Profit after Tax Considerations and Adjustments	165.7	(29.6)	25.4	(21.5)	(55)
Retained Earnings—Beginning of Period	167.8	333.5	303.9	329.3	308
Retained Earnings—End of Period	333.5	303.9	329.3	307.8	253
Gross Profit Percentages	7.3%	5.9%	3.8%	1.9%	3.7%

EXHIBIT 2

B. J. GUNNESS CONSTRUCTION COMPANY
Comparative Balance Sheets
(thousands of dollars)

		May 31		Nov. 30
ASSETS	1974	1975	1976	1976
Current Assets				
Cash and certificates of deposit	493.7	246.9	241.6	68.9
Contract receivables				
Current	907.2	639.9	1452.8	1104.9
Retention	462.6	382.6	696.3	397.3
Receivables from federal & state tax refunds	—	—	—	41.4
Officers notes & accrued interest	75.2	221.6	51.3	30.5
Other receivables	17.2	6.3	7.8	8.8
Costs & estimated earnings in excess of billings on uncompleted orders	4.8	27.5	15.0	4.3
Prepaid expenses, deposits, and cash value of life insurance	23.6	34.6	42.7	38.7
Investment and advances to joint venture	118.9	63.5	29.0	8.0
Total	2103.2	1622.9	2536.5	1702.8
Property, Plant & Equipment				
Land	—	37.6	38.9	33.7
Buildings & improvements	—	90.3	95.3	92.3
Transportation equipment	92.1	111.9	138.0	138.0
Construction equipment & machinery	137.4	133.3	144.0	146.8
Office furniture and equipment	27.2	26.9	28.9	34.0
Leasehold improvements	19.5	22.5	22.5	22.5
	276.2	422.5	467.6	467.3
Less accumulated depreciation	161.4	177.8	216.4	232.0
Net Property, Plant & Equipment	114.8	244.7	251.2	235.3
TOTAL ASSETS	2218.0	1867.6	2787.7	1938.1

EXHIBIT 2 (continued)

B. J. GUNNESS CONSTRUCTION COMPANY

EQUITIES	1974	May 31		Nov. 30 1976
		1975	1976	
Current Liabilities				
Subcontracts payable				
Current	880.4	550.1	1204.6	940.0
Retention	268.3	276.2	500.6	275.5
Current portion of mortgage payable	—	18.2	2.5	2.7
Billings in excess of cost & estimated earnings on uncompleted contracts	331.0	245.7	457.2	187.1
Accrued liabilities	59.3	208.7	69.2	39.2
Taxes payable	278.3	144.5	107.6	70.6
Total	1817.3	1443.4	2341.7	1515.1
Long Term Liabilities				
Mortgage payable (net of current portion)	—	53.1	49.5	48.0
Deferred taxes	48.7	48.7	48.7	48.7
Total Liabilities	1866.0	1545.2	2439.9	1611.8
Stockholders Equity				
Common stock	18.5	18.5	18.5	18.5
Retained earnings	333.5	303.9	329.3	307.8
Total	352.0	322.4	347.8	326.3
TOTAL EQUITY	2218.0	1867.6	2787.7	1938.1

EXHIBIT 3

Gunness Construction Company Overhead Account

	Budget Category	Current Operating Expenses	Projected Reductions	Projected Operating Expenses	
1	Salaries & payroll taxes	285 960	⟨76 942⟩	209 018	1
2	Depreciation	47 550	⟨22 444⟩	25 106	2
3	Equip. repair & maint.	27 500	⟨5 000⟩	22 500	3
4	Legal & accounting	25 000	⟨15 000⟩	10 000	4
5	Pension and profit sharing	25 000	⟨25 000⟩	—	5
6	Rent	19 500	⟨9 500⟩	10 000	6
7	Telephone	19 000	⟨8 000⟩	11 000	7
8	Insurance	28 570	⟨2 194⟩	26 376	8
9	Office expense	18 750	⟨8 000⟩	10 750	9
10	Travel & entertainment	17 500	⟨11 500⟩	6 000	10
11	Training & recruiting	16 000	⟨13 500⟩	2 500	11
12	Property tax	10 000	—	10 000	12
13	Utilities	8 000	—	8 000	13
14	Gas & oil	7 160	⟨2 160⟩	5 000	14
15	Advertising	6 640	⟨4 140⟩	2 500	15
16	Interest	4 450	6 500	10 950	16
17	Vehicle licenses	5 370	⟨2 970⟩	2 400	17
18	Data processing	4 500	⟨1 500⟩	3 000	18
19	Building maintenance	4 400		4 400	19
20	Group insurance	3 300	⟨690⟩	2 610	20
21	Radio	3 470	⟨2 520⟩	950	21
22	Shop supplies	3 480	⟨1 230⟩	2 250	22
23	Dues & subscriptions	3 340	⟨840⟩	2 500	23
24	Other	1 000	⟨1 000⟩	—	24
25					25
26					26
27					27
28					28
29					29
30	Total operating expenses	595 440	⟨207 630⟩	387 810	30
31					31
32					32
33	Allocations to job cost				33
34	Equipment	⟨65 024⟩	⟨20 024⟩	⟨45 000⟩	34
35	Insurance	⟨20 916⟩	⟨5 916⟩	⟨15 000⟩	35
36					36
37					37
38	Net operating expenses	509 500	181 690	327 810	38
39					39
40					40

EXHIBIT 4

B. J. GUNNESS CONSTRUCTION COMPANY
Profit Planning Worksheet
Six Months Periods Ending
(thousands of dollars)

Date and gross profit percentage	November 30 1977	March 31, 1978			November 30, 1978			March 31, 1979		
		5%	4½%	4%	5%	4½%	4%	5%	4½%	4%
Bonding capacity—start of period (annual)	6000	6000	6000	6000	7650	7650	7650	7808	7614	7421
Bonding capacity—end of period (annual)	6000	7650	7650	7650	7808	7614	7421	8332	7828	7339
Average	6000	6825	6825	6825	7729	7632	7536	8070	7721	7380
Annual sales rate (1.3 times average)	Not applicable	8872	8872	8872	10048	9922	9796	10491	10037	9594
Sales available in six months' period	4050	4436	4436	4436	5023	4960	4898	5246	5019	4799
Gross profit	202.5	221.8	199.6	177.4	251.2	223.2	195.9	262.3	225.8	191.9
Operating expenses	175.0	188.9*	176.4#	163.9+	200.0	187.5	175.0	212.5	200.0	187.5
Income before taxes	27.5	32.9	23.2	13.5	51.2	35.7	20.9	47.8	25.8	4.4
Taxes to be paid		—	—	—				(13.1)	(6.8)	(1.1)
Bank loan payment	(25.0)	(25.0)	(25.0)	(25.0)	(25.0)	(25.0)	(25.0)	(25.0)	(25.0)	(25.0)
Working capital addition	2.5	7.9	(1.8)	(11.5)	26.2	10.7	4.1	11.7	(6.0)	(21.7)
Net surety allowed at beginning of period	380.0	382.5	382.5	382.5	390.4	380.7	371.0	416.6	391.4	366.9
Net surety allowed at end of period	382.5	390.4	380.7	371.0	416.6	391.4	366.9	428.3	385.4	345.2
Bonding capacity at 20:1 (annualized) available for next six months	7650.0	7808	7614	7421	8332	7828	7339	8566	7708	6904

* ½ 327,810 + 25,000
\# ½ 327,810 + 12,500
+ ½ 327,810

EXHIBIT 4 (continued)

B. J. GUNNESS CONSTRUCTION COMPANY

Date and gross profit percentage	November 30, 1979			March 31, 1980			November 30, 1980		
	5%	4½%	4%	5%	4½%	4%	5%	4½%	4%
Bonding capacity—start of period (annual)	3332	7828	7339	8566	7708	6904	8956	7600	6370
Bonding capacity—end of period (annual)	8566	7708	6904	8956	7600	6370	9312	7264	5329
Average	8449	7768	7122	8761	7654	6637	9134	7432	5850
Annual sales rate (1.3 times average)	10938	10098	9258	11389	9950	8628	11874	9662	7604
Sales available in six months' period	5492	5049	4629	5695	4975	4314	5937	4831	3802
Gross profit	274.6	227.2	185.2	284.7	223.9	172.6	296.9	217.4	152.1
Operating expenses	212.5	200.0	187.5	225.0	212.5	200.0	225.0	212.5	200.0
Income before taxes	62.1	27.2	(2.3)	59.7	11.4	(27.4)	71.9	4.9	(47.9)
Taxes to be paid	(17.6)	(7.6)	.7	(16.9)	(3.2)	.4	(21.6)	(1.5)	—
Bank loan payment	(25.0)	(25.0)	(25.0)	(25.0)	(25.0)	(25.0)	(25.0)	(25.0)	(25.0)
Working capital addition	19.5	(5.4)	(26.7)	17.8	(16.8)	(52.0)	25.3	(21.6)	(72.9)
Net surety allowed at beginning of period	428.3	385.4	345.2	447.8	380.0	318.5	465.6	363.2	266.5
Net surety allowed at end of period	447.8	380.0	318.5	465.6	363.2	266.5	490.9	341.6	193.6
Bonding capacity at 20:1 (annualized) available for next six months	8956	7600	6370	9312	7264	5329	9819	6832	2904**

**Multiple lowered to 15:1

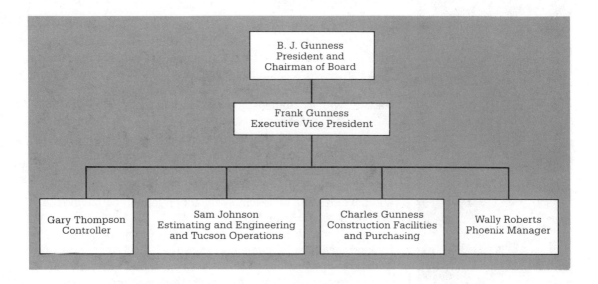

EXHIBIT 5
**B. J. Gunness Construction Company Organization Chart
1977**

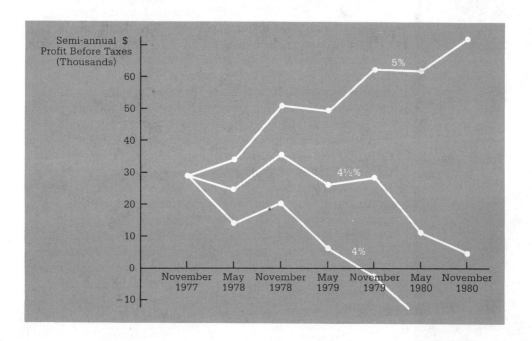

EXHIBIT 6
**Planning Projections,
22 March 1977**

FIRST CHICAGO CORPORATION

Hugh O. Hunter

PART I
THE BANKING ENVIRONMENT OF THE 1970S AND 1980S

Over the past several decades, subtle but important changes have been occuring in the U.S. commercial banking industry. These included a gradually increasing reliance by banks on "purchased" funds—short term liabilities acquired in the money markets, with a commensurate decrease in "core" (demand and passbook time) deposits.

Another evolving trend is the increasing international character of banking in the U.S. Foreign banks have found easy access to U.S. markets, introducing new competition; and large U.S. banks have expanded into overseas markets, and have become increasingly reliant on foreign borrowings to support domestic loan demand.

The McFadden Act, which prohibits interstate banking, has been so amended to allow virtually all phases of banking to operate interstate, the sole exception being the taking of core deposits. Thus, especially the large "money center" banks lend, lease, purchase funds and raise capital without regard to state boundaries. This too has had the effect of increasing competition.

All of these trends were well developed by the beginning of the 1970s, and contributed to the profound changes which were to occur in banking in the decade. The catalyst for change was a relatively new phenomenon, one which began in the late 1960s, and accelerated to a totally unexpected degree in the 1970s. This was the abrupt and simultaneous increase in both the level and volatility of interest rates. Bank core deposits shrunk because of the federally mandated rate ceilings attached to these deposits. These lost deposits were replaced by increasingly expensive purchased funds. Suddenly, interest expense became the largest single expense for the banks. Competition for "cheap" core deposits intensified. Many banks caught with fixed rate loans booked at lower historical rates found themselves losing money, and "net interest margin" became an item of prime importance.[1] Loan rates rose and banks competed actively for these high yielding loans. Not only were they competing against each other, but they faced customer resistance to the high rates, and increasingly lost ground to the encroachments of leasing and commercial paper.

During the 1970s two major U.S. banks and scores of smaller banks failed as the shakeout in the industry

Copyright 1981 Hugh O. Hunter

This case was prepared from published information. The Company in no way participated in its preparation began. It continues today, and with passage of the *Depository Institutions Deregulation and Monetary Control Act of 1980,* the Federal Government has, in effect, increased levels of competition. The Act gradually removes interest rate deposit ceilings, weakens usury laws, and allows "thrift" institutions to compete more directly with commercial banks.[2] In addition, pressure mounts to further dismember the McFadden Act to allow limited interstate branching.

PART II
FIRST CHICAGO CORP. AND CONTINENTAL ILLINOIS CORP., 1971–75.

Succumbing to the competitive pressures of the 1970s, and to a natural rivalry, Chicago's two largest banks began, in 1971, a race for growth which lasted for four years and left one bank seriously weakened and the other positioned to assume clear dominance. Chicago is one of the three money centers in the United States (the other two being New York and California). In the money centers reside the truly national and international banks. Chicago's two money center banks are First Chicago and Continental Illinois.[3] These two banks were nearly identical in size and earnings, and were the dominant banks in the lucrative midwest market. The backbone of any large commercial bank is its commercial (business) lending. Here, First Chicago had an edge, one that had been painstakingly developed over the Bank's 108 years in the City. In the 1940s and 1950s, First Chicago emerged as one of nation's premier industrial lenders. The Bank pioneered the use of specialized industrial lending divisions. Under its chairman, Gaylord Freeman, First Chicago achieved much of its growth in the early 1970s by giving virtually free rein to its commercial lending officers. This policy of decentralization creates lending departments which can aggressively market loans and respond quickly to customer demands. In doing this, the bank gives up much of its control, and in the volatile 1970s, this lack of control cost First Chicago dearly.

In the period 1971–75, First Chicago was the fastest growing major U.S. bank. The price it paid was booking huge volumes of questionable loans. With the recession of 1974–75, First Chicago charged off $92.9 million in loan losses, with a great many other "non-performing" loans still on the books.

Nearly matching First Chicago in growth during this period was rival Continental Illinois. Both banks doubled their assets and deposits in the period 1971–75. Continental was not unaffected by the 1974–75 recession, but it ended this period with a relatively solid loan portfolio, charging off $20.2 million in loan losses. This was reflected in a turnaround in operating profit. In 1973–74 combined, First Chicago reported about $13 million more profit; but in 1975 alone, Continental's operating profit was $14 million higher.

During this period, Gaylord Freeman had planned for his succession by appointing four executive vice presidents, one of whom would be chosen Chairman and C.E.O. One of these was A. Robert Abboud, a diminutive, pugnacious ex-Marine—Harvard Law, and Harvard M.B.A. graduate. In late 1975, Abboud acceded to the chairmanship of the troubled bank. Abboud was Freeman's choice, but reportedly not the choice of the Board of Directors. A predictable contest for power had developed between the four, an internecine fight which merely added to the turmoil at First Chicago.

One of the four, Richard L. Thomas, became president and remains in that position today. The other two left to assume top positions in two California banks, and took with them a number of key executives. It was the beginning of a talent drain which would last for five years.

PART III
FIRST CHICAGO UNDER ABBOUD, 1975–80

Abboud's Management Style   When Abboud took over, he perceived a bank in desperate trouble; one whose excesses of lending and lack of control had to be sharply curtailed. He centralized management in what had traditionally been a decentralized organization. The focus of all major decisions, especially those involving lending, was Bob Abboud. His "hands-on" management style was accompanied, some say, by an almost tyrannical treatment of subordinates. Abboud claimed later that he had to save the Bank almost by himself, because to involve others, and let the seriousness of First Chicago's plight leak, would have caused a "worldwide financial panic."[4]

Until late 1979, there was in essence no strategic planning at First Chicago. Continental Illinois, starting the second half of the decade with a strong financial base, developed a comprehensive five year strategic plan. Abboud busied himself with saving First Chicago. In this, he claimed success. "Look, this is the biggest turnaround in banking history."[5]

Abboud's tactics and motives were questioned by many in the bank. Once during his tenure, he took personal control of the Bank's "money desk" and negotiated transactions in the international money markets.[6] Some claim that he was angered over low trading profits. He says that he was keeping a desperately illiquid bank afloat by negotiating with foreign central banks to honor First Chicago's international clearings.

Morality also became a factor in Abboud's management. Twice he withheld loans from companies whose managers were accused of criminal activities. The companies were the Lockheed Corporation and Playboy Enterprises. He accused many of his executives of lacking in loyalty to the organization. He accused his loan officers of accepting favors (expecially whiskey) from their business customers. And after the wealthy Pritzker family (Hyatt Corp. and Marmon Group) withdrew business from First Chicago, Abboud said, "I just didn't like the nature of some of the businesses (the Pritzkers) were in."[7]

Loan Policies   Determined not to make any more low quality commercial loans, and to extract profits from those loans made, Abboud applied tough credit standards and raised the cost of borrowing from First Chicago. He forced delays in approving loans, and he demanded high fees or compensating balances for loan commitments.[8]

Abboud was a tough bargainer. Once, he withdrew a $20 million letter of credit from a refining company, forcing it into bankruptcy. When a $60 million line of credit to a "theme park" was in jeopardy, Abboud forced conversion of the loan into equity.

In his zeal, Abboud applied his tough policies more or less equally to all commercial customers, losing some good ones in the process.

The Branching Fight   Shortly after becoming Chairman, Abboud reversed a tradition at First chicago and began to concentrate on retail banking—consumer lending and branching—at the expense of corporate banking.

Illinois is a unit banking state (not allowing branching or group banking). Stifled by their inability to branch, and thus attract low cost core deposits, both First Chicago and Continental Illinois, in 1975, opened EFT terminals in the Chicago area.[9] The State forced closure, but Abboud, in April 1976, challenged the law by opening ten "community offices" around Chicago. When he lost in the courts, Abboud began to vigorously campaign for a change in the State banking laws. He used a close relationship with Chicago's Mayor Daly to elicit political support. Illinois is still a unit banking state.

Asset-Liabilities Management   In 1977, after three years in which the commercial loan portfolio fell from $5 billion to less than $4 billion, First Chicago began a partial reversal of its stringent lending policies and began to solicit loans. In an effort to attract business, loans were made at fixed rates and for longer than normal periods—some as long as five years. These loans were financed with purchased funds, carrying short maturities. The loan portfolio began to grow.

In 1979, interest rates rose dramatically. First Chicago had not been successful in refinancing its fixed rate loan portfolio with longer term fixed rate liabilities before rates rose. As a result, its net interest income fell by $20 million in nominal dollars or $77 million in inflation adjusted dollars.

The reasons for the Banks's failure to re-finance are not clear. Certainly, some financial institutions simply failed to see the rise in rates in time. It is also possible that the defection of key managers left First Chicago unable to respond in time.[10]

Results   In the first year and a half of the Abboud era, First Chicago lost 12% of its executives. Throughout the entire era, executives and loan officers left because of differences with Abboud, and because the once exciting period of growth at First Chicago had ended. A no-growth environment does not satisfy the more aggressive managers. Also, in steady-state, not as many are needed. Indeed, many who left were not replaced.

In his effort to improve First Chicago's balance sheet (by 1979 the asset/equity ratio was a very low 22/1), Abboud lost some important corporate customers.[11] These included Inland Steel, Co., Gould, Inc., the Pritzkers, and Marshall Field. To add to the embarrassment, two of these firms were represented on the Bank's Board of Directors, and most went to Continental Illinois.

By the end of 1979, Continental Illinois had solidified its number one position in Chicago. From 1975–79, Continental's commercial loans doubled, while First Chicago's fell by 6%, in spite of its renewed efforts to attract loans. During the same period, Continental's profits grew some 73% while First Chicago's grew by 4% in nominal (current) dollars.

In the early 1970s, First Chicago held a commanding position in energy and commercial real estate lending. By the end of the decade, both markets had been taken over by Continental Illinois. Continental emerged as perhaps the nation's leading energy bank, and it held a dominant market share of new high rise construction in Chicago. (See exhibit 1 for comparative 1980 data.)

During the Abboud years, First Chicago's earnings per share grew at a compound rate of 3.7%, the lowest of the top ten U.S. banks. Net income, which had fallen in 1979 because of high interest rates, fell even more sharply in 1980. The reasons cited by the Bank were the continuing decline in net interest income due to high interest rates, increased loan losses, and higher inflation induced operating expenses.

Abboud had managed to reduce the Bank's non-performing loans from $1.4 billion in 1976 to $831 million in 1980. Nonperforming loans proportioned to total loans were twice the national average at First Chicago in 1976. By 1980, they were still above average.

PART IV
EXIT ABBOUD, ENTER SULLIVAN

In May 1980, a dispute between Abboud and his chief operating officer forced the Board's hand, and Abboud was fired. After a search, the Board selected Barry F. Sullivan, from Chase Manhattan Corp., as Chairman. Sullivan came with strong "people" skills and with a penchant for strategic planning. The Board had selected Bob Abboud's opposite, a man with many of the strengths of Abboud's predecessor, Gaylord Freeman.

By early 1981, Sullivan had done the following:

1 Decentralized the commercial lending function to allow quicker decisions, and announced an aggressive lending policy.

2 Arranged to sell $150 million of real estate loans, most of them nonperforming, at a $7 million loss.

3 In August 1980, when interest rates were relatively low, refinanced $400 million of liabilities with longer term deposits.

4 Articulated a goal of closely balancing asset and liabilities maturities.

5 In October 1980, presented to the Board a five-year strategic plan.

PART V
EXCERPTS FROM FIRST CHICAGO CORP.'S
FIVE-YEAR PLAN, 1980–85[12]

Part 1 Environmental Assessment   Relative to the last five years, the world's economies will generally have higher rates of inflation, slower real economic growth, and greater volatility in business cycles and interest rates.

The legislative and regulatory processes are unlikely to produce either major problems or major opportunities, but the prospects for changes in interest rate ceilings and interstate banking restrictions will present some strategic challenges.

A number of social trends that have affected the banking industry, including ever-rising expectations of the work force and increased turnover, are likely to continue.

Competition in the banking industry will remain intense, but corporations will use fewer banks as principal or "first tier" providers of banking services.

Part 2 Essence Statement   "The mission of First Chicago is threefold: to be a world class money center bank with national and international reach, to be the premier bank serving the Midwest, and to be the leader in bringing banking services to the Chicago community.

"We are dedicated to earning a preferred position with each of our customers by consistently delivering high quality service on a competitive basis. Such service will be provided in a spirit of long-term partnership whereby we commit to make the customer's interests our interests.

"The cornerstone of that service will be professional competence and focused resources. Both will be explicitly directed only at those markets, industries and products in which we can excel.

"The development of close working partnerships with financial institutions will be a key focus and specialization of First Chicago. We strongly believe that this approach will best serve the institutions themselves, their customers, and ours as well.

"First Chicago's commitment to serve our customers requires a physical presence in financial and commercial centers of the world and wherever else such a presence is important to the effective delivery of our services.

"Two commitments are essential to our mission—first, to attract, develop and retain people of the highest character and competence; second, to develop and provide creative financial products and services, with particular emphasis on emerging technology.

"First Chicago starts from a base that is strong and financially sound. We will enhance that strong base through increasing profitability at acceptable rates of return with resultant benefit to our shareholders, customers and employees.

"The challenge in accomplishing this mission is considerable, but we are committed to its achievement."

Part 3 Financial Objectives   With regard to capital policy, management reaffirmed its intention that First Chicago remain among the better capitalized of the major U.S. bank holding companies. Dividend recommendations to the Board of Directors will be consistent with this objective, but will also reflect the desire to generate periodic increases in per share dividends. Further reflecting this conservative policy, limitations were placed on the use of long-term debt as an element of capital structure.

The continuous maintenance of strong liquidity is a key priority in the Corporation's financial objectives. Because First Chicago relies heavily on purchased funds markets worldwide, achieving this liquidity objective will require careful management of funding operations as well as effective management of liquid assets on the balance sheet.

As discussed in the Letter to Shareholders, the great volatility in market interest rates over the past two years has resulted in fluctuating earnings for the

Corporation in part because of a mismatch between longer-term fixed-rate assets and liabilities. Management expects interest rates to remain volatile, and has therefore set as an objective the establishment and maintenance of a balance sheet structure that will insulate the Corporation's net interest income from changes in interest rates to the maximum degree possible.

Finally, to ensure adequate ability to absorb credit losses, the Corporation will maintain a strong ratio of loan loss reserves to total loans.

Part 4 Priority Markets, Products, and Geographic Areas   The next task in the construction of the strategic plan was to identify those markets, products, and geographic areas tht present the greatest opportunities for profitable growth and that are consistent with the Corporation's overall mission. This process involved extensive market research and careful assessment of the Corporation's own capabilities.

Although a basic outline has been completed and areas of initial emphasis selected, the scope of this task is so large, and the design of marketing programs for its implementation is so complex, that it will not be completed until late in 1981.

Implementation   After extensive study in late 1980, management concluded that the Corporation's existing organizational structure needed revision to accomplish the goals of the strategic plan. Therefore, in January of 1981, significant changes were made in the Corporation's business unit structure and management reporting responsibilities.

The objective of this reorganization is to focus the considerable talent within the Corporation, and that of the additional personnel to be recruited from outside, on the customer-oriented objectives that the corporation has set for itself in its strategic plan. Throughout the strategic planning process, management has recognized that the Corporation's success will depend ultimately on the ability to serve customer needs better than its competitors. With this strategic plan as a guide, and the efforts of thousands of employees as the driving force, management is confident that success will be achieved.

Barry Sullivan seems determined to revive the Bank, buffeted by inconsistent management over the past decade. As the Bank's management looks to the future, a number of questions remain:

1   Did Bob Abboud "turnaround" First Chicago?

2   Were his actions necessary, or did he overreact to a less than desperate situation?

3   Could First Chicago have avoided being caught by high interest rates in 1979?

4   Why was Continental Illinois able to prosper during the uncertain 1970s?

5   How likely is First Chicago, under Sullivan's leadership, to re-establish itself alongside Continental Illinois?

6   Does the new five-year plan include a realistic assessment of First Chicago and its environment, and does it chart the proper course for the bank?

ENDNOTES

1 Net interest margin is the difference between the average yield on assets and the average cost of liabilities.

2 Thrift institutions include Savings and Loan Associations, Mutual Savings Banks and Credit Unions.

3 This case involves First Chicago Corp. and Continental Illinois Corp., holding companies for the First National Bank of Chicago and Continental Illinois National Bank & Trust Co., respectively. Nearly all large banks have formed holding companies of which the bank is the primary subsidiary.

4 Abboud quoted in *Forbes*, September 1, 1980, 34.

5 Abboud quoted in *Forbes*, September 1, 1980, 34.

6 The money desk is the trading room for investment securities and purchased funds.

7 Abboud quoted in *Forbes*, September 1, 1980, 34.

8 A loan commitment is an informal agreement by the bank to have money available to a commercial customer. The customer then may or may not borrow the entire amount of the commitment.

9 EFT—Electronic Funds Transfer.

10 In banking, almost all purchased liabilities are short term (one year or less). Banks are able to acquire funds in maturities ranging from overnight to one year. The average maturity of a bank's liabilities can have a great impact on earnings when interest rates are volatile.

11 Not all of these customers withdrew entirely from the Bank. Some substantially reduced their borrowings and deposits.

12 These excerpts are taken from the First Chicago Corp., *Annual Report 1980*, pp. 6–11, 13, 17.

EXHIBIT 1*

First Chicago Corp. and Continental Illinois Corp. COMPARATIVE DATA, 1980 (millions)		
	First Chicago	Continental
Rank	10	6
Total Assets	$28,699	$42,089
Total Deposits	21,361	27,314
Loans	16,939	26,784
Growth Measures (Average Annual Rates)		
Assets 1976–80	11.5%	17.7%
1979–80	12.4	19.0
EPS 1976–80	− 12.2	12.2
1979–80	− 43.8	15.2
Profitability		
Return on equity		
1977–80 (avg. annual)	10.0%	16.0%
Net Interest Margin, 1980	1.77%	2.55%

*Forbes, April 13, 1981, 136–39.

	December 31, 1980	
Interest Sensitivity of Loans* (In Thousands)	Fixed Rate	Variable Rate
Domestic		
Due in one year or less**	$1,387,519	$ 2,938,292
Due in one to five years	1,295,855	1,948,419
Due after five years	582,174	426,433
Total domestic	$3,265,548	$ 5,313,144
Foreign		
Due in one year or less**	$ 687,943	$ 2,747,557
Due in one to five years	151,179	2,311,233
Due after five years	81,047	568,325
Total foreign	$ 920,169	$ 5,627,115
Total loans	$4,185,717	$10,940,259

*Excludes domestic consumer and residential mortgage loans
totaling $1,841,655.

**Includes demand loans.

Domestic time certificates of deposit of $100,000 and over, at December 31, had maturities as follows (in thousands):

	1980	1979	1978
Less than three months	$3,319,681	$2,672,187	$2,692,250
Three to six months	626,152	689,465	1,255,895
Seven to twelve months	126,062	190,765	477,107
Over one year	399,781	195,507	111,169
Total	$4,471,676	$3,747,924	$4,536,421

	December 31, 1980		
Maturity Distribution of Loans* (In Thousands)	One Year or Less**	One to Five Years	Over Five Years
Domestic			
Commercial	$2,271,531	$1,814,832	$ 546,330
Secured by real estate	528,833	699,426	241,214
Financial institutions	598,132	524,680	136,474
Other	927,315	205,336	84,589
Total domestic	$4,325,811	$3,244,274	$1,008,607
Foreign	3,435,500	2,462,412	649,372
Total loans	$7,761,311	$5,706,686	$1,657,979

*Excludes domestic consumer and residential mortgage loans
totaling $1,841,655.

**Includes demand loans.

EXHIBIT 2

First Chicago Maturity Distribution and Interest Sensitivity of Loans, and Time Certificates of Deposit

	1980	1979	1978	1977	1976
As Reported					
Net interest income (millions)	**$373**	$406	$426	$384	$383
Dividends declared, per share	**1.20**	1.15	1.05	0.98	0.96
Market price of common stock at year end	**15⅝**	15½	19	18½	22⅞
As Adjusted					
Net interest income (millions)	**$373**	$461	$538	$523	$555
Dividends declared, per share	**1.20**	1.31	1.33	1.33	1.39
Market price of common stock at year end	**14⅞**	16⅝	23⅛	24½	32⅜
Consumer Price Index, average (1967 = 100.0)	**246.8**	217.4	195.4	181.5	170.5

Loans—Composition

December 31 (In Thousands)	1980	1979	1978	1977	1976
Domestic					
Commercial	**$ 4,632,693**	$ 4,689,302	$ 4,225,066	$ 3,744,019	$ 4,051,411
Secured by real estate*	**2,308,637**	1,970,402	1,618,688	1,440,121	1,166,915
Real estate investment trusts	**143,566**	212,700	287,254	386,718	566,524
Other financial institutions	**1,115,720**	1,201,841	1,277,506	1,023,600	947,958
Consumer	**1,002,491**	1,103,267	962,302	732,710	556,314
Other	**1,217,240**	1,105,582	973,579	1,080,409	922,840
Total domestic	**$10,420,347**	$10,283,094	$ 9,344,395	$ 8,407,577	$ 8,211,962
Foreign	**6,547,284**	5,453,587	4,438,284	4,489,772	3,507,577
Total loans	**$16,967,631**	$15,736,681	$13,782,679	$12,897,349	$11,719,539

*Includes residential and other mortgages.

Analysis of Net Charge-Offs

Charge-Offs	1980	1979	1978	1977	1976
Domestic					
Commercial	**$ 56,476**	$ 56,387	$ 25,620	$ 21,880	$ 40,097
Secured by real estate	**5,036**	10,264	30,173	20,137	48,580
Real estate investment trusts	**—**	4,069	8,661	32,226	35,376
Consumer	**36,276**	30,655	20,204	11,035	9,186
Other	**1,562**	2,477	3,691	6,009	7,966
Foreign	**22,244**	3,718	18,547	12,878	12,483
Total charge-offs	**$121,594**	$107,570	$106,896	$104,165	$153,688

Recoveries	1980	1979	1978	1977	1976
Domestic					
Commercial	**$ 6,147**	$ 15,789	$ 3,668	$ 1,498	$ 3,728
Secured by real estate	**2,272**	2,208	188	906	1,276
Real estate investment trusts	**2,031**	2,297	50	117	2
Consumer	**6,466**	5,007	3,316	2,881	2,502
Other	**1,483**	1,636	339	179	231
Foreign	**1,348**	3,944	1,813	181	135
Total recoveries	**$ 19,747**	$ 30,881	$ 9,374	$ 5,762	$ 7,874
Net charge-offs	**$101,847**	$ 76,689	$ 97,522	$ 98,403	$145,814

Nonperforming Assets December 31 (In Thousands)	1980	1979	1978	1977	1976
Loans					
Nonaccrual loans	**$397,460**	$455,814	$ 593,960	$ 805,984	$1,058,504
Renegotiated loans*	**294,731**	309,006	382,820	351,995	206,376
	$692,191	$764,820	$ 976,780	$1,157,979	$1,264,880
Other real estate	**139,033**	139,395	159,075	153,673	95,783
Total	**$831,224**	$904,215	$1,135,855	$1,311,652	$1,360,663
Nonperforming assets as a percentage of total loans and other real estate	**4.9%**	5.7%	8.2%	10.1%	11.5%

*Includes only those renegotiated loans which are not classified as nonaccrual loans.

Nonperforming assets are comprised of 1) those loans on which the Corporation does not accrue interest but recognizes interest as income only as collected ("nonaccrual loans"), 2) those loans which bear a rate of interest which has been reduced below market rates due to the deteriorating financial condition of the borrower ("renegotiated loans"), and 3) real estate assets acquired in satisfaction of debt ("other real estate"). The table below shows a five year summary of the Corporation's nonperforming assets.

EXHIBIT 3
Interest Income and Selected Dividends, with Loans—Composition

Consolidated Statement of Condition
First Chicago Corporation and Subsidiaries

December 31 (In Thousands)	1980	1979
Assets		
Cash and due from banks—non-interest bearing	$ 2,769,859	$ 2,458,364
Due from banks—interest bearing	5,007,651	6,714,241
Securities		
Investment (market values—$1,381,027 in 1980 and $2,004,751 in 1979)	1,621,175	2,132,715
Bond trading account	103,063	177,062
Other short-term investments	435,056	662,761
Loans, net of unearned discount	$16,939,150	$15,703,782
Less Allowance for possible loan losses	150,577	140,424
Loans, net	$16,788,573	$15,563,358
Lease financing, net	362,966	377,236
Premises and equipment	287,517	260,372
Accrued income receivable	402,618	415,921
Customers' acceptance liability	578,497	977,756
Other real estate	139,033	139,395
Other assets	203,433	302,619
Total assets	$28,699,441	$30,181,800
Liabilities		
Deposits—domestic		
Demand deposits	$ 3,259,524	$ 3,371,078
Time deposits		
Savings passbook	$ 711,718	$ 798,571
Other savings-type	1,493,159	1,302,007
Other time	4,224,330	3,545,638
Total time deposits	$ 6,429,207	$ 5,646,216
Total deposits—domestic	$ 9,688,731	$ 9,017,294
Deposits—overseas branches and subsidiaries	11,672,423	12,088,766
Total deposits	$21,361,154	$21,106,060
Funds borrowed	4,461,606	5,613,458
Notes payable	247,512	318,640
Acceptances outstanding	586,245	980,519
Other liabilities	838,405	976,603
Total liabilities	$27,494,922	$28,995,280
Capital		
Preferred stock—without par value, authorized 5,000,000 shares, none issued	$ —	$ —
Common stock—$5 par value	200,768	200,768

	1980	1979
Number of shares authorized	54,000,000	54,000,000
Number of shares issued	40,153,640	40,153,640
Number of shares outstanding	39,806,598	39,633,073

	1980	1979
Surplus	698,492	548,558
Undivided profits	310,638	445,264
Total	$ 1,209,898	$ 1,194,590
Less Treasury stock at cost, 347,042 shares in 1980 and 520,567 shares in 1979	5,379	8,070
Total capital	$ 1,204,519	$ 1,186,520
Total liabilities and capital	$28,699,441	$30,181,800

The accompanying notes to financial statements are an integral part of this statement.

EXHIBIT 4

Consolidated Statement of Condition
First Chicago Corporation and Subsidiaries

Consolidated Statement of Earnings
First Chicago Corporation and Subsidiaries

For the Year (In Thousands)	1980	1979	1978
Interest Income			
Interest and fees on loans	**$2,152,179**	$1,655,008	$1,229,825
Interest on bank balances	**774,735**	550,109	235,900
Interest on investment securities			
United States Government and Federal Agency	**66,020**	70,092	91,338
States and political subdivisions	**37,916**	36,130	43,406
Other (including dividends)	**31,342**	33,112	24,946
Interest on other short-term investments	**63,479**	70,828	57,252
Interest on bond trading account securities			
States and political subdivisions	**3,750**	2,606	1,776
Other	**18,402**	13,554	8,533
Lease financing income	**25,872**	24,942	29,283
Total	**$3,173,695**	$2,456,381	$1,722,259
Interest Expense			
Interest on deposits	**$2,170,316**	$1,507,118	$ 988,823
Interest on funds borrowed	**610,638**	521,754	283,820
Interest on notes payable	**19,786**	21,667	23,594
Total	**$2,800,740**	$2,050,539	$1,296,237
Net Interest Income	**$ 372,955**	$ 405,842	$ 426,022
Provision for loan losses	**112,000**	84,000	118,000
Net Interest Income After Provision for Loan Losses	**$ 260,955**	$ 321,842	$ 308,022
Other Operating Income			
Bond trading profits	**$ 8,225**	$ 5,980	$ 5,809
Foreign exchange trading profits	**21,808**	11,195	13,079
Trust department revenue	**44,211**	36,171	33,488
Service charges on deposit accounts	**10,678**	10,651	6,944
Other service charges and commissions	**89,114**	74,593	62,396
Other income	**67,056**	50,992	61,621
Total	**$ 241,092**	$ 189,582	$ 183,337
Other Operating Expense			
Salaries	**$ 188,952**	$ 157,807	$ 136,778
Profit-sharing	**10,649**	9,659	8,866
Other employee benefits	**28,508**	23,368	19,069
Occupancy expense of premises, net	**41,644**	29,465	27,646
Equipment rentals, depreciation and maintenance	**28,272**	24,146	21,030
Other expense	**149,258**	122,245	107,462
Total	**$ 447,283**	$ 366,690	$ 320,851
Income Before Income Taxes and Security Gains or Losses	**$ 54,764**	$ 144,734	$ 170,508
Applicable income taxes (benefit)	**(11,733)**	29,286	39,463
Income Before Security Gains or Losses	**$ 66,497**	$ 115,448	$ 131,045
Security Gains or (Losses)			
Before taxes	**$ (6,756)**	$ (6,493)	$ (1,409)
Applicable income taxes (benefit)	**(3,267)**	(3,086)	(763)
After taxes	**$ (3,489)**	$ (3,407)	$ (646)
Net Income	**$ 63,008**	$ 112,041	$ 130,399
Earnings per Common and Common Equivalent Share			
Income Before Security Gains or Losses	**$1.68**	$2.91	$3.30
Net Income	**$1.59**	$2.83	$3.29
Average Number of Common and Common Equivalent Shares Outstanding	**39,651,996**	39,632,576	39,670,511

The accompanying notes to financial statements are an integral part of this statement.

EXHIBIT 5

Consolidated Statement of Earnings
First Chicago Corporation and Subsidiaries

Consolidated Statement of Changes in Financial Position
First Chicago Corporation and Subsidiaries

For the Year (In Thousands)	1980	1979	1978
Sources of Financial Resources			
Provided from operations			
Net income	$ **63,008**	$ 112,041	$ 130,399
Provision for loan losses	**112,000**	84,000	118,000
Deferred income taxes	**(39,800)**	6,800	9,200
Depreciation and amortization of leasehold improvements	**21,114**	18,971	17,290
Resources provided from operations	$ **156,322**	$ 221,812	$ 274,889
Increase in:			
Deposits	**255,094**	3,639,619	412,337
Funds borrowed	**—**	1,745,944	751,119
Decrease in:			
Due from banks—interest bearing	**1,706,590**	—	—
Investment securities	**511,540**	527,874	108,545
Bond trading account securities	**73,999**	—	—
Other short-term investments	**227,705**	—	—
Other, net	**36,333**	101,545	—
Total	**$2,967,583**	$6,236,794	$1,546,890
Applications of Financial Resources			
Increase in:			
Cash and due from banks—non-interest bearing	$ **311,495**	$ 376,962	$ 83,149
Due from banks—interest bearing	**—**	3,589,770	119,507
Bond trading account securities	**—**	48,257	7,065
Other short-term investments	**—**	111,540	208,588
Loans	**1,337,215**	2,025,833	983,991
Decrease in:			
Funds borrowed	**1,151,852**	—	—
Notes payable	**71,128**	—	56,439
Additions to premises and equipment, net	**48,259**	38,855	24,841
Cash dividends declared	**47,634**	45,577	41,606
Other, net	**—**	—	21,704
Total	**$2,967,583**	$6,236,794	$1,546,890

The accompanying notes to financial statements are an integral part of these statements.

EXHIBIT 6

**Consolidated Statement of Changes in Financial Position
First Chicago Corporation and Subsidiaries**

726

Historical Financial Summary
First Chicago Corporation and Subsidiaries

Selected Financial Data

(Dollars in Thousands except per share data)	1980	1979	1978	1977	1976
For the Year					
Net interest income	$ **372,955**	$ 405,842	$ 426,022	$ 384,290	$ 383,085
Provision for loan losses	**112,000**	84,000	118,000	109,000	126,500
Income before security					
gains or losses	**66,497**	115,448	131,045	111,099	92,928
Per share	**1.68**	2.91	3.30	2.80	2.35
Net income	**63,008**	112,041	130,399	114,113	105,640
Per share	**1.59**	2.83	3.29	2.88	2.67
Dividends declared per share	**1.20**	1.15	1.05	0.98	0.96
At Year-End					
Total assets	**$28,699,441**	$30,181,800	$24,066,073	$22,613,959	$19,834,052
Total deposits	**21,361,154**	21,106,060	17,466,441	17,054,104	14,063,432
Loans, net of unearned					
discount	**16,939,150**	15,703,782	13,754,638	12,868,169	11,695,067
Total capital	**1,204,519**	1,186,520	1,120,004	1,030,886	955,563
Financial Ratios					
Income before security gains					
or losses as a percentage of:					
Average capital	**5.55%**	9.98%	12.17%	11.19%	10.08%
Average assets	**0.23**	0.45	0.58	0.53	0.50
Average interest earning					
assets	**0.27**	0.52	0.67	0.60	0.56
Total capital at year-end as					
a percentage of:					
Total assets at year-end	**4.2**	3.9	4.7	4.6	4.8
Total net loans at year-end	**7.2**	7.6	8.2	8.1	8.2
Total deposits at year-end	**5.6**	5.6	6.4	6.0	6.8
Average capital as a					
percentage of:					
Average assets	**4.2**	4.5	4.8	4.7	5.0
Average net loans	**7.6**	8.3	8.4	8.3	8.2
Average deposits	**5.9**	6.5	6.6	6.8	7.1
Common Stock and Shareholder Data					
Market price					
High for the year	$ **16⅝**	$ 19⅞	$ 25¾	$ 22⅞	$ 23¾
Low for the year	**10¾**	14⅜	16¾	16⅞	16½
At year-end	**15⅝**	15½	19	18½	22⅞
Dividend payout ratio	**75.47%**	40.64%	31.91%	34.03%	35.96%
Price earnings ratio					
(year-end market)	**9.3**	5.3	5.8	6.6	9.7
Shareholders' equity per					
share (at year-end)	**$30.26**	$29.94	$28.26	$26.02	$24.12
Number of shareholders	**15,524**	14,922	14,642	15,314	15,819

EXHIBIT 7

Historical Financial Summary
First Chicago Corporation and Subsidiaries

Average Balances/Interest Differential/Rates
First Chicago Corporation and Subsidiaries

Year Ended December 31	1980			1979		
(Income and rates on tax equivalent basis) (Dollars in Thousands)	Balance	Interest Income/ Expense	Average Rates Earned/ Paid	Balance	Interest Income/ Expense	Average Rates Earned/ Paid
Assets						
Due from banks—interest bearing* (A)	$ 5,810,914	$ 774,735	13.33%	$ 5,019,216	$ 550,109	10.96%
Investment securities*						
United States Government						
and Federal Agency	740,768	66,020	8.91	829,522	70,092	8.45
States and political subdivisions**	655,312	68,859	10.51	661,442	65,376	9.88
Other**	382,892	38,714	10.11	442,826	39,528	8.93
Bond trading account securities*						
States and political subdivisions**	56,696	6,945	12.25	47,554	4,826	10.15
Other	156,007	18,402	11.80	143,746	13,554	9.43
Other short-term investments*	507,907	63,479	12.50	646,294	70,828	10.96
Loans, net of unearned discount (B)						
Domestic**	10,135,009	1,355,464	13.04	9,281,489	1,101,108	11.52
Foreign	5,866,017	811,717	13.77	4,736,480	563,251	11.82
Total*	$16,001,026			$14,017,969		
Less Allowance for						
possible loan losses	149,376			142,468		
Loans, net	$15,851,650			$13,875,501		
Lease financing* ** (C)	370,522	33,032	16.44	386,989	36,070	15.72
Cash and due from banks—						
non-interest bearing	1,993,565			1,749,322		
Other assets	2,180,282			1,731,524		
Total assets/ Total interest income (D)	$28,706,515	$3,237,367		$25,533,936	$2,514,742	
Liabilities and Capital						
Deposits—domestic						
Demand deposits	$ 2,768,674			$ 2,582,155		
Time deposits						
Savings passbook	$ 752,240	$ 39,708	5.28%	$ 859,602	$ 44,310	5.15%
Other savings-type	1,369,596	137,179	10.02	1,225,304	100,889	8.23
Other time	3,451,799	446,934	12.95	3,548,452	365,826	10.31
Total time deposits	$ 5,573,635			$ 5,633,358		
Total deposits—domestic	$ 8,342,309			$ 8,215,513		
Deposits—overseas offices (E)	12,144,467	1,546,495	12.73	9,466,375	996,093	10.52
Total deposits	$20,486,776			$17,681,888		
Funds borrowed	4,767,657	610,638	12.81	4,740,945	521,754	11.01
Notes payable	277,440	19,786	7.13	315,954	21,667	6.86
Other liabilities	1,975,831			1,637,792		
Capital	1,198,811			1,157,357		
Total liabilities and capital/Total interest expense	$28,706,515	$2,800,740		$25,533,936	$2,050,539	
Earning Assets	$24,682,044			$22,195,558		
Interest Income/Earning Assets		$3,237,367	13.12%		$2,514,742	11.33%
Interest Expense/Earning Assets		2,800,740	11.35		2,050,539	9.24
Interest Differential		$ 436,627	1.77%		$ 464,203	2.09%

*Indicates earning asset.

**Includes tax equivalent adjustment based on 46% Federal income tax
rate in 1980 and 1979, and 48% in 1978 and prior years.

(A) Principally balances in overseas offices.

(B) Includes fees on loans of $37,990,000 for 1980; $35,126,000 for 1979;
$23,128,000 for 1978; $18,010,000 for 1977; and $20,715,000 for
1976. Rates are calculated exclusive of fee income.

EXHIBIT 8

Average Balances/Interest Differential/Rates
First Chicago Corporation and Subsidiaries

	1978			1977			1976		
	Balance	Interest Income/ Expense	Average Rates Earned/ Paid	Balance	Interest Income/ Expense	Average Rates Earned/ Paid	Balance	Interest Income/ Expense	Average Rates Earned/ Paid
	$ 3,012,318	$ 235,900	7.83%	$ 2,804,529	$ 173,778	6.20%	$ 1,864,388	$ 126,068	6.76%
	1,218,572	91,338	7.50	1,341,181	85,975	6.41	1,591,890	107,050	6.72
	833,509	81,438	9.77	1,025,644	98,974	9.65	810,428	80,849	9.98
	311,762	30,272	9.71	233,025	19,459	8.35	173,530	15,423	8.89
	38,252	3,415	8.93	39,366	3,448	8.76	27,736	2,558	9.22
	112,128	8,533	7.61	99,753	6,488	6.50	94,389	6,007	6.36
	728,180	57,252	7.86	575,132	28,872	5.72	394,045	21,396	5.29
	8,595,179	821,558	9.33	8,131,727	630,318	7.57	8,108,800	617,185	7.38
	4,398,853	413,830	9.33	3,972,773	332,534	8.29	3,239,766	284,256	8.71
	$12,994,032			$12,104,500			$11,348,566		
	125,179			124,913			129,580		
	$12,868,853			$11,979,587			$11,218,986		
	414,012	46,114	16.48	361,548	37,784	15.58	345,312	29,405	11.52
	1,516,061			1,320,554			1,221,861		
	1,375,819			1,152,484			859,350		
	$22,429,466	$1,789,650		$20,932,803	$1,417,630		$18,601,915	$1,290,197	
	$ 2,528,558			$ 2,502,674			$ 2,570,202		
	$ 963,308	$ 48,484	5.03%	$ 1,051,457	$ 52,864	5.03%	$ 976,435	$ 49,132	5.03%
	1,175,863	82,861	7.05	1,202,267	79,118	6.58	1,287,368	84,817	6.59
	4,355,202	328,177	7.54	3,634,947	207,655	5.71	3,469,209	204,171	5.89
	$ 6,494,373			$ 5,888,671			$ 5,733,012		
	$ 9,022,931			$ 8,391,345			$ 8,303,214		
	7,167,523	529,301	7.38	6,301,592	380,160	6.03	4,672,320	301,648	6.46
	$16,190,454			$14,692,937			$12,975,534		
	3,634,933	283,820	7.81	3,899,106	219,485	5.63	3,694,047	196,301	5.31
	327,044	23,594	7.21	373,478	26,390	7.07	280,030	18,899	6.75
	1,200,616			974,344			730,376		
	1,076,419			992,938			921,928		
	$22,429,466	$1,296,237		$20,932,803	$ 965,672		$18,601,915	$ 854,968	
	$19,662,765			$18,584,678			$16,650,284		
		$1,789,650	9.10%		$1,417,630	7.63%		$1,290,197	7.75%
		1,296,237	6.59		965,672	5.20		854,968	5.13
		$ 493,413	2.51%		$ 451,958	2.43%		$ 435,229	2.62%

(C) Includes tax equivalent adjustments, primarily amortization of investment tax credits on a tax equivalent basis, of $7,161,000 for 1980; $11,128,000 for 1979; $16,831,000 for 1978; $11,553,000 for 1977; and $5,941,000 for 1976. Rates are calculated on balances reduced by deferred liability for taxes and deferred investment tax credits.

(D) Includes tax equivalent adjustments based on 46% Federal income tax rate in 1980 and 1979, and 48% in 1978 and prior years of $63,672,000 for 1980; $58,361,000 for 1979; $67,391,000 for 1978; $67,668,000 for 1977; and $52,144,000 for 1976.

(E) Includes balances of Edge Act corporations.

EXHIBIT 8 (continued)

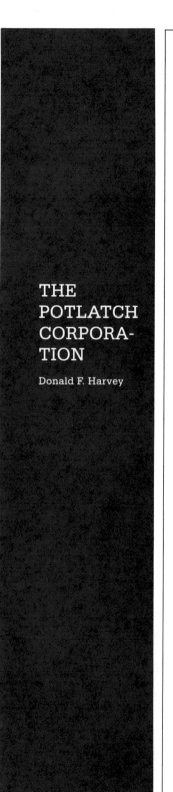

Following is a statement of Potlatch's business philosophy and company purpose, dated September 8, 1972.

"Potlatch will be a company characterized by a growing profit and reasonable rate of return; achieved by talented, well trained and highly motivated people; properly supported by a sound financial structure; and with a keen sense of social responsibility to all of the publics with whom the company has contact.

"Within the framework of the business philosophy, the company will strive to:

a. Achieve a growing profit and a reasonable rate of return, giving proper recognition to the inherent cycles in the economic climate.

b. Establish a balance between a disciplined drive for current profits and a broad-gauged program for long-term growth.

c. Utilize efficiently all human, financial, physical, and natural resources.

d. Develop a decentralized group of businesses, fully competitive within their own operating environments, which can capitalize upon their own strengths as well as utilizing the overall capabilities of the company, while operating within the parameters established by total company objectives and policies established for coordination and control.

e. Provide quality products and services within the competitive limits of each product line.

f. Be sensitive to the needs and desires of employees.

g. Maintain a sound financial structure, flexible enough to finance unique opportunities or unforeseen difficulties without adversely affecting the shareholder's interests.

h. Ensure ethical standards, open and forthright relationships with all publics, and deep concern for the environment.

I INTRODUCTION

In the ten years since he became president of the forest products company, Potlatch Corp., Richard B. Madden has applied his personal passion for balance to every phase of the com-

Copyright 1981 by Donald F. Harvey

This case was prepared from published information. The company in no way participated in its preparation.

pany's operations—from the mix of its major product lines to the composition of its board of directors. The results to date have been impressive. Potlatch's earnings had tumbled to a ten-year low of $1.4 million in 1971, Madden's first year on the job; it shot up to a record $45.3 million, or $6.20 a share, on sales of $487.9 million in 1974. Then in recession-ridden 1975, the company managed a highly respectable net of $37.5 million, or $5.03 a share, on sales of $504.3 million.

When Madden joined San Francisco-based Potlatch, he found a company that was not only foundering financially but seemed to have lost almost all sense of proportion. For one thing, his predecessor had launched a series of ill-fated acquisitions that took Potlatch far from its basic lumber and paper business. For another, the company was run by the seat of its pants, concentrating all its management on day-to-day operations and giving little thought to planning for the future.

Madden's first order of business was to dump several of the acquisitions that had turned sour, including a home-building firm, a modular-building division and a lumber mill in Columbia. The cost was heavy: $23 million in losses and write-offs. But it restored Potlatch to its primary business: solid-wood products, such as lumber and plywood, and bleached-paper products, such as packaging, business and printing papers and tissue.

Then he took on the toughest job: instilling in a totally operations-oriented management the essential lessons of long-range planning. The lack of any long-term strategy had been a major drag on profits. For example, Potlatch owns an unusually large amount of timber land for a company its size, some 1.3 million acres in Idaho and Arkansas. But it was making poor use of this valuable asset. While competitors were cutting timber on twenty-to-forty-year cycles, much of Potlatch's low-cost timber was on a seventy-year cycle—limiting the amount it cut each year. The company was also wasting another valuable resource, the wood chips left over from its sawmill operations, which provide a rich source of raw material for making pulp and paperboard. With no mill of its own to convert them, Potlatch was selling the chips to other companies.

II POTLATCH OPERATIONS IN IDAHO

The *Inland Empire* is the name for the region of the Pacific Northwest located roughly between the Rockies and the Cascades. First explored by Lewis and Clark in the early 1800s, it embraces great forests, vast stretches of open country, fertile prairies, deep valleys, mountain ranges, numerous lakes and river systems, and even desert. Its rich natural resources support major farming, mining, and forest products industries.

Within this domain, northern Idaho has a heavy concentration of timberland. It was here that Potlatch Corporation got its start early in this century. Today, its Idaho forests and related mills comprise one of the company's three regional operating systems.

The others are in Arkansas and Minnesota, and all three differ markedly in climate, forest cover, plant facilities, product mix, and proximity to markets. But Potlatch's operating goal, as a tree farming and wood-converting company, is the same everywhere—to capitalize on the relationships among what its forests will grow, what its plants will produce, and what the markets will buy.

The essential link here is its manufacturing capability, which adds dollar value to wood as it flows from the stump to the customer's end use. By choosing the most suitable products and by producing and distributing them efficiently, Potlatch generates capital for the continual new investment necessitated by changes in technology, markets, competition, and its business environment.

Potlatch's Idaho system is diverse and highly developed, reflecting both the character of the forest and the duration of its presence there. They operate in an area roughly 100 miles long by 80 miles wide, encompassing 518,000 acres of company lands and nine manufacturing sites. Approximately 4,700 Potlatch employees work in the state.

The forest in North Idaho is virtually all softwoods, principal commercial tree species being grand fir, Douglas fir, inland red cedar and Idaho white pine. The climate and growing conditions in this area stimulate natural regeneration and a timber crop rotation period shorter than most other interior sites. Forest management can add to this natural productivity.

Of the 21 million acres of timberland in Idaho, some 14 million are capable of growing trees as a crop and are available for this purpose. Approximately 70 percent of this commercial forest is under the control of state and federal agencies. Consequently, Potlatch and the state's other wood-based manufacturers must depend on public lands for at least a part of their needs, the proportions varying from company to company.

With extensive holdings, Potlatch can rely on its own lands for much of its timber supply. But these valuable properties are more than simply a "woodpile" from which the mills draw raw material; land is regarded as a basic resource, an asset to be wisely managed for a perpetual return.

Potlatch's goal is to optimize earnings from tree farming, and—as with most agricultural undertakings—this can be realized by efficiently raising the most suitable crops in the right amounts for harvest at the most appropriate times. Forest management must, over the long term, take into account new manufacturing technologies and the changing realities of the marketplace.

To raise the productivity of the Idaho lands, foresters are altering the tree population. Currently, many sites are occupied by overmature timber whose development has slowed or stopped altogether. This dense, dark environment also has negative effects on wildlife populations and on watershed values, both of which benefit from a variety of environments. Over a period of time, Potlatch is harvesting these old growth stands to allow vigorous new stems to take their place. With more acreage taking advantage of the rapid growth rates of younger trees, the forest's overall yield—in terms of cubic feet of wood fiber added per acre per year—will be significantly increased.

Meanwhile, as they convert to a younger forest, they are also intensifying forest management through a variety of silvicultural techniques to further encourage regeneration and growth.

This major undertaking on forest lands is most significant to Potlatch's Idaho operations. Large logs gradually are giving way to smaller ones which have become commercially usable because of both changes in the economic value of wood and advances in processing.

Purchased timber always has been an important raw material source, usually accounting for somewhat less than half of total log requirements. Most of this wood is obtained through competitive bidding at Forest Service and state timber sales.

Besides whole logs, Potlatch purchases a significant volume of wood by-products from other companies operating in the general area, recovering what otherwise would be waste. Chips, made from the residue of lumber and plywood manufacture, and sawdust are raw materials for pulp manufacture, and shavings are used to make particleboard. They also are buying other waste materials, including bark, which serves as an excellent fuel.

The key to profitable conversion of the tree crop is a family of manufacturing facilities which convert the logs and residuals to their best economic end uses. This assignment is a complex one because of the varied harvest (considering the different species, sizes, and grades of logs) and the large geographic area from which it is gathered. Accordingly, Potlatch operates a network of plants strategically located near available wood supplies, highly diverse in processing capability and designed and maintained to be cost-competitive.

The centerpiece of this system is the operation at Lewiston, one of the largest and most highly integrated forest products complexes in the world. It receives both logs and residuals, turning these into lumber, specialty wood products, plywood, kraft pulp, bleached paperboard, and household tissue products. It processes two-thirds of the total Idaho raw material throughput.

More than 50 percent of the whole logs entering the Idaho system are processed at one of the six sawmills. Besides a very large unit at Lewiston, the western wood products division has sawmills at Spalding, Kamiah, Potlatch, St. Maries and Coeur d'Alene. Some are specialized as to log size, species cut, or end product. Together they manufacture dimension (framing) lumber, boards, decking, and other laminated wood products.

Other primary log users are the three plywood plants, at Lewiston, Jaype, and St. Maries. All of them concentrate on sheathing grades for construction, and two produce *Plystran*™, Potlatch's proprietary plywood having a reconstituted wood core.

Both the sawmills and plywood plants generate residuals, which go to Lewiston for pulping.

Other users of logs are two split cedar operations at Jaype and Santa, which make fencing products.

Rounding out the wood products operations is a plant at Post Falls which produces particleboard underlayment from planer shavings.

At Lewiston, the Idaho pulp and paperboard division's mill manufactures bleached kraft pulp largely from residual chips and sawdust. Rated capacity is 1,100 tons of pulp per day, and about 80 percent of this fiber is run across the mill's two paperboard machines. Potlatch's Idaho paperboard grades are particularly noted for their physical strength, a quality owed to the long softwood fibers used, and are sold mostly to manufacturers of folding cartons and dairy packaging.

Most of the pulp not used in paperboard is piped to the adjacent tissue mill of the consumer products division. There, two paper machines produce bulk rolls, which are converted into private-label facial and bathroom tissues, toweling or napkins and then packaged for shipment to retail outlets and distributors in the western states. This is one of the highest value-added operations in Potlatch.

Together, the forest lands and facilities in Idaho provide an integrated structure, but can it be managed to evolve and endure against its competitors?

Constant change is another fundamental characteristic of Potlatch in Idaho, and a quiet, gradual transformation is taking place there, sparked both by opportunity and necessity. Change is happening almost everywhere, not necessarily in dramatic fashion, but rather through a large number of medium-sized and small undertakings. Their nature varies tremendously—from new forestry techniques, to more modern logging equipment, to elimination of production bottlenecks, to more sensitive and responsive process controls, to improved ways to convert wood into useful, marketable products.

Potlatch is managing its forests better. It is utilizing more of the tree and is adding more dollar value to wood. It is doing a better job of protecting the environment and is becoming more energy self-suficient. The plants are becoming increasingly cost-effective, and customers are getting better quality and service. And, in recent years, until the 1980 recession, the earnings generated from essentially the same land base have increased. (See Exhibit 1.)

III PRODUCT SEGMENTS

While Idaho remains the single most important operations base for Potlatch, the company also has extensive timber resources and manufacturing facilities in Arkansas and Minnesota (see Exhibit 2). Following is the recent performance of the company's various product segments.

Wood Products

$ (in thousands)	1980	1979	1978
Sales	$233,576	$285,518	$283,759
Shipments			
lumber (board feet)	505,825	574,240	600,258
plywood (sq. ft., ⅜" basis)	398,236	447,118	439,430
particleboard (sq. ft., ¾" basis)	58,817	65,923	66,375

While housing starts declined slightly in 1979, demand for lumber and plywood remained relatively strong. In the first half of 1980, housing starts declined sharply to a post-World War II low, and forced closing of eleven mills in North Idaho. There was some recovery in the second half, but the situation remained tenuous because of continuing high interest rates.

Ten-Year Record[1]

Potlatch Corporation and Consolidated Subsidiaries
(Dollars in thousands–except per-share amounts)

For the years ended December 31	1980	1979
Ten-Year Summary of Consolidated Operations		
Net sales	$819,593	$809,059
Costs and expenses		
Depreciation, amortization and cost of fee timber harvested	44,984	40,454
Materials, labor and other operating expenses	652,784	611,415
Selling, administrative and general expenses	54,354	53,367
	752,122	705,236
Earnings from operations	67,471	103,823
Interest expense	(17,756)	(22,348)
Interest income	7,743	12,631
Other income (expense), net	4,875	(268)
Earnings before taxes and extraordinary items	62,333	93,838
Percent of net sales	7.6%	11.6%
Provision for taxes on income	12,926	22,838
Percent of pretax income	20.7%	24.3%
Earnings before extraordinary items	49,407	71,000
Extraordinary items, net of taxes	–	–
Net earnings	$ 49,407	$ 71,000
Financial returns, before extraordinary items		
Percent return on equity[4]	10.2%	16.5%
Percent return on net sales	6.0%	8.8%
Per common share[2]		
Earnings before extraordinary items	$ 3.25	$ 4.69
Extraordinary items	–	–
Net earnings	$ 3.25	$ 4.69
Cash dividends	$ 1.34	$ 1.20
Stockholders' equity[3]	$ 33.88	$ 31.94
Shares outstanding, net of treasury stock (in thousands)[2][3]	15,230	15,164
Number of stockholders[3]	5,277	5,516
Price range of common stock[2]		
High	45	39
Low	29	29
Average daily trading volume (shares)[2]	11,010	8,392
Employment		
Number of employees[3]	10,214	10,181
Wages, salaries and cost of employee benefits	$261,850	$250,735
Selected production statistics (in thousands)		
Lumber, domestic (board feet, dry)	515,043	603,170
Plywood, domestic (square feet, ⅜" basis)	398,961	447,502
Particleboard (square feet, ¼" basis)	59,720	65,909
Pulp (air-dry tons)	708	711
Paperboard (tons)	492	488
Printing and business papers (tons)	234	237
Tissue paper (tons)	86	70

(1) When acquisitions have been accounted for as poolings of interests or when certain
accounts have been reclassified, only the year preceding has been restated.
(2) Adjusted for 2-for-1 stock split in 1976.

44

EXHIBIT 1

1978	1977	1976	1975	1974	1973	1972	1971
$787,036	$688,424	$624,056	$504,294	$487,868	$442,407	$377,433	$356,024
38,095	26,846	26,095	21,488	20,115	18,594	18,019	18,535
580,203	514,353	475,320	383,844	359,511	329,194	298,844	285,540
51,731	47,115	46,405	43,357	39,382	36,579	32,129	30,610
670,029	588,314	547,820	448,689	419,008	384,367	348,992	334,685
117,007	100,110	76,236	55,605	68,860	58,040	28,441	21,339
(16,243)	(12,720)	(9,551)	(8,088)	(8,168)	(7,688)	(4,874)	(5,301)
4,884	512	621	668	5,139	4,405	1,768	1,487
(8,887)	(3,333)	221	3,646	909	(1,947)	(1,621)	(626)
96,761	84,569	67,527	51,831	66,740	52,810	23,714	16,899
12.3%	12.3%	10.8%	10.3%	13.7%	11.9%	6.3%	4.7%
32,599	22,756	19,813	14,364	21,451	18,831	7,129	6,184
33.7%	26.9%	29.3%	27.7%	32.1%	35.7%	30.1%	36.6%
64,162	61,813	47,714	37,467	45,289	33,979	16,585	10,715
–	–	–	–	–	–	–	(9,312)
$ 64,162	$ 61,813	$ 47,714	$ 37,467	$ 45,289	$ 33,979	$ 16,585	$ 1,403
16.8%	18.6%	16.1%	14.2%	19.8%	16.8%	8.4%	5.3%
8.2%	9.0%	7.6%	7.4%	9.3%	7.7%	4.4%	3.0%
$ 4.24	$ 4.09	$ 3.17	$ 2.51	$ 3.10	$ 2.33	$ 1.12	$ .72
–	–	–	–	–	–	–	(.62)
$ 4.24	$ 4.09	$ 3.17	$ 2.51	$ 3.10	$ 2.33	$ 1.12	$ .10
$ 1.04	$ .88	$ .7725	$ .7125	$ .625	$ .525	$ .50	$ .50
$ 28.47	$ 25.29	$ 22.10	$ 19.74	$ 18.12	$ 15.64	$ 13.85	$ 13.20
15,141	15,116	15,068	15,003	14,596	14,602	14,590	14,919
5,479	4,936	4,557	4,571	5,213	5,134	4,599	4,687
39¼	39⅝	35½	25¾	17⅝	16⅝	15¾	19⅜
23⅝	26⅛	24⅛	12	10⅛	9¾	10¾	10⅜
8,548	6,890	9,280	12,380	6,020	8,680	7,440	5,760
10,350	10,174	10,055	10,242	10,229	10,855	10,788	11,194
$231,647	$210,323	$193,773	$165,997	$149,547	$129,106	$124,410	$118,158
589,861	620,602	617,471	517,251	453,858	494,268	554,220	598,785
437,452	449,763	433,696	401,056	393,704	430,512	418,370	424,944
66,401	62,352	55,838	16,176	–	–	–	–
675	534	532	480	501	483	468	445
454	313	309	284	283	272	241	244
290	317	302	264	298	302	290	247
72	73	69	67	69	57	51	53

(3) At year-end.
(4) Calculated on stockholders' equity at the beginning of the year.

EXHIBIT 1 (continued)

Pulp and Paperboard

$ (in thousands)	1980	1979	1978
Sales	$226,932	$194,364	$164,448
Shipments			
pulp (tons)	108,399	91,609	96,003
paperboard (tons)	481,605	484,231	446,615
	590,004	575,840	542,618

Potlatch is the second largest producer of bleached kraft paperboard, a packaging material widely used for milk and other food products, pharmaceuticals, toiletries and other consumer necessities. These end uses call for a variety of paperboard weights and finishes, including extruded plastic coatings and clay coatings for enhanced printing qualities.

The pulp and paperboard group has two manufacturing facilities. The larger, at Lewiston, utilizes softwood fiber only, received almost entirely in the form of wood residuals from sawmills and plywood plants. The McCehee, Ark., facility is able to use both hardwoods and softwoods originating from residuals, tree tops and pulpwood. The properties of this fiber mix make for a broadened overall line of paperboard grades. The locations of these two plants enable them to serve markets nationwide, and to carry on an export business.

In 1980, dramatically increased prices helped make this the most profitable of the company's divisions.

Printing and Business Papers

$ (in thousands)	1980	1979	1978
Sales	$186,625	$174,455	$186,619
Shipments			
coated paper (tons)	150,227	145,434	132,573
uncoated paper (tons)	84,173	91,922	166,697
	234,400	237,356	299,270

Demand for the higher quality coated paper has remained strong, forcing the Northwest Paper Division to allocate production. In 1980, profits were eroded slightly by higher costs, but this was partially offset by high average prices.

Consumer Products

$ (in thousands)	1980	1979	1978
Sales	$69,456	$59,686	$64,340
Shipments			
tissue products (tons)	72,627	66,116	70,122
paper plateware (tons)	—	170	8,238
	72,627	66,286	78,360

1980 Sales, Capacities, Production and Fiber Flow (Capacities as of September 30, 1980)

Land Bases   **Solid Wood Converting**   **Pulp Manufacturing**

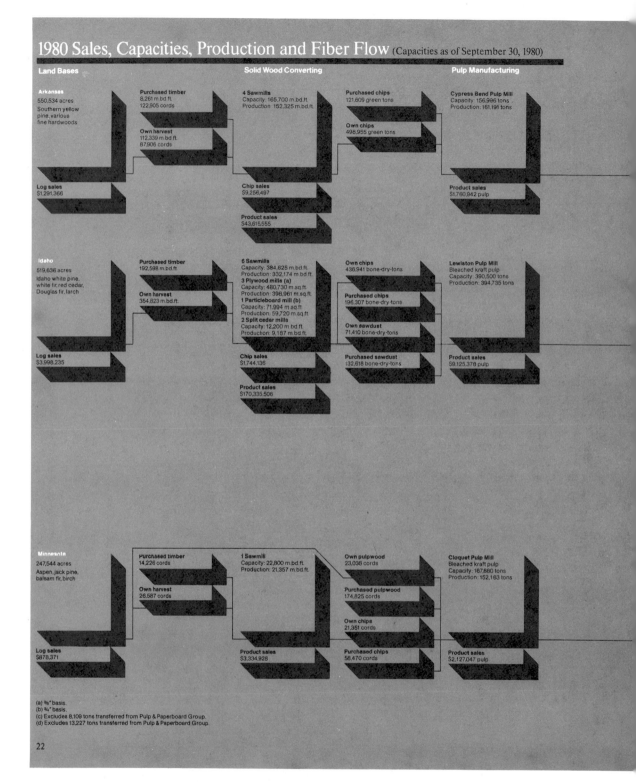

Arkansas
550,534 acres
Southern yellow
pine, various
fine hardwoods

Purchased timber
8,261 m.bd.ft.
122,905 cords

Own harvest
112,339 m.bd.ft.
87,906 cords

4 Sawmills
Capacity: 165,700 m.bd.ft.
Production: 152,325 m.bd.ft.

Purchased chips
121,609 green tons

Own chips
498,955 green tons

Cypress Bend Pulp Mill
Capacity: 156,996 tons
Production: 161,191 tons

Log sales
$1,291,366

Chip sales
$9,256,497

Product sales
$43,615,555

Product sales
$1,760,942 pulp

Idaho
519,636 acres
Idaho white pine,
white fir, red cedar,
Douglas fir, larch

Purchased timber
192,598 m.bd.ft.

Own harvest
354,823 m.bd.ft.

6 Sawmills
Capacity: 384,625 m.bd.ft.
Production: 332,174 m.bd.ft.
3 Plywood mills (a)
Capacity: 480,730 m.sq.ft.
Production: 398,961 m.sq.ft.
1 Particleboard mill (b)
Capacity: 71,994 m.sq.ft.
Production: 59,720 m.sq.ft.
2 Split cedar mills
Capacity: 12,200 m.bd.ft.
Production: 9,187 m.bd.ft.

Own chips
436,941 bone-dry-tons

Purchased chips
196,307 bone-dry-tons

Own sawdust
71,410 bone-dry-tons

Purchased sawdust
132,618 bone-dry-tons

Lewiston Pulp Mill
Bleached kraft pulp
Capacity: 390,500 tons
Production: 394,735 tons

Log sales
$3,998,235

Chip sales
$1,744,136

Product sales
$170,335,506

Product sales
$9,125,378 pulp

Minnesota
247,544 acres
Aspen, jack pine,
balsam fir, birch

Purchased timber
14,226 cords

Own harvest
26,587 cords

1 Sawmill
Capacity: 22,800 m.bd.ft.
Production: 21,357 m.bd.ft.

Own pulpwood
23,038 cords

Purchased pulpwood
174,825 cords

Own chips
21,351 cords

Cloquet Pulp Mill
Bleached kraft pulp
Capacity: 187,880 tons
Production: 152,163 tons

Log sales
$878,371

Product sales
$3,334,928

Purchased chips
58,470 cords

Product sales
$2,127,047 pulp

(a) ⅜" basis.
(b) ¾" basis.
(c) Excludes 8,109 tons transferred from Pulp & Paperboard Group.
(d) Excludes 13,227 tons transferred from Pulp & Paperboard Group.

22

EXHIBIT 2

738

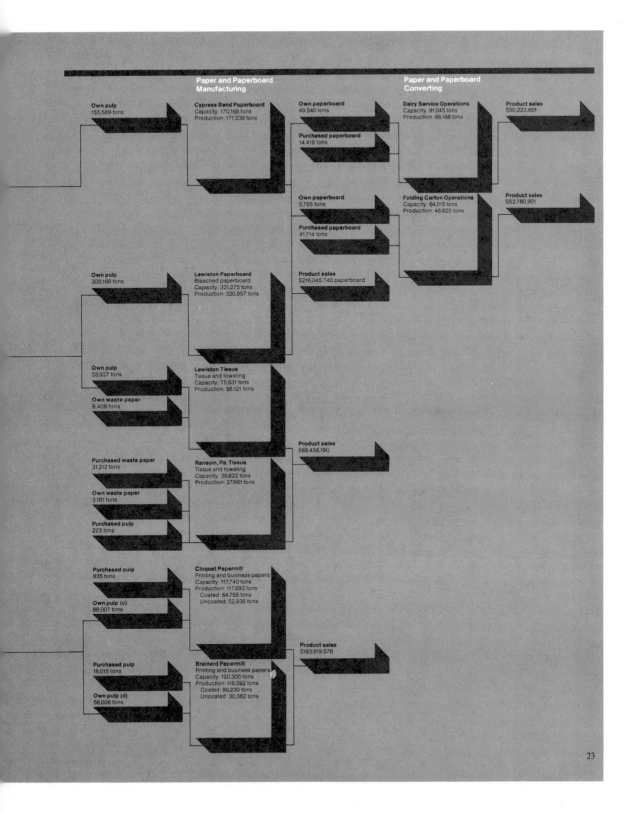

Paper and Paperboard
Manufacturing

Paper and Paperboard
Converting

Own pulp
155,589 tons

Cypress Bend Paperboard
Capacity: 170,168 tons
Production: 171,238 tons

Own paperboard
49,540 tons

Purchased paperboard
14,416 tons

Dairy Service Operations
Capacity: 91,045 tons
Production: 68,168 tons

Product sales
$50,222,661

Own paperboard
5,795 tons

Purchased paperboard
41,714 tons

Folding Carton Operations
Capacity: 64,015 tons
Production: 48,625 tons

Product sales
$52,780,901

Own pulp
303,166 tons

Lewiston Paperboard
Bleached paperboard
Capacity: 321,275 tons
Production: 320,957 tons

Product sales
$216,045,740 paperboard

Own pulp
53,927 tons

Own waste paper
9,409 tons

Lewiston Tissue
Tissue and toweling
Capacity: 75,631 tons
Production: 58,121 tons

Purchased waste paper
31,212 tons

Own waste paper
3,181 tons

Purchased pulp
223 tons

Ransom, Pa. Tissue
Tissue and toweling
Capacity: 39,822 tons
Production: 27,861 tons

Product sales
$69,456,190

Purchased pulp
835 tons

Own pulp (c)
88,007 tons

Cloquet Papermill
Printing and business papers
Capacity: 117,740 tons
Production: 117,693 tons
  Coated: 64,755 tons
  Uncoated: 52,938 tons

Purchased pulp
18,015 tons

Own pulp (d)
58,006 tons

Brainerd Papermill
Printing and business papers
Capacity: 120,300 tons
Production: 116,592 tons
  Coated: 86,230 tons
  Uncoated: 30,362 tons

Product sales
$183,619,578

23

Potlatch operates paper manufacturing and converting facilities which produce a full line of household tissue items. Serving markets in the East, Southeast, Midwest and the eleven western states, the plants are located in California, Idaho and Pennsylvania. Wood pulp required for the western operation comes primarily from the Idaho pulp and paperboard division's mill at Lewiston; the eastern operation gets its bleached fiber mainly from recycling high-grade waste paper and paperboard.

The consumer products division manufactures facial and bathroom tissues, towels and napkins. These products are sold under the proprietary brand names of a variety of retail distributors, including supermarket, variety and drug chains as well as the cooperative buying services that supply independent grocers. Consumption of proprietary-branded tissue products accounts for 20.0 percent of the national total.

Packaging

$ (in thousands)	1980	1979	1978
Sales	$103,004	$ 95,036	$ 87,830
Shipments			
folding cartons (tons)	43,911	42,900	42,035
liquid-tight containers (tons)	64,002	66,587	63,897
	107,913	109,487	105,932

Potlatch's packaging division, with its focus on converting, differs from its other businesses, all of which are engaged in primary manufacturing. The packaging operations start with paperboard rolls or sheets, which are printed, cut, and formed into finished products ready for use by customers. Bleached paperboard is the principal raw material, and more than half of the packaging plants' requirements are supplied by the company's pulp and paperboard group.

This division operates within two segments of an extremely large and diverse market for consumer and industrial packaging; folding cartons and liquid-tight containers. The two areas, although broadly related, are distinctly different in production and marketing requirements. Therefore, the division is managed as two separate profit centers, having roughly equivalent dollar sales volumes.

In Exhibit 3, Product Segment financial data are presented.

IV CONCLUSION

Says Madden, "We are optimistic about the future. Our basic strategy, which remains unchanged, centers on the improved utilization of fiber available in the company's three operating regions, from both our own holdings of 1.3 million acres and other nearby ownerships. Well into the 1990s, we will be building out our resource base, adding productive assets and, in turn, expanding Potlatch's cash generating capability, the foundation of our investment planning.

As a consulting firm called in to design a new strategy for Potlatch in the 1980s, what would you recommend?

Potlatch is an integrated forest products company with substantial timber resources. It is engaged principally in the growing and harvesting of timber and the manufacture and sale of wood products, printing and business papers, and other pulp-based products. Its timberlands and all of its manufacturing facilities are located within the United States.
Following is a tabulation of business segment information for each of the past three years 1980-1978:

	1980	1979	1978
Sales to Unaffiliated Customers:[1]			
Wood products	$ 233,576	$285,518	$283,759
Lumber	164,731	211,840	198,571
Plywood	55,258	63,734	69,848
Other	13,587	9,944	15,340
Printing and business papers	186,625	174,455	186,619
Other pulp-based products	399,392	349,086	316,658
Bleached kraft pulp and paperboard	226,932	194,364	164,488
Tissue	69,456	59,686	64,340
Folding cartons	52,781	47,633	43,792
Liquid-tight containers	50,223	47,403	44,038
Total sales	$ 819,593	$809,059	$787,036
Intersegment Sales or Transfers:[2]			
Wood products	$ 61,429	$ 36,924	$ 29,316
Printing and business papers	3,077	2,916	2,452
Other pulp-based products	513	128	157
Total intersegment sales	$ 65,019	$ 39,968	$ 31,925
Operating Income:			
Wood products	$ 19,108	$ 42,321	$ 59,915
Printing and business papers	24,194	27,606	25,751
Other pulp-based products	41,872	48,844	46,247
	85,174	118,771	131,913
Less corporate items:			
Interest income	(7,743)	(12,491)	(4,709)
Administration expense	13,662	13,833	13,667
Interest expense	17,756	22,348	16,243
Other[3]	(834)	1,243	9,951
Earnings before taxes on income	$ 62,333	$ 93,838	$ 96,761
Identifiable Assets:[2]			
Wood products	$ 292,975	$279,052	$211,212
Printing and business papers	199,417	165,098	146,225
Other pulp-based products	435,757	375,357	326,744
Corporate	93,495	157,427	81,649
Total	$1,021,644	$976,934	$765,830
Depreciation, Amortization and Cost of Fee Timber Harvested:			
Wood products	$ 16,049	$ 16,294	$ 14,699
Printing and business papers	7,443	6,956	7,030
Other pulp-based products	20,685	16,432	15,731
Corporate	807	772	635
Total	$ 44,984	$ 40,454	$ 38,095
Capital Expenditures:			
Wood products	$ 56,457	$ 83,289	$ 28,278
Printing and business papers	44,291	38,523	33,099
Other pulp-based products	48,604	59,768	41,267
Corporate	81	708	522
Total	$ 149,433	$182,288	$103,166

[1]While export sales to foreign customers are less than 10 percent of consolidated sales, sales to U.S. brokers who ship to foreign countries combined with foreign sales total 11.2 percent of 1980 net sales. Sales to any single customer are less than 10 percent of consolidated sales.
[2]Intersegment sales for 1978-1980 consist primarily of chips and other fiber sales to the pulp and paperboard facilities, the majority of which are based on prevailing market prices. The company's timber, timberlands and related logging facilities have been allocated to the segment that is the primary consumer of the raw material in its geographical location.
[3]Includes for 1978 a $9,760 charge from settlement of legal actions involving alleged violation of antitrust laws relating to paper packaging products and fine papers.

42

EXHIBIT 3

Potlatch Corporation and Consolidated Subsidiaries
(Dollars in thousands)

At December 31	1980	1979
Ten-Year Summary of Consolidated Financial Position		
Current assets	$200,731	$196,429
Current liabilities	105,902	137,482
Working capital	94,829	58,947
Capital assets, at cost		
Buildings, machinery and equipment, net	683,075	586,306
Timber, timberlands and logging facilities, net	81,974	76,459
Unexpended revenue bond funds	23,021	69,773
Other noncurrent assets, net	32,843	47,967
Total net assets	$915,742	$839,452
Capitalization		
Long-term debt, less current installments	$329,937	$302,976
Deferred taxes	69,854	52,106
Stockholders' equity	515,951	484,370
Total capitalization	$915,742	$839,452

For the years ended December 31	1980	1979
Ten-Year Summary of Consolidated Funds Flow		
Source of funds		
Net earnings before extraordinary items	$ 49,407	$ 71,000
Depreciation, amortization and cost of fee timber harvested	44,984	40,454
Deferred taxes	17,748	9,458
Proceeds from new long-term debt	41,000	120,269
Other, including extraordinary items	2,181	12,832
Total source of funds	$155,320	$254,013
Application of funds		
Cash dividends paid	$ 20,346	$ 18,185
Additions to plant and properties	149,433	182,288
Increase (decrease) in investments of unexpended revenue bond funds	(46,752)	65,328
Reduction of long-term debt	14,039	10,868
Other	(17,628)	12,662
Total application of funds	$119,438	$289,331
Addition to (reduction of) working capital	$ 35,882	$(35,318)

(1) When acquisitions have been accounted for as poolings of interests or when certain
accounts have been reclassified, only the preceding year has been restated.

EXHIBIT 4
Ten Year Financial Summary

R. LIBRARY LETTERKENNY

742

1978	1977	1976	1975	1974	1973	1972	1971
$192,780	$174,395	$153,094	$134,844	$139,914	$149,676	$121,010	$109,136
98,515	66,322	65,290	56,671	51,924	52,790	45,419	44,106
94,265	108,073	87,804	78,173	87,990	96,886	75,591	65,030
463,578	402,237	337,117	259,590	217,415	187,458	173,814	158,616
68,041	64,750	62,005	58,967	52,784	44,136	41,381	39,532
4,445	–	–	–	–	–	–	–
36,986	27,968	18,879	20,251	23,238	21,203	21,135	19,630
$667,315	$603,028	$505,805	$416,981	$381,427	$349,683	$311,921	$282,808
$193,574	$187,989	$151,942	$103,090	$100,971	$108,066	$ 95,994	$ 70,075
42,648	32,775	20,822	17,793	15,976	13,203	13,901	15,792
431,093	382,264	333,041	296,098	264,480	228,414	202,026	196,941
$667,315	$603,028	$505,805	$416,981	$381,427	$349,683	$311,921	$282,808

1978	1977	1976	1975	1974	1973	1972	1971
$ 64,162	$ 61,813	$ 47,714	$ 37,467	$ 45,289	$ 33,979	$ 16,585	$ 10,715
38,095	26,846	26,095	21,488	20,115	18,594	18,019	18,535
9,873	11,953	3,029	1,817	2,772	(697)	(1,891)	(737)
13,386	59,556	56,347	10,032	–	16,500	33,500	–
1,288	5,926	3,558	14,662	7,324	6,685	9,188	11,798
$126,804	$166,094	$136,743	$ 85,466	$ 75,500	$ 75,061	$ 75,401	$ 40,311
$ 15,738	$ 13,290	$ 11,616	$ 10,582	$ 9,126	$ 7,664	$ 7,406	$ 7,354
103,166	98,980	108,053	76,222	59,810	38,428	38,319	21,582
4,445	–	–	–	–	–	–	–
7,801	23,509	7,495	7,913	7,095	4,428	7,581	9,640
9,462	10,046	(52)	567	8,365	4,273	11,198	(229)
$140,612	$145,825	$127,112	$ 95,284	$ 84,396	$ 54,793	$ 64,504	$ 38,347
$(13,808)	$ 20,269	$ 9,631	$ (9,818)	$ (8,896)	$ 20,268	$ 10,897	$ 1,964

47

EXHIBIT 4 (continued)

(In millions of average 1980 dollars except per-share and historical amounts)	1980	1979	1978	1977	1976
Net sales in historical dollars	$819.6	$809.1	$787.0	$688.4	$624.1
Net sales in constant dollars	819.6	918.5	994.0	936.1	903.4
Historical cost net earnings	$ 49.4	$ 71.0	$ 64.2	$ 61.8	$ 47.7
Constant dollar data:					
Net earnings from continuing operations	$ 15.9	$ 50.9	$ –	$ –	$ –
Purchasing power gain from holding net monetary liabilities	39.5	36.2	–	–	–
	$ 55.4	$ 87.1	$ –	$ –	$ –
Current cost data:					
Net earnings from continuing operations	$(30.5)	$ 3.1	$ –	$ –	$ –
Purchasing power gain from holding net monetary liabilities	39.5	36.2	–	–	–
Gain due to increase in current cost over increase in constant dollars	16.3	23.0	–	–	–
	$ 25.3	$ 62.3	$ –	$ –	$ –
Per common share:					
Historical cost net earnings	$ 3.25	$ 4.69	$ 4.24	$ 4.09	$ 3.17
Constant dollar net earnings from continuing operations	$ 1.05	$ 3.36	$ –	$ –	$ –
Purchasing power gain from holding net monetary liabilities	2.60	2.39	–	–	–
	$ 3.65	$ 5.75	$ –	$ –	$ –
Current cost net earnings from continuing operations	$(2.01)	$ .20	$ –	$ –	$ –
Purchasing power gain from holding net monetary liabilities	2.60	2.39	–	–	–
Gain due to increase in current cost over increase in constant dollars	1.07	1.52	–	–	–
	$ 1.66	$ 4.11	$ –	$ –	$ –
Cash dividends in historical dollars	$ 1.34	$ 1.20	$ 1.04	$ .88	$.7725
Cash dividends in constant dollars	1.34	1.36	1.31	1.20	1.12
Year-end data:					
Stockholders' equity:					
In historical dollars	$ 516.0	$ 484.4	$ 431.1	$ 382.3	$ 333.0
In constant dollars	817.0	811.3	–	–	–
In current cost dollars	1,628.3	1,604.9	–	–	–
Market price per common share:					
In historical dollars	38	30	30	29	36
In constant dollars	36	32	36	38	50
Average consumer price index	246.8	217.4	195.4	181.5	170.5

32

EXHIBIT 5
Five Year Financial Summary (Inflation adjusted)

Potlatch Corporation

Directors

James G. Affleck
*Chairman of the Board and
Chief Executive Officer
American Cyanamid Company
(diversified chemical products)
Wayne, New Jersey*

John F. Bonner
*Executive Consultant
Formerly President and
Chief Executive Officer
Pacific Gas and Electric Company
(public utility)
San Francisco, California*

Frederick W. Davis
*Investment management
Kirkland, Washington*

C. Jackson Grayson, Jr.
*Chairman
American Productivity Center
(nonprofit organization
to improve productivity)
Houston, Texas*

George F. Jewett, Jr.
Vice Chairman of the Board

Richard G. Landis
*Chairman of the Board
and Chief Executive Officer
Del Monte Corporation
(food products and
related services)
San Francisco, California*

Richard B. Madden
*Chairman of the Board and
Chief Executive Officer*

John J. Pascoe
*Chairman of the Board
Arcata Corporation
(printed products and
redwood lumber)
Menlo Park, California*

Toni Rembe
*Partner
Pillsbury, Madison & Sutro
(law firm)
San Francisco, California*

Reuben F. Richards
*Executive Vice President
Citibank, N.A.
(commercial banking)
New York, New York*

Robert G. Schwartz
*Vice Chairman
of the Board
Metropolitan Life Insurance
Company
(life insurance)
New York, New York*

Langdon S. Simons, Jr.
*President
Langdon Simons Associates, Inc.
(corporate planning consultants)
Seattle, Washington*

Roderick M. Steele
*President and
Chief Operating Officer*

Frederick T. Weyerhaeuser
*President
Conwed Corporation
(diversified manufacturer
of specialized industrial
and interior products)
St. Paul, Minnesota*

Audit Committee
John F. Bonner
C. Jackson Grayson, Jr.
George F. Jewett, Jr.
Richard G. Landis

Principal Officers

Richard B. Madden
*Chairman of the Board and
Chief Executive Officer
Age 51/With company 10 years*

Roderick M. Steele
*President and
Chief Operating Officer
Age 55/With company 18 years*

Richard N. Congreve
*Group Vice President
Pulp, Paperboard & Packaging
Age 52/With company 18 years*

Richard V. Warner
*Group Vice President
Wood Products
Age 51/With the company 28 years*

George C. Cheek
*Senior Vice President
Public Affairs
Age 50/With company 3 years*

John M. Richards
*Senior Vice President
Finance
Age 43/With company 16 years*

Harold W. Arnold
*Vice President and
Tax Manager
Age 50/With company 14 years*

F. Andrew Bayer
*Vice President
Industrial Relations
Age 44/With company 8 years*

C. Larry Bradford
*Vice President
Pulp and Paperboard
Arkansas Division
Age 44/With company 8 years*

Frances M. Davis
*Vice President and
General Counsel
Age 55/With company 6 years*

Edwin F. Erickson
*Vice President and
General Manager
Northwest Paper Division
Age 52/With company 27 years*

Irwin W. Krantz
*Vice President
Employee Relations
Age 54/With company 9 years*

R. Steven Mason
*Vice President
Consumer Products Division
Age 50/With company 9 years*

James R. Morris
*Vice President
Western Division
Wood Products Group
Age 48/With company 25 years*

Charles L. Neuner
*Vice President
Planning and Business Development
Age 55/With company 9 years*

Richard C. Nordholm
*Vice President
Community Relations
Age 53/With company 30 years*

Hubert D. Travaille
*Vice President
Government Relations
Age 41/With company 4 years*

George E. Pfautsch
*Controller
Age 45/With company 18 years*

Clifford W. Woodward
*Secretary
Age 64/With company 30 years*

Robert F. Wulf
*Treasurer
Age 43/With company 7 years*

48

EXHIBIT 6
Principal Officers and Directors

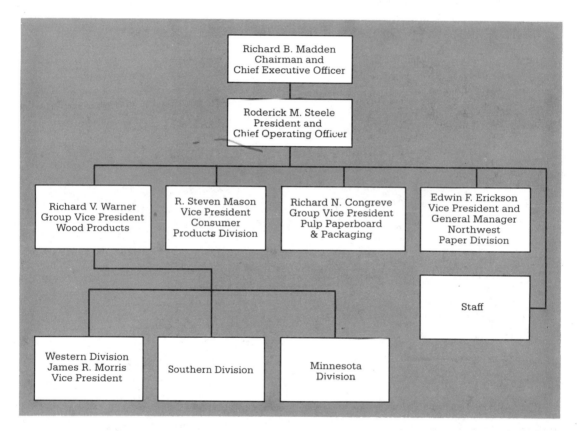

EXHIBIT 7
Potlatch Corporation Organization Structure

AUTHOR INDEX

TOPIC INDEX

R.T.C. LIBRARY, LETTERKENNY

R.T.C. LIBRARY, LETTERKENNY